Margot E. Fassler is Robert S. Tangeman Professor of Musicology and Director of the Institute of Sacred Music at Yale University.

Rebecca A. Baltzer is Professor of Musicology at the University of Texas, Austin.

THE DIVINE OFFICE
IN THE LATIN MIDDLE AGES

Frontispiece: A sainted bishop and two clerics copying, beginning Jerome's general prologue to the Old Testament. Plate from f.1r of Beinecke MS. 206, a Northern French Bible from the late thirteenth century. Published with the permission of the Beinecke Rare Book and Manuscript Library, Yale University.

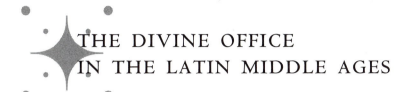

THE DIVINE OFFICE
IN THE LATIN MIDDLE AGES

Methodology and Source Studies,
Regional Developments,
Hagiography

Written in Honor of Professor Ruth Steiner

Edited by

MARGOT E. FASSLER

REBECCA A. BALTZER

OXFORD
UNIVERSITY PRESS

2000

OXFORD

UNIVERSITY PRESS

Oxford   New York
Athens   Auckland   Bangkok   Bogotá   Buenos Aires   Calcutta
Cape Town   Chennai   Dar es Salaam   Delhi   Florence   Hong Kong   Istanbul
Karachi   Kuala Lumpur   Madrid   Melbourne   Mexico City   Mumbai
Nairobi   Paris   São Paulo   Singapore   Taipei   Tokyo   Toronto   Warsaw

and associated companies in
Berlin   Ibadan

Published by Oxford University Press, Inc.
198 Madison Avenue, New York, New York 10016

Oxford is a registered trademark of Oxford University Press

Library of Congress Cataloging-in-Publication Data
The Divine Office in the Latin Middle Ages : methodology and source
studies, regional developments, hagiography : written in honor of
Professor Ruth Steiner / edited by Margot E. Fassler
and Rebecca A. Baltzer.
p.   cm.
Includes bibliographical references and index.
ISBN 0-19-512453-7
1. Church music—Catholic Church—500–1400.   2. Divine office.
3. Divine office (Music)—History and criticism.   I. Steiner, Ruth.
II. Fassler, Margot Elsbeth.   III. Baltzer, Rebecca A. (Rebecca Anne), 1940–   .
ML3080.D58   2000
264'.02015'0902—DC21   99-19507

9 8 7 6 5 4 3 2 1

Printed in the United States of America
on acid-free paper

This volume is dedicated to Ruth Steiner, in gratitude for her scholarship and her generous spirit, which have shaped not just this book but the field of chant studies as a whole.

Preface

Having catalogued the several hours of the Divine Office, supplying scriptural justifications for each of them, Basil the Great spoke of the importance of rendering daily praise at set times throughout the day:

> Not one of these times is to be overlooked by those who have earnestly dedicated their lives to the glory of God and Christ himself. Moreover I think it useful to have diversity and variety in the prayer and psalmody at these appointed times, because somehow the soul is frequently bored and distracted by routine, which by change and variety of the psalmody and prayer at each hour its desire is renewed and its concentration restored. (*MECL*, 68)

The quotation begins with the warning that "not one of these times is to be overlooked," and they were not: for over one thousand years every monk, nun, canon, or friar in the Christian West sang some form of the hours of daily prayer; through books of hours and other devotional materials, the Office was brought to the laity in later centuries as well. To be "a religious" meant, first and foremost, to be a person who joined in formal and set communal prayer, the *opus dei,* which was at the heart of the monastic vocation and incumbent upon clerics as well. The fear of boredom Basil mentions was an ever-present problem for those who prayed the Office: medievals not only were attentive to the psalmody that is basic communal Christian prayer, they embroidered it with thousands upon thousands of new texts and chants, not only in the Carolingian period, but long after. All these readings, prayers, chants, and chant texts were preserved in codices from the tenth century onward, making the production of Office books a major activity of scriptoria throughout the Middle Ages, and often calling upon the creativity of illuminators and calligraphers as well, for the books ranged from the rude to the deluxe. The Office was not only central to medieval modes of religious life, it was also a subject of perpetual and powerful influence upon exegetes and theologians, who were familiar with the Bible through the ways of organizing and presenting Scripture and scriptural commentary found in the Office. It is not to be wondered at that large numbers of medieval authors included commentaries upon the Office in their writings; beyond these, as the art, drama, and poetry of the Middle Ages demonstrate, the medieval imagination itself was shaped by the performance style and content of the Office.

Any debate about the centrality of the Office to defining life and learning in the Middle Ages would be easy to win. Yet surprisingly, the Office has been very little studied in our own age, and this in spite of the great explosion of scholarly work on the medieval period in this century. The Office is, when one considers the Latin West at least, the last great relatively unexplored frontier. Liturgiologists in this century have not been particularly interested in the Latin Middle Ages, but have tended to concentrate on the early Christian period, finding there the best models for the restoration of public prayer in contemporary churches. For medievalists in disciplines besides musicology, the very "diversity and variety" of the subject have made it seem dauntingly difficult. Yet there is nothing that better embodies the paradoxical culture of the Latin Middle Ages: its stable consistency, and at the same time its ferment, regional diversity, and penchant for change.

This volume attempts to draw students of the Middle Ages, both scholars and nonspecialists, more deeply into this vast, little-explored terrain, demonstrating something of the broad dimensions of the territory and of the tools and methods used to chart it, and pointing to the several kinds of knowledge that can be gained from its study. Our book falls into five parts, each of which coheres around a particular period, aspect of the Office, or theme. The opening section forms a two-part introduction to the volume. The first chapter explores the variety of materials used to form the Office in the Carolingian period and explains how to use them; the second chapter presents some of the thorny problems scholars encounter when attempting to "read an Office book." It is easy to be fooled, and scholars must often consult several representatives of a single tradition for the best answers to certain questions. The second section of the book contains three chapters on the pre-Carolingian Office. Because the problems encountered when dealing with early Offices are very different from those met in the later Middle Ages, they need to be approached with special tools. James McKinnon's chapter focuses on the kinds of work that need to be done and are being done, concentrating on the first centuries. The next two chapters deal with the period immediately after this.

The rest of the book is primarily concerned with the tenth century and later. These chapters have been divided into four sections, each of which represents a vital field of current research; in every case, the opening chapter will form a kind of introduction to the section as a whole. The first of these parts has to do with sources—the manuscripts, their contents and natures—and it points to several of the ways they are commonly used to study the texts and music of the Office. The second concentrates on regional developments and variations, moving between the Office and the Mass, and the ways in which the Office related to other ceremonies and musical repertories. Some chapters in this section demonstrate the importance of establishing contexts for materials found in the Office, given that they so often reach beyond the confines of the *opus dei* and the choir. (The phrase *opus dei* is discussed in the appendix to Benedict of Nursia, ed. Frye, 105–6.) In the third section we present a collective argument for the centrality of Office sources to the study of medieval hagiography. Christian communities knew the saints primarily through the Office, for it was there, even more than in the Mass, that liturgical materials were particularized and individual *vitae* shaped for communal celebration. The propers of the Mass were standardized: tropes and sequences, although far more malleable, usually belonged to regional traditions; but the Office varied community by community, in at least some of its aspects. The concluding section of the book highlights the technological advances made in recent decades in handling the enormous amount of surviving evidence surrounding the medieval Office and its praxis. New tools only recently developed hold keys never before available for unlocking the treasure chest of the Divine Office.

Ruth Steiner has been the great pioneer in driving the scholarly community toward the collaboration necessary for successful study of this boundless and complicated subject, her zeal for this work coming of age alongside electronic databases and the World Wide Web. It is she who has, almost single-handedly at first, led the way for chant scholars worldwide to contribute their own indexes and studies to the cumulative effort, and in some cases to launch projects of their own. Through CANTUS, the database she established with her students at the Catholic University of America, detailed inventories of over 40 manuscripts deliberately chosen from a variety of uses and geographic regions are now "on line," their contents available throughout the globe to any scholar who knows enough about the Divine Office to use them profitably. The CANTUS project, which recently moved from the Catholic University of America to the University of Western Ontario, where it is headed by Terence Bailey, shows the genius Steiner has for creating an open-ended collaborative project, which would not stop with the work of a single generation.

Many of us who acknowledge a great debt to Ruth Steiner in our scholarly work were trained, as was she, as musicologists, and have grown used to CANTUS and the opportunities it and other electronic tools offer, and the potential for scaling even greater heights in the future. With this book, we hope to introduce a wider range of scholars to these materials, and also to promote the study of the Divine Office among scholars of every discipline in medieval studies, for it pertains immediately to every subject, from art history, to canon law, to biblical studies and hermeneutics, to gender studies and historiography. Finding ways of studying it with ever greater sophistication will be up to each discipline, but it is satisfying to report that significant new tools necessary for beginning the work are now available.

The many students who worked with Professor Steiner at the Catholic University of America for over a decade were her helpmates in the beginning of a collaborative dream that has since become virtual reality. In order to use CANTUS, and to read this book, it is essential that a readily accesssible plan of the Office be available. Yet it is difficult to capture such a complex and varying structure in a simple series of charts. Lila Collamore, one of the most experienced members of Steiner's team at the Catholic University, has generously supplied a set of plans that are keyed to the workings of CANTUS, and which form a part of her own forthcoming publication on how to use CANTUS and structure files for it. We are most grateful to her for sharing this part of her work, and providing information that forms a fitting introduction both for the reader and for a book dedicated to Ruth Steiner.

N.B.: All biblical citations follow the Vulgate.

New Haven, Connecticut   M. E. F.
Austin, Texas   R. A. B.
In festo annuntiationis BMV, 1999

Acknowledgments

This book has taken years to edit and produce, as might be expected of a complicated work by an international team of authors, each of whom has striven in her or his own way to write about a highly technical subject for medievalists who are not necessarily trained in liturgy and musicology. Our first debt is to the authors: for their painstaking work, for their patience with the editors, and for their unfailing love of the subject. The various stages of production were dependent upon the resources of the Yale Institute of Sacred Music, the Yale Divinity School and its library, and the School of Music and libraries of the University of Texas at Austin; we are grateful for the support of these institutions. The numerous musical examples for this volume were all prepared and edited by Rebecca Baltzer. Ruth Steiner, the dedicatee of this book, has served as an able consultant upon several occasions, and we are grateful for her advice and support.

We especially thank John Leinenweber, research fellow at Yale Divinity School, whose work on the bibliography, notes, and indexes has been exemplary, and Gale Pollen, senior administrative assistant at the Yale Insitute of Sacred Music, who has worked on formatting and other clerical details throughout. We are grateful for the assistance of those scholars who prepared translations and redactions: Susan Boynton, Barbara Haggh, Lori Kruckenberg, and Philip Zimmermann. Harry Attridge of Yale Divinity School helped with the several printings and formattings of the bibliography. Extensive editorial work was supported by grants from other institutions, and so we offer thanks to the Mellon Foundation and to the Institute for Advanced Study, Princeton. Early versions of some chapters were presented in May 1994, in a group of four sessions on the Office organized through the auspices of the International Congress on Medieval Studies sponsored by the Medieval Institute of Western Michigan University. We thank all who took part in these sessions and contributed to our initial conversations about the book.

We are grateful for the advice and support of Maribeth Payne, music editor at Oxford University Press, who has shepherded the project since its conception, and for the editorial skills and keen intellect of Bonnie Blackburn who, as copyeditor, helped immensely with the final stages of production.

The frontispiece is printed with the permission of the Beinecke Library at Yale University; we also acknowledge the permission to print other photographs given by the British Library and the Bibliothèque nationale de France.

Contents

List of Illustrations

List of Tables

List of Musical Examples

Contributors

Wulf Arlt is professor of music at the University of Basel. From 1971 to 1978 he was director of the Schola Cantorum Basiliensis. His publications have focused on questions of genre and the interrelation of music and text and include important sources of medieval music in facsimile, and he has collaborated with Dominique Vellard on recordings of medieval music. His edition of the Le Puy Circumcision Office is in preparation.

Terence Bailey is professor of musicology at the University of Western Ontario in London, Ont. He has written a number of books and articles on the early medieval liturgy and on ecclesiastical chant, most of them concerned with the Ambrosian rite of Milan. He is a Fellow of the Royal Society of Canada.

Rebecca A. Baltzer, professor of musicology at the University of Texas, Austin, has published studies on the music, manuscripts, theory, and musical culture of the Notre-Dame School and the Ars Antiqua. She edited vol. 5 of the *Magnus Liber Organi* edition (1995) and is editing the liturgy and music for two complete medieval feast-days at Notre-Dame of Paris.

Gunilla Björkvall received her Ph.D. from Stockholm University, where she is senior lecturer in Latin. She is involved in editions of medieval Latin liturgical tropes and prosulas within the *Corpus Troporum* project, and is presently editing Latin versus from twelfth-century France. She is also involved in an interdisciplinary project with Andreas Haug on early medieval verse and music.

James Boyce, O.Carm. received his Ph.D. in Historical Musicology from New York University. Ten of his published articles on Carmelite liturgy and chant have recently been collected into a book entitled *Praising God in Carmel: Studies in Car-*

melite Liturgy (1999). He teaches in the department of art history and music at Fordham University in New York.

Lila Collamore is the course director of the program in chant performance at the Irish World Music Centre, University of Limerick. As a graduate student at the Catholic University of America she was part of the CANTUS team under the direction of Ruth Steiner; many of her publications have been connected with this project. Her doctoral dissertation concerns Office manuscripts from southern France and Spain.

László Dobszay is chief member of the Hungarian Academy of Sciences Institute for Musicology and professor at the Liszt Ferenc Music Academy (University) in Budapest. Among his publications are *Catalogue of Hungarian Folksong Types* (1990, with J. Szendrei), *Corpus Antiphonalium Officii Ecclesiarum Centralis Europae* (1988, 1990), *A History of Hungarian Music* (1993), *Handbook of Gregorian Chant* (1993), *After Kodály* (1993), and *The History of Congregational Hymnody in Hungary* (1995).

Joseph Dyer teaches music history at the University of Massachusetts, Boston. His special interest is the liturgy and music of Rome during the Middle Ages. He has published on a variety of medieval topics: Old Roman chant, monasticism, the singing of psalms, medieval performance practice, and chant theory in the Carolingian period and the thirteenth century.

Margot Fassler is the Robert S. Tangeman Professor of Music History and director of the Institute of Sacred Music at Yale University. Her numerous publications include *Gothic Song: The Victorine Sequences and Augustinian Reform in Twelfth-Century Paris* (1993) and *Making History at Chartres: The Virgin's Cult in Liturgy and Art, and the Sense of the Past* (forthcoming). She is writing a book on Hildegard of Bingen.

James Grier is professor of music history at the University of Western Ontario in London, Ont. He is the author of numerous studies of music and liturgy in eleventh- and twelfth-century Aquitaine, and *The Critical Editing of Music: History, Method, and Practice* (1996).

Barbara Haggh is associate professor of music at the University of North Texas. She has written on the history of medieval sacred music, music theory, and music in late medieval towns, and has edited Marian offices by Guillaume Du Fay and for the order of the Golden Fleece, and music for St Elizabeth of Hungary.

Andreas Haug received his Ph.D. from the University of Tübingen. Formerly lecturer and director of the Bruno-Stäblein-Archiv at the University of Erlangen-Nürnberg, in 1999 he became professor at the Center for Medieval Studies at the University of Trondheim. He is the author of numerous studies, mainly on medieval music.

David Hiley received his Ph.D. from King's College, University of London, and is professor of music at Regensburg University. He is author of numerous studies of medieval plainchant, in particular of English chant traditions, and has edited several facsimiles of chant manuscripts. His *Western Plainchant: A Handbook* appeared in 1993.

Andrew Hughes has degrees from Oxford and is currently a university professor at the University of Toronto and first vice-president of the Mediaeval Academy of America. He has produced bibliographies and editions of medieval music; electronic databases, videotapes, and texts relating to the medieval liturgy and its manuscripts, including *Medieval Manuscripts for Mass and Office* and *Late Medieval Liturgical Offices.*

Michel Huglo taught at the Université Libre de Bruxelles from 1973 to 1987 and is emeritus director of research at the CNRS, Paris. He is the author of *Les Tonaires* and *Les Processionaux manuscrits* (RISM B/XIV/1, forthcoming) and numerous studies on medieval chant, theory and theorists, and early polyphony.

Gunilla Iversen is professor of Latin in the department of classical languages at Stockholm University. In the *Corpus Troporum* she has edited tropes to the Proper and Ordinary chants of the medieval Mass. She has published numerous studies on medieval liturgical poetry, drama, and Hildegard of Bingen. Her study *Chanter avec les anges: Poésie dans la messe médiévale* (2000) is in press.

Ritva Maria Jacobsson is a professor in the Institute of French and Italian at Stockholm University. A Latinist and a liturgist, she has published versified Offices, tropes, and sequences, and is the founder of the *Corpus Troporum* project. She is also a peace and human rights activist.

Peter Jeffery, professor of music at Princeton University, is author of *Re-Envisioning Past Musical Cultures: Ethnomusicology in the Study of Gregorian Chant* (1992) and *A New Commandment: Toward a Renewed Rite for the Washing of the Feet* (1992), co-author (with Kay Kaufman Shelemay) of *Ethiopian Christian Liturgical Chant: An Anthology* (1993–97), and editor of *The Study of Medieval Chant: Paths and Bridges, East and West* (forthcoming).

Lora Matthews received her Ph.D. from the University of Western Ontario and teaches in the School of Cultural Studies, Carleton University, and the music department of the University of Ottawa. Her work includes articles on Johann Kuhnau's rhetoric and seventeenth- and eighteenth-century sacred music, on Josquin Desprez and music in Milan in the late fifteenth century, and a book on the latter, co-authored with Paul Merkley.

James W. McKinnon was Richard H. Fogel Professor of Music at the University of North Carolina, Chapel Hill. His books include *Music in Early Christian Literature* (1987), *Antiquity and the Middle Ages* (ed., 1990), *The Early Christian Period and the Latin Middle Ages* (ed., 1998), *The Temple, the Church Fathers and Early Western Chant* (1998), and *The Advent Project: The Later Seventh-Century Creation of the Roman Mass Proper* (2000). He died in early 1999.

Paul A. Merkley received his Ph.D. from Harvard University and is a professor in the music department of the University of Ottawa. He has written books on tonaries, Ambrosian chant, and most recently he has published articles on Josquin Desprez and co-authored a book with Laura Matthews on music in Milan in the late fifteenth century.

Hartmut Möller received his Ph.D. from Mainz University, Germany, and is professor of music at the Staatliche Hochschule für Musik, Freiburg. He is the author of studies of medieval music and of contemporary music, including *Die Musik des Mittelalters* (1991; Neues Handbuch der Musikwissenschaft, vol. 2) and *The Zwiefalten Antiphoner: A CANTUS Index* (1996).

Susan Rankin read music at Cambridge University, taking her doctorate there with a dissertation on medieval liturgical drama. She is reader in medieval music at Cambridge University and a fellow of Emmanuel College. Publications on a variety of monophonic and polyphonic medieval repertories include the jointly authored (with Wulf Arlt) study and facsimile *Stiftsbibliothek St. Gallen 484 und 381* (1996).

Anne Walters Robertson received her Ph.D. from Yale University and is professor of music at the University of Chicago. She has written on medieval music and its liturgical, architectural, and philosophical contexts, including *The Service Books of the Royal Abbey of Saint-Denis: Images of Ritual and Music in the Middle Ages* (1991).

Janka Szendrei, Ph.D., is a professor at Liszt Ferenc Music University and head of department in the Hungarian Academy of Sciences Institute for Musicology in Budapest. Her publications include *Notated Manuscripts of Medieval Hungary* (1981), *The History of Hungarian Chant Notations* (1983), *Catalogue of Hungarian Folksong Types* (1990, with L. Dobszay), *Graduale Strigoniense s. XV/XVI* (2 vols., 1990–1993), and 40 recordings as conductor of the Schola Hungarica.

Craig Wright received his Ph.D. from Harvard University and is professor of the history of music at Yale University. Among his numerous studies of medieval and Renaissance music and musicians are *Music at the Court of Burgundy: 1364–1419* (1979) and *Music and Ceremony at Notre Dame of Paris, 500–1550* (1989).

THE DIVINE OFFICE
IN THE LATIN MIDDLE AGES

Prelude

Charting the Divine Office

LILA COLLAMORE

Saint Benedict opens chapter 16 of his rule with a quote from the book of Psalms: "septies in die laudem dixi tibi" ("Seven times a day have I praised you"; Ps. 118:164). The Divine Office forms a continuous cycle of daily prayer, sacred reading, and meditation in the life of the church.[1] This cycle never ends—the Office from one day leads without a break into the Office of the next. Each day has eight hours: Matins (or Vigils, now known as the Office of Readings or the Night Office), Lauds, Prime, Terce, Sext, None, Vespers, and Compline:

Hour	Time celebrated	Clock time for 21 March
Matins	the eighth hour of the night	2:00 A.M.
Lauds	daybreak	about 5:30 A.M.
Prime	the first hour of the day	6:00 A.M.
Terce	the third hour of the day	9:00 A.M.
Sext	the sixth hour of the day	12:00 noon
None	the ninth hour of the day	3:00 P.M.
Vespers	before dark	about 5:30 P.M.
Compline	before retiring	

Note: The Romans divided the day and the night into twelve unequal hours each. Consequently, the length of the hour depends on the length of the day (or night). At Rome (lat. 41°54′ N), an hour ranges from 45 to 75 minutes in length.

The daily Office may follow either the monastic cursus or the Roman cursus. (The monastic cursus is that used in monastic communities, especially those that follow the Rule of St. Benedict.) The Roman cursus is used in cathedrals, secular and parochial churches, and by some religious orders, such as the friars and canons, and is also known as the secular cursus, the cathedral cursus, or the canons' cursus. The main elements of the Office are the same in both cursus, but the number and arrangement of these elements is different.

3

On Sundays and major feasts,[2] the Office (and its cycle of proper chants) begins with Vespers on the eve of the feast (known as First Vespers), continues through Vespers on the day of the feast (Second Vespers), and ends with Compline. The most important feasts also include a celebration on the Octave (the day a week after the feast), within the Octave, and so on. Feasts of this rank take the festal form of Matins, with nine or twelve lessons and the Te deum to mark their dignity.

Feasts next in importance are celebrated from Matins to Compline on the day of the feast. This Office also takes the festal form. Less important feasts have Matins in the ferial format, a shortened version of the hour with only one nocturn with lessons. (The more important of these in the Roman cursus include the Te deum in Matins.) The least important saints are commemorated only with a Memorial. On days on which no feast falls (that is, no feast that is celebrated with part of the regular Office), the Ferial Office is sung.[3] Weekdays of the Ferial Office are celebrated from Matins (in the ferial format) to Compline.

In addition to the regular Office, there are other hours that fall outside the formal Office cycle: in practice, these do not displace the daily Office, but may be celebrated in addition to it. Some of these Offices are identical in structure to the regular Office (such as the Office of the Dead), others are variants (the Little Hours of the Virgin; see chap. 20 below), or scaled-down versions (Memorials).

Sundays and major feast days usually have a fairly complete set of proper chants from First Vespers through Second Vespers. Lesser feasts have proper chants for only part of this cycle, with the rest supplied from the Commons or the Ferial Office. An antiphoner includes such proper chants as antiphons, responsories, and versicles; a breviary also includes hymns, readings, and prayers. Those elements that are unchanging (such as the blessings at each reading of Matins, and the opening and closing versicles at each hour) are rarely included in these books, and for the most part are omitted from this discussion.

Matins

Matins is the longest hour and, along with Lauds and Vespers, the most important musically. Matins has three parts: the opening; a middle section consisting of one to three nocturns; and a closing section. The opening section is invariable (opening versicles, invitatory, and hymn), with a few exceptions.[4] The nocturns vary in number and structure depending on the cursus, the rank of the feast, and the time of year, as does the structure of the closing section. The festal form of Matins is used on Sundays and major feast days. The ferial form is used for lesser feasts, or on weekdays on which no feast falls.

A festal Roman Matins includes three nocturns of equal structure, thus: three antiphons with psalms (indicated by the psalm incipit), a versicle, and three lessons, each followed by a great responsory. Lessons are readings drawn from Scripture, the Lives of the Saints, or some other suitable source. The last responsory of a nocturn has the *Gloria patri* (the lesser doxology) as a second verse.

Festal Matins in the monastic cursus also has an opening section, three nocturns, and a closing section, but apart from the opening section it differs in structure from the Roman version. The first and second nocturns contain six antiphons with psalms, and four lessons and responsories. The third nocturn contains a single antiphon sung with three Old Testament canticles, followed by four lessons and responsories.

The nocturn in festal Matins

	Roman cursus	Monastic cursus	Monastic cursus
		first and second nocturn	third nocturn
1	antiphon + psalm	antiphon + psalm	antiphon + 3 Old Testament canticles
2	antiphon + psalm	antiphon + psalm	
3	antiphon + psalm	antiphon + psalm	
4		antiphon + psalm	
5		antiphon + psalm	
6		antiphon + psalm	
	versicle	versicle	versicle
1	lesson	lesson	lesson
	responsory	responsory	responsory
2	lesson	lesson	lesson
	responsory	responsory	responsory
3	lesson	lesson	lesson
	responsory	responsory	responsory
4		lesson	lesson
		responsory	responsory

The ferial form of Matins is less elaborate and lengthy than festal Matins. Roman ferial Matins is shortened by reducing the number of nocturns and the amount of material in each nocturn. The three nocturns are reduced to one, which has six antiphons rather than three, sung with twelve psalms.[5]

Matins of the Roman cursus

	Festal format	Ferial format
opening section	v. *Deus in adjutorium* invitatory + Ps. 94 hymn	v. *Deus in adjutorium* invitatory + Ps. 94 hymn
first nocturn	3 antiphons + 3 psalms versicle 3 lessons + 3 responsories	6 antiphons + 12 psalms versicle 3 lessons + 3 responsories
second nocturn	3 antiphons + 3 psalms versicle	3 lessons + 3 responsories
third nocturn	3 antiphons + 3 psalms versicle 3 lessons + 3 responsories	
closing section	Te deum collect v. *Dominus vobiscum* v. *Benedicamus dominus* v. *Fidelium animae*	collect v. *Dominus vobiscum* v. *Benedicamus dominus* v. *Benedicamus dominus* v. *Fidelium animae* Versicle[7]

Note: The collect, a prayer also known as the oration (*oratio*), is in practice preceded by the versicle *Dominus vobiscum*.

Monastic ferial Matins omits the entire third nocturn, and the lessons and responsories of the second nocturn. The first nocturn is shortened to only three lessons and responsories. The alleluia antiphon of the second nocturn (sung to the melody of one of the texted antiphons provided for that nocturn), is used with all of the psalms of that nocturn. The three texted antiphons replace the alleluia antiphon during Lent; as Lent is a penitential season, the word "alleluia" is avoided.[6]

Matins of the monastic cursus

	Festal format	Ferial format
opening section	v. *Deus in adjutorium* invitatory + Ps. 94 hymn	v. *Deus in adjutorium* invitatory + Ps. 94 hymn
first nocturn	6 antiphons + 6 psalms versicle 4 lessons + 4 responsories	3 antiphons + 6 psalms versicle 3 lessons + 3 responsories
second nocturn	6 antiphons + 6 psalms versicle 4 lessons + 4 responsories	Alleluia antiphon (3 antiphons in Lent) + 6 psalms chapter versicle
third nocturn	antiphons + 3 canticles versicle 4 lessons + 4 responsories	
closing section	Te deum Gospel *Te decet laus*	
		Kyrie
	collect	collect
	v. *Dominus vobiscum*	v. *Dominus vobiscum*
	v. *Benedicamus domino*	v. *Benedicamus domino*
	v. *Fidelium animae*	v. *Fidelium animae*

The night is longer in winter than in summer, allowing more time for Matins without loss of daylight hours for work. In the summer season, from Easter to 1 November, the hour is further abbreviated in the monastic cursus: the first nocturn is shortened by replacing the three lessons and great responsories with a chapter (a short reading from Scripture) and short responsory.[8]

Weekday ferial Matins of both the monastic and Roman cursus normally has two psalms with each antiphon. In the monastic cursus, however, a "psalm" may be only a portion of an actual psalm, as the Rule of Benedict divides the larger psalms into two or more sections for liturgical use. The monastic Ferial Office also has some variations in the standard numbers of antiphons in each hour. On Monday and Thursday, the first nocturn of Matins has four antiphons rather than three.[9]

The Te deum (*Hymnum Ambrosianum*) is sung in Matins on Sundays and major feasts, and on weekdays during Christmas Time and Paschal Time to mark the joyfulness of those seasons. It is omitted during Advent and from Septuagesima through Easter Eve except on saints' days.

A distinctive feature of Paschal Time (*tempore paschale,* or T.P.) is the substitution of the word "alleluia" for the text of an antiphon. When this is the case, rather than having a series of three or more antiphons, all with the text "alleluia," it is common to find only one antiphon intended to be used with all the psalms of a nocturn (or for all the psalms of Lauds or Vespers). "Alleluia" is also added to the end of chants, or at the ends of the phrases within a chant. Matins of Easter Sunday, Easter Week, and Pentecost Sunday have only one nocturn.

Lauds

Lauds
v. *Deus in adjutorium*
1 antiphon + psalm
2 antiphon + psalm
3 antiphon + psalm
4 antiphon + Old Testament canticle
5 antiphon + psalm
chapter
responsory
hymn
versicle
antiphon + Benedictus
(the Canticle of Zacharias; Luke 1:68–79)
collect
v. *Dominus vobiscum*
v. *Benedicamus domino*
v. *Fidelium animae*

Lauds has the same structure in both the monastic and the Roman cursus. The fourth "psalm" of Lauds is an Old Testament canticle. On Sundays, this is the Canticle of the Three Boys (Dan. 3:57–58, 56), known as the *Benedicite.* Other canticles are used on weekdays. The fifth "psalm" of Lauds consists of Pss. 148, 149, and 150 (known as the *Laudate* psalms) treated as a single psalm with one antiphon. Lauds on Saturday of the monastic Ferial Office lacks the fourth antiphon.[10]

The responsory of Lauds is usually a short responsory; however, on major feast days, the responsory may be a great responsory, often drawn from Matins for that feast. The Roman Ferial Office has no responsories for Lauds and Vespers on weekdays. During Easter Week the Mass Gradual and Alleluia are sung at Lauds and Vespers, and there are Memorials for the Holy Cross and processions to the baptismal font.

After the Gospel Canticle (the Benedictus), *Kyrie eleison* is added on feast days, and on Wednesdays and Fridays during the penitential seasons of Advent and Lent. At Lauds and Vespers, this *Kyrie,* referred to as the preces, normally consists only of the refrain "Kyrie eleison, Christe eleison, Kyrie eleison."

Tenebrae

The three days before Easter—Maundy Thursday, Good Friday, and Holy Saturday—are known together as the *Triduum*. During the *Triduum* there are many
special features in the Office, including the omission of all hymns from Matins on
Maundy Thursday through None on the Saturday after Easter. Matins for the *Triduum* is combined with Lauds and this new service is known as *Tenebrae*. *Tenebrae*
follows the Roman arrangement of the nocturns (even in manuscripts of the monastic cursus). Omitting the opening portion of Matins, *Tenebrae* begins directly
with the first antiphon and psalm of the day. The lessons for the first nocturn on
each day are drawn from the Lamentations of Jeremiah, and are sung to special
tones used only for the Lamentations. From the end of the third nocturn, *Tenebrae*
proceeds directly into the first antiphon and psalm of Lauds. After the psalms of
Lauds, it also departs from the usual form for Lauds. Although local traditions
vary, manuscript S (Silos) of *CAO* concludes the hour with the Benedictus with its
antiphon, followed by the *Kyrie eleison* with the *versus in triduo*.

The Little Hours

The Little Hours of Prime, Terce, Sext, and None

Prime	Terce, Sext, and None
v. *Deus in adjutorium*	v. *Deus in adjutorium*
hymn	hymn
antiphon + 3 or 4	antiphon + 3 psalms
psalms	
chapter	chapter
short responsory	short responsory
versicle	versicle
preces (on some feasts)	
collect	collect
v. *Dominus vobiscum*	v. *Dominus vobiscum*
v. *Benedicamus domino*	v. *Benedicamus domino*
	v. *Fidelium animae*

After the hour as outlined above, Prime continues with the reading of the Martyrology, followed by a series of set versicles, prayers, and other material. On some
Sundays the Athanasian Creed (*Quicumque vult*) is said in Prime after the psalms
but before the repeat of the antiphon. In the Sarum Use a separate antiphon is
provided for the Creed. The preces are said at Prime on some feasts, and consist
of *Kyrie eleison*, various petitions, the Confiteor, and some prayers. They may be
shortened (as in Lauds and Vespers) to the *Kyrie eleison* only.

The "psalms" in the Little Hours are portions of Ps. 118. This psalm consists of
176 verses, divided into 22 sections of eight verses each. Each section is treated in
the Office as a single psalm.

Vespers

Vespers

	Roman cursus	Monastic cursus
	v. *Deus in adjutorium*	v. *Deus in adjutorium*
1	antiphon + psalm	antiphon + psalm
2	antiphon + psalm	antiphon + psalm
3	antiphon + psalm	antiphon + psalm
4	antiphon + psalm	antiphon + psalm
5	antiphon + psalm	
	chapter	chapter
	responsory	responsory
	hymn	hymn
	versicle	versicle
	antiphon + Magnificat	antiphon + Magnificat
	(the Canticle of Mary; Luke 1:46–55)	
	collect	collect
	v. *Dominus vobiscum*	v. *Dominus vobiscum*
	v. *Benedicamus domino*	v. *Benedicamus domino*
	v. *Fidelium animae*	v. *Fidelium animae*

Vespers of the Roman and monastic cursus differ only in the number of psalms (and consequently antiphons): the Roman cursus has five while the monastic cursus has only four.[11] When First Vespers of Easter Sunday follows the Easter Vigil, the dismissal is *Ite missa est,* rather than the usual closing versicles.

As at Lauds, the preces are added at Vespers on Wednesdays and Fridays during Advent and Lent, and on feast days, and the responsory at Vespers may likewise be a great responsory.

Compline

Compline

v. *Deus in adjutorium*
antiphon + 3 psalms
hymn
chapter
short responsory
versicle
antiphon + *Nunc dimittis*
(the Canticle of Simeon; Luke 2:29–32)
preces (on some feasts)
collect
v. *Dominus vobiscum*
v. *Benedicamus domino*
blessing

Compline is preceded by a short lesson and examination of conscience. It is followed by a Memorial to the Blessed Virgin Mary. In the monastic cursus, the three psalms of Compline are the same every day (Pss. 4, 90, and 133); in the Roman cursus the psalms vary according to the day of the week. Compline rarely has proper chants for a feast, although it does have seasonal variations.

Memorials

Memorials are mini-hours that are often attached to the end of Lauds and Vespers, after the collect.[12] A Memorial consists of an antiphon sung without a psalm (or, more rarely, a responsory) followed by a versicle and a collect.

Memorials may occur on specific days, or they may be movable. Fixed-day Memorials are often for a saint whose feast falls on the same day as a more important saint. The more important feast suppresses the Office of the less important saint, reducing it to a Memorial. Memorials may also occur on the days within the Octave following the feast of a very important saint. For example, it is common to find a Memorial for St. Peter on 30 June, which is celebrated as the feast of St. Paul: 29 June is the feast of SS. Peter and Paul, and the next day, when the Office is devoted to Paul, Peter receives a Memorial. Memorials intended to be sung throughout the year are votive offices. Memorials of this type are common for the Virgin Mary, the Holy Cross, All Saints, or a local patron saint.

Notes

1. The arrangement of the elements in the Divine Office is not the same everywhere: the structure presented here is based on the sources that have been indexed by CANTUS. This schema works well for understanding the manuscripts, but it is not complete in detailing the variants among the various uses that do not appear in these sources. For example, the manuscripts only provide a single antiphon to be used with all of the psalms in each of the Little Hours so that the number of psalms intended in the hour is not clear. This text and tables have been adapted from *The CANTUS Algorithm* (Washington, D.C.: Catholic University of America, 1996, rev. 1998), used by permission. This work was carried out as part of the CANTUS Project at the Catholic University of America, under the direction of Ruth Steiner. CANTUS was supported by grants from the Dom Mocquereau Foundation and the National Endowment for the Humanities.

2. Medieval chant manuscripts usually do not indicate the degree of the feast. The modern calendar recognizes four ranks: feasts of the first class (festive) that run from First Vespers to Compline; feasts of the second class (semifestive) that are celebrated from Matins through Compline; feasts of the third class (ordinary) from Matins to Vespers, with the Te deum in Matins but utilizing the ferial Matins format; and ferial days on which no feast falls.

3. The Ferial Office includes Sunday, which is festal in form and runs from First Vespers on Saturday to Compline on Sunday. The chants and prayers of the Ferial Office are sung continuously throughout the year, unless they are replaced by proper chants and prayers for a particular feast.

4. Matins of Epiphany lacks the hymn and, in the Roman cursus, the invitatory. Matins for the Office of the Dead lacks both the hymn (at the opening) and the Te

deum (at the closing), and is arranged according to the Roman cursus, regardless of the cursus of the book.

5. The modern breviary calls for nine psalms with nine antiphons.

6. The Farewell to the Alleluia, a special ceremony that appears on Septuagesima Sunday in some manuscripts, marks the suppression of the word "alleluia" from Septuagesima until Easter. In this ceremony, Matins is distinguished by the use of the word "alleluia" in most of the responsories, and other chants at Vespers, Matins, or Lauds also begin with "alleluia" or consist entirely of repetitions of this word.

7. The exact liturgical position of this versicle is not clear. Usually the manuscripts have no rubrics for this item, but Paris, BNF lat. 15181 and 15182 offer "versus sacerdotum." Cambridge, UL Mm.ii.9 (the Barnwell Antiphoner) is more specific: "Iste versus dicitur in omnibus feriis ante laudes quoniam preces dicuntur nisi adventum et quadragesimam." The most common text of the versicle is "Fiat misericordia tua domine super nos."

8. The short responsory (*responsorium breve*) in summer ferial Matins in the monastic cursus is the only short responsory that ever appears in Matins. All of the other responsories of Matins are great responsories (*responsoria prolixa*).

9. The cursus of psalms for the Ferial Office and the antiphons with which they are sung is laid out in Claire (1975).

10. Two of the sources indexed by CANTUS actually do have an antiphon, "Ignis suc-," for this position in Lauds: Karlsruhe, Landesbibl. Aug. LX, and Florence, Laurenziana, Conv. Sopp. 560.

11. In the monastic Ferial Office, Vespers of Thursday and Friday have three antiphons.

12. Processions have the same form as Memorials but, unlike Memorials, are placed after the end of the hour.

I ✦ A METHODOLOGICAL INTRODUCTION

Sermons, Sacramentaries, and Early Sources for the Office in the Latin West

The Example of Advent

MARGOT E. FASSLER

The Office is daily prayer, rooted in the cyclical changing of light marking out the steady passage of day to night and back again. But days are parts of years, and the Office increasingly, in both the East and the West, contained texts that changed with (were proper to) feasts and seasons. Students of the Office, then, are ever cognizant both of motion through the hours of the day, and through the year, needing to understand not only the development of individual Office hours and their components, but also of the larger rhythms of the calendar. The Christian year unfolded in the Middle Ages in two vast cycles of feasts: the Temporale and the Sanctorale. Feasts "of the time" are those feasts celebrating the coming, birth, life, death, resurrection and ascension of the Messiah, and many of these are movable feasts, dependent upon the calculation of Easter. Feasts of the Sanctorale commemorate the lives of the saints, and although these are all fixed feasts, nonetheless they interact with feasts of the Temporale, and complicated regulations existed by the central Middle Ages for determining what happened when important feasts from one cycle coincided with those of the other.[1] It is no coincidence that there are comparatively few major feasts of the Sanctorale in Lent and Eastertide: because the complexities of daily services would have crowded out or at least minimized the presence of sanctoral feasts celebrated during these times, hagiographers often looked outside of the period from Lent to Ascension when establishing new saints' feasts. Another major difference between feasts of the two cycles is the nature of the Office readings: although lengthy readings from the Bible are prominent in both, often comprising the readings for at least the final nocturn of Matins, readings for feasts of the Temporale are dependent upon sermons, whereas feasts of the Sanctorale draw their readings from both sermons and hagiographical materials.[2] Hence, feasts of the Temporale tend to exhibit less variety than those for the Sanctorale, especially, of course, in regard to saints of local cults.

The subject of this chapter is Advent, the pre-Christmas season, a part of the temporal cycle, and its rise and early development in the West up to the late eighth century.[3] The chapter was written especially for this volume to demonstrate the ways in which liturgical scholars traditionally study the Office and its history, laying out the common source materials, here using Advent as a test case for working with the various kinds of tools and other indexes currently available.[4] The purpose is not only to outline the liturgical significance and early history of Advent in the West, but also to show to nonspecialists how significant problems for research emerge, and the ways scholars acquire a sense of the dimensions of these problems in working with early liturgical materials. There are many works available for introducing researchers to the sources, but few try to show how to use them interactively to define and solve problems. This chapter, then, is as much about using the sources as it is about the sources themselves.

To study the many intricacies of the medieval Office, the scholar needs to look not only at one type of materials, not just at prayers, or not only at chants, or at readings. Medieval Offices were made of every liturgical element: a variety of texts, various genres and layers of music, numerous ceremonies continually evolving with the times, many types of performing forces, from the brilliant to the pedestrian, to choirs of all shapes and sizes. Moreover, Offices unfolded within certain areas of ecclesial space, surrounded by particular kinds of furniture and decorative arts. All these require study from scholars representing a broad range of approaches and disciplines. At the close of this particular exploration, which demonstrates how to use a select number of materials useful for all students of the Office, new questions will be posed for the study of Advent specifically. However, the modes of inquiry presented here would work equally well for any feast or season, depending, of course, upon the state of the sources and of the previous scholarship. This chapter demonstrates the kinds of questions commonly asked of liturgical sources from the period, and what the expectations may be when they are raised.

The fifth through the eighth centuries are the formative period for the Divine Office in the Latin West. Although the centuries under discussion in this chapter have received the least attention in our book, during this period the bulk of the materials from which the medieval Office would be fashioned were created, that is, the sermons and saints' lives, prayers, organized cycles of scriptural readings, and many chant texts and families of melodies as well.[5] The kinds of sources one consults to deepen understanding of the medieval Office depend not only upon the type of feast, but also on chronology and location, with materials being far scarcer in the pre-Carolingian and early Carolingian periods than in later centuries. James McKinnon has outlined in this volume the nature of knowledge concerning assigned Offices of monastic and public prayer from late antiquity, especially in the East, where the Office first developed; Joseph Dyer and Peter Jeffery have consulted early rules and other materials to offer varied pictures of the shapes of early monastic Offices in the West. It has been demonstrated in this work that no matter what the subject, the student of Western liturgical practices begins, however cursorily, in the East, for it is here that most Western feasts, seasons, and liturgical practices had their beginnings.

It comes as something of a surprise, then, to consult the standard sources and find that the liturgies of both Jerusalem and Constantinople have no extensive or highly developed Advent feasts or season. The rise of Christmas as a feast in the late fourth century hastened a development of some sort of Advent in a few regions, but in Jerusalem Christmas developed late, and was not firmly in place until the sixth century.[6] Instead, the feast of Epiphany, a time for revealing and explaining the mysteries of Christ's appearance on earth, rather than the commemoration of the birthday itself, received major emphasis. Even in Constantinople, where Christmas was established by the early fifth century, only the week before the feast formed an Advent of sorts. Readings from the major prophets during the weeks before Christmas/Epiphany were found in the early liturgies of Jerusalem and Constantinople, however, as was the case in early Western pre-Christmas seasons as well.[7]

Extensive Advent cycles are found in both the East Syrian and West Syrian rites, but the actual dates of the establishment of these cycles are difficult to ascertain, especially given that opening leaves in early sources are often later additions.[8] Nonetheless, it enhances understanding to know that both Syrian traditions developed from the fifth through the eleventh centuries, presenting church years beginning with extensive Advent cycles, and that these cycles emphasized the Annunciation. The East Syrian cycle was dominated by Old Testament prophecies concerning the Messiah, and celebrated the multifaceted significance of his coming; the West Syrian cycle followed the New Testament events in chronological order, moving from the Annunciation to Zacharia through that to Mary, the Visitation, Joseph's dream, the birth of the Baptist, and the awaiting of and immediate prediction of Christ's birth. Moolan contrasts the two as follows:

> In summary, then, one may say that the West Syrian tradition, in agreement with the greater emphasis on *historia* over *theoria* noted in Antiochene exegesis and mystagogy, presents the more *historically ordered sequence* of liturgical propers, whereas the East Syrian propers continually revolve around a few basic *theological themes.*[9]

Christmas came early and decisively to Rome, however, being established there in the mid-fourth century, and this provided the occasion for liturgical speculation upon preparation for the birth of the Messiah.[10] In the case of Advent, then—and in this it differs from any other major unit of liturgical time in early medieval Christian practice—one looks as much to the West as to the East for origins and development. This makes the rise of Advent a particularly good subject for a volume on the Office in the West (see esp. Geir Hellemo 1989). The Eastern sources will remain helpful guides for this work, but they do not have the central importance here that they do for investigating other seasons and many other major feasts. Clearly, the Council of Ephesus and the Christological controversies of the late fourth and early fifth centuries placed a new emphasis on Mary and the Annunciation, and this manifested itself in each of the Eastern traditions and in the West as well. In the East, sermons such as those by Proclus of Constantinople established exegesis upon Luke and Isaiah in particular as central to Christian Messianism; some of these discussions were translated into Latin and known in the West.[11] Equally important, however, were the fifth-century sermons written by Western writers, some of whom are well known to us, and others of whom remain anonymous.[12] The work on Advent here will lead directly to the chapters of two other scholars in this volume, Ritva Jacobsson and James Grier, both of whom discuss materials falling in this season, demonstrating the variety to be expected in ninth- and tenth-century sources. This chapter is concerned with the pre-history of the shifting liturgical circumstances that produced this variety.[13]

Early Sermon Literature

There are several bodies of information one uses to understand liturgical development in the West during the early Middle Ages, and choosing among them will depend upon the topic and the particular questions addressed. Full explanation will require examination of sermons and other exegetical literature, the proclamations of church councils, hagiographical writings, and liturgical books themselves, with the greatest importance assigned to lectionaries, sacramentaries, homiliaries, and ordinals.[14] Ultimately, one must work simultaneously with many groups of materials, playing one against the other, and this process makes the work complicated, but also, ultimately, rewarding. In an introductory study such as this, it will only do to lay out the materials genre by genre, choosing those deemed central to the subject at hand. Many types of liturgical practices flourished side by side in the West before the Carolingian reforms; it is not to be wondered at that the evidence remaining is contradictory. The process of standardization taking place north of the Alps and familiar to us from the ninth century forward was not known for the most part in earlier times, even in Rome itself, where there is evidence that competing traditions functioned simultaneously.[15]

Once the usual review of the secondary literature has been made and the preliminary consultation of select Eastern sources carried out, the standard place to begin study for any aspect of the Western liturgy is with sermon literature from the fifth and sixth centuries, some of which was arranged in liturgical cycles during the fifth century by Western liturgists, especially men from southern Gaul, and in Rome by the late sixth century.[16] The poverty of early sources is less keenly felt because significant preachers from the era were sometimes liturgical preachers, who deliberately mentioned texts delivered during the day, and who, in preparing their words for specific occasions, expressed their attitudes toward individual feasts and seasons.[17] Because the preachers introduced here were so well respected in later centuries, it became common to write new works in their names, or to ascribe unidentified works to them, thus making problems in dating and attribution especially keen. Only critical editions of many fifth- and sixth-century sermon writers have helped solve these pseudepigraphical difficulties. Although many problems remain in need of solution, the work of modern editors has contributed to liturgical studies immensely, given that much research in early periods depends directly upon sermon literature, especially as it found its way into liturgical homiliaries. In addition, the great number of critical editions found in the series Corpus Christianorum can be explored with keyword and other searches useful for monitoring changes in common liturgical topoi.[18] Sermons written in the fifth and sixth centuries are not only important, then, for the evidence they contain about these centuries themselves. They also are the foundation upon which all future liturgical development took place, especially in the Office, where readings from early sermon literature shaped feasts and seasons as they were introduced in later periods.

Augustine's teacher Ambrose wrote several series of sermons that provide crucial information for understanding attitudes toward various liturgical themes and toward the sacraments. His exegesis did not, however, provoke the mentioning of specific chant texts and readings to the degree found in Augustine's homiletic literature, and so has not been as extensively mined by liturgical historians as has that of his famous disciple. Ambrose's exposition on the Gospel of Luke, a central exegetical text throughout the Middle Ages, treats the subjects of Advent and Nativity in its opening chapters (as the Lucan account was central to the liturgical sense of these events); excerpts from this commentary came to play a role in medieval homiliaries at Advent, especially those days of the season where incarnational themes were emphasized.[19]

Ambrose's sermons and exegetical treatises were major sources for the writings of Maximus of Turin, who died sometime between 408 and 423, and who wrote many short sermons later anthologized in medieval homiliaries. Until recently his work had been difficult to sort out: there were two bishops Maximus in Turin during the fifth century, and our author is apparently the earlier of the two; much has been attributed to Maximus that he did not write and many of his own works were long assigned to other authors. The new edition of Maximus by Mutzenbecher in the Corpus Christianorum has put the identification of this author and his writings on surer ground.[20] At least for now it seems that his three pre-Christmas sermons do indeed demonstrate a sense of the season in early fifth-century northern Italy; it is clear from the texts themselves that they form a small cycle of cross-referenced works. The first of them makes parallels between the birthday of a secular ruler, with all its lavish trappings, and the various purifications fitting as preparation for the birthday of the Lord. The Gospel text referred to in the sermon is Matt. 22, the parable of the wedding feast. In Maximus' treatment, the wretch without a proper garment is likened to a person who has not lived rightly, not only in fasting and prayer, but also in charity toward others. The second sermon refers strongly and three times to Matt. 11:12, enough for us to claim that this, and surrounding verses, probably comprised the Gospel of the day. Hence we find reference here to the Forerunner, John the Baptist. The third sermon was preached very soon before Christmas, and in it Maximus made reference to the approaching equinox, and the gradual lengthening of the light:

> the extreme conclusion of the cycle of days has anticipated my preaching. For by this very brevity the world tells us that something is about to happen by which it will be restored to a better state, and with increasing longing it wishes for the brilliance of the shining sun to cast light on its darkness. While it dreads to have its course come to an end because of the shortness of the hours, it shows by a kind of hope that its year is to be formed anew.[21]

The sermons of Augustine, perhaps to an extent because of his own proclivities and acknowledged sensitivity to music, often mention the texts sung or intoned, and have been a goldmine for generations of liturgical scholars. He has no sermons for an Advent season—as there must not have been one in early fifth-century northern Africa. In his Christmas and Epiphany sermons, however, one finds themes concerning the paradox of divinity mixed with human flesh that dominate in comparable exegesis in the East as well:

> Christ has been born: as God of the Father, as man of His mother; of the immortality of His Father, of the virginity of His mother; of His Father without a mother, of His mother without a father; of His Father as the beginning of life, of His mother as the end of death; of His Father as the Ruler of all days, of His mother as the Sanctifier of this day. (*Sermons,* no. 12, p. 121)

Augustine's Christmas and Easter sermons were sources for authors who did compose for the pre-Christmas season, including Caesarius of Arles and numerous later exegetes. Of particular importance for the developing character of the Christmas vigil in the later Middle Ages was the tract "Contra Judaos, Paganos et Arianos" by Augustine's disciple the Carthaginian Quodvultdeus. This was a Western response to the triumph of Ephesus and Chalcedon and an indictment of Arianism.[22] Many other sermons written in northern Africa in the fifth century were also of major importance, as will be seen later in this chapter, in the development of Western sermon cycles that made up the Office readings. The bulk of these sermons, usually ascribed to Augustine in the Middle Ages, is, by and large, still without secure attribution, but they testify to the central role of north African churchmen upon the development of feasts and seasons in the Western, and especially in the Roman, liturgy.

Among Augustine's near contemporaries, Pope Leo I is of special importance. His sermons survive in a series of annual cycles, which scholars have dated with some precision. A small group preached for the Ember Days of December provide interpretations of the liturgical period before Christmas.[23] Leo's sermons emphasize a time of fasting and charity before Christmas, and selections from these works can be found in the medieval Advent Office in various guises, with the passage below from the Roman breviary as an example.[24] An early compiler of the text has reshaped the sermon passage to emphasize the coming of the Lord in the opening sentence:

> Let every man then make himself ready against the coming of the Lord, so that He may not find him making his belly his god, or the world his chief care. Dearly beloved brethren, it is a matter of everyday experience that fulness of drink dulleth the keenness of the mind, and that excess of eating unnerveth the strength of the will. The very stomach protesteth that gluttony doth harm to the bodily health, unless temperance get the better of desire, and the thought of the indigestion afterward check the indulgence of the moment.[25]

Peter Chrysologus, bishop of Ravenna and a contemporary of Leo I, wrote several sermons that develop themes of advent and incarnation, although in a less complicated exegesis than is found in the East. His emphasis on the Virgin and the long-awaited coming into human flesh suggest a fifth-century pre-Christmas feast in honor of the Virgin in Ravenna in the fifth century. Suitbert Benz, in his book-length study of a seventh-century Ravennate sacramentary fragment (which contains only Advent and part of Epiphany), demonstrates the ways in which Chrysologus' ideas were translated into actual liturgical texts (Benz 1967).

Caesarius of Arles, writing across the Alps and two generations after Leo, Peter, and Maximus, does not know the seasonal four periods of fasting celebrated in early fifth-century Rome, and yet he does commemorate in his sermons (three of which were written for a pre-Christmas period) a time of fasting in preparation for the feast of Christmas, known as St. Martin's Lent, which is frequently cited in the literature.[26]

The sermons of Leo and Caesarius show that sufficient liturgical space for Advent had been carved out and that certain themes and biblical passages were established as appropriate to the season. As with Maximus, Caesarius' works are filled with banquet imagery, and urge the proper kinds of preparation needed to meet the bridegroom, to enter the feast when he knocks and calls:

> If an earthly king or the head of a family invited you to his birthday celebration, with what kind of garments would you endeavor to adorn yourself when you approached? Surely with new and shining ones, costly ones whose age or cheapness or ugliness could not offend the eyes of the one who invited you. Therefore, with Christ's help strive as much as you can with a like zeal, so that your soul may with an easy conscience approach the solemn feast of the eternal king, that is, the birthday of our Lord and Savior, if it is adorned with the decoration of various virtues. Let it be adorned with the jewels of simplicity and the flowers of temperance, gleaming chastity, shining charity, and joyful almsgiving. For if Christ the Lord recognizes that you are celebrating His birthday with such dispositions, He Himself will deign to come and not only visit your soul, but also rest and continually dwell in it. As it is written: "I will dwell with them and walk among them," (2 Cor. 6:16); and again, "Here I stand knocking at the door; if anyone rises up and opens the door, I will enter his house and have supper with him, and he with me" (Rev. 3:20). (*Sermons*, 9)

The juxtaposition of ideas of fasting and preparation, when imported into the Advent Office lectionary, dominated as it was by readings from the Prophet Isaiah, would generate yet other meanings for the season. In the fifth century, then, in Gaul and in Rome, and in northern Italy, there was a place for Advent, and, at least in the sermons of Maximus and Caesarius, an emphasis upon preparation for the feast of Christ as the approaching Bridegroom.

The Gospel homilies of Pope Gregory the Great, if they are authentic (as is now believed), present an early view of the stational liturgy in Rome.[27] Although the captions for the sermons must be later additions, and although the precise ordering of the works requires further study, it is clear that there were three distinct sermons for Sundays before the Nativity as well as a sermon for Ember Week in December, and that Advent has received a thematic elaboration in Gregory's homilies not found in Leo or Maximus. Gregory's sermons are commentaries upon the Gospel texts of a specific lectionary; thus the emphases within them arise from the readings themselves. But he elaborates upon these texts to bring forth themes of judgment and the Second Coming, with Advent as a season of preparing to leave the world and its ways behind. These ideas were found as well in Maximus, Leo, and Caesarius, but the fasting and preparation called for were not controlled by tightly drawn parallels between self-denial and the Second Coming. Gregory, who wrote as one century was drawing to a close and another beginning, believed the world was old, tired, and soon to die. The Lord came first in "the fullness of time"; he would return when time was ripe, like a fig tree laden with fruit (see, for example, Homily 3, pp. 17–19). In the homily probably written for the week before Christmas, Gregory develops the tree imagery, with Christ as the axe laid to the root of the tree from Luke 3:1–11.[28]

The emphasis in three of Gregory's four sermons centers upon John the Baptist, in each case the subject of the probable Gospel readings themselves.[29] Gregory uses the Baptist to promote the themes of fasting, good will toward others, and especially of humility and plain living, which had been appropriate in Rome during the pre-Christmas weeks for centuries before he wrote. The Baptist is the angel who goes before the Lord, the one who brings him in, as a good Christian would help a friend; his humility is apparent from his realization that he was lesser, and would decrease as the Lord increased. But he is also a prophet, and Gregory explains the suggestion that he might be Elijah by saying that he is the forerunner of the Redeemer, as Elijah will be the forerunner of the Judge. Here is the emphasis on prophecy that would develop further in the hands of later liturgists and sermon writers.[30] Gregory's sermons, not only quoted at length in homiliaries, also were the major source for the sermons of Bede, which came to be frequently excerpted in their own right, forming as they do complimentary Office readings for the earlier sermons of Gregory himself.[31] Bede's collection appears to be close to the homiliary of Cuthbert, itself based on a system of readings brought from Naples to England, which will be discussed below (see *HML*, 72–73, and Morin 1891).

Sermon writers of the fifth and sixth centuries spun out the materials for the Advent liturgies then developing in the West. We leave the early seventh century with a multifaceted body of sermons for the season from many regions and with a repertory of characteristic themes emphasizing preparation and fasting, the prophecies of the Old Testament and of John the Baptist, and calls to meet the Bridegroom clothed in the charity appropriate to the occasion of judgment. Advent was well established in the West by the death of Gregory I, in Ravenna, in Gaul, in Rome. Collections of liturgical materials themselves would now slowly arise, codified in the wake of interaction between sermon texts written in the fifth and sixth centuries, standardized series of biblical readings, and prayer texts composed in the late sixth and seventh centuries. The earliest layers of Western liturgical books, those compiled in the sixth century itself, do not contain Advent; books from the seventh century forward generally do.[32]

Sacramentaries

This early type of liturgical book contains collections of the texts needed by a celebrant to conduct the Mass and other services, and thus is primarily, although not exclusively, comprised of prayers. Sacramentaries are essential to the researcher, even when the subject is the Office rather than the Mass: they are arranged, for the most part, by feasts, and thus provide guideposts for charting liturgical change within seasonal cycles and the liturgical calendar. Furthermore, the prayers of the sacramentaries, although frequently first developed in a Eucharistic context, were adapted for service in the Office and for private devotion as well.

The first surviving Western sacramentaries fall into several well-known categories, explained in detail in Cyrille Vogel's *Medieval Liturgy: An Introduction to the Sources;* with this book, a complicated subject is made managable for the nonspecialist, laid out by a master who spent his life with the sources themselves. When reading Vogel, one keeps at the elbow Klaus Gamber's *Codices liturgici Latini antiquiores (CLLA)*; whatever its particular faults and omissions, this annotated catalogue of primary sources is the standard reference book in the field. It lays out liturgical materials in a way that is instructive in itself, demonstrating the many kinds of books available for consultation, categorizing them according to the several traditions in the Latin West, and providing bibliography on each source. In addition, the several volumes describing liturgical sources found in the series Typologie des sources du moyen âge occidental are useful for updating the bibliographies in *CLLA*.[33] Clear from this array of sources is the need for interregional study, especially in the formative decades just before and during the Carolingian Renaissance; scholars have assumed the interdependence of Mass and Office texts, but the lines linking them are, we will see, not neatly drawn. In fact, the views of scholars concerning the early Roman liturgy, no matter what the field or subject, are based on study of the sacramentaries. To evaluate anyone's ideas and to develop theories of one's own, to know what they are, where they came from, and the nature of their contents is essential.

The sacramentaries provide layers upon layers of prayer texts, emanating from northern Italy, Rome, Gaul, Spain, Anglo-Saxon England, Ireland, and other areas, but virtually all Roman books themselves were copied and edited in the North, and samplings from some of the most important types of these books are offered here. The dating of the sources depends primarily upon noting which feasts they contain, and benchmark Roman feasts are conveniently listed in the back of Klauser's *Das römische Capitulare Evangeliorum.* With so much material circulating, and in various states of redaction, chronology is vexingly difficult, and can only be attempted by experts close to the sources. Antoine Chavasse, who has written more about sacramentaries than any other scholar, is such a person.[34] To trace out Chavasse's ideas regarding Advent, one works through the families of sacramentaries as outlined by Vogel (and to an extent, Vogel's explanations are dependent upon Chavasse!), consulting Gamber's *CLLA* and the appropriate volumes in the Typologie series for bibliography on individual manuscripts. The prayers themselves are conveniently tabulated in Deshusses's *Concordances et tableaux pour l'étude des grands sacramentaires,* with listings and comparative tables for each major family of sources and a very useful word index (Deshusses and Darragon, *Concordances,* 6 vols.). The *Concordances* is one of the most important tools to have been produced in the field of medieval liturgical studies in this century, and with it a scholar can keep fairly tight control over a very complex field of materials.[35] A significant omission in the book is independent listings for non-Roman sources, especially those of the Gallican and Old Spanish rites, this latter being left out completely.[36]

Chavasse's writings on Advent are representative of his research as a whole.[37] Using the sacramentaries and other early liturgical books in a comparative study, he attempts to outline a chronological development of feasts and seasons in Rome, and to show how they were or were not received in other regions as well. The broad outlines of historical development are often filled in with minute details regarding the sources, and the only way to critique these would be through careful analysis of the sources themselves, a task that will not be attempted here. Chavasse's stages in the development of the Advent season in Rome are neatly argued, presenting a tripartite scheme.[38] He believes that the first Advent cycle was in place before the time of Gregory I, and had six Sundays, resembling the traditions found in the Old Spanish, Milanese, and Gallican sources. In Rome, however, Ember week of December, which came to occupy the days just before Christmas, offered an intense culmination of the themes of fasting stressed throughout the season. Thus, the final Sunday of Advent was left vacant, the solemn Saturday Vigil service serving instead for the celebration of the day. Therefore, there were actually six Sundays in Advent, but liturgies for only five of them. Subsequently, a four-Sunday cycle became the norm, but this cycle was developed in two different ways, depending upon the fashion in which the final Sunday was treated. Some Roman churches kept the fourth Sunday before Christmas vacant, the elaborate readings of Saturday's Vigil service serving instead for the celebration of the day. With the placement of the Vigil earlier and earlier in the day, the empty Sunday apparently came to seem like an omission in many churches, and eventually the vacant Sunday was provided with its own liturgy. Some churches had three actual Sunday liturgies, with the fourth Sunday left vacant; some had four actual liturgies, as the fourth Sunday had been supplied with texts, music, and readings.

Chavasse's picture of Advent depends upon study of prayer concordances, with some attention to textual variants; it finds a strong level of support in other kinds of liturgical collections as well, in some homiliaries, and in early collections of chant texts for the Mass. But his views can at least be tempered by a different kind of study: consideration of thematic ideas within the various families of prayer texts. Working through the types of sacramentaries, beginning with the Roman books and ending with the Gallican and Old Spanish, we will seek to know in what ways the traditions are different in emphasis and design.

The earliest Roman sacramentary, the *Veronensis* (L), while having no Advent per se, does have series of prayers for Ember Days.[39] These sixth-century prayers had some impact on the development of Advent formularies, especially as found in the Old Gelasian sacramentary (V).[40] This development was reflected in the state of the Mixed Gelasian sacramentaries (G)[41] as well as in the Sacramentary of Milan (Be).[42] Still, these early Ember Day prayers, although powerfully influential in later Ember Day formularies in the sources mentioned above, were only infrequently adapted for Sundays in Advent. The earliest Roman layer had no apparent influence on Advent prayers as found in the Gallican sources considered here;

although two of the tenth-month (December) Ember Week prayers are found in Gallican sources, they are not used as Advent prayers.[43]

The themes of prayers found in L are, as would be expected, penitential, and generically so, enough to make them usable for Lent or other seasons of the year. The kinds of prayers written for Advent and found in V are more specifically thematic than those found for Ember Days in L. The prayers are arranged in five formularies for Sundays, the last of which is followed by a long series of prayers for the season. Following in immediate succession are the three formularies for Ember week: Wednesday, Friday, and Saturday. The Advent formularies themselves are, in many instances, proper to the season, with emphasis upon themes of begging indulgence for sins, and on preparation through purification, with the introductory prayers 1121, 1122, and 1126 serving as good examples (using the numbering system found in Deshusses and Darragon, *Concordances;* see 5:169–70). But another set of themes proper to the season plays out as well, with allusions to waking and sleeping, as found in the parable of the wise and foolish virgins of Matt. 25, to the wedding feast of Matt. 24, and to the knocking of Christ on the door found in Rev. 3; all of these themes are drawn together in Luke 12:35–37 as well. The imagery of preparation for the feast, the Advent coming, is reminiscent especially of the sermons of Caesarius of Arles, where the subject of banqueting and imagery similar to some of these prayer texts abounds.

The Gregorian sacramentary (H) contains several of the Ember prayers also found in L, but fewer of them than are found in V and G, and never for Advent, but rather usually for Lent.[44] In other words, the liturgical prayers developed for December Ember Days in the sixth century were used later to form the materials for this same week as part of Advent, but only as the season was known in the so-called Gelasian traditions represented by V and G, and in the Milanese use. In fact, the Gregorian Sacramentary, the core of which is now thought to be contemporary with the Old Gelasian Sacramentary, reflects a different liturgical practice from that found in V: prayers in the Gregorian tradition are three in number for most formularies, and the texts demonstrate the succinctness long associated with Roman liturgical expression, in general, but in actuality more a part of a particular stripe of the Roman use.[45] A cursory study of this material suggests that the Gregorian Advent prayers are, for the most part, rearrangements of materials found in Old Gelasian and Gallican sources, with frequent Milanese correspondences as well. However, the thematic cast of the prayers in H is quite different from these other uses. Gone from the Advent prayers in H are any with thematic allusions such as those found in V and G. These are stark calls for preparation from those who pray, and requests for help from God.

The characters of many Advent formularies found in the Gallican and Old Spanish rites are both more elaborate and more strongly topical than those of the Gregorian rite. The formularies found in the Bobbio Missal, an important witness to the Gallican tradition, offer themes of major importance, with emphasis on John the Baptist, and they demonstrate yet again the regional variety found in early layers of Advent prayers.[46] Although there are many correspondences between the Advent prayers in Bobbio and V, the second set in Bobbio did not make its way into either of the Gelasian types. Filled with allusions to the Baptist, this group of prayers is also found as the first set in the Old Spanish rite, with certain modifications. A search for comparable emphasis on the Baptist in Advent formularies in the Gelasians and the Gregorian yields sparse results, with prayer 1522 (Deshusses), an opening prayer, as a possible example:

> Lord, stir up our hearts for preparing the ways of your only Only-begotten, so that we may be deserving to serve throughout His Advent with purified minds.

This prayer opens the second Advent Mass in both the Old Gelasian and the Gregorian sacramentaries.

Given the development of Advent in the wake of the Councils of Ephesus and Chalcedon, Marian and incarnational themes would be expected in prayers for Advent (see Fassler forthcoming and Constas 1994). There are hints of such themes in the Gelasian traditions, but none in the Gregorian. In the Bobbio Missal, however, in the third Mass (there are three Advent formularies, four counting the Vigil of Christmas), the first preface to the Canon refers to Mary and Gabriel's announcement, and this prayer is also found in the so-called Missale Gallicanum Vetus. The Mass of the Christmas Vigil found in the Bobbio Missal has Luke 12:35–37 as the Gospel reading, asking for the watchfulness of those waiting for their master to return from the wedding banquet. The prayers for this feast, not found elsewhere, are Marian and incarnational in nature. The only formularies in V with a Marian emphasis are found in Ember Wednesday. In the Mixed Gelasian tradition, one of these prayers shifts to the third (of five) Sundays in Advent, and the other was left in its Wednesday position. An emphasis on Mary and the incarnation in mid-Advent is not reflected in the sermons studied above, but it was a part of the works brought into the homiliaries from northern Africa and Spain, as will be seen below.

Edmund Bishop has written about the Old Spanish rite as the first in the West to develop a profound Marian emphasis, and here we see its apparent influence in the writing of Advent prayers, many of which, unlike the Advent formulary shared with the Bobbio Missal, are incarnational in tone.[47] Compilers of the Old Spanish rite, however, were not alone in promoting a Marian emphasis within Advent. Thematic development there resembles that of the Ravennate fragment described briefly above, but, as Benz demonstrates in his analysis, close connections between this and the tradition as it developed in Rome, Gaul, or Spain are not to be found.[48] The Leofric Collectar, a prayer book representing the use of Anglo-Saxon England, was strongly influenced by southern Italian liturgical practices. It too demonstrates a strong emphasis upon John the Baptist, Incarnation, and the Virgin Mary in several of its texts.[49]

It is as well to close this section with attention to the location of Advent in these sources. In Gallican, Milanese, and Old Spanish sources, Advent was placed at the beginning of surviving books. In all early Roman sources, however, Advent was found at the end of the yearly cycle of feasts and seasons, a location picked up by the compilers of the first surviving Gregorian sacramentaries. We may now suspect that the Roman location was not, as some have hypothesized, a deliberate statement concerning Advent as the end of the church year with reference to the apocalyptic end of time. Rather, this position may have developed in some Roman sources simply because it was the location of the December Ember Days, the original liturgical kernel of the season in this tradition.

The Gospel Readings

Early sermons with their themes and exegetical treatments are the first witnesses to liturgical development; they, in turn, are followed first by early collections of prayers, and by standardized series of Gospel readings.[50] These latter two kinds of materials must always be used together when studying the early medieval Mass and Office. I have discussed sacramentaries in this chapter first as a matter of convenience: I wished to lay out Chavasse's theories early in the analysis. But, it should be noted, Chavasse worked with the Gospel lectionaries too, and could not have painted the picture of Advent he did without their evidence. In fact, a cardinal rule for the study of the medieval Latin liturgy is: identify the Gospel reading for the feast (or the series of readings for the season) to be studied. This reading will be the first determinable item in many cases, and, furthermore, if fixed, it will govern (or at least color) much other development. The Gospel reading at Mass was commonly read in the Office too, within the third Nocturn of Matins, and is very often the liturgical text from which much of the rest of the liturgy emanates, both Mass and Office, including other readings, prayers, and chant texts. Once a Gospel text is established for any day in a given rite, it becomes, at least for a time, the foundation upon which all else is chosen or composed. When this appears not to be true, one wonders why, and seeks to locate points of change or other influences. In working with any other feast or season besides Advent, one would determine these readings in the Eastern rites as well—in Jerusalem, Constantinople, and as many others as possible. But in Advent, as explained at length above, it is appropriate to begin with the Western sources themselves.

There are basically three kinds of sources that identify Gospel readings.[51] Among the earliest are Bibles themselves, which sometimes contain marginal notes of liturgical significance; when working with marginal notations the scholar must discern if their dates are contemporary with the texts themselves.[52] A second kind of source, often found at the back or front of the Gospel books or Bibles themselves, is listings of chapters that were read liturgically (pericopes). Such a grouping of pericope headings is often called a Capitulary. They were of two types, those listing readings from the Gospel, and those listing readings from non-Gospel parts of the Bible.[53] Another kind of book contains the readings themselves, extracted and sometimes placed in liturgical order, thus making up a primitive lectionary.[54] Frere made the point long ago that capitularies are often much more archaic than the liturgical lectionaries themselves, which were prepared at great expense and energy for actual use. Capitularies, on the other hand, were readily copied even when they were no longer strictly followed, and thus tended to have a long "shelf life" (Frere 1930, Introduction). Thus the shadows of older traditions coexisted in many centers alongside newer practices, ready to challenge the historically astute practitioner.

In the case of the Roman liturgy, establishing the Gospel reading for a given feast is a relatively easy matter, at least for one strain of Roman liturgical development. Klauser's classic study, *Das römische Capitulare Evangeliorum*, lays out the readings in various chronological stages, beginning with a pure Roman state from the mid-seventh century and working through to two mid-eighth-century uses, one Roman, and other Franco-Roman.[55] Table 1.1 compares the Gospel readings for feasts of Advent and indicates the common rubrics used for the days within the season, which shift from early to later sources. Along with the Gospel readings found in Klauser, it is important to compare the sermons of Gregory the Great, who preached at a late sixth- or early seventh-century stage within the Roman tradition. Table 1.1 suggests (and this was important evidence for Chavasse) that the Roman Gospels in some churches were laid out in fixed pericopes by the time of Gregory, but the number of Sundays within the season was in flux. It can be seen that the readings on which Gregory preached his Advent sermons form a kind of core for the development of the festal cycle, with three sermons for Sundays of Advent and one sermon for the Saturday of Ember Week. Some sources show five Sundays, and some four or three.

The Roman Advent readings Klauser presents are very consistent from the mid-seventh through the mid-eighth century, as can be seen in table 1.1. Readings for Wednesdays, Fridays, and Saturdays were added by the mid-eighth century to the unchanging core of Sunday and Ember Week readings. The first reading that Chavasse considered for a Sunday in Advent is John 6:5–14. The feast and reading may not be a true part of the season, called as it is "for the seventh week after St. Cyprian." Still, with its mention of Andrew (whose feast falls right at this time—30 November), and the final verse of the passage, "This is indeed the prophet who is to come into the world," the reading provides a festal duality. The reading for the fourth week before Christmas is Matt. 21:1–9, the story of Jesus' triumphal entrance into Jerusalem. The third week before Christmas was dominated by Luke 21:25–33, with the powerful image of the Second Coming, pregnant with signs, human trembling, and a brief quotation from Dan. 7:13–14 embedded within verse 27: "Then they will see 'the Son of Man coming in a cloud' with power and great glory." John the Baptist dominates in the readings of the second and first weeks before Christmas; the readings of the Ember Days bring forth texts describing the Annunciation and the Magnificat, with John's cry from Isa. 40:3–5 heard within the final reading on Ember Saturday. There is no Sunday after Ember Week in this tradition, but the missing Sunday is not called *vacat* ("empty"), as it was in some stages of Roman Advent.

A second important southern Italian use was present in Naples and the surrounding Campania from the late sixth century. The tradition was established in Anglo-Saxon England as well by a series of missionaries from Italy, most importantly by the Abbot Hadrian.[56] Hadrian, who originated in Greek-speaking Africa, was head of a monastery in Naples for over twenty years, and had become a highly trusted advisor of Pope Vitalian and of the Emperor Constans II before his last

Table 1.1 Gospel readings for Advent in the Roman tradition: selected sources

Pure Roman ca. 645 Gospel readings		Roman Frankish after 750 Gospel readings		Gregory the Great Scriptural sources of Advent Homilies	Paul the Deacon		Naples/Anglo-Saxon Würzburg 68, ca. 700 (for comparison)	
Rubric	Scripture	Rubric	Scripture		Rubric	Scripture	Rubric	Scripture
Eb 7 post sci cypriani	John 6:5–14	item in adventus Domini	John 6:5–14		Eb 5 ante natale domini	John 6:5–14	de Adventum	Luke 21:25
						John 1:19		
Fer. 4	Matt. 8:14–22	Fer. 4 item ut supra	Matt. 8:14–22			Luke 1:26–27	Fer. 4	Luke 12:32
			Luke 10:3–9					
Fer. 6	Luke 12:13–31	Fer. 6 item ut supra	Luke 12:13–31				Fer. 6	Luke 12:39
			Mark 13:33–37					
Fer. 4	Mark 8:15–26	Fer. 4	Mark 8:15–16					
Eb 4 ante natale Domini	Matt. 21:1–9	Eb 4 ante natale Domini	Matt. 21:1–9		Eb 4 ante natale domini	Matt. 21:1–9	Dom. 2	Matt. 11:2
		Fer. 4	Matt. 3:1–6				Fer. 4	Matt. 3.1
		Fer. 6	Luke 3:7–18				Fer. 6	Matt. 24:3
Eb 3 ante natale Domini	Luke 21:25–33	Eb 3 ante natale Domini	Luke 21:25–33	Luke 21:25–33	Eb 3 ante natale domini	Luke 21:25–33	Dom. 3	Luke 1:26
		Fer. 4	Matt. 11:11–15				Fer. 4	Matt. 24:23
		Fer. 6	Mark 1:2–8				Fer. 6	Matt. 24:34

(continued)

Table 1.1 (*continued*)

Pure Roman ca. 645 Gospel readings		Roman Frankish after 750 Gospel readings		Gregory the Great Scriptural sources of Advent Homilies	Paul the Deacon		Naples/Anglo-Saxon Würzburg 68, ca. 700 (for comparison)	
Rubric	Scripture	Rubric	Scripture		Rubric	Scripture	Rubric	Scripture
Eb 2 ante natale Domini	Matt. 11:2–10	Eb 2 ante natale Domini Fer. 4 Fer. 6	Matt. 11:2–10 Matt. 3:7–11 Luke 7:18–28	Matt. 11:2–10	Eb 2 ante natale domini	Matt. 11:2–10	Dom. 4 Eb. 4 de Adventum	Luke 3:1 Mark 13:18
Eb 1 ante natale Domini	John 1:19–28	Eb 1 ante natale Domini	John 1:19–28	John 1:19–28	Eb 1 ante natale domini infra Eb item	John 1:19 "Legimus . . ." "Vos in-quam . . ."	Dom. 5 Eb. 1	Luke 4:14 John 1:19
Fer. 4 ad scam Mariam	Luke 1:26–38	Fer. 4 ad scam Mariam	Luke 1:26–38		Fer. 4 ad scam Mariam	Luke 1:26–38		
Fer. 6 ad apostolos	Luke 1:39–47	Fer. 6 ad apostolos sabbato ad scum petrum in XII lectiones	Luke 1:39–47		Fer. 6 ad apostolos	Luke 1:39–47 Luke 3:1		
Fer. 7 ad scum Petrum	Luke 3:1–6		Luke 3:1–6	Luke 3:1–6				

mission (Bischoff and Lapidge 1994, 130–31). He reached England in 670, via Gaul, where he had already sojourned twice before. This international figure, fluent in both Greek and Latin, well informed concerning liturgical circumstances in some regions of Gaul, and a promulgator of Neapolitan monastic liturgy, shaped liturgical practices in the formative seventh century, in his case, finally in England.

Liturgies were transmitted through such powerful persons, who had not only books, but also the understanding of how to implement the liturgies the books contained. Several famous manuscripts relate to the use of Naples as transplanted to England, including the Lindisfarne Gospels, a book studied as a representative of the Neapolitan liturgical tradition even in the early part of this century (Morin 1891).[57] The so-called Burchard Gospel Book, the contents of which are listed in table 1.1 in the far right column, represents the Neapolitan use, as it was brought to England, and from there to Würzburg. It is a book that may have been influenced by the Roman tradition outlined from Klauser's book in table 1.1 as well.[58] Among the many differences between this southern Italian Advent and that of Rome are the position of Luke 21 as first in the series; Matt. 21, which describes the triumphal entrance into Jerusalem, is not present; and the Annunciation reading from Luke is in the center of the season. With so many traditions in evidence, clearly there would have been considerable confusion regarding Advent (and other feasts and seasons as well) in early eighth-century Gaul. Texts for the Office of all types, including chant texts, would have varied in order, and even in nature, from region to region.

As table 1.2 shows, non-Roman lectionaries demonstrate varying numbers of Sundays and none of them follows the Roman tradition, although certainly there were some common texts. The Gallican sources, as tabulated by Pierre Salmon in his introduction to the Luxeuil lectionary, provide spotty information as to what the readings were.[59] Tragically, the leaves containing Advent are missing from the Luxeuil lectionary itself. One finds Old Testament readings in the source at Schlettstadt, and Epistles in the earlier section of the manuscript;[60] Vatican, BAV Vat. lat. 5755 from the seventh century provides notations for Epistles as well; but the list of Gospels compiled from Paris, BNF lat. 256 and lat. 10863 offers the only surviving Gallican five-Sunday cycle of Advent Gospels.[61] That readings from Isaiah were well established during the season is clear from the study of other series of Advent readings attested by the sources. The Bobbio Missal represents yet another tradition, with three Sundays and a Vigil Mass. The sources testify to the long-acknowledged understanding of variability within the Gallican traditions.[62]

The Milanese readings for Advent, found in a source from the second half of the ninth century, present yet another order of Epistle and Gospel readings.[63] They also show that there were six Sundays of Advent in Milan. The Old Spanish sources, rich in prayer texts, testify less frequently to the Gospel and other readings. Although Advent is frequently lost, falling as it did at the beginning of liturgical books, the *Liber commicus*, as found in a modern edition, contains the full cycle.[64] Here too, as with the other non-Roman traditions, the series of readings is unique. As would be expected, many of the readings are common in other regions, but the numbers of verses and the order of the readings themselves reveal no standardization from tradition to tradition.

Table 1.2 Gospel readings for Advent in the non-Roman tradition: selected sources

Paris, BNF lat. 256 St. Denis?, early 8th c.		Bobbio Missal Paris, BNF 13246		Bergamo, S. Alexandri 9th c. (2)		Bede Scriptural sources Advent homilies	Old Spanish Liber Commicus	
Rubric	Scripture	Rubric	Scripture	Rubric	Scripture	Scripture	Rubric	Scripture
De Primo Aduento	John 1:35–51	Incipiunt liccionis de aduentum dni	Matt. 11:2–5	Dom. 1	Matt. 24:1–44		Primo Dom.	Matt. 3:1–11
Secunda dnica in Aduentum	Matt. 24:15	In aduentu dni. 2	Matt. 3:1–12	Dom. 2	Luke 3:1–18		Secundo Dom.	Matt. 11:2–15
Tercia dnica aduentum	Matt. 11:2	In aduentu dni. 3	Matt. 24:27–44	Dom. 3	Matt. 11:2–15		Tercia Dom.	Matt. 21:1–9
Quarta dnica de Aduentum	Luke 3:2			Dom. 4	Matt. 21:1–9	Mark 1:4–8	Quarta Dom.	Mark 1:1–8
Quinta dom de Aduentum	Matt. 3:1			Dom. 5	John 1:15–28	John 1:15–18	Quinta Dom.	Luke 3:1–18
Sexta dnica aduentum	Matt. 21:1			Dom. 6 missa in ecclesia	Luke 1:39–45	Luke 1:26–38		
				Item ad Scam Mariam	Luke 1:26–38	Luke 1:39–55		
				missa in Vigil Natal Dni	Matt. 1:18–25	Matt. 1:18–25		

It is worth pointing out that Matt. 24, a text of importance in the sermons of Caesarius, and perhaps referred to in some prayers of the Old Gelasian sacramentary, is present as a reading in all non-Roman traditions, including the Neapolitan, and is found in both Gallican sources tabulated here. Matt. 21:1–9, the entrance into Jerusalem, is found in both Paris, BNF lat. 256 and the Milanese use, but later in the series than in Rome. Luke 21, however, part of the Roman lectionary by the late sixth century, as witnessed by Gregory's Advent sermon on the text, is present in none of the Gallican sources, nor in the Old Spanish rite, nor in Milan. It is found as a reading "De Adventu" in the Gospel book of Burchard, however, and may have served there as the reading for the first Sunday in Advent. The contents of the Roman readings are the one consistent strain in the development of Advent in the West; Gregory's sermons, it is to be noted, might have served for the Neapolitan use as well, if, as has sometimes been speculated, it existed early in Rome and was favored by certain monastic communities there.

Homiliaries

The third important type of liturgical evidence from the late sixth, seventh, and eighth centuries are the liturgical collections of sermons for the Office compiled for a variety of uses, but, as far as the Roman rite is concerned, demonstrating a central tradition with many stripes, at least in regard to Advent; these, we will see, were combined in the late eighth century in the Office homiliary of Paul the Deacon.[65] It is the homiliaries which provide the first picture of Advent as it was celebrated in the Office, where readings from sermons were of central importance, particularly to the elaborate night Office of Matins. Scholarship on the homiliaries has been greatly advanced in recent decades, especially through the work of Réginald Grégoire, whose carefully tabulated analyses of medieval liturgical homiliaries makes comparison of the various traditions, at least on a simple level, a possibility (of special importance here is his *HLM*) and through the thoughtful study of Raymond Étaix, who has concentrated upon later redactions of earlier traditions. A representative collection of his many studies has recently been published.[66] Even a short time spent with these two authors will demonstrate to the reader that the homiliaries and their traditions are both as complicated and as important to liturgical history as the sacramentaries and Gospel books, and that they are the first great body of liturgical books prepared specifically for Office use, taking the researcher to the heart of this subject more directly than any other body of early liturgical materials.

Grégoire (*HLM*) has discussed the major witnesses of the Roman homiletic tradition in great detail, summarizing much earlier scholarship in the process, and inventorying contents of the sources. Of the several witnesses, we will compare briefly three, all of them closely related. The Homiliary of Alan of Farfa (d. 769 or 770) actually represents in its core a seventh-century Roman collection emanating from St. Peter's on the Vatican, corresponding to the scheme of biblical readings laid out in Ordo Romanus XIV, with certain changes.[67] The Roman homiliary of the scribe Agimundus was used in the basilica of SS. Philip and James by the early

eighth century, and survives as Vatican, BAV Vat. lat. 3835 and 3836, its first volume
having been lost. The parentage of the book in its primitive layers is African and
from the sixth century; these were the works forming the original core of the homiliary of St. Peter's.[68] Vatican, BAV San Pietro C 105 is a liturgical homiliary from
the Basilica of St. Peter's itself, the handwriting dating from the second half of the
tenth century. This fragmentary book, the surviving contents of which represent
the first part of the church year, is very close to the homiliary of Alan of Farfa
mentioned above; Alan's is based on an even earlier tradition. The study of the
earliest Roman homiliaries suggests that, in regard to the earliest layers of the
Office liturgy, all roads lead to St. Peter's.

What is Advent like in these three Roman Office collections? The sermons for
Advent found in the so-called Homiliary of Alan of Farfa are not divided into
pericopes or provided with titles, piece by piece, in the inventory Grégoire presents. Instead, they are a collection of complete works (not excerpts, in most cases)
to be read at the Office during the season, and these fall into large sections. Thus
it is not easy to claim centrality for particular biblical passages, although some of
the themes present have been discussed above. First are five so-called homilies
of St. Augustine, none of which is actually by the designated author. The series
commences with a magnificent treatise long attributed to St. Augustine, "Legimus
sanctum Moysen." In actuality the sermon is a composite work: the first half is
taken from a letter written in 437 by the African Antonius Honoratus, and the rest
from a Pseudo-Augustinian sermon "Sanctus Hic."[69] The sermon presents early
versions of themes that would be central to the later medieval Office, and to the
understanding of Advent, with emphasis upon the significance of the flowering
rod of Aaron (Num. 17:6–8) as a type of the Virgin Mary who would bear at once,
contrary to nature, both flower and fruit. The association of Christ with Aaron the
priest is also developed here, with reference to the order of Melchisedech. Excerpts
from Caesarius' three Advent sermons follow, and then an Advent sermon from
Maximus of Turin, and a sermon by Pseudo-Maximus which Morin believed may
have been of Spanish origin. This latter work, "Ecce ex qua tribu," like the "Legimus sanctum Moysen," emphasizes the prophetic voices predicting the coming of
the Messiah, here with emphasis upon the "stirps Jesse," the shoot of Jesse.[70] As
with some non-Roman prayer texts mentioned above, the sermons of this collection resonate with the themes that will dominate in the fully developed medieval
Office of Advent.

The next work is a composite sermon, fashioned from Ambrose's commentary
on Luke, but called here a sermon on the incarnation of the Lord by St. Ambrose.
Next is an excerpt from a letter by Pope Leo, this too called "de incarnatione."
Excerpts from Pope Leo's three sermons for Ember Week of Advent finish out the
cycle. Except for the final group, this is a series with a powerful incarnational thrust
and a strong Marian emphasis. The collection as a whole appears quite different
in character from the prayers and readings in the Gregorian tradition, but reso-
nates instead with the southern Italian, Ravennate, and Spanish liturgical materials
described above. To be noted is the absence of sermons by Gregory the Great.

Many of the sermons presented in the Homiliary of Alan of Farfa are found in the other Roman homiliaries mentioned above as well, but with modifications and certain additions. The homiliary of St. Peter's at the Vatican shows "Legimus sanctum Moysen" broken out of the Pseudo-Augustinian group and placed after the excerpts by Ambrose; in addition the book includes in the final position, even after the Ember Days sermons by Pope Leo, a sermon by the fifth-century Carthaginian Quodvultdeus, "Vos inquam convenio." This sermon became the basis for the tradition of prophets' plays in the Middle Ages, and we witness here how it first came into the Roman liturgical sources.[71]

The homiliary of Agimundus is even more varied, and organized in a different way. A series of three sermons, two by Caesarius and one by Maximus, is followed by the four Advent sermons of Gregory I, the third of which is supplied with a Gospel reading: Luke 3:1–11. The works are designated for the first through the fourth Sundays in Advent. This set is followed by three sermons on the Incarnation, "Ecce ex qua tribu," the excerpt from the letter by Leo I, and "Legimus sanctum Moysen." Following this set are the three Advent sermons of Leo I. Thus the Marian/incarnational material is less emphasized here, and placed just before Ember Week, while the sermons of Gregory have come to have an important position in the center of the materials. The sets of sermons would have been used simultaneously, it seems, except for the Ember Day offerings. Thus each week in Advent might have something by Caesarius, something from Gregory, and something from the Marian group. In addition, two of the series seem set up for a three-Sunday Advent, but the series of Gregory's sermons is definitely for four Sundays.

Clearly in the materials for Advent in the Roman homiliaries we move in a different world from the Gregorian sacramentary, even from the lectionaries tabulated by Klauser. In the homiliaries, the sense of the season has a balance between two types of equally represented thematic material: around half of the works are incarnational and Marian, and these are found first in the various series; the rest of the sermons, from Caesarius, Leo I, and, eventually, although not always, from Gregory I, interweave the themes of penance, fasting, and a focus on John the Baptist that are already familiar from the fifth century onward.

The final work to be discussed here is the homiliary of Paul the Deacon. Paul the Deacon (ca. 720–ca.799), a Lombard by birth, was educated in Pavia, and came to Monte Cassino in around 773–74.[72] He was a visitor at the court of Charlemagne for several years, and was commissioned to compile the homiliary that was later promulgated in the king's *Epistola generalis*.[73] This, the official Office book of the Carolingian reformers, contains an Advent very different in structure and content from the Roman homiliaries discussed above. It is organized into five "weeks before the Birth of the Lord" and shows strict adherence to the Roman Gospel readings tabulated in Klauser (see table 1.1). In order to accommodate the readings, beginning with John 6:5, the Deacon has brought in sermons not found in the tradition discussed above, and reorganized the common sources he does use, getting rid of Caesarius, and of much of the material containing incarnational and Marian themes. Thus, the first week has a reading from the corresponding place in Augustine's *Treatise on the Gospel of John*. The reading for Week 2, Matt. 21, depicts the triumphal entrance into Jerusalem, and Paul the Deacon has used a

homily by Pseudo-Chrysostom, "Opus imperfectum in Matthaeum."[74] For the remaining three weeks, sermons by Maximus are used in conjunction with the three
by Gregory. "Legimus sanctum Moysen" is assigned to "within the week before the
Birth of the Lord," and "Vos inquam convenio" by Quodvultdeus appears as an
alternate. Not only are there five weeks before Advent, there is also an Ember Week,
which is assigned homilies by Bede, the Ember Week sermon of Gregory, and one
work by Maximus.

It should be emphasized that the readings from John 6:5–14, for the fifth week
before Christmas, and Matt. 21:1–9, for the fourth week before Christmas, have
the appearance of being recent additions to the ancient system of Office readings
established in Rome from the sixth century onward. Paul the Deacon was bringing
the Office tradition more closely in line with that of the Mass books studied above,
in particular with that of the Gospel lectionary as tabulated by Klauser. In the case
of Advent, they must not have been well syncronized at the time he did his work—
seated, we might imagine, amid books he understood very well, and others he did
not, and consulting with other scholars at the court of Charlemagne. His task was
to standardize these materials, and it is clear that, at least for the season of Advent,
he decided to coordinate Mass and Office liturgies as closely as possible. In the
process of synchronizing these readings, some materials for the Office would seem
suited to the Gospel of the day, others would not. There must have been great
consternation on the part of liturgists as Gospels were altered, and their powerful
pull upon preexistent liturgical materials for the Office was felt in the widespread
areas adopting the standarized Roman liturgy as promulgated by the Carolingians.
The process itself caused disrupture and disjunction, as will be demonstrated in
the concluding section of this chapter.

Conclusion: An Advent of Confusion

Amalarius of Metz's *De ecclesiasticis officiis* is the greatest Carolingian liturgical
commentary, a source that dominates the tradition of the genre for all centuries
onward.[75] It is also a work marked by doubt and confusion, as its author, a scholar
of the highest rank, admits openly that the sources he has before him simply do
not agree, even on basic points. This same attitude can be found in his *Liber de
ordine antiphonarii,* the preface to his lost antiphoner.[76] Here, some two generations after the work of Paul the Deacon, Amalarius discusses moving Office chants
around during the liturgical planning process so that they would agree with the
Gospel of the day, or the substitution of one so-called Roman piece for a better-
fitting work from the so-called Messine tradition, or vice versa. In both of these
liturgical treatises, agony is ameliorated through allegory, the latter functioning
more as an antidote to the scholar's pain than as a self-indulgent flight of fancy.[77]
Amalarius knew too much, and his task was to make sense of a tradition that
claimed to be uniform and ancient and was instead hopelessly varied, some of it
old, some of it fairly new. The passage describing liturgical sources for the Advent
liturgy is representative both of the kinds of problems he faced and the allegorical
solutions he sometimes resorted to in his work as both liturgist and liturgiologist:

In ancient Mass books and lectionaries is found written: "five weeks before the birth of the Lord." Indeed just as many readings are contained in the lectionary, and just as many in the Gospel book, for the time period mentioned for Sundays up to the birth of the Lord. The antiphoner [of the Mass] contains three daily services, and four for Sunday, which is *vacat* [empty] after the Saturday of twelve readings (Ember Saturday); but the night office, as I said above, has four services for Sundays.

The author of the lectionary stirs our faith to recall the proclamation of our Lord Jesus Christ when about to come throughout the five ages of the world; the author of the missal which is called Gregorian and of the antiphoner moves us that we might recall the festive birth of our Lord through three types of books, to whit the law, the prophets, and the psalms, and through a fourth, that is the beginning of the Gospel in which is described Gabriel the archangel sent to Zachary, clearly the one bringing the announcement of the birth of the precursor of the Lord, and also the prophecy of Zachary concerning the coming of the Lord; and Gabriel sent to Mary the Virgin, telling her about the conception of Our Savior, and certain other things right on up to the nativity itself.[78]

Amalarius' difficulty with liturgical books and the discrepancies between them in the early ninth century is symptomatic of his times, a crucial period for the development of the Office in the West. A second chapter would now take up the many types of materials described here and study the ways in which they were combined to fashion Advent in the form we know it from later medieval books. We can only point the way here, mentioning some of the themes that emerge from study of the materials above and looking briefly at some chant texts in this context. Amalarius knew of differences in the counting of Sundays before Advent, and these are manifested in the first collections of Mass texts, which date from about the year 800; six early examples have been tabulated by Hesbert.[79] The sources Hesbert used for the *AMS* all contain texts for the Proper of the Mass, and they demonstrate that three different plans for Advent circulated in the ninth century (see table 1.3). MS R from Rheinau contains five Sundays "ante natale Domini," formulating the season in a fashion resembling the manner of early Gospel books and the homiliary of Paul the Deacon. James McKinnon and others have written about the correspondence that Offertory antiphons frequently have with the Gospel of the day. In R the fifth Sunday before Christmas bears no discernible relationship to John 6, read on that day in the Roman tradition.[80] But none of the other early Mass books tabulated by Hesbert refers in its texts to this Gospel either; they all begin with the fourth Sunday before Christmas, and this is called (in all but the Rheinau source) the "First Sunday in Advent." The rest of the Sundays, including the chants sung on them, are fairly uniform until the end of the Advent series. The last Sunday shows great variance: R contains the fifth Sunday, but all the chants have been borrowed either from the previous Sunday or from Ember Days. In this tradition, a fifth Sunday was desired, but there were not unique chants for it. Three of the sources contain only three Sundays in Advent (M, B, and K). The famous Antiphoner of Compiègne, Paris, BNF 17436 (C) contains a full set of chants for the last Sunday in Advent, but the Sunday is labeled "vacat."[81] The antiphoner of Senlis

Table 1.3 Rubrics for early Mass formularies in Advent compared

M	R	B	C	K	S^a
—	D5 ante Nat. D.	Heb 23 post Pent.	—	Heb 23 post Pent.	Heb 23 post Pent.
D1	D4 ante Nat. D.	—	D1 ad S. Andream	D1 ad S. Mariam	D1
D2	D3 ante Nat. D.	D2 ad Hierusalem	lacuna	D2 ad Hierusalem	D2 ad Hierusalem
D3	D2 ante Nat. D.	D3 ad S. Petrum	D3 ad S. Petrum	D3 ad S. Petrum	D3 ad S. Petrum
[Ember Weekdays]					
F4	F4 ad S. Mariam	F4 ad S. Mariam	F4 ad S. Mariam	F4 ad S. Mariam	F4 ad S. Mariam
F6	—	F6	F6 ad Apostolos	F6 ad Apostolos	F6
Sa 12 L	S 12 L ad S. Petrum	Sa 12 L ad S. Petrum	Sa 12 L ad S. Petrum	Sa 12 L ad S. Petrum	Sa 12 L ad S. Petrum
—	D1 ante Nat. D.	—	D Vacat	—	D4

D = Dominica; Heb = Hebdomada; F = feria; L = Lectionibus; Sa = Sabbato; — = no rubrics or liturgical materials

^a Manuscripts as in *AMS*.

has the same chants for this feast as in Compiègne, except that the introit differs (see esp. *AMS*, 10–11). This divergence helps to explain the situation in R. The compilers of this source knew the Roman Gospel series, and wanted an Advent to match it. But they only had chants for three Sundays in Advent. Others were borrowed and developed to fill the gaps. These sources indicate the three stages Amalarius mentioned: three Sundays, four (with one labeled "vacat"), and the four-Sunday series that would come to dominate, but all within sources containing Mass texts (*antiphonalium missarum*).

A closer look at the texts reveals yet another subject worthy of independent investigation. As table 1.1 demonstrates, Gospel readings for Advent in the Roman use as tabulated by Klauser present Matt. 21:1–9, the triumphal entrance into Jerusalem, as the Gospel for the fourth Sunday before Christmas; in early Mass books after the Carolingian standardization, this became the Gospel for the Mass and Office of the first Sunday in Advent. The chants sung for this Sunday at Mass and in the Office, however, have little resonance with this Gospel. If the homiliaries are any indication, then Matt. 21:1–9 was fairly new to the Office tradition as standardized in the homiliary of Paul the Deacon.

Yet more evidence bearing on this confusion is present in the chants, both for Mass and Office, sung on the second Sunday of Advent, beginning with the introit *Populus Sion*. Jerusalem dominates in the chant texts, with the Communion antiphon *Hierusalem surge* as a good example, and the station in three of the Sextuplex manuscripts for the second Sunday is "Ad Hierusalem."[82] But if we turn back again to table 1.1 and early lists of Gospel texts, the reading for the second Sunday in

Advent was Luke 21:25–33; although the earlier part of chapter 21 has reference to Jerusalem, the section read at Advent does not. The themes are rather apocalyptic, with reference to the "Son of Man coming in a cloud," the text that dominates in the Office chants not on this, the second Sunday of Advent, but on the first Sunday, which begins with the famous responsory *Aspiciens a longe*. Somehow, the Gospel readings and the chant texts for the first two Sundays in Advent became seriously out of line. This is true for books containing Office chants as well. Examination of texts for antiphons and responsories in *CAO*, both in the secular and the monastic use, reveal the same disjuncture, and testify to the links that liturgical materials employed for the first Sunday in Advent have with the Gospel for the second Sunday, Luke 21:25–33, whereas Office chant texts for the second Sunday often extol the name of the Holy City of Jerusalem.

The connection of Office chant texts for the first Sunday in Advent with the Gospel of Luke, read on the second Sunday, is demonstrated in a series of antiphon texts for the Magnificat found in Hesbert's *CAO* MS E, from Ivrea, an eleventh-century source.[83] The texts of the group refer to the major themes embodied in Office texts for the first Sunday in Advent: the prophetic coming of the Messiah; the signs of his coming and the cloud imagery; and incarnation motives, including strong reference to Mary and the angelic pronouncement. Although several of the texts found here are present in the other sources tabulated in this volume of *CAO*, the most specific among them is not—"Erunt signa in sole et luna." This text, which is a direct quotation from Luke 21:25–33, demonstrates even more strongly than the others the connection the series once had with this Gospel text.

It would be a worthy endeavor to try to understand this disjuncture between Gospel of the day and Office chant texts in a more complete way. One could begin by examining the situation within ancient uses both north and south of the Alps, and studying Amalarius' revisions of Office chants in this light as well. Charts in the back of Hassens's edition compare Office chants as discussed in Amalarius and as found in both "Roman" and "Old Roman" uses.[84] A useful collection of chant texts compiled by Knud Ottosen, *L'Antiphonaire latin au moyen-âge*, offers the kind of evidence that must be compiled for every season. The book presents the great responsories of Advent as found in the manuscripts listed by Hesbert in *CAO*.[85] Ottosen's work points the scholar in the direction of chant databases such as CANTUS, but without the searching capabilities we have grown used to having available. Even a cursory examination of Ottosen's data suggests that the still-forming Advent found in the late eighth century had settled down considerably in the years after Amalarius. Yet, although the Advent responsories are relatively stable as a group, one finds them used in various orderings, and (especially within the monastic uses, which required more of them) in various combinations with other material.[86] All of these permutations invite further study.

The subject of the Old Roman Office, with its connection to St. Peter's, points back to the homiliaries described above. We saw that there was a particular tradition of sermons and themes that pervaded the Roman Office liturgy for centuries, and that this tradition, for Advent at least, was transformed dramatically in the eighth century north of the Alps. Yet another mode of investigation, then, would be to examine the Office chants, both from the Roman and Old Roman traditions—which, we have said, are very closely related—for the vestiges of early development. Were the chants created, at least some of them, in the midst of the early sermon tradition? Even a cursory look is suggestive of the possibilites. Incarnational and Marian themes, for example, dominate in chant texts for the first Sunday in Advent, just as they did in the early homiliaries of Rome. Can this be a coincidence, or were some of these chants first formed to suit the readings found as part of that tradition? This mode of study underscores the importance of the Office as made up of many strains of material, each having its own history. Through the Office, sung by the educated classes of Europe for centuries, the sermons of the past were kept alive and in liturgical context. Scholars have only begun to explore the interactive relationships between these sermons and many other aspects of the Office, the chants, the prayers, the Gospel readings.

In addition, it must be observed that discordance between Gospel readings and chant texts described here was excised in the modern Roman liturgical books, which were put in final form in the sixteenth century. Consultation of breviaries and missals will demonstrate that the Gospels for the Sundays of Advent are closer to the texts implied by the early homiliaries; the triumphal entrance into Jerusalem is not present.[87] The synchronization between Gospel readings and Mass and Office chant texts is improved. Compare the following Gospel readings for Sundays in Advent with those in tables 1.1 and 1.2:

> Dominica 1: Luke 21:25–33
> Dominica 2: Matt. 11:2–10
> Dominica 3: John 1:19–28
> Dominica 4: Luke 3:1–6

This is a warning to us not to rely on these later books for study of the medieval liturgy, even though, more often than not, they reflect the shape of early practice.

The complexities and richness of the Advent Office as formed in the late eighth and early ninth centuries were shaped, in many cases, through adaptations of the ancient materials described in this chapter. The Office of Advent, through the interaction of homiletic texts, Gospels, prayers, and chant texts, reveals the diversity and genius of Western liturgy in its formative state, and raises an array of questions for further study, especially given that themes of "Adventus" would come to dominate in many liturgical genres of the central Middle Ages (see Fassler 1993b and 1994). The creative genius of the tenth and eleventh centuries was lavished upon the Office, as each region and religious community refashioned a large body of broadly circulating materials to suit its particular needs and tastes. The process of understanding how this happened is crucial to knowing how religious cultures evolved in the Latin Middle Ages.

Notes

1. The ordinals of Chartres cathedral, for example, begin with pages of instructions for the celebration of Advent and what happens when days important to the season coincide with Sundays or important saints' days. See Delaporte, *L'Ordinaire chartrain.*

2. Detailed plans comparing the structure of the monastic day as it evolved in both

monastic and cathedral liturgies of the Roman rite by the ninth century are found in Huglo (1988), 83, Harper (1991), 86–97, Reynolds (1984), and Dubois and Lemaître (1993). The plans of the Divine Office designed by Lila Collamore (see the Prelude to this volume) are simple guides for the reader, and reflect the state of affairs in the central Middle Ages and later. The actual situation varied in its details from time to time and place to place, and to try to capture "the" liturgical day in a single chart or diagram is impossible.

3. The shape of Advent was little affected by the changing date of Easter because Christmas, although part of the Temporale, was fixed. However, the dates of Sundays in Advent changed every year, as did the specific dates of Ember week, and these days might coincide with a number of saints' feasts.

4. The scholarship on the season of Advent is surprisingly sparse. Thomas Talley (1991) was criticized for not paying enough attention to the season. But, to be fair to his work, it should be acknowledged that Advent was not fully developed in the early period, the focus of his study. Other scholars' works are popular rather than scholarly in nature, for example, Jean Daniélou (1951), Wilfrid Harrington (1935, repr. 1988), and, more recently, J. Neil Alexander (1993). Another important group of studies treats the theme as it arose in classical civilization and related to ceremonial, as in, for example, Pierre DuFraigne (1994) and Michael MacCormick (1986). The subject has had great importance for art historians, with classic treatment in the writings of André Grabar, who has been followed by numerous others, including Erich Dinkler (1970) and, more recently, Geir Hellemo (1989). The standard single article on the subject remains Ernst Kantorowicz (1944). My forthcoming book on the Cult of the Virgin in medieval Chartres contains extensive discussion of the sense of *Adventus* in the medieval liturgy.

5. General introductions to the Divine Office are not difficult to come by, but quality varies. One of the best such discussions to appear in recent years forms part of Martimort (1992). The introductory bibliography includes standard works such as Pierre Salmon (1962) and also a list of documents and writings concerning the Office since the Second Vatican Council.

6. For a brief, but useful, overview of the rise of Christmas, which includes discussion of all major areas in the East and West, see Botte (1932).

7. For discussion of liturgical themes associated with the pre-Christmas season in fifth-century Constantinople, see Fassler (forthcoming).

8. Moolan (1985), a revised version of the author's doctoral dissertation, has received criticism for its treatment of the manuscripts and for the choice of sources: see, for example, Winkler (1987a).

9. Moolan (1985), 270. The terms and polarities used here are as laid out by Robert Taft (1986).

10. See Talley (1991) and n. 21 below for discussion of the dependency of the date of Christmas upon an understanding of the spring equinox as the time of Jesus' conception.

11. For translations of the sermons of Proclus and extensive commentary, see Constas (1994).

12. The massive *Clavis patristica pseudepigraphorum medii aevi*, edited by Iohannis Machielsen, summarizes the results of recent investigations into misattributed works author by author, and helps researchers gain a better sense not only of which works were misattributed, but to whom. Volume 1, parts A and B, is devoted to "Opera homiletica."

13. Advent is also the subject of a forthcoming book by James McKinnon that is concerned primarily with the formation of chant texts and melodies of the Mass propers for this season.

14. This chapter, for the sake of space and time, concentrates on only three major

types of evidence—sacramentaries, capitularies, and homiliaries—with some reference to ordines and sources of chant texts at the end. Missing here is analysis of the work of church councils, which would have to be offered to complete the discussion. The documents of early Gallican councils have been edited by Munier; the standard collection for council documents remains Mansi. Hagiography and its relevance to the Divine Office do not arise to a great degree in the study of Advent; an invaluable introduction to the study of hagiographical sources, including legendaries and martryologies, is Dubois and Lemaître (1993). Also missing in this chapter is psalmody, a subject treated in some detail in the chapters of this volume by Peter Jeffery and Joseph Dyer. A good introduction to several interrelated subjects as they apply to Carolingian liturgical reforms can be found in Jacobson (1996), especially his chap. 1, "The European Liturgy in Ninth-Century Francia," 16–60.

15. The various pre-Caroline liturgies and chant repertories have been of great interest to scholars in recent decades. For an introduction to the problems as currently defined, and for bibliography, see Jeffery (1992).

16. For introductions to these very early collections, see *HLM*. As Vogel (1986), 34–37, points out, the authors and attributions are tantalizing, for none of the works survives: Musaeus of Marseilles, who died around 460, prepared a lectionary, a responsorial, a sacramentary, and, perhaps, even a book of sermons; Mamertus, archbishop of Vienne, composed a lectionary around 450; Sidonius Apollinarius, who died around 480, as bishop of Clermont, composed prayers for the Mass, perhaps even compiling a collection of these. Although this collection from Gaul remains the most substantial, other names from other regions are also connected with liturgical books in the fifth century; among them are: in Spain, Priscillian and Peter of Lérida; in Italy, Paulinus of Nola; in Milan, Bishops Simplicianus and Eusebius.

17. See Jeffery (forthcoming) for the thesis that there was a shift in the ways chant texts were cited from the fifth to the sixth centuries.

18. The *Clavis patrum Latinorum* (1995) is the standard source for authors and individual works from the early centuries of the Common Era. See also n. 12 above.

19. Liturgical historians have prized Ambrose most highly for his contribution to the evolution of prayers and understanding of the sacraments. See, for example, August Jilek (1992).

20. See CCSL 23; the sermons have been translated recently by Boniface Ramsey. References are to these volumes, with English translations taken from the latter.

21. See Sermon 61A, opening, p. 150. Because the conception of John the Baptist as described in the Bible was believed to have taken place in the fall, and it is known that Jesus was conceived some six months after him, then Jesus would have been conceived roughly at the time of the spring equinox, and born at the winter solstice; John was conceived around the time of the fall equinox and born at the summer solstice. These biblical foundations for the festive cycles are treated at length in Talley (1991).

22. This, the most studied of Quodvultdeus' works, has recently appeared in a modern edition in CCSL.

23. The introduction to the new English translation provides a description of the ways in which the sermons have been dated.

24. The extent to which sermon writers of the period were writers of prayer texts is evaluated in N. W. James (1993). He answers in the affirmative for a small group of prayers by Leo, but points to many of the difficulties in such attributions. Oftentimes prayers may have been used as sources for sermons rather than the other way around.

25. See the Latin edition of Leo's sermons in CCSL, with this as a quotation from Sermon 19. The sermons are newly translated into English (Fathers of the Church series, vol. 93). For the passage in context in the Tridentine books, see *The Roman Breviary*, 1:216.

26. The idea of readiness in the period before the feast of Christmas is exemplified by the following passage:

> Know truly that the man who has willed to guard those two virtues, namely, humility and charity, will be able to approach the Lord's birthday with assurance. Therefore let us strive to devote ourselves to the Lord in such a way that we can gather together, in these few days, what may suffice us for the entire year. For we believe that the Lord himself spoke about those days of His coming through the prophet: "On the days of your festivities you shall mortify yourself" (Lev. 16:29).

Translation from Caesarius of Arles: *Sermons*, 3, Sermon 189, p. 15. The period of fasting before Christmas in sixth-century Gaul is referred to in Gregory of Tours, *History of the Franks*, Book X, sect. 31, p. 472; the Second Council of Tours (567) defined periods of fasting as observed by monks. See Clercq, *Les Canons*, 2:363.

27. Gregory the Great, *Forty Gospel Homilies*. All translations are from this work, based on the Latin in PL 76, with some corrections and emendations. The four advent homilies are found on pp. 15–49, the last having been preached on Luke 3:1–11.

28. As in Homily 6, p. 42: "The tree is the entire human race in this world. The axe is our Redeemer. His humanity is like the axe's handle and iron head. It is his divinity which cuts. The axe is now laid at the root of the tree because, although he is waiting patiently, what he will do is nonetheless apparent."

29. Only the first Advent sermon, Homily 3, based on Luke 21:25–33, is not concerned with John the Baptist.

30. See esp. Homily 5, based on Matt. 11:2–10, pp. 28–33.

31. Bede's Advent sermons are published with the rest of his homilies in a critical edition in CCSL 122. A table at the beginning of the volume compares his scriptural sources, which are idiosyncratic for Advent, with those of other traditions. These readings will be discussed briefly below.

32. A system of liturgical readings from northern Italy contained in a sixth-century source (Milan, Ambrosiana SP 45; *olim* C.39.inf.) provides a single reading "In adnuntiatione aduenti." The reading, John 1:6–17, describes John the Baptist and is not found as an Advent reading in the several uses included in table 1.1. See Morin (1903).

33. See, for example, Huglo (1988), Martimort (1991) and (1992), and Metzger (1994).

34. His writings on Advent are primarily in two locations: *Le Sacramentaire*, 412–26 and 641–43; and (1953).

35. With so many numbers in columns, the potential for error is great. I have found several typographical errors, and the concordances should be checked against the editions themselves.

36. Of course, to have included them, as I have suggested here, might have overloaded the apparatus and complicated the work enough to have postponed its appearance. The Gallican correspondences are noted to the far right for every major Roman source type, and this is of tremendous usefulness for the researcher.

37. His scholarly oeuvre is in the midst of reevaluation at the present time. Especially in question is his propensity to invent early and now lost archetypes and to use them as the bases for his arguments. See, for example, an evaluation of the scholarship on the sacramentaries in Vogel (1986).

38. See especially his article on Advent (1953) and the summaries on the season in *Le Sacramentaire Gélasien* (1958), 412–26.

39. The *Veronensis* (Verona, BC 85) is not an official book but a personal collection of libelli made by a clergyman in late sixth-century Verona; Vogel calls the book a "presacramentary." The book represents Roman use, but through a Veronese lens. It does establish that there was a core of Roman prayers in circulation by its date, and their

appearance in other later sources proves the longevity of this tradition. For detailed discussion of the various theories regarding this famous source and a table of contents, see Vogel (1986), 38–46, and Metzger (1994), 38–56.

40. The so-called "Old Gelasian" sacramentary is a unique example, but more likely to represent a type than is the *Veronensis*. (The fragmentary liturgical index of Saint-Thierry of Reims corresponds to this use. The source breaks off just as Advent begins.) Vatican, BAV Reg. lat. 316, fols. 3–245, was copied around 750 in the nunnery of Chelles, just outside of Paris. The book has two main layers, one of which is Roman, and represents incorporated small collections (or libelli) from seventh-century Rome (between 628 and 715), specifically the "presbyteral Sacramentary of the Roman *tituli*." The other part contains Frankish revisions and supplementary materials. Although there is disagreement among scholars regarding which and to what extent the additions are Frankish, Vogel counts the five sets of Advent prayers among the materials believed to be of Frankish origin. See Vogel (1986), 74. For contents of the source and their natures, see Metzger (1994), 81–106.

41. The Gellone Sacramentary (G), Paris, BNF lat. 12048, is representative of the type of the "mixed Gelasian" or Frankish sacramentary, or, as they are also known, the "eighth-century Gelasian." The Frankish Gelasian, to be distinguished from the "Old Gelasian," is a book prepared in Gaul from Roman sources of two types: (1) a papal sacramentary, but revised to suit the liturgical practices of the presbyteral use at St. Peter's on the Vatican, and (2) the "Old Gelasian" itself described here, which, it is to be remembered, was also of a presbyteral character. The most recent scholarship terms the type, of which many examples survive, the "Sacramentary of Flavigny," reflecting the theory that a now-lost archetype was prepared for the Benedictine monks of this place "late in the reign of Pepin III (751–768), and not too long after the momentous residence of Pope Stephen II in *Francia* (754–755)." See Vogel (1986), 76, Metzger (1994), 107–13, and also Moreton (1976). Dumas, *Liber sacramentorum Gellonensis*, is a critical edition.

42. The first complete Milanese sacramentary is the late ninth-century *Sacramentarium Bergomense*, edited by Paredi, and used as a basis for many comparative studies.

43. As the books testify, there were Gallican liturgies of many types, and these are yet to be sorted out by liturgiologists, perhaps for the reason that there may not be sufficient surviving sources to do so in a systematic way. They are:

1. Siglum: Ga/G. The Missale Gothicum, Vatican, BAV Reg. lat. 317, dated to the early eighth century (leaves containing Advent are lost).
2. Siglum: Ga/V. The so-called Missale Gallicanum Vetus, BAV Pal. lat. 493, which is actually three books, or fragments of books, all dating from the early to mid-eighth century. The second of these contains sets of Advent prayers, and these prayers probably fell at the end of the book to which the collection orginally belonged.
3. Siglum: Ga/B. The Bobbio Missal, Paris, BNF lat. 13246, a lectionary plus a sacramentary, which comes from upper Italy, perhaps from Bobbio itself, and dates from the eighth century.
4. Siglum: Ga/F. The so-called Missale Francorum, Vatican, BAV Reg. lat. 257, another eighth-century Gallican source.

44. The so-called Gregorian Sacramentary: its core is now believed to have been compiled and put in order during the reign of Pope Honorius I (625–38). See Vogel (1986), 81 for discussion. Although the original *Hadrianum* does not survive, a copy of it does: the *Sacramentary of Hildoard of Cambrai*, Cambrai, BM 164, fols. 35–203, was commissioned by Bishop Hildoard, who also stands behind the copying of the *Sacramentary of Gellone* and the *Lectionary of Alcuin*. Paul the Deacon, who prepared the

lectionary that is a standard source for the history of the Office, was directly involved in attempting to procure the *Hadrianum* for Charlemagne and his advisors. The collection circulated in several types:

1. Siglum: H. Type I is the *Hadrianum,* the prototype of which is the book sent from Rome to Charlemagne by Pope Hadrian I. The edition used is that of J. Deshusses, *Le Sacramentaire grégorien,* prepared from Cambrai 164.
2. Siglum: P. Type II (as found in the Sacramentary of Padua, BC Codex D.47) is the papal sacramentary of type I, but adapted to presbyteral use at St. Peter's basilica on the Vatican in the late seventh century. This is not the first time such an adaptation produced a new variant.
3. Siglum: H/Sp. Another type is the *Hadrianum* plus supplement, and this represents the expansions and additions of the Carolingian liturgical reformer Benedict of Aniane in the early ninth century. There are several representative examples: see Vogel (1986), 90–93. His work was needed because the *Hadrianum* itself was a disappointment to Frankish liturgists: it was neither complete nor well suited to their purposes. Benedict made his revisions not out of lack of respect for Roman liturgical practice, but from necessity.

45. See, for example, the classic article by E. Bishop (1918a), "The Genius of the Roman Rite," which was first printed in 1899.

46. See Lowe, *Bobbio Missal: Notes and Studies.* Mass readings are also found in this source, and one can see immediately how the prayers and the readings go together. Systems of readings will be discussed in the section below, directly following this.

47. See, for example, E. Bishop (1918b), as well his notes to the *Book of Cerne* (1902). From the mid-seventh century, the Feast of Mary the Virgin was celebrated on 18 December in the Old Spanish rite, and this doubtless influenced the character of Advent as it developed in the region. For understanding the thematic complexity of Advent as found in the earliest Old Spanish sources, one would need a second study, including paleographic analyses of crucial codices. The sacramentary now in the library of Verona is counted as the oldest extant source, comparable to the eighth-century prayer books mentioned above from other areas. Its contents may date from the very early eighth century, and represent the work of two liturgical reformers, Ildefonsus of Toledo (ca. 607–ca. 667) and Julian of Toledo, who died in 690.

48. The kinds of connections Benz explores in his detailed analyses of individual prayers show parallels in language and vocabulary rather than sharing of specific blocks of text. He also says there are not deeply ingrained "Spanish symptoms" in this collection.

49. See Frederick Warren, *The Leofric Missal.* This prayer book has been the object of frequent modern study.

50. The readings for the Epistles, although not as central in setting the tone for the day or the season, are nonetheless very important. In a study of greater length, I would include a section on these readings for Advent; suffice it to say that they are variable from center to center, and can be investigated with many of the tools described in this section.

51. Vogel (1986) explains the differences between the three with characteristic clarity (314):

> Of thirty-eight *codices* (Roman and non-Roman) before 800, nineteen indicate the pericopes (liturgical readings of set length) by marginal notes to the text of a New Testament; eight *codices* by marginal notes and lists of *incipits* and *explicits* for each reading—often of different periods and origins—; three *codices* provide the readings *in extenso,* i.e., they are lectionaries properly speaking; and two *codi-*

ces give the pericopes in full in the context of a sacramentary. We can at least learn from such statistics that, in the oldest documents we have, the use of marginal notes was more frequent than the use of lists of pericopes, lectionaries or sacramentaries with readings included. It would be a mistake, however, to conclude that these four ways of providing readings were simply four consecutive stages of a gradual evolution . . . these four systems coexisted side by side for hundreds of years until, finally, the lectionary with full readings won the day.

52. These types of books are indexed in *CLLA;* Gamber also provides an introduction to them.

53. The listings of Gospel readings were far more common: whereas only a handful survives from the ninth century or earlier, there are over 140 Gospel capitularies from the eighth and ninth centuries and around another 100 from the tenth century. See Vogel (1986), 317–18.

54. These are of two types, and catalogued individually in *CLLA:* those for non-Gospel readings are often called a *comes,* a *liber comitis,* or an *Epistolary,* and those for Gospel readings, an *Evangeliary.*

55. The writings and indexes of Frere (1930, 1934, 1935), although now out of date, are still useful for his opinions and insights.

56. For full discussion of this extraordinary transmission of learning and liturgical emphases, which accounts, among other things, for the influence of Antiochene exegesis upon Bible study in England, see Bischoff and Lapidge (1994).

57. For brief discussion of the sources with liturgical scholarship, see *CLLA,* 226–38, Gamber (1962), and Bischoff and Lapidge (1994), 155–72.

58. Burchard was of Anglo-Saxon origin, but became Bishop of Würzburg in 743. See Morin (1893) and Bischoff and Lapidge (1994), 158–60. For sources representing the Roman use in Würzburg, see Morin (1911).

59. See also the comparative table that forms part of his introduction.

60. See Vogel (1986), 322–23. Further bibliography and discussion are found in G. Morin (1908) and *CLLA,* 179.

61. All these sources are discussed, with relevant bibliography, in *CLLA.*

62. For discussion of these texts, see the notes to the edition by Lowe et al.

63. The Milanese sacramentary in Bergamo has been edited by Paredi; two earlier fragments of Milanese sacramentaries, one from the seventh century and the other from the eighth, are described in *CLLA,* 262–63.

64. I am grateful to Don Randel for having supplied this reference and copies of the texts. See *Liber commicus,* ed. Justo Pérez de Urbel and Atilano González y Ruiz-Zorrilla, 3–25. The unedited fragment of the tenth-century *Liber misticus* from San Millán, not available to me, also contains Advent readings.

65. The words "sermon" and "homily" will be used interchangably here, as were their Latin counterparts throughout most of the Middle Ages.

66. Étaix, *Homéliaires;* many of the studies contain invaluable inventories of early homiliaries.

67. See *HLM,* 127. For further discussion of this key witness, see Salmon (1962), 67–70. *OR* XIV is edited in Andrieu, *Les Ordines,* 3:30–41.

68. See *HLM,* 343–44 for bibliography, especially the article of Chavasse (1955).

69. For analysis and discussion, see Barré (1957). It should be noted that the citation for this article is faulty in *HLM,* 183.

70. This sermon is discussed in my forthcoming book on the cult of the Virgin Mary at Chartres.

71. The most recent work on the plays of the prophets is Evitt (1992).

72. His most famous writings are histories, most notably the *History of the Lombards,* which has been translated into English by William D. Foulke. Events are chron-

icled through 744, and much knowledge of the seventh and early eighth centuries in northern Italy is dependent upon this work.

73. See Jacobson (1996), chap. 2, "Examination, Education, Exhortation and Exegesis," especially the section on homiliaries, 71–80. The homiliaries were not only central to the night Office, they were also texts to be used by preachers in explaining the liturgy and its significance.

74. See *CPL* 707, where the sermon is attributed to an unidentified Arian bishop of the mid-sixth century.

75. The thirteenth-century treatise on the liturgy by Durandus of Mende, now being edited in CCCM, is largely dependent upon Amalarius, as are many works in between the two authors. For a recent listing of medieval liturgical commentators, see Fassler (1995).

76. See Hesbert (1980) for speculation as to the probable nature of this source.

77. The modern denigration of Amalarius' talents is discussed and critiqued in the opening pages of Jacobson (1996).

78. For the Latin, *LO* 3, c. 40, 374–75. An analogous passage is found in *LO* 4, c. 30, 500–1.

79. For a summary of information regarding these six manuscripts, see *CAO*, Vogel (1986), 359–60, and Huglo (1988). Advent is tabulated on pp. 2–11.

80. This series of chants was mentioned in the theoretical treatise *Musica et Scolica enchiriadis*, ed. Hans Schmid, 221. I am grateful to Peter Jeffery for this reference. The series is commonly found late in the year for Sundays after Pentecost.

81. As table 1.3 shows, an unfortunate lacuna limits the usefulness of Compiègne for study of the Advent Office. The nature of this source is discussed in chap. 6 in this volume.

82. For discussion of stational liturgies, see Baldovin (1987) and Brooks-Leonard (1988).

83. Hesbert notes some unique features of the source in *CAO*, 1:xx–xxi.

84. The so-called Old Roman liturgical tradition has been much studied. This use, usually studied from later manuscripts, as these are what survives, represents the liturgical practice of Roman basilicas; it was, even in the late stage in which we know it, different from the so-called Gregorian tradition. The Office chants are readily available in a facsimile edition of the most important source. See Bonifacio Baroffio et al., *Biblioteca Apostolica Vaticana Archivio S. Pietro B 79*, 2 vols. The bibliography, vol. 1, pp. 11–15, is thorough and useful.

85. Michel Huglo, in a talk at Princeton University (March 1997), estimated that Hesbert's listing of Office MSS in *CAO* contains about half of the surviving notated medieval Office manuscripts. There is much work to be done in identifying, dating, and placing the rest. In spite of its incompleteness, Hesbert's listing is still the standard place to begin when searching for sources from a given region of Europe.

86. The secular office, that of cathedrals, of Augustinian canons, and of Dominicans, required nine responsories; the monastic office required twelve (see the chart in the Prelude to this volume). The greatest instability is in the "extra" responsories needed for the monastic Office; the nine responsories that were used for the secular Office and supplemented in the monastic Office are much more stable. On "extra" responsories, see chap. 2 in this volume.

87. An English translation of the Tridentine Roman breviary is *The Roman Breviary* (1908); this little-known source can be very useful for undergraduates and others who do not have sufficient command of Latin to work with the originals.

Reading an Office Book

LÁSZLÓ DOBSZAY

Compared with the Mass, the order of chants for the medieval Office is more complex and diverse, depending upon the traditions of single dioceses, religious orders, or individual monasteries. It is just this diversity that can teach us much about the history of liturgical music, too. The boundaries and mutual relationships of liturgical rites give firm evidence for discernible institutions, and because they do so, this hint can be followed when the assignment of musical traditions and musical influences is to be localized. In this respect, the Temporale of the Office plays an outstanding role since it represents a deeper and more stable layer in the usage of a single institution than the Sanctorale does.

These characteristics can relate to (1) the chant repertory, (2) its distribution among the various points of the service, and (3) some general features of the Office structure as well. Since the peculiarities of a given usage may occur at *various* points of the rite, the method of *sondage* ("testing") is not adequate for identifying a manuscript or a rite; the full Office must be analyzed in each source. Unfortunately, there are few published Office lists available for comparative analyses, and any attempt to increase their number requires international cooperation. Following the publication of some alphabetical indexes as appendices to source editions,[1] and Dom René-Jean Hesbert's compilation of twelve early manuscripts (*CAO;* cf. Möller 1987), the first systematic venture in this field was the CANTUS project directed by Ruth Steiner. Indexes of well-selected codices are partly published, partly available on disk, and now consultable on the Internet for interested scholars.[2]

The *CAO–ECE* program launched in 1986 at the Budapest Institute for Musicology has slightly different aims, in that rather than individual manuscripts, "typical forms" of the individual usages are documented as they can be found in relevant groups of manuscripts (Dobszay and Prószéky 1988 and Dobszay 1988). A great number of antiphoners and breviaries have been taken into consideration,[3] and not only the "early" ones (difficult to check because of the lack of control sources), but also relatively late sources, which might be just as good a witness of old traditions as the early ones, and which can be easily checked with the other sources of the same provenance.

Provenance in this respect means more than the place where the codex was made. The church institution, that is the diocese, archdiocese, order, monastery, or congregation, the liturgical use of which is reflected in a manuscript, is regarded as the place of provenance for a given source (Dobszay and Prószéky 1988, 12–13). The definition of provenance in this sense is often not easy. The presence of local saints and the names of scribes or owners is, in the best case, the first indication of a local (or regional) attribution. But the decisive factor can only be the full contents of the Office rite as revealed by comparative analysis. In this respect it is easier first to define the rite of the secular (diocesan) institutions, and then that of early monastic houses, since the former followed a strict regulation that was valid for a well-circumscribed area and was stable for a longer time (Dobszay and Prószéky 1988, 48).

However helpful an index of a codex may be, an *interpretation* of the manuscripts is needed for understanding of a codex and its rite. The relationship between individual sources and the rite reflected by them may often be influenced or disturbed by several factors, so that a given source can only be taken as a perfect description of a rite after its entries have been subjected to control. Moreover, the scribe followed his own strategy in recording a living practice and supposed the user would be able to read his work correctly—which is not the case today. The key to the correct interpretation lies hidden partly in the codex itself, in that one aspect of a given source may be used for a better understanding of another (in terms of analogies, information supplied, consistent rubrics, etc.). An additional aspect is the witness of additional sources made for the identical use. These can clear up what is obscure in the individual sources and help distinguish essential features from unique phenomena or plain errors. The widest horizon for interpretation is the entire complex of medieval Office books: they reveal what was generally accepted, possible, rare, or exceptional in the Roman rite, and what must simply be excluded from the sphere of possible readings (unless there exists very strong argument to the contrary).

I wish to present some types of such interpretations, illustrated with simple and clear examples.

Deceptive Omissions

The Utrecht Antiphoner begins with the responsory *Ecce dies* and its verse *In diebus*.[4] The antiphons for the psalms, which stand at the beginning of Vespers, are not mentioned here, because the scribe supposed the reader knew that his church used the *per annum* series of antiphons (*de psalterio*) at Vespers in Advent.

A survey of several antiphoners puts the situation in proper light. A great number of medieval churches adhered to an ancient tradition of singing Vespers of

Advent (and also the Advent weekday Matins and Lauds, except for the last week) with antiphons from the annual psalter (*de psalterio*). The first item in the series of Vespers antiphons is *Benedictus Dominus*—that is, words identical with the appropriate psalm (143). When an antiphoner records *a. Benedictus,* its readers are presumed to know that the word refers to five antiphons, or the whole series of the ordinary Saturday Vespers. But it means the same even if no rubric is given at all and the first recorded item is the responsory, as it is in our case. (See table 2.1.)

As table 2.1 demonstrates, Salzburg, Wrocław, Passau, and Bamberg adhered to the ancient tradition of singing Advent Vespers (and also the Advent weekday Matins and Lauds, except for the last week) with antiphons *de psalterio.* In a great majority of manuscripts no rubric is given in cases such as these. On the other hand, Prague made an exception for First Vespers of Sundays, and offers a special *antiphona sola super psalmos.* Aquileia does the same, but the item itself is different in the 1st–2nd and the 3rd–4th weeks. Gniezno assigns another antiphon for the same function, but only on the first Sunday, which is the beginning of Advent. The same is true of Mainz, with the difference that each of the five psalms has its own antiphon. A curious usage can be found in the Hungarian dioceses. In Esztergom all the weekdays are sung with the antiphon *de psalterio,* except the last seven days. These have a proper antiphon that is of Hungarian origin. First Vespers of Sunday has a special series of five antiphons, while Second Vespers is sung with the antiphons of Lauds. The five-antiphon series found in Esztergom has also been adopted in Kalocsa province, but all the other days are provided with a special *antiphona sola.* These liturgical practices are marked irregularly in the sources, and can only be understood by a comparative study of manuscripts.

In preparing a survey of a manuscript, philological accuracy must, of course, be observed (notes, signs). The historically exact reading requires, however, that the scholar interpret what is happening and what an omission means. In order to portray the situation in Utrecht 406 accurately, the scholar would need to supply missing information based upon an understanding of both general and regional practices. It would be problematic simply to show an "omission," for, in this case, none was intended.[5]

Missing Items

After the responsory *Ecce dies* and its verse, the Utrecht manuscript records the versicle *Rorate caeli* and the antiphon for the Magnificat, *Ecce nomen Domini,* whereas the hymn that a scholar might expect between the responsory and the versicle is missing. Is this a *real* omission, or should the lack of the hymn be attributed to the practice of designing this Office book? As is well known, the *cursus saecularis* of the Roman rite (contrary to St. Benedict's monastic Office) received the hymn relatively late, and there were differences among local liturgies regarding the inclusion of the hymns for given liturgical days and Hours.[6] Approximately half of the dioceses, for example, did not sing a hymn at Matins until the late Middle Ages.[7] Other sources are witness to an inverted order of the *capitulum* (the short reading) and the hymn at Lauds;[8] some churches sang the same Hour with

Table 2.1 Antiphons for psalms in Advent Vespers

Day	Aquileia	Salzburg, Wrocław	Gniezno	Passau, Bamberg	Prague	Mainz	Esztergom	Kalocsa
HEBDOMADA I								
Dca, V1	Veni et libera	de psalterio	Gabriel angelus	de psalterio	Gaude et laetare	1. Hora est / 2. Veni et libera / 3. Nox prae / 4. Salvatorem / 5. Scientes quia	1. A diebus / 2. Dnm Salvatorem / 3. Gabriel angelus / 4. Maria dixit / 5. Respondit angelus	1. A diebus / 2. Dominum . . . / 3. Gabriel . . . / 4. Maria dixit / 5. Respondit . . .
Dca, V2	de psalterio	de psalterio	de psalterio	de psalterio	de psalterio	de psalterio	de laudibus	Veni et libera
feriae	de psalterio	de psalterio	de psalterio	de psalterio	de psalterio	de psalterio	de psalterio	Veni et libera
HEBDOMADA II								
Dca, V1	Veni et libera	de psalterio	de psalterio!	de psalterio	Gaude et laetare	de psalterio!	A diebus, etc.	A diebus, etc.
Dca, V2	de psalterio	de psalterio	de psalterio	de psalterio	de psalterio	de psalterio	de laudibus	Veni et libera
feriae	de psalterio	de psalterio	de psalterio	de psalterio	de psalterio	de psalterio	de psalterio	Veni et libera
HEBDOMADA III								
Dca, V1	Levabit dominus	de psalterio	de psalterio	de psalterio	Gaude et laetare	de psalterio	A diebus, etc.	A diebus, etc.
Dca, V2	de psalterio	de psalterio	de psalterio	de psalterio	de psalterio	de psalterio	de laudibus	Veni et libera
feriae	de psalterio	de psalterio	de psalterio	de psalterio	de psalterio	de psalterio	de psalterio	Veni et libera
HEBDOMADA IV								
Dca, V1	Levabit dominus	de psalterio	de psalterio	de psalterio	Gaude et laetare	de psalterio	A diebus, etc.	A diebus, etc.
Dca, V2	de psalterio	de psalterio	de psalterio	de psalterio	de psalterio	de psalterio	de laudibus	Veni et libera
feriae	de psalterio	de psalterio	de psalterio	de psalterio	de psalterio	de psalterio	Dicite pusillanimes	Veni et libera
Vigilia Vigiliae	Levate capita	de psalterio	de psalterio	Quomodo fiet	de psalterio	de psalterio	Dicite pusillanimes	Veni et libera

Key: Hebdomada I, II, etc. = 1st, 2nd, etc. week of Advent

Dca = Dominica (Sunday); feriae = weekdays; V1, V2 = 1st/2nd Vespers; "Vigilia Vigiliae" = Vespers on 23 December or without a hymn depending on the given day, or other factors.[9] In addition, antiphoners frequently do not contain those genres (for example, hymns) recorded in other readily available liturgical books (for example, a *Psalterium-Hymnarium*).

In view of the variability described above, the lack of this item in Utrecht 406 may or may not be interpreted as an actual omission of the hymn at Vespers. A more precise understanding of this omission can only be found if Vespers of this codex is examined throughout the entire antiphoner and also if the order of the Advent Office in Utrecht 406 is compared with other Utrecht sources. In fact such comparison reveals that *no* hymn was sung in Utrecht during First and Second Vespers of Advent Sundays, but that one was sung on weekdays (just the opposite of the custom of some other churches). This is why the proper hymn of Advent Vespers (*Conditor alme siderum*) is written out in full for Monday Vespers while the hymn of Compline is recorded on the first folio. A hymn is consistently missing at Matins throughout the codex. The omission of the hymn at First Vespers of Advent reflects *actual* practice:

Day	Office	Genre	Incipit
D1	V1	a 1–5	[de psalterio]
		R	Ecce dies veniunt
		V	In diebus illis
		H	—
		v	Rorare caeli
	C	a	de psalterio?
		H	Christe qui lux es
		v	?
		AN	Qui venturus est
	Inv	a	Dominum qui venturus
	M	H	—
	N1	a 1–3	Hora est

Key: D1 = 1st Sunday; V1 = 1st Vespers; C = Compline; Inv = Invitatory; M = Matins; N1 = 1st Nocturn

a = antiphon; R = responsory; V = verse; H = hymn; v = versicle; AN = antiphon to the Nunc dimittis

The Question of Multiple or Surplus Items

It is not rare that a source offers surplus items at a given point within a feast, for example, more chants than could be sung for a particular service. The cause of this abundance of items is frequently the "preservationist" nature of the scribe (or the person commissioning the work), who did not want to leave out any chants or texts found in the books from which he was copying, even if the works were no longer part of the liturgy. This sometimes happened, for example, when a monastic Office with twelve responsories was translated into a secular Office with nine responsories. In this or similar cases, the manuscript and the actual liturgical practice were not in accordance, and the manuscript serves instead as witness to the practice of an earlier time or a different church, rather than to the liturgy for which the source was copied. Those using the book in the Middle Ages would have understood the situation; modern scholars looking at the manuscript out of context might well be perplexed. More frequently, however, surplus items have their special place in the celebration even if the manuscript contains no remarks explaining how to use them. In many such cases the item is recorded not at the actual liturgical place where it was used.

The first responsory of Advent (*Aspiciens a longe*) had three verses almost everywhere in the Roman church, and we know from other books (for example, from ordinals) that these verses were actually sung in a very solemn way, with a repeated section of the respond ("repetenda"), which was shortened again and again after each verse.[10] The case is not so clear with the ninth responsory (i.e. the third responsory of the third Nocturn) of the first Sunday in Advent. Here the Utrecht Antiphoner displays two verses.

Day	Office	Genre	Incipit
D1	N3	R3	Laetentur caeli
		V3	Tunc exsultabunt
		V3+	Orietur in diebus

Key: D1 = 1st Sunday of Advent; N3 = 3rd nocturn; R3 = 3rd responsory; V3 = its verse; V3+ = second verse

In fact, a few churches adopted responsories with two verses.[11] In other cases the second verse was to substitute for the first when the responsory was repeated on subsequent days.[12] In the case tabulated above from Utrecht, however, no indication for the use of the second verse can be found. Thus the responsory must be assumed to have been performed with two verses, probably for the sake of solemnity on the first day of the liturgical year, and to provide a balance for the multiverse first responsory, *Aspiciens*.

Some manuscripts record four, five, or more responsories at the third Nocturn of certain Sundays.[13] Since the number of readings, and consequently of responsories, was fixed at Nocturns, it would be absurd to suppose that the church community actually sang more responsories than three for any given Nocturn. Even if we take into consideration the possibility of a "preservationist" scribe or commissioning body, several other explanations can be offered for the presence of these surplus pieces here. In some dioceses surplus items were sung during the procession before the Mass.[14] More frequently, however, surplus responsories replaced the regular Sunday set during the week, either in a predetermined order or according to the decision of the choirmasters. A decisive answer in each case can be given only after comparing a problematic manuscript with other sources of the same tradition, especially books of differing functions such as a breviary, or an ordinal. From studying the Lenten responsories in the Esztergom liturgy, we have been able to determine which were sung for particular Sundays, and which for weekdays (see also Dobszay and Prószéky 1988, 322–23):

Day	Office	Genre	Incipit
D3	N1	R1	Videntes Joseph
		R2	Dixit Judas fratribus
		R3	Videns Jacob vestimenta
	N2	R1	Joseph dum intraret
		R2	Memento mei
		R3	Tollite hinc vobiscum
	N3	R1	Iste est frater vester
		R2	Dixit Ruben fratribus
		R3	Salus nostra
3f2	M	R1	Merito haec patimur
		R2	Dixit Joseph undecim
		R3	Nuntiaverunt Jacob

Key: D3 = the 3rd Sunday of Lent; 3f2 = Monday in the third week; N1 = 1st Nocturn; M = Matins; R1 = 1st responsory.

An interesting case is that of surplus antiphons *in evangelio,* chants sung with the intoning of the Benedictus at Lauds and the Magnificat at Vespers. In an early stage, we may assume that a set of antiphons contained an indeterminable number of pieces taken from the text of the pericopes without any strict assignment.[15] When the liturgical order of an ecclesiastical center was stabilized, however, two of the antiphons were designated as *antiphonae maiores* while the rest were neglected or used at a less important part of the Office (e.g. added to the psalms of the Lesser Hours).[16] The decision concerning which pieces were assigned to which functions may have been left to those in charge; the distribution was determined by local customs (*consuetudines*) and, finally, the antiphons could have grown integrally into the order of the local Office.[17] These transitions and uncertainties are reflected in the sources of one and the same institution. (Sometimes antiphons are simply listed; in other cases, they are recorded with additional instructions; or their order is restructured.)

Problems of Redaction; Format and Method of Compilation

Very often the different ways of redaction in composing an antiphoner obscure the picture, and make the correct reading of the manuscript difficult.[18] For example, all the antiphons of the Christmas octave (*commemorationes*) might be notated continuously in one source and distributed among Lauds and Vespers of the subsequent days in another. The difference between the sources is here, of course, only apparent.[19] The order of antiphons during Eastertide is rather confused in the Salzburg sources because of the different methods of redaction, and only a careful comparison can demonstrate that the practices behind the surface of the supplied details are almost the same in all sources from this diocese. In other words, a stable Salzburg order has been recorded, but with different formats (*CAO–ECE* I/A, 166, 178).

Without a careful study of many sources, changes and differences might be assumed where none actually occurred.

Changes in the Course of Time

Where the tradition of a diocese is documented by a chain of sources over several centuries, a striking stability of rite often emerges in spite of additions, minor modifications, and, perhaps, "reforms." This is why the main requirement is, in my opinion, to work with a coherent group of manuscripts, rather than with individual sources. Comparison can then bring to light what is essential in a local usage and what is not. As a result, minor differences and temporary changes can be understood as such more easily.

During Advent a special set of antiphons (*Veni et libera; Tuam Domine excita; In tuo adventu*) and *responsoria brevia* (*Veni ad liberandum; Ostende nobis; Super te*) were sung at the Lesser Hours all over Europe. The sources of the Esztergom diocese (Strigonium), however, take the antiphons for the Lesser Hours of Sunday from Matins (*Hora est; Scientes; Nox praecessit*), and, in a unique practice, the texts of the short responsories are identical with those of the *versicles* at the three Nocturns, transformed, in each case, to the shape and melody of a *responsorium breve* (see example 2.1).[20]

The "seasonal" antiphons and responsories are introduced in Esztergom only on the first Advent *Monday*. There are only a few manuscripts (e.g. the thirteenth-century breviary Zagreb MR 67 and the fifteenth-century antiphoner Bratislava, Archív Mesta, EC. Lad. 2 = Knauz 2, both following the Esztergom rite) that change this disposition: in these cases, the seasonal pieces are introduced on Sun-

Example 2.1. The versicles of Matins adapted to the responsoria brevia of the Lesser Hours (use of Esztergom)

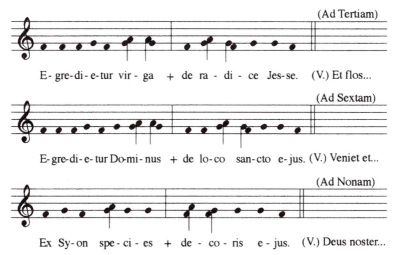

day and remain unchanged during the entire season of Advent. This arrangement is unknown in other fifteenth-century Esztergom sources, but is identical with that of the twelfth-century Codex Albensis (Graz, UB 211) and (in regard to the responsories) with the sources of Kalocsa province (cf. Dobszay and Prószéky 1988, 237, 238, 242, 256, 267, 272). What this means is that in Hungary a widespread (European) arrangement was in general use until the fourteenth century, when a new order was introduced in Esztergom, and the diocese adhered to this new order steadfastly over the subsequent centuries. The source Knauz 2, on the contrary, represents a *local* variant of the Esztergom Office (Pozsony/Bratislava, collegiate chapter) that preserved the earlier usage.

Ritus and *Consuetudo*

There are no sharp borderlines between the fixed local liturgy (*ritus*) and the rules of its everyday adaptation; many components that might exist in earlier times as unwritten or written customs (*consuetudo*) later became incorporated into the proper rite of a church or diocese. And yet the "correct reading" of the sources may require the separation of the two.

Comparison of responsories for Eastertide in Passau and Salzburg sources reveals confusion concerning the number and distribution of the pieces among the various days—so much so, in fact, that one is inclined to speak of entirely different rites (see table 2.2).[21] For the correct interpretation of the table, the following facts must be taken into consideration: the Easter season is divided into three subsections in all areas following the Roman rite. The words of the responsories were taken from the events of the Resurrection and of the Acts of the Apostles during the first period; from Revelation during the second period or section; and from the Psalms during the third.[22] This clear disposition is, however, disturbed by three changes (on the level of *consuetudines* or unwritten/written rules): (1) From about the eleventh century Matins during Eastertide was celebrated with only one Nocturn in most dioceses; consequently the nine responsories of Sundays had to be distributed among the weekdays.[23] (2) From the same time, the Sundays of Eastertide were celebrated repeating the liturgy of the day of Resurrection, and the proper texts of the single Sundays themselves were shifted to the appropriate subse-

Table 2.2 Responsories for the fourth Sunday after Easter in Passau and Salzburg sources

	Antiphonale Pataviense	Breviarium Pataviense	Ordinarius Salzburgiensis	Aquileian Antiphoner
R1	Si oblitus fuero	Angelus domini descendit	Dignus es domine	Si oblitus fuero
V1	Super flumina	Angelus domini locutus	Parce domine	Super flumina
R2	Viderunt te aquae	Angelus domini locutus	Ego sicut vitis	Hymnum cantate nobis
V2	Illuxerunt	Ecce praecedet	Ego diligentes	Illic interrogaverunt
R3	Narrabo nomen	Dum transisset	Audivi vocem	Viderunt te aquae
V3	Qui timetis	Et valde mane	Vidi angelum	Illuxerunt

quent Mondays (a custom that caused many disturbances in the liturgical ordering of Saturday and Sunday Vespers).[24] (3) The turning point from one period to the other might be shifted over from one week to the other "secundum consuetudinem ecclesiae." All these changes touched the "how" and not the "what" in the celebration of the Office. Liturgical books might give instructions for the celebration, each in its own way.

Returning to the Passau and Salzburg sources, it turns out that these books contain practically the same system of responsories. The Passau Breviary (second column) presents the responsories of the Resurrection days and introduces the *Si oblitus* series only on Monday. The Ordinarius Salzburgiensis still keeps the responsories of the second section and makes the turn from the *Dignus es* "historia" to the *Si oblitus* not earlier than the fifth Sunday. Thus the differences in columns 1 to 3 derive from nothing other than the influence of the above-mentioned *consuetudines*. Two rites can be said to be truly different only when the actual repertory, the ordering of the repertory, and the assignments of verses are divergent between them (as is the case with Aquitaine versus Passau/Salzburg in table 2.2).

Conclusion

If the primary agents of chant history are the communities that performed, preserved, transmitted, enriched, or modified a tradition, the sources must be regarded not only as elements in a textual stemma, products of scribal activity, but also as views of particular everyday practices. The test of understanding a manuscript would be to be able to pray or sing through the entire liturgy as it was performed at the church for which the codex was written.

So we need a *full* form of the Office, even if the codex recorded only a portion of it explicitly, and at the same time a *typical* form of it, in order to eliminate the contingencies of single manuscripts and arrive at the community's usage. The procedure that leads to this is neither a creation of an "Urform" nor an arbitrary compilation from several manuscripts. The reconstruction of the typical form is based on a thorough analysis of the sources, and the documentation must be accompanied with accurate references to individual manuscripts (see e.g. Dobszay and Prószéky 1988, 281–370). Temporal or local variations of the tradition have to be taken into consideration, and the scholar can be forced by new experiences to modify his view.

The procedure is similar to the operation of the human mind in constructing a concept, gathering essential elements from individual phenomena, and separating them from *accidentalia*. In so doing, the risk of failure is not greater than that in any other historical undertaking that transcends a mere positivistic description. During comparative study, single manuscripts—useful and necessary as they are—can often mislead. In the end, only the description and comparison of the *traditions* themselves produce satisfying conclusions. All scholarly effort relies on nothing other than the sources—and yet our primary concern is not about the *sources* but about the *life* they represent.

Notes

1. *Antiphonaire monastique . . . de Lucques* (PM 9), *Antiphonaire monastique . . . de Worcester* (PM 12); Froger, ed., *L'Antiphonaire de Hartker* (PM II/1); Frere, *Antiphonale Sarisburiense.* Cf. Karnowka (1983). Some late medieval rhymed offices have recently been published and cataloged in Andrew Hughes, *LMLO.*

2. For example, CANTUS 1990, 1992, and 1993.

3. *CAO–ECE* I/A (Salzburg) is based on thirteen manuscripts (twelfth to fifteenth centuries); *CAO–ECE* II/A (Bamberg) on eight sources (twelfth to fifteenth centuries); *CAO–ECE* III/A (Prague) on twelve sources (thirteenth to sixteenth centuries). For the Advent section the program used fourteen sources in the following distribution: from the eleventh century: 1; twelfth: 8; thirteenth: 11; fourteenth: 24; fifteenth: 53; sixteenth: 7. From Germany (and the Netherlands): 39, Hungary: 36, from Poland and Czechoslovakia: 21, others: 8.

4. Utrecht, Rijksuniversiteit 406 (3.J.7; *olim* Eccl. 318): fol. 4r–v. (The main body of the codex is from the 12th century; fol. 4v is a 14th-century copy of the first folio, now lost.) See the facsimile edition by Ruth Steiner, *Utrecht, Bibliotheek der Rijksuniversiteit, 406 (3.J.7),* with Introduction by Ike de Loos (Ottawa, 1997).

5. Reference to the psalm antiphon(s) is missing in all six sources published in *CAO* I. A hymn is recorded only in the Bamberg source. The responsory is missing in four of the six sources, while the Ivrea manuscript lists *before* Vespers all the versicles that should be distributed among the Hours.

6. Apel (1958), 423. *NG* 8:838. For more detailed recent discussion of these issues, see Dobszay (forthcoming).

7. On a random selection of 23 dioceses (Cambrai, Beauvais, Aquileia, Augsburg, Bamberg, Freysing, Mainz, Hildesheim, Regensburg, Trier, Utrecht, Salzburg, Passau, Brixen, Erfurt, Linköping, Kulm/Chełmno, Gniezno, Wrocław/Breslau, Kraków, Prague, Olomouc, Transylvania, Kalocsa, Esztergom/Gran) only nine include a hymn in Matins.

8. For example, in the printed breviary of Eichstätt of 1483.

9. For example, in the Passau Office. The rubric of the Passau printed breviary of 1490 says that at Vespers during the pre-Lenten season "hymnus non dicitur nec dominicis diebus nec ferialibus nisi sabbatinis noctibus, tunc dicitur hymnus 'Dies absoluti' usque ad dominicam primam Quadragesimae"; nor did Passau sing a hymn at Lauds during Eastertide.

10. *CAO* 4, no. 6129. For the performance see, e.g., the Ordinary Book of Eger Cathedral (1509): "Item primum responsorium hac die habet quattuor versus cum Gloria Patri. Primum versum canunt duo pueri. Secundum similiter duo. Tercium similiter duo. Repetitiones autem semper fiunt in choro. Gloria Patri omnes sex pueri canunt ante altare maius. Et repetitio responsorii ab ante fit per capellanos chori" (Kandra, *Ordinarius,* 2). (On this day the first responsory has four verses, the Gloria Patri included. The first verse is sung by two boys, and the same with the second and third verse; after the verse, the repetitive part of the responsory is always performed by the choir. The Gloria Patri is sung in front of the main altar by all six boys, and the responsory is started from its beginning by the choir chaplains.)

11. For example, in Salzburg: *CAO–ECE* I/A, 90–91.

12. For example, the verses *In principio* and *Puer natus* in the responsory *Verbum caro;* see *CAO–ECE* I/A, 117.

13. For example, CANTUS 1992, p. 6, fol. 6, fol 5r–v; pp. 25–26, fols. 66v–67r; p. 28, fol. 174r–v; CANTUS 1993, p. 14, fol. 297r; p. 18, fol 304r–v; p. 19, fol. 306r; p. 22, fols. 312r–313r; p. 23, fol. 315r–v; Dobszay and Prószéky (1988), 32, nos. 15741–44; *CAO–ECE* I/A, 82, no. 2152; *CAO–ECE* II/A, 77, no. 15041, p. 115; no. 22260, and other examples following.

14. Antiphonarium Pataviense (thirteenth c.): Munich, BS 16141, rubric at the first Sunday after Epiphany.

15. For example, on the weekdays of Lent. Cf. *CAO* 1:134–67.

16. Compare the surplus "antiphonae in evangelio" during the Lenten weekdays in Piacenza, BC 65 (CANTUS 1993, 21–25) and in Salzburg (*CAO–ECE* I/A, 138–48).

17. "Antiphonae ex evangeliis assumptae in psalmos Benedictus et Magnificat prima ad matutinum secunda ad vesperas, si vero plures sunt in medio quae restant dicantur ad horas" (The antiphons taken from the (daily) Gospel for the psalms of Benedictus and Magnificat: the first (is sung) at Matins, the second at Vespers; if there are more, the remaining between the first and the last ones are sung at the Lesser Hours); from the twelfth-century *Liber Ordinarius* of Salzburg Cathedral, Salzburg, UB II. 6, fol. 52. Almost the same words occur in the breviary (1490). In fact, the Salzburg sources themselves list and distribute these surplus antiphons in rather different ways.

18. *CAO* intended to reproduce the order of entries as they actually follow each other in the manuscripts. Doing so, unfortunately, generated quantities of empty space on the pages, and frequent references were required to hint at the analogous places that cannot be read in parallel columns.

19. These particular chants are fully written out at the appropriate days in the Salzburg *Liber Ordinarius* (Salzburg II. 6; similarly in the antiphoner Vorau, SB 287, the printed Salzburg breviary, and in the breviaries Szombathely, Püspöki Könyvtár lat. 10 and 14). The same series is gathered together in the "Dominica infra octavam" in the thirteenth-century Salzburg Antiphoner (Szombathely lat. 1). A similar gathering can be found in the Klosterneuburg antiphoners Klosterneuburg, Augustiner-Chorherrenstift Ccl 1010 and Ccl 1013. The same series of commemorative antiphons is collected at the end of the feast of the Nativity in the Esztergom sources.

20. *Breviarium Strigoniense* (1484); cf. Dobszay and Prószéky (1988), 273. The examples are taken from the Paulite Antiphoner (Zagreb, Cathedral Library, MR 8, pp. 7–8). These responsories are not found in *CAO* 4.

21. The sources are Munich, BS clm. 16141; *Breviarium Pataviense* (1490); Salzburg II. 6; CANTUS 1992, 40.

22. *CAO* 1, nos 76a, 88a, 78a, 79, 822, 85a, 88, 89. Cf. *CAO–ECE* I/A. nos. 30550–600, 30800–600, 30960–31010, 31430–720, 32200–430.

23. "Sed quia quamplures omnes dies hinc usque in octava pentecostes cum tribus psalmis et lecionibus observare volunt . . .; illi qui cotidianis diebus iii psalmos et iii tantum lectiones videntur agere non ex regula sanctorum patrum sed ex fastidio et negligentia comprobantur agere. Romani autem diverso modo agere ceperunt maxime a tempore quo teutonicis concessum est regimen nostre ecclesie. Nos autem et ordinem investigantes et antiquum morem nostre ecclesie statuimus fieri sicut prenotavimus antiquos imitantes patres" (*Liber Ordinarius,* Salzburg II. 6, fol. 70v). (But since there are many people who wish to celebrate all days from this day until the end of the Octave of Pentecost with three psalms and three readings only . . . those who pray all days (of the Easter season) with only three psalms and three readings, do this not by following the rules of the holy Fathers, but because of fatigue and neglect. The Romans, however, began to follow (this) diverse practice, mainly from the time in which our church was given over to the Germans. We, however, seeking both the right order and the ancient usage of our church, decree as above, imitating our ancient fathers.) Cf. Bäumer 1895, 312.

24. "Dominica prima imponitur feria secunda, et sic de aliis dominicis usque ad ascensionem Domini." (The first Sunday is placed on Monday and the same way until the Ascension of our Lord (*Breviarium Strigoniense* [1484], fol. 146). "Secundis feriis usque ascensionem Domini secundum consuetudinem huius regni semper hore canonice cum missa servantur et imponuntur de dominica eo quod dominicis diebus nihil

dicitur de dominica sed per totum de resurrectione domini ut supra." (According to the use of this country, on Mondays until the Ascension of our Lord, the Canonical Hours, together with the Mass, are taken and placed from the Sunday, so, that on Sundays themselves nothing is said from the proper of the Sundays but everything from the Resurrection day, as above.) *Ordinarius . . . Agriensis ecclesiae* (= Kandra, *Ordinarius*, 78).

II ✦ THE PRE-CAROLINGIAN OFFICE

The Origins of the Western Office

The origins of the Divine Office, the Church's system of corporate worship outside of the Mass, is a story that has become well known in recent times, thanks
especially to the work of Paul Bradshaw (1981) and Robert Taft (1986).[1] Still it is
worth recounting—from its beginnings to its classic Western manifestation in the
Rule of St. Benedict—from the peculiar point of view of the music historian. Such
retelling, moreover, provides the opportunity to offer some slight qualification,
again, from the viewpoint of a music historian, to the conventional wisdom on
the subject.

The Office is a creation of the fourth century; it came about by a merger of the
morning and evening services of the urban cathedral with the daily round of monastic offices to create a horarium roughly commensurate with the medieval Western Office. It has a prehistory, however, of considerable interest, even if one of the
most interesting questions of that prehistory—the question of synagogue origins—must be answered in the negative. In 1944 the Anglican scholar Clifford
Dugmore made the claim that the morning and evening offices of the early church
were directly derived from morning and evening synagogue services, which were,
in turn, derived from the morning and evening sacrificial services of the Temple
in Jerusalem (Dugmore 1944). This is an idea of considerable appeal and plausibil-
ity, but it has been abandoned in recent decades.[2] There is no need here to rehearse
the numerous points of detail that speak against it, but two broad considerations
are worthy of mention. The first is that the very existence of formalized morning
and evening prayer services in the synagogue, before the destruction of the Temple
by the Romans in A.D. 70, is doubtful, while it is all but certain that public morning
and evening Christian prayer services were not a practice of the primitive church.
The Christian debt to Judaism in this respect is more general than the inheritance
of specific services; it is the broad tendency to single out certain hours of the day
as times set aside for prayer.

The central point to be borne in mind is that during the first three centuries of

Christianity, before its emancipation by Constantine in 312, such hours of prayer were observed privately rather than publicly. The hours so designated were: morning and evening; the third, sixth, and ninth hours of the day; and the middle of the night. It is perfectly legitimate to see in these times six of the eight that would come to make up the medieval Office, with nighttime prayer corresponding to Matins (referred to hereafter as Vigils); morning prayer to Lauds; prayer at the third, sixth, and ninth hours to Terce, Sext, and None; and evening prayer to Vespers. Only Prime and Compline are not accounted for. Still one must not assume that most early Christians observed all six of these hours every day, let alone that a sort of private breviary existed at the time. For one thing, different patristic authors cite different combinations of hours: most notably the earlier third-century Alexandrians, Clement and Origen, appear to favor morning, noon, and evening, while their Carthaginian contemporaries, Tertullian and Cyprian, recommend the third, sixth, and ninth hours (in addition, needless to say, to morning and evening).[3] In the view of the present author the patristic evidence is too sparse and scattered to establish the actual practice of Christians in any particular region, but it is agreed that it is sufficient to demonstrate that the six Office hours that would come to be observed publicly in the course of the fourth century were already sanctified, at least in conception, by the third century.

To be distinguished from these times of private prayer are a number of public gatherings that are mentioned in the pre-fourth-century sources. In addition to descriptions of the Eucharist, there are references to instructional meetings in the morning, instructional meetings on Wednesday and Friday at the ninth hour, when the fast for these days comes to an end,[4] and the evening *agape* (or love feast).[5] These meetings, however, are not the direct ancestors of the Office. A service of the Office is not a catechetical meeting, but rather a liturgical gathering for prayer and worship (noteworthy in this respect is the almost total exclusion of scriptural readings from the fourth-century Office). Nor does any Office hour take the form of a community meal like the *agape*, although it must be said that the description of the third-century Roman *agape* given in the *Apostolic Tradition* of Hippolytus includes the *lucernarium,* the ceremony of lamp-lighting that is the hallmark of fourth-century cathedral Vespers.

The Change from Private to Public Prayer Hours

Liturgical historians are unanimous in associating the change from private to public observation of prayer hours with the emancipation of the Church under Constantine in 312. As a formerly persecuted minority grew in number and status, and as great stone basilicas were erected in virtually every town of the Mediterranean basin, it became the custom to celebrate morning and evening prayer (referred to hereafter as Lauds and Vespers) in the presence of the local bishop. The earlier fourth-century evidence is distressingly sparse, but Eusebius of Caesarea (d. ca. 340) assures us that "throughout the whole world in the churches of God at the morning rising of the sun and at the evening hours, hymns, praises, and truly divine delights are offered to God" (Taft 1986, 33). It seems fair enough to take the words of Eusebius as a reference to what has come to be known as the "cathedral Office," so called because in the centuries before the development of the parochial system the bishop's church was the center of each Christian community.

The cathedral Offices of Lauds and Vespers, as reconstructed from later fourth-century sources,[6] were characterized by ceremony and symbol that reflected the time of day, and by a choice of hymns, psalms, and prayers that were particularly appropriate to the occasion. A typical cathedral Lauds would begin at sunrise and include Ps. 62,[7] "O God, my God, to thee do I watch at break of day," as well as Pss. 148–50, the three psalms of praise from which Lauds eventually derives its name. The ceremony might also include the hymn *Gloria in excelsis,* and would generally include a series of intercessory prayers, possibly in the form of a litany, and a concluding blessing by the bishop. Vespers would open with the ceremony of lamp-lighting, which might be accompanied by *Phos hilarion,* the ancient hymn that celebrates Jesus as the Light, and by Ps. 140, which includes the verse "Let my prayer be directed as incense in thy sight, and the lifting up of my hands as an evening sacrifice." Like Lauds, Vespers would also include intercessory prayers and a concluding blessing by the bishop. The symbolism of light was present in both ceremonies, and while the mood of Lauds was characteristically one of praise, the idea of contrition for one's failings during the day generally figured prominently among the vesperal themes.

It is best, perhaps, to leave the description of the fourth-century cathedral Office at that, that is, as a composite of the elements and tendencies that appear most often in the later fourth-century sources. Robert Taft, however, has gone much further, attempting to reconstruct the probable sequence of events in the individual offices of the principal Eastern and Western ecclesiastical centers. No other scholar in the field could have come so close to succeeding in such an attempt; no one else combines the same breadth of learning, sure judgment in interpreting sources, and ability to construct a compelling larger historical view. But there is an inherent danger in creating the sorts of reconstructions that are involved here: one can too easily grant them a greater concreteness, specificity, and fixity than the available evidence warrants. For one thing, there are no sources for individual churches from the first two-thirds of the fourth century, only Eusebius' general remark about the widespread custom of morning and evening hymns and prayers in the churches. We do not know, for example, which churches led the way in establishing the daily observance of Lauds and Vespers. We do not know the process by which one church might have influenced another in this respect, which churches might have been more successful than others at it, and which less inclined to participate. As for the content of the earlier fourth-century cathedral Offices, we must settle for the assumption that they used by and large the same sort of material that appears in the later fourth-century documents.

But the later fourth-century evidence is itself not so full as one might wish. For St. Basil's Caesarea Taft had little more to go on than Basil's frequently quoted Epistle 207 of A.D. 375, which describes a nighttime vigil of psalmody and prayer:

Among us the people arise at night and go to the house of prayer; in pain, distress and anguished tears they make confession to God, and finally

getting up from prayer they commence the singing of psalms. . . . After thus
spending the night in a variety of psalmody with interspersed prayer, now
that the light of day has appeared, all in common as if from one mouth and
one heart offer the psalm of confession [Ps. 50?] to the Lord, while each
fashions his personal words of repentance. (*MECL,* no. 139)

Taft (1986, 39–41) attempts to reconstruct the cathedral Vigils and Lauds of Cappadocia (the region of Asia Minor that includes Caesarea) from this passage, even
though it appears to describe a single service, not two, and to cite only one specific
item in the service, the "psalm of confession." He is at pains, moreover, to argue
against monastic involvement in the service, whereas it seems unlikely that Basil's
quasi-monastic communities of men and women, who were described in the previous paragraph of the letter as "persevering in prayer night and day" and "continuously chanting hymns to our God," would be excluded from such a vigil. Everything we know about the later fourth-century urban Office, as Taft would be the
first to agree, speaks for a celebration of the Office in common between urban
ascetics and the more typical laity.

Taft's reconstruction of the Cappadocian cathedral Office may be the most tenuous that he attempts; the evidence for Antioch, for example, is much more substantial, with the material from the *Apostolic Constitutions* and a number of references from the works of St. John Chrysostom. I raise the case of Cappadocia to
illustrate that even the most historically responsible of contemporary liturgiologists can appear to grant a greater stature, universality, and stability to the fourth-
century cathedral Office than can be supported by the sources. It is presented,
moreover, as something that achieved maturity free from monastic contamination,
even if overwhelmed by the monastic Office in the final decades of the fourth
century. The monastic Office is, as we shall see, something of an embarrassment
to modern liturgical scholars.

The Monastic Office

The monastic Office originated in the early fourth century among the first Christian monks, earnest souls who fled the temptations of the city for the harsh solitude of the deserts, most notably those of Egypt.[8] The two outstanding figures of
the Egyptian movement were St. Antony (d. 356), who settled in Lower Egypt,
north of Cairo, and St. Pachomius (d. 346), who worked far to the south in the
region of the Upper Nile, near Thebes. The monasticism of Lower Egypt is generally characterized as eremitic, that is, a form of monasticism in which the monks
live as hermits, even if in close proximity to a charismatic leader like Antony. The
monasticism of Upper Egypt tended more toward the cenobitic variety, that is, a
living together in community, again, under the guidance of a charismatic leader
like Pachomius.

And what sort of office did the Egyptian monks pursue?[9] Fundamental to the
early monastic Office, indeed fundamental to the entire early monastic life, was
the attempt to take as literally as possible the scriptural counsel "to pray without

ceasing" (1 Thess. 5:17). Of considerable interest to the music historian is that the primary device adopted by the Egyptian monks to realize this attempt was the chanting of the psalms continuously, that is, not occasionally and selectively as in the cathedral Office, but in numerical order for extended periods of time.[10] This chanting, moreover, was not so much a form of praise to God as a vehicle for meditation, and as such it was usually interspersed with prayer, as often as not with a pause for prayer after each psalm.

While there is abundant testimony to the chanting of psalms by individual monks in a variety of circumstances—including the recitation of the entire Psalter in a single night (*MECL*, nos. 126 and 127)—liturgical historians have tended to ignore such practices and to concentrate instead upon the monastic Office in the narrow sense. In doing so, perhaps, they have tended, just as in the case of the cathedral Office, to reify and to fix what must have been subject to considerable variation from time to time and place to place. It can be said, however, that two services a day was the norm, roughly similar to the cathedral Office in this respect, with one in the morning and one in the evening, although the first of the two might often take place before daybreak and the second in the later afternoon. The eremites of Lower Egypt are said to have observed these hours in their private cells during the week and to have assembled together only on weekends. Palladius, who visited Lower Egypt in about 388, described his impression of the afternoon office: "Indeed one who stands there at about the ninth hour can hear the psalmody issuing forth from each cell, so that he imagines himself to be high above in paradise" (*MECL*, no. 117).

In the cenobitic colonies of Upper Egypt the monks met in common for their two daily offices. Armand Veilleux has sifted through the various layers of the Pachomian documents in an effort to establish the original form of the Office as prescribed by the master before his death in 346 (Veilleux 1968, 117–58, 276–323). The basic structure of the Office, both morning and evening, appears to have been that of the so-called "six prayers." Each of these six "prayers" consisted of a scriptural reading recited by an individual monk while the others sat in silence, after which they stood, crossed themselves, and said the Lord's Prayer with arms extended, and then prostrated themselves for silent penitential prayer, finally to rise again, cross themselves, and to pray once more in silence. Veilleux and those who have treated the subject after him emphasize how a careful reading of the most primitive Pachomian documents has refuted the long-standing interpretation of the "six prayers" as "six psalms," an interpretation that can be found as early as St. Jerome: in his Latin translation of the *Precepta* of Pachomius, he added *psalmosque* after the phrase *sex orationes* (Veilleux 1968, 296).

Modern liturgical historians have seized upon this paraphrase of Jerome as evidence that the authentic Pachomian weekday Office was not necessarily psalmic,[11] but surely this is focusing upon a single tree at the expense of the forest. Aside from the circumstance that the scriptural recitations of the six prayers might very well have included psalms, and aside from the further circumstance that the Sunday morning Pachomian Office was most definitely a service of psalmody, the evidence that psalmody was a pervasive practice of fourth-century Egyptian monks— whether during nighttime Vigils (*MECL*, nos. 118, 120, 127), while on journeys

(*MECL*, no. 119), when visiting fellow monks (*MECL*, nos. 127, 128), or while at funerals (*MECL*, nos. 111, 113)—is so overwhelming as to make any attempt to downplay its importance quite futile.[12] And one must ask why Jerome, himself a monk in Palestine, would have thought it advisable to add the phrase *psalmosque* if he did not assume from his own experience, rightly or wrongly, that the Pachomian Office was psalmodic. The point has been brought out here to illustrate what was referred to above as an embarrassment on the part of contemporary liturgical historians with regard to the monastic Office. The specific point of embarrassment is the practice of continuous psalmody as opposed to the carefully selective psalmody of the cathedral Office. W. Jardine Grisbrooke represents the modern viewpoint well when he writes: "Long habituation to forms of the office including this *recitatio continua* of the psalms has until very recently prevented recognition of its intrinsic absurdity; it would hardly be sillier to use a modern hymnbook in the same way" (Grisbrooke 1992, 415, n. 4).

Be that as it may, the music historian must simply observe that continuous psalmody did not seem an absurdity to fourth-century desert monks. Nor did it seem an absurdity to contemporary urban monks and nuns. Little is known about urban monasticism in the earlier fourth century; one tends to assume that it originated as desert monasticism that spread in the course of the century from its remote solitudes to the principal ecclesiastical centers. It is true, certainly, that many of the outstanding ecclesiastical leaders of the time visited Egypt to learn the ways of the desert monks, and true also that urban monastic groups found an inspiring example in these fabled ascetics. But it is arguable also that the impetus for idealistic men and women living in the cities to come together into communities devoted to prayer and self-deprivation was a natural outgrowth of tendencies already manifested in earlier Christian centuries.

But whatever its origins, urban monasticism showed itself as devoted to psalmody as its desert counterpart; it is scarcely an exaggeration to say that psalmody was its defining characteristic. Chrysostom writes of his monastic brothers in Antioch: "As soon as they are up, they stand and sing the prophetic hymns. . . . Neither cithara, nor syrinx, nor any other musical instrument emits such sound as is to be heard in the deep silence and solitude of those holy men as they sing" (*MECL*, no. 187). And similarly the Pseudo-Chrysostom: "In the monasteries there is a holy chorus of angelic hosts, and David is first, middle and last; in the convents there are bands of virgins who imitate Mary, and David is first, middle and last" (*MECL*, no. 195).[13]

The Cathedral Office

The psalmody of urban monasticism had a profound, indeed overwhelming, influence on the cathedral Office; it transformed the morning and evening offices, and it filled the intervening hours of the day with additional offices. The city where this is best observed is Jerusalem, the one location for which we have a full and detailed description of the daily Office, thanks to the narrative of Egeria, the Spanish nun who visited the Holy Land in the late fourth century. The morning monastic and cathedral Offices were combined at Jerusalem by the simple expedient of retaining both and performing them successively, the monastic psalmodic Vigil followed by the cathedral service of praise, a pattern still recognizable in Western medieval Vigils and Lauds. Egeria describes the monastic Vigil in these words:

> Each day before cockcrow, all the doors of the Anastasis are opened, and all the *monazontes* and *parthenae*, as they are called here, come down, and not only they, but also those lay people, men and women, who wish to keep vigil at so early an hour. From that hour until it is light, hymns are sung and psalms responded to, and likewise antiphons; and with every hymn there is a prayer. For two or three priests, and likewise deacons who say these prayers with every hymn and antiphon, take turns to be there each day with the *monazontes*. (*MECL*, no. 242)

The service is one of extended psalmody sung exclusively by the monks and nuns, even if in the presence of the admiring laity. After each psalm there is a prayer, according to the time-honored monastic practice; the prayers, however, are said by members of the local clergy, assigned on a daily basis, and apparently bringing a sort of diocesan sanction to the monastic service. The bishop himself is not present, for this is an essentially monastic service. He made his appearance only at the beginning of Lauds: "As soon as it begins to grow light, they start to sing the morning hymns, and behold the bishop arrives with the clergy" (*MECL*, no. 243). Egeria continues by describing prayers led by the bishop, who eventually leaves the sanctuary and goes among the faithful, allowing them to kiss his hand before his concluding blessing. Lauds, then, unlike Vigils, appears to be an essentially cathedral service, even if it is the monks and nuns who sing "the morning hymns," which include in all probability those chants specific to Lauds, such as Ps. 62, Pss. 148–50, and perhaps *Gloria in excelsis*. Indeed Lauds is the service that manages best to retain some semblance of its cathedral character, even in the medieval West, where the absorption of the cathedral Office by the monastic Office was near total.

Sext and None are sung during the course of the day (with Terce reserved for Lent at Jerusalem). Egeria's description reveals these services to be made up exclusively of monastic psalmody, brought to a close when the bishop enters to recite a concluding prayer and to bless the faithful: "Again at the sixth hour all come down to the Anastasis in the same way, and sing psalms and antiphons until the bishop is called in. He likewise comes down . . . and again he first says a prayer, then blesses the faithful. . . . And at the ninth hour they do the same as at the sixth" (*MECL*, no. 244).

With Vespers, the monastic and cathedral elements, although remaining distinct, combine in one service. The service begins in the absence of the bishop: the lamps are lit—the traditional rite of the *lucernarium*—amid the monastic singing of the specific evening psalms, followed by extended psalmody; when the bishop arrives, finally, the psalmody is continued. In Egeria's words:

> But at the tenth hour—what they call here *licinicon*, and what we call *lucernare*—the entire throng gathers again at the Anastasis, and all the lamps and candles are lit, producing a boundless light. . . . And the *psalmi lucernares*, as well as antiphons, are sung for a long time. And behold the

bishop is called and comes down and takes the high seat, while the priests also sit in their places, and hymns and antiphons are sung. And when these have been finished according to custom, the bishop arises. (*MECL,* no. 245)

A series of prayers, including a litany, follows, and the service concludes with the bishop administering separate blessings to the catechumens and the faithful. What is striking about the service from the perspective of the medieval Western Office is that the overall shape of Vespers appears already present, that is, a period of continuous psalmody followed by a series of disparate events.

The six Offices at Jerusalem—Vigils, Lauds, Terce, Sext, None, and Vespers—comprised the typical daily pattern of the time; Prime and Compline were the only members of the medieval horarium not regularly present. The latter made its appearance first. There was a period of time between Vespers and bedtime, so that it was only natural that the end of the day would come to be observed within some monastic circles by a short service of psalmody and prayer in common. Basil, for example, describes a sort of proto-Compline in his so-called *Longer Rules* when he writes: "And again as night begins, we must ask that our rest will be free from sin and evil phantasy; Ps. 90 must be recited at this hour" (*MECL,* no. 137). Ps. 90, with its verses 5 and 6, "thou shalt not fear the terror of the night . . . nor that which walks about in darkness," will find its way into St. Benedict's Compline. Prime was the last of the Office hours to make its appearance, and it was, as we shall see present, in Western sources that it did so.

The Western Office

The documents cited up to now were exclusively Eastern for the good reason that virtually nothing of the sort exists for the contemporary West. This is true especially for the cathedral Office and most especially true for the cathedral Office of Rome. In the view of the present author the lack of sources describing the late fourth-century cathedral Office of Western cities may simply reflect the circumstance that it was very little developed at the time.[14] And the fact that the Western medieval Office has so little trace of the cathedral Office may simply reflect the fact that the original development of the Western Office took place primarily under monastic auspices. It is true that Western Lauds, with its use of selected psalms like Ps. 62 and Pss. 148–50, appears to be utilizing cathedral material. But while the monastic early morning Vigil was certainly characterized by continuous psalmody, there is no reason why monastic groups, independent of cathedral example, could not have chosen to greet the new day with appropriate psalms of praise. It is not historically plausible to deny to monks completely the ability to use appropriate psalms at key points in the Office. So when Cassian (d. 435) tells us that his monastery near Marseilles, as well as the monastery in Bethlehem where he spent his youth, closes Vigils with Pss. 148–50, we need not insist that this is a borrowing from the cathedral Office (*MECL,* no. 348).

Cassian's rule, the *De institutis coenobiorum,* written sometime after 415, purports to be a description of the Egyptian monastic Office, while it is clearly an adaptation of Eastern practices to the circumstances of his own Gallican communities of monks and nuns. It is only the first in a series of full descriptions of Western monastic Offices—including the Gallican rules of Caesarius of Arles (d. 542) and Aurelian of Arles (d. 551), and the central Italian *Rule of the Master*—that precede the classic formulation of Benedict, written for his monks at Monte Cassino in about 530. There is obviously not the space here to survey the provisions of these rules. Rather three points will be treated, the first two very briefly, the third at slightly more length.

The first concerns the origins of Prime. Traditionally it was attributed to Cassian, who spoke of a new office of "three psalms and prayers, according to the custom established long ago at the offices of Terce and Sext" (*MECL*, no. 347); the office was instituted, as Cassian explains, to prevent the slothful from returning to bed before Terce, and to bring the number of day offices to seven, in accord with the precept of the psalms: "Seven times a day I have given praise to thee" (Ps. 118:164). Taft has argued forcefully that Cassian was speaking not of Prime but of Lauds, a view that has persuaded many, but not all.[15] In any event Prime appears in the rule of Caesarius of Arles and in all subsequent Western rules.

A second point worthy of mention is the inclusion in the Western Office of hymns—hymns, that is, in the new metrical manner of St. Ambrose. Cassian does not mention them, but Caesarius, Aurelian, the Master, and Benedict do, with Benedict, in fact, referring to them as *ambrosiana*. It comes as something of a surprise that these worthy ascetics would welcome such creations after the fourth-century church appeared to have adopted so restrictive a position on the so-called *psalmi idiotici*.

The final point involves the preoccupation of Western monastic Offices with a strictly symmetrical and numerical apportionment of the Psalter. One detects in the development of Christian liturgies a gradual movement from ad hoc arrangement (dare one use the word improvisation?) to permanently fixed ones. This is observable first, perhaps, in overall liturgical structures; the permanent shape of the Eucharist, for example, including the pre-eucharistic service of the word, is clearly visible already in Justin Martyr's (d. ca. 165) frequently quoted description of Sunday morning Eucharist at Rome (see *MECL*, no. 25). Secondly, it would appear, Ordinary prayers and chants become fixed; thus we have in the later fourth century the widespread use of the Sanctus at the Eucharist, Pss. 148–50 at Lauds, and the appearance of the medieval text of the Latin eucharistic prayer in St. Ambrose's *De sacramentis*. And finally there follows the larger project of fitting out the entire church year with permanently assigned Proper prayers, readings, and chants.[16]

I believe that the monastic concern with the precise apportionment of the Psalter is a peculiar phase of this broad liturgical movement toward fixity. Thus, while the fourth-century Cappadocian *De virginitate* prescribes for Vigils: "Say as many psalms as you can while standing" (*MECL*, no. 153), a few decades later Cassian insists upon exactly twelve psalms for Vigils (the standard medieval number, one should note) (*MECL*, no. 338). Modules of three also figure prominently in early monastic rules: one recalls that in Egeria's description of Sext and None the monks and nuns "sing psalms and antiphons until the bishop is called in," whereas Cassian specifies precisely three psalms for the same offices.

Such examples can be multiplied indefinitely, but particularly worthy of mention are the intriguing speculations of Joseph Pascher (1957b, 255–67) about the makeup of Roman Vespers before the time of Benedict. Pascher, followed by Adalbert de Vogüé (1967c, 195–99), argues from certain Holy Week Vespers that retain six psalms, and from the fact that Sunday Vespers begins with Ps. 109 in all early medieval arrangements, that the fifth-century monastic Vespers of the Roman basilicas used six psalms each day. The 42 psalms from Ps. 109 to Ps. 150 were simply apportioned in numerical order over the seven days of the week. At some point, the medieval Roman number of five psalms each day was achieved by eliminating the seven psalms that were sung at other hours; these were Ps. 117 for Sunday Lauds, 118 for the Little Hours, 133 for Compline, 142 for Friday Lauds, and 148–50 for daily Lauds. This reform must have taken place, Pascher argues, sometime before Benedict's stay in Rome in the early sixth century, thus paving the way for his own reform, which further refined the process already underway. Benedict reduced the number of psalms at Vespers to four, doing so not only to avoid singing the same psalm more than once each week, but to provide some variety at the Little Hours, which hitherto had only portions of Ps. 118 assigned to them. He called for the psalms of Vespers to be taken in order from Ps. 109 to Ps. 147, omitting those set aside for other hours, namely, Ps. 117 to 127 for the Little Hours, 133 for Compline, and 142 for Saturday Lauds. This left him three psalms short of the required 28 (only two short, had he not combined the short Ps. 115 and 116 into one). He made up the deficit by dividing three longer psalms (138, 142, and 144) into two psalms each.[17]

The process was clearly not one motivated by selecting thematically appropriate psalms. There was a measure of that only at Lauds and Compline. Rather the process was, in Vogüé's words, a "mechanical" one, "a matter of a very modest task of arithmetic."[18] Surely this is precisely the sort of thing that so disturbs contemporary liturgical historians. It is not for the music historian, however, to pass any such judgments, but simply to record the monastic commitment to the weekly recitation of the Psalter that so decisively shaped the character of the Western Office.

Notes

1. A particularly cogent summary of the subject is Grisbrooke (1992).
2. See especially P. Bradshaw (1981), 1–71; McKinnon (1986); Taft (1986), 11; P. Bradshaw (1992a), and (1992b), 186–87.
3. The relevant sources are cited in P. Bradshaw (1981), 47–71, and Taft (1986), 13–30.
4. For these instructional meetings, see P. Bradshaw (1981), 66–68.
5. On the *agape*, see P. Bradshaw (1981), 55–57.
6. On the fourth-century cathedral office, see P. Bradshaw (1981), 71–92; Taft (1986), 31–56; and Grisbrooke (1992), 407–9.
7. The Greek and Latin numbering of the psalms is used here throughout.
8. For a highly readable account of early Christian monasticism, see Chitty (1966).
9. On the fourth-century Egyptian monastic office, see P. Bradshaw (1981), 93–110, and Taft (1986), 57–74. More specifically on the office of Upper Egypt, see Veilleux (1968).

10. On the psalmody of desert monasticism, see Dyer (1989), 44–47, and McKinnon (1994), 505–10.

11. See especially Taft (1986), 64–65.

12. For other passages associating desert monasticism with psalmody, see *MECL* 105, 106, 110, 112, 114, 115, 124, 125.

13. For other passages associating psalmody with monks and nuns, other than those of Egypt, see *MECL* 138, 146, 152, 180, 196, 197, 199, 242–49, 289, 294, 295, 300, 327, 336–50, 375, 379, 387.

14. I have, for example, assembled more than two hundred references to liturgical psalmody from the sermons of St. Augustine without finding any material unambiguously descriptive of cathedral Lauds or Vespers; see McKinnon (forthcoming).

15. See Taft (1986), 206–9. Grisbrooke (1992) upholds the traditional view, p. 416, n. 17.

16. On the process of achieving liturgical fixity, see McKinnon (1995).

17. Benedict of Nursia, *Regula*, chap. 18.

18. "un process mécanique"; "il s'agit d'un très modeste travail d'arithmétique": Vogüé (1967c), 197.

4

Observations on the Divine Office
in the Rule of the Master

JOSEPH DYER

The written rules that governed monastic life from the end of the fourth through the mid-ninth century are survivals of what must have been a much larger literary production. They range in comprehensiveness from a few disconnected precepts to scrupulous directives covering many aspects of personal and communal behavior.[1] The reasons for this variety can be traced to the function of the written rules; they were never expected to stand alone or act as a substitute for the abbot's authority to determine the norms of the common life in the monastery. In fact, many small monasteries probably had no written rule whatsoever. In such houses monastic life was shaped by the traditions of the monastery as interpreted by the abbot or abbess, who had probably passed most of their lives in the same cloister.

The hegemony of local tradition manifests itself most clearly with regard to the monks' prayer life. Though monks spent many hours of the day and night in communal prayer, very few of the monastic rules offer detailed information about the arrangement of psalms, readings, responses, and prayers that constitute what came to be known as the Divine Office. Even when a monastery accepted the disciplinary components of a new rule that originated outside the community, local traditions of celebrating the Office might still have continued to prevail. It is for this reason that the liturgical observances found in a specific rule can be of only modest value in establishing the locale where that rule might have been followed.[2] During the eighth century, the era of the "regula mixta," components of various rules (often those of Columban and Benedict) were combined to establish norms for newly founded or reformed monasteries. Only the eventual dominance of the rule of Benedict (hereafter RB) brought this practice to an end.

Beginning in the early sixth century, some of the surviving rules furnish information sufficient to permit a satisfactory realization of the structure, if not always the precise content, of the Divine Office in monasteries where those rules were observed in their entirety. St. Benedict (480–555) stands out for the clarity and completeness of his instructions about what psalms were to be sung at each of the hours of prayer, day and night. The anonymous abbot known only as the "Master," most likely a slightly older contemporary of Benedict, is less specific in his rule (hereafter RM), but he probably furnished to his contemporaries—if not to us— sufficient information for carrying out the daily round of prayer.[3] Two bishops from southern Gaul, Caesarius of Arles (bishop, 502–42) and his successor Aurelian (bishop, 546–51), proposed for the nuns and monks under their jurisdiction much longer offices than either Benedict or the Master had done.[4] The Irish abbot Columban (d. 615) imposed even heavier demands on those who observed his rule.[5] He made the number of psalms chanted at night depend on the length of the period of darkness: the entire Psalter was recited over the course of Nocturns on Saturdays and Sundays during the winter. The burden of psalmody on the shortest weekday nights of summer was lighter: only 24 psalms.

Table 4.1 lists in chronological order the monastic rules that provide information about (1) the structure of the Office, (2) the number of times the monastic community gathered for prayer in common, and (3) the location within the rule of the chapters that concern the Office. About half of these rules devote no more than a single chapter, sometimes just a single paragraph, to any of these topics. The anonymous seventh-century rule known as the *Regula cuiusdam patris ad monachos,* requires no more than four sentences to legislate the number of prayer times, the number of psalms (12), prayers and lessons (two) at the night office of Nocturns, and the termination of the weekend Nocturns "ad gallorum cantus."[6] Although Columban and his imitator, Donatus of Besançon, dedicate only a single chapter to the Office, they compress a considerable amount of information into this small space.[7] Abbot Ferreolus merits a place in table 4.1 solely on the basis of his admonition that the psalms should be recited in the order of the Psalter, a refrain familiar from the rule of the Master.[8] The *Regula Tarnantensis* mentions the Divine Office merely as one element of the monastic horarium.[9] If monastic rules

Table 4.1 The Divine Office in the monastic rules

Rule	Date	Chapter(s)
Augustine: *Ordo monasterii*	ca. 400	No. 2 of 11 sections
Regula Magistri	500–25	Chaps. 32–55 of 95
Caesarius of Arles: *Regula virginum*	512–34	Chaps. 66–69 of 73
Benedict: *Regula monachorum*	530–55	Chaps. 8–18 of 73
Caesarius of Arles: *Regula monachorum*	534–42	Appendix
Aurelian of Arles: *Regula monachorum*	546–51	Appendix
Regula Tarnantensis	551–73	Chap. 9 of 23 (from Augustine, Caesarius, Aurelian, *Regula Secunda Patrum*)
Ferreolus: *Regula*	553–73	Chap. 12 of 39
Columban: *Regula monachorum*	ca. 600	Chap. 7 of 7
Isidore of Seville: *Regula monachorum*	615–19	Chap. 6 of 24
Fructuosus of Braga: *Regula complutensis* (*Regula communis*)	646	Chaps. 2–3 of 22
Donatus of Besançon: *Regula ad virgines*	ca. 650	Chap. 75 of 77
Regula cuiusdam patris ad monachos	7th c.	Chap. 30 of 32

refer to the Office in greater detail, it is often to legislate the number of daily psalms, an obligation that might vary according to the season of the year or the liturgical rank of the day—ferial or festal. Although the psalmody imposed by the rule of Benedict does not vary seasonally, the Master allowed a slight reduction in the number of psalms between early spring and the autumnal equinox.

Rarely do the liturgical portions of the rules, other than those of Benedict, Caesarius, Aurelian, and the Augustinian *Ordo monasterii,* assign specific psalms to fixed hours of the daily or weekly Office. The brief guide to the Office in the *Ordo monasterii* prescribes Pss. 62, 5, and 89 for Matins (the hour known as "Lauds" in the later medieval Office).[10] The outline of Sunday Matins in the rule for nuns by Caesarius of Arles cites the psalm *Confitemini* (117), which was to be sung after the introductory "directaneum parvulum," presumably an abbreviated psalm sung without a refrain, and before "*Cantemus domino* [Exod. 15:1] et omnes matutinarii [psalmi] cum alleluiis."[11] He mentions only one other psalm, *Miserere mei deus* (50), at the beginning of the second nocturn in winter. His successor as bishop of Arles, Aurelian, lists the specific psalms to be sung at Matins.[12] The absence in many rules of references to specific psalms may be easily explained. Apart from the notable exception of Benedict, most of the monastic legislators assumed that the old monastic custom of *psalmodia currens,* the recitation of the psalms of the Psalter in strictly numerical order, would prevail. The practice is explicitly ordained in the rule of Ferreolus, but implied in most of the other rules that mention the psalmody of the Office.[13] The Master insistently demands that this venerable custom be assiduously respected. Only a few psalms assigned by long-standing tradition to certain offices (Matins, Vespers, Compline) were fixed, though assignment to these hours would not necessarily mean that the psalms in question were omitted from their normal place in the *psalmodia currens.*

The position of the chapter(s) dealing with the Office in each rule is also worthy of note. Column 3 of table 4.1 shows that in about half of the rules the description of the Office comes at or near the end of the text, almost as an afterthought. Aurelian's treatment of the Office actually occurs after the *explicit* that concludes his rule. The chapters in Ferreolus, Isidore, and the *Regula Tarnantensis*—close to the middle of these rules—contain so little information that they can hardly be considered substantial descriptions of the Office. The Master, on the other hand, places the Divine Office at the heart of his rule.[14] This could be symbolic or merely accidental, but the anonymous abbot lavishes considerable attention on the format of the Office and the discipline with which it is to be observed. In this respect he stands close to the "father" of Western monasticism, Benedict of Nursia, and remote from the other early monastic lawgivers, who record only random notes on the Divine Office.

The Master's Office, important for the richness of its detail, harbors mysteries that have yet to be clarified. Doubt has been cast, for example, on the coherence of the two descriptions of the Office found in the rule. The Master's successive directives for the office of Matins, the monastic morning prayer, have not been convincingly integrated. While solutions to many of these problems will remain elusive, in the following pages that honor the scholarly achievements and career of Ruth Steiner, I hope to be able to present observations that will contribute to a better understanding of the Divine Office in the longest of all Western monastic rules.

The rule of the Master has aroused the interest of scholars not only because of its treatment of the Divine Office, but also because of its connections with the dominant monastic rule of the Middle Ages, the rule of Benedict. Until the 1930s it was assumed that the Master had borrowed passages from Benedict. The contrary claim—that Benedict of Nursia borrowed heavily from the rule of the Master in composing his own rule—caused considerable consternation in monastic circles.[15] The relative dating of the two rules carries obvious implications for the treatment of the Divine Office in each. If Benedict knew the teachings of the Master, his own rule shows that he accepted many of the Master's principles of the spiritual life, but adopted a critical stance toward the structure of the Master's Office, with its insistence on the *psalmodia currens*.[16] If, on the other hand, Benedict were the model for the Master, the latter would have ignored or rejected the careful planning of psalmody that marks the Benedictine Office. The current view, largely formed by the many studies of Adalbert de Vogüé, holds that the rule of the Master originated in central Italy somewhere between Rome and Naples during the first quarter of the sixth century and that it did indeed provide the source for some of Benedict's legislation on the monastic life.[17] This dating and localization explains how the rule of the Master could so easily have become a model for Benedict, writing in the same region a few years later.

In a study of the relationships between the two rules that appeared a few years ago Marilyn Dunn sought to reverse the currently accepted chronology of the two rules and place the rule of the Master under the influence of both Benedict and the Irish abbot Columban (Dunn 1990). According to her theory, the rule of the Master was written not in the vicinity of Rome or in Campania, but in northern Italy, where Columban was active and influential as a monastic founder. According to Dunn's theory, then, the origins of the rule of the Master would need to be situated nearly a hundred years later than the early sixth-century date defended by Vogüé and accepted by most scholars and localized in an entirely different region of Italy.[18] The arguments that she has brought forward to support this new hypothesis will be weighed carefully by experts on the monastic rules; indeed Adalbert de Vogüé has already responded with a defense of his position.[19] A brief discussion of one of Dunn's arguments that touches on an aspect of the localization question and on the distribution of psalms in the Master's Office must, however, be examined here.

As "definitive proof of Irish influence on RM," Dunn pointed to the Master's remark that the longer winter cursus of Nocturns should extend "from the winter [*sic*] equinox to the vernal equinox, that is, from 24 September to 25 March, or better still until Easter, because the nights are long" ("ab aequinoctio hiemali usque aequinoctium vernum, id est ab VIII Kalendas Octobris usque ad VIII Kalendas Aprilis, sed melius usque ubi [*sic*] fuerit Pascha, quia noctes maiores sunt," RM 33.27–28). In this passage the Master seems to be associating the vernal equinox not with the 21 March date generally used in the ecclesiastical calculation of Easter (at least from the early fourth century, when it was fixed on that date by the Council of Nicaea), but with 25 March, the date of the vernal equinox in the Julian calendar. Dunn observed that in his rule for monks Columban also placed the vernal equinox on 25 March ("in vernali aequinoctio, id est VIII Kalendas Aprilis"). She regarded this congruence as a strong argument in favor of the Master's dependence on Columban, since she argued that this date "was part of the Irish system of calculating the date of Easter, a system discarded centuries earlier in Italy and Gaul where 21 March was recognized as the date of the spring equinox."[20] Is the 25 March date a uniquely Irish phenomenon, as Dunn maintains, or does it fit other contexts as well? The answer to this question can best be elucidated by a brief discussion of medieval calendric lore.

Julius Caesar's reform of the Roman calendar in 46 BC fixed the vernal equinox on the eighth day before the Kalends of April (25 March), but even this reformed "Julian" calendar incorporated a calculation error of a little more than eleven minutes per year, or about one day every 130 years.[21] This error caused the true vernal equinox gradually to anticipate the 25 March date. By the early fourth century, when the Council of Nicaea convened and discussed a uniform practice for setting the date of Easter, Alexandrian astronomers had calculated that the vernal equinox had moved to 21 March.[22] Though as a practical matter Rome and most other churches had abandoned the Julian equinox in favor of the ecclesiastical equinox on 21 March, the traditional date of the equinox fixed by the Julian calendar (25 March) was not entirely forgotten. Bede (672/3–735), the greatest medieval authority on the calendar in the West, cited both dates, though in different contexts, in his definitive *De temporum ratione* (725). The 25 March date held a special importance for Bede, because of the tradition that on that date (viii Kal. Apr.) "the Lord was conceived and suffered" ("dominum conceptum et passum [est]").[23] He noted approvingly, however, that the Alexandrian experts ("quos calculandi esse peritissimos constat") had fixed 21 March (xii Kal. Apr.) as the date to be used for the calculation of Easter, a date that benefited from "non solum auctoritate paterna, sed et horologica consideratione." Following a rule "confirmed" by the Council of Nicaea, Bede concluded that Easter must fall between 22 March and 25 April.

As late as the seventh century the Irish clung tenaciously to a system of Easter calculation by then outmoded. This involved both the 25 March equinox and the celebration of Easter within the period *lunae xiv–xx,* that is, during a period bounded by the day of the full moon (*luna xiv*) and the six days thereafter.[24] Columban carried these idiosyncratic practices with him from Ireland to the Continent. He disputed with Gallic bishops on the question and, in a rather impertinent letter to Gregory the Great (written "magis procaciter quam humiliter," according to his own estimate), he heaped ridicule on the Easter table followed by the Roman and the Gallican churches. He also criticized the Gallic bishops for celebrating Easter as late as *luna xxi* and *xxii,* and he asked Gregory to enforce the limits *luna xiv–xx* (Ep. 1. In *Opera,* 2–5). Columban did not directly bring up the question of the date of the equinox, but he did take a swipe at those who celebrate "the Lord's resurrection . . . before his passion,"[25] most likely an allusion to the celebration of Easter before 25 March, a date sometimes regarded as the anniversary of the Passion. Only the Irish objected to the celebration of Easter before 25 March.

The fact that both the Master and Columban used the Julian calendar to identify 25 March as the date of the vernal equinox would appear to be a slim basis for

positing Irish influence on the Master. The Master makes no connection whatsoever between the 25 March date and the controversial questions of paschal calculation. Though the Master's observation about the winter cursus of psalmody
(quoted above) might be read to imply that Easter must fall sometime *after* 25
March, he in fact draws no connection between the equinox and Easter, though of
course Easter would most often occur after 25 March. He merely proposes two
alternative dates for reducing the number of psalms at Nocturns from 16 (the winter *pensum*) to 12 (the summer *pensum*): either the Julian calendar's equinox on 25
March or ("melius," the preferable and more symbolic date) Easter, whenever that
might occur. Columban cites 25 March as the date of the vernal equinox in his
Regula monachorum, but he makes no mention of Easter, nor was there any need
for him to do so.[26] Apart from the fact that both the Master and Columban divide
the year into two parts and adjust the number of psalms to the length of the nights,
there is little in common between their schemes for the Office.[27] The Master's citation of the date of the Julian equinox does not place him within an Irish sphere
of influence.

On the basis of similar calendric arguments Adalbert de Vogüé has argued that
the Master's activities should be placed within a Roman sphere of influence. He
noted the presence in the *Liber diurnus* (a book of model letters believed to have
been used by the papal chancery from about the late sixth century onward), of
a document known as the *cautio episcopi,* which seems to parallel the Master's
ambivalence about the date for terminating the long winter cursus of psalmody.
The *cautio* required a bishop-elect to promise that he would celebrate daily Vigils
with his clergy beginning at cockcrow.[28] On the shorter nights of spring and summer (Easter to 24 September) three lessons, three antiphons, and three responsories were prescribed. With the arrival of the autumn equinox on 24 September,
however, he and his clergy were obliged to observe Vigils of four lessons with their
responsories and four antiphons. This obligation extended "from the [autumnal]
equinox to the other, vernal equinox and to Easter" ("a vero aequinoctio usque ad
alium vernale equinoctium et usque ad pascha").[29] The division of the year into
two parts and the alternative division points—the vernal equinox *or* Easter—were
interpreted by Vogüé as "un nouvel appoint à la localisation de notre Règle dans
la région de Rome."[30] The fact that the office prescribed by the *cautio* assumes a
variable number of psalms according to the seasons of the year places it in opposition to what is known of the customs observed in the Roman basilica monasteries.
(Benedict, who based his Office on the observance of the urban monasteries, made
no provision for varying the psalmody according to the season of the year.) If one
grants that the *cautio* transmits genuine Roman material—a conclusion that is by
no means certain—then one would be compelled to assume that it describes a
Roman clerical, rather than monastic, practice. Unfortunately, virtually no information has survived from the early sixth century about the obligations of the Roman clergy in regard to the Office or parts thereof. It seems unlikely, moreover,
that the Master, profoundly rooted in the old monastic tradition, would have resorted to clerical practice for any part of his Office. For this reason alone the relevance of the prescriptions found in the *cautio episcopi* seems unlikely. Benedict, on
the other hand, adopted the custom of the clerical "ecclesia romana" in the choice

of the variable canticles of Matins (RB 13.10), but he made an exception for Saturdays. He divided the canticle of Moses (Deut. 32:1–43) into two parts, thus departing from the Roman custom, which never divided long psalms or canticles.

Neither of the hypothetical reconstructions of the sixth-century Roman Office devised by Camillus Callewaert and Joseph Pascher points to similarities between the Divine Office in the rule of the Master and the contemporary Roman basilical Office. Callewaert assumed that a weekly distribution of the Psalter prevailed among the monastic communities serving the Roman basilicas and that the Psalter was divided into a "vigil" block (Pss. 1–108) and a "vesper" block (Pss. 109–47[–150]). Underlying his paradigm was the assumption that these blocks of psalms were derived (at least in principle) from the monastic *psalmodia currens* that remained intact in the "primitive" form of the Roman Office that prevailed until the end of the fifth century. Callewaert's brilliant reconstruction depends on a complicated series of realignments that remove certain psalms from the strict numerical succession of the Psalter and assign them to other hours of the day.[31] The process by which these psalms (4, 5, 42, 50, 53, 62, 64, 66, 89, 90, 91, 94, 117, 142) were removed from the numerical sequence in successive waves of displacements remains inevitably speculative.

Joseph Pascher criticized Callewaert's assumptions as unhistorical, though he did not develop an explanation quite as comprehensive and systematic as Callewaert's.[32] Noting that the medieval Roman Vigils included Pss. 1–20 with the omission of Pss. 4 and 5, Pascher proposed a decimal base for Sunday Vigils (originally Pss. 1–25). On ordinary feriae (weekdays) his scheme calls for twelve psalms with the subtraction of certain psalms (42, 53, 62, 66, 89, 90, 91, 92, 99) for other hours. The 25 psalms of primitive Roman Sunday Vigils would have included Pss. 4 and 5, a view that Pascher supported by observing that (1) the 21 psalms (7 × 3) of Easter week Matins (i.e., Vigils) include these two psalms while omitting Pss. 9, 17, 21, 24;[33] (2) the nocturnal office for martyrs includes both Pss. 4 and 5; and (3) the responsories for the Sundays after Epiphany draw their texts from the psalms sung during the Nocturns. Since these responsories include texts drawn from Pss. 1–25, these same psalms must have once been sung at Nocturns.

The principle underlying the Master's distribution of psalms differs fundamentally from models of the sixth-century Roman practice (as elaborated by Callewaert and Pascher) that influenced Benedict. The Master's frequent insistence that the Psalter be recited in strictly numerical order ("currente semper psalterio") would have permitted neither a weekly distribution of the psalms nor the daily recitation of Ps. 118, both practices customary at Rome. Callewaert's calculations were based on the assumption, derived from the traditions of Egyptian monasticism, that the dominical and ferial morning office had a duodecimal base. This foundation is absent from the Master's winter Nocturns with their idiosyncratic 13 antiphonal psalms and from his summer Nocturns that contain nine antiphonal psalms. While seasonal variation in the number of psalms does indeed reflect older monastic traditions, the absence of readings at Nocturns cannot be associated with either the early monastic or the early Roman Office.[34] In the final analysis, however, it appears that neither Callewaert's nor Pascher's reconstructions of sixth-century

Roman Nocturns bears much resemblance to the same office in the rule of the Master.

Pascher's proposed model for Roman Matins (i.e., "Lauds") and Vespers suggests at least one point of contact with the rule of the Master (to which Pascher makes no reference). The Master's Matins (RM 35 and 39) has six psalms as does the corresponding evening office, Lucernarium (RM 36 and 41, the latter by inference).[35] Pascher believed that at Rome both Matins and Vespers formerly had six psalms, not five (or four, in the case of the Benedictine Office) (Pascher 1957b and Vogüé 1968, 122, 155–57). Roman Matins would have consisted of six invariable psalms: 50 (replaced by 92 on Sundays), 62, 66, 148, 149, 150. According to Pascher, the reduction to five "psalms" maintained the opening psalm, grouped Pss. 62+66 as a single psalm in second place, inserted a variable psalm in third place and an Old Testament canticle in fourth place, while the traditional morning Pss. 148–50 stood in last place as a single psalm. Pascher's arguments for six psalms at Vespers seem to be much stronger than his argument for this number at Matins.[36] He observed that the "vesper block" of psalms (108–50) contains 42 psalms—exactly the number needed for six psalms on each day of the week. Observations from the earliest preserved antiphoners and the special Roman Easter Vespers make his case plausible, at least from the standpoint of an intriguing but inevitably speculative calculation. This numerical correspondence, one term of which is hypothetical, does not link the structure of the Master's Office unequivocally to Rome. Though he probably lived in a region not far from Rome, the Master ignored not only clerical but also non-urban monastic traditions in drawing up the structure of his Office.

The treatise on the structure and discipline of the Divine Office in the rule of the Master extends from chapter 32 to chapter 55, and it is clearly divided into two separate but complementary discussions: chapters 33–37 and chapters 39–44. Saturday Vigils are mentioned summarily in chapter 49.[37] Additional chapters are devoted to psalmody at mealtime (38, corresponding to 43), the use of alleluia (45), the discipline of psalm singing and reverence in prayer (46–48), deportment between times of communal prayer (RM 50), and a *regula quadragesimalis* (RM 51–53).[38] Chapters about prompt arrival for the Office (RM 54) and observance of the appointed times of prayer while on a journey (RM 55) complete the Master's treatment of the Office.

The two discussions are, to be sure, complementary, and for this reason analyses of the Master's Office have generally amalgamated the information found in related chapters.[39] While this coordination undoubtedly facilitates comprehension of each prayer hour, it obscures certain distinctive features that can be revealed only by careful attention to the order in which the Master presents the *opus dei* to his disciples.[40] The two layers of composition need to be discussed separately. Table 4.2 compares the summary presentation of the Office in chapters 33 through 37 with its subsequent elaboration in chapters 39 to 44.[41] Only with the assistance of the second presentation could one arrive at an adequate reconstruction of the Divine Office as celebrated in the Master's monastery.

The first treatment of the Office establishes (1) the number of daily "imposi-

Table 4.2 The Divine Office in the Rule of the Master

Winter Nocturns	Chap. 33.27–34	Chap. 44.1–4 versus apertionis [1] responsorium hortationis
	[13] antiphons	[9] antiphons without alleluia
	3 responsories	1 responsory without alleluia [4 antiphons with alleluia] 1 responsory with alleluia
	lectiones	lectio apostoli [praepositus] lectio evangelii (abbot)
	versus	versus
	rogus dei	rogus dei
Summer Nocturns	Chap. 33.35–40	Chap. 44.5–8 versus apertionis [1] responsorium abbatis
	9 antiphons	6 antiphons without alleluia
	3 responsories	1 responsory without alleluia 3 antiphons with alleluia 1 responsory with alleluia "ut fiant duodecim inpositiones"
	lectiones	lectio apostoli [praepositus] lectio evangeliorum (abbot)
	versus	versus
	rogus dei	rogus dei
Vigils (Saturday)		Chap. 49 "Omni sabbato debent in monasterio exerceri vigiliae a sera usque dum secundo fuerit gallus auditus, et iam fiant matutini. Sed propter quod vigiliae dicuntur, a somno se fratres abstineant et psallant et legentes audiant lectiones."
Matins (ferial)[a]	Chap. 35.1	Chap. 39.1–4 "Matutini psalmi cum antifanis semper psallantur":
	6 psalms	4 psalms without alleluia 2 psalms with alleluia
	1 responsory	1 responsory
	versus	versus
	lectio apostoli [praepositus]	lectiones [praepositus]
	evangelia (abbot)	evangelia (abbot) without

Table 4.2 (*continued*)

		alleluia except on Sundays (Easter to Epiphany)
	rogus dei	
Prime, Terce, Sext, None	Chap. 35.2–3	Chap. 40
	3 psalms	2 psalms with antiphons 1 psalm with alleluia
	1 (short) responsory	1 (short) responsory
	lectio apostoli [praepositus]	lectio apostoli [praepositus]
	lectio evangelii (abbot)	lectio evangeliorum (abbot) versus
	rogus dei	rogus dei
Lucernarium (winter and summer)	Chap. 36.1–6	Chap. 41 "Psalmi lucernariae cum antifanis psalli debent"
	6 psalms	[4 psalms with antiphons] 2 psalms with alleluia
	1 responsory	1 responsory
	versus	versus
	lectio apostoli [praepositus] evangelia (abbot)	lectio apostoli [praepositus] evangelia (abbot) without alleluia except on Sundays (Easter to Epiphany)
	rogus dei	
Compline	Chap. 37	Chap. 42 "Psalmi conpletorii omni tempore cum antifanis psallantur"
	3 psalms	2 psalms with antiphons 1 psalm with alleluia
	1 (short) responsory lectio apostoli [praepositus] lectio evangeliorum (abbot) rogus dei versus clusoriae	

a See table 4.3 for Sundays and feasts.

tions," (2) the proportion of antiphonal psalms to responsorial psalms in each hour, and (3) certain devotional and disciplinary guidelines. An "imposition" in the Master's terminology is either a complete psalm (antiphonal or responsorial) or one of the canticles sung at Matins and Lucernarium.[42] The Master's "law of the 24 impositions" (according to the phrase coined by Dom Adalbert de Vogüé) requires that there be exactly this number of psalms sung during the night (Nocturns and Matins) and day (little hours and Lucernarium) offices. This number symbolizes for the Master the number of elders wearing golden crowns and playing harps who offer their praise before the throne of God in the book of Revelation (4:4, 5:8–9). Although Compline is counted as one of the "seven times a day" that the psalmist praises God, its psalms are not counted toward the sum of 24 impositions, perhaps because the choice of psalms was fixed and not variable from day to day.[43] Nocturns does not count as part of the sevenfold praise "that the Scripture might be fulfilled that says: 'From the rising of the sun to its setting—it does not say *after* its setting*—praise the name of the Lord'" ("ut conpleatur scriptura dicens: *A solis ortu usque ad occasum*—non enim dixit post occasum—laudate nomen domini," RM 34.7).[44] The psalms of Nocturns are, nevertheless, reckoned among the required 24 impositions.

The Master's summary information about the number of impositions proves of value in reconstructing winter Nocturns, an office rendered obscure because of lacunae in the manuscript tradition of chapters 33 and 44. (The brackets in table 4.2 indicate the missing material.) The first modern editor of the rule of the Master, Hugh Ménard, observed that only the unusual number of 13 antiphonal psalms (here called "antiphons") would satisfy the total of 16 impositions specified by the Master for winter Nocturns in RM 33.[45] The number 16 is confirmed by an allusion to the 16 prophets of the Hebrew Scriptures. The 12 impositions of the shorter summer nights are justified by a not unexpected reference to the 12 apostles. In the latter instance the proportion of antiphonal psalms to responsories (9:3) is clearly stated. The other elements of Nocturns ("lectiones et versum et rogus dei") are mentioned almost in passing in this chapter, just to exclude them from the impositions. The first description of the night Office contains no mention of the Vigils described later in RM 49.

In addition to providing a cursory outline of winter and summer Nocturns, chapter 33 also regulates the discipline of the night Office. Since it must be completed before cockcrow, the *terminus noctis*, the Master warns that the *praepositi* (monastic officials subordinate to the abbot) assigned to watch throughout the night must remain alert, so that the call of the cock "does not get ahead of or catch up with the Nocturns" (RM 33.3).[46] In summertime this does not seem to matter because of the shortness of the nights. At that time of year, moreover, Nocturns does not begin until cockcrow, and it leads directly into Matins without a pause. The material on Nocturns presented in table 4.2 comes from the central portion of RM 33, which closes with a warning that the doxology terminating each psalm should never be omitted, save in cases of "gravior necessitas," when it is permitted to say only a part of each required psalm, followed by a single doxology. The absence in RM 33 of the "versus apertionis" (*Domine, labia mea aperies*) and the "responsorium hortationis" (*Venite exultemus domino*, Ps. 94) is only apparent:

both are mentioned at the close of the previous chapter. The later redaction of Nocturns incorporates the versus and the responsory, led by the abbot, into its description (cf. RM 32.12 and 14 with RM 44.1).

Just as the explanation of the number of psalms at Nocturns in RM 33.27–34 was preceded by an instruction (nos. 1–26), so too are the treatments of Matins and the day hours (RM 35) and Lucernarium (RM 36) preceded by general regulations on the times these hours are to be observed (RM 34). Matins must be sung when the rays of the sun can be seen; Lucernarium must take place *before* sunset for, as the Master reminds us, the Lord is to be praised "from the rising of the sun to its setting" (Ps. 113:3), not after! Because of the exhausting nature of manual labor in the summer, Lucernarium may be sung somewhat earlier during the warmer months of the year, so that the brothers can enjoy sufficient rest.

The initial description of the morning office of Matins in the RM is compressed into a single sentence (RM 35.1). I have added to the list of items in table 4.2 the information that one of the *praepositi* reads a brief excerpt from one of the epistles, an assignment made also in RM 46: "the deans [*praepositi*] in turn always say the lesson from the apostle. The abbot, if he is present, always says the lessons from the Gospel; if he is absent, the deans in turn do so."[47] The assignation seems a logical one for the monastic officers immediately lower in rank than the abbot, to whom is always granted the prerogative of reading or singing from the Gospel both the "lectio evangeliorum" and the "evangelia," the latter term to be discussed below.

The terse description of the other hours in the first outline of the Office parallels that of Nocturns. The comment about summer Lucernarium, that there must be eight impositions (RM 36.7), seems superfluous, unless as a cautionary remark that only Nocturns undergo a change in content from season to season. Compline, an hour parallel in structure to Prime, Terce, Sext, and None, closes the monks' day. The *versus clusoriae* comes at the end of Compline (not earlier as do the usual *versus*) and initiates the monastic great silence that lasts until the beginning of Nocturns the next day.[48] The following chapter on the psalmody at mealtime (RM 38) might seem either out of place or an afterthought. Its position can be regarded as logical, however, for two reasons: (1) it concerns psalmody "not included in the number of the day's seven canonical praises" (RM 38.3), and (2) it does not interrupt the integrity of chapters 33–37 on the Divine Office. Inserted within the second treatment of the Office (RM 39–44) there is a parallel chapter (RM 43) that responds to the disciple's question about psalmody in the refectory.

Although the second treatment of the Office in the rule of the Master is not quite a complete blueprint for its celebration, it does clarify essential details about the inner structure of the hours. Much of what was left unclear in the earlier treatment can be supplemented with information from the later chapters, which analyze the blocks of psalms into those with and without alleluia.[49] Only Compline receives a fuller description in the first treatment of the Office (RM 37) than it does in the second (RM 42).

The second description of the liturgical day in the Master's monastery begins not with Nocturns but with Matins, an office that in wintertime immediately follows cockcrow.[50] RM 39.1 subdivides the six Matins psalms of RM 35 into a group

of four psalms with antiphons and two with alleluia.[51] This is the ferial arrangement; on Sundays and feasts alleluia was sung with all the psalms and responsories
that followed the singing of the "benedictiones," the Canticle of the Three Children
(Dan. 3), whose location within the Office is not further specified.[52] Though the
Master places the two groups of psalms in a successive relationship ("after these
four [psalms] two with alleluia"), it has been argued that the model of the little
hours should be followed by dividing the six psalms into two groups of three
psalms—that is, two psalms sung with antiphons followed by a single psalm with
alleluia.[53] The *responsorium* that follows the psalms at Matins (as well as at Nocturns and Lucernarium) consists of an entire psalm ("psalmi perexplicentur").[54]
The single "lectio apostoli" of RM 35.1 has become plural ("lectiones"). The Gospel
canticle (Benedictus at Matins and Magnificat at Lucernarium) followed, presumably sung with an antiphon throughout the year, though the Master's rubrics mention only that it was sung with an alleluia on Sundays from Easter until Epiphany.[55]
The six psalms added to the responsory and canticle bring the total number of
impositions at Matins to eight, parallel to the number at Lucernarium.

The description of Matins in RM 39.1–3 thus supplements the information provided in RM 35, but the Master seems then to contradict his statement about
"psalms at Matins" by requiring that, apart from Ps. 50 and the *laudes* psalms
(148–50), Matins should consist entirely of canticles.[56] The critical sentence (RM
39.4) reads as follows:

Sed matutini extra quinquagesimo	But let Matins, apart from Ps. 50
psalmo et laudes de canticis fiant	and the *laudes,* consist of canticles;
dominica vero vel aliis diebus festis	on Sundays or other feasts if it
vel si aliquis fuerit natalis sancto-	should be a sanctoral feast, the
rum benedictiones dici oportet.	"benedictions" must be said.
(RM 39.4)	

These two passages, following so closely upon one other as they do, cannot be
contradictory, nor does RM 39.4 intend to draw a distinction between the structure
of ferial Matins and that reserved for Sundays and feasts. Otherwise, we should
have expected the sentence to begin with the phrase "dominica vero." While the
traditional Gospel canticles are prescribed for Matins and Lucernarium, there is
no explicit provision for the use of the Old Testament canticles in the Master's
Office. Benedict prescribed three of these for the third nocturn of Sundays and
feasts and a variable Old Testament canticle at Matins just before Pss. 148–50. He
recommended that the custom of the Roman church be followed for the variable
Old Testament canticle of weekday Matins, but he permitted the abbot to choose
the nocturn canticles presumably because there was no long-standing tradition,
monastic or clerical, on this matter.[57] Like the Master, Benedict insisted that the
"benedictiones" serve as the canticle for Sundays.

A reconstruction of Matins as presented in the rule of the Master must take
into account not only the complementary information provided by RM 35 and
39.1–4 but also the specification that the sung items must add up to eight "impositions." Corbinian Gindele (1956) and Eoin de Bhaldraithe (1977) have proposed
two entirely different reconstructions of the Matins office in the rule of the Master.

Gindele's reconstruction was based on his idiosyncratic interpretation of the terms "antiphon" and "psalm" in the monastic rules.[58] According to Gindele, Ps. 50 stands for the first of a group of three psalms, the two latter of which go unmentioned in the rule. The *laudes* count as a single psalm, which, combined with the preceding three psalms of the Psalter (145–47), constitute the "two psalms with alleluia" (RM 39.1). This makes room for four canticles (not counting the Gospel canticle Benedictus). Thus, according to Gindele, the required eight "impositions" of Matins would actually consist of nine psalms and four canticles in addition to the responsory (a complete psalm) and the *evangelia*. Evidence internal to the rule of the Master renders Gindele's assumptions more than questionable, and his suggestion that the word "antiphona" stands for three psalms, not just one, has encountered substantial resistance. It appears, moreover, that he has abandoned this premise (Gindele, 1974). Since his reconstruction of Matins in the rule of the Master was largely based on this assumption, it is no longer tenable.

The reconstruction the Master's Matins proposed by Eoin de Bhaldraithe raises fundamental questions about their place in the historical context of the Western monastic Office.[59] First of all, he denied that the Master's reference to "evangelia sancta" meant the Gospel canticles, Benedictus and Magnificat, both of which he assigned to a place just before the singing of the *laudes* psalms, not after, as is commonly the case in the Western monastic Office. He interpreted the *evangelia* as the combination of an antiphon with a Gospel reading. De Bhaldraithe's argument rests on two pieces of evidence. He observed that the Master introduced a comparison from secular ecclesiastical practice—the reading of the epistle by a cleric in minor orders and the Gospel by a deacon—to explain why, at Matins and Lucernarium, the *praepositus* reads the "lectio apostoli," but that the "evangelia" is assigned to the abbot himself.[60] Second, he pointed to a decree of a Roman council held in 595 under Gregory I—and hence nearly a century after the Master—that forbade deacons to chant anything other than the Gospel at Mass. Putting these two texts together, he concluded that, just as the singing of the alleluia and the chanting of the Gospel at Mass were both at one time the "duty" of a deacon, so too the "evangelia" in the RM must signify the combination of a chant (in this case an antiphon) with a Gospel reading.

The first piece of evidence occurs in a chapter entitled "De inponendis psalmis in oratorio quovis tempore," in which the subject of readings is not the central point. (Aside from the weekly Vigil, readings form a minor part of the Master's Office anyway.) Most likely, the Master's attention focused on the comparative rank of those performing a service rather on what they were doing. It provided a justification for one of the abbot's prerogatives, in this case the intoning or singing of the Gospel canticle. With respect to the decree of the Roman council, it is unknown to what extent deacons of the time, other than the Roman ones who were the target of the decree, assumed the cantor's role, nor is it entirely clear what they were singing. The decree mentions only "psalmos vero et reliquas lectiones" (not the alleluia) as charges that would henceforth be removed from the deacons' responsibilities: it makes no necessary connection between this disciplinary measure and the deacon's prerogative of chanting of the Gospel at Mass.[61] Whatever Roman deacons took upon themselves to sing, their custom cannot have been a "duty" associated with the diaconal office. If "evangelia" does indeed mean a reading from the Gospels, as de Bhaldraithe maintains, it still remains unexplained how "alleluia" or any antiphon was supposed to be combined with it.[62] The Master's "evangelia" must have possessed some of the qualities of song, since he always figures it among the impositions along with the psalms and responsories. It must have resembled in some manner the chanted antiphonal or responsorial psalms, which are always counted as impositions, while Scripture readings are never so counted.[63]

The word *evangelia* itself is peculiar in the Master's rule. It cannot be construed invariably as a neuter plural (sg. *evangelium*). In an extensive study of the liturgical vocabulary of the monastic rules Elisabeth Kasch came to the conclusion that "evangelia" had become an invariable noun, signifying not an excerpt from the Gospels, but the Gospel canticles of Matins and Lucernarium.[64] The word occurs without grammatical inflection in the phrase "cum responsorio et evangelia" (RM 36.2, 7 and 39.3: "cum evangelia"). The Master uses the correct relative pronoun for the neuter plural form in the phrase "evangelia, *quae* semper abbas dicat" (RM 35.1, 41.3, and 39.2, in the latter case without the word *semper*).[65] In the phrase that precedes the comparison with the epistle and Gospel readings at Mass cited above, the Master ordains that "after the reading from the apostle has been recited, the abbot always, if he is present, follows with the Gospel" ("postquam lectionem apostoli fuerit recitata, evangelia semper abbas praesens sequatur," RM 46.5). Here the word appears to be in the accusative case, but singular in meaning.[66] There is an echo of the Master's terminology in the rule of Benedict: both the *vespertina synaxis* and the *matutinorum solemnitas* contain a "canticum de evangelia," the identity of which can hardly be in doubt.[67] It seems safe to conclude that the Master is indeed referring to the Gospel canticles, Benedictus and Magnificat, at Matins and Lucernarium, respectively, not to a hybrid form of Gospel reading plus antiphon proposed by de Bhaldraithe. Whenever the Master clearly means a reading from the Gospels ("lectio evangeliorum") the word is always inflected according to its appropriate grammatical form.

My own proposal for a reconstruction of the Master's Matins attempts to reconcile the fragmentary and apparently contradictory information provided by his rule. One of the eight impositions of Matins (RM 33.31, 37) must have been the introductory Ps. 50 and, since the Master manifests little affection for the grouping of psalms under one antiphon with a single *Gloria* (RM 33.42–45), Pss. 148–50 must be counted as three separate items.[68] The responsory and the *evangelia* count as two more impositions. Once these obligatory items of the Office have been accounted for, there remains space for two additional impositions: the canticles mentioned in RM 39.4. On ordinary weekdays Ps. 50, the two canticles, and the first of the *laudes* psalms were sung without alleluia. Then would follow the two psalms with that refrain, exactly doubling the module of the day hours in RM 40 (4+2 instead of 2+1). On Sundays and feasts all of the psalms following the *benedictiones* receive an alleluia refrain (RM 41.4), and the brothers are exempted from the requirement of kneeling for the prayer at the conclusion of each psalm.[69] Finally, it cannot be accidental that the Master does not insist that the chanted "psalms" of Matins be chosen "currente semper psalterio," as he does in both descriptions of Lucernarium (RM 36.1 and 41.2), the hour whose structure closely parallels that of Matins. Thus it seems that the variable parts of Matins in the rule of the Master were Old Testament canticles, not psalms. A hypothetical scheme that attempts to make sense of the Master's plan for Matins might resemble the one shown in table 4.3.

The Master's very detailed instructions for the use of alleluia (RM 45) with psalms and responsories does not affect the overall structure of Matins. In brief, from Easter to Pentecost and from Christmas to Epiphany all antiphons and responsories are sung with alleluia. Beginning with Lucernarium on Epiphany the alleluia is "locked up" (*claudatur*), but an exception appears to be made for all Sundays of the year, when in honor of the Resurrection alleluia is sung with all of the antiphons and responsories that follow the *benedictiones*. The celebration of the feast of the titular saint of the monastic oratory follows the Sunday practice.

The little hours (Prime, Terce, Sext, None) present fewer problems. The second treatment of the these hours (RM 40) gives clear evidence of what Vogüé has called "the law of two-thirds." Two psalms with antiphons are succeeded by a psalm with alleluia as its refrain (whether or not the psalm carries this title in the Hebrew Psalter).[70] This practice prevails throughout the year except that alleluia is not sung between Epiphany and Easter. The position of the *versus*, probably omitted inadvertently in RM 35.3, has been supplied in table 4.2.

The second treatment of Lucernarium (RM 41.1–4) adds to the information provided earlier only the fact that the last two of the six antiphonal psalms receive the alleluia refrain, a parallel with Matins. As at Matins, the *evangelia* of Lucernarium is sung with alleluia on Sundays during the period when alleluia is used in the Office.

The second discussion of Nocturns (RM 44.1–8) clarifies the structure of that office, revealing details that could never have been deduced from the first traversal (RM 33.27–34). The "versus apertionis" is none other than "Domine, labia mea aperies" (Ps. 50.17), which the monks—led by the abbot according to RM 44.1—chant upon entering the oratory for the night Office. This verse is also mentioned in RM 32.12, where it is directed to be sung three times, as it is in the Benedictine Office (RB 9.1). The text of the "responsorium hortationis" (RM 44.1) is identified in the first treatment of the Office (RM 32.14).[71] The name given to it by the Master

Table 4.3 The Office of Matins in the Rule of the Master

Sunday and Feasts	Ferial
Ps. 50 [+ antiphon]	[Ps. 50] + antiphon
canticle 1 [+ antiphon]	canticle 1 + antiphon
canticle 2 (Dan. 3) [+ alleluia?]	canticle 2 + antiphon
Ps. 148 + alleluia	Ps. 148 + antiphon
Ps. 149 + alleluia	Ps. 149 + alleluia
Ps. 150 + alleluia	Ps. 150 + alleluia
responsory + alleluia	responsory
versus	versus
reading(s)	reading(s)
Gospel canticle + alleluia	Gospel canticle (without alleluia)
Rogus dei	Rogus dei

signals the psalm inviting the community to prayer: "Venite, exultemus domino" (Ps. 94). It has sometimes been claimed that Benedict introduced this psalm, allegedly not present in the contemporary Roman Office, but it cannot be established beyond doubt that Ps. 94 was unknown at Rome as an introduction to Nocturns.[72] Since Benedict borrowed so much from the Master, the source of the inspiration for the invitatory psalm might reasonably be sought in the Master's "responsorium exhortationis ad laudes Domini" led by the pastor-abbot to encourage his flock at the beginning of the night Office.

Unfortunately, lacunae in the manuscript transmission of RM 44 prevent us from clarifying the unusual number of impositions (16) specified by RM 33.31 at winter Nocturns. The number of responsories remains constant at three. Nocturns begins with one, the "responsorium hortationis." The other two are not linked to readings, but distributed at two separate points in the Office. The defective text of RM 44 implies that the block of 13 antiphonal psalms must somehow be split. The reconstruction of Nocturns in table 4.2, proposed by the first editor of the rule of the Master, Hugh Ménard, has been followed by Vogüé and other commentators on the RM.[73] The distribution of the antiphonal psalms is the only speculative feature, since the other elements of Nocturns (readings, verse, rogus dei) were already mentioned in RM 33. The summer Nocturns (RM 44.5–8) not only agree with the earlier description, but also furnish a retrospective paradigm, though not a flawless model, for the distribution of the antiphonal psalms in winter Nocturns. The "law of two-thirds" rules the proportions of the summer psalms in a way it cannot do in wintertime, since 13 is not divisible into three equal parts.

Vigils (RM 49) are observed in the night between Saturday and Sunday, obviously as a substitute for Nocturns, since Matins follows immediately upon the second cockcrow.[74] The vagueness of the description of how the monks pass the night between dusk (*sera*) on Saturday and Sunday morning reflects the origin of the practice in the ancient Vigils of the Eastern monks. Watching through the night could be either a personal pious exercise or, as is the case here, a communal preparation for the weekly commemoration of the Resurrection.[75] The structure of the hours occupied in psalmody and listening to scriptural readings (probably including patristic texts) would have been governed by monastic custom and the abbot's discretion. These weekly Vigils supplied to some extent for the absence of long readings from Scripture at Nocturns or any other hour in the rule of the Master. The short *lectiones* prescribed during the week were recited from verses the monks had memorized, but at Vigils they were long enough to require reading "ex codice" (RM 44.9).

The two treatments of the Divine Office in the rule of the Master naturally give rise to questions about the existence of successive stages of composition and reorganization. Although it is virtually certain that the rule must be attributed to a single author, that author probably did not compose this extremely long document all at once, but in subsequent redactions and interpolations. Given this likelihood, the desirability of elaborating simple directives about the *opus dei* with fuller information later in the rule is not difficult to understand. A rhetorical device unifies the elaborated treatment of the Office in chapters 39–45 of the rule. Information is presented in response to the disciple's questions, introduced by "qualiter" (or "quomodo" in the case of chapter 45). Nothing in the "response" implies that the question format was genuinely necessary. There are, curiously, no obvious cross-references from one section on the Office to the other, except the "currente semper psalterio" refrain.[76]

I have tried to demonstrate the integrity and coherence of the liturgical code in the rule of the Master. Some scholars have maintained, however, that certain chapters are "out of place" and disruptive to the putatively original and allegedly more coherent structure of the rule. François Masai, who published a diplomatic edition of the RM, doubted the unity of the Master's teaching on the Office and believed that he could perceive "a much older foundation comprising chapters 34, 47, 48, and 49" (Masai 1949, 433). These chapters treat, respectively, the day hours, reverence in psalmody and prayer, and Vigils. Masai regarded RM 34 as the chapter that most appropriately introduces the entire section on the Office, even though in the received text of the rule chapter 33 ("De officiis divinis in noctibus") can also be considered to begin that discussion. Adalbert de Vogüé agreed with Masai that RM 34 served this introductory role, and he believed that RM 33 stood "primitivement" after RM 38 (psalmody in the refectory).[77] Both the second treatment of the Office and the *regula quadragesimalis* (RM 51–53) commence with Matins, as does the Master's listing of the "seven times a day" (RM 34.2).

I would argue that the received arrangement of the chapters makes sense without hypothesizing any dislocations. First of all, RM 33 follows quite logically upon the previous two chapters (RM 31–32) regulating the sleep of the brethren and the responsibilities of the "vigigalli" charged with waking them. RM 32.12 ff. actually marks the true beginning of Nocturns with the "versum apertionis" and the invitatory. The opening of RM 33 thus stands in an intimate relationship with the preceding chapter. The first half of this chapter (RM 33.1–26) legislates the time of awakening, summer and winter, the separation of Nocturns and Matins in winter, and sleep as it impinges on attentiveness during the Office. The second half of the chapter (RM 33.27–54) is devoted to the psalmody of Matins and prohibitions against "pairing" the psalms and omitting the doxology at the conclusion of each psalm. Chapter 33 thus occupies an appropriate place in the wider context of the monastic day and does not imply an ordering of daily times of prayer inconsistent either with the second treatment of the Office or with the *regula quadragesimalis*.[78] In the second treatment of the Office the Master has no need to link the hours of prayer with the monks' nightly repose, a subject adequately covered already, so he begins with Matins, the first hour of the "seven times a day." The Master ends the second treatment with Nocturns, an office that stands outside the "seven times" framework, as we have seen above in the discussion of RM 34.6–7.

In the foregoing pages I have reviewed several aspects of the Divine Office as presented in an early sixth-century monastic rule that has continued to attract the attention of scholars, not least of all because of its relationship with the rule of Benedict. Nothing in the rule of the Master pertaining to the Office—certainly not calendric considerations—requires us to date its composition later in the sixth century or place it under the influence of Irish monasticism. The Master's Office is, moreover, entirely inconsistent in spirit and structure with the Office imposed by Columban on his monasteries.[79] The Office described by the Master is, as I have tried to demonstrate, entirely coherent across the two presumably successive redactions undergone by this part of the rule. The succinct first description (RM 33–37) resembles those encountered in the "primitive" orders of fifth-century monastic rules.

A wider dissemination of the rule, perhaps for a monastery outside the immediate jurisdiction of the Master, or a desire to solidify existing practice for his successors would explain the need for a more precise description of each Office, a need supplied by RM 39–44. Not only are the treatments compatible with each other, but their content implies a chronology. It is inconceivable that the generally less detailed RM 33–37 could have arisen after RM 39–44 or be placed after it in the text of the rule. The Divine Office in the rule of the Master occupies an important position in the history of liturgical prayer. While it insists on the venerable monastic custom of singing the psalms strictly in the order of the Psalter ("currente semper psalterio"), it does so within a framework marked by moderation. This latter aspect and certain structural features of the Master's Office influenced Benedict as he prepared the great rule that was destined to shape Western monasticism and its life of prayer.

Notes

1. The clearest overviews of the monastic rules and their interconnections are Vogüé (1977) and Vogüé (1985b). All of the known rules were collected by Benedict of Aniane in the early ninth century in the great *Codex Regularum* (Bouillet 1965). This collection formed the foundation of the Holstenius–Brockie edition of the rules (1759), which was in turn reprinted by Migne in the nineteenth century (PL 103:393–700). Modern editions of the rules are cited in the bibliography. In dating the rules I have followed Adalbert de Vogüé and other modern editors.

2. François Masai in his contribution to a discussion of the monastic rules in *RB Studia* (1977) called their liturgy "the last of the indications that permits the localization of a complete monastic rule" ("Il s'en suit que la liturgie est vraiment le dernier des indices à permettre la localisation de l'ensemble d'une législation monastique"; 1:224).

3. The lengthy monastic *florilegium* in the manuscript Paris, BNF lat. 12634, attributed by Adalbert de Vogüé to the Neapolitan abbot Eugippius, incorporates many selections from the RM. The only matters relating directly to the Office concern prompt arrival (from RM 54–55). CSEL 87 is an edition of the manuscript; see also Vogüé (1965a).

4. Heiming (1961) compares the Office in the Western monastic rules with John Cassian's description of the monastic Office in the East. See also P. Bradshaw (1981) and Taft (1986).

5. *Regula monachorum,* in *Opera,* ed. Walker, 128–30.

6. Villegas, ed., "La 'Regula cuiusdam Patris ad monachos,'" chap. 30, p. 34.

7. For Columban see n. 5 above; Donatus, *Regula* 75, ed. Vogüé, 308–10.

8. "Ut omni tempore psalmi usque ad finem psalterii in ordine decantentur." Ferreolus, *Regula* 12, ed. Desprez, "La *Regula,*" 131 and trans. Desprez, *Règles,* 305.

9. Villegas, ed., "La 'Regula Monasterii Tarnantensis,'" chap. 9, pp. 26–27.

10. Ed. Lawless, 74. Cassian says that Pss. 50, 62, and 89 were sung by the Bethlehem monks as part of a "novella solemnitas" (*Instit.* 3.6), a morning office that followed Nocturns. On the *Ordo monasterii* and Cassian see Taft (1986), 94–100. (The numbering of the psalms follows the Vulgate.) Throughout the present essay the older monastic

terminology, Nocturns and Matins, will be preferred to Matins and Lauds for the night and morning offices, respectively.

11. *Regula virginum* 69.11; ed. Vogüé, 262. In the *Regula monachorum* Caesarius identifies the "direct" psalm (without the modifier) as Ps. 144; ed. Morin, 153. See also Heiming (1961), 116–17.

12. *Regula monachorum* 56.12–19. In Holstenius, *Codex,* 1:153. The numbering follows the translation in Desprez, *Règles,* 244.

13. Cassian, the *Ordo monasterii,* Caesarius, Aurelian, *Regula Tarnantensis,* Columban, Donatus, Fructuosus, and Isidore. For a discussion see the chapter "The Sequential Cursus in the Early Christian Liturgy" in Bailey (1994). Gindele (1956) reconstructs weekday Matins and dates the responsory as an independent chant in a questionable manner.

14. The early placement of chapters on the Office in the *Ordo monasterii* and Fructuosus does not seem to imply undue prominence.

15. Most of the articles and monographs relevant to the dispute are cited in the bibliographies of Cappuyns (1964) and Jaspert (1977). The most readable overview of the theories that have been presented is Knowles (1963), 135–95.

16. Benedict's indebtedness to the contemporary Roman basilical Office was first demonstrated in Camillus Callewaert's studies on the genesis of the Western Office (Callewaert, 1940); see also Benedict of Nursia, *Regula,* ed. Fry, 398–400, and ed. Vogüé, vol. 5.

17. The author outlines his views in *La Règle du Maître,* 1:221–33, 2:519, 3:501–2, and Vogüé (1965b). Despite its many interesting observations, Vogüé (1966) seems forced in its attempt to situate the RM in the vicinity of Subiaco on the basis of information about the monasteries in this region contained in the *Dialogues* of Gregory the Great. Nevertheless, linguistic studies have pointed to this region as the likely point of origin; see Pratesi (1951–52) and Lentini (1967), 56–57.

18. The arguments are presented in Vogüé's editions of the two rules: *RM* (1964–65), 1:221–33; *RB* (1971–72), 1:149–72. Payr (1959, 83–84) dates the composition of the rule of the Master in the 870s in northern Italy.

19. See Vogüé's challenge (1992) to the weak points of Dunn's position and her subsequent rejoinder (1992).

20. Dunn (1990), 583. The passage from Columban's rule reads: "in quo similitudo synaxeos est sicut in vernali aequinoctio, id est in VIII Kalendas Aprilis" (Columban, *Regula monachorum* 7; *Opera,* 130).

21. Comprehensive discussions of medieval chronology may be found in H. Leclercq (1937), Pedersen (1983), and Ware (1992); for a briefer overview see the chapter "solar Calendars" in A. Kelly (1993), 45–47. Both the autumnal equinox and the two solstices, summer and winter, occupied symmetrical locations in the calendar, falling on the eighth day before the Kalends of October, July, and January (24 September, 24 June, 25 December), respectively.

22. The date chosen was not based on direct astronomical observations, according to Newton (1972), 26. The revised Julian calendar with this "ecclesiastical" equinox remained in effect until the correction ordered by Pope Gregory XIII in 1582.

23. Bede, *De temporum ratione* 30 ("De aequinoctiis et solstitiis"), ed. Jones, 374. Talley (1991) provides a stimulating general treatment of this view in the early Church. Bede chronicled the friction between the Irish church and Roman practice concerning the observance of Easter in the *Historia gentis Anglorum ecclesiastica* 2.4, 2.19, 3.4, 3.25; ed. Colgrave and Mynors, 146, 198–203, 224, 294–309. See also the chapter "Easter in the British Isles" in Bede, *Opera de temporibus,* 78–81.

24. Rome had generally celebrated Easter between *luna xvi* and *luna xxii,* though the principles used to calculate the equinox and the tables that incorporated them were

a not infrequent subject of dispute. H. Leclercq maintained that Rome deviated from this practice and kept *luna xiv–xx* as the boundaries for the celebration of Easter from the end of the third century to 343 (1937, 1551–52), an opinion shared by Grumel: "Il me semble bien que durant ce temps le règle du *xvi lunae* pour le célébration de Pâques ait subi une éclipse" (p. 168, n. 13). Leclercq further hypothesized that the Irish practice had been derived from Rome during this period (1937, 1557). That the Irish system derived rather from Sulpicius Severus has been demonstrated by McCarthy (1994). I am grateful to Leofranc Holford-Strevens for this reference and for reviewing this section of my essay.

25. "Quippe qua ratione utraque stare possunt, ut scilicet resurrectio Domini ante suam celebretur passionem." Ep. 1.3. In *Opera*, 4. The other practice to which Columban refers ("ratione utraque") is an Easter observance bounded by *luna xiv–xx*.

26. See n. 20 above; for a general discussion of Columban's office see Heiming (1961), 125–31.

27. Columban's seasonal arrangement is more nuanced than the Master's; see the chart in Walker's edition of the *Regula monachorum,* in *Opera,* 131.

28. In winter the Nocturns of the Master's monastery were chanted before cock-crow, but from Easter to the autumn equinox (24 September) the Nocturns begin at cockcrow (RM 32.1–10; ed. Vogüé, 2:172–74, trans. Eberle, 194–95).

29. Sickel, ed., *Liber diurnus* 74, p. 77 (one is tempted to read "or" in place of "and"). The *cautio,* whose provisions were supposedly imposed on bishops of *Italia suburbicaria* and wherever the bishop of Rome exercised metropolitan authority, does not specify the date of the vernal equinox. Doubt has been cast on the exclusively Roman contents of the collection. Taft (1986, 186) dates the *cautio* before 559, since Pope Pelagius I seems to refer to it in one of his letters (44.12). For Benedict "winter" begins on 1 November and extends until Easter (RB 8.1).

30. Vogüé, *La Règle du Maître,* 3:501. Vogüé argued strongly that the origin of the rule of the Master is to be sought "selon toute vraisemblance dans le voisinage de Rome" (ibid., 3:222). On the similarity between the Master's description of the use of alleluia "in ecclesia" and Roman practice see Vogüé (1965b) and (1968), 155–57.

31. Callewaert (1939), 51–57; and Callewaert (1940b–e). Callewaert's research forms the basis for the first table ("Ordo psallendi romanae ecclesiae ante s. VII") in Gibert Tarruel (1973), 331. It is generally assumed that Pss. 148–50 always occupied a place of honor at the close of Matins in the Western Office; see Hanssens (1952), 81, 105–6, and Taft (1986), 193–209; a contrary perspective is offered by Froger (1946 and 1952) and Bradshaw (1981), 106–10.

32. Pascher (1958) and (1965a), who sometimes omits accurate citation of evidence.

33. *Ordo Romanus* 30A.21–22, in *Ordines Romani,* ed. Andrieu, 3:457–58.

34. The "lectiones" of RM 34.30 are identified in RM 44.4 as the two short readings drawn from the epistles and the Gospels, respectively.

35. The term "Lucernarium" originated by the late fourth century as a name for the office observed as the evening lamps (*lucernae*) were being lit. Egeria used the term *lucernare* many times in the report of her pilgrimage to the Holy Land (ed. Pétré; see also Kasch [1974]), and the "hora lucernarii" terminates afternoon labor in the Augustinian *Ordo monasterii* (3; ed. Lawless, 74). The sixth-century rule of Caesarius for virgins equates it with *vespera* (66), and the same usage prevails in the rule of Aurelian (Holstenius, *Codex,* 1:393, 395) and the *Regula Tarnantensis* (9; ed. Villegas). The Master invariably uses the neuter plural *lucernaria* (Cappuyns 1964, s.v.; Kasch, 58–61). "Vespera" in the RM is employed even outside the liturgical code as an expression virtually the equivalent of Lucernarium, when it does not mean simply "evening" (RM 59.2–3, 61.18).

36. Pascher (1957b and 1965b), summarized in Pascher (1958) and Becker (1965). The (second) table in Tarruel (1973), 332, gives a more lucid view of Pascher's reconstruction than can be found in that author's works.

37. For an overview of the Office see Vogüé, *La Règle du Maître*, 1:49–63.

38. This calls for suspension of the Office on Good Friday and Holy Saturday; see Wathen (1986).

39. Heiming (1961), 90–102. Discussions of the Master's legislation on the Divine Office may be found in Vogüé, *La Règle du Maître*, 1:49–63, Vogüé (1968), 153–54, P. Bradshaw (1982), 139–49, Taft (1986), 122–30, Gindele (1960), Vogüé (1960), Janeras (1960), Gindele (1974), revising views found in Gindele (1961). The rule of Benedict also has a double presentation, but of a very different type. Chapters 8–17 of the RB cover the structures of Nocturns, Sunday Vigils, Matins on Sundays and weekdays, Vigils for the feasts of saints, the use of alleluia, the day hours, and Vespers. Benedict's second treatment of the Office (RB 18) covers the order of psalmody, devising a weekly distribution of the Psalter (*psalterium per hebdomadam*) that would have been irrelevant to those who followed the old monastic *psalmodia currens* so strongly defended by the Master. For a comparison of the RM Office with that of the RB see *Regula*, ed. Fry, 378–98, 478–93.

40. Both *opus dei* and *divinum officium* are terms used by the Master for the daily course of psalms; see the index volume (3) of Vogüé's edition of the RM. On the tradition of the term *opus dei* see Hausherr (1947).

41. The table does not show the parallel between RM 38 and 43, chapters about psalmody in the refectory. The Master specifically excludes these psalms from those chanted as part of the Divine Office: "non est in numero septem laudum canonicarum diei" (RM 38.3).

42. Summer Lucernarium is described thus: "in summer there must be eight impositions at Vespers, counting the responsory and the Gospel [canticle] but not the verse and the readings" (RM 36.7). See Kasch (1974), 113–15 ("inpositio"); Heiming (1961), 92–98; Vogüé (1961b). The meaning of this technical term in the liturgical language of the Middle Ages awaits a thorough investigation; it usually means more than just an "intonation," as usually translated by Eberle, *The Rule;* see Dyer (1989). "Antiphona" is a shorthand designation for a psalm with a refrain sung by singers divided into two groups. A "responsorium" also has a choral refrain, with which the entire community responds to the verses sung by the soloist. It is not exactly clear how the two historical modes of performance were distinct from each other, nor how many times the soloist's chanting of the psalm text was interrupted by the antiphonal or responsorial refrain. For the most recent review of the question see Nowacki (1995). It is interesting to note that the rule of the Master is the first monastic source to mention that, while singing the Office in the oratory, the monks are divided into two "choirs," each with ten members (RM 22.13–14, 92.35, 93.64).

43. The Master omits his refrain "currente semper psalterio" in regulating Compline (RM 37 and 42), probably because the phrase "psalmi completorii" denotes invariable psalms.

44. Benedict distinguished between "septies in die laudem dixi tibi" and "media nocte surgebam ad confitendum tibi" [Ps. 118:164, 62] (RB 16).

45. Ménard's edition of the text (Paris, 1638) was reprinted by Migne (PL 103). Adalbert de Vogüé's reconstructions have followed his lead, both in the new edition of the RM (1:49 ff.) and earlier in Vogüé (1960).

46. Two *praepositi* were assigned to supervise groups of ten monks (see RM 11 for their duties). RM 31.7 assigns to them the responsibility of watching the *horolegium* night and day. This is probably a generic term for a time-monitoring device, a sundial

on sunny days (RM 56.21) and a marked candle or hourglass during the night. The Master does not require the *praepositi* to be skilled in observation of the stars and constellations.

47. "Lectiones apostoli praepositi semper vicibus dicant; evangelii lectiones, si praesens fuerit, abbas semper dicat, si absens, praepositi vicibus." RM 46 reads like a series of footnotes to the preceding chapters on the Office.

48. RM 37. Cf. RM 30.12: "factis conpletoriis, in ultimo dicant hunc versum: 'Pone, domine, custodiam ori meo et ostium circumstantiae labiis meis' (Ps. 140:3)." In his edition of the rule of the Master, Vogüé calls attention to a parallel passage in *OR* 18.10 (Andrieu, 3:206) in which this verse closes Compline sung in the monastic dormitory.

49. On the basis of antiphons in the León Antiphoner, Gindele (1974) concluded that these "alleluia" antiphons consisted of texts to which the word was attached, not antiphons that consisted of this word only.

50. The description of the Office in the Augustinian *Ordo monasterii* also begins with Matins (ed. Lawless, 74).

51. An additive process seems to be implied in the contrast between "antiphonae sex sine alleluia … deinde tres antiphonae cum alleluia" at summer Nocturns (RM 44.6–7).

52. The canticle is so called because each line begins with the imperative "benedicite" (bless). For a comprehensive survey of the liturgical use of this text see Bernard (1993).

53. See Gindele (1960 and 1974). This configuration is a familiar feature in the rules of Caesarius ("psalmi duodecim cum alleluiaticis suis," chap. 66) and Aurelian (56.2, 10, 51–52). An alleluia psalm was the twelfth and last psalm in the Vespers of the Egyptian monks according to Cassian (*Instit.* 2.5), but this had to be one of the alleluia psalms of the Psalter (*Instit.* 2.11). This does not seem to be the case in the RM. For Terce, Sext, and None the *Ordo monasterii* has a threefold grouping: one responsorial psalm followed by two antiphons (ed. Lawless, 74).

54. At the little hours the responsory consists of only two psalm verses ("bína capita") followed by the doxology, so that the brothers can more quickly return to their work (RM 46.8–10).

55. RM 39.2. The monastery, "dedicated to the divine service in a special way" ("quasi in peculiari servitio dei," RM 28.47), continues to sing alleluia after the feast of Pentecost, during the period when "alleluia is restricted in the churches" ("ecclesiis clauditur alleluia," RM 28.46), at least for those churches—Rome among them— known to the Master. Cf. RM 45.8–9 and Vogüé (1965b). The practice noted by the Master corresponds to that cited in the letter of Johannes Diaconus (d. 526), a Roman cleric contemporary with the Master, to Senesius (PL 59:406). The Master seems to date the beginning of a stricter monastic program of fasting from Sexagesima Sunday (28.8–12).

56. This is the unique occurrence of the word "canticle" in a liturgical context in the RM.

57. RB 11.6 and 13.10; *RB 1980*, 206 and 208. For Saturday Benedict specifies that the canticle from Deuteronomy (32:1–43) be divided into two halves, presumably because the Roman church did not divide it. Benedict's reference to the Roman church implies that those likely to read his rule would have no difficulty ascertaining what it was, presumably because they lived in the vicinity—another indication helpful in localizing the rule of Benedict.

58. Gindele's views were challenged by Heiming (1961), 94–98, and Vogüé (1961b), reacting to Gindele (1957).

59. De Bhaldraithe's conclusions are summarized and generally accepted in Taft (1986), 128–30.

60. "Ut eo ordine quo missae a clericis celebrantur, id est, cum minor clericus apostolum perlegerit, sequitur maior diaconus evangelia sancta lecturus" (thus in the order in which Mass is celebrated by the clergy, that is, after a lower-ranking cleric has read the apostle [i.e., epistle], a deacon, higher in rank, follows with the reading of the holy Gospel). RM 46.6; Eberle, *The Rule*, 205.

61. Gregory the Great, *Registrum*, 362–63. For an interpretation of this decree in the Roman context see Dyer (1993), 28–32. De Bhaldraithe assumes that the alleluia before the Gospel was the chant in question.

62. See RM 36.2 (Lucernarium) and RM 39.3 (Matins).

63. See RM 36.2 (Lucernarium) and RM 39.3 (Matins).

64. Kasch (1974): "es lässt sich vermuten, daß die Form 'evangelia' in der liturgischen Sprache bevorzugt wurde und daher vielleicht zur Formel erstarrte" (109). Cf. "semper *in opus Dei* dicant hunc versum" (RM 45.14; p. 208 [italics added]). Corbett (1958) is the fullest treatment of the Master's language. See also Heiming (1961), 100–1; Vogüé, *La Règle du Maître,* 2:192 (note).

65. Cf. RM 35.2: "lectionem evangelii quam . . . dicat."

66. I have followed Eberle's translation (p. 205), though the passage is not without syntactical problems. The Master's less than perfect command of Latin has been noted elsewhere. As Lentini (1967, 59) remarks, "tutta la costruzione involuta o maldestra ci rendono perplessi sull'abilità stilisticamente letteraria del redattore."

67. Benedict of Nursia, *Regula*, 12.4 and 17.8; ed. Fry, 206 and 212. For the structure of Benedict's *matutini* with parallels to the RM see Fry, 392–3 and 405. De Bhaldraithe does not note the presence of these passages in the RB.

68. Robert Taft (1986, 128) observes that only Cassian disagrees with this placement of Ps. 50. Cassian claimed that throughout Italy in his day Ps. 50 was sung at the end of Matins ("consummatis matutinis hymnis," *Instit.*, 3.6; CSEL 17:41. With some misgivings, Taft concludes (correctly, I think) that Cassian, who lived a century before the Master, must have been mistaken. The Benedictine Office calls for this psalm daily at Matins, inserted after Ps. 66 and before the variable psalm (RB 12.3), but in the Roman secular Office Ps. 50 is used only on feriae. De Bhaldraithe suggested that the canticle from Daniel replaced Ps. 50 on Sundays and feasts, but nothing in the rule of the Master compels that arrangement.

69. "Nam omnes antifanae ipso die [Sunday] a benedictionibus [Dan. 3] dictis cum alleluia psallantur et genua non flectantur usque ad secundae feriae futuros nocturnos" (RM 41.4 and 45.12). Vogüé has argued that the omission of the alleluia between Epiphany and Easter extended to the entire Office (*La Règle du Maître*, 1:55).

70. The biblical alleluia psalms are 104–6, 110–18, 134–35, 145–50 (Vulgate numbering). On the "loi des deux tiers" see Vogüé, *La Règle du Maître,* 1:51–63.

71. "Post quem versum [Domine, labia mea aperies] ab omnibus dictum invitet et suscitet pastor oves suas per responsorium ad laudes Domini, dicens: 'Venite, exultemus Domino, iubilemus Deo salutari nostro'" (RM 32.14).

72. Bäumer (1905), 1:247; Callewaert (1939), 56, 172, and Callewaert (1940f), 139. Baumstark (1957) says that "Psalm 94 dürfte auf Gemeindevigilien Italiens zurückzuführen sein" (p. 93). In his note to Baumstark's discussion in *Nocturna Laus* Odilo Heiming sees the Benedictine Office as the model for Rome in this instance.

73. Eberle's translation of the passage, incorporating Vogüé's emendations, reads as follows: "At the nocturns the abbot must say the opening verse, then the hortatory responsory [Ps. 94]. Then, in winter [nine] antiphons without alleluia, then a responsory without alleluia, [then four antiphons with alleluia], in any case always in the sequence of the psalter, then another responsory this time with alleluia, so that there are sixteen intonations, a reading from the apostle, a reading from the Gospel, which is always made by the abbot or, if he is absent, by the deans in turn, then a verse

and the prayer to God (Oportet in nocturnis ab abbate dici versum apertionis, deinde responsorium hortationis, deinde in hieme <novem> antifanas sine alleluia, deinde responsorium sine alleluia, <deinde quattuor antifanas cum alleluia,> currente dumtaxat semper psalterio, deinde alium responsorium iam cum alleluia, ut fiant sedecim inpositiones, lectionem apostoli, lectionem evangelii, quam semper abbas dicat, si absens fuerit, praepositi vicibus, versum et rogus dei, RM 44.1–4)."

74. Cf. RM 33.1. See table 4.2 for the text, which concludes with the instruction that "after Matins they take repose [repausent] in their beds." Sunday is a day of complete rest (RM 75.3–7) in the Master's monastery.

75. This is not the usual meaning of "vigilia(e)" in the monastic rules, which use the term as an equivalent to "nocturni." See Kasch (1974), 83–88. "La vigile antique était essentiellement un exercice ascétique, une veillée, dont la première obligation était celle de rester éveillé, tout en s'adonnant à la psalmodie et à la lecture, mais aussi en s'aidant de gestes multiples, de travail manuel, voire d'exercices violents au grand air" (Hanssens 1952, 35). A midnight Office is mentioned in the rule of Fructuosus (Holstenius, *Codex,* 1:201) and Friday–Saturday Vigils in the *Itinerarium* of Egeria (27.8) and Cassian, *Instit.* 3.8. Baumstark (1957) draws attention to the Byzantine *pannychís* and the Russian "all-night vigil" (134–37). See also Benedict of Nursia, *Regula,* ed. Vogüé, 5:453–63). On the history of the monastic Vigil see Marcora (1954), 137–51 and 225–29.

76. The "renvois" (cross-references) cited by Vogüé in his edition of the RM (1:179) are not convincing, but the repetition of 47.21 at 48.7 is a genuine curiosity!

77. According to Vogüé, RM 34.1 "sonne comme un exorde" (*La Règle du Maître,* 1:183). The learned editor's attempt to demonstrate that "similiter" in RM 33.32 once referred to a topic in RM 36 that preceded it in an earlier version of the rule is not convincing.

78. After the latter section—an interpolation—the RM returns to prayer legislation (RM 54–55) and instructions about saying the Office while traveling.

79. Gindele (1961, 295) makes the same claim with respect to Benedict and Columban.

Eastern and Western Elements in
the Irish Monastic Prayer of the Hours

PETER JEFFERY

The Divine Office of the early Irish church is one of the more recondite subjects in the study of Western liturgical history—but therefore one of the more interesting. With the famous exceptions of the Stowe Missal and the Bangor Antiphoner, the surviving Irish liturgical books are all fragmentary. No later sources are available that could help us interpret these fragments, because the Irish liturgy was one of the many lesser traditions that was swept away by the liturgical reforms of the Carolingian period. Instead, we must rely on other kinds of evidence beyond the liturgical books and fragments. First, there is the liturgical information that can be gleaned from Psalter and Gospel manuscripts of Irish provenance, and from anthologies of material for private prayer.[1] Equally important, however, is the large corpus of medieval Irish literature, both in Latin and in the vernacular—for it is replete with references to, and descriptions of, liturgical practices of all kinds. Finally, our interpretations must be informed by comparative liturgiology, for the known history of the liturgical office in the early Eastern and Western churches is the only corrective available to ensure the validity of our reconstructions.

It has been more than a century since Frederick Edward Warren made the first and only attempt to identify, assemble, and interpret all the relevant passages, allusions, fragments, and sources in a thorough and comprehensive study of the medieval Irish liturgy.[2] Warren's book incorporated so much information that it is still helpful today, even though his own synthesis is completely outdated. Of course, many of the medieval texts Warren used or edited himself are now available in better editions, and have been subjected to a century's further scrutiny. The corpora of Irish and Hiberno-Latin literature are much more adequately catalogued, dated, and localized.[3] More than that, however, Warren's views were inevitably shaped by the ecclesiastical polemics of his time, which put an exorbitant value on anything that could be interpreted as a hint of "independence from Rome."[4] Fortunately this kind of concern is no longer a problem for serious scholars (but see B. Bradshaw 1989), though it still survives, tragically, in the Catholic/Protestant strife that sunders modern Ireland.

The relationship of the early Irish church to Rome and other churches is in fact one of the major questions we face in seeking to re-imagine its liturgy, for the leading figures of Irish Christianity certainly considered themselves loyal to Rome, even as they fought to maintain practices that were incompatible with Anglo-Saxon and Continental expressions of *Romanitas*. Relationships to the Eastern churches are also an issue. The Irish liturgy is full of striking parallels to Eastern Christian practices, which surely appealed to the love of the exotic and apocryphal that is so evident in the literary culture of medieval Ireland (cf. Dumville 1978). Yet many of these can be shown to be derived from Western European sources rather than direct Eastern contacts. At the same time, efforts to isolate Roman or Eastern or other influences and borrowings quickly run afoul of the fact that it is equally difficult to establish which elements are genuinely Irish. The travels of Irish missionary-pilgrims all over Europe are legendary, and the monks of Ireland encountered and contributed to ecclesiastical traditions everywhere they went. Much of the extant material that we regard as "Irish" or "Celtic," in fact, we do so only because it had an Irish author, or is preserved in a manuscript in Insular script: neither characteristic guarantees that either the physical manuscript or its textual content ever circulated in Ireland itself, and there is much that was clearly created and remained on the European continent (Gamber 1982, Schneiders 1996, and, more generally, Bieler 1963). From our perspective, then, the Irish liturgy looks much like that of the Ethiopian church at the opposite corner of medieval Christendom, full of unexpected enigmas and motley surprises (cf. Jeffery 1993). Each tradition, like a "hall closet"[5] on the farthest frontier of the medieval Christian world, has attracted an eclectic profusion of texts, traditions, and practices from an astonishing range of locales, reformulating much according to its own native genius, yet preserving disparate items in a kind of creative tension, rather than forcing everything into a single, unitary composition. This is nowhere more true than in the case of the Office, one of the least researched areas of the medieval Irish liturgy.

Finally, considerable advances have been made in the field of liturgical studies that compel us to revise almost all of Warren's interpretations. This is particularly true with the evidence relating to the Liturgy of the Hours or Divine Office, which in the Irish tradition is especially problematic and therefore particularly neglected.[6] We now have access to more material than Warren knew, and we know that the histories and interrelationships among these sources are far more complex and variegated than he could have imagined.[7] Basic to our contemporary understanding is the distinction between two different approaches to daily prayer, which began to emerge in the fourth century out of the older traditions of the Christian house churches (P. Bradshaw 1990): The "monastic Office," originally fostered by communities of lay ascetics in the Egyptian desert, was based on the ideal of "unceasing prayer" (1 Thess. 5:17). It was austere, limited in music and ceremonial, exhaustive and repetitious. The notion of reciting the entire Psalter over the course of a week, or some other fixed period of time, is its most obvious legacy (P. Bradshaw 1995). On the other hand the "cathedral Office," celebrated in urban settings under the leadership of the diocesan clergy headed by a bishop, was hierarchical and ceremonious, grandiose and musical, celebrating the daily alternation of darkness and light and the annual progression of feasts and seasons with all the resources the local Christian community could muster. These two kinds of Office are best imagined as ideals, however, for in practice most liturgical traditions actually combine elements of both. The cathedral Office, which aimed to include every element of the local Christian population, inevitably incorporated the urban communities of monks as well. Nor could the monks outside the cities resist for too long the twin temptations of clerical ordination and liturgical elaboration. Thus in the study of any liturgical tradition, including the Irish, the best approach is to seek to identify cathedral and monastic tendencies or elements, to assume that every source we enounter stands somewhere on a continuum between the two ideals.

The cathedral and monastic Offices each looked back to a prestigious homeland, and these two liturgical centers were the places most frequently visited by pilgrims and most widely imitated all over the Christian world. One of these was Egypt, the legendary home of monasticism, and the original source of many of the practices that define the monastic Office; its tradition survives most faithfully today in the Coptic Orthodox Church. The other center was Jerusalem, where monks and ordinary laity, locals and pilgrims, and all ranks of the clergy celebrated a lavish and complicated round of services that emphasized the relics and "holy places" in and around Christianity's Holy City. Elements of this tradition are preserved most fully in the liturgies of the "West Syrian" group: the Byzantine rite celebrated in the Greek and Russian Orthodox Churches, and the rites of the Armenian Orthodox and Syrian Orthodox ("Jacobite") Churches.[8] Both Egyptian and Syro-Palestinian liturgies exerted much influence on the early local traditions of the West, notably the complex of liturgical traditions we lump together as "Gallican," which were in use throughout the area of France and northern Italy up to the Carolingian period, when they were suppressed in favor of the Roman Office (a heavily monasticized cathedral Office that became the basis of the medieval and Tridentine Roman Breviary) and the closely-related Benedictine Office (celebrated wherever monastic life is governed by the Rule of St. Benedict). Because of this suppression, which began in the eighth and ninth centuries, most of these pre-Carolingian local traditions are poorly attested; they have to be reconstructed from conciliar decrees, sermons, and analogies with the Mozarabic traditions of Spain, which survived under Muslim rule until the Reconquista of the eleventh century (Jungmann 1962). Only from three Gallican centers do we have substantial evidence regarding the structure of the Divine Office: (1) the city of Tours in northwestern France,[9] (2) the Mediterranean island monastery of Lérins in the bay of Cannes, which provided the basis for the tradition of Arles,[10] and (3) the monastery of St. Maurice at Agaune, east of the Lake of Geneva.[11] But among the most interesting sources that do survive, there are some connected with Ireland or with Continental Irish activity. The time is ripe for a new and detailed consideration of this Irish material, and the purpose of the present chapter is to outline some of the major directions in which new investigation will lead.

The Irish Office of the Three Fifties

The Rule of St. Benedict (*CPL* 1852), written in the early sixth century, sternly warns that "monks who sing less than the complete psalter . . . in the course of a week render a lazy service of devotion, for we read that our holy fathers energetically achieved this in a single day."[12] Benedict was doubtless thinking of the Fathers of the Desert, the heroes of the earliest period of Egyptian monasticism, who were said to have performed astonishing feats of ascetical endurance. For instance, in a collection of stories about extended fasting and food deprivation, we read:

> A certain other old man came to a certain one of the Fathers. He cooked a morsel of lentils, and said, "Let us do the Work of God [i.e., the Divine Office], and [then] let us taste [the food]." And a certain one of them completed the whole Psalter, but another recited by heart [the biblical books of] two major prophets in the manner of a reader (*lectoris ordine*). And when it was morning the old man who had come parted, and they forgot to eat the food.[13]

However common this sort of thing may have been as an ascetic exercise, it is unusual to find a formal liturgical office in which all 150 psalms are sung over the course of a single night. However, an eleventh-century Antiochene collection of monastic stories records an instance that seems to straddle the line between monastic exuberance and structured liturgy. Known as the *Narration of John and Sophronios,* this tale purports to recount the experience of two seventh-century Palestinian monks visiting Egypt, though in fact the true provenance and dating of this document is very difficult to determine.[14] In the Office they observed, as shown in table 5.1, the psalms were performed through the night into the early morning, divided into three groups of fifty, with each group followed by prayers (*Pater noster, Kyrie eleison*) and readings. A Western Office with a similar arrangement can be found in the rite of twelfth-century Milan, where this type of vigil was celebrated only a few times a year.[15] In the Milanese tradition, where parallels to Syro-Palestinian usages are frequent, the three groups of fifty psalms were separated by readings and the singing of responsories.

In Ireland, however, the recitation of the entire Psalter in three parts seems to have been practiced daily. Ninth-century monastic rules written in Irish, associated with the movement of the Céli Dé or Culdees, take this practice for granted—a monk was forbidden to eat until he had said all 150 psalms. Thus the rules are concerned not to establish the practice itself, but to regulate such details as whether one should stand throughout or sit sometimes, how often to genuflect, and what to do after each of the "three fifties." Two of the methods advocated are shown in the third column of table 5.1: In the first, which resembles the Office of John and Sophronios, the monk stands for the first and third group but sits for the second, saying a *Pater noster* each time he changes position. In the second, one or three canticles (psalm-like texts from books of the Bible other than the Psalter) are read after each fifty psalms.[16] This is in fact the arrangement found in many Irish manuscripts of the Psalter, in which canticles are placed after Pss. 50 [RSV 51], 100 [RSV 101], and 150.[17] Interestingly, the canticles in these manuscripts tend to be the same

Table 5.1 The Irish Office of the Three Fifties, with some Eastern and Western parallels

Milan (Beroldus) (Magistretti 1894, 57–58)	"John and Sophronios" (Longo 1965–66, 251–52)	Ireland (Tallaght Rules) (Gwynn & Purton 1911–12, 128–41)	Irish Psalters (Mearns 1914, 68–70)
litany & procession			
Te deum	(standing)	(standing)	
	Pater noster	*Pater noster*	
Pss. 1–50	**Pss. 1–50**	**Pss. 1–50**	**Pss. 1–50**
	Pater noster	*Pater noster*	
		1–3 canticles	3 canticles
	50 *Kyrie eleison*		
	(sitting)	(sitting)	
reading of saint's life responsory	reading of James's epistle		
	(standing)	(standing)	
Pss. 51–100	**Pss. 51–100**	**Pss. 51–100**	**Pss. 51–100**
	[*Pater noster*]	*Pater noster*	
	[50 *Kyrie eleison*]	1–3 canticles	3 canticles
	(sitting)		
reading of saint's life responsory	reading of Peter's epistle		
	(standing)	(standing)	
Pss. 101–150	**Pss. 101–150**	**Pss. 101–150**	**Pss. 101–150**
	Pater noster	*Pater noster*	
	50 *Kyrie eleison*	1–3 canticles	1 canticle
	(sitting)		
	reading of John's epistle		
	(standing)		
Mass	nine odes	*Beati* and canticles	additional canticles

ones that were sung at Lauds in the medieval Roman Office.[18] As the liturgical traditions of those times varied greatly in the number and ordering of the Old Testament canticles, this is a clear indication of early contact with Rome on the part of the Irish church.[19] But this is not so surprising since the Irish, with their love of biblical studies, also seem to have preferred the Vulgate text with its "Gallican" Psalter[20]—imbued as it was with the authority of St. Jerome and his mentor Pope Damasus—over the local Old Latin texts that circulated in much of Europe.[21] One of the earliest witnesses of this Psalter text is also one of the most prized relics of the Irish church, a sixth-century manuscript allegedly written by St. Columba of Iona.[22]

The many variations in the Céli Dé documents make clear that we are not dealing with a unified liturgical cycle, but with a complex of related practices. At least part of the reason for this diversity seems to be that, in many cases, the Three Fifties were evidently conceived as more of an individual ascetic or penitential exercise than a public office celebrated by a community. Thus one Irish metrical rule, datable before 800, advises monks "to sing the three fifties from tierce to tierce, if it be possible, by the ordinances of the ancients." The phrase "if it be possible" gives the impression that this is only a recommendation to an individual, like the other penances proposed in the same text: a hundred prostrations each morning and evening, two hundred prostrations every day except Sunday, one hundred or (in another passage) two hundred blows on the hands every Lent, three hundred prostrations every day and three at every canonical hour.[23] The "ancients," however, are not the Fathers of the Egyptian desert, but the great saints of the early Irish church.

If the extraordinary stamina of the Desert Fathers was proof of their devotion or holiness, the Irish practice called for something more. Irish asceticism had a strong expiatory character that is spelled out, for instance, in an Irish penitential of the eighth century or earlier, representative of a type of literature that was one of the major Irish contributions to medieval Western Christianity (*CPL* 1881–84; Kenney 1968, 72–77): "The three fifties every day, with their conclusion of the *Beati*, to the end of seven years, saves a soul out of hell," we are told at the beginning. But to accomplish the same feat in only one year requires "365 paternosters and 365 genuflections and 365 blows with a scourge on every day to the end of the year, and fasting every month." The purpose of this text, in fact, is to list equivalent penances that may be substituted for harsher ones. In place of "'black fasting' [i.e., no dairy products] after a great crime" a holy man may substitute "the three fifties with their hymns and with their canticles" or "one hundred blows with a scourge." A series of 365 Paters "while standing up, the arms unwearied towards heaven . . . the elbows must not touch the sides at all," will substitute "for a year for sudden repentance," but in place of "a year of hard penance" one must spend "three days and three nights at it in a dark house," with "a three days' fast save three sips of water every day," during which one should "sing 150 psalms every day while standing up without a staff, and a genuflexion at the end of every psalm, and a *Beati* after every fifty, genuflexion between every two chapters (?) and a *Hymnum dicat* after every *Beati* . . . and he must not let himself down into a lying posture. . . ." In place of a more ordinary fast, "for any one that can read: the three fifties with their canticles while standing up, and celebrating every canonical hour, and twelve genuflexions and the arms stretched out towards God at the hours of the day, with earnest thought towards heaven." For the illiterate were prescribed such things as "300 genuflections and 300 honest blows with a scourge," "a night without sleeping, without sitting down, except when he lets himself down for genuflexion," with multiple repetitions of the Pater noster, the Credo, and certain songs in Celtic.[24]

There are even stories of the Psalter being recited more than once a day, as in the legend of a young cleric who, after impregnating a nun and thus assuring her death and damnation, built a hut by her grave, recited the psalms and the *Beati* seven times a day with a hundred prostrations, and after a year received a vision in which she told him that she was almost freed (Stokes, *Lives*, p. x). How it must have felt to inhabit a world that valued such stories, in which no amount of atonement was ever quite enough, is proclaimed in a ninth-century Irish poem:

> The high knowledge feeds me, the melodious song of the believers. Let us sing the song which the ancients have sung, the course (?) which they have sounded forth. Would that I could expel from my flesh what they have expelled. . . . God's love demands His fear. . . . A load of devotion with gentleness, pure . . . without sorrow. The mind towards bright eternal heaven.[25]

Yet even as a penitential practice, the recitation of the Three Fifties could retain some connection to the communal office. For example the "Rule of Patrick," a document of Céli Dé background, refers to "the singing of the three fifties every canonical hour" (O'Keeffe, "Rule," 223, para. 12). The "Rule of Ailbe of Emly," an Irish poem (Kenney 1968, 123), quite clearly places the Three Fifties in the context of the canonical hours celebrated by the whole group. From it we can partially reconstruct the monastic day shown in table 5.2 (O'Neill, "The Rule," 98–105). The day began and ended with 100 genuflections; in the morning these were linked to the recitation of the *Beati* and the three groups of fifty psalms. Other groups of psalms, the *Hymnum dicat,* and the *Deus in adjutorium* (Ps. 69:1 [RSV 70:1]) were also prescribed for various times of the day. There is a parallel with the fifth-century Gallican monastic rules of Lérins, in that silence is mandated between the Morning Office and Terce (the third hour), work between Terce and None (the ninth hour).[26] Particularly striking is the passage, found only in some of the manuscripts, describing the morning reading of the Gospel followed by a procession to the cross. This is a clear parallel to the Resurrection Vigil that originated in the Church of the Holy Sepulchre in Jerusalem and was widely imitated elsewhere (Egeria, trans. Wilkinson, 124–25). Additional parallels to the Resurrection Vigil will be discussed in due course.

The Office in the Rule of Ailbe has some similarities to an Office described in an Irish text known as "The Second Vision of Adamnan" (Kenney 1968, 627). Adamnan's Office clearly had a penitential purpose, for it is specified for use during three-day fasts paralleling the Ember days of the familiar Roman liturgical calendar. Such fasts are alleged to be efficacious in preventing plague and invasion by Danes. But it would seem that this Office could also be used for communal public prayer, for at the end "they lift their hands up to heaven, and they give a blessing to God and Patrick with the saints of Ireland, and to every soul that is in the

Table 5.2 The liturgical day in the Rule of Ailbe of Emly, with Eastern and Western parallels

Rule of Ailbe of Emly 16–39 (O'Neill, "Rule," 98–105)	Parallels
(beginning of day:) 100 genuflections at *Beati* three groups of fifty psalms	Tallaght rules: 3 groups of 50 psalms, multiple genuflections (Gwynn 1927, 51–55)
[in some MSS only: prayer confession without ceasing (litany?) reading of Gospel and monastic rule procession to cross]	Jerusalem: Resurrection Gospel procession to Golgotha (Egeria, *Travels,* 124–25)
30 psalms each morning versicle *Deus in adjutorium* after each	Tallaght: 30 Paternosters after 150 psalms
silence until Terce: washing, sewing, private prayer	Lérins: silence until Terce for reading and study (Vogüé, *Les Règles,* 1:131–35)

bell rung for Terce:
   Hymnum dicat sung
	Tallaght: *after* Terce
	   Beati
	   Hymnum dicat
	   Unitas in trinitate

brothers wash and dress 3 genuflections on entering church [for Mass?]	
receive work assignments, work till None	Lérins: work from Terce to None
None: psalms, prostration, *Beati*	Byzantine rite: Typica with Beatitudes after None (Arranz 1965, 416–17, 444)
bell rung for call to refectory	Tallaght: bell rung for call to refectory, singing of Pater noster, psalm verses, *Beati*
Vespers: 100 genuflections	Tallaght: varying numbers of genuflections at each hour
Midnight: 12 psalms	Rule of Columban: 12 psalms at midnight office (Walker 1957, 130)

assembly of these triduans, whether alone or in a multitude" (Stokes, *Lives,* 432–33). As shown in table 5.3, this Office included the familiar 100 genuflections at the *Beati,* followed by canticles, psalms, and hymns, with many genuflections and a cross vigil (a period of kneeling with arms out in the form of a cross) (Gougaud 1927, 10–14; Godel 1963, 314–21). Almost the same series of texts has been copied onto the last verso of the seventh-century Gospel codex known as the Book of Mulling,[27] and this helps to clarify, among other things, the identity of the ubiquitous *Beati,* a text frequently mentioned in Irish literature but rarely identified (e.g., Gwynn, "The Rule of Tallaght," 51–55 and *passim*). Though many editors of Irish texts have included footnotes identifying the *Beati* with Ps. 118 [RSV 119], *Beati immaculati in via,* its frequent use as a kind of appendix to the Psalter suggests it is more likely to be a canticle. The text *Beati pauperes in spiritu* found in the Book

Table 5.3 An office of intercession against pestilence

Adamnan's Second Vision (Stokes, *Lives*, 432–33)	Book of Mulling (Lawlor 1897, 146–47; Lawlor 1897–99, 212; LS = Lapidge and Sharpe)
	alleluia [?]
100 genuflections	
Beati [Celtic: *Biait*]	
Magnificat	*Magnificat*
Benedictus	*Benedictus* [in *saecula*] [= part of hymn *Noli pater;* LS 590]
	Videns ihesus turbas ascendit in montem [Gospel: Matt. 5:1 ff.]
Miserere mei Deus [= Ps. 50] cross vigil	
Patrick's hymn	*Christus illum* [= end of hymn *Audite omnes*; LS 573] *Memoria aeterna* [additional stanza?] *Patricius episcopus* [= stanza also in Bangor Antiphoner]
Hymn of the Apostles	*Invitiata quo feramus* [= LS 292] *Exaudi donec dicis peccata plurima* [additional stanza?]
smiting of hands	
Hymnum dicat	*Maiestatem immensam* [= end of hymn *Hymnum dicat*] *Unitas usque in finem* [additional stanza?]
Michael's hymn	*In trinitate spes mea* [?][LS 588]
	Credo in Deum *pater noster* *Ascendat oratio* [?]
3 genuflections after each hymn 3 breast strikes at each genuflection with a Celtic prayer	

of Mulling, namely the Beatitudes from the Sermon on the Mount (Matt. 5:1–12), is a more plausible candidate. It is recited as a canticle in the Byzantine rite,[28] and was also known as a canticle to St. Ambrose of Milan (Franz 1994, 366). The fact that it is much shorter than Ps. 118 [RSV 119] makes the Irish reports of numerous repetitions somewhat more plausible.[29]

The ambiguous character of this type of office, which can be either a common celebration or an individual act of penitence, recalls the ethos of the Desert Fathers:

We are in the habit of distinguishing between "private" prayer and "liturgical" prayer, but for the early monks there was but one prayer, always personal, sometimes done in common with others, sometimes alone in the secret of one's heart. . . . It was the same prayer which was performed in the cell as in the community gathering, and neither setting was seen as superior to the other. There was nothing inherently corporate in the worship, nothing which might not be done equally well alone as together. Although a communal assembly offered an element of mutual encouragement in the work of prayer, . . . nevertheless the presence or absence of other people was ultimately a matter of indifference.[30]

But the ambiguity also calls to mind the important role that Irish monasticism played in the formation of Western penitential discipline. Irish monasticism is frequently credited with—or blamed for—introducing the practice of private, auricular confession in place of the more ancient practice, whereby penitents were expelled from and subsequently reconciled to the Church as a group, in public ceremonies.[31] The obsessive character of the Irish penances associated with the Office of the Three Fifties, with their numerous repetitions and punitive exercises, certainly left their mark on later European religious customs[32]—perhaps they also contributed to the shift away from the communal celebration of the choral Office, toward the private recitation of the breviary (Taft 1993, 297–306). Certainly the medieval anxiety to pile up large numbers of Masses on one's own behalf was one of the factors in the emergence of the private Mass—a purely Western innovation like the private Office (Vogel 1986, 156–59). Echos of the Irish Office of the Three Fifties survived in such medieval monastic customs as the *trina oratio,* in which three groups of psalms were recited in penitence while kneeling or prostrate before the altar.[33]

Offices Derived from Cassian

The eighth-century *Navigatio Sancti Brendani,* recording a fictional voyage of St. Brendan, includes two descriptions of liturgical offices. The more famous one is outlined in full in chapter 17, when the Irish saint stops at the Isle of the Three Choirs (one each of boys, youths, and men). But another office with the same structure is evidently sung by birds in chapter 11, though fewer specific texts are identified (see the first two columns of table 5.4).[34] In this Office it is possible to detect parallels with both Palestinian and Egyptian methods of celebrating the Divine Office, as these were reported in the early fifth-century *Monastic Institutions* (CPL 513) of St. John Cassian (fl. ca. 415–30), the founder of two monasteries in Marseilles and one of the most important writers of Western monasticism. For Irish monasticism in particular, "the great teacher in matters appertaining to prayer was certainly Cassian" (Ryan 1972, 328 ff.). In opposition to the multifarious Gallican practices of his time, Cassian published idealized and selective descriptions of the Egyptian and Palestinian uses, as he remembered them from his own sojourns in monasteries at Bethlehem and in Egypt. The Egyptian night Office, described in his Book II, featured the recitation of 12 psalms before dawn and 12 more in the evening; the Palestinian Office of Cassian's Book III included the recitation of the last three psalms (148–50) in the morning, and three psalms at each of the other hours (Cassian, ed. Guy, 64–65, 95–115). Though modern scholars do not fully trust Cassian's accounts of the Egyptian and Palestinian Office traditions,[35] in the centuries after his death they became very influential in the formation of the Western monastic Office (Heiming 1961).

Table 5.4 The Offices of the *Navigatio Sancti Brendani,* and the Egyptian and Palestinian Offices according to Cassian

Navigatio S. Brendani (ed. Selmer 1959, 22–28, 49–53)		Cassian, *De institutis coenobiorum* (ed. Guy 1965, 56–117)	
Isle of Birds (chap. 11)	Isle of 3 choirs (chap. 17)	Egypt (2:4)	Palestine (3:1–6)
Tercia vigilia noctis	*Vigiliae matutinae*	*Nocturnae solemnitates*	*Matutina solemnitas*
			Pss. 62, 118, 147
Domine labia mea aperies prayer			
Ps. 148	**Pss. 148–50**		**Pss. 148–50**
	12 psalms "per ordinem psalterii"	**12 psalms** Old Testament reading New Testament reading	
Aurora	*Dies*		*Novella solemnitas*
Ps. 89	**Pss. 50, 62, 89**		**Pss. 50, 62, 89**
Tercia hora	*Tercia*		*Tertia*
Ps. 46	**Pss. 46,** 53, 114 "sub alleluia"		3 psalms
	[*Mass,* including communion antiphon *Hoc sacrum corpus Domini*]		
Sexta	*Sexta*		*Sexta*
Ps. 66	**Ps. 66,** 69, 115		3 psalms
Nona	*Nona*		*Nona*
Ps. 132	**Pss.** 129, **132,** 147		3 psalms
Vespertina hora	*Vesperi*	*Vespertinae solemnitates*	[Vespers not described]
Ps. 64	**Pss. 64,** 103, 112	**12 psalms**	
	15 gradual psalms [= **119–33**]		
	(The three choirs sang through the night until Matins)		

The Offices presented in the *Navigatio* conflate Cassian's two traditions into a single ordo. First, in the vigil before dawn one finds the three morning psalms 148–50, followed by twelve psalms "per ordinem psalterii," perhaps meaning that the complete Psalter was read at this point in groups of 12 over a period of days. This arrangement is somewhat unusual, for though most other Christian traditions make use of Pss. 148–50 in the morning, these three psalms, which come from the end of the Psalter, tend to serve as the conclusion of the liturgical psalmody, after the other psalms rather than before them. But this odd placement is understandable if the intent was to combine the two traditions reported by Cassian: the three psalms of the Palestinian tradition followed by the 12 of the Egyptian tradition. Similarly, the next Office in the series, though it corresponds to Prime, is not actually named in the *Navigatio,* but is simply said to have taken place at dawn (*aurora*) or daybreak (*cum dies illucessisset*). This too shows the influence of Cassian, who describes this Office as a recent innovation, and, having no name for it, calls it simply "the new celebration" (*novella solemnitas;* Taft 1993, 191–209). The three psalms Cassian assigns to this hour (50, 62, 89 [RSV 51, 63, 90]) are also those of the *Navigatio* (some of the psalms are misidentified in the footnotes of the Selmer edition). The three psalms assigned to Vespers, an hour mentioned but not described in detail by Cassian, may be due to simple extrapolation of what Cassian prescribes for the other hours. The evening recitation of the gradual psalms or "songs of ascents" may answer to the 12 psalms of Cassian's Egyptian vespers, though there are 15 of them rather than 12. The duplication of a three-psalm Palestinian pattern and a 12-psalm Egyptian pattern in the evening has a parallel in another Office derived from Cassian, outlined in a pseudonymous monastic rule entitled *Regula Cassiani.*[36] There the two night hours of 12 psalms, one variously called Nocturns and Matins, the other called Vespers, are combined with five daylight hours of three psalms each: Prime, Terce, Sext, None, and Duodecima—the last said at the twelfth hour or end of the day (*terminatio diei*) (Ledoyen, "La 'Regula Cassiani,'" 171, 177). In effect there were two evening hours, Duodecima with three psalms and Vespers with 12. Similarly, in the Gallican Office that was celebrated at Arles, the Office called Duodecima had 12-plus-three psalms, but this was at times increased to 18 or more, including Ps. 103 [RSV 104], as in chapter 17 of the *Navigatio S. Brendani* (Taft 1993, 107).

We do not know whether the Offices described in the *Navigatio S. Brendani* were ever actually celebrated by anyone, since the work is a fiction. But the tension evident at Vespers, between the prescriptions of Cassian on the one hand and the practices of known Gallican centers on the other, can also be seen in the usages of the seventh-century Irish monasteries on the Continent. The *Navigatio* Offices and the Continental monastic Offices have another feature in common: neither exhibits any trace of the Three Fifties, so central to sources written in the Irish language.

The Offices of the Irish Monasteries
on the Continent

Of the many Irish *peregrini,* the most important was St. Columban, who, after completing his monastic formation at Bangor in Ireland, came to the Continent about the year 590. After founding several monasteries, notably Luxeuil in eastern France, his repeated quarrels with the Gallican bishops over the legitimacy of Irish practices led to his exile. He wound up in northern Italy, where he founded the monastery at Bobbio in 613; it was at Bobbio that he died in 615. Columban's Office is outlined in chapter 7 of his *Regula monachorum* (table 5.5).[37] Columban, like Cassian, was very aware of a multiplicity of traditions, though he insisted his own prescriptions were in agreement "with our elders" (*cum senioribus nostris*). He ac-

Table 5.5 The Office according to the Continental Irish monastic rules

Columbanus, *Regula monachorum* (chap. 7 ed. Walker 1957, 128–33); Donatus, *Regula* (chap. 75, ed. Vogüé 1978, 308–10)	"quidam catholici" (acc. to Columban, ed. Walker 1957, 132–33)	*Regula cuiusdam patris ad Monachos* (ed. Villegas 1973, 34)
(*Saturdays and Sundays*) **12–25 chorae of 3 psalms**	(*Saturdays and Sundays*) **36 psalms**	(*Saturdays and Sundays*) vigils until cockcrow
(*other days* 12 chorae (36 pss.) in winter 8 chorae (24 pss.) in summer		
(*feasts of martyrs in winter*) 15 chorae (15 pss.) [Donatus only]		
	(*cockcrow*) 3 psalms	
	matutinum 3 psalms	(*at dawn*) missa
per diurnas horas **3 psalms each hour** versicles of intercession		(*three daytime gatherings*) **3 psalms each hour**
Initium noctis	*Initium noctis*	(*three nighttime gatherings each with:*)
12 psalms	3 psalms	**12 psalms** prayers Old Testament reading New Testament reading
Medium noctis **12 psalms**	*Medium noctis* 3 psalms	

tually described one alternative tradition with which he did not agree, which he ascribed to "certain catholics" (*quidam catholici;* see Vogüé 1988).

Columban's Rule is not a complete description of the Office, for it takes a certain amount for granted. It does not, for instance, state how many hours there were during the day, but focuses on the elements that he thought required correction or emphasis. His major concern was to ensure that the number of psalms in the night Office should expand and contract as the length of the night varied over the course of the year—a Gallican practice[38] that contradicted Cassian's fixed number of 12 psalms at each hour. The unit of psalmody in Columban's night Office was the chora, consisting of three psalms, the last of which was sung antiphonally.[39] On the nights leading up to Saturday and Sunday mornings, the number of chorae varied, from 12 (i.e., 36 psalms) on the shortest summer nights to 25 (i.e., 75 psalms) on the longest winter nights. Thus in the dead of winter it was possible to complete the entire Psalter of 150 psalms in the two nights of a single weekend. Winter weekdays had 12 chorae, while summer weekdays had twenty-four psalms, apparently eight chorae. Each of the day hours (it is not stated how many day hours there were) had three psalms, the Palestinian number according to Cassian. Two other night hours, *initium noctis* at nightfall and *medium noctis* at midnight, had 12 psalms each, the Egyptian number for night hours according to Cassian. Columban's "certain catholics," on the other hand, sang only 12 psalms per night. No matter how long or short the night was, these were split among four services, at nightfall, midnight, cockcrow, and morning. The "catholics" agreed with Columban's tradition, however, in especially emphasizing the nights leading into Saturday and Sunday morning, when 36 psalms were sung.

Columban's prescriptions are essentially repeated (with the addition of 15 *chorae* on feasts of martyrs) in the *Regula ad virgines* (*CPL* 1860) of Donatus (d. 660), a bishop of Besançon who had been a monk at Luxeuil. Since Donatus stated that this Office was "according to the norm of our rule" (*juxta normam regulae nostrae;* Donatus, *Regula,* 237), it seems likely that Columban's Office was actually celebrated at least at Luxeuil. If so, another *Regula ad virgines,* by Waldebert, abbot of Luxeuil (*CPL* 1863), may also be allied to the Columbanian tradition, though it contains little liturgical information. Another Irish monastic rule, anonymously entitled "The Rule of a certain Father" (*Regula cuiusdam patris*) (*CPL* 1862) presents a tradition indebted to Columban's rule, though we do not know where it may have been written or followed. It appears to agree with Columban in having three hours during the night, though each has the Cassianic arrangement of 12 psalms and two readings. A vigil of possibly variable length was held on the nights leading up to Saturday and Sunday mornings, but little is said about it in contrast to the heavy emphasis Columban gave to it. There was also a *missa* at cockcrow (whether a Mass or a morning Office is not clear), a practice not mentioned by Columban. The number of day hours, with three psalms each, is fixed at three to equal the number of night hours, in contrast to the lack of specificity in the rules of Columban and Donatus (Villegas, "La 'Regula cuiusdam,'" 34).

Thus there appears to have been a range of related traditions in the Continental Irish monasteries, each of which stood somewhere in the spectrum between contemporary Gallican practices and the prescriptions of Cassian. Three of these traditions are represented by (1) the Office of Columban and Donatus (and Waldebert), (2) the Office of "certain catholics," and (3) the Office of "a certain father." It is not clear whether any of these traditions was known in Ireland itself, where the extant documents are related instead to the Office of the Three Fifties. How Irish, then, were the traditions of the Continental Irish monasteries? At the crux of this question lies the most extensive and important source of information about the medieval Irish Office: the manuscript known as the Bangor Antiphoner.

The Bangor Antiphoner and Its Allies

As the largest extant source of Irish hymns, canticles, prayers, and antiphons for the Irish liturgy of the hours, the Bangor Antiphoner and its allied fragments deserve extended treatment in any investigation of the Irish Office.[40] The Antiphoner is among the earliest surviving monuments of Irish paleography (*CLA* 3, 311), a cornerstone of Julian Brown's classification of Insular scripts, in which it exemplifies the set and cursive minuscule of "Phase I" (Brown 1993, 118, 147, 190, 206, 211, 224). The manuscript is supposed to have originated at Columban's original monastery of Bend-Chor or Bangor in Ireland—not to be confused with the now better-known Bangor in Wales[41]—because it contains three hymns honoring the founder, the rule, and the abbots of that monastery (Kenney 1968, 92). Because the hymn honoring the Bangor abbots names all of them from Comgall, the founder, down to Cronan, who is described as still reigning (*nunc sedet*), the manuscript is regarded as firmly dated to the period of Cronan's reign, 680–91.[42]

However, this argument applies at best to the authorship of the hymn, not necessarily to the provenance of the manuscript containing it—particularly as the codex is written in more than one hand. There can be no doubt that the scribes were Irish, and Irish provenance would be confirmed by the fact that the folios consist of "normal insular membrane" (Brown 1993, 236). But it was at Bobbio that the manuscript was discovered in the sixteenth century, and the textual content offers reasons to think that the Irishmen who created it were actually working on the Continent, if not at Bobbio itself. First of all, several texts in the manuscript suggest closer relationships to Continental liturgical traditions—notably the Gallican tradition of southern France at Arles, and the "Ambrosian" liturgy of Milan—than to contemporary Ireland. Second, the Office of the Bangor Antiphoner represents a developed form of the tradition going back to the Rule of Columban; thus the natural home of such a manuscript would seem to be one of Columban's Continental foundations, unless it can be shown that Columbanian monasticism was introduced into Ireland itself. Third, and particularly interesting, is the fact that certain texts of the Bangor Antiphoner recur in a later manuscript from the Bobbio library (now in Turin),[43] but rearranged in a way that shows some historical and liturgical development. This seems a strong indication that it was at Bobbio that the texts were actually used, and at Bobbio that the developments in the Turin fragment took place, whether or not these texts were also known at Bangor or elsewhere in Ireland.

Table 5.6 outlines the contents of the Bangor Antiphoner.[44] The manuscript is not in fact an antiphoner in the modern sense, for it does not contain a complete repertory of Proper Office chants arranged according to the liturgical year. It would be more accurate to consider it a supplement or appendix to the Psalter, containing examples of the kinds of non-psalm material needed to celebrate the Office. This material is in fact only very loosely organized. The first major section (fols. 1r–17v), indeed, contains the two kinds of material most frequently appended to Psalters: canticles and hymns.[45] The second section (fols. 17v–31v) is a collection of collects or prayers to be said at the different liturgical hours, or after the psalms and canticles of the Office, according to a widespread Eastern and Western practice that was followed in the Columbanian tradition, though it did not survive into the familiar Roman Breviary.[46] This section includes three cycles of collects for the daily round of Offices (fols. 17v–22r), seven sets of collects following the canticles of the morning Office (fols. 22r–29v), and a brief appendix of miscellaneous material, including the hymn celebrating the rule of Bangor and an exorcism prayer (fols. 30r–31r). The third section contains antiphons, that is, the texts of the musical refrains that were sung with the psalms and canticles (fols. 31v–33r), including fourteen sets of antiphons for the morning Office, and smaller collections of antiphons for Ps. 89 [RSV 90], for martyrs, and for communion. Finally there is a supplement of

Table 5.6 The Bangor Antiphoner

First gathering (five bifolia + three inserted leaves): fols. 1–6, 7–9, 10–13
I. Canticles and hymns
    1r–3r [1] *Canticum Moysi.* Audite coeli quae loquor [Deut. 32]
    3r–4v [2] *Hymnus sancti Hilarii de Christo.* Hymnum dicat turba fratrum
    4v–6v [3] *Hymnus Apostolorum ut alii dicunt.* Precamur patrem
    6v and 10r [4] *Benedictio sancti Zachariae.* Benedictus dominus deus Israel

Three inserted single leaves: fols. 7–9
    7r–8v [5] *Canticum.* Cantemus domino [Exod. 15]
    8v–9v [6] *Benedictio puerorum.* Benedicite omnia opera domini [Dan. 3]

First gathering (continued): fols. 10–13
    10r–v [7] *Hymnus in die Dominica.* Laudate pueri dominum. . . . Te deum laudamus
    10v–11r [8] *Hymnus quando communicant sacerdotes.* Sancti venite
    11r–v [9] *Hymnus quando cereus benedicitur.* Ignis creator igneus
    11v–12v [10] *Hymnus mediae noctis.* Mediae noctis tempus est
    12v–13r [11] *Hymnus in Natali Martyrum, vel Sabbato ad matutinam.* Sacratissimi martyres
    13r–v [12] *Hymnus ad matutinam in Dominica.* Spiritus divinae lucis gloriae
    13v [13] *Hymnus Sancti Patricii magistri Scotorum.* Audite omnes amantes

Second gathering (four bifolia): fols. 14–21
    14r–15v [13] *Hymnus sancti Patricii* (continued)
    15v–17v [14] *Hymnus Sancti Comgilli Abbatis nostri.* Recordemur justitiae
    17v [15] *Hymnus Sancti Camelaci.* Audite bonum exemplum

II. Collects for the Divine Office, with an appendix
  A. Collects for the cycle of daily hours
      17v [16] one *Collectio ad secundam*
      18r–v [17]–[26] one cycle of metrical collects for the hours
      18v–22r [27]–[56] one cycle of prose collects and other prayers for the hours
Third gathering (seven bifolia + one inserted slip): fols. 22–36
      22r–v [57]–[61] one cycle of prose collects for the night hours

  B. Collects for the canticles of the Sunday morning office
      22v–28v [62]–[93] seven cycles of prose collects for the Sunday morning office
      28r [94] one collect *Super cantemus domino*
      29r (inserted slip) end of collect [94]

  C. Appendix of miscellaneous texts
      30r–v [95] Bangor hymn: *Versiculi familiae Benchuir.* Benchuir bona regula
      30v–31r [96] exorcism prayer, *Collectio super hominem qui habet diabolum*
      31r [97] collect for the morning office, *Oratio de Martyribus*

III. Antiphons
  A. One antiphon for Ps. 89 at Secunda on Christmas
      31r–v [98] *Incipit antiphona in natali domini super Domine refugium ad secundam*
  B. Ten sets of antiphons for the morning canticles
      31v [99.1]–[99.6] three pairs of antiphons for *Cantemus* and *Benedicite*
      32r [99.7]–[100] one set of antiphons for *Cantemus, Benedicite,* and Pss. 148–50
      32r–v [99.9]–[99.20] six pairs of antiphons for *Cantemus* and *Benedicite*
  C. Antiphons for feasts
      32v [101]–[104] four antiphons *De martyribus*
  D. Antiphons for Ps. 89 at Secunda
      32v [105]–[107] three Sunday antiphons *Super Domine refugium in dominico die*
      32v [108] one ferial antiphon, *Alia cotidiana*

Table 5.6 (*continued*)

　E. Communion antiphons
　　　32v–33r [109]–[115] seven antiphons *Ad communionem*

IV. Miscellaneous Supplement
　A. One canticle
　　　33r [116] *Ad vesperam et ad matutinam*. Gloria in excelsis deo
　　　33v (1)–(12) Eastern continuation of the Gloria in excelsis: Cotidie benedicimus te
　B. Prayers and antiphons
　　　34r [117]–[119] *Ad horas diei oratio communis*
　　　34v–35r [120]–[122] three collects: *Ad matutinam, Ad horam nonam, Ad secundam*
　　　35r [123] Te deum continuation: *Post Laudate pueri dominum in dominico*
　　　35r [124] one collect *De martyribus*
　　　35v [125]–[126] two more Te deum continuations: *Item alia post laudate*
　　　36r [127] collect for blessing the candle, *Ad cereum benedicendum*
　　　36r [128] another Te deum continuation
　C. Hymn honoring abbots of Bangor
　　　36v [129] *memoriam abbatum nostrorum*. Sancta sanctorum opera

---

further material (fols. 33r–36v), arranged in essentially the same order as the rest of the manuscript: first a canticle (the *Gloria in excelsis*),[47] then more prayers and collects, then more antiphons, ending with the hymn honoring the abbots of Bangor.

　　Thus, to the degree that there is any organization at all, the texts in the Bangor Antiphoner are collected by genre or type, not in the daily or annual order they would have been used in the liturgy, or according to any other overarching schema. If the manuscript was intended to support actual liturgical celebration, it would have been useful only to someone who already knew a great deal about when and how to perform the canticles, collects, and antiphons that are found there. Paleographical study shows that in fact this collection was assembled gradually, with little or no prior plan as to the ultimate content. The main hand (called A in Warren, *Antiphonary,* 1:xx) wrote the first fascicle and began the second one, through folio 24. A second hand (B), inserted the extra leaves 7–9, and alternates with hand A on folios 25 and 26. "But the latter part of the MS. from fol. 25 *v.* onwards, and more especially from fol. 30 *r.,* has been executed by an extraordinary number of different scribes. No fewer than fifteen different people seem to have written down collects, anthems [i.e. antiphons], hymns, etc. in no special sequence, and without any close connexion" (Warren, *Antiphonary,* 1:xx). In this manuscript, then, we may well be witnessing one of the very first attempts to put the Irish Office into written form.

　　A detailed study of the physical manuscript with a view to tracing the growth of the collection would be beyond the scope of this chapter, but such a study would provide one of the few available opportunities to observe a medieval chant tradition at this watershed moment. The general outlines of the process can be marked, however. First, though the texts are arranged in little collections, subcollections, and appendices, these should not be considered liturgical *libelli,* since that word properly refers to small collections in unbound gatherings that circulate independently (Gy 1991). The textual organization of the Bangor Antiphoner is not reflected in its fascicle structure, for each of the three major sections overlaps two of the unequal-sized fascicles. Codicologically speaking, the entire manuscript must be considered a unit. Its primitive organization, plus the fact it was written in a still-undetermined number of hands, indicate that the textual content was not fully planned from the beginning, but grew over time, with more than one individual playing a role in assembling the material. After the first hand had written the first fascicle and part of the second, the next hand added some leaves to the first fascicle and continued writing in the second fascicle, with other hands soon joining in. In the next stage, after many of the texts had been entered, but when the manuscript was still quite young, someone added liturgical rubrics above almost every text to show what its liturgical usage was. A logical further step in the direction toward becoming a true antiphoner is represented by the Turin fragment—there the canticles and collects, rather than being arranged in separate collections, are interspersed in a practical liturgical order (see table 5.7 below). The transition from the limited organization of the Bangor Antiphoner to the liturgically more usable Turin fragment is easily accounted for if both manuscripts reflect the usage of Bobbio, at two different stages in its development.

For reconstructing the Office of the Bangor Antiphoner, it makes sense to begin with the second collection of texts, for the three cycles of collects or prayers for the hours of the day (fols. 18r–22v) will show us what the daily services were in the milieu (be it Bangor or Bobbio) where the Bangor Antiphoner was assembled. The first of these cycles is made up of metrical collects (an unusual genre) that may well have been composed as a set. The second series is the most comprehensive and contains the most material. The third series extends only from the midnight Office through the morning. In addition, other stray collects for the various hours will be found throughout the manuscript, identified by their (subsequently added) rubrics.

The first hour of the day was evidently called Secunda, though it corresponded to Prime. The collects for this hour speak of the morning light [16–17, 122], and one of them beseeches God to hear the prayers "we offer in this first hour of the day" ([27]: *qui in hac prima diei referimus*). This hour evidently included Ps. 89 [RSV 90], the third psalm of Cassian's *novella solemnitas* and in the dawn hours of the *Voyage of St. Brendan*, because the Bangor Antiphoner includes antiphons for it, to be sung on Christmas [98], on Sunday [105–7], and on weekdays [108]. It would be logical that antiphons be supplied only for the third psalm if the Bangor Antiphoner emerged in a milieu that followed the chora system of Columban's rule, in which only the third psalm of each group was sung with an antiphon.

We know less about the content of Terce, Sext, and None—the collects focus instead on biblical events associated with each of these hours: the descent of the Holy Ghost at the third hour on Pentecost [28] (Acts 2:1–15), the Crucifixion at the sixth hour [19, 29] (Mark 15:33), the conversions of Cornelius [20] (Acts 10:30) and of the Good Thief [121] (Luke 23:39–43) at the ninth hour. These associations were reported by Cassian (ed. Guy: 94–100), though such interpretations of the hours can be traced back as far as the third century.[48] The Irish also had access to them through several vernacular treatises (Kenney 1968, 550), and a Latin text attributed to St. Jerome[49] preserved in the Bobbio Missal, a Gallican Massbook written in

France or northern Italy that, like the Bangor Antiphoner, was discovered in the Bobbio library (*CLLA* 220, Kenney 554). One is reminded also of the troparia for Terce, Sext, and None in the Byzantine and Egyptian horologia.[50] The Bangor Antiphoner includes another text that seems to have been intended for use at the little hours, for it is called "Common prayer at the hours of the day" (*Ad horas diei oratio communis* [117–19]). It consists of series of psalm versicles[51] alternating with collects and ending with the Pater noster, and somewhat resembles the intercessory versicles that were mandated for each hour "by our elders" (*a senioribus nostris*) according to Columban's Rule (*Opera*, 1957: 130–31).

The evening hour of *Vespertina* [*hora*] may have included the recitation of Ps. 140 [RSV 141], alluded to in one of the collects for this hour. This is the Vespers psalm par excellence in most of the Eastern rites, though this Eastern usage has no unambiguous attestation in the West (Taft 1993, 394). The *Gloria in excelsis* could be sung *ad Vesperum et ad matutinum* [116] according to the rubric; in most other traditions it was part of the morning Office.[52]

Next in the collect series we find one or two prayers *Ad initium noctis,* which was evidently a distinct celebration from Vespers. The *initium noctis* collects [22, 32, 33] not surprisingly refer to the oncoming darkness of night. Because the same theme dominates the collect *Ad cereum benedicendum* [127] and the "Ambrosian" hymn *Ignis creator igneus* [9] sung "when the candle is blessed" (*Hymnus quando cereus benedicitur*), it would appear that there was a lucernarium or lamplighting ceremony at this hour. The *Regula coenobialis* ascribed to St. Columban (Kenney 1968, 45, II), more a penitential than a monastic rule since its main purpose is to prescribe punishments, actually mentions a lamplighting of some sort, though not necessarily part of a communal Office: "If he has not blessed the lamp, that is, when it is lighted by a younger brother and is not presented to a senior for his blessing, . . . six blows" (Columban, *Opera*, 146–47).

Many have observed that the Passover and paschal themes in the collects and in the hymn *Ignis creator* recall the language of the paschal praeconia—the genre of hymns honoring the Easter candle that is represented in the Roman rite by the text *Exsultet iam angelica* (T. Kelly 1996; Fuchs and Weikmann 1992; *CLLA* 043, 485–99, *CPL* 1906a, 1932). This has led some to conclude that the Bangor Antiphoner texts were intended, not for a daily or weekly evening service, but for the annual Easter Vigil on Holy Saturday (McLoughlin 1969; Curran 1984, 59–64), even though the Bangor Antiphoner is a collection of material for the daily and weekly cycles that includes very few texts restricted to specific days of the year. But to make this distinction is to view the evidence anachronistically: In the formative period of the Christian liturgy, every Sunday had a paschal character as a celebration of the Resurrection.[53] The annual blessing of the Easter candle was originally only a special instance, though it became the sole survival in the West, of the lucernarium that took place every Saturday night (MacGregor 1992, 431–39, cf. Vives et al., *Concilios,* 194).

In the second of the collect cycles, the prayers *Ad initium noctis* are followed by a series of versicles and collects *Ad pacem celebrandam* [34] which ask for forgiveness of sins and "that we may not fear from nocturnal fear" (*ut non timeamus a timore nocturno*), a typical Compline sentiment. The *Ad pacem,* which apparently corresponds to the *oratio communis* of the day hours, is followed by a form of the Apostles' Creed and the Pater noster [35–36]. It was evidently at this point that the nightly monastic silence began, for the *Regula coenobialis* prescribes fifty lashes "if he has made a sound after the peace" (*Si post pacem sonaverit*, Columban, *Opera*, 162–63). The *Regula ad virgines* of Waldebert, Abbot of Luxeuil (*CPL* 1863) also emphasizes the importance of maintaining silence (PL 88, 1061).[54]

The difference between the Rule of Columban, which has a single evening hour, and the Bangor Antiphoner, which has both a Vespers and a Compline-like *initium noctis* with lucernarium, suggests that in the Antiphoner we have a later and more developed, perhaps "Gallicanized," form of the Columbanian tradition. The Office of Arles, according to St. Caesarius (d. 542), included a lucernarium celebration (part of the cycle of the cathedral Office) followed by a service called *Duodecima* [*hora*] ("twelfth hour," part of the monastic Office). Like the Vespers in chapter 17 of the *Navigatio Sancti Brendani*, Duodecima could include as many as 15 or 18 psalms or more. On top of these two services, Caesarius' successor Aurelian of Arles (d. 551) added a Compline hour (Taft 1993, 107, 155–56). If the multiple evening services of the Bangor Antiphoner owe something to the Arles arrangement, this would tend to locate the Antiphoner on the Continent, as a witness to the later development of the Columbanian tradition at Bobbio, rather than in Ireland as an authentic liturgical book of Bangor. The fact that the only other known manuscript of the lucernarium hymn *Ignis creator* also comes from the Bobbio library[55] would be consistent with this. The chronology of this hypothetical "Gallicanization," however, would depend in part on the authenticity of the *Regula coenobialis* ascribed to Columban (cf. Charles-Edwards 1997). A passage therein states that the punishment for negligently losing monastery foodstuffs is to lie prostrate and immobile during all 12 psalms of Duodecima, evidently corresponding to the service that Columban's *Regula monachorum* had called *Initium noctis* (Columban, *Opera*, 146–47), and perhaps to the Vespers hour in the Bangor Antiphoner. The punishment passage was reiterated by Donatus of Besançon (*Regula*, 269). Waldebert of Luxeuil also directed that 12 psalms *super cursus seriem* be sung by anyone who came late to the Office (PL 88, 1060–61).

The next hour in the collect series, *Ad nocturnam* [*horam*], was evidently the midnight hour mentioned in the rule of Columban. The collects [23, 37, 57], like the hymn *Mediae noctis* [10], refer unequivocally to the middle of the night. As the hymn was also assigned to the midnight hour in the Office of Arles,[56] this could be seen as another Gallican element in the Bangor Antiphoner. There is, however, another possible explanation. *Mediae noctis* was also the midnight hymn in what students of Latin hymnology call the Old Hymnal, a small cycle of about 15 Office hymns, thought to have circulated widely in early medieval Europe. At the core of the collection stood the genuine hymns of St. Ambrose of Milan (339–97); the others, including *Mediae noctis*, closely imitate his iambic dimeter stanzas, and thus are appropriately called "Ambrosian" hymns. The Old Hymnal is best attested in early Anglo-Saxon sources, which raises the possibility that the collection ultimately came from Rome.[57] But though some of the hymns are mentioned by Cassiodorus, and the Benedictine Rule refers to "Ambrosiani" without citing specific hymn incipits,[58] this is not sufficient to confirm Roman origin. The cycle of hymns used in the Office of Arles was related to but not identical with the Old Hymnal, as is the core hymn repertory of the Ambrosian Rite of Milan. Nor is the presence of *Mediae noctis* in the Bangor Antiphoner the only sign of contact with the Ambrosian hymn tradition: The lucernarium hymn *Ignis creator,* though attested only in the Bangor Antiphoner and another manuscript from the Bobbio library, is a good enough imitation to have been considered a genuine work of Ambrose by some, while the metrical collects of the Bangor Antiphoner resemble early Gallican hymns created in the Ambrosian tradition (Curran 1984, 59–65, 93–96). The Ambrosian hymnodic language and stanzaic structure make them quite different from the more demonstrably Irish hymns that are the main reason for linking our manuscript to Bangor: the three Bangor hymns, with their repeated refrains and tedious rhymes, also the Pseudo-Hilarian *Hymnum dicat* and the hymns for St. Patrick and St. Camelacus in trochaic tetrameter.[59] Opinions differ as to whether the Ambrosian type of hymn was known and imitated in Ireland at this period.[60] Even the eleventh-century "Irish Liber Hymnorum" (Kenney 1968, 574) includes only one such hymn (Bernard and Atkinson, *The Irish,* 1:197). But we do know that Ambrosian hymns were composed in seventh-century Bobbio, where *Nostris sollemnis saeculis,* in honor of St. Columban, was incorporated in the *Vita Columbani* compiled by Jonas of Bobbio within decades of the saint's death (Krusch, *Ionae,* 227; Kenney 1968, 48; *BHL,* 1898).

Two of the collect series in the Bangor Antiphoner, the first and third, continue with three [24–26, 58–60, cf. 120] prayers *Ad matutinam* [*horam*], suggesting this hour was divided into sections, like the three nocturns of Roman and Benedictine Matins. In one series, the first collect refers to waking by night in words that echo Ps. 62 [RSV 63], "God our God, to you we ought to keep vigil from the light, and you awaken us from deep sleep, and deliver our souls from slumber, that in our bedrooms we may feel remorse, and may merit to be remembered by you" [58]. In the third series the second collect refers explicitly to the time of cockcrow (*Gallorum . . . cantibus*) and the third to sunrise (*Adventum . . . luminis*). All this suggests that the three nocturns were timed to coincide with midnight, cockcrow, and sunrise—traditional prayer times to be sure, but times that may have been especially emphasized in the rigorous Irish tradition. The pseudo-Jerome treatise in the Bobbio Missal, in fact, connects the first nocturn with such midnight events as the slaying of the Egyptian firstborn (Exod. 11:4), the earthquake that freed Paul and Silas from prison (Acts 16:25–26), and the coming of the heavenly Bridegroom in the parable of the Wise and Foolish Virgins (Matt. 25:6). The second nocturn it connects with the cock that crowed after Peter denied the Lord (Matt. 26:74–75). There is apparently no third nocturn as such in this source; the next celebration, called *Matutinas,* took place at dawn, the time of the Resurrection (Luke 24:1, John 20:1). In the second set of collects in the Bangor Antiphoner, the prayers *ad matutinam* [38–39, and possibly 54; 39 is the same as 59] are accompanied by an extensive series of "Common prayer of the brothers" (*Oratio communis fratrum,* [40–56]): versicles and collects for forgiveness, for the baptized, for priests, for the abbot, for the brothers, for various kinds of sinners and penitents, for travelers, those who give alms, and for the sick. The series resembles a longer form of the *oratio communis* for the day hours [117–19], and the content closely parallels the versicles that

Columban directed to be said at every hour.[61] Two of the collect series in the Bangor Antiphoner end with prayers of supererogation, that the petitioners may benefit from the merits of the martyrs and saints [52, 55, 61]. These may have formed
part of the common prayer also, or they may have been used on feasts.

The bulk of the material in the Bangor Antiphoner is for the morning Office
corresponding to Lauds, particularly as this was celebrated on Sunday. Though the
name of this hour was not clearly indicated, it was evidently celebrated at sunrise,
corresponding to *matutinas* in the Pseudo-Jerome treatise or the last section *Ad
matutinam* in the three Bangor Antiphoner series of collects for the daily cycle.
The seven sets of prayers for this hour in the Bangor Antiphoner [62–94] show
that its structure was relatively consistent, and this is partly confirmed by the Turin
fragment and a fragment in Paris (Kenney 1968, 573; Bannister, "Liturgical," 422–
27); see table 5.7. Each of the seven Bangor sets begins with three collects, one to
follow each of the three major chants of Matins: the song of Moses at the Red Sea
(*Cantemus domino,* from Exod. 15), the Song of the Three Children in the fiery
furnace (*Benedicite,* from Dan. 3), and the Lauds psalms 148–50 (called *Tres psalmos*
[64] or *Laudate dominum*). The texts of the *Cantemus* and *Benedicite* are found in
the first section of the Bangor Antiphoner, but on an inserted bifolium (fols. 7r–
8v)—yet they are written in the second of the two hands that are most prevalent
in the manuscript, an indication of how this "antiphoner" was assembled gradually
and without a preconceived plan. The Bobbio fragment in Turin, on the contrary,
is dominated by the *Cantemus* and *Benedicite* texts. Each of them, as well as the
incipit of Ps. 148, is followed by collects from two of the series in the Bangor Antiphoner, as well as one unknown collect.[62] Thus the fragment represents a relatively
organized collection that is liturgically more useable, an obvious advance over the
haphazard, piecemeal arrangement of the Bangor Antiphoner. In both the Bangor
Antiphoner and the Turin fragment, the texts of the *Benedicite* and *Cantemus* canticles reflect an Old Latin, pre-Vulgate tradition, also found in certain Irish Psalters, the Irish *Liber hymnorum,* and the Gallican lectionary of Luxeuil (*CLLA* 255).[63]

Table 5.7 Canticles, hymns, and collects for the dawn hour

Turin, BN 882 n. 8	Paris, BNF lat. 9488
Exod. 15	
3 collects	
Dan. 3	
2 collects	
incipit of Pss. 148–50	
3 collects	
Hymnum dicat turba fratrum	*Hymnum dicat turba fratrum*
2 collects	
Spiritus divine lucis glorie	*Spiritus divine lucis glorie*
2 collects	
Laudate pueri . . . Te deum	*Laudate pueri . . . Te deum*
3 collects	
1 collect for Sundays	

The antiphon section of the Bangor Antiphoner is dominated by a series of ten pairs of antiphons for the *Cantemus* and *Benedicite* [99]—one pair also includes an antiphon for the three *Laudate* Psalms [100]. The abbreviation *dominus con* following the *Cantemus* in the Turin fragment (Meyer 1903, 183) may be the incipit of one of these antiphons, *Dominus conterens bella* [15]—if so it is the only antiphon in the fragment as it now stands. The pairing of *Benedicite* with the Laudate psalms in the Sunday morning Office has parallels in many liturgical traditions, and it is not unusual to find *Cantemus* preceding them as well.[64] *Cantemus* and *Benedicite* (or one of the other canticles from Dan. 3) are also fixtures of the ancient 12-reading vigils modelled on the Easter vigil at Jerusalem.[65] But the possibility of singing them even on weekdays is suggested by the Bangor *Cantemus* collect addressed to "God, who daily absolve your people from the yoke of Egyptian servitude . . ." [68]. Psalms 148–50, the Lauds or *Ainoi,* are a universal component of the dawn Office in Christian liturgy. The theme of universal praise that dominates these psalms is taken up in the collects with an explicitly musical vocabulary, suggesting that this was one of the musical high points of the daily Office.

To the God of Thunder say a new hymn, . . . make a loud noise with diverse modes of spiritual melody [*diversis spiritalis melodiae modis*] . . . [70].

May the angels, forces, stars, powers praise you O Lord, and those things which owe you their origin exult in an office of your praise, that by singing together with you the harmony of the universe, your will may be done on earth as in Heaven . . . for according to the multitude of your magnitude we praise you, Lord, by the favor of your praise, shown forth in immolation by the psaltery, in mortification by the tympanum, in the congregation by the chorus, in exultation by the organ, in jubilation by the cymbalum, that always we may merit to have your mercy, Christ, Savior of the World . . . [93].

This exalted musical terminology, convinced of the unity of human and celestial singing, is once again more readily tied to Bobbio than to Bangor, given the present state of the known sources. It is reminiscent of the life of St. Columban written by Jonas, who became a monk at Bobbio within three years of Columban's death, and who obtained his information by interviewing people who had actually known Columban at Bobbio and Luxeuil, including St. Gall (Kenney 1968, 48). Morbidly fascinated by deathbed accounts of angelic singing, accompanied by unearthly lights and sweet odors, Jonas wrote of a certain nun Landberga, who in delirium saw a dense cloud bright with lightning, and heard heavenly voices "singing and exulting" the *Cantemus* canticle (Krusch, *Ionae,* 275–76). He wrote of Domma, another nun, in whose mouth a trembling fireball was seen as she sang *Hoc sacrum corpus* (Krusch *Ionae,* 266–67), the communion antiphon that occurs in the *Navigatio S. Brendani,* the Bangor Antiphoner [112], and other sources (Gamber, "Ein ägyptiches," 228). Two young girls who witnessed this died after singing "songs unheard by human ears and sweet modulations" (*inaudita auribus humanis carmina ac dulcia modulamina*) from the None office one day to None the next (Krusch, *Ionae,* 267–68). Others heard angelic voices singing various psalm texts

(Krusch *Ionae*, 264), while the monk Theudualdus, upon receiving the viaticum, intoned the antiphon *Ibunt sancti* (Krusch *Ionae*, 292), for which a medieval melody actually survives (Stäblein 1973).

Suggestions of an affinity between the contents of the Bangor Antiphoner and the liturgical life of Bobbio are not the only hints that the manuscript originated in northern Italy. Many of the antiphons of the Bangor Antiphoner are textually similar to antiphons with comparable liturgical functions in the "Ambrosian" chant repertory of Milan. Among the Bangor Office antiphons for the *Cantemus* and *Benedicite*, for instance, are three that have essentially the same text,[66] four that have similar texts,[67] and three that have the same incipit as Ambrosian antiphons with the same liturgical functions.[69] The communion antiphon *Corpus domini accepimus* [109] differs by only one word from the Milanese communion antiphon *Corpus Christi accepimus* (Ratti and Magistretti, *Missale*, 357). Like many other texts in the Ambrosian repertory, the first half of *Corpus domini* has close parallels in some Palestinian Greek communions, while the second half paraphrases Ps. 22:4 [RSV 23:4] (Baumstark 1958, 97). But the fact that *Corpus domini* occurs in none of the other collections of Irish communion antiphons[69] suggests it was not really part of the Irish liturgical tradition, though it obviously is the sort of thing that might have found its way from Milan to nearby Bobbio. The presence of the canticle of Zachary (*Benedictus dominus deus*, Luke 1:68–79) and the second canticle of Moses (*Audite*, Deut. 32:1–43) in the Bangor Antiphoner can also be interpreted as an Ambrosian parallel (Curran 1984, 186–88; cf. table 5.8 below).

After the two canticles (*Cantemus* and *Benedicite*) and the *Laudate* psalms, the Office of the Bangor Antiphoner had a Gospel reading, at least on Sundays when, as the collects *post evangelium* make clear, the theme of the reading was the Resurrection [65, 74, 79, 85]. In the collect texts, much is made of the fact that the Resurrection happened at dawn.

> Exulting in joy for the light given to us this day, we offer praise and thanks to God, begging his mercy that, to us who solemnly celebrate the day of the Lord's resurrection, he may deign to grant peace, tranquility, and joy, that from the morning vigil even to the night, protected by the favor of his mercy, exulting in perpetual gladness we may rejoice. [65]

One of the collects *post evangelium* [84] refers to the singing of hymns: "Delighted by spiritual canticles, sounding together we sing hymns to you O Christ." That hymns actually followed the Gospel reading is clear from the fact that every collect *super evangelium* is followed by a collect *super hymnum*, which often reiterates the Gospel themes of light and resurrection [66, 80, 86]. In the Turin fragment we actually find three hymns at this point, *Hymnum dicat turba fratrum*, *Spiritus divine lucis*, and the Te deum. These three also occur in the same order in the Paris fragment (see above, table 5.7). In the first part of the Bangor Antiphoner, though the hymns do not occur in any particular order, they clearly were regarded as hymns for Sunday morning: *Spiritus divine* has the rubric *Hymnus ad matutinum in dominica*, and Te deum the rubric *Hymnus in die dominica*. *Hymnum dicat*, dubiously attributed to Hilary of Poitiers (*CPL* 464), also fits the context, for it traces the life of Christ, and in its final stanzas it becomes a dawn hymn. *Spiritus divine lucis* is Christological in content also, with a strong light theme. Some of the collects following these hymns in the Turin fragment are also found in the Bangor Antiphoner, though this placement differs somewhat from what is indicated in the Bangor rubrics,[70] suggesting that the use of three hymns at this point is a more recent development, whereas the collectors of the Bangor Antiphoner material still envisioned only one hymn. The *Regula coenobialis* ascribed to Columban also speaks of a single hymn to be sung on the Lord's Day and on Easter (Columban, *Opera*, 158–59). Any one of these three could perhaps be used, as could the Christological *Precamur patrem* [3], which the rubric calls "Hymn of the apostles, so they say" (*Hymnus apostolorum ut alii dicunt*).[71] Perhaps the *Gloria in excelsis* could be used at this point as well, since the rubric says it could be sung in the morning.

But there is much to suggest that the preferential Sunday hymn was the Te deum [7].[72] For one thing, this hymn has its own collects, while *Hymnum dicat* and the other texts do not [123, 125, 126, 128]. These collects happen to be very similar to, indeed virtually interchangeable with, some of those for the morning Pss. 148–50, which echo the language of the Te deum itself and take up the theme of universal praise [64, 73, 78, 93].

> Te dominum de coelis laudamus,
> tibi ut canticum novum cantare mereamur.
> Te dominum in sanctis tuis venerabiliter deprecamur . . . [64][73]

In fact the text of the hymn itself has been brought closer to these morning *Laudate* psalms; in the Bangor Antiphoner its familiar incipit, *Te deum laudamus*, is preceded by the first verse of Ps. 112 [RSV 113], "Laudate pueri dominum: laudate nomen domini."[74] Such parallelism is easier to understand if the Te deum were regarded as an integral part of the Sunday morning Office, comparable to the *Laudate* psalms. There may also be a hint of this in the fact that the extra bifolium containing *Cantemus* and *Benedicite* was tipped into the Bangor Antiphoner right in front of the folio on which the Te deum begins, as if to assemble the three major Sunday canticles in their liturgical order.

The morning collect cycles generally include collects *de martyribus* [61, 67, 87, 97, 124]. Perhaps there was a commemoration of martyrs and saints at the end of Sunday Lauds. More likely these collects were for feast days, when the Resurrection reading and hymns of Sundays could have been replaced by hagiographical readings and hymns.[75] In fact most of the hymns in the first part of the Bangor Antiphoner that are not paschal in character are devoted to saints: to St. Patrick, "teacher of the Irish" [13], to Camelacus [15], to "Comgall our abbot" (the founder of Bangor) [14], and the "In memory of our abbots" [129] that lists the abbots of Bangor. The rubric of *Sacratissimi martyres*, "Hymn on feasts of martyrs, or on Saturday at Matutinum" [11], appears to confirm that the Sunday arrangement could be adapted on other days. The most problematic item is the hymn in honor of Bangor itself, *Benchuir bona regula*, [95] unless there was a feast celebrating the founding or dedication of this monastery. In this hymn Bangor is called "a true vine, brought over from Egypt" (*vinea vera ex Aegypto transducta*), attesting to the Irish monks' sense of continuity with the Egyptian founders of monasticism (cf. Ps. 79:9 [RSV 80:8]).[76]

The structure of the morning Office in the Bangor Antiphoner is full of familiar elements found in other liturgical traditions. In table 5.8 the Resurrection Vigil of fourth-century Jerusalem and the night and morning Offices of the Egyptian monastic horologion are outlined in the extreme left and right columns. Four other traditions are arranged on the page according to their relative similarity to these two seminal traditions. According to Egeria's account of the Office at Jerusalem, the monastic communities spent much of the night singing hymns or psalms, corresponding to the nocturns or staseis of the other later traditions. At cockcrow, they were joined by the clergy and ordinary worshippers, and everyone entered the Anastasis (on the site of what is now the Church of the Holy Sepulchre) for the Sunday morning Office of the Resurrection. Three psalms were sung, commemorating the three days that Christ lay in the tomb. A prayer was said after each, then the Prayer for All. Incense was burned, and an account of the Resurrection was read from one of the Gospels. Then there was a procession to Golgotha where the Crucifixion had taken place; another psalm was sung and a prayer said, after which came the dismissal.[77] At Milan[78] and in the Palestinian monastic Office,[79] now celebrated in all churches of the Byzantine rite, most of these elements were preserved. Some of them can also be discerned in the early sixth-century Office of Arles, based on that of the monastery at Lérins.[80] The Egyptian monastic Office, on the other hand, preserves no trace of the Resurrection Gospel or the procession.[81]

In the Palestinian tradition that became the Byzantine Office, the three psalms were shortened to the final verse, Ps. 150:6 (Jeffery 1991, 68, 75). In the Ambrosian Office we find a group of canticles that could arguably be presented as a parallel to the three psalms of Jerusalem, since they precede the biblical readings or (in *Breviarium Ambrosianum*) the homilies on the Gospel of the day (which was not usually a Resurrection account). The third canticle varied between Jonah and Habakkuk depending on the season, but on Saturdays all three canticles were replaced by the *Cantemus* and two sections of Ps. 118 [RSV 119]; the later *Cantemus* was then omitted (Magistretti, *Manuale* pt. 1, 54, 58). Thus the three canticles preceding the readings of the Ambrosian morning Office are a close parallel to the *Cantemus*, *Benedicite*, and Pss. 148–50 of the Bangor Antiphoner and the Egyptian *Psalmodia*, though the Bangor Antiphoner preserves the Resurrection Gospel while the Egyptian Office has no reading at this point.

On the other hand the procession to Golgotha, which might seem the most difficult feature to export outside the original Jerusalem venue, is relatively well preserved in Milan as a procession with crosses and lights. At Arles, on the other hand, it seems to have become merely a procession out of doors (Golgotha was outdoors in Egeria's time). Ironically, the Palestinian tradition, the most direct descendent of the rite of Jerusalem, dropped the procession altogether, perhaps because it was felt this could only be done at Golgotha itself. Though there is no evidence of a procession in the Bangor Antiphoner, the Rule of Ailbe of Emly (see table 5.2) indicates that this practice was known in Ireland.

At Milan and Arles the procession was followed by the singing of the morning canticles and psalms, including the familiar threesome of *Cantemus* (Exod. 15), *Benedicite*, and Pss. 148–50 that the Egyptian Office and the Bangor Antiphoner

Table 5.8 The Sunday morning office of the Bangor Antiphoner compared with other traditions (psalm numbers follow Vulgate/Septuagint)

Jerusalem (Egeria)	Milan (Beroldus)	Palestine (Byzantine Horologion)	Arles/Lérins (Caesarius & Aurelian)	Bangor Antiphoner (ed. Warren 1893–95)	Egypt/Ethiopia (Psalmodia/Saʿātāt)
		Orthros	*Nocturnos*		*Midnight Office*
hymns at night		6 psalms, litany	1 or 2 nocturns	3 nocturns	3 nocturns
		2 staseis of the psalter gradual pss. 118–32			
cockrow: entry into Anastasis	*Matutinum* hymn canticle: Dan. 3:26–56			*Matutinam*	*Psalmodia*
3 psalms, prayer after each	3 canticles: Isa. 26:9–20 1 Kgs./Sam. 2:1–10 Jon. 2:2–9 or Hab. 3 (or **Cantemus** + Ps. 118 in two parts)			**Cantemus** + collect	**Cantemus** Ps. 135
				Benedicite + collect	**Benedicite** *Magnificat*
		Ps. 150:6		**Pss. 148–50** + collect	**Pss. 148–50** **Gloria in excelsis** trisagion
Prayer for All			*Matutinales*		*Morning Prayer*
incense					
Resurrection Gospel	readings or homily on **Gospel of day**	**Resurrection Gospel**	**Resurrection Gospel**	**Resurrection Gospel**	
	canticle: Luke 1:68–79 or Deut. 32		5 other readings	collect	

(continued)

Table 5.8 (*continued*)

Jerusalem (Egeria)	Milan (Beroldus)	Palestine (Byzantine Horologion)	Arles/Lérins (Caesarius & Aurelian)	Bangor Antiphoner (ed. Warren 1893–95)	Egypt/Ethiopia (Psalmodia/Saʿātāt)
procession to Golgotha with singing psalm at **cross**	**procession** with candles & **crosses** *antiphona ad crucem*		**procession** outside		
		Ps. 50	Ps. 135 or 117		**Psalm 50**
	Cantemus + prayer	9 odes + kanon	**Cantemus**		12 psalms
					Gospel
		hymn of light			hymn of light
	Benedicite or **Ps. 50** + prayer		**Benedicite**		
	Ps. 148–50, 116 psalmus directus (variable)	**Pss. 148–150**	**Pss. 148–150** Te deum	Te deum or hymn collect	
	Gloria in excelsis hymn	**Gloria in excelsis**	**Gloria in excelsis**		**Gloria in excelsis** *Sanctus*
blessings & dismissal	dismissal	litany & dismissal		intercessions	*Pater noster* + prayers

had placed earlier. The *Cantemus* and *Benedicite* would also be among the nine odes of the Byzantine canon sung at this same point, just before Pss. 148–50.[82] A hymn on the theme of light and/or the *Gloria in excelsis* will also be found in most of these traditions, as they are in the Bangor Antiphoner.

Given all these Eastern and Western parallels, should we conclude that the Bangor Antiphoner shows us the Office of Bangor in Ireland, or a developed form of St. Columban's Office as it was celebrated at Bobbio? Let it be said, first of all, that this is not necessarily a choice between antitheses, for the Bangor Office, the Rule of Columban, and the Bobbio Office could well represent three points on the same chronological line. Columban's rule repeatedly states that its prescriptions for the Office have been handed down "from our elders" (*senioribus nostris*), and this may refer to older Irish traditions of the sort that Columban knew at Bangor, to which we no longer have direct access. Certainly the Rule of Ailbe of Emly (table 5.2) shows that such features as a Jerusalem-like Gospel with cross procession, the minor hours of Terce, Sext, and None, a lengthy Vespers and a midnight Office of 12 psalms could all be combined with the recitation of the Three Fifties that seems to have stood at the core of insular Irish practices. On the other hand, though it is possible that a post-Columbanian practice rife with Gallican and north Italian features could have been imported back into Ireland, the Irish sources we have examined, some of which date as late as the ninth century, do not encourage this view. All things considered, then, the Bangor Antiphoner as we have it does seem to represent St. Columban's Office as it developed after his time at a Continental center, under the influence of Gallican and north Italian traditions such as we might expect to find at Bobbio. It was at Bobbio, therefore, that I believe the Irish scribes of the Bangor Antiphoner (or at least some of them) did their work. In the discussion of such questions, however, there is a potential wild card in the "Spanish symptoms" that have been discerned in some of the Bangor Antiphoner texts (Curran 1984, 12, 73, 113–14, 133, 137, 151–54). Significant relationships to the Mozarabic liturgical traditions of Spain could, ironically enough, support Irish rather than Continental origin, for there are scholars who believe they can trace a direct "line of transmission running from Syria and Egypt in the sixth and seventh centuries to Visigothic Spain and thence to Brittany, to Cornwall, to South Wales and to Ireland" (Crehan 1976, 87). The paradoxes encountered by anyone seeking to account for Continental or oriental elements in Ireland are exemplified by the work *De locis sanctis* (*CPL* 2332, Kenney 1968, 112, Lapidge and Sharpe 1985, 304) by Adomnán (d. 704), abbot of the island monastery of Iona in Scotland, and a descendant of its founder St. Columcille or Columba (not St. Columban!). The work is a detailed and often seemingly accurate description of the churches and shrines in Jerusalem and the Holy Land—yet Adomnán himself had never been there. He derived his information from a returning pilgrim who just happened to have been shipwrecked near Iona: a person about whom, but for Adomnán's writing, we would know nothing at all. The path by which any foreign element found its way into the Irish liturgy could often have been equally circuitous and fortuitous.

The Coming of the Roman Office

The two most influential liturgical centers in the early Christian period were Jerusalem and Egypt, and traditions from both these places found their way into the Irish Offices through Cassian and other Western sources. But by the eighth century a new center was emerging in the West, and the liturgical situation in Europe was beginning to change radically, as the various local traditions of the Gallican churches were beginning to be suppressed in favor of the rite of the city of Rome. The importation of the Roman rite was a complex affair: though authorized by King Pepin himself about the year 754 (Vogel 1979) the effort had many champions, who operated more or less independently of each other, both before and after that date. The typical procedure seems to have been to obtain books or texts from Rome, and to attempt to follow their prescriptions within the familiar context of traditional Gallican practices. As a result, the Roman texts that were brought north were soon hybridized, affirming fealty to Rome while actually transmitting Roman material that had been adjusted, expanded, or mixed with Gallican material. The process can be observed clearly in the "eighth-century Gelasian" sacramentaries, Frankish adaptations of the Roman "Gelasian" sacramentary of the seventh century, and in the textual history of the Ordines Romani, descriptions of the Roman liturgical usages that were gradually revised and rewritten. What really happened, in short, was the creation of a new liturgical tradition—an amalgam of Roman and non-Roman texts and customs, forged by Frankish smiths in a Gallican workshop. It was this new creation that, after being reintroduced into Rome itself, passed into history as the medieval Roman rite we know.

Irish monks and scribes surely played a role in this liturgical synthesis. For instance, two of the earliest (ninth century) manuscripts of the so-called New Hymnal, a Gallican product that replaced the Old Hymnal and was incorporated into the medieval Roman Breviary, were copied by Irish scribes.[83] Fragments of Irish manuscripts at St. Gall, a Swiss monastery founded by and named for one of St. Columban's companions, include parts of a twelfth-century notated antiphoner and an early copy of Augustine's *De musica* (Duft 1982, 930–31); an Irish role in the formulation of Carolingian music theory has been alleged also (Münxelhaus 1982). More importantly, Columban's own followers and spiritual descendants played a significant part in promoting the Roman monastic rule of St. Benedict, first alongside the rule of Columban in various "mixed rules," then ultimately as the only rule (Moyse 1982; Prinz 1965, 263–92; Löwe 1982, 120–37, 171–374). But perhaps the best glimpse of the Romanizing mentality is to be seen in the collection of liturgical materials preserved in the MS St. Gall 349, including the texts published by Andrieu as Ordines Romani 15, 16, 18, and 19.[84] These were evidently written about the mid-eighth century by a monk in eastern France, perhaps within the orbit of the Columbanian monastery of Luxeuil.[85] The anonymous author missed no opportunity to emphasize the authority of the Roman tradition, as is clear from the title of Ordo Romanus 16:

In the Holy Name of our Lord Jesus Christ, here begins the Instruction of Ecclesiastical Order, how those who are faithfully serving the Lord in monasteries, both according to the authority of the Catholic and Apostolic Roman Church and according to the disposition and Rule of St. Benedict, ought to celebrate, with the help of the Lord, in the solemnity of the Mass or the feasts of saints or also in the divine offices of the entire year, day and night, as was handed on to us by wise and venerable Fathers in the Holy and Roman Church (*OR* 3:147).

The collection ends, in fact, with a list of the many Roman popes and fathers who created the Roman liturgical tradition, possibly the earliest document to credit Pope Gregory the Great explicitly with editing a chant repertory (*OR* 3:222–24). The author closed his collection with the direst of warnings:

If anyone, once he knew these things, were to neglect to keep and celebrate [them], insofar as he was able with the help of God, or if he perhaps threw [them] out, [as if] knowing better or having accepted an example from elsewhere, there is no doubt that he is deceiving himself, and is unfortunately plunging himself into the darkness of error, having dared to despise and derogate so many and such fathers and holy authors (*OR* 3:224).

Lest anyone wonder what sort of reprobate might claim to "know better or have accepted an example from elsewhere," our author was ready to be more specific: he was speaking of those who invoked the fathers and saints of the Gallican, non-Roman Western churches, to whom the alternative liturgical traditions were ascribed, but whom our author knew to have been faithful disciples of Rome. "I don't know by what cheek or presumptuous temerity of spirit they dare [to invoke] blessed Hilary and Martin or Germanus or Ambrose, or many saints of God," he fumed, "whom we know were sent into this Western land from the Holy Roman See by blessed Peter the Apostle and his successors, who shone with wonders and miracles, and who deviated in nothing from the Holy Roman See or from the synod of 318 catholic fathers gathered at Nicaea together with the Holy Spirit, or from the other three principal councils." Those partisans of non-Roman liturgies who dared to invoke these non-Roman saints, saying, "As they held or kept, so also we seem to hold or keep," were actually as distant from these fathers in life and morals as heaven is from earth, for "we know" that "these resplendent confessors of Christ whom we named above frequently went to Rome and had discussions with the blessed papacy or with Christian emperors, or, if any of them deviated from the Holy Roman See, it is obvious that they were often corrected among us" (*OR* 3:225). For this author it made no difference that the ecumenical Councils said nothing about the Roman liturgy—by invoking them he ventured to the point of saying that his opponents' insubordination descended even to heresy: "For six heresies have arisen in the world from the eastern part against the Holy Roman Church, but aided by the grace of Christ, the Holy See of Blessed Peter the apostle broke and mastered all those heresies. A seventh still remains, and the elders and wise ones and doctors of the Holy See of the Roman Church have handed down that it is waiting to rise from this western and northern part [of the world]" (*OR* 3:226–27).[86]

But these apocalyptic rantings ultimately fail to make up for what our author lacked in factual knowledge. His Latin is poor, and his information about the Roman liturgy second-hand at best. He had evidently not been to Rome himself, and his major sources were typical of what was in circulation north of the Alps, including Ordo Romanus 1 with its Frankish interpolations, and the recension of Ordo Romanus 11 that is preserved in the eighth-century Gelasian sacramentary of Gellone (*OR* 3:59–92, 131–44). Even to these sources, however, he was surprisingly unfaithful, and his own Ordines are full of non-Roman practices and vocabulary. His ideal liturgy was one in which the Annunciation was celebrated in Advent (*OR* 3:95; see Jeffery 1991, 57), baptisms took place on Epiphany,[87] the eucharistic bread was brought out in vessels shaped like towers (cf. Gamber, *Ordo,* 33; Gamber, *Die Messfeier,* 34), during an offertory chant that he called "offerenda [the Milanese term], which the Franks call 'sonum' [the Gallican term]" (*OR* 3:123). He would have witnessed none of these things in Rome.

What is most interesting for our purposes, however, is what this author had to say about the Office. Whether or not he realized it, his prescriptions clearly attempt to fit Roman material into a foreign framework—a framework much like the Irish one we have just surveyed. Like the collect cycles in the Bangor Antiphoner, his day began with Prime, though—again as in the Bangor Antiphoner—it could be sung at either the first or second hour of the day. The other hours too are carefully matched to the same times as in the Continental Irish monastic traditions: Compline when the sun goes down (*Initium noctis*), Nocturns at midnight, Lauds not until the daylight has actually appeared (*OR* 3:205–7). Non-Irish sources of the period, notably the Benedictine Rule that our author claimed to be following, begin the office with the night hours rather than with Prime. The Benedictine Rule is generally less rigorous about timing the liturgical celebrations to specific points during the day, and it explicitly contradicts our author by stating that the night Office is to begin two hours after midnight (8.1–2). Particularly striking, however, is the way Nocturns was to end. "According to the Rule of St. Benedict," we are told, "always on Sundays, the reading of the Holy Gospel is read according to the time [of year] in which it may be; and the hymn *Te deum laudamus* follows, and the verse with *Kyrie eleison,* and the nocturnal vigils are finished" (*OR* 3:149). But this is not correct: in fact the Rule of St. Benedict directs that the Te deum be sung after the last responsory, *before* the abbot reads the Sunday Gospel. After the Gospel the Rule mandates a different hymn, *Te decet laus* (*OR* 3:134–35, 149, n. 16; Benedictine Rule 11.8–10). What our self-righteous author presented as the authentic Roman and Benedictine tradition was actually an echo of the arrangement in the Bangor Antiphoner, wherein the Te deum was indeed sung after the Gospel. The structure of the Bangor Office was so deeply ingrained that it could not be overcome, even by as determined a Romanizer as our author, whose uncompromising attitude toward his opponents may itself owe something to the harsh punishments and unrelenting strictness of Columbanian monasticism.

Other witnesses show that the Irish encounter with the Roman Office persisted into the next century. Fragments of an antiphoner in a ninth-century Insular hand offer our most detailed glimpse of what such an office could look like (Morin 1905; Kenney 1968, 570). As in the Bangor Antiphoner, the preponderance of texts appear to have been intended for the Office of Lauds, though they are collected into little cycles and groups that are not necessarily identified by adequate rubrics. Unlike the Bangor Antiphoner, however, this manuscript followed the general progression of the liturgical year. A distinctly un-Roman trait is the direction to read the Passions from the four Gospels on the first four Sundays of Lent (Morin 1905, 346). However, the absence of a preparatory period from Septuagesima to the beginning of Lent, with the result that the suspension of the alleluia is pushed back to Epiphany, does suggest a Roman or quasi-Roman background, for its closest parallel is in the central Italian *Rule of the Master.*[88] Yet what is particularly striking about the fragment is its many near-agreements with the familiar Roman tradition. Antiphons are grouped in fives, just as at Roman Lauds and Vespers. When the psalms accompanying the antiphons are indicated, their arrangement is close to that of the Roman and Benedictine Psalters (table 5.9).[89] Thus the psalms for what is evidently the feast of the Presentation (2 February) and for the Sundays of Lent essentially correspond to the psalms of Sunday Lauds in the Roman and Benedictine cursus, while the psalms for weekdays in Passiontide are also close to those of the Roman ferial Psalter.[90] The Benedictus and Magnificat are the Gospel canticles, responsories frequently but inconsistently end with the *Gloria patri,*[91] and the only surviving collect is from the Gregorian Sacramentary. Moreover, a significant number of antiphon, responsory, and versicle texts are familiar from the Gregorian chant repertory. "En somme, c'est encore avec le fonds romain que notre liturgie offre le plus de ressemblance" (Morin 1905, 333).[92]

One would very much like to know the provenance of this fragment. The best that its discoverer, Germain Morin, could do was to link it to the monastery of St. Benedict at Fleury, on the basis of a partially erased ex libris he found on one leaf.[93] After viewing it under ultraviolet light, however, I am convinced that this twelfth-century ownership mark, probably written on the fragment after it had been turned into flyleaves, actually read *Ex libris Sancti Benigni,* not *Benedicti.* This suggests it was once at Saint-Bénigne in Dijon, the medieval library of which is now widely scattered (cf. Auger 1985). Where the fragment may have been before that is at present impossible to say.

No doubt there were many for whom the adoption of the Roman Office represented progress and improvement. But there were also some who regretted the loss of the Irish tradition, and one of them has left us his views in the only surviving statement of dissent. The anonymous writer of this eighth-century Latin tract, "An Account of the Cursus: Who were its authors?"[94] was clearly just the sort of person that the author of the *Ordines Romani* in St. Gall 349 so detested—the kind who would invoke the authority of non-Roman fathers and saints to uphold the preservation of non-Roman liturgical practices. Rather than admit legitimacy only to the Roman tradition, the writer of the "Account" purports to trace the apostolic origins of all of the traditions by which the liturgy of the hours was then celebrated. "If we carefully investigate the authors," he began, "we immediately find out that [the Office] was sung, not as certain inexpert people have put forth with false and varying objections, and as many people round about still presume." He demonstrated this with each cursus individually, dutifully beginning with the *Cursus Romanus.* The Roman Office was really nothing new, for it had been used in Gaul

Table 5.9 Lauds psalms in Paris, BNF n.a.l. 1628 and the Roman and Benedictine breviaries

	Paris BNF n.a.l. 1628		Roman Breviary		Benedictine Breviary	
	(2 Feb.)	(Lent)	(usual)	(Septuagesima)	(usual)	(Eastertide)
S					66	66
U	92	21	92	50	50	92
N	117	90	99	117	117	99
	62	62	62+66	62+66	62	62
	Dan. 3	Dan. 3	Dan. 3	Dan. 3	Dan. 3	Dan. 3
	148–50	148–50	148–50	148–50	148–50	148–50
	(Passiontide)					
M					66	
O	50		50		50	
N	5		5		5	
	62		62+66		35	
	90		Isa. 12		Isa. 12	
	148–50		148–50		148–50	
T					66	
U	50		50		50	
E	42		42		42	
	62		62+66		56	
	90		Isa. 38		Isa. 38	
	148–50		148–50		148–50	
W					66	
E	50		50		50	
D	64		64		63	
	62		62+66		64	
	68		1 Kgs. 2		1 Kgs. 2	
	148–50		148–50		148–50	
T					66	
H	50		50		50	
U	89		89		87	
	62		62+66		89	
	108		Exod. 15		Exod. 15	
	148–50		148–50		148–50	
F					66	
R	50		50		50	
I	142		142		75	
	62		62+66		91	
	90		Hab. 3		Hab. 3	
	148–50		148–50		148–50	
S					66	
A	50		50		50	
T	91		91		142	
	62		62+66		Deut. 32:1–21	
					Deut. 32:22–43	
	34		Deut. 32		148–50	
	148–50		148–50			

since disciples of St. Peter brought it to Lyons, as Eusebius and Josephus report.[95] One gets the impression that its contemporary proponents, therefore, were advocating the unnecessary. On the other hand, the *Cursus Gallorum,* the Gallican Office, also had apostolic origin, for it was first sung by St. John the Evangelist, and passed down to his disciple Polycarp, from whom it was brought to Gaul by St. Irenaeus.[96] With this tradition the anonymous writer was evidently more familiar, for he had more to say about it than for the Roman Office: "Thenceforth, the writings of the Old and New Testaments and of many prudent men [were performed] in modulations, [as they] composed reciprocal antiphons and responsories or *sonus* and alleluias, not from their own material, but from the Sacred Scriptures." And after this Gallican cursus, based as it was on writings of unimpeachable authority, had spread throughout the world, it was further put in order by no less a figure than St. Jerome, the great authority on biblical study and the supposed author of the pseudonymous text on the symbolism of the hours in the Bobbio Missal.

This writer also knew of a *Cursus Orientalis,* edited by St. Athanasius and by SS. Chromatius and Paulinus of Aquileia, but not used in Gaul. It had an office for each of the 12 hours of the day, and was sung by a certain St. Macarius, probably the well-known desert father, though the name was also identified with Lérins.[97] Also listed are the cursus written by St. Ambrose and mentioned by his disciple St. Augustine (i.e., the Milanese "Ambrosian" tradition), and the cursus of St. Benedict, outlined in his rule and authorized for monks by Pope Gregory the Great. But the writer of this treatise devoted the most space to the Irish tradition, for which he clearly had the greatest affection, "which at the present time is called the *Cursus Scottorum,*" but which was now being "thrown away through false opinion." It is the only tradition for which the writer emphasized the vast numbers of holy people who followed it, and the genealogy he provided is impressive indeed: This was the Office, he wrote, citing Eusebius and Josephus, that was prayed by St. Mark the Evangelist in the days when all Egypt and Italy were as one church. "So united was his preaching that all, both men and women, sang *Sanctus* or *Gloria in excelsis deo* or the Lord's Prayer and *Amen.*" After writing down the Gospel dictated to him by St. Peter,[98] St. Mark brought this cursus from Rome to Egypt, where it spread both through the Egyptian monasticism of Antony, Paul, and Macarius, and through the Cappadocian monasticism of Gregory of Nazianzus and Basil the Great. From Egypt Cassian brought it to Lérins, whence Caesarius brought it to Arles and it spread throughout Gaul. Germanus of Auxerre and Lupus of Troyes used it in their monasteries and brought it to Britain,[99] where they taught it to St. Patrick. Patrick sang it throughout his long life of 153 years, and after him it passed to St. Comgall, the founder of Bangor, where it was used by three thousand monks. It was Comgall who sent Columban into Gaul, and he established the Irish cursus at Luxeuil. From there many monasteries of men and women were gathered, all of them receiving from St. Columban the very Office that St. Mark himself had sung so many centuries before. This Office was thus imbued with the authority of both Rome, where St. Peter had dictated the Gospel to St. Mark, and Egyptian monasticism, over which Mark had presided as the first patriarch of Alexandria. "And if you do not believe, look in the Life of Blessed Columban and the life of Blessed

Abbot Eustasius, and you will find it more fully in the sayings of Blessed Attala, Abbot of Bobbio."[100]

Of course we do not believe this fantastic story, this preposterous claim that a single uniform tradition, going back to the earliest days of the Church, was followed in Rome and Egypt and Palestine and Gaul and Britain and Ireland and Gaul again. Yet the writer was not completely wrong, for the Irish monks did make use of varying combinations of elements and traditions from most of these places, and the number of religious men and women who had once followed Irish usages may indeed have been as great as he claimed it was. But we who have lived through another era of liturgical upheaval, with its own excesses of competing and fanciful historical claims, can look back with sympathy on the anonymous writer who, in solitary defiance of the spirit of his age, sat down to pen, against an irresistible wave of Romanizing uniformity, a final protest on behalf of the tradition of Cassian and Columban and all those saintly monks—the last desperate defense of the Irish monastic Office.

Notes

1. The sources are conveniently catalogued in *CLLA*, 1968, 130–52, and *CLLA*, 1988, 21–23. Liturgical sources cited in this article will be identified by Gamber's numbering preceded by the abbreviation *CLLA*. For liturgical and literary sources identified by *CPL* number, see Dekkers, *Clavis*.

2. Warren (1881). A second edition, Warren (1987), is an attempt to bring this book up to date with a new introduction and bibliography by Jane Stevenson. For my review see Jeffery (1989).

3. For Irish writings in Latin, the indispensable guide is Lapidge and Sharpe (1985). Sources written in both Irish (Celtic) and Latin are described in Kenney (1968/1993). Both these catalogues are cited in the present article by number rather than by page. Irish and Latin monastic rules are also listed and discussed in Gougaud (1908), 167–84, 321–33. Ó Maidín (1996), unfortunately, did not come to my attention until after I had written this chapter.

4. Note how much space Warren (1881) devoted to the topics of "Independence of Rome," 29–46, "Eastern Origin," 46–57, "Gallican" and "Spanish Connection," 57–63, and "Points of Difference between the Roman and Celtic Church," 63–82—nor is this concern absent from other sections of the book as well.

5. I owe this felicitous simile to a conversation with my fellow Benedictine Aidan Kavanagh.

6. Warren himself dealt with the Office only very briefly as a subtopic of the "choral service" (1881, 125–27). Jane Stevenson's lengthy introduction to the reprint of Warren (1987) devotes little more, pp. xx–xxii, lxxxi–lxxxii.

7. The fullest synthesis of this research is Taft (1993). Note that there was little modern literature for Taft to cite on the Irish Office beyond an early draft of the present chapter; see p. 115, n. 44. See also P. Bradshaw (1983); reviews and discussion of Bradshaw's first edition include Winkler (1982a), P. Bradshaw (1982), Winkler (1982b).

8. Of great interest to modern scholars, though it exerted little influence beyond its homeland in the Middle Ages, is the East Syrian or Chaldean Office, celebrated in the ancient Persian empire in what is now Iraq. The only ancient tradition that developed outside the Hellenistic culture of the Roman Empire, it is the one in which the distinction between monastic and cathedral elements is particularly clear and instructive. Winkler (1970 and 1974) and Matéos, *Lelya-Ṣapra*.

9. We know this tradition mainly from the writings of St. Gregory of Tours (*CPL* 1023–26) and from the decrees of local councils. (Taft 1993, 147–50, 182–83). C. de Clercq, *Concilia*, 182–83.

10. This tradition is known from the monastic rules and other literature emanating from Lérins (*CPL* 1841–43a, 1859–59b), ed. Vogüé, *Les Règles*, but more fully from the monastic rules issued by former Lérins monks who became bishops of Arles: Caesarius (*CPL* 1009, 1012), Aurelian (*CPL* 1844–46), and John (*CPL* 1848). See also Taft (1993): 102–13, 150–56, 180–82. A valuable monograph could and should be written on this material. On the history and physical remains of the monastery, see Antier (1973).

11. This Office was distinctive in the way it exemplified the ideal of unceasing prayer: it was carried out by monks organized into shifts, so that it literally never ended! See Gindele (1959); Masai (1971); Zufferey (1988), 32–33. For the histories of the Gallican monastic traditions of Tours, Lérins, Agaune, and elsewhere, see Prinz (1965), 19–120.

12. 18.24–25. The latest edition of the Benedictine Rule with commentary is Benedict of Nursia, *Regula*, ed. Vogüé and Neufville, together with Vogüé (1961a). The same Latin text is reproduced with an English translation and commentary in *RB* 1980, ed. Fry. In the present chapter the text will be cited by chapter and verse numbers so that one may consult either edition. These numbers are not found or are not the same in all the earlier editions, however.

13. PL 73:871. From the *Verba Seniorum,* a Latin translation of a Greek collection of sayings of the Desert Fathers (*BHL* 6527; *CPG* 5570).

14. Longo (1965–66). See also Baumstark (1957/1967): 145–46, 156–59; Husmann (1973). John and Sophronios actually existed, and left behind a significant corpus of writings (*CPG* 7376–77, 7635–81). The *Narration,* however, is not by either of them. See Chadwick (1974), 44.

15. Magistretti, *Beroldus,* 57–63. Magistretti, *Manuale,* pt. 1, 41–47. This type of office was performed only on the vigils of the feasts of saints who had important churches in Milan, notably SS. Gervasius and Protasius, Lawrence, Ambrose, Stephen, John the Baptist, Peter. The liturgy of the vigil included a stational procession to the relevant church, with the clergy carrying relics and lamps.

16. Kenney (1968), 266. Gwynn and Purton (1911–12): 140, 128–29, 138–39, 140–41. Gwynn, "The Rule." On the background of these texts see O'Dwyer (1981).

17. Bannister (1911), 280–84; Mearns (1914), 68–70; Kenney (1968), 476; Schneider (1960); McNamara (1973), 269–70; McNamara (1983).

18. Following the procedure used throughout this chapter, the canticles will be identified first by their Latin incipit, then by their chapter and verse numbering in the Latin Vulgate, then (where there is a difference) by the numbering in the New Revised Standard Version, a modern English translation in the Protestant tradition. Following Ps. 50 [RSV 51] in the Irish Psalters: the Song of the Three Hebrew Children (*Benedicite,* Dan. 3:57–88 [RSV Additions to Daniel: Song of the Three Jews 35–66]), the song of Isaiah (*Confitebor,* Isa. 12:1–6), the song of Hezekiah (*Ego dixi,* Isa. 38:10–20). Following Ps. 100 [RSV 101]: the song of Hannah (*Exultavit,* 1 Kings 2:1–10 (RSV 1 Sam. 2:1–10), the song of Moses at the Red Sea (*Cantemus,* Exod. 15:1–19), the song of Habakkuk (*Domine audivi,* Hab. 3:2–19). Following Ps. 150, the second song of Moses (*Audite caeli,* Deut. 32:1–43). After this, the material is more varied from one manuscript to another.

19. See Mearns (1914), 51–53. Schneider, *Die altlateinischen,* 94–96; Schneider (1949).

20. McNamara (1973), 260–64; Doyle (1976), 32–33; McNamara (1984), 68; McNamara (1993), 117–18.

21. Tov (1992), 153; Würthwein (1995) 91–99; Marsden (1995), 7–9, 21, 27.

22. Lawlor (1916); Kenney (1968), 454; Bullough (1982), 84, 97–98; Lapidge and Sharpe (1985), 506; Lambert (1991), 159–61.

23. Kenney (1968), 268 (i); Strachan (1904–5) 1:196, 193, 197. This text is attributed

in one manuscript, but implausibly, to St. Comgall, the founder of the monastery at Bangor. See Gougaud (1908), 182–83.

24. Kenney (1968), 76; Meyer, "An Old Irish," 492–98; the question mark is Meyer's. The texts of the *Beati* and *Hymnum dicat* will be identified below.

25. Kenney (1968), 268 (v); Strachan (1904–5) 2:63, 64, 65. The question mark is Strachan's, but one wonders if the Irish word translated "course" could have meant "cursus" or liturgical office. On early Irish monastic spirituality, see Vogt (1982).

26. The quiet period was used for spirtual reading. Vogüé, "La 'Regula Orientalis,'" 262; Vogüé, *Les Règles*, 1:131–35; Ferreolus, *Regula monachorum*, 117–48, esp. 138. Other monastic rules had different provisions, however: Villegas, "La 'Regula cuiusdam,'" 58–59; Vogüé, *La Règle du Maître*, 224–27, 234–37; Benedict of Nursia, *Regula* 48:3–23 (Vogüé and Neufville, 2:598–605).

27. Lawlor (1897), 145–66; Lawlor (1897–99); Bernard and Atkinson, *The Irish*, 1:xxi–xxvi; Lapidge and Sharpe (1985), 536; Kenney (1968), 562. Three of the hymns are cited by their final stanzas rather than by the first line, a practice also attested in the Irish Liber Hymnorum (Bernard and Atkinson, *The Irish,* 1:14–15 and 2:xxix–xxx, 8); two of these, plus another hymn, apparently have extra stanzas appended, a practice also found in the Bangor Antiphoner (see table 5.6, below), where they seem to parallel the collects and antiphons appended to some of the psalms. See also Ní Chatháin (1976), 230–31.

28. The Beatitudes are the predominant feature of the Office of the Typika, recited after None; they are also frequently sung as the Third Antiphon at the beginning of the Byzantine Divine Liturgy. Arranz, *Le Typicon*, 416–17, 444; Black, *A Christian*, 6–8, 81–82. Mercenier, *La Prière*, 189–98, 234, 282. They also occur as a canticle in West Syrian traditions and those that had Byzantine contact: Mearns (1914), 17, 29, 44–47. The antiphon that is customarily sung with them in Byzantine usage, based on Luke 23: 42, is also sung in the Good Friday service of the Mozarabic rite (but with Ps. 50 [RSV 51]) and the Ethiopic rite (with no psalm or canticle). See Brou and Vives, *Antifonario*, 273–74; Shelemay and Jeffery, *Ethiopian*, 2:54–55.

29. On the other hand, the so-called Psalter of St. Caimin, Kenney (1968), 479; Lapidge and Sharpe (1985), 512, contains only Ps. 118 [RSV 119] in its present fragmentary form. If there was an Irish practice of copying this psalm independently of the other psalms, that would indeed suggest that there was also a practice of reciting it outside the Psalter, perhaps as a substitute for the entire Psalter. See also Brou and Wilmart, *The Psalter*, 237–45.

30. Taft (1993), 68; see also P. Bradshaw (1990), 129; Kok (1992); Vogüé (1989, 1995).

31. A classic and influential statement of this Irish role will be found in Amann (1933), 845–948, part of a much larger article, "Pénitence," by Amann and others. That the Irish "brought a new system of penance to the Continent" is also stated in Vorgrimler (1978), 93–103. This view gave rise to a modern historiography that emphasizes "conflict" between Irish and "Mediterranean" patterns or approaches, as exemplified by Orsy (1978), 27–51. A cautious attempt to nuance this view will be found in Dallen (1986), 100–38. On the early and later history of public penance rites see Favazza (1988) and Mansfield (1995). For further bibliography, especially on Eastern Christianity, see Taft (1988), 2–21.

32. Gougaud (1927), 10–14, 147–204. K. Hughes (1970), 48–61. The obsessiveness of these medieval Irish practices—so unlike the feel-good mushiness purveyed by some contemporary books on "Celtic spirituality"—is preserved in the fasting, vigil, and stational exercises still carried out by pilgrims to the island known as St. Patrick's Purgatory, "the Mecca of the Gaelic people." See De Breffny (1982), 139–41. Though the psalms are not part of these ceremonies, there are frequent repetitions of the Pater noster, Ave Maria, Credo, and the rosary. Much of current writing on "Celtic spiritual-

ity" looks back to the folklore collected in Scotland and published in Carmichael, *Carmina*. This is an important collection of valuable material which, as Carmichael recognized (1:xxv, xxxiii–xxxiv), appears to look back in some respects to the pre-Reformation culture. But whether it can be said to breathe the same spirit as early medieval Celtic monasticism remains to be demonstrated.

33. Sometimes the seven penitential psalms, or the fifteen gradual psalms, or a group of thirty psalms. The three sections were said for oneself, for others, and for the faithful departed. An early and particularly explicit source is the Anglo-Saxon *Regularis Concordia* of about 972 (CCCM 7/3:81–82), but the private practice became an official part of the Office in the Cluniac tradition (CCM 7/4:16).

34. Selmer, *Navigatio*, 25–26, 50–52. Lapidge and Sharpe (1985), 362; *BHL*, 1436. A relationship to the Céli Dé is alleged by Bray (1995). The communion antiphon *Hoc sacrum corpus domini* can also be found in other Irish liturgical sources; see the items cited in n. 69.

35. Though Cassian personally visited both Egypt and Palestine and was thus an eyewitness, "he says himself he no longer trusts his memory," and in any case his intention was to present an idealized summary of the variegated Egyptian tradition in order to promote "a reform of Gallic monasticism along Egyptian lines" (Taft 1993, 58). On the possibility of confirming elements of Cassian's description from Egyptian sources, see: Veilleux (1968), 146–54; [Mitchell] (1981), 379–414, esp. 383–86; Kok (1992).

36. *CPL* 1874; text edited in Ledoyen, "La 'Regula Cassiani.'" On its historical context, see Vogüé (1985a).

37. Kenney 45, I. *CPL* 1008; Columban, *Opera*, 128–33. Lapidge and Sharpe (1985), 641. Today only chapters 7, 8, and 9 are considered to go back to Columban himself, but this includes the chapter on the Office; see *CPL* 1108. For a detailed study see Heiming (1961), 125–31.

38. See the traditions of Tours and Arles outlined in Taft (1993), 109, 149. Italian traditions also changed the length of the night office in different seasons, but did this by changing the number of readings as well as the number of psalms: an early Roman oath for newly appointed bishops (in *CPL* 1626) has them promising to celebrate vigils with their clergy every day, from cockcrow to dawn, with three readings, three antiphons, and three responsories on the short summer nights, four readings, responsories and antiphons on long winter nights, but always with nine readings, responsories and antiphons on Sundays (Foerster, *Liber*, 135; Taft 1993, 186–87). Alternate groupings of threes and fours and their multiples also occur in Italian monastic rules: see Heiming (1961), 110; Taft (1993), 125, 135; [Mitchell] (1981), 390–91.

39. Heiming (1961), 128–30. Similar triple groupings of psalms were used in many other liturgical traditions, including the Office of Tours (Taft 1993, 149) and in the Italian *Regula Magistri* (*CPL* 1858); see Vogüé, *La Règle*, 1:51–54. Evidence for antiphonal alternating choirs is adduced from some Irish hymns in Stevenson (1996), 113.

40. Ed. Warren, *The Antiphonary*. A recent study is Curran (1984), reviewed in Jeffrey (1985). For more on the Bangor Antiphoner and its allied fragments, see *CLLA* 150–63; Lapidge and Sharpe (1985) 532, 534, 572–77, 786–88; Kenney (1968), 568–70. *CPL* 1938. I do not cite the more recent edition, Franceschini, *L'antifonario*, because for the purposes of this article it is best to stay close to the facsimile of the manuscript in Warren's edition, even though Warren's normalized Classical spelling distorts the rough Latin of the manuscript.

41. See the map of Irish foundations in the back of Löwe (1982), after p. 1084.

42. Thus the date "not after 680–691" is given for this "earliest datable piece of Irish calligraphy" in O'Neill (1984), 62. But see Morrish (1988), 515–16.

43. Ed. Meyer, "An Old-Irish," *CLLA* 151; Lapidge and Sharpe (1985), 786. Kenney (1968), 569. The script is classified as "Phase II half-uncial" according to the terminol-

ogy of Brown (1993), 210–11. For plates and description see Cipolla, *Codici,* 1:96–97; 2, pl. XXXIV; *CLA* 4, 454.

44. The numbers in brackets are those assigned to each item in Warren, *The Antiphonary,* even though I would have numbered the contents somewhat differently. Obviously my reconstruction of the liturgy behind the Bangor Antiphoner differs significantly from that of Curran (1984).

45. For examples of Latin Psalters with supplements that include canticles and/or hymns, see *CLLA* 352, 353, 358, 590, 591, 592, 1612, 1613, 1615, 1617, 1618, 1619, 1622, also Mearns (1914). An Irish example (Kenney 1968, 571) is published in facsimile in Bieler, *Psalterium:* see pp. xv–xvi of the introduction. An interesting comparison can be made with the Orationale of Verona (*CLLA* 330, cf. 331), the earliest substantial collection of Mozarabic chant, which dates from about the same period as the Bangor Antiphoner. It too contains collects and antiphons to be used with the liturgical psalms, but unlike the Bangor Antiphoner it is an organized, planned collection.

46. The *Regula Coenobialis* attributed to Columban refers to "prostration" (*humiliatio*) and "bending the knees in prayer" after each psalm of the Office (Columban, *Opera,* 146–47, 158–59). The practice of ending every psalm (sometimes also readings) with kneeling or prostration in silent prayer, followed by a collect said by the leader, was widespread if not universal in early Eastern and Western Christianity; see Taft (1993), 153–54, 169, 176–77, 180–81, 189–90, 213. It was, however, particularly prominent in Egyptian monasticism, whence it spread to monastic traditions elsewhere; ibid., 58–65, 67, 88–89, 102, 114–17, 120, 122, 124, 129–30, 211. Texts for the collects in several Western traditions are published in Brou and Wilmart, *The Psalter;* see especially their pages 230–37 on the Bangor Antiphoner prayers.

47. The Bangor Antiphoner is often cited as the earliest witness to the Latin text of the *Gloria in excelsis* (*CLLA* 041). Possibly earlier, however, is the seventh-century fragment of the Milanese Mass ordo in St. Gall MS 908 (*CPL* 1906; *CLLA* 501); for bibliography see Bourque (1958), 424–25, no. 555. The Bangor Antiphoner, however, along with the eleventh-century Irish *Liber hymnorum* (Bernard and Atkinson, *The Irish,* 1:50–51), agree with the Milanese Office (Magistretti, *Manuale,* pt. 2, 416) in that they include (differing forms of) the continuation that is typically attached to the *Gloria* in Eastern traditions, which begins "Daily we bless you . . ." See Quecke (1970), 416–21; Mercenier, *La Prière,* 126–29. However, this continuation is missing in the earliest manuscript of the Greek and Coptic texts, the fourth- or fifth-century Codex Scheide in Princeton (Schenke, *Das Matthäus,* 30–31, 128–31, plates 16–17), as well as in the unorthodox fourth-century text in the *Apostolic Constitutions* (Metzger, *Les Constitutions:* 3:112–13).

48. See Bradshaw (1983), 47–71; Chadwick (1972).

49. Lowe, *The Bobbio* (1920), 180–81; *CPL* 633c; Godel (1963), 280–81.

50. The series includes at least the three troparia: Κύριε, ὁ τὸ πανάγιόν σου Πνεῦμα ("Lord, who at the third hour sent your All-Holy Spirit") for Terce, Ὁ ἐν ἕκτῃ ("Who on the sixth day at the sixth hour were nailed to the Cross") for Sext, and Ὁ ἐν τῇ ἐνάτῃ ("Who at the ninth hour tasted death") for None. See Mercenier, *La Prière,* 163, 173, 182; Black, *A Christian,* 77, 79–80, 83; *The Coptic Morning Service,* 143, 146, 149.

51. On the early use of psalm versicles in the Western Office, see Martimort (1995).

52. Taft (1993), 393; P. Bradshaw (1983), 82, 103. In some of the earliest witnesses to the Greek text, notably the fifth-century Codex Alexandrinus, the *Gloria in excelsis* is entitled "morning hymn." Rahlfs, *Septuaginta,* 1931, 364–65; 1979, 2:181–83.

53. See the bibliography in Rordorf (1981), 111, n. 18.

54. For further bibliography on the peace in the Bangor Antiphoner, including an apparent parallel in the East Syrian Office, see Verbraken (1988), 611.

55. Turin, BN G. V. 38; see Curran (1984), 216–17. The fact that Alcuin quoted the

hymn, however, shows that it did circulate more broadly. The Turin MS, which contains the monastic rules of both Benedict and Columban as well as hymns and antiphons, appears to be a valuable source of information about worship in "mixed rule" monasteries a few centuries after the era of the Bangor Antiphoner; the MS is dated to the late ninth or early tenth century in Cipolla, *Codici*, 1:141, with some facsimiles printed in 2: plates LVI–LVII. An eleventh-century hymnal from Bobbio, Vatican, BAV Vat. lat. 5776 (see *CLLA* 1676), has received little study but evidently lacks *Ignis creator;* no doubt it reflects an even later stage in the integration of this originally Irish monastery into mainstream medieval liturgical practice.

56. Taft (1993), 104. On the hymns of the Arles Office, see Bulst, *Hymni*, 91–98, 163–66.

57. *CPL* 2009; Gneuss (1974); Ambrose, *Hymnes,* 104–14, 696–701; Franz (1993–94 and 1994); Milfull, *The Hymns*, 1–5.

58. Attempts to identify the hymns known to Benedict include: Berlière (1908); Blume (1908); Vogel (1958); see also Ilàri (1980).

59. Curran (1984), 81–83, 22–46; Kenney (1968), 87–88; Lapidge and Sharpe (1985), 572–77.

60. Kenney (1968), 89; Bulst (1976), 92–93. It is significant that *Ignis creator* is not listed in Lapidge and Sharpe (1985), who evidently did not consider it a Hiberno-Latin composition. Yet one who was convinced of the manuscript's origin in Ireland could logically conclude, "The hymns in the Bangor Antiphonary (680–91) show that not all the Latin poetry of Ireland at this time was written in the Hisperic style" (J. Brown 1993, 147).

61. ". . . three psalms at each of the day-time hours, . . . together with an addition of versicles which intercede first for our own sins, then for all Christian people, then for priests and the other orders of the holy flock that are consecrated to God, finally for those that do alms, next for the concord of kings, lastly for our enemies . . ."; *Opera*, 130–31.

62. Following *Cantemus* is an unknown collect, then the collects Warren numbered [81] and [62]. Following the *Benedicite* are [82] and [63]. Following the *Laudate* psalms are [83], an otherwise unknown collect, and [64]. Meyer (1903), 188 suggests the Irish rubric *ibfelib* may mean "an Festtagen," connecting it with the word *féil*. See Royal Irish Academy *Dictionary,* 3:66.

63. Mearns (1914), 68–69; Meyer (1903), 175–77, 180 n; Salmon, *Le Lectionnaire,* 1:lxix–lxx, 105, 110–11, 113–115. Apart from the canticles, however, the Luxeuil lectionary contains the Vulgate text. Fragments of another early Vulgate manuscript from Luxeuil are identified and listed in Ganz (1991).

64. That the canticles from the book of Daniel were in universal use was already asserted by Rufinus (d. 410; see Taft 1993, 144). Traditions known to have used it in conjunction with Pss. 148–50 and other canticles such as *Cantemus* include: the Gallican Offices of Tours (P. Bradshaw 1983, 118; Taft 1993, 146) and of Arles (Taft 1993, 112, 154), the Mozarabic Office (Taft 1993, 118, 159, 162), Italian monastic rules and the Roman Office (Taft 1993, 128–29, 135), the Coptic and Ethiopic Offices (Taft 1993, 255, 265), the Armenian and Syrian traditions (Taft 1993, 222, 232, 241), the fragmentary Latin antiphoner discovered on Mt. Sinai, perhaps representing a north African tradition (Fischer 1964, 285–87).

65. Zerfass (1968), 100–1; Bertonière (1972); Winkler (1987b); Winkler (1988–89).

66. The *Benedicite* antiphon *Sancti et humiles corde* [99.14] has the same text as Bailey and Merkley (1989), 222, no. 1191, Bailey and Merkley (1990), 419; Magistretti, *Manuale,* pt. 2, 387, line 3. It is based on Dan. 3:87. The *Cantemus* antiphon *Dominus conterens bella* [99.15] has the same text as Bailey and Merkley (1989), 180, no. 417, Bailey and Merkley (1990), 487; Magistretti, *Manuale,* pt. 2, 403, line 9. It is based on the Old

Latin text of Exod. 15:3. The antiphon to Ps.89, *Respice in servos tuos* [106], and the Ambrosian psallendum with the same text are in Bailey and Merkley (1989), 220, no. 1162; Magistretti, *Manuale,* pt. 2, 268, line 12. It is based on the Gallican Psalter text of Ps. 89:16.

67. Of the *Cantemus* antiphons: *Gloriosus in sanctis mirabilis* [99.5] resembles *Gloriosus in sanctis faciens mirabilia* in Bailey and Merkley (1990), 493. *Cantemus domino gloriose enim* [99.17] resembles *Cantemus domino gloriose quia* in Bailey and Merkley (1990), 478; *Filii autem Israel* [99.19] resembles three Ambrosian *Filii Israel* antiphons in Bailey and Merkley (1990), 485–86. Among the *Benedicite* antiphons, *Benedicite omnia opera* [99.16] resembles antiphons in Bailey and Merkley (1990), 415, 436, 437.

68. The antiphon pair *Gubernasti domine populum tuum* [99.11] for the Exodus 15 canticle *Cantemus,* and *Tres pueri cantabant* [99.12] for the Daniel 3 canticle *Benedicite,* have the same incipits as the Ambrosian antiphon pair *Gubernasti iustitia tua populum tuum* for the *Cantemus* and *Tres pueri testimonium* (Bailey and Merkley 1990, 445), sung together on the third Sunday of Lent. See PM 6 (1900), 228. The antiphon *De coelis dominum laudate* [100] to Pss. 148–50 has almost the same incipit as *De caelis dominum laudemus,* Bailey and Merkley (1990), 349; Bailey and Merkley (1989), 172, no. 299; Magistretti, *Manuale,* pt. 404.

69. Irish communion antiphons are relatively well attested, since they can be found both in the Stowe Missal and allied fragments (ed. Warner, *Stowe Missal; CLLA* 101–25; *CPL* 1926; Kenney 1968, 555–57; Lapidge and Sharpe 1985, 537; Gamber, "Ein ägyptisches," 228; Duft 1982, 928–29; O'Briain 1946, 224) and in the Irish rite of visiting and bringing communion to the sick (Warren 1881, 164–65, 170–71, 173, 177–79). On the Mass and communion in Columbanian monasticism see Stevenson (1997).

70. After *Hymnum dicat* is a collect [84], continuing the series of [81] through [83] found after the canticles and psalms, but the second collect is unknown. After *Spiritus divine lucis* are collects [87] and [67]. After Te deum are [126], an unknown collect, [29], and another unknown collect. According to the rubrics of the Bangor Antiphoner, however, [87] and [67] are for (feasts of?) martyrs, while [29] is for the hour of Sext.

71. That it is actually a work of Columban is proposed in Lapidge (1997).

72. The author and original context of this hymn remain unknown. It is listed among the dubia of Nicetas of Remesiana in CPL 650.

73. Cf. Mearns (1914), 68.

74. There is a possible Eastern precedent in a Greek hymn preserved in the fourth-century *Apostolic Constitutions,* which begins with this same psalm verse, continues with the *Laudamus te* segment of the *Gloria in excelsis,* then the *Te decet laus* (a canticle also preserved in the Benedictine Office), ending finally with the *Nunc dimittis* (Metzger, *Les Constitutions,* 3:114–15).

75. On Irish sources regarding the veneration of saints, see Hennig (1965), 69–70, 74–87.

76. For further bibliography on these hymns see Lapidge and Sharpe (1985), 572–77, and pp. 146–47.

77. Taft (1993), 52–55. The earliest description of the Resurrection Vigil at Jerusalem is in the account of the Latin pilgrim Egeria, written about the year 383, ed. Maraval, *Égérie,* 242–45; English translation by Wilkinson, 124–25. On the later history of this service, see Jeffery (1991), especially Table III on p. 74.

78. Magistretti, *Beroldus,* 36–46, 158–71; Magistretti, *Manuale,* pt. 2, 24–26 and throughout; Magistretti, *Manuale,* pt. 1: 52–63; W. C. Bishop (1924), 98–108; *Breviarium Ambrosianum.*

79. [Hambourg] and Ware, *The Festal,* 75–76; Matéos, "Un horologion," 47–76; Taft (1993), 279–82.

80. Taft (1993), 111–12. See also the sources listed in n. 10 above.

81. Quecke (1970); Burmester, *The Horologion*, x–xi, 140–56, etc.; Turaev, *Časolov*, 110–75; Getatchew and Macomber (1982), 8–10, 205–8; Taft (1993), 255–56.

82. The nine odes of the Byzantine/Palestinian Office, which are often found appended to Greek Psalters that reflect this liturgical milieu, are: Exod. 15:1–19 [= *Cantemus*], Deut. 32:1–43 [= *Audite caeli*], 1 Kings [Sam.] 2:1–10 [= *Exultavit*], Hab. 3:2–19 [= *Domine audivi*], Isa. 26:9–20, Jon. 2:3–10, Dan. 3:26–45 [= *Benedictus es*], Dan. 3:52–88 [= *Benedicite*], Luke 1:46–55, 68–79 [= *Magnificat + Benedictus dominus*]. Mearns (1914), 7–14; Rahlfs, *Septuaginta* (1931); Rahlfs (1979) 2:151–78. As shown in table 5.8, the Milanese/Ambrosian Office uses the same set of canticles, but in a different order; they are also found in Milanese order appended to the Ambrosian Psalter (Magistretti, *Manuale*, pt. 1, 164–77; Mearns 1914, 53–55). This is one of many striking parallels between the Milanese Office and the Syrian and Palestinian traditions. Others include the appending of Ps. 116 [RSV 117] to Pss. 148–50 (Taft 1993, 232, 241) and the alternation of the *Benedicite* on Sundays with Ps. 50 [RSV 51] on weekdays (Taft 1993, 232). Certain remarks of St. Ambrose indicate that Isa. 26:9–20 (which is in the Palestinian list but not the Roman) was already used as a liturgical canticle in Milan of his time (Taft 1993, 142), and this recalls the similar parallel in Ambrose's use of the Beatitudes as a canticle (Franz (1994), 366; see n. 28 above).

83. Gneuss (1974), 412; Kenney (1968), 572. An edition of an early recension of the New Hymnal is Wieland, *Canterbury Hymnal*. See also Milfull, *The Hymns,* 5–15.

84. *CPL* 1998. *OR* 3:3–21, 45–154, 197–227. Much of the text is reprinted with an extensive commentary by Joseph Semmler in Hallinger, *Initia,* 3–75.

85. Ordo Romanus 17, derived from Ordines Romani 15 and 16, exhibits even stronger associations with the Irish foundations of Luxeuil and Bobbio. See *OR* 3:157–93, esp. 170–72. An alternative view was published by Hallinger (1960). Hallinger argued that many of the allegedly non-Roman traits in Ordines Romani 15–19 can be shown to have parallels in Italian sources, notably the Rule of the Master, so that perhaps these Ordines are better witnesses to Roman usage than Andrieu believed. I reply that: (1) Hallinger has a point that some of these were widely used ancient customs, and that in the age of the "mixed rules," before the general acceptance of the Benedictine Rule, texts and practices based on them were transmitted far and wide, and may well have been used even in Roman monasteries. (2) Hallinger seems to think that the "Gallican" liturgical realm excluded Italy, whereas in fact most local Italian uses exhibit traits that are closer to transalpine (Gallican and Mozarabic) traditions than to the liturgy of Rome. (3) In any case, the argument is limited to specific points where Hallinger knows of parallels in other monastic literature—other non-Roman liturgical traits that are not particularly monastic, such as the practice of baptizing on Epiphany, go unmentioned or are not really dealt with.

86. The fact that this author knew only six ecumenical councils has been taken to indicate that he must have been writing before the seventh, the second council of Nicaea, which met in 787 and condemned iconoclasm (*OR* 3:12–13). But in fact, as the history of the *Libri Carolini* makes clear, it was not until well into the ninth century that this council was generally accepted in the West as ecumenical.

87. *OR* 3:110–12. This practice of performing baptisms on Epiphany was opposed by Rome from the fifth century on, in favor of what became the standard practice of baptizing on Easter. At Rome, baptisms were also performed on Pentecost, though this practice has not survived in the other liturgical traditions. See P. Bradshaw 1993.

88. Morin (1905), 344 shows what are evidently Epiphany antiphons, all of which have the word *alleluia* at the beginning, middle, and end. This is the sort of thing one finds in the Gregorian chant repertory at Septuagesima, just before the "farewell to the alleluia." On the early Roman practice of emphasizing *alleluia* on Septuagesima just before suspending it until Easter, see *OR* 2:462. The *Rule of the Master*, on the other

hand, says that at Epiphany "let all antiphons and responsories be sung with alleluia, and from that day let alleluia be closed and immediately subtracted from the oratory." See Vogüé, *La Règle*, 1:55–56 and 2:206–9. See also Gindele (1974). The "Old Roman" chant tradition is close to the *Rule of the Master,* for it has the alleluia emphasized and then suspended on the Octave of Epiphany.

89. The arrangement of the Benedictine Psalter is spelled out in the Rule of St. Benedict, chapters 8–18; see [Mitchell] (1981), 390–97. It was clearly drawn up against the background of an already traditional Roman arrangement, no longer attested in any known witness. The earliest source that does give us the Roman arrangement is Amalarius of Metz (early ninth century), *Opera* 3, ed. Hanssens: 22–23, 26–30, 141. See also Raffa (1971), 207–17. However, the practice of substituting Pss. 92 [RSV 93] and 99 [RSV 100] for Pss. 50 [RSV 51] and 117 [RSV 118] in the Benedictine Office is first attested in an eighth-century ordo of Monte Cassino; see Hallinger, *Initia*, 114, 116, 122. For general discussions see also Pascher (1954); Pascher (1958); H. Schmidt (1960), 438–56; Pascher (1971), 267–8; Gibert Tarruel (1973).

90. The first psalm in the fragment is Ps. 92 [RSV 93], as in the Roman and Benedictine cursus. The second is Ps. 117 [RSV 118], as in the Benedictine cursus for Sundays and the Roman cursus for Sundays in Lent. The fragment states that, during Lent, these two were to be replaced by Pss. 21 [RSV 22] and 90 [RSV 91], both of which have Passion associations. The third psalm according to the fragment was Ps. 62 [RSV 63], as in the Benedictine cursus for Sundays. In the Roman cursus this psalm was used every day at this point, combined with Ps. 66 [RSV 67] as a single psalm with one antiphon. The fifth "psalm" in the fragment and in the Roman and Benedictine traditions consisted of Pss. 148–50, performed as a single psalm with one antiphon. It is in the fourth position, where the Roman and Benedictine Offices used the same sequence of Old Testament canticles, that the fragment is most different. On Sunday, the fragment has the usual *Benedicite* canticle from Daniel (see also n. 18 above). On the weekdays of Passiontide, however (the only weekdays for which psalm information is given in the fragment), we find a series of four psalms with Passion themes, 108 [RSV 109], 90 [RSV 91], 34 [RSV 35], and 68 [RSV 69], the first three of which are then repeated for the last three days of the week. Though such substitutions are not a known Roman or Benedictine practice, the Roman liturgy does prominently feature these psalms in other contexts during Passiontide. Even here, then, some sort of Roman relationship seems plausible.

91. The verse incipit *Gloria* at the end of many responsories in the fragment presumably refers to the *Gloria patri* in its familiar Roman form, whereas at least some non-Roman rites used the form *Gloria et honor patri . . .* , authorized by the Council of Toledo in 633 (Vives et al., Concilios, 196–98), and found throughout the liturgical books of the Mozarabic tradition. That the *Gloria et honor* form circulated in Ireland is evident from the fact that it is found (in Greek translation!) on an eighth-century stone cross in County Donegal (Berschin 1988, 96, 104, pl. 16) The presence of the *Gloria* following some responsories in the fragment but not others seems random, consistent with the chaotic history of this practice in the Roman rite itself. Neither Benedict's rule of restricting the *Gloria* to the last responsory of each nocturn (9.5–7, 11.3), nor the proposal of the Council of Toledo to use it only with cheerful texts, seems to have been followed here. The Roman Breviary issued after the Council of Trent and in use up to the 1970s still preserved some variety from one occasion to another, as indicated in the *Rubricae Generales:* "At the end of the last responsory of each nocturn *Gloria patri* is said . . . unless it is indicated otherwise in particular places" (13:4, cf. 27:2).

92. One is tempted to compare this manuscript with the fragmentary missal in Irish script edited in Bannister, "Liturgical," 412–21. Here too we find familiar Roman prayers and Gregorian chant texts interspersed with unfamiliar material in a unique arrange-

ment. For instance, the introit text *In excelso throno,* usually assigned to the first Sunday after Epiphany, is here assigned to Epiphany itself, while an apocryphal Gospel is to be read on Circumcision.

93. Morin (1905), 329. Nothing new was added in Morin (1913), 51 or in Verbraken (1988), 612.

94. *Ratio de cursus qui fuerunt eius auctores,* ed. Joseph Semmler in Hallinger, *Initia,* 1:77–91. The treatise is also frequently cited from an earlier edition: Legg, *Ratio;* Kenney (1968), 548.

95. Eusebius of Caesarea, "The Father of Church History," quoted extensively from a document showing that there was an early Christian community that suffered persecution and martyrdom in second-century Lyons and Vienne. He did not explicitly link these people to St. Peter, and of course said nothing about their liturgical offices. See Stevenson, *A New,* 34–44. Josephus, a Jewish historian of the first century A.D., did not report this information at all, and it is obvious that the writer of the *Ratio de cursus* had not actually read him.

96. For what St. Irenaeus himself wrote regarding his relationship to Polycarp and John, see Stevenson, *A New,* 114–17, esp. 115.

97. The writer was evidently thinking of the Egyptian Office, which did emphasize the 12 hours of the day and night; see Taft (1993), 72. Hence the attribution to St. Athanasius of Alexandria. Though writings about the Egyptian St. Macarius circulated in Latin (*BHL* 5093–95), the name was also used as a pseudonym in some of the monastic rules of Lérins (Vogüé, *Les Règles*). I do not know why this tradition was connected with Aquileia, a north Italian see that, admittedly, was at times independent of Roman ecclesiastical and liturgical authority.

98. On the tradition that the Gospel of Mark was written in Rome and based on the reminiscences of St. Peter, see: Stevenson, *A New,* 47–49; Brown and Meier (1983), 191–201; Koester (1990), 273–75.

99. On the activities of these individuals see Thompson (1984).

100. The life of Columban referred to is no doubt the work of Jonas, which we have already cited so many times in this chapter (Krusch, *Ionae, BHL* 1898). The second volume of Jonas' work, dealing with Columban's saintly disciples, includes sections on Abbot Eustasius of Luxeuil (*BHL* 2773) and Abbot Attala of Bobbio (*BHL* 742); presumably these are the texts to which our writer refers. They do not support his historical claims any better than the writings of Eusebius and Josephus do, but our writer's respect for them does place him within the environment of Columbanian monasticism.

III ✦ MANUSCRIPT STUDIES

6

The Antiphoner of Compiègne

Paris, BNF lat. 17436

RITVA JACOBSSON

Scholars who work on the Divine Office, both in the East and in the West, are able to glean much information concerning their subject from sources dating from the third and fourth centuries up through the dawn of the Carolingian Renaissance (see chap. 3 above and Taft 1986). The main elements of the Office as it evolves later in the West are already apparent in the late fourth-century diary of the nun Egeria and in the earliest monastic rules from the East—the Psalms, the readings, and the prayers. Ancestors of antiphons and great responsories are mentioned in sixth-century Western rules as well, those of the Master and of St. Benedict. These later sources, however, as shown in the chapters by Joseph Dyer and Peter Jeffery—although they include instructions for singing and for plans of the psalmody, are very poor in actual liturgical texts. Indeed, it is not until very late, in the ninth century, that we are able to have the actual Office chant texts before our eyes. These come with the production of the first liturgical books for the Office, the earliest of which is the subject of this chapter.[1]

The oldest existing Latin Office book is the antiphoner of Compiègne, or the so-called antiphoner of Charles the Bald, perhaps copied around 870, seemingly by a single scribe, and, as myth has it, for presentation to the emperor himself (Paris, BNF lat. 17436).[2] One of the difficulties in studying early chant texts for the Office is discerning the various chronological layers. Antiphons and responsories mentioned, in incipit form, by Amalarius of Metz and also by his adversaries Florus and Agobardus of Lyons, are known to have been sung at the beginning of the ninth century,[3] whereas it seems that texts for the Offices of local saints, St. Vedast (Vaast), St. Médard, and others were created around the same time that the antiphoner of Compiègne was compiled.[4] The chant texts are taken from the *Vitae* and *Passiones* of these saints, and the style is not biblical. What of the other texts? Offices of widely celebrated saints are doubtless older than those of local saints: Benedict, Lawrence, Martin, Cecilia, and Lucy. Ruth Steiner has shown the ways in which responsories for many popular saints were extracted from their Lives and transformed into Matins chants (Steiner 1986). But in most cases, the oldest layers of chant texts are thought at present to be those for feasts of the Lord.[5] Even in the oldest saints' feasts and temporal feasts, however, it is striking that almost every Office contains at least some nonbiblical material. Furthermore, even the texts actually taken from the Bible are themselves centonized, reworked, and readapted in several ways.[6] Understanding this process of reworking scriptural text is of primary importance, and suggests questions concerning when, where, by whom, and why these texts were gathered into this particular book.

Although the present chapter, dedicated as it is to the Office for the feast of the apostle Andrew, cannot answer the broader questions alluded to above, it will demonstrate how in one particular case the texts of the antiphons and of the responsories were chosen, reworked, and organized in the oldest extant Latin liturgical book containing Office texts. It should be underscored at the outset that the nature of this particular Office, like many others in the Compiègne book, testifies to a state of great fluidity. The source reveals that the organization of the Liturgy of the Hours in the late ninth century was far from being set and complete. Instead, the book demonstrates that whereas an established stock of Office texts is already present, the shape of single texts, their number, and their ordering are very different from what is found in the later sources tabulated in *CAO*. The Compiègne book bears witness to a grandiose conception of the Divine Office, one to be celebrated daily throughout the year, but likewise to the chaotic state of the materials extant to be incorporated into the plan.

The Character of the Compiègne Book

The nature of the Compiègne book helps explain why it has been associated with Charles the Bald: it is deluxe, written in a particularly elegant script, and heavily decorated with more than 3,000 gold initials; originally the book was doubtless bound within precious ivory plaques. Yet, ironically, and in contrast to its lavish nature, the text of the codex is itself very poor.[7] It contains many uncorrected mistakes, and was neither prepared for musical notation, nor later supplied with neumes: as Hartmut Möller, and Gunilla Björkvall and Andreas Haug demonstrate in their chapters in this volume, setting neumes to text demands control of the words, at least on some level. The many irregularities and inadequacies concerning rubrics, contents of individual feasts, general layout, and mode of organization must be broached before proceeding to the study of the feast of St. Andrew in particular.

The problematic nature of the book itself affects the understanding of its contents. Its rubrics are irregular: sometimes there are no rubrics where one would expect them; in other places their Latin forms are incorrect, and there is no consistent system guiding the use of rubrics.[8] For example, "Responsoria unde supra" (responsories from which place above), occurs over 50 times, but this statement actually has nothing to do with references to texts already used. Such references do, however, occur, but they are expresssed as "Require retro ut supra" or "Require in feria II istius ebdomade" or "require a Pascha usque in Octabam" (rubrics on fols. 59v and 60). ("Seek as above" or "seek in Monday of this week" or "seek from Easter until the octave.") The "responsoria unde supra" occur in all kinds of feasts (with the exception of Lent), and the rubric is used both when the number of responsories is regular, small, or very large; it is also used both for biblical and for nonbiblical texts. However, this rubric is found in other early manuscripts as well, and there the words "unde supra" seem to relate to the readings from which the responsories—and also the antiphons—were taken.[9] Other idiosyncrasies abound. There are gaps in the Compiègne manuscript, places where empty spaces occur, sometimes exceeding three lines.[10] There are also problems with the ordering of pieces. Some are clearly misassigned: at the "dominica V post Epiphaniam" (fifth Sunday after Epiphany) there is one responsory *Vere famulus Dei* (fol. 43), without a rubric, but which belongs to the feast of St. Peter's chair (22 Feb.). On fol. 44, "in natale S. Valentini" (14 Feb.) after the rubric "Antiphonas in eodem," the first of the three antiphons, *Beata progenies unde Christus,* belongs to a feast of the Blessed Virgin Mary. At the feast of the apostles SS. Philip and James (1 May), after 18 antiphons (without rubrics), on a new page (fol. 63v) is written the responsory *Nomen et gloriosi Georgius* (*CAO* 7222; its textual form is strange). The feast of St. George (23 Apr.), however, has been copied before that of SS. Philip and James. Also the number of antiphons and responsories is highly irregular from feast to feast. For less important feasts, one might expect only a few pieces, with the rest to be taken from commons; it is not surprising then, that St. Brice (fol. 84) has only five antiphons, all for Lauds, "in matutinis laudibus." However, with great frequency one finds that after the rubric "In vigilia . . ." there is only a single antiphon and a verse for First Vespers, and thereafter the invitatory with the three nocturns begins. In each one of the nocturns there are three antiphons and three (or four) responsories, except in the last nocturn where the number of chants can be quite large. "In matutinis laudibus" (which always means "Lauds" in the Compiègne book) there are most often five regular antiphons, followed by a shifting number of antiphons "in evangelio" (for the Benedictus, the canticle of Zachary). At the feast of Epiphany (fols. 41v–42), for example, the third nocturn offers ten responsories and Lauds fifteen antiphons "in evangelio." If Second Vespers is represented, the antiphons are almost always five, but those *in evangelio* (for the Magnificat canticle) can be of differing numbers. The numbers of these chants are so utterly irregular that there seems to be no pattern as to their numbers or positions, as the following tabulation of select examples shows.

In vigilia octavas domini (Christmas octave, fols. 40v–41), there are three nocturns with the customary three antiphons, but with no responsories at all. The feast of St. Benedict (21 Mar., fols. 70v–71v) follows the monastic cursus with six antiphons in two nocturns each but none in the third nocturn, and seven Lauds antiphons. In the feast of St. Lawrence (10 Aug., fols. 71v–72v) there are eight Lauds antiphons and thereafter six more for Benedictus. The feast of St. Médard (5 June, fols. 65v–66v) offers three antiphons for First Vespers, and after the three regular nocturns, four further antiphons are supplied, under the rubric *Antiphonas unde supra ad nocturnum* (see above). Thereafter follow six antiphons for Lauds, with nine more for the Benedictus (Jonsson 1968, 60–61). The Assumption (fols. 73v–75) contains first 17 responsories without any special rubric; thereafter the rubric *antiphonas unde supra* with three nocturns having three antiphons each but no responsories, then five Lauds antiphons and twenty-nine antiphons *in evangelio*.

In virtually all the Offices in the Compiègne book, the same pieces, or parts or variants of them, occur, but frequently not gathered together. It seems probable that the large numbers of very similar texts in the oldest chant books may indicate different ways of singing. The idea for a piece was clear, the biblical or hagiographical source chosen, the most important words were selected—but the exact textual shape would be decided according to the various melodic formulas and styles operating within the many chant genres. One example, taken from the feast of Purification (fols. 43v–44), illustrates the many formulations of the text "Accepit Simeon":

Responsum accepit Simeon (verse *in vigilia ad vesperos*);
Responsum accepit Simeon ab Spiritu sancto, non visurum se mortem, nisi
   videret Christum domini (I noct., resp. 3);
Suscipiens Iesum . . . V. Responsum accepit Simeon ab Spiritu sancto, non
   visurum se mortem, nisi videret Christum domini (II noct., resp. 1);
Responsum acceperat Simeon ab Spiritu sancto, non visurum se mortem,
   nisi videret Christum domini. Et benedixit eum et dixit: Nunc dimittis,
   domine, servum tuum in pace, quia viderunt oculi mei salutare tuum,
   domine. (II noct., resp. 2);
Responsum acceperat, ut supra (only incipit, III noct., V belonging to resp.
   Simeon iustus);
Responsum accepit Simeon ab Spiritu sancto, non visurum se mortem, nisi
   videret dominum (Lauds, ant. 1) ;
Responsum accepit Simeon (Lauds, verse)

If we stand back from the array of materials to be found in the Compiègne source, and their several modes of presentation, we wonder what sort of book this is. In one place with an overwhelming fifty antiphons, we encounter the rubric "Item antiphonas de resurrectione domini ubicumque volueris" (fol. 60v) ("Likewise antiphons for the Lord's resurrection, wherever you want"). Further, "Responsoria de dominica V et sunt canendi [*sic*] usque in Ascensione Domini" (fol. 62v) ("responsories for the fifth Sunday and they should be sung until the Lord's Ascension") is the rubric for sixteen responsories. Although the rubrics, the numbers of pieces, and the irregularities of the Compiègne book can easily be studied by comparison with *CAO* 1, yet there is a problem in doing so: the Compiègne book is around 100 years older than all other books containing the texts of the Office, and the "norm" that has become the basis for scholarly discussions may have stood behind this source, or it may not have been present in exactly the way we know it. Because no other complete books of the same age are extant, it is impossible to know if they might have offered a more regularized state of materials. The kind of work described by László Dobszay for the proper "reading of an Office book" (see chapter 2) requires other books of the same use and date, and they do not exist to provide a context for this special source.

The nature of the source suggests that it may well be an anthology, a treasury of chant texts. If it were prepared for liturgical use, or at least for consultation in the rendering of the Office, then, following the dicta of the cantor, the use of the texts might have been different at different occasions. Indeed, no exact instruction concerning their selection, nor a clear indication concerning their precise function, exists. The next oldest books, the Hartker Codex and the Mont-Renaud antiphoner, while not in as fluid a state as Compiègne, do have irregular numbers of pieces.[11] For liturgical use, a selection of what should be sung and what should be left out apparently has to be made for every occasion of celebration. David Hiley writes: "It looks as if the manuscripts all select responsories from a common pool of favourite compositions, practically all of which were already available early in the ninth century (at least in time for the Compiègne source to include them)."[12] The Compiègne book is special, prepared for a particular person, perhaps for a king. It contains both general material and local texts for saints from the north of France, such as Vedast, Quentin, and, above all, Médard, a saint of special importance to King Charles the Bald. This suggests that different sources must have been used in the preparation of the book. In addition, the anthology-like state of the book might help account for its preservation: it was not precisely tied to any single liturgical use; and it was not pored over incessantly in the day-to-day tasks of liturgical singing.

But if the Compiègne manuscript is an anthology, has it no liturgical underpinnings at all? Was it a source merely to be used as a tool for supplying materials for Divine Office upon any particular occasion? The answer is not "either/or," but "both/and," and this will be clarified in the discussion to follow. On the one hand liturgical structures are alluded to throughout the source. Most often the single Hours to be celebrated are indicated by rubrics, and there are many cases where we find a regular number of pieces, most consistently regarding antiphons for Lauds. On the other hand, the superfluous numbers of pieces, particularly for the Benedictus, but often in other contexts as well, characterize the book as an anthology. This helps account for the strange repetitions of texts and its generally confused state. What we witness here is probably the work of a liturgical compiler who had not been able to—or, perhaps, had not even wanted to—insert all the materials, taken over from what seems to be several sources, within a polished, well-organized structure. Probably this state also testifies to a semi-oral culture where liturgical books did not prescribe but rather proposed what should be sung in the Office, and offered choices to those responsible for planning the services. It has recently been suggested that the book was prepared from a collection of libelli, and that this accounts for its particular nature, for the repetitions, and for the out-of-order pieces, and for the great variety it exhibits (see Jeffery 1995, 221–22). If it is true that the scribe made a deluxe book, but from a group of booklets containing many different liturgical sources, this would account for many of the features of the book described above.

The extent to which the scribe and others involved chose pieces carefully is a matter for further consideration. It is clear that the antiphoner was produced under rushed circumstances and also that it was never actually completed, as testified by the many gaps within its text. Perhaps the book had to be finished in order to be presented on a certain day: the solemn dedication of the octagonal chapel of the royal Abbey of Saint-Médard in Soissons, on 5 May in the year 877 has been offered as a possibility (cf. Huglo 1993a). However, in some ways, it is fortunate for us that the scribe worked in the ways he did, not standardizing materials and merely, and sometimes seemingly mechanically, reproducing what was before his eyes, for this provides a precious kind of evidence: in the case of St. Andrew, two different recordings of what is in essence the same feast.

Two Offices for St. Andrew

The two presentations of the Office of Andrew falling at the end of the book may well be the result of successive copying from two different sources, both of which contained the feast, and the similarities of whose textual traditions will be evaluated below. As the tabulated list of the two versions (see table 6.1 below) demonstrates, this double presentation once made it appear to scholars as though one of the Offices was celebrated on an earlier date, reasoning which seemingly no longer holds.[13] It now appears more likely that the position has to do with the nature of the book itself, apparently compiled as it was from a group of libelli, sometimes with little thought about repetitions and inconsistencies.[14] The position of the Feast of St. Andrew elsewhere in the source would seem to confirm this. The Compiègne manuscript is a double book, the first 30 folios containing a Gradual, called the *Liber Antiphonarius* and written more or less at the same time, in the same place, by the same hand, and with the same type of decorations, but originally a separate book and only later bound with the *Liber Responsalis* treated here. However, a comparison between the two books shows that the Gradual contains the feast of St. Andrew (*vigilia* and *natalis*) at the end, only one time, and after the feast of St. Chrysogonus (24 Nov.) but before *in ordinatione pontificis*.[15] Thus internal evidence seems to indicate that Andrew's feast, even in this unique source, was probably a celebration for 30 November, with a vigil on the 29th.[16] In regard to the Office of St. Andrew, further close analysis will suggest that the scribe's work was not to revise or to make sure that the book was standardized and uniform, but rather to preserve the sources from which he copied. In spite of minor discrepancies between them, the two Offices are astonishingly similar, so much so that there was little reason to go to such trouble to record them both, unless for the reasons we have already suggested. If the scribe, or those who supervised his work, had been careful students of the material being copied, they might well have used incipits for pieces already present in the book and written out those not found elsewhere, but there is no systematic use of any system of abbreviation in the copying of the two Offices.[17]

The basic appearances of the two copies are as follows:
On fol. 84, the opening rubric is displayed:

> *Antiphonas et Responsoria in vigilia sancti Andreae apostoli ad vesperas,* followed by:
> one antiphon;
> the rubric *Responsoria unde supra* and sixteen responsories with verses;
> five antiphons *in matutinis laudibus;*

eighteen antiphons *in evangelio* (for the Benedictus);
six antiphons *in die ad vesperas;*
one antiphon *in evangelio* (for the Magnificat)

However, immediately after (fol. 85v) follow *antiphonas et responsoria in vigilia sanctae Caeciliae virginis*—an entire office for St. Cecilia (22 Nov.)—and right after that a somewhat shortened office for St. Clement (23 Nov.). Thereafter appears, a second time, on fol. 87v, a second office for St. Andrew:

In vigilia sancti Andree.
Its first rubric says *ad vesperas,* with one antiphon; thereafter follow:
the rubric *Ad invitatorium* with its antiphon;
the first nocturn with three antiphons and four responsories;
the second nocturn with three antiphons and three responsories;
the third nocturn with three antiphons and seven responsories;
the *Antiphonas in matutinis laudibus* (the expected five antiphons);
in evangelio (for the Benedictus); five antiphons;
in die ad vesperas; six antiphons;
finally three antiphons *in evangelio* (for the Magnificat)

Even if the presentation of two Offices for St. Andrew, and the anomalous location of one of them, is merely the result of copying from two sources successively, the situation offers the scholar a unique opportunity to view two differing ninth-century versions of an Office for the same saint. It is crucial first to compare the contents of the two Offices, and then to examine the elements comprising them with great care. Table 6.1 provides incipits of the first Office, fols. 84–85v (hereafter called Off. A) and the Office following the feasts of St. Cecilia and St. Clement, fols. 86v–88 (hereafter called Off. B) in parallel columns. The rubrics are abbreviated, and the responsory verses and the psalms are not marked. The table will be useful for following the brief comparison of the two renditions of the Office that follows.

The ways in which the texts have been entered are also worthy of observation, not only for what they reveal about the scribe and his intentions, but even more importantly for what they show about the sources from which he copied. In Off. A, the responsories are written one after the other, but on fol. 85 the antiphons for Lauds are displayed as verses, each new item beginning a new line, in most cases. Also in order to make the antiphon texts fit, they are heavily abbreviated, and this distinguishes the copying of this Office from most others in the Compiègne manuscript. In Off. B, this crowded appearance is less apparent, visible only in the copying of a few of the Lauds antiphons and in the biblical Vespers antiphons. Off. B starts, after the office of St. Clement, with the rubric falling in the middle of a line, and not announcing the office of St. Andrew in a clear way. Off. A has after the rubric "AD VESP" a versicle, *In omnem terram,* and only one antiphon, *Venite post me.* Thereafter follow sixteen responsories before the Lauds antiphons. If we regard their positions within the other manuscripts in the *CAO,* it can be seen that these responsories always are assigned to nocturns of Matins. In Off. B the first eight texts are exactly the same as in Off. A, distributed over the nocturns, and of the other eight of Off. A, six occur in the third nocturn of Off. B, although the

Table 6.1 Comparison of the two Offices for St. Andrew in the
Compiègne manuscript

Office A	Office B
ANS ET RESP. IN VIG. S. ANDREAE APOST. AD VESP.	IN VIGILIA S. ANDREE AD VESP.
V In omnem terram	V In omnem terram
A Venite post me	A dum perambularet
	AD INVITATORIUM Regem apostolorum
	In I NOCTURNO A Vidit dominus = 11A A Venite post me = 18A A Relictis retibus = 12A V In omnen terram
RESP. UNDE SUPRA	RESP. UNDE SUPRA
1R Dum perambularet	R Dum perambularet
2R Venite post me	R Venite post me
3R Mox ut vocem	R Mox ut vocem
4R Oravit sanctus Andreas	R Oravit sanctus Andreas
	IN II NOCTURNO A Dilexit Andream = 13A A Dignum sibi dominus = 5A A Salve crux quae = 14A V Dedisti hereditatem
	RESP. UNDE SUPRA
5R Homo Dei ducebatur	R Homo dei ducebatur
6R O bona crux	R O bona crux
7R Doctor bonus	R Doctor bonus
	ANT. IN III NOCTURNO A Accipe me ab hominibus = 15A A Tu es Deus meus = 16A A Non me permittas = 3A V Adnuntiaverunt
	RESP. UNDE SUPRA
8R Expandi manus	R Expandi manus = 8R
9R Vir iste in populo suo	R Salve crux quae = 14R
10R Dilexit Andream	R Dilexit Andream = 10R
11R Beatus Andreas de cruce	R Vir iste in populo suo = 9R
12R Beatus Andreas apostolus	R Cum vidisset beatus Andreas = 13R
13R Cum videret beatus Andreas	R Dum penderet beatus Andreas = 15R
14R Salve crux quae	R Videns crucem = 16R
15R Dum penderet beatus Andreas	
16R Videns crucem	
ANT. IN MAT. LAUDIBUS	ANT. IN MATUTINIS LAUDIBUS
1A Salve crux pretiosa	A Salve crux pretiosa
2A Beatus Andreas orabat	A Beatus Andreas orabat
3A Andreas Christi famulus	A Andreas Christi famulus
4A Christo amabilis	A Christo amabilis
5A Qui persequebatur iustum	A Qui persequebatur iustum
V Constitues	V Constitues

Table 6.1 (*continued*)

Office A	Office B
IN EVANGELIO	IN EVANGELIO
1A Unus ex duobus	A Unus ex duobus = 1A
2A Christus me misit	A Videns Andreas crucem = 9A
3A Non me permittas	A Ego si patibulum
4A Biduo vivens	A Non me permittas = 3A
5A Dignum sibi dominus	A Christus me misit = 2A
6A Sanctus Andreas apostole	
7A Andreas apostole domini	
8A Dixit Andreas Symoni	
9A Videns Andreas crucem	
10A Continuo relictis retibus	
11A Vidit dominus Petrum	
12A Relictis retibus suis	
13A Dilexit Andream	
14A Salve crux que	
15A Recipe ab hominibus	
16A Tu es Deus meus	
17A Dum perambularet	
18A Venite post me	
IN DIE AD VESP.	IN DIE AD VESP.
1A Iuravit dominus	A Iuravit dominus
2A Potens in terra	A Potens in terra
3A Collocet eum	A Collocet eum
4A Disrupisti domine	A Disrupisti domine
5A Confortatus est	A Confortatus est
V Nimis honorati	V Constitues
IN EVANGELIO	IN EVANGELIO
A Concede nobis	A Concede nobis
	A Biduo vivens = 4A
	A Andreas apostolus domini = 7A

order is not exactly the same; two of the responsories (11, *Beatus Andreas de cruce,* and 12, *Beatus Andreas apostolus*), appear only in Off. A. In Off. A only one antiphon, *Venite,* occurs in First Vespers, but all the responsories apparently belonging to the three nocturns are written together, ready for division into different nocturns, although there are no antiphons for Matins supplied at all.[18]

Further comparison shows that the antiphons of Lauds are exactly the same in Off. A. and Off. B. Thereafter, *in evangelio* (for the Benedictus), there are eighteen antiphons in Off. A. All the nine antiphons of the nocturns in Off. B figure among these eighteen, just as do four of the five Benedictus antiphons of Off. B.[19] We find also two Magnificat antiphons from the eighteen in Off. A among the antiphons of Second Vespers in Off. B (4, *Biduo vivens,* and 7, *Andreas apostolus*) and, finally, three antiphons, figuring only here in Off. A (6A *Sanctus Andreas,* 8A *Dixit Andreas,* and 10A *Continuo relictis*). Second Vespers is comprised of exactly the same antiphons in both offices; however, Off. B offers *in evangelio,* thus for the Magnificat, both the one—and same—as in Off. A, and two more antiphons, already mentioned above.

The main difference between the two offices is the lack of organization in Off. A. In this source, after one First Vespers antiphon, there is no invitatory and no distribution in nocturns, only sixteen responsories without a rubric—they might as well belong to Vespers. After five regular Lauds antiphons follow eighteen antiphons *in evangelio.* Second Vespers contains six biblical antiphons, common for a feast of the apostles. Quite clearly, Off. A represents an earlier stage in the organization of the Office. A large stock of pieces is presented, but the organization of the main office, the *vigiliae* (or Matins service), is not laid out. All texts found in Off. B exist also in Off. A, except two, the invitatory and Benedictus antiphon *Ego si patibulo.* However, a few pieces in Off. A were not used in Off. B.[20] As can easily be seen from table 6.1, the order of some pieces varies. There are also textual variants between the pieces found in the two versions, allowing us to conclude that they were certainly copied independently. However, as many of the errors found in the texts of the two copies are identical, and this holds true both for responsories and for antiphons, the two Offices belong to the same textual tradition. Off. A, however, is without question the more accurate of the two. There is not sufficient evidence to go beyond this understanding of the nature of the two Offices when compared with each other. Details regarding differences between variants will be considered further in the discussion of individual responsory and antiphon texts. In order to explore the natures of these liturgical texts in greater detail, it is first essential to understand the primary sources from which the texts were fashioned.

The Office of St. Andrew: Introduction and Background

In general, the *Passiones* or the *Vitae* form the principal source for the chant texts of individual saints' Offices. This is the case also with the apostles, since the Bible does not provide information regarding their life of ministry, or details concerning their suffering and death.[21] Andrew is a case in point. He is mentioned in the Bible together with the other apostles, but he does not play an individual role. Rather, although his name figures a dozen times in the New Testament, it is mostly in the context of group action. A fisherman, together with his brother Simon Peter, he was called by Jesus at the lake of Galilee to be a follower (Matt. 4:18–19); in one version of the feeding of 5,000 men, he drew attention to the boy with the five loaves of bread and the two fish (Joh. 6:9). There is not enough material here to understand character, to nourish cult, or, eventually, to fashion a *historia* for the Office.

Thus Andrew acquired a legendary character, based upon both widely circulating stories and the growth of his cult within particular regions and cities of the East and West. Although the relics of apostles Luke, Timothy, and Andrew are referred to as being present in the basilica of the Holy Apostles by Constantinopolitan bishops such as John Chrysostom (398–404) and Proclus (434–47), these men underscored the apostolic importance of St. Peter. However, the Latin bishop Paulinus of Nola (d. 431) claims in his *Carmen* 19 that emperor Constantius transferred the body of the apostle Andrew from Patras to the basilica built by Constantine the Great in Constantinople. Since it had not been possible to obtain the remains of St. Peter, or St. Paul, Paulinus stresses the importance of providing Constantinople with the relics of an apostle in order to sustain comparisons to Rome, which possessed the relics of both Peter and Paul (Paulinus of Nola, PL 61, 672). Perhaps from this time forward, the middle of the fourth century, a feast of St. Andrew would have been coming into Eastern liturgies. In the West the feast was established in the fifth century, and the cult spread rapidly after this time. It seems that Gregory the Great was important for instituting the cult in Rome, having founded a monastery in the name of St. Andrew (article "André," *DACL* 1:2031–34). The legend that the see of Constantinople was founded by Andrew seems to have come in during the sixth century, and to have been intensified in the seventh century. Thus, the Sixth Ecumenical Council held in Constantinople in 680 declared this city an "apostolic see."[22]

As is the case with many of the apostles, Andrew's legends emphasize his travels, the result of missionary zeal. Gregory of Tours (d. 594), who apparently had a deep devotion to Andrew, provides detailed accounts of Andrew's powers in his *Liber de miraculis Beati Andreae Apostoli,* which he wrote shortly before his death.[23] The apocryphal Acts of St. Andrew were used by Manicheans and other heretical movements in the early centuries, and had to be revised to promote orthodox ideas; the earliest versions were transmitted only as fragments.[24] The oldest such Latin reworking, "The letter of the Presbyters and Deacons of Achaia," probably from the sixth century, contains only the end of the *Acta,* namely the martyrdom of the apostle.[25] As would be expected, the apocryphal *Acta Andreae* were crucial to the development of the Office.[26] In these acts, the missionary work of Andrew in Patras is described, and special attention is focused upon his martyrdom. Although, as the notes to this chapter attest, there has been long and complicated discussion concerning the origins, relative ages, and interrelationships between the various redactions and fragments of the acts, legends, and miracles of St. Andrew, nonetheless, the following details emerge as central to the versions that sustained the Office liturgy in the West.

To promote the sense of authenticity, the acts are cast in the form of a letter written by the priests in Achaia, eyewitnesses of the death of the apostle Andrew. The text is highly rhetorical, a feature relished by those who selected the texts used for the Office, and it contains a long dialogue between Aegeas, the proconsul in Patras, and St. Andrew, who describes the history of salvation and invites Aegeas to believe in Christ. The proconsul refuses, and Andrew is brought to the cross, where he is to be fastened with ropes, not with nails, in order to make him live longer and thus suffer more. The people protest against his crucifixion and come close to forcing a reprieve from the proconsul. But the apostle yearns to follow his master on the cross, addresses a highly emotional speech to the cross, is crucified, and subsequently hangs two days upon the cross, preaching all the while to the people. After his death, his body is taken care of by Maximilla, one of his followers, ironically the wife of the proconsul Aegeas who was his principal adversary.[27] The ways in which the legendary material was used in the liturgy require careful study of the antiphons and responsories for the feast.

First Vespers and (Vigil) Responsories in Office A

The vast numbers of Office texts in honor of the apostle Andrew found in the manuscript are difficult to sort out and to study in a systematic way. Because many pieces are similar, certain expressions recur in various contexts, making it crucial to examine the texts carefully, and in comparison with their scriptural and other sources, always with an eye to the ways in which the texts were fashioned and the materials from which they were made were transformed in the process. The following commentary concentrates upon all the responsories of Off. A. Numbering systems refer to table 6.1.[28]

The opening text, the verse *In omnem terram,* occurs frequently in the common office of apostles.[29] The only antiphon, *Venite post me,* is a literal quotation from Matt. 4:19, the Gospel for the feast of St. Andrew, attested as early as the time of Gregory the Great (Willis 1994, 112–13). The responsories will, however, be examined particularly closely, since, as Ruth Steiner emphasized, their form is so important to the ultimate nature of the musical setting itself (Steiner 1986). It will be seen that the responsories have been shaped to emphasize two themes, and their sources are primarily two. The theme of the opening three is the calling of the apostles, as expressed in the Gospels of Matthew and Mark; the thirteen following responsories all treat the death of St. Andrew, and as depicted in the *Acta* of the apostle. In both instances, however, the source texts have been shaped to better suit their liturgical purposes:

Responsory 1	Matt. 4:18	Mark 1:16
Dum perambularet dominus	Ambulans autem	Et praeteriens
supra mare	iuxta mare	secus mare
secus litus Galileae	Galileae	Galileae
vidit	vidit duos fratres	vidit
Petrum	Simonem qui vocatur Petrus	Simonem
et Andream	et Andream	et Andream
	fratrem eius	fratrem eius
retia mittentes	mittentes rete	mittentes retia
et in mare	in mare erant autem piscatores	in mare erant enim piscatores
vocavit eos dicens	et ait illis	et dixit eis Iesus
venite post me	venite post me	venite post me
faciam vos	et faciam vos fieri	et faciam vos fieri
piscatores hominum	piscatores hominum	piscatores hominum

"When the Lord walked by the sea, at the shore of Galilee, he saw Peter and Andrew, his brother, casting nets into the sea and he called them saying: 'Come after me, I will make you fishers of men.'"[30] Although the responsory appears to conflate the two Gospels of Matthew and Mark, the words from an older Latin version of

Matt. 4:18 might have been influential as well in the shaping of the opening, "Dum transiret," echoing the ancient "Cum praeteriret."[31] This structure provides a temporal clause instead of the present participle, and the word "dominus" is added, lending a more distinct role to the Lord in this call. The geographical setting of the action is also expanded (*secus litus* added). In other places, the text is shortened and simplified, save for the exhortation "Venite. . . ." And the manner of introducing this utterance is worthy of observation. Whereas the Gospel versions offer one simple verb for "saying," "ait" or "dixit," the responsory has the double "vocavit eos dicens." "Vocavit" becomes the key word in this text concerned with the vocation of an apostle. (The expression "vocavit eos" is, in fact, used in Matt. 4:21, concerning the calling of James and John, a little later in the same chapter.) These small but significant modifications all show how the biblical text has been adapted for its liturgical purpose. The liturgical style of the responsory is strengthened by its verse, *Exaudi deus,* taken from Ps. 54:2–3—a favored psalmodic expression for liturgical use. The final words of the verse, "a finibus terrae," "from the ends of the world," are very well adapted to the second half of the responsory, "vocavit eos dicens. . . ."

Responsory 2, "Come after me, I will make you fishers of men, and they, leaving the nets and the boat, followed him," repeats Jesus' words "Venite post me," for the third time in this Office. The statement is balanced here by the apostles' action: "At illis relictis retibus . . ." ("and these leaving their nets . . ."). The opening emphasis upon Christ is followed by a shift of attention to the dramatic action of the apostles. Both Gospels contain an adverb emphasizing speed: "continuo" in Matt. 4:20, "protinus" in Mark 1:18, "at once." Whereas these are omitted in the liturgical text, other things are added. The "et nave" (leaving the nets) "and the boat," may be an echo of Luke 5:11: "et subductis ad terram navibus relictis omnibus secuti sunt illum" ("And having brought their ships to land, leaving all things, they followed him"); through this subtle allusion, the singer may become mindful as well of the miraculous fishing present in the very different account of Luke, and this adds depth to the text.[32] The replacement of "eum" with "dominum" makes the language more in keeping with liturgical tradition. The verse repeats literally the text of the first responsory, with two modifications: the biblical "duos fratres" is added, but the "retia mittentes in mare" is omitted. The nets are already mentioned in the responsory, and so the expression "duos fratres" was sufficient to make the connection.

Responsory 3 has one subject, the protagonist Andrew, here depicted in close contact with his Lord: "As soon as the blessed Andrew heard the voice of the Lord preaching, he left the nets, by whose use and function he had lived, and followed the giver of the eternal life, as if a reward." This is still evangelical, its theme being the vocation of the apostle. But the language is not biblical. The verse is a quotation from the homily of Gregory the Great, found in Carolingian lectionaries for this feast.[33] Instead of borrowing most expressions directly from the Bible, whoever was responsible for this text wrote in a rhetorical style: "praedicantis domini" ("the Lord preaching"), "quorum usu actuque vivebat" ("the use and function by which he lived"), added *beatus,* an expression typical of the hagiographical genre, and the final expression "aeterne vitae secutus est premio largitorem."[34]

The remaining responsories are all composed of expressions taken both directly and as paraphrases from the account of the *Acta Andreae*.[35]

Responsory 4, "Saint Andrew prayed while he looked up to heaven, shouted with loud voice and said: 'you are my God whom I have seen, do not let me be taken down by the impious judge, because I know the virtue of the holy cross. V. You are my Master, Christ, whom I loved, whom I recognized, whom I confessed.[36] Only listen to me in this voice.'" This is, however, not an exact quotation. The first verb, "oravit," "he prayed," belongs to the language of liturgical formulas: several antiphons and responsories begin with it, or with "orabat," or "orante";[37] several also include the expression "oravit sanctus N voce magna et dixit" ("Saint N. prayed with loud voice and said"). The "looking up to heaven" is borrowed rather from Scripture: it is found when Jesus blessed the bread at the miracle of the loaves and fishes,[38] and was adopted in the Canon of the Mass at the consecration: "with the eyes lifted up to you, God Father."[39] St. Stephen also looked up to heaven.[40] However, the circumstances described here are as found in the *Acta*. Most of the responsory verse is a literal quotation: "Tu es magister meus domine, quem dilexi, quem vidi, quem secutus sum, quem cognovi, quem in ista cruce confiteor ... sic modo in isto verbo me exaudi" ("You are my Master, Lord, whom I loved, whom I saw, whom I followed, whom I knew, whom I confess in this cross ... so listen to me now in this word").[41] This responsory concludes with allusion to martyrdom, and, with its generally liturgical character, places the mystery of the cross at its center.[42]

Responsory 5, *Homo dei*, "God's man was led away that they should crucify him. But the people cried out with loud voice saying: 'His innocent blood is condemned, without reason.'" The text contains both biblical and liturgical elements.[43] The text reflects parts of the *Acta:* "Iustus homo et amicus dei, quid fecit ut ducatur ad crucem," p. 24, 3–4 ("The righteous man and God's friend, what did he do to be led to the cross?"); "cruci eum affigi praecepit," 23, 8 ("He ordered him to be fastened to the cross"); "exclamavit voce magna dicens," p. 24, 8 ("he exclaimed with loud voice saying"). The expression "innocent blood" ("innocens sanguis") is frequent in the Vulgate, particularly in the prophetic books, and the verse "Filii alieni" is found in Ps. 17:46. Consequently, this responsory, although having narrative content and referring to the relation between the apostle and the people, is liturgical in its character, permeated as it is with biblical–liturgical expressions such as "Homo dei," "innocens sanguis," and the psalm verse.[44]

Responsory 6, "O good cross, you who have received the grace and beauty from the limbs of the Lord, receive me from the human beings and give me back to my Master, so that he, through you, might receive me, he who saved me through you." And the verse, "Hail, cross which is dedicated in the body of Christ and from his limbs decorated as if with pearls," is an invocation to the cross. Both expressions are quotations from the *Acta*, present as exclamations from St. Andrew himself. The text is characterized through its vocative ("O bona crux"), and its imperative verb forms ("Accipe, salve"). Not only do we encounter words describing beauty ("decorem," "pulchritudinem," "tanquam margaretis ornata"), belonging to cross poetry like that of Fortunatus, but, above all, the close relationship between the apostle and his Master is underlined ("per te me" twice). A number of the responsories for the Feast of the Exaltation of the Cross, appearing also in the Compiègne book, consist of this kind of exclamation: "O crux benedicta . . ." (*CAO* 7265); "O crux gloriosa, o crux adoranda . . ." (*CAO* 7266); "O crux admirabilis . . ."; V. "O laudabilis crux quae in corpore Christi dedicata es . . ." (*CAO* 7264).[45]

Responsory 7, "The good doctor and God's friend Andrew is brought to the cross; watching from far away he sees the cross. Hail, cross . . ." is a paraphrase of a passage in the *Acta* (p. 25, 1–6). *Doctor* is frequently used to refer to the apostles: St. Paul talks about himself as the *doctor gentium* (1 Tim. 2:7). In another passage from the *Acta*, St. Andrew is said to be *bonum doctorem, pium modestum* (p. 28, 3). The verb *videns* from the source is here changed to *aspiciens,* which echoes the responsory from Advent I, *Aspiciens a longe, ecce video Dei potentiam* (*CAO* 6129, "Seeing from far away, lo, I see God's power"). Responsory 8 also contains the same invocation to the cross as the previous responsory: *salve, crux suscipe.*

Responsory 8, "I have spread forth my hands all the day in the cross, to a people not believing but contradicting me, who walk ways which are not good, but follow after their sins," is a quotation from Isa. 65:2, and which, significantly, is quoted in part in Rom. 10:21, a text read in the Andrew Office.[46] Here we find the text in a form from an earlier Latin version of the Bible, with only the expression "in cruce" added.[47] The verse text contains a quotation from Ps. 93:1–2: "The Lord is the God to whom revenge belongs." The focus of this responsory is entirely placed upon the evil people, those responsible for the crucifixion, and forms a parallel to the condemnation of those who kill Christ, particularly as in the Gospel of John.

Responsory 9, *Vir iste in populo suo mitissimus apparuit* ("This man appeared as the mildest within his people"), offers a liturgical formula often adapted for a martyred saint, and reflects as well the Christlike state of those who die for the faith. It is not surprising that this responsory is sung also on the feast of St. Stephen—parts of it are adapted from his story in Acts—and for St. Otmar. The text is a biblical mosaic, a text in praise of the saint, which concentrates upon his holiness and prayers.[48] Although a standard type, this particular text has special resonance within the Andrew Office.

Responsory 10, "The Lord loved Andrew in the odor of sweetness. When he (Andrew) hung on the cross, he (the Lord) found him worthy of being his martyr, whom he called (to be) an apostle when he was at the sea; and therefore he was called God's friend." The beginning of this text figures as an alleluia verse in the Mass of St. Andrew, but not in the manuscripts edited in *AMS* (CT 2:39). It is possible that the alleluia verse was modeled upon this Office responsory. The text is a pastiche of biblical quotations, and has allusions both to the Lord's calling of his apostles at the sea and to the crucifixion, both of Jesus and of Andrew.[49] The short text contains six verbs, starting with one, "dilexit"; the next two verbs refer to his death; thereafter follow two verbs for the calling at the sea and, finally, the summation: therefore he was called God's friend.

Responsory 11, "The blessed Andrew cried out from the cross, saying: Lord Jesus Christ, do not let me be released from this cross, if you do not first receive my spirit," is almost a quotation from the *Acta* (p. 33, 1–3), but most words are slightly changed. The words *beatus Andreas* instead of *sanctus Andreas* are a *variatio sermonis,* the words *de cruce* having been added before *clamabat dicens* so that *de cruce* figures twice in this short piece. The passage from the *Acta*, "if you do not first receive my spirit" (*nisi prius accipias spiritum meum*) reflects of course the words of Jesus on the cross, *In manus tuas domine commendo spiritum meum* (Luke 23:46; Ps. 30:6). This expression is also the second half of the following verse, "Since you are my protector" (*Quoniam tu es protector meus*), whose first half is a psalm quotation (Ps. 30:5). The biblical character is also emphasized through the first verse *Domine exaudi* (Ps. 101:2).

Responsory 12 is formed from different parts of the *Acta*. After the liturgical presentation, *Beatus Andreas,* follows the moment when he sees the cross (p. 24, 8 ff.) and greets it, asking the Lord to receive him, his disciple (p. 25, 8 ff.), combined with the moment when he refuses to be taken down from the cross (p. 29, 5 ff.).[50] But words are added that do not belong to the *Acta* text: "with pure heart" (*mundo corde*), a biblical expression (Ps. 23:4; Matt. 5:8) or *laetus pergo ad te,* which is a reworking of *gaudens venio ad te,* "joyful I come to you" (p. 25, 5–6). And *secretum (crucis)* might reflect the *mysterium crucis* that figures many times in the conversation between St. Andrew and his judge Aegeas. The verse (*Vidit crucem . . .*) *Suscipe sancta crux* is a nonliteral reworking of the *Acta* (p. 125, 5 ff.).

Responsory 13 contains the same theme as the previous one: Andrew sees the cross, greets it, and asks it to receive him as it received his Master. The text is a quotation from the *Passio* (*BHL* 429): "Salve crux quae diu fatigata" (variant *fatigare*) "requiescis expectans me. Certissime enim scio te gaudere suscipiens discipulum eius . . ." (*An. Boll.,* p. 376, ll. 3–5) ("Hail cross, who for a long time has been waiting vexed, expecting me. I know for sure that you enjoy receiving His disciple . . .").[51] This is one of the strongest cross expressions in this office: here the cross is totally personified, literally suffering in its waiting for St. Andrew. The phrase appearing in the *Acta,* "suscipias me discipulum eius qui pependit in te" (p. 25, 6) ("receive me, the disciple of Him who hanged on you") is reflected in the verse.

The words of responsory 14, once more a hailing of the cross, have already been used in previous pieces, especially in responsory 6 (with its verse) and 7; the text is a faithful quotation from the *Acta* (p. 24, 8–25, 2; 6).

Responsory 15 echoes the *Acta:* "(quia iam secunda die) in cruce positus veritatem praedicare non cessat" (p. 29, 2–3) "(since, already the second day) put on the cross, he does not cease to preach the truth", combined with an expression coming just before: "Interea vadit omnis populus cum clamore ad domum Aegeae; omnes pariter clamantes dicebant: virum sanctum, pudicum, ornatum moribus . . . non debere hoc pati" (p. 28, 1–3; 29, 1) ("Meanwhile all the people come with shouts to Aegeas' house; all together they said crying out: the holy man, chaste, decorated with good morals, should not suffer this"). Although a free paraphrase, the text follows rather closely the events and the utterances of the *Acta.* The verse is distorted and, as far as I can discern, without direct models, although *praedicare verbum Dei die ac nocte* has biblical parallels (Acts 13:5; 1 Thess. 2:9). "That also we will be worthy of a fatherland and that every fatherland might have peace, I was sent to preach in all (fatherlands), so that those being righteous in their hearts might know the secrets of my Lord's cross."[52] The theme of peace and of *patria* are unique to this responsory.[53]

The last responsory, 16, which has the same contents as 12 and 13, is particularly focused upon the cross. Two parallel participles: *Videns crucem Andreas exclamavit dicens* ("Seeing the cross, Andrew exclaimed, saying") correspond to the introduction of the verse, *Vivens pendebat* ("he hung alive upon the cross").[54] These participles and also the verbs in the imperfect (*pendebat* and *docebat*) provide a contrasting backdrop for the exclamation with its imperative forms. The words *crux admirabilis* figure in a responsory for the Exaltation of the Cross, also found in the Compiègne antiphoner (*CAO* 7264). To the "shining over the whole world" (*per totum mundum fulgida*) there are not any exact parallels in the *Acta*, but it could point to the famous cross hymn *Vexilla regis* by Fortunatus, *arbor decora et fulgida* (Walpole, *Early*, no. 34, 17).

Observations made concerning the texts of the sixteen responsories in Office A can be summarized as follows:

1. The presentation of responsories is irregular: a verse may be omitted, or repeated as an incipit, or doubled. The linguistic state of many texts is quite poor.

2. The same topic is treated in several ways in two or sometimes in even more responsories, and the same words and expressions are frequently repeated.

3. Both narrative elements in the third person and direct speech, in the first person, with invocations, are found; shifts in person may occur in the same piece. Two ways of beginning a responsory and a verse predominate: either a verb or a "liturgical presentation," the latter referring to the type *Beatus Andreas, Vir iste,* etc. There is also frequent variation between present and past tense.

4. The majority of the responsories have a highly rhetorical style.

5. Although the many responsories treating the crucifixion of St. Andrew are drawn from or inspired by the *Acta,* there are both whole pieces derived from Scripture, and a number of singular biblical expressions and allusions.

6. The most important feature of these texts is the clearly dominating theme of the cross, figuring in twelve of sixteen responsories, in some of them more than once.

7. Comparison with the *Acta* shows that the dialogue between the apostle and his judge, comprised of very long speeches, was not used for these liturgical texts. This means that the whole beginning of the *Acta* is absent from the chants of the Office. Instead, expressions referring to the cross were those deemed appropriate for liturgical use.

Other Chant Texts and Their Relationships to the Responsories

The five Lauds antiphons

The first of the five Lauds antiphons, *Salve crux,* repeats in a shorter form the cross texts of the responsories (resp. 7, 12, 14). The second presents the same theme, although in a slightly different form: "The blessed Andrew prayed, saying: 'Lord, king of eternal glory, receive me, hanging on the cross.'" The expression "domine rex aeterne gloriae" (frequent in various liturgical genres and originally found in Ps. 23:10, as well as in the Te deum) and *pendentem in patibulo* (with its alliteration) do not figure in the *Acta,* although the words *crucis patibulum* occur there. The use of these expressions intensifies the liturgical character of the texts, as has been shown earlier: there is a particular language found in the liturgy. The third antiphon, *Andreas Christi famulus,* "Andrew, Christ's servant, God's worthy apostle, brother of Peter and companion in suffering," seems to be a fragmentary imitation of iambic dimeter, a case found also in a text for St. Benedict: *Benedictus Dei famulus / magnum fecit miraculum* ("Benedict, God's servant, worked a great miracle").[55]

The fourth antiphon is the only text in the entire Office to mention Maximilla. She was, according to the *Acta,* the wife of the proconsul Aegeas, one of the most important of the followers of St. Andrew, and among those who buried the apostle. The text of this antiphon contains one expression borrowed from the *Passio,* namely *optimo in loco sepelivit.*[56] The fifth antiphon is without any concrete model, as far as could be determined. There might be some slight reminiscences of Wisd. of Sol. 10:19 and Matt. 5:10. The words *in ligno crucis* "in the wood of the cross" are added before the biblical words *dux iusti fuisti,* "you were the leader of the righteous." The antiphons of Lauds contain nothing concerning Andrew's early calling, however; they come the closest to a traditional *historia:* the first two describe the situation before the cross, the third sums up the significance of martyrdom, the fourth treats the burial, and the fifth and the last antiphon denounces the evil man responsible for the apostle's death.

The eighteen antiphons for the Benedictus

The pattern formed by the eighteen antiphons for Benedictus is not unlike the responsories treated above.[57] The first one, *Unus ex duobus,* is a slightly reworked version of John 1:40 and states simply, without any rhetorical flourishes, that Andreas followed the Lord. The second one, *Christus me misit,* quotes the place in the *Acta* where, in the dialogue with the judge, Aegeas, Andrew mentions his missionary success (*Acta,* p. 19, 6–7). The third and fourth antiphons, depicting Andrew on the cross, are also taken from the *Acta,* containing variations upon the words of responsories 4 and 15. In the third, however, appears an expression from the *Acta,* here used only in this text, "It is time that you commend my body to the earth" (*Acta,* p. 33, app. crit.). The fourth antiphon text is very simple:

> Biduo vivens
> pendebat in cruce
> pro Christi nomine
> beatus Andreas
> et docebat populum.

"Living two days, he hung on the cross, for Christ's name, the blessed Andrew, and taught the people." The text is constructed out of small units, each one containing five to seven syllables, with *pro Christi nomine* figuring predominantly in the middle.[58]

The fifth antiphon is a shortened form of responsory 10:

Responsory 10	Antiphon 5
Dilexit Andream dominus in odorem suavitatis. Dum penderet in cruce dignum sibi computavit martyrem quem vocavit apostolum dum esset in mari	 Dignum sibi dominus computavit martyrem quem vocavit apostolum dum esset in mari alleluia

"The Lord loved Andrew in the odor of sweetness. When he hung on the cross, he judged him worthy as a martyr, him whom he called as an apostle when he was in the sea." The sixth antiphon belongs to a category not encountered so far, constituting a direct prayer to the saint.[59] The seventh antiphon has the same theme as the second, missionary work, and also echoes literally the antiphon *Benedictus dei famulus / magnum fecit miraculum:* "Andreas apostolus domini magnum operatus est miraculum" ("the Lord's apostle Andrew worked a great miracle").[60]

Dixit Andreas, antiphon 8, presents a quotation from the Gospel (John 1:41–42), and is in fact an important text since it mirrors the words of Andrew to his brother Simon: "We have found the Messiah." Antiphon 9, *Videns Andreas,* is basically the same as responsory 12 and 16, Andrew seeing the cross and expressing his love for it ("I have always been your lover"). Antiphons 10–12 are all about the calling at the sea, and are similar in function to the first three responsories. Antiphon 13 is the same as the first part of responsory 10, *Dilexit Andream,* followed by an alleluia. Antiphon 14 is exactly the same as the verse of responsory 6, and antiphon 15 as the last part of this same responsory: both are greetings to the cross and taken from the *Acta.*

Antiphon 16 contains expressions similar to those found in responsory 4:

Responsory 4	Antiphon 16
Oravit sanctus Andreas, dum respiceret caelum, voce magna clamavit et dixit: tu es Deus meus, quem vidi; ne me patiaris ab impio iudice deponi, quia virtutem sanctae crucis agnovi. V Tu es magister meus, Christe, quem dilexi, quem cognovi . . .	 Tu es deus meus, in quo complacui et dilexi, quia virtutem sanctae crucis agnovi.

"St. Andrew prayed while he looked up to heaven, cried with a loud voice, and said: 'You are my God whom I have seen, do not permit me to be taken down by the impious judge, since I know the power of the holy cross. V. You are my master, Christ, whom I loved, whom I recognized. . . .'" Antiphons 17 and 18, concern Christ's calling at the sea, and are biblical; both texts parallel the first responsory, *Dum perambularet.*

The eighteen antiphons to be used for Benedictus constitute a veritable florilegium. Half of them contain the name Andrew or the title *apostolus:* these reiterate the specific character of the apostle's feast. Present as well is a kaleidoscopic panorama of speech: utterings in the first person, statements in the third, one direct prayer to the saint, one short, partly versified piece, eight texts commencing with a verb, some followed by alleluia. Yet none of these antiphon texts is directly related to the text of the Benedictus canticle itself, Zachary's proclamation of recognition.

The five antiphons of Second Vespers

The five antiphons of Second Vespers are of a different character than those for Lauds: all are biblical, made up of verses from the psalms they accompany. All these psalms, as well as the antiphons, are often used in saints' feasts, particularly for apostles, forming a traditional common stock, any of which may be adapted readily to apostles' feasts.[61] The antiphon for the Magnificat, *Concede,* contains the expression from the *Passio:* "Concede nobis hominem iustum, redde nobis hominem sanctum, ne interficias hominem deo carum . . . mansuetum et pium" (*An. Boll.,* 376–77, l. 25–1), but is also a paraphrase of a passage in the *Acta* (p. 24, 4–5; 28, 2–3) where the people ask that the righteous man not be delivered. Above all, *iustum, sanctum, carum, mansuetum et pium* are all honoring words, figuring in the Bible and added to the antiphon text to lend a scriptural character. Finally, in Off. B, all the texts are the same as those also appearing in Off. A, with two exceptions: (1) the invitatory, *Regem apostolorum,* which belongs to the common stock of invitatories (*CAO* 1125), in the Compiègne book also figuring in the office of St. Peter; and (2) the Benedictus antiphon *Ego si patibulum crucis,* a refined text with its chiastic parallelism *patibulum crucis / crucis gloriam,* its parallel and opposing verbs, and its strong beginning, *Ego.*

The Antiphons and Their Psalms

Office B allows for exploration of a subtly difficult and elusive subject, the relationship of antiphon texts to psalmody in general, and here, to the particular psalms assumed to be present for accompaniment by the particular antiphons in question. These antiphons were selected and arranged from the stock of various Andrew antiphons already studied above, and they were combined with a rather limited number of psalms suitable for the feast of an apostle. Are there discernible principles being followed in such work?

The first three antiphons in the first nocturn are all narrative, biblical, and very simple. The first one, *Vidit Dominus Petrum et Andream et vocavit eos* ("The Lord saw Peter and Andrew and called them"), is without any ornamentation whatsoever. The psalm *Caeli enarrant* (18), concerning God's power and glory, also contains a passage concerning God's law, testimony, and justice: "Lex domini immaculata convertens animas, testimonium domini fidele, sapientiam praestans parvulis . . ." (8; "The law of the Lord is unspotted, the testimony of the Lord is faithful, giving wisdom to little ones"); "Etenim servus tuus custodit ea" (12; "For your servant keeps them"), which suits the text of the antiphon well. The second antiphon is a direct address: *Venite post me, dicit dominus, faciam vos fieri piscatores hominum* ("Come after me, I will make you fishers of men"), and its psalm is *Benedicam dominum* (33). The psalm contains the same expression, "venite (filii, audite me)" (12), but the different themes in the psalm are about God's help and support, about the pious who will be blessed and liberated from evil. The third antiphon, *Relictis retibus suis secuti sunt dominum Iesum Christum* ("They left their nets and followed the Lord Jesus Christ"), would have been sung with Ps. 44, *Eructavit,* which was commonly employed for feasts of apostles and martyrs through verse 17: "Constitues eos principes super omnem terram" ("You shall make them princes over all the earth"). It is a psalm interpreted in a messianic way: the bridegroom and hero is Christ, and all follow him, "Memores erunt nominis tui in omni generatione et generationem" (18; "They shall remember your name throughout all generations").

In the second nocturn the two first antiphons are about God's love for his apostle. The first one, *Dilexit Andream in odorem suavitatis, alleluia* ("He loved Andrew in the odor of sweetness"), belongs to the psalm *Omnes gentes* (46), which has been sung at the apostles' feasts mostly because of verse 10: "Principes populorum congregati sunt" ("The princes of the people are gathered together"). Above all, it is a text of praise. In this case, a literal echo is heard in verse 5: "Elegit nobis hereditatem suam, speciem Iacob quam dilexit" ("He has chosen for us his inheritance, the beauty of Jacob which he has loved"). The second antiphon in this nocturn consists of *Dignum sibi dominus computavit martyrem quem vocavit apostolus dum esset in mari* ("The Lord judged him worthy as his martyr, whom he called as an apostle when he was at the sea"), used for Ps. 60, *Exaudi Deus deprecationem.* The connection here to the antiphon, dealing with the vocation of the apostle, would particularly concern the expressions "factus es spes mea, turris fortitudinis" (4; "for you have been my hope; a tower of strength") and "dedisti hereditatem timentibus nomen tuum" (6; "you have given an inheritance to those who fear your name"). The third and last antiphon in this nocturn is a greeting to the cross, *Salve crux.* That the psalm *Exaudi Deus orationem meam* (63) belongs to the apostles' feasts is surely due to its verse 10: "Et annuntiaverunt opera Dei et facta eius intellexerunt" ("And they declared the works of God and understood his doings"). However, the linking of the cross antiphon *Salve crux* and this psalm is prepared by the use of the psalm for the passion of Christ. The laments about evil things and the prayer for God's protection are well suited to the cross theme.

The first antiphon of the third nocturn, *Accipe me,* is an address to the cross; the psalm *Confitebimur* (74) treats the theme of God the judge. The connection is not immediate, and the same can also be said about the antiphon *Tu es deus meus* and psalm *Fundamenta* (86), which praises Jerusalem. The last antiphon, *Non me permittas,* and the psalm *Dominus regnavit* (98) seem to fit well together, the close relationship between the Lord and his servants being the main theme.

Is it really worth trying to see connections between these antiphons and the psalms we can suppose they were sung with in the Office? Only a certain number of psalms were possible to use at an apostle's feast, and the number of antiphons is also restricted. However, when we compare all antiphons figuring in Off. A with those nine selected out for the three nocturns and the nine psalms in Off. B, it seems that some adaptation took place. Although it would not be possible to make sweeping claims, nonetheless there seems to be an intelligence behind the process. I have also tried to see whether the choice of antiphons has been directed to fit the psalms of Lauds; however, this seems not to be the case.[62] On the other hand, the fact that the Lauds psalms of every feast Office were the same could be a reason to contrast these solemn psalms of praise to antiphon texts, which reveal specific events about the saint celebrated. This same mode of expression has been observed in other Offices besides the one for St. Andrew.

Sources and Liturgical Pieces of the Andrew Office

As already been shown, the same sources have been used to generate a large number of pieces for this Office, many of which overlap and restate each other. It is crucial to be aware of this process of restatement to understand the St. Andrew Office, and the texts for other Offices as well: this process of restatement is how the Bible and other sources were learned and ruminated in the liturgy during the Middle Ages. The following examples are offered to demonstrate the various forms this "art of restatement" took.

Source

(Iesus) ambulans autem iuxta mare Galilaeae vidit duos fratres, Simonem, qui vocatur Petrus, et Andream, fratrem eius, mittentes rete in mare; erant enim piscatores. Et ait illis: venite post me et faciam vos fieri piscatores hominum, at illi continuo relictis retibus secuti sunt eum (Matt. 4:18–20).

Liturgical pieces

A   Venite post me, faciam vos piscatores hominum. (*CAO* 5357)

R   Dum perambularet dominus supra mare secus litus Galileae, vidit Petrum et Andream retia mittentes et in mare vocavit eos dicentes: venite post me, faciam vos fieri piscatores hominum. (*CAO* 6554)

R   Venite post me, faciam vos piscatores hominum; at illi relictis retibus secuti sunt dominum.

V   Dum perambularet dominus supra mare secus litus Galileae, vidit duos fratres Petrum et Andream et vocavit eos. (*CAO* 7835)

R   Mox ut vocem . . . relictis retibus . . .

V   Ad unius iussionis vocem Petrus et Andreas relictis retibus secuti sunt redemptorem. (CAO *7182*)

A   Unus ex duobus, qui secuti sunt dominum, erat Andreas Simonis Petri. (*CAO* 5279)

A   Continuo relictis retibus et patre secuti sunt salvatorem. (*CAO* 1908)

A   Vidit dominus Petrum et Andream et vocavit eos. (*CAO* 5413)

A   Relictis retibus suis secuti sunt dominum Iesum Christum. (*CAO* 4607)

A   Dum perambularet dominus supra mare secus litus Galileae. (*CAO* 2464)

A   Venite post me, dicit dominus, faciam vos fieri piscatores hominum. (*CAO* 5357)

If we count the responsory verses as separate items, no fewer than twelve pieces are made out of these three Gospel verses. Everything from the source is present somewhere, but various words are added as well, and the source text is steadily reshaped and changed. The expression "relictis retibus" is repeated in these pieces five times. If all texts were sung in one feast, this expression would have been strongly emphasized.

Source

Cumque pervenisset ad locum, ubi crux parata erat, videns eam a longe exclamavit voce magna dicens: Salve crux (pretiosa), quae in corpore Christi dedicata es, et ex membrorum eius margaritis ornata. (*Acta*, p. 24, 7–25, 2.)

. . . gaudens venio ad te, ita ut et tu exultans suscipias me, discipulum eius, qui pependit in te, quia amator tuus semper fui et desideravi amplecti te. O bona crux, quae decorem et pulcritudinem de membris domini suscepisti, diu desiderata, sollicite amata . . . accipe me ab hominibus et redde me magistro meo, ut per te me recipiat, qui per te me redemit. (*Acta*, p. 25, 5–26, 1; cf. app. crit.)

Liturgical pieces

R 6   O bona crux quae decorem et pulchritudinem de membris domini suscepisti. Accipe me ab hominibus et redde magistro meo, ut per te me recipiat, qui per te me redemit.

V   Salve crux, quae in corpore Christi dedicata es, et ex membris eius tanquam margaretis ornata. (*CAO* 7260)

R 7   . . . ducitur ad crucem, aspiciens a longe vidit crucem . . . (*CAO* 6484)

R 12   . . . vidit crucem, exclamavit ad eam: suscipe discipulum eius, qui pependit in te, quem vidi, quem amavi, quem secutus sum . . .

V   Vidit crucem Andreas, exclamavit et dixit: suscipe, beata crux, humilem propter dominum, suscipe discipulum eius. (*CAO* 6196)

R 13   Cum videret beatus Andreas crucem, exclamavit et dixit: Salve crux
         . . .

V   Suscipe, beata crux, humilem propter dominum, suscipe discipulum
        eius qui pependit in te. (*CAO* 6376)

R 14   Salve crux, quae in corpore Christi dedicata es, et ex membris eius
        tanquam margaretis ornata es, suscipe discipulum eius, qui pependit
        in te.

V   Salve crux pretiosa, suscipe discipulum eius, qui pependit in te,
        magister meus Christus. (*CAO* 7563)

R 16   Videns crucem Andreas exclamavit dicens: O crux admirabilis, o
        crux, quae per totum mundum fulgida es, suscipe discipulum
        Christi. (*CAO* 7855)

A   Salve crux pretiosa, suscipe discipulum eius, qui pependit in te,
        magister meus Christus. (*CAO* 4693)

A   Beatus Andreas . . . suscipe me pendentem in patibulo . . . (*CAO*
        1610)

A   Videns Andreas crucem cum gaudio dicebat, quia amator tuus sem-
        per fui et desideravi. (*CAO* 5383)

A   Salve crux, quae in corpore Christi dedicata es et ex membris eius
        tanquam margaretis ornata. (*CAO* 4694)

A   Recipe me ab hominibus et redde me magistro meo, ut per te me
        recipiat qui per te me redemit. (*CAO* 4575)

The *Acta* text is sometimes changed to the extent that only the main idea remains, not the literal expression (cf. Berschin 1986–91, 1:88–94). There might also
have been other versions of the *Acta* that have played a role in the literal stock of
texts composed for this Office. Nevertheless, it is obvious how much a rather restricted number of words, expressions, and ideas from the *Acta* model are repeated
in these liturgical texts.

Conclusions

The Office of St. Andrew is not a "historia," presenting in a logical order of events
the life of the saint. Rather the texts develop a consistent focus upon two themes:
the vocation of the apostle, drawn from the biblical source, and the martyrdom,
namely the crucifixion, of the apostle, as told in the apocryphal *Acta*. Only one
text mentions his missionary activity and another what happened after his death,
but no miracles whatsoever are mentioned (cf. Berschin 1986–91, 1:88–94). Only
one text is a prayer of intercession. A number of texts are psalm quotations.

    Several texts are identical or similar. The same passage from the Gospel or from
the *Acta* has been repeated or reworked in different ways. When the melodies of
similar texts in later books containing the musical notation are compared, the tendency is that all these similar texts have different melodies. The melodies are

strictly bound to their genres, whether these are responsories, verses, or antiphons, or relate to the modes and their specific formulas (cf. Berschin 1986–91, 1:88–94).

Like other saints' offices in the Compiègne book, that of St. Andrew contains a number of formulas belonging to the genre of "liturgical presentations." The beginning of a piece is important, and so is the repetition of the saint's name.[63]

Two connected phenomena dominate the Office, the relation between the apostle Andrew and his Master and the role of the cross. Again and again the words of "the nets left behind" (*relictis retibus*) occur. This is the beginning of an absolute following of Christ, the scene where Andrew just drops what he has in his hands to accept the call of Christ. The opposite pole of this following of Christ is the end of his life, his martyrdom. St. Andrew greets the cross, praises it, shows frustration and disappointment when the people almost succeed in getting him released from it, insists on being fastened to it, and preaches for two days while hanging on it. The word "cross" figures in the majority of pieces, often as the subject.[64]

A comparison with the Peter Office in the same source (fols. 68–69v) permits the following observations: All the vigil antiphons in the St. Peter Office are taken from their psalms. In the texts a great number of biblical passages have been used, many of which underline the position of Peter as the shepherd of souls and the rock of the church; also texts from the Acts are used. The vocation at the sea is mentioned only in the responsory *Simon Petre, antequam de navi vocarem te, novi te* (*CAO* 7674) ("Simon Peter, before I called you from the ship, I knew you"). A few pieces have nonbiblical sources, among them the famous *Domine, quo vadis* (the antiphon of First Vespers) and the three last antiphons for Benedictus, taken from the Apocrypha:

> *Cum respexisset Petrus crucem, lacrymas fundebat prae gaudio. Non sum dignus.* (*CAO* 2030; "When Peter had seen the cross, he shed tears in joy. I am not worthy.")

> *Petrus et Paulus militantes Romam venerunt. Circumdantes Simonem invenerunt cum Nerone. Fidem permanserunt Salvatorem.* (*CAO* 4288; "Peter and Paul came fighting to Rome. Surrounding they found Simon with Nero. They remained in faith with the Redeemer." The text defective, as so often in the Compiègne manuscript.)

> *Beatus Petrus, dum penderet in cruce, alacri vultu dominum deprecabat: Domine Iesu Christe, commendo tibi oves quas tradidisti mihi.* (*CAO* 1657; "The blessed Peter prayed with happy face to the Lord while he hung on the cross: Lord Jesus Christ, I commend to you the sheep that you entrusted to me.")

These texts have clear parallels with those in the Office of St. Andrew: the joy before the cross and the speech from the cross. There are even literal concordances. What in the Peter Office occupies a small part, is, however, much more developed in the Andrew Office. The purpose must have been to create bonds between the Prince of the Apostles and his brother, to give some of the glory of Peter also to Andrew. It should also be remembered that St. Peter is mentioned three times in the Office for St. Andrew.

The office of the Exaltation of the Cross (14 Sept.) also contains a number of pieces similar to the Andrew texts (cf. p. 00 above), together with texts from the story of how Helena, Constantine's mother, found the cross, and, to a similar degree, with strophes from Fortunatus' cross hymns:

> *O crux benedicta . . . (CAO 7265)*
> *O crux gloriosa, o crux adoranda (CAO 7266)*
> *O crux admirabilis . . .*
> V *O laudabilis crux . . . (CAO 7264)*
> *Super omnia ligna cedrorum, tu sola excelsior, in qua vita mundi pependit, in*
>   *qua Christus triumphavit, et mors mortem superavit (CAO 5061; cf. 7724,*
>   "Above all cedar trees, only you are more elevated, on which the life of the
>   world hung, in which Christ triumphed and death conquered death.")
> *Crucem tuam adoramus . . . (CAO 1952–53)*

If a relationship between the legend of the finding of the cross and the apocryphal Acts of St. Andrew exists, it is a subtle one, and hard to discern. It does seem, however, that there are at least connections between the liturgy of the cross and the liturgy of St. Andrew. The cross theme strengthens the celebration of both feasts. It also lends a unique character to the feast of St. Andrew when compared to other apostles' feasts, making it almost another cross feast. The intimate relation between St. Andrew and the cross, finally, makes him a follower of Jesus in a special way.[65]

With its combination of biblical and legendary material, the Andrew Office stands between the many great feasts of biblical saints, the Virgin Mary, John the Baptist, the Apostle Peter, and local saints, whose Offices depended upon later materials. Of primary importance here is the ways in which a clear liturgical theme, that of the cross, is emphasized in rhetorical form. Most of the items contained in the Compiègne book were later used in all Latin Office books, although a few responsories and antiphons did not survive. However, the material has usually been organized in other ways, as can easily be seen from the *CAO*.

The repetitions, the variants, and the confused organization of the pieces in the Office of St. Andrew as it appears in the Compiègne book give a hint of a culture where not all liturgical texts were written down. It seems quite probable that what is offered in this luxurious liturgical book, perhaps compiled for a king, mirrors a reality of formulas, of ideas, of expressions prepared for a process of reformulation, of expansion, of truncation, and of variance, according to the cantor's will and ability. Later the pieces were stabilized and their order standardized, but the shapes of the texts in the Compiègne manuscript offer evidence from before the process had firmly taken hold. Thus the book is a unique key to understanding how liturgies were made in the Latin Middle Ages, and to the great accomplishment and talent exibited by those—for the most part—unnamed individuals who created new liturgical texts for the Office from the Bible and many other sources, always with a sophisticated understanding of their contexts.

Appendix: The Authorship of the Office

The Office of St. Andrew, as it appears in the Codex Hartker, has been attributed by Walter Berschin to Ekkehart I of St. Gall, "the Deacon" (d. 973), a writer of liturgical texts (Berschin 1981, 13–47). The reason is a passage from Ekkehart IV (d. around 1060) in his chronicle *Casus S. Galli* (chap. 80): "Scripsit enim doctus ille . . . antiphonas 'Ambulans Hiesus,' 'Adoremus gloriosissimum.'" ("Then this learned man wrote the antiphons . . . .") Berschin thinks that these two incipits refer to the whole Office, which he edits from the Hartker Codex as a creation of Ekkehard I. However, it is clear that only the two antiphons mentioned above, those found in the beginning of the Office, and the last piece, the antiphon *in evangelio* for Second Vespers (Magnificat), *Cum pervenisset beatus Andreas,* are not already present in the Compiègne book. Ekkehard I lived between 910 and 973, and the Compiègne book was written before 877 (Notker of St. Gall, *Notker,* 1:439–40). The entire Andrew Office is at least 60 years older, probably even much older than the time of its recording in Compiègne.[66] However, Ekkehard IV may well be revealing accurate information. The pieces mentioned by him do not occur in Compiègne, and, therefore, might very well have been composed by Ekkehard I himself.[67] In his analysis Berschin emphasizes what in the *Acta* was *not* used in the Office: "nichts von der typisch apokryphen Staffage des Apostellebens . . . sondern allein der ergreifende Ausdruck der Kreuzesmystik" (Berschin 1981, 22). The *mysterium crucis* has, however, a dominant place in the whole *Acta,* and the word *crux* occurs there more than 30 times.

David Hiley chose the 30 November Office of St. Andrew to demonstrate ways in which the comparison of the order of responsories may allow scholars to trace the origin of a manuscript. He thus shows that the Office in the antiphoner of Saint-Denis is identical with that of the book of Mont-Renaud (Hiley 1993, 337–38). However, not one but two responsory lists could have been extracted from the Compiègne book, the 30 November Office (Off. B) but also the Office recorded earlier (Off. A), which would show that the same pieces have a different ordering in the same source. At present, more work needs to be done in trying to trace the affiliations of these two Offices with other sources or family of sources.

Finally, there is a curious piece of information in a manuscript containing the translation of the body of St. Cyricus from Nevers to Saint-Amand (Paris, BNF lat. 2717): four compositions, attributed to Hucbald of Saint-Amand, are mentioned. One of them is *de S. Andrea modulamen antiphonarum.* Rembert Weakland states briefly that "since no further clues are given by the author," we have no possibility of identifying these antiphons. Hucbald of Saint-Amand was born not earlier than 840. While theoretically possible, it seems unlikely that he is the author of the Compiègne Office.[68]

The name of the person—or perhaps the persons—who composed the Office for St. Andrew, or rather, the many different antiphons and responsories, variously arranged in the various liturgical books, as is the case for most early Offices, is apparently not recoverable.[69]

Notes

1. The literary shape of these chant texts—and their musical forms as well—remain unknown until the first surviving written sources. In many cases, it is clear that the texts are much older than the dates of the early sources. How old they might be has been discussed by many scholars, including Hourlier (1973) and Hucke (1973), who refer to early layers dating from the fifth century.

2. In Huglo (1993a) and Jeffery (1995) there is both a good overview of the most important bibliography concerning the manuscript and the most recent opinions regarding date, origin, destination, and provenance. See also Steiner (1986).

3. It is also possible to find witnesses to some early Office chants through tonaries predating the first liturgical sources. Cf. Huglo (1971).

4. For the office of St. Vedast, see Brou (1961), and for the office of St. Médard, Jonsson (1968), 54–63.

5. The office of John the Baptist is biblical, just as are those of St. Paul, containing mostly material from the Epistles, and that of St. Michael, where texts from the Psalms and from the book of Revelation predominate.

6. The libretto-like quality of certain chant texts is discussed in Levy (1984).

7. The Compiègne book is not the only one where an elegant script and decoration are matched by a poor text. Another example is the Cotton Caligula Troper (London, BL Cotton Caligula 14). Cf. Teviotdale (1991) and Jacobsson (1993).

8. Cf. Odelman (1975) and CT 5, chapter 6, "Rubriques," 104–18.

9. Jonsson (1968), 190, 218. I have discussed the phenomenon with Michel Huglo, whom I thank for his interesting ideas. An explanation could be that the responsories were copied from at least some libelli not containing the whole office but only the responsories. The rubric might be a reference to the texts of the readings. Its appearence in the Compiègne book is probably due to some sources where this rubric is appropriate. It should be added that, in two cases, we also find the rubric "Antiphonas unde supra," for the feast of St. Médard and for the Exaltation of the Cross. Certainly sources from the period were often divided by genre. Amalarius writes two different books in the Roman use, the *responsoriale* containing responsories and the *antiphonale* containing antiphons. However, this would not fully explain the arrangement in Compiègne, compiled as it was from so many sources. See Amalarius, *Prologus antiphonarii* 18 (*Opera* 1:363, l. 26 ff.): ". . . apud Romanos: . . . Pars quae continet responsorios, vocatur responsoriale, et pars quae continet antiphonas, vocatur antiphonarius. Ego secutus sum nostrum usum et posui mixtim responsoria et antiphonas secundum ordinem temporum, in quibus sollemnitates nostrae celebrantur."

10. See, e.g., fols. 24–25v, 44, 44v, 62v, 63, 63v, 65v, 76v, 77, 78v, 79, and following.

11. St. Gall, SB 390–391, "Hartker antiphonary" (PM II/1); *Le Manuscrit du Mont-Renaud* (PM 16).

12. Hiley (1993), 337–38; see also Möller, *Das Quedlinburger Antiphonar, passim.*

13. Dom Hesbert had no doubts: in the preface to *CAO* 1 he claimed "pure distraction" for the scribe. When the scribe discovered that he had written the office at the wrong place, that is before St. Cecilia (22 November) and St. Clement (23 November), he simply wrote it down once more, on the correct day, 30 November. In the edition of the Maurists, the explanation is that there were perhaps two days, *unus ob martyrium, alter propter corporis translationem* ("the one for the martyrdom, the other for the translation of the body"); PL 78, 817, n. a. (In the year 1705, the Maurists had included both the gradual and the antiphoner from Paris 17436 among the works of Gregory the Great, and their edition was reprinted by Migne.)

14. However, it should be noted that the Antiphonary of Silos (GB:Lbl Add. 30850) from the eleventh century, edited in *CAO* 2, *cursus monasticus*, also contains the office

of St. Andrew, exactly at the same place as in the first copying of the Compiègne codex, that is "before" St. Cecilia and St. Clement, but only there, not repeated at its correct place. Dom Hesbert had no other explanation for the position of the first St. Andrew Office in Compiègne, other than random error: "Jusqu'à plus ample informé, on peut penser que la coïncidence est fortuite; il fallait pourtant la signaler." *CAO* 2, p. xix.

15. The last layer of the manuscript is now missing, but it was still there when the Maurists edited it 1705. Thus, the text now missing can be supplied through PL 78, col. 709, but not through the *AMS,* where it is marked as a lacuna. Cf. Froger (1980), 338 and Huglo (1993a).

16. Various older calendars and other liturgical books examined did not show any trace whatsoever of a St. Andrew feast in November *before* the 29th. The only information given by Amalarius is that there are double night offices, a tradition he adopted in his antiphoner. Amalarius Ant 63 (*LO* 3:98): "In vigilia S. Andreae inveni, ut supra, duplicia nocturnalia, quod secutus sum in nostro antiphonario."

17. There is, in fact, one example in the Compiègne book of an office where the majority of pieces consist only of incipits, namely the feast of All Saints, fol. 82. Instead of the specific antiphons and responsories for this feast, figuring in the later manuscripts, the Compiègne book, representing an earlier stage, offers mainly pieces already used in various other feasts. Many of these are biblical, particularly the antiphons. But nonbiblical texts also appear. In fact, it is a mosaic, a selection of texts from the feasts of the Blessed Virgin, of martyrs and virgins, of apostles and confessors, and even one antiphon addressing the sacred Trinity is represented: *Te trina deitas,* the doxology of the hymn *Sanctorum meritis* (*CAO* 5125). Since most of the texts are presented only as incipits, it means that for the celebration, the antiphons or the responsories must be found in several different places throughout the book. In the Andrew office, the few pieces presented as incipits refer only to texts figuring in the same feast. Above all, no incipit in Office B refers to a text existing only in Office A.

18. This arrangement has at least one similar case, for the feast of the Assumption (fol. 73).

19. The antiphons *Respice ab hominibus* and *Accipe me ab hominibus* are one and the same although the incipits are different.

20. Resp. 11 and 12 and ant. *Sancte Andreas, Dixit Andreas,* and *Continuo relictis.*

21. An overview concerning literature and editions of the Apostles' legends is given by Berschin (1986–91), 1:88 ff.

22. For the development of the Andrew cult, see particularly Dvornik (1958), 138–80.

23. *BHL* 430–32; see MGH, *Scriptores rerum Merovingicarum* (1884), I, 1, pp. 821–46. Cf. Berschin (1986–91), 296.

24. *BHL* 428, with the incipit "Passionem sancti Andreae apostoli . . ." or "Quod oculis nostris vidimus . . ." (428a) or "Diacones ecclesiarum Achaiae . . ." (428b). See Dvornik (1958), 181–223. Another fragmentary Latin Passion is found in *BHL* 429, *Analecta Bollandiana,* 13:374–78. See also *BHL, Novum supplementum* (1986).

25. For the editions of the *Acta Andreae,* see Bonnet, *Acta.* The Latin *Acta,* as far as I know, is not represented in any more recent edition than Bonnet. The same text, however in a less good version, is also contained in Mombritius (1910).

26. See Dvornik (1958); Schneemelcher, *Neutestamentliche;* Bovon, *Les Actes,* containing the *Liber de miraculis beati Andreae apostoli* by Gregory of Tours (*BHL* 430); Flamion, *Les Actes.*

27. In the following, all the references to the *Acta* are given to pages and lines of the Bonnet edition.

28. The texts are found in *CAO* and in PL 78, cols. 813–18 (defective).

29. This quotation of Ps. 18:5 is found in the Pauline Epistles (Rom. 10: 18).

30. R1 *Dum perambularet . . . vidit Petrum et Andream*

　　Off. A *retia mittentes et in mare vocavit eos*

　　Off. B *retia mittentes in mari vocavit eos.*

Apart from the fact that the accusative and ablative (*in mare/i*) are interchangeable in this period of Latinity, the crucial problem is the word *et*. The only place where the word *et* really would fit is before *vocavit*. However, the version in Off. B is acceptable: "He saw Peter and Andrew. When they were throwing nets in the sea, he called them." The version in Off. A is most likely an error.

31. *Versio antiqua*, Sabatier, *Bibliorum*, Matt. 4:18, *cum praeteriret;* Jülicher, *Itala*, 17.

32. ". . . vidit alios duos fratres Iacobum Zebedaei et Iohannem fratrem eius in navi" (Matt. 4:21); "vidit Iacobum Zebedaei et Iohannem fratrem eius et ipsos in navi componentes retia" (Mk. 1:19).

33. Gregory the Great, *In evangelia*, 1.5 (*BHL* 428g; PL 76), col. 1093A: "ad unius iussionis vocem Petrus et Andreas relictis retibus secuti sunt redemptorem . . . nihil ab eo de praemio aeternae retributionis audierant. D: Valuit Petro et Andreae dimissis retibus et navi." See *HML*, 181 and *passim*.

34. This expression, however, offers difficulties, as can be seen from the many variants in Hesbert's edition (*CAO* 4, 7178). The best Latin solution is without doubt "aeternae vitae praemia largientem," but I think it is possible to keep this Compiègne version, "he followed the giver of the eternal life, through (or "as") a reward." If so, we must think that "praemio" belongs to "giver." Another solution is to change to the word to "praemii." Cf. Bruylants, *Les Oraisons*, no. 874: ". . . et aeternae vitae praemia largiatur."

The difficult passage already mentioned has two different versions in Off. A and Off. B:

　　A *aeternae vitae secutus est premio largitorem*

　　B *aeternae vitae secutus est premia largitori*

In the first case, the original *premia* in the manuscript was changed to *premio*, and this is also the form figuring in the repetition of the responsory after the verse. The A version is best. However, there might is a possibility that the B version simply used a dative after *sequi*. Cf. Hofmann and Szantyr 1965, II/2, p. 89. Perhaps the scribe used a model having the version *praemia largitorem*, which he changed to *premio* in order to obtain a better sense, "he followed, for a reward, the giver of the eternal life" (Off. A). In the second case, Off. B, I cannot find any sense—perhaps the scribe had *largitoris* in mind, "he followed the rewards of the giver of the eternal life." A sound rendering is found in the Hartker codex: "aeternae vite secutus est premii largitorem." Cf. Berschin (1981), 17.

35. Bonnet, *Acta*, 1–37. Observe the variants given in the apparatus criticus.

36. *confessum* MS = *confessus sum*.

37. *CAO* 4172–74; 4177–81; 4186–88; 7328–30; 7334–36.

38. "Respexit in caelum et benedixit illis" (Luke 9:16).

39. "elevatis oculis in caelum ad te deum Patrem . . ." (Canon of the Mass), Deshusses, *Le Sacramentaire*, 1:89.

40. Acts 7:55: "cum autem esset plenus spiritu sancto intendens in caelum, vidit gloriam Dei."

41. Bonnet, *Acta*, 33, app. crit. We also find the following words in different places in the *Acta* (from Bonnet: "exclamavit voce magna dicens" (p. 24, 8); "Tu es magister meus quem dilexi quem vidi" ("you are my Master whom I loved, whom I saw") (33, app. crit.); "voce magna sanctus Andreas dixit . . . iube me de ista cruce non deponi" ("let me not be taken down from this cross") (33, 1–2).

42. The words "ab impio iudice" ("by the impious judge") seem to reflect the ex-

pression "the righteous man suffers this through an impious judgment" ("iniusto iudicio sanctum virum hoc pati," p. 27, 1). Cf. Berschin (1988), 2:85.

43. Cf. e.g. Deut. 33:1; 2 Tim. 3:17; cf. also the expression "vir Dei" (*CAO* 5429–32; 7889–92), and the Italian introit, taken from the *Dialogues* of Gregory the Great, *Vir dei Benedictus;* cf. Codex 123 from the Biblioteca Angelica, Rome, fol. 56v (PM 18).

44. Responsory 5 contains a variant between the two versions of the text, and that of Off. B is less acceptable: "innocens eius sanguis sine causa dampnavit," whereas in Off. A the verb is "damnatur," with the translation, "his innocent blood has without reason been condemned."

45. Cf. the hymns by Venantius Fortunatus to the Holy Cross; Walpole, *Early,* nos. 33–35. The Office for the Holy Cross in the Compiègne book is found on fols. 76v–77v.

46. Responsory 8 contains a textual variant. In Off. B, *Expandi,* contains a "constructio ad sensum," "populum . . . qui ambulant . . ." ("a people that walks . . ."), whereas Off. A has the correct form of the verb, "ambulat."

47. "Expandi manus meas tota die ad populum incredulum, et contradicentem, qui non ambulaverunt in via bona [vias non bonas, app. crit.], sed post peccata sua." (Sabatier, *Bibliorum,* 2:631.)

48. ". . . erat enim Moses vir mitissimus super omnes homines" (Num. 12:3); "Stephanus autem plenus gratia et fortitudine" (Acts 6:8); "pro eo ut me diligerent detrahebant mihi; ego autem orabam" (Ps. 108:4).

49. "Et ambulate in dilectione sicut et Christus dilexit nos et tradidit se ipsum pro nobis oblationem et hostiam Deo in odorem suavitatis" (Eph. 5:2); the last words "in odore/m suavitatis" is a common biblical expression. Cf. also "et amicus dei appellatus est" (James 2:23).

50. "Liturgical presentation" is a technical term, used for liturgical set phrases concerning saints, such as: "Beatus vir N," or "Sanctissimus episcopus N," etc. Cf. Jonsson (1968), 60, 123, 161.

51. Responsory 13 offers more examples of variants in which Off. A has better readings than those found in Off. B: Off. A "Cum videret" and in Off. B "Cum vidisset;" Off. A "fatigaris expectans" and in Off. B "fatigaris expectas."

52. I suggest the following version: "Ut et nos mereamur patria<m> et omnis patria habe<a>t pacem, missus sum praedicare in omnibus, ut cognoscant (MS cognoscar) recti corde secreta crucis domini mei."

53. Indeed, Responsory 15 does not occur in any other of the *CAO* sources. Its verse contains a number of errors in language that are exactly the same in both versions of the Office. It seems that the source, or at least the tradition, must have been the same for the two versions.

54. Comparing the two versions of responsory 16 reveals that Off. B gives an incorrect reading with "non dimittis errare" instead of "non me dimittas errare" as found in Off. A.

55. *CAO* 1714; Jonsson (1968), 67. Cf. also a much later hymn, but which could have a model common to the Office and the hymn (*AH* 19:51).

56. See *Analecta Bollandiana,* 378, l. 5, and Bonnet, *Acta,* 36, app. crit.

57. This is true regarding variants as well, with Off. A consistently containing the better readings. "Beatus Andreas orabat" (*CAO* 1610) in Off. A contains "domine rex," whereas in B "domine" is lacking. Antiphon 1 for Benedictus, *Unus ex duobus* (*CAO* 5279) contains the word "frater" ("Andreas frater Simonis Petri"), which in Off. B has fallen out. In Antiphon 2, *Christus me misit* (*CAO* 1795), Off. B follows the model, "parvum populum," whereas Off. A presents "parvulum populum." It might be a scribal slip—or a "lectio difficillior." Antiphon 3, *Non me permittas* (*CAO* 3923), offers the more correct form "commendas" in Off. B, but Off. A follows the *Acta* model, with

"commendes." Antiphon 7, *CAO* 1395, not found in the other *CAO* sources, contains a number of differences, and none of the versions is good:

Off. A: *Andreas apostolus domini magnum operatus est miraculum templum Dei praedicando iugiter convertit populum Myrmidonem.*

Off. B: *in templo; praedicandum; Mirmidonium.*

In 9, *Videns Andreas* (*CAO* 5383), the expression *amator tuus* in Off. A is represented in Off. B by the less appropriate version *amor tuus.*

Two different versions exist of *CAO* 4575, Off. A: *Recipe ab hominibus;* Off. B: *Accipe me ab hominibus.* Further, 16, *Tu es Deus meus* (*CAO* 5202) has the word *alleluia* added in Off. A, but not in Off. B.

58. The expression is not found in the *Acta*, 29, 2–3; the word *biduo* is found in the shorter Passion, *An. Boll.*, 377, l. 1; see also the version used in the Roman breviary (*Itaque cruci affixus est, in qua vivus pendens et Christi fidem praedicare numquam intermittens, ad eum migravit*).

59. Notice the double *deprecare pro nobis/intercede pro nobis;* cf. *CAO* 4023, 4718, 4721. Also, I have kept the mixture of nominative and vocative of the source, *sanctus/apostole.*

60. The people of the *Myrmidones* here mentioned are not referred to in the *Acta.* Cf. the first chapter of *De miraculis beati Andreae apostoli* by Gregory of Tours: "De Mattheo apostolo et quae in Myrmidona acta sunt" (Prieur, *Acta*, 2:569 ff.).

61. In *CAO*, these antiphons occur from four to 11 times in different feasts for the apostles.

62. The traditional Lauds psalms are 92, 96, 62, the canticle Benedicite, and Pss. 148–50. See Eisenhofer (1941) 2:518–21.

63. Examples are *Homo dei; Doctor bonus et amicus dei Andreas; Vir iste; Beatus Andreas; Andreas Christi famulus; Sancte Andreas apostole Christi.* In the same way a number of liturgical pieces within the other Offices in the Compiègne book start with a liturgical presentation, giving the name of the saint. See *CAO* 1597, 1599, 1617, 1633, 1640–44 (*Beatus* XX), etc.—the list can be long. (See n. 51 above.)

64. The importance of the cross is reflected as well in the preface (*contestatio*) for the Mass of St. Andrew as found in Gellone Sacramentary (Dumas and Deshusses, *Liber*), no. 1667: "nec pendens taceret in cruce . . . eius exemplo ipse patibulo figeretur."

65. It is not unusual that a particular theological theme is emphasized in a saint's Office. For example, the Holy Trinity is emphasized in the Office of SS. John and Paul; see PL 78:788.

66. Peter Ochsenbein has repeated the attribution, "wie Walter Berschin überzeugend nachweisen konnte"; see Berschin, Ochsenbein, and Möller (1991), 28. However, in the same book Hartmut Möller has observed that the St. Andrew Office also exists in the Compiègne manuscript (p. 35, n. 37). The incipits of the Andrew office are also found, as Möller mentions, in the tonary from Metz; cf. Lipphardt (1965), 170 ff.

67. This gives increased credibility to other attributions made by him, such as the tropes composed by Tuotilo (cf. Rankin 1993).

68. The Offices known to have been written by Hucbald provide hardly any grounds for comparison regarding style or type. For instance, Hucbald's *historia* "In plateis ponebantur" in honor of St. Peter is strictly biblical. Cf. Weakland (1959), 155–62.

69. I thank Professor Walter Berschin, who read the manuscript and offered valuable perspectives.

7

The Divine Office at Saint-Martial in the Early Eleventh Century

Paris, BNF lat. 1085

JAMES GRIER

From the time of its reform under the Benedictine rule in 848, the Abbey of Saint-Martial in Limoges rapidly rose in importance to become not only the preeminent ecclesiastical institution in the city, but also one of the most powerful and influential monasteries in Aquitaine, numbering some 50 daughter houses at the time of its takeover by the Cluniacs in 1062–63.[1] By the end of the tenth century, the monks at Saint-Martial had developed a sophisticated musical culture as part of their liturgical observance.[2] A number of happy accidents conspired to preserve many of the manuscripts that transmit that musical culture and its liturgical environment. First, the librarians of the Abbey took the unusual step of retaining virtually all the music manuscripts produced there from at least the late tenth through the end of the eleventh century. Second, they collected music and liturgical manuscripts from a number of other abbeys in Aquitaine, which enable us to create a context within which to appreciate the musical accomplishments of Saint-Martial. And third, the Abbey's library was sold to King Louis XV in 1730–32, with the result that some 200 manuscripts from Saint-Martial are today housed in the Bibliothèque Nationale de France.[3]

Among those manuscripts are two that attest to a thorough revision and codification of the Abbey's liturgical music during the first decades of the eleventh century, probably under the supervision of Roger de Chabannes, the Abbey's cantor.[4] Those manuscripts are Paris, BNF lat. 1085 and 1120, which, between them, transmit virtually all the music necessary for the performance of the Divine Office and Mass, respectively. The former, which may have been written by Roger himself, is one of the earliest extant monastic sources for Office chants.[5] Moreover, it shows that, in the context of contemporary Office manuscripts and the comments of the Carolingian liturgists, the monks at Saint-Martial celebrated a unique and distinctive form of the Office, which subsequent events, however, curtailed before the end of the eleventh century.

Specifically, Paris lat. 1085 exhibits a unique mixture of what contemporaries would have regarded as Roman and Frankish elements. Many of the responsories it preserves employ a compositional technique wherein passages from different books of Scripture are combined and adapted to create a single liturgical text. Some scholars suggest that this technique is typical of the Gallican liturgy. Another Frankish element appears to be the use of multiple verses with responsories, particularly on feasts of greater importance. In contrast, the manuscript calls for the singing of the Doxology after every responsory of Matins, as in the Roman tradition, and it would appear that the entire respond was to be sung after the Doxology, again following Roman custom. Finally, Paris lat. 1085 departs from both usages by including a significant number of unique verses for the responsories, and by indicating that the longer form of the Doxology (including the phrase that begins *sicut erat*) is to be sung, a practice unattested in any other known Office manuscript.

The date of Paris lat. 1085 is fixed by a firm *terminus post quem non*, namely the absence of the Dedication of 18 November, which took place in 1028. The Dedication feasts that are present fall on 2 May (*Dedicatio basilice quam dedicauit in honore sancti Petri beatissimus Martialis in Lemouicas ciuitate*, fols. 65r–66r) and 13 October (*Dedicatio ecclesie sancti Saluatoris in monasterio beatissimi Martialis fundatum in Lemouice ciuitatis*, fols. 91v–93v). These agree with the Dedication feasts present in the Kalendar of Paris lat. 1240 (fols. 11r–16r), the tenth-century troper from Saint-Martial. In fact the list of feasts in Paris lat. 1085 (see appendix A) offers only one significant difference from the Kalendar of Paris lat. 1240, and that is the presence of the feast of Mary Magdalene (22 July, fol. 78v), the addition of which suggests that Paris lat. 1085 postdates Paris lat. 1240.

Evidence for a *terminus ante quem non* is less definite. The last gathering of Paris lat. 1085 (fols. 105–10) is a palimpsest, of which enough of the lower text is legible to identify it as a fragmentary libellus of processional antiphons. Moreover, both the text and music hands (especially the latter) are similar to those of the fragmentary troper preserved as the endleaves of Paris, BNF lat. 1834 (fols. 1–2, 151–52).[6] Therefore, I would assign approximately the same date to both fragments. Alejandro Planchart shows that Paris lat. 1834 preserves an intermediate stratum of the trope repertory, between the tenth-century version in Paris lat. 1240 and the eleventh-century state in Paris, BNF lat. 1120 (Planchart 1981, 357–60; see also Grier 1995, 70, 109–14).

Furthermore, Danielle Gaborit-Chopin dates Paris lat. 1834 to the beginning of the eleventh century on the basis of its initials (Gaborit-Chopin 1969, 65, 190). The date of the palimpsest in Paris lat. 1085, therefore, stands as the *terminus ante quem non* for the main body of the codex, and, by association with Paris lat. 1834, the palimpsest would also seem to belong to the first years of the eleventh century. Gaborit-Chopin also dates the main body of Paris lat. 1085 to the beginning of the century because of two drawings, a finding consistent with the other evidence presented here (Gaborit-Chopin 1969, 68, 184–85).

One significant aspect of this dating of the main body of Paris lat. 1085 is that the Office of Mary Magdalene, although unremarkable in content, is the earliest on record for this saint. Matins contains a single nocturn (with only three responsories), and most items are borrowed from either the Common of Virgins or the

Assumption (*CAO* 3 and 4 contain the full texts of the Office chants). (See table 7.1.) Nevertheless, no other source that can be safely dated before Paris lat. 1085 transmits an Office for this feast. Victor Saxer notes that the liturgy for Mary Magdalene began to appear in manuscripts during the eleventh century, but he does not demonstrate that either of his earliest sources (from Orléans and Reims), although both eleventh-century books, dates from the first quarter of the century (Saxer 1959, 1:153–82, esp. 159–60, 169–70).

Codex Paris lat. 1085 represents a systematic attempt to record the texts of the Divine Office as celebrated at Saint-Martial in the first decades of the eleventh century. The only precedent for it from the Abbey is the very brief antiphoner in Paris lat. 1240 (fols. 66r–78v). For most Offices, this contains items for Lauds only (Emerson 1993, 206–8). In view of the comparable age of Office books from other institutions, Paris lat. 1085 might be product of the first efforts at Saint-Martial to preserve a complete record of the Office, and I consider this the most likely explanation for its compilation. A second possibility arises, however, from two misfortunes suffered by the Abbey in the tenth century. In 953 and again shortly after the beginning of Guigo's reign as abbot in 974, fire swept the monastery.[7] Both Adémar de Chabannes, nephew and pupil of Roger, and Bernard Itier, the Abbey's librarian in the early thirteenth century, particularly note that the second fire destroyed

Table 7.1 The Office of Mary Magdalene in Paris, BNF lat. 1085

Incipit	CAO 3/4
VESPERS	
A. In diebus illis mulier	3224
MATINS	
SVPER VENITE Regem uirginum	1150
FIRST NOCTURN	
A. Nominabitur quod fecit	—
R. Diffusa est gratia	
V. Contempsisti enim	6446
R. Veni electa mea	
V. Audi filia	7826
R. Ista est speciosa	
V. Ista est quae ascendit	6994
LAUDS	
A. Veni sponsa	5328
A. Haec est uirgo sapiens quam	3007
A. Veniente	5332
A. Benedico te	1703
A. Prudentes	4404
R. Specie tua	7679
V. Intende	
V. Inuenta bona	
IN EVANGELIVM	3822
A. Mulier quae erat	
A. Optimam partem	4167
A. Maria autem unxit	3696bis/3699

books. Hence it is possible that Paris lat. 1085 was compiled to replace a book lost in one of these fires.

Although Paris lat. 1085 presents a complete set of Offices for the liturgical year, and within each Office the full complement of sung items, the items themselves are abbreviated. In the usual format, each sung item is represented by its incipit, above which the musical incipits occasionally appear. In addition, a roman numeral, signifying the modal classification of the melody, precedes all items that include a verse or psalm to be sung to a tone (i.e., every invitatory, antiphon, and Matins responsory). As Michel Huglo notes, these numbers were added sometime after the original compilation of the codex (Huglo 1971, 111). In the next generation of Aquitanian music scribes, Roger's nephew, Adémar, used the same type of modal numbers in Paris, BNF lat. 909 and 1978, during the period 1028–34, and so it is likely that they were entered into Paris lat. 1085 not long after its completion.[8]

A cue to the lesser Doxology (*Gloria patri*) appears, where appropriate, between the modal number and the incipit. Here the practice of Paris lat. 1085 directly contradicts the Rule of St. Benedict, and presents the first of several pieces of evidence that indicate the idiosyncratic nature of the liturgy it records. St. Benedict stipulates that the Doxology is to be sung as part of the last responsory of each nocturn.[9] But Paris lat. 1085 calls for the Doxology at the end of each responsory, in keeping with what Carolingian liturgists understood to be Roman, as opposed to Frankish, practice.[10] The presence of Paris lat. 1085 in a Benedictine house makes this discrepancy with the Rule of St. Benedict all the more noteworthy. Moreover, the cue to the Doxology (*Gloria seculorum amen*) suggests that the entire text, including the section beginning *sicut erat,* was to be sung.[11] Both Amalarius and the twelfth-century ordo for Guido of Castille indicate that the Doxology after a responsory ends with the words *spiritui sancto.*[12] Finally, no repetendum is indicated after the Doxology, and from this absence I infer that the entire respond is to be performed after it, again consistent with Amalarius' description of Roman custom.[13]

Its manner of presentation resembles that of St. Gall, SB 359, the tenth-century Mass book from Saint Gall (reproduced in facsimile in PM 1924). Here only graduals, alleluias, and tracts are written out in full, with complete neumation; all other items are represented by incipits, some with music. Again, the pieces presented in complete form are those of most interest to the soloists, who sang the tracts and the verses of the graduals and alleluias. To be sure, both St. Gall, SB 359 and Paris lat. 1085 include music that was sung chorally, namely the choral responds of graduals and alleluias (in the former), and of Matins responsories (in the latter). Nevertheless, in both codices, the pieces that are indicated by their incipits only are those in which a solo singer would have no responsibilities beyond starting the choir by intoning the first few words. And so both St. Gall, SB 359 and Paris lat. 1085 could well have served as the reference book during those sessions when the cantor and weekly cantor planned the week's liturgy, writing down the incipits of the sung items and choosing the monks who were to sing or begin them.[14]

Matins in the Office for Holy Innocents (28 Dec.), fols. 21r–22v, illustrates the typical arrangement. It begins with the incipit of the Invitatory and a cue to *Venite,* Ps. 94, followed by the incipits for the six antiphons of the first nocturn and cues to their accompanying psalms. In Holy Innocents, as is the case throughout the manuscript, the texts most often written out in full are the verses for Matins responsories. At the top of fol. 21v, for example, the first responsory is represented by its incipit, *Sub altare dei.* The verse *Vidi sub altare* then follows, written in full, with a cue to the repetendum, *Quare non,* the second verse, *Audivi enim voces,* again in full, and a final cue for the repetendum, *Et acceperunt.* Here, subsequent cues to the repetendum indicate a progressive shortening of the respond after each verse, which Amalarius characterizes as a Frankish practice.[15] With the antiphons and psalms of the second nocturn, and the antiphon *ad cantica* at the beginning of the third nocturn, the scribe returns to identification by incipit only.

Four responsories from Matins of this feast are given complete. Table 7.2 gives the full list of responsories. To judge from Hesbert's tables, the four complete responsories knew a much more restricted circulation than the other eight, whose responds are represented by incipit only; these latter occur in all six of the manuscripts Hesbert presents as witnesses of the monastic cursus of the Office.[16] In contrast, three of the four responsories given complete appear each in only one of Hesbert's monastic witnesses.[17]

The fourth responsory, *Vidi sub altare,* is found in two of the manuscripts edited by Hesbert, each time varying slightly.[18] Table 7.3 shows the two varying forms, along with the version in Paris lat. 1085, which combines elements of both, and the biblical source of the passage. All four responsories occur in the eleventh- or early twelfth-century Aquitanian antiphoner Toledo, BC 44.1.[19] Most of this feast is missing from Toledo, BC 44.2, but the last responsory of Matins is *Hi empti sunt* (CANTUS 1992, p. 9).

Furthermore, the scribe of Paris lat. 1085 has entered the music for these four items, including that for the verse. The latter are formulaic and determined by the modal classification of the respond melody, just like the psalm tones in antiphonal psalmody; the responsorial tones, however, are more elaborate.[20] They constitute the most extensive repertory in the body of Office chant that is sung entirely by soloists. (Aside from the incipits of the choral items, the soloists also sing the verses of the invitatory; these are not written out in Paris lat. 1085.) With the subsequent addition of the modal numbers, this music became redundant, and it is clear that whoever added the numbers was especially concerned to make assured the modal classification of these melodies. Therefore there seem to be two criteria for the inclusion of a complete text in Paris lat. 1085, with or without neumation: first, those texts sung by the soloists; and second, those items in more restricted circulation, and so probably less well known.

The repertory and usage recorded in Paris lat. 1085 show unique characteristics when compared with other Office manuscripts of the same age. We have already noted its distinctive treatment of the lesser Doxology with Matins responsories, among which other unusual features occur. Although all the responsories for its Office of Holy Innocents appear in at least one of the six monastic manuscripts edited by Hesbert, and eight of the responsories occur in all six, none of the six presents exactly the same list as Paris lat. 1085. The distinction sharpens when we broaden our sample by considering the responsories for the four Sundays of Advent, for which Hesbert assembled the data from some 800 medieval and early

Table 7.2 Responsories for the Office of Holy Innocents in Paris, BNF lat. 1085

Folio	Incipit	CAO 4	Text	Music
FIRST NOCTURN				
21v	R. Sub altare dei	7713	incipit	no
	V. Vidi sub altare		complete	no
	V. Audiui enim uoces		complete	no
21v	R. Vidi sub altare	7879/7880	complete	yes
	V. Sub trono dei		complete	yes
	V. Euangelius fulgidus		complete	yes
21v	R. Effuderunt sanguinem	6624	incipit	no
	V. Posuerunt mortalia		complete	no
	V. Splendent Bethleemitici		complete	no
21v	R. Isti sunt sancti qui passi sunt	7022	incpit	partial
	V. Mendaces et uani		complete	no
	V. Vindica domine		complete	no
SECOND NOCTURN				
22r	R. Vidi turbam magnam	7881	complete	yes
	V. Et clamabunt		complete	partial
	V. Coronauit eos		complete	no
22r	R. Adorauerunt uiuentem	6050	incipit	no
	V. Venientes autem		complete	no
	V. Et ceciderunt		complete	no
22r	R. Isti sunt sancti qui non	7021	incipit	partial
	V. Hi sunt qui		complete	no
	V. Virginei propter castitatem		complete	no
22r	R. Ecce uidi agnum	6617	incipit	no
	V. Et cantabant quasi		complete	no
	V. Insignum passionum		complete	no
THIRD NOCTURN				
22r	R. Cantabant	6266	incipit	no
	V. Sub trono dei		complete	no
	V. Audita est uox		complete	no
22r–v	R. Hi sunt qui	6816	complete	yes
	V. Hi empti sunt		complete	yes
	V. O quam gloriosum est		complete	no
22v	R. Hi empti sunt	6812	complete	yes
	V. Et nemo poterat		complete	yes
	V. Hi sunt qui		complete	no
22v	R. Centum xliiii milia	6273	incipit	no
	V. Hi empti sunt		complete	no
	V. Corporeae integritatis		complete	no

Table 7.3 Responsory *Vidi sub altare*

Rev. 6:9–10	*CAO* 4, no. 7879	*CAO* 4, no. 7880	Paris, BNF lat. 1085, fol. 21v
9 uidi subtus altare	Vidi sub altare dei	Vidi sub altare dei	Vidi sub altare dei
animas interfectorum	animas interfectorum	animas interfectorum	animas interfectorum
propter uerbum dei,	propter dei,	propter uerbum dei	propter uerbum dei
et propter testimonium	et propter testimonium		
quod habebant,	quod habebant;	quod habebant;	quod habebant;
10 et clamabant	et clara voce	et voce magna	et magna uoce
uoce magna dicentes:	dicebant:	clamabant:	dicebant:
Vsquequo domine			
(sanctus et uerus),			
non iudicas, et non			
uindicas	Vindica, domine,	Vindica, domine,	Vindica, domine,
sanguinem nostrum de iis	sanguinem nostrum	sanguinem sanctorum	sanguinem nostrum
qui habitant in terra?	qui effusus est.	tuorum qui effusus est.	qui effusus est.

Renaissance Office manuscripts.[21] Appendix B gives the complete list of responsories for Advent in Paris lat. 1085.[22] The sequence of responsories for the second, third, and fourth Sundays matches none of the monastic manuscripts consulted by Hesbert.[23] The first twelve responsories for the first Sunday (Paris lat. 1085 includes five responsories in the third nocturn for a total of thirteen) agree with Hesbert's group G, comprising nine manuscripts, all a century or more younger than Paris lat. 1085, and all but one of which are Cistercian in origin.[24] I consider this agreement to be inconsequential.

More important is the accord between Paris lat. 1085 and what Hesbert defines as the Roman, or secular, cursus. A substantial core of secular Office manuscripts agree in the identity and order of the nine responsories for each of the Sundays of Advent (*CAO* 5:27–31).[25] Paris lat. 1085 retains these pieces, in order, as the first nine responsories for each feast. This arrangement is by no means unique among monastic manuscripts, as Hesbert's tables show, and its presence in Paris lat. 1085, one of the earliest sources of the monastic Office, further substantiates Hesbert's assertion that the monastic cursus derives from the secular Office (*CAO* 5:28–31, 233–58). The parallel between the repertory of Paris lat. 1085 and the secular cursus does not persist throughout, however. In the Office of Holy Innocents, for example, agreement in the identity of the responsories does not bind the six secular manuscripts edited by Hesbert, in the first place, and, in the second place, Paris lat. 1085 differs from all of them: its second and fifth responsories, *Vidi sub altare* and *Vidi turbam magnam*, respectively, occur in none of the six.[26] These differences illustrate the independence that individual monastic institutions exercised in shaping their liturgies in this period.

The independence of Paris lat. 1085 further emerges from a consideration of its treatment of verses for the Matins responsories. As tables 7.3 and 7.5 show, Paris lat. 1085 regularly lists two or more verses for each responsory: every item for Holy Innocents includes two (table 7.2), and 44 of the 49 responsories sung on the four

Sundays of Advent incorporate two or more verses (appendix B). Three of the Advent pieces list three verses, and one, *Hierusalem cito* for the second Sunday, gives no fewer than five verses. The sheer quantity of verses in the responsories of Paris lat. 1085 far outstrips that of any other known Office manuscript readily available for consultation. Of the 800 manuscripts surveyed by Hesbert, only MR, containing 31 Advent responsories with multiple verses, comes close to the prolixity of Paris lat. 1085.[27]

Peter Wagner suggested that multiple verses were only exceptional in older manuscripts, and more common in younger sources.[28] His first observation, however, is based on St. Gall, SB 390–91, a source that Hesbert finds unusual in that it follows the secular form of Matins in giving nine responsories for most feasts instead of the monastic form with twelve (*CAO* 2:vi–ix). The arrangement of verses, then, may also accord more closely with secular than monastic usage. Certainly Amalarius regards the use of one verse to be the norm in secular Matins. In the Prologue to his commentary on the Antiphoner, he suggests that, when two or three verses are supplied for a responsory that is to be sung two or three times in the week, a different verse is used on each occasion.[29] If this were the case, however, there would be no need to mark a different point of departure for the repetendum after each verse, usually effecting a progressive shortening of the respond, as the example cited above from *Sub altare dei,* the first responsory for Holy Innocents, shows.

The number and arrangement of the responsorial verses in Paris lat. 1085 suggest that they served to increase the solemnity of the most important feasts at Saint-Martial (just the reason that Amalarius attributes to his Roman informant [*Propter honorem magnae festivitatis*] but subsequently dismisses in favor of the explanation advanced above). For example, when Adémar de Chabannes adapted the existing episcopal liturgy for the Abbey's patron to create an apostolic version, he doubled the number of verses for each responsory to two.[30] And, in a later version of the apostolic liturgy, he contemplated using as many as four verses for each responsory (Paris, BNF lat. 1978, fol. 103r–v). Other Offices compiled by Adémar show that, in his mind, the quantity of responsorial verses indicated the importance of the feast. St. Cybard, the patron of Adémar's home abbey in Angoulême, and SS. Valery and Austriclinian, companions of St. Martial, all held inferior stations to the newly-coined apostle Martial, and the responsories in their Offices are supplied with one verse each, with the exception of the twelfth responsory in Valery's office, which is furnished with two verses.[31]

Beyond sheer quantity, however, the verses in Paris lat. 1085 exhibit the manuscript's independence in another way: the number of Advent verses that are apparently unica. Of the 99 verses listed for the season in Paris lat. 1085, 27 are unknown in the 800 manuscripts consulted by Hesbert.[32] These verses are marked with an asterisk in appendix B. In contrast, the source with the greatest number of unique verses in Hesbert's survey, a thirteenth-century breviary from San Rufo, contains only five verses that are otherwise unattested (Hesbert's source 534; see *CAO* 5:17). Neither MR nor St. Gall, SB 390–91, on the other hand, contains any unica among its verses for Advent. Again, Paris lat. 1085 stands out as the witness of a singular liturgical practice.

How singular? Do the unique verses represent a regional or even institutional practice, or do they belong to a broader tradition that does not survive in sources elsewhere? An examination of the verses' literary structure suggests that the unica in Paris lat. 1085 belong to the same milieu as the more widely disseminated texts. The verses fall into three categories: quotations from Scripture, nonscriptural texts, and texts that paraphrase or combine several passages from Scripture.[33] The first two categories need not long detain us. Although none of the verses in Paris lat. 1085 that are attested elsewhere is nonscriptural, several of the Advent responds are, most notable among which is the first, *Aspiciens a longe.* Nonbiblical texts occur frequently in the responsories throughout the liturgical year, especially in the feasts of the Sanctorale, which often use the saints' *vitae,* but also in some Temporale feasts, such as Christmas.[34]

The last category, texts that use scriptural sources in paraphrase and combination, is of greater significance. (On responsorial texts, see Alfonzo 1936, especially 30–47.) The verse *Ecce cum virtute* provides a good example of the technique. Sung as part of the responsory *Ecce dominus veniet,* in the first nocturn of the second Sunday of Advent, it is found in nearly 500 of Hesbert's sources (*CAO* 6:20–21). The verse combines passages from the extremes of the Bible (one of the Judaeo-Hebrew historical books and a New Testament epistle), with a commonplace exhortation to create a new text suitable for the liturgical season:

Paris lat. 1085, fol. 6r	Biblical sources
Ecce cum uirtute ueniet,	2 Chr. 17:5: Confirmavitque dominus
et regnum in manu eius	regnum in manu eius
et potestas et imperium.	Jude 25: imperius et potestas ante omne saeculum

A similar adaptation occurs in the verse *Propter nimiam karitatem* (Responsory *Ecce iam venit,* fourth Sunday of Advent, second nocturn), which is also widely known (*CAO* 6:33–34). The responds in Paris lat. 1085, all of which were widely circulated, exhibit the same technique of composition in several instances. Perhaps the most extreme example is *Ecce apparebit,* the first responsory on the third Sunday of Advent:[35]

CAO 4, no. 6578	Biblical sources
Ecce apparebit dominus super nube candidam	Rev. 14:14: Et vidi et ecce nubem candidam
et cum eo sanctorum millia,	Deut. 33:2: et cum eo sanctorum millia.
et habens in vestimento et in	Rev. 19:16: Et habet in vestimento et in
femore suo scriptum: Rex regum et	femore suo scriptum: Rex regum et
dominus dominantium.	dominus dominantium.

Pio Alfonzo, who worked primarily on the Hartker antiphoner, St. Gall, SB 390–91, felt that respond texts of this type were infrequent (Alfonzo 1936, 37–38). Several of the unique verses in Paris lat. 1085 follow the same pattern. One example is *Gressus rectos facite,* from the responsory *Confortamini,* in the third nocturn of the first Sunday of Advent. Here passages from one of the didactic books of the Old Testament and a Pauline epistle are combined, with slight modifications to retain the sense:

Paris lat. 1085, fol. 5r	Biblical sources
Gressus rectos facite pedibus uestris et uacillantes confirment sermones uestri.	Heb. 12:13: et gressus rectos facite pedibus vestris Job 4:4: Vacilantes confirmaverunt sermones tui.

Two conclusions result from these observations. First, the unique verses in Paris lat. 1085 agree in literary style with the better-known Advent verses. But do they represent the original work of monks at Saint-Martial, like Roger de Chabannes, who adopted for new compositions the techniques they observed in the central tradition? Or did these unique verses originally form part of that mainstream tradition that has otherwise perished? The second conclusion helps to answer these questions, and that is that this technique of composition very closely resembles that observed by Kenneth Levy in certain offertories whose texts derive from scriptural books other than the Psalter.[36] The creators of these texts adapted scriptural language with the purpose of providing literary material suitable for musical setting. Levy further hypothesizes that this type of offertory might have originated in the Gallican liturgy. With this suggestion in mind, it is striking to note that the two widely circulated Advent verses that evince this technique, *Ecce cum virtute* and *Propter nimiam karitatem,* occur in Paris lat. 1085 and MR, two early west Frankish sources, but not in St. Gall, SB 390–91, an early east Frankish witness, which also, according to Alfonzo, rarely uses responds of this type.[37] Even more striking is the juxtaposition of this apparently Gallican technique of composition with the Roman characteristics seen elsewhere in Paris lat. 1085.[38] It is possible, then, that the usage to which this codex attests is a unique blend of Gallican and Roman practices.

The abundance of multiple verses in Paris lat. 1085 permits a speculation on the history of responsorial singing in the Western liturgy. Many scholars state that, in its earliest form, the responsory consisted of an entire psalm, sung by a soloist, with a choral refrain repeated after each verse, and that the use of a single verse in the Carolingian liturgy constitutes an abbreviation of the original practice.[39] This reconstruction is based upon the vaguely worded descriptions of liturgical singing in patristic writings.[40] Augustine offers the most specific comments about responsorial singing in two passages, couched in nearly identical words, from his commentary on the Psalms, which indicate that the entire psalm was sung in his time.[41] Frankish evidence from the sixth century suggests that the style of performance known to Augustine persisted into that period. Gregory of Tours, when discussing a late sixth-century Frankish context, refers to the *psalmus responsorius,* without defining or describing it.[42] A Gallican source from the sixth century, Paris, BNF lat. 11947, the Psalter of Saint-Germain, contains the mark R beside individual verses, which is taken to indicate the choral refrain in a responsorial setting of a complete psalm (Gastoué 1937–39, 41:104–5; and Huglo 1982).

Isidore of Seville, writing around A.D. 600, describes the responsory as an ancient practice, but does not mention the use of multiple verses or indicate that the responsorial texts are drawn from the Psalter.[43] His description, then, contradicts neither Augustine nor Amalarius. Pierre Batiffol understood the texts of the tenth-century responsories to represent a composite state, perhaps originating in the seventh century, despite the presence of readings from an early form of the Latin Bible, predating the translations of St. Jerome.[44] This evidence led him to express grave reservations about the historical connection between the *psalmus responsorius* of late antiquity and the Carolingian responsory.[45] If such an association did exist, the multiple verses in Paris lat. 1085 should betray at least some vestiges of the practice.

The bulk of evidence from the Advent verses in Paris lat. 1085 weighs against accepting this link. First there is the question of the texts, of both responds and verses, that are either nonscriptural or consist of adaptations of scriptural passages, as illustrated above. Second, many of the texts that are quotations from the Bible come from books other than the Psalter. In both these cases, it is difficult to imagine a complete psalm as the historical antecedent (Crocker 1990b, 136–37). In the second instance, however, the possibility remains that a chapter, or part of one, substituted for a psalm, a point that receives further discussion below. Moreover, the verses, no matter what their origin, exercise a certain amount of mobility. *A solis ortu,* for example, drawn from Ps. 106:3, appears in Paris lat. 1085 with two responsories during the Advent season, and, among the sources surveyed by Hesbert, with a total of 22 different responsories, including the two in Paris lat. 1085.[46] In fact, the whole question of the verses' variability speaks strongly against the historical connection with the fourth-century *psalmus responsorius.*[47]

Other evidence presents equally strong arguments. In many cases, respond and verses are drawn from different books of the Bible. The responsory *Salvatorem exspectamus,* for example, occurs in virtually all the manuscripts consulted by Hesbert, and it exhibits considerable stability in the tradition.[48] Hesbert encountered a total of three different verses with it, but the overwhelming majority of sources (751 out of the 756 manuscripts that include it) present one or both of the two verses that occur in Paris lat. 1085. (Five manuscripts, including MR, give both verses.) Furthermore, all three texts (respond and the two verses) are exact quotations of Scripture. But they occur in three different books of the Bible: two Pauline epistles and the Psalter. Again it is difficult to reconcile this item with Augustine's description of responsorial psalmody.

The responsories give the impression, in general, that they are the result of a careful and deliberate selection and combination of texts that are appropriate to the season. *Salvatorem exspectamus* serves as a typical example:[49]

Resp.   Salvatorem exspectamus Dominum Jesum Christum, qui reformavit corpus humilitatis nostrae, configuratum corpori claritatis suae. (Phil. 3:20–21)

Verse	Preoccupemus faciem eius in confessione, et in psalmis iubilemus ei, (Ps. 94:2)
Resp.	Qui reformavit corpus humilitatis nostrae, configuratum corpori claritatis suae.
Verse	Sobrie et iuste et pie uiuamus in hoc seculo expectantes beatam spem et aduentum glorie magni dei, (Titus 2:12–13)
Resp.	Qui reformavit corpus humilitatis nostrae, configuratum corpori claritatis suae.
Verse	Gloria patri, et filio et spiritui sancto. sicut erat in principio, et nunc, et semper, et in saecula saeculorum, amen.
Resp.	Salvatorem exspectamus Dominum Jesum Christum, qui reformavit corpus humilitatis nostrae, configuratum corpori claritatis suae.
Resp.	We await the savior, the Lord Jesus Christ, who reformed the body of our humility, configured according to the body of his clarity.
Verse	Let us come before his face in confession, and let us rejoice in psalms for him,
Resp.	Who reformed the body of our humility, configured according to the body of his clarity.
Verse	Let us live soberly, justly and piously in this age, awaiting the blessed hope and coming of the glory of the great God,
Resp.	Who reformed the body of our humility, configured according to the body of his clarity.
Verse	Glory be to the Father, the Son and the Holy Ghost. As it was in the beginning, so it shall be now and always, forever and ever, amen.
Resp.	We await the saviour, the Lord Jesus Christ, who reformed the body of our humility, configured according to the body of his clarity.

Preoccupemus, the verse from Ps. 94, does not specifically mention the theme of Christ's Advent, although it does exhort the rejoicing that will accompany that event. The two Pauline texts, however, are centrally concerned with the anticipation of the season, and the verse neatly echoes the respond with the key word *expecto* ("I await"). The whole forms a satisfying literary unit. Moreover, the repetenda create logical grammatical units, a matter of some importance to Amalarius.[50] It is to preserve grammatical sense, therefore, that the repetenda after both verses are the same, instead of the second repeat's being shortened, because no suitable place to begin the second repetendum is available.

The accumulated evidence suggests that, at some time after the late antique period, and possibly not before the seventh century, liturgical responsories were introduced that differed significantly in textual form from the fourth-century *psalmus responsorius*. One example from the Advent responsories in Paris lat. 1085, however, might preserve a trace of the earlier practice. *Docebit nos dominus* is assigned to the last nocturn of the third Sunday of Advent, where it is presented with two verses, *Venite ascendamus* and *Domus Iacob venite* (see appendix B). The respond was widely circulated, appearing in over 700 of the manuscripts in Hesbert's survey, and both verses in Paris lat. 1085 are attested, although only fourteen manuscripts present *Domus Iacob* (*CAO* 6:47). No manuscript known to Hesbert, however, preserves the form of the responsory found in Paris lat. 1085: seven manuscripts give two verses, but all join *Venite ascendamus* with *Ex Sion species*, a verse taken from Ps. 49:2–3.

Aside from its uniqueness, the arrangement in Paris lat. 1085 is also noteworthy for the fact that it combines three texts all taken from the same scriptural passage, Isa. 2. The first five verses of this chapter describe the new home of God, perched on a mountaintop, to which all nations will come for judgment. By analogy, the coming of this new home can be associated with the Advent of Christ, and so the passage can be made to suit the Advent season. Paris lat. 1085 uses verses 3 and 5 for its version of *Docebit,* and verse 4 occurs in one of the unique responsorial verses in Paris lat. 1085, with the responsory *Descendet dominus* in the second nocturn of the same Sunday (see appendix B). It is not beyond the realm of possibility that somewhere in the prehistory of *Docebit* lies a responsorial form similar to that which Augustine describes, which used the first five verses of Isa. 2. The nonpsalmodic nature of the text makes the connection with Augustine's account all the more noteworthy.

Nevertheless, the isolation of *Docebit* in Paris lat. 1085 lessens the weight of its testimony. No other source preserves precisely this combination of texts, and no other Advent responsory in Paris lat. 1085 duplicates the selection of multiple texts from the same passage of Scripture. Where two texts share origins, either the responsory uses a single verse (e.g., Responsory *Missus est,* first Sunday of Advent, first nocturn, where Luke 1 is the source of both respond and verse), or it combines two excerpts from the same passage with texts from other sources (e.g., Responsory *Aspiciens a longe,* first Sunday of Advent, first nocturn, which combines two verses from Ps. 79 with a third verse from Ps. 48 and a nonscriptural respond). These examples indicate that when two or more texts derive from the same scriptural source, their combination is more likely the result of compositional planning than the abbreviation of an earlier, fuller responsorial form.

Codex Paris lat. 1085, therefore, preserves a repertory of responsories that is remarkable on a number of counts. Several of the pieces exhibit a compositional technique (namely the combination and adaptation of passages from different books of Scripture) that some scholars, principally Kenneth Levy, would associate with the Gallican liturgy. It shares this feature with MR (but not St. Gall, SB 390–91), as it does, too, an abundance of multiple verses in the Offices of important feasts, like the Sundays of Advent and Holy Innocents. This connection, together with Amalarius' apparent unfamiliarity with the practice, and the nearly total absence of such multiple verses in St. Gall, SB 390–91, suggests two hypotheses. First,

the usage may be monastic in origin: both MR and Paris lat. 1085 come from Benedictine houses, and Amalarius seems more conversant with the secular liturgy;
St. Gall, SB 390–91, though monastic, reflects secular usage in other ways (e.g.,
by giving nine responsories for many feasts). And second, it could also reflect an
older, Gallican practice, dating back to pre-Carolingian times.

Finally, its treatment of the Doxology is unique: it calls for the longer form of
the text, which usually occurs in antiphonal psalmody, and for which there is no
parallel among readily available Office manuscripts; it requires the Doxology to be
sung after every responsory, in the Roman custom; and it seems to indicate that
the entire respond be sung after the Doxology, again in keeping with Roman, as
opposed to Frankish, usage. The preference for Roman customs is indeed strange
in a house that claimed its origins in a donation of the Frankish emperor Louis
the Pious.[51] Whatever the origins of this mélange of practice, it is clear that Paris
lat. 1085 reflects a highly idiosyncratic liturgy in comparison with other monastic
sources of comparable age. The liturgical independence of Saint-Martial became
one of first victims after the purchase and forcible takeover of the Abbey by the
monks of Cluny in 1062–63.[52] Subsequent books for the Office, namely Paris,
BNF lat. 743 (an eleventh-century Breviary) and Paris, BNF lat. 1088 (a thirteenth-
or fourteenth-century Antiphoner) both exhibit a completely uniform Cluniac
liturgy.[53]

The main purpose of Paris lat. 1085 is to preserve a comprehensive list of the
sung items of the Divine Office for the entire liturgical year, probably to serve as a
reference list for the cantor. Along the way, several features that indicate a unique
liturgical usage were recorded, but I would be reluctant to ascribe a great deal of
independence to the compiler of the codex, who may have been Roger de Chabannes. The unique responsorial verses, for example, may be traces of an older way of
singing the responsories, rather than original compositions at Saint-Martial. The
one exception to this pattern is the Office for Mary Magdalene: the feast was introduced at Saint-Martial not long before the compilation of Paris lat. 1085, and the
Office in this codex is the earliest known version. Codex Paris lat. 1085 was compiled, therefore, to preserve and record the existing Office liturgy at Saint-Martial
rather than to innovate.

Appendix A: Feasts and rubrics in Paris, BNF lat. 1085

Folios	Date		Feast or Rubric
3v–5v			[First Sunday of Advent]
5v			Feria ii, iii, iiii, v, vi, Sabbato
5v–7r			Dominica ii [of Advent]
7r–v			Feria ii, iii, iiii, v, vi, Sabbato
7v–9r	10 December	4 Ides Dec	Festus Sancte Valerie
9r–v	13 December	Ides Dec	Natale Sancte Lucie
9v–11r			Dominica iii [of Advent]
11r			Feria ii, iii, iiii, v, vi, Sabbato
11r–12v			Dominica iiii [of Advent]
12v–13r			Responsoria infra eadem ebdomada
13r–14r			Feria ii, Feria iii, iiii, v, vi, Sabbato
14r–v			Antiphone maiores de aduentu domini
14v–15r	24 December		In uigilia natalis domini
15r–18r	25 December		In nocte sancta
18r–19v	26 December	7 Kal Jan	Solempnitas prothomartyris Stefani
19v–21r	27 December	6 Kal Jan	Assumptio sancti Iohannis euangeliste
21r–23r	28 December	5 Kal Jan	Natale Innocentium
23r	1 January		In octabas domini
23r			Dominica i post natalem domini
23v–25r	6 January		In uigilia epyphanie
25r–v	13 January		In octabas epyfanie
25v			Dominica i post epyphaniam
25v			Dominica ii
25v–26r			Dominica iii
26r–27v			Responsoria de psalmis canenda ab octabas epifanie usque in septuagesimam
27v–28r			Feria ii
28r–29r			Feria iii
29r–v			Feria iiii
29v–30v			Feria v
30v–31r			Feria vi
31r–32r			Sabbato
32r–33v	20 January	13 Kal Feb	Festus sancti Sebastiani martyris
33v–35r	21 January	12 Kal Feb	Passio sancte Agnetis uirginis
35r–35bis	25 January	8 Kal Feb	Conuersio sancti Pauli
36r–37r	2 February	4 Nones Feb	Purificatio sancte Marie
37r–38v	5 February	Nones Feb	Passio sancte Agathe uirginis
38v–39r	22 February	8 Kal Mar	Cathedra sancti Petri
39r–40r	21 March	12 Kal Apr	Transitus sancti Benedicti abbatis
40r–v	25 March	8 Kal Apr	Adnuntiatio sancte dei genetricis
40v–42r			Dominica in septuagesima
42r			Infra ebdomada
42r–43r			Dominica in sexagesima
43v–44v			Dominica in quinquagesima
44v–45r			Feria ii, iii, iiii, v, vi, Sabbato
45r–46r			Dominica i in quadragesima
46r			Feria ii et per omnes ferias usque in passionem domini semper dic hunc uersum
46r–v			Feria ii, iii, iiii, v, vi, Sabbato
46v–47v			Dominica ii in quadragesima

(*continued*)

Folios	Date		Feast or Rubric
47v–48r			Feria ii, iii, iiii, v, vi, Sabbato
48r–49r			Dominica iii in quadragesima
49r–v			Feria ii, iii, iiii, v, vi, Sabbato
49v–50v			Dominica iiii in quadragesima
50v–51r			Feria ii, iii, iiii, v, vi, Sabbato
51r			In cantu non cantetur Gloria; Seruetur autem eo modo usque in dominicam sanctam pasce, qualiter non cantetur gloria in inuitatoriis neque in responsoriis; sed semper a capite repetitur antiphona superposita
51r–52r			Dominica v in quadragesima de passione domini
52r–v			Feria ii, iii, iiii, v, vi, Sabbato
52v–53v			Dominica vi in quadragesima qua uocatur ramis palmarum
53v–54r			Feria ii
54r–v			Feria iii
54v			Feria iiii
55r–56r			Feria v in cena domini
56r–57r			Feria vi in parasceuen
57v–58v			Sabbato sancto
58v–60r			Dominica sancte resurrectionis
60r–v			Feria ii
60v			Feria iii
60v–61r			Feria iiii
61r			Feria v
61r			Feria vi
61r–v			Sabbato
61v			Dominica octabas pasce
61v			Item antiphone de resurrectione
62r			Dominica i, ii, iii, iiii post octabas pasce
62r–63r			Responsoria in resurrectione de apocalipsin
63r–64r			Idem responsoria in resurrectione de psalmis
64r	23 April	9 Kal May	Natale sancti Georgii martyris
64r–65r	1 May	Kalends May	Festiuitas Philippi et Iacobi
65r–66r	2 May	6 Nones May	Dedicatio basilice quam dedicauit in honore sancti Petri beatissimus Martialis in Lemouicas ciuitate
66r–67r	3 May	5 Nones May	Inuentio sancte crucis
67r	3 May		Ipso die natale sanctorum Alexandri, Euenti, et Deodori de quibus oportet agere in ii nocturno sicut de plurimis martyriis
67r–68r			In uigilia ascensionis domini
68r			Feria vi infra octabas ascensionis domini
68r			Sabbato
68r			Dominica i post ascensione
68r			Feria ii, iii, iiii, v octabas ascensionis, vi post octabas ascensionis
68r–69v			Sabbato sancto in uigilia pentecostes
69v			Feria ii, iii, iiii, v, vi, Sabbato
69v			Dominica in octabas pentecosten

Folios	Date		Feast or Rubric
70r–72v			[Trinity]
72v			Antiphona de pentecosten
73r	2 June		In natale sanctorum Marcellini et Petri
73r	8 June		In natale sancti Medardi
73r–74v	24 June	8 Kal Jul	Natiuitas sancti Iohannis Baptiste
74v	26 June	6 Kal Jul	Festus Iohannis et Pauli matryrium
74v–76r	29 June	3 Kal Jul	Passio Petri apostoli terminatur cruce; in festo ipsius
76v	29 June		Eodem die beatus Paulus capitalem subiit [s]ententiam; in solempnitate illius
76v–77r	30 June	Pri Kal Jul	Natale sancti ac beatissimi patroni nostri domini Martialis praesuli[s] Lemouicensis
77r–v	6 July	2 Nones Jul	Octabas apostolorum
77v–78r	7 July	Nones Jul	Octabas sanctissimi Marcialis episcopi et confessoris ciuitate Lemouici
78r–v	11 July	4 Ides (*sic*) Jul	Sollempnitas beatissimi Benedicti
78v	22 July	11 Kal Aug	Natale sancte Marie Magdalene
79r	1 August	Kalends Aug	Machabei martires transierunt ad gloriam et Petrus liberatur a uinculis; in festiuitate ipsius
79r	1 August		In secundo nocturno agatur de plurimis martyriis repperitur
79r–v	3 August	3 Nones Aug	Inuentio beati Stephani prothomartyris
80r–81v	10 August	4 Ides Aug	Beatus Laurentius super craticulam spiritum emisit; in uigilia eiusdem martyris
81v	11 August	3 Ides Aug	Natale sancti Tiburtii martyris
81v–82v	15 August	18 Kal Sep	In adsumptione sancte dei genetricis
82v–83v			Item antiphone in ueneratione sancte Marie ad uigilie
84r	22 August	11 Kal Sep	Passio sancti Symphoriani nostri martyris
84r–85r	29 August	4 Kal Sep	In passione beati baptiste Iohannis
84v	29 August		In secundo nocturno de sancto Sabina sicut de uirginum celebretur
85r–86r	8 September	6 Ides Sep	In natiuitate sancte marie
86v–87v	14 September	18 Kal Oct	Exaltatio sancte crucis; in eadem enim festiuitate
87v	14 September		Eodem die passio sanctorum Corneli et Cipriani martyrium expletur de quibus in secundo nocturno agatur
87v–89r	22 September	10 Kal Oct	Martyrium consumauit sanctus Mauricius cum sociis; in ac autem festiuitate
89r	27 September	5 Kal Oct	De sancto Cosme et Damiano
89r–90v	29 September	3 Kal Oct	In onore arcangeli Micaelis
90v–91v	9 October	7 Ides Oct	In festiuitate sancti Dionisi et sociorum eius
91v	10 October	6 Ides Oct	In translatione sanctissimi presuli[s] Martialis antiphone et responsoria sicut in octabas eiusdem antistitis repperitur quod est nonas Iulii
91v–93v	13 October	3 Ides Oct	Dedicatio ecclesie sancti Saluatoris in monasterio beatissimi Martialis fundatum in Lemouice ciuitatis

(*continued*)

Folios	Date		Feast or Rubric
93v	14 October	Pri Ides Oct	In natale sancti Calixti episcopi
93v–94r	1 November	Kalends Nov	Solempnitas omnium sanctorum. In geiunio eandem festiuitatem
94r–95r	11 November	3 Ides Nov	Migrauit beatus Martinus ex hoc mundo ad celis; in cuius festa
95r	13 November	Ides Nov	In depositione beati Brictioni episcopi
95r–96r	22 November	11 Kal (*sic*) Dec	In festiuitate sancte Cecilie
96r–97r	23 November	10 Kal (*sic*) Dec	In festiuitate sancti Clementis martyris
96v	23 November		In secundo nocturno de sancta Felicitate
97r–98r	30 November	2 Kal Dec	Beatus Andreas de cruce migratur ad celis; in cuius uigilia
98r–99v			In solempnitatibus sanctorum apostolorum
99v–101r			In festiuitatibus sanctorum martyrium
101r–2r			In ueneratione unius martyris
102r–3v			In natale unius episcopi et confessoris
104r–v			[Added pieces]
105r–6r			Responsoria de regum
106r–v			Responsoria de sapientia
106v–8r			Responsoria de Iob
108r–v			Responsoria de Tobi
108v–9r			Responsoria de Iudith
109r			Responsoria de Hester
109r			De Ezram
109r–10r			Responsoria de Machabeorum
110r–v			Responsoria de Prophetis

Appendix B: Responsories in Paris, BNF lat. 1085 for the four Sundays of Advent

Folio	Incipit (* = unique)	Source	CAO 4(5)

FIRST SUNDAY OF ADVENT

First Nocturn

Folio	Incipit (* = unique)	Source	CAO 4(5)
3v–4r	R. Aspiciens a longe	—	6129(11)
	V. Quique terrigene	Ps. 48:3	
	V. Qui regis Israel	Ps. 79:2	
	V. Excita domine	Ps. 79:3	
4r	R. Aspiciebam	Dan. 7:13–14	6128(12)
	V. Ecce dominator	Isa. 40:10	
	V. Potestas eius	Dan. 7:14	
4r	R. Missus est	Luke 1:26–27, 29–32	7170(13)
	V. Aue Maria gratia	Luke 1:28	
4r	R. Aue Maria	Luke 1:28, 35	6157(14)
	V. Quomodo in me	Luke 1:34–35	

Second Nocturn

Folio	Incipit (* = unique)	Source	CAO 4(5)
4r	R. Saluatorem	Phil. 3:20–21	7562 (15)
	V. Preoccupemus	Ps. 94.2	
	V. Sobrie et iuste	Titus 2:12–13	
4r	R. Audite uerbum	Jer. 31:10, Isa. 62:11	6149(16)
	V. A solis ortu	Ps. 106.3	
	V. Adnunciate	Jer. 4:5	
4v	R. Ecce uirgo	Isa. 7:14, 9:6	6620(17)
	V. Super solium Dauid	Isa. 9:7	
	V. Tollite portas	Ps. 23:7	
4v	R. Obsecro domine	Exod. 4:13, 3:7–8	7305(18)
	V. Ecce domine	Exod. 4:10, 13	
	*V. Deus qui sedes	Ps. 9:5	
	V. Qui regis Israel	Ps. 79:2	

Third Nocturn

Folio	Incipit (* = unique)	Source	CAO 4(5)
4v	R. Laetentur caeli	Isa. 49:13	7068(19)
	V. Orietur in diebus	Ps. 71:7	
	V. Tunc Exultabunt	Ps. 95:12–13	
4v	R. Alieni non transibunt	Joel 3:17–18	6066(62)
	V. Ecce ego ueniam dicit dominus et sanabo	Hos. 14:5	
	*V. Non transibit per eam	Isa. 35:8, Wisd. 7:25	
4v–5r	R. Montes Israel	Ezek. 36:8	7177(60)
	V. Rorate caeli	Isa. 45:8	
	*V. Frondete et date	Sir. 39:19	
5r	R. Confortamini	Isa. 35:3–4	6321(61)
	*V. Gressus rectos facite	Heb. 12:13, Job 4:4	
	V. Ciuitas Hierusalem	Tob. 5:26	

(continued)

Folio	Incipit (* = unique)	Source	*CAO* 4(5)
5r	R. Ecce dies ueniunt	Jer. 33:14–16	6583(63)
	V. In diebus illis	Jer. 33:16	
	*V. Veniet qui eripiat	Rom. 11:26	

SECOND SUNDAY OF ADVENT

First Nocturn

6r	R. Hierusalem cito	Mic. 4:8–9	7031(21)
	V. Ego enim dominus deus	Isa. 41:13–14	
	V. Quare dicis Iacob	Isa. 40:27	
	V. Popule meus Israel	Isa. 41:8, 43:5	
	*V. Gaude et laetare Syon	Amos 4:12	
	V. Israel si me audieris	Ps. 80:9–11	
6r	R. Ecce dominus ueniet	Zech. 14:5–6, 8–9	6586(22)
	V. A solis. ortu	Ps. 106:3	
	V. Ecce cum uirtute	2 Chr. 17:5, Jude 25	
6r	R. Hierusalem surge	Bar. 5:5, 4:36	7034(23)
	V. Leua in circuitu	Isa. 49:18/60:4, Num. 27:12	
	V. Dilataberis ad orientem	Gen. 28:14	
6r	R. Ciuitas Hierusalem	Isa. 40:10	6290(24)
	V. Ecce dominator dominus	—	

Second Nocturn

6r–v	R. Ecce ueniet dominus protector	Isa. 43:14, Rev. 14:14	6613(25)
	V. Et dominabitur a mari	Ps. 71:8	
	*V. Veniet in nubibus caeli	Matt. 24:30/Mark 13:26	
6v	R. Sicut mater	Isa. 66:13–14	7660(26)
	V. Dabo in Syon	Isa. 46:13	
	*V. Ecce ueniet dominus quem	Mal. 3:1	
6v	R. Hierusalem plantabis	Jer. 31:5–7	7033(27)
	V. Exulta satis	Zech. 9:9	
	V. Sion noli timere	John 12:15	
6v	R. Egredietur dominus de Samaria	Isa. 16:5	6639(28)
	V. Et preparabitur in misericordia	Isa. 16:5, Mal. 3:3	
	*V. Preparabitur solium iustitiae	—	

Folio	Incipit (* = unique)	Source	CAO 4(5)
Third Nocturn			
6v	R. Rex noster	John 1:29	7547(29)
	V. Ecce agnus dei	Isa. 52:15, 11:10	
	V. Super ipsum continebunt	—	
6v–7r	R. Ecce ab [A]ustro	Hab. 3:3	6570(73)
	V. Aspiciam uos et crescere	Lev. 26:9	
	*V. Ecce uenio cito	Rev. 22:12	
7r	R. Festina ne	Ps. 39:18	6728(92)
	V. Veni domine et noli tardare	Hab. 2:3	
	*V. Tuam domine excita potentiam	Ps. 79:3	
7r	R. paratus esto	Amos 4:12–13	7351(94)
	V. De radice Iesse	Isa. 11:1	
	*V. Ecce ueniet cum uirtute magna	Isa. 40:10, 1 Cor. 4:5	

THIRD SUNDAY OF ADVENT

First Nocturn

Folio	Incipit	Source	CAO 4(5)
9v	R. Ecce apparebit	Rev. 14:14, Deut. 33:2, Rev. 19:16	6578(31)
	V. Apparebit in finem	Hab. 2:3	
	V. Dominus de Syna ueniet	Deut. 33:2, Isa. 63:1	
9v	R. Bethleem ciuitas	Mic. 5:2, 4–5	6254(32)
	V. Deus a Libano ueniet	Hab. 3:3	
	V. Loquetur pacem gentibus	Zech. 9:10	
9v	R. Qui uenturus	Heb. 10:37	7485(33)
	V. Ex Syon species	Ps. 49:2–3	
9v–10r	R. Suscipe uerbum	—	7744(34)
	V. Paries quidem filium	Isa. 7:14/Matt. 1:21/ Luke 1:31	
	*V. Salue semper sancta uirgo	—	

Second Nocturn

Folio	Incipit	Source	CAO 4(5)
10r	R. Aegipte noli	—	6056(35)
	*V. Gaude et letare Iacob	—	
	V. Ecce ueniet dominus exercituum	Isa. 3:1	
10r	R. prope est ut ueniat	Isa. 14:1	7438(36)
	V. Qui uenturus est	Heb. 10:37	
	V. Reuertere uirgo	Jer. 31:21	

(*continued*)

Folio	Incipit (* = unique)	Source	*CAO* 4(5)
10r	R. Descendet dominus	Ps. 71:6–7	6408(37)
	V. Et adorabunt eum	Ps. 71:11	
	V. Et conflabunt gladios suos	Isa. 2:4	
10r	R. Veni domine et noli	Hab. 2:3	7824(38)
	V. Excita domine	Ps. 79:3	
	*V. Miserere templi sanctificationis tuae	Sir. 36:15	

Third Nocturn

Folio	Incipit (* = unique)	Source	*CAO* 4(5)
10r–v	R. Ecce radix Iesse	Isa. 11:10	6606(39)
	V. Dabit illi dominus deus	Luke 1:32	
	V. Radix Iesse qui exsurget	Rom. 15:12	
10v	R. Docebit nos dominus	Isa. 2:3	6481(70)
	V. Venite ascendamus	Isa. 2:3	
	V. Domus Iacob uenite	Isa. 2:5	
10v	R. Egredietur uirga	Isa. 11:1,5	6641(81)
	V. Et requiescet super eum	Isa. 11:2	
	*V. Egressus eius erit	Mic. 5:2, Isa. 52:15	
10v	R. Ecce ueniet dominus princeps	—	6612(71)
	V. Veni domine et noli tardare	Hab. 2:3	
	*V. Propterea expectat dominus	Isa. 30:18	

FOURTH SUNDAY OF ADVENT

First Nocturn

Folio	Incipit (* = unique)	Source	*CAO* 4(5)
11v	R. Canite tuba in Syon	Jer. 4:5, Isa. 62:11	6265(41)
	V. Adnunciate illut in finibus	Jer. 31:10	
	*V. Properate et clamate	Jos. 6:10	
11v	R. Octaua decima die	Isa. 19:20, Exod. 23:20, Deut. 31:7/Judg. 2:1	7309bis/ 7886(42)
	V. Inuocabitis me et ibitis	Jer. 29:12	
	V. Ego sum dominus deus uester	Exod. 20:2/Lev. 19:36/ 25:38/Deut. 5:6	
11v	R. Non auferetur	Gen. 49:10	7224(43)
	V. Pulcriores sunt oculi eius	Gen. 49:12	
11v	R. me oportet	John 3:30, 1:27	7137(44)
	V. Hoc est testimonium	John 1:15	
	V. Ego quidem baptizaui uos	Mark 1:8	

Appendix B (*continued*)

Folio	Incipit (* = unique)	Source	*CAO* 4(5)
Second Nocturn			
11v	R. Ecce iam uenit	Gal. 4:4–5	6596bis/ 6596(45)
	V. Prope est ut ueniat	Isa. 14:1	
	V. Propter nimiam karitatem	Eph. 2:4, Rom. 8:3	
11v–12r	R. Virgo Israel	Jer. 31:21–22	7903(46)
	V. In karitate perpetua	Jer. 31:3	
	*V. Gaude et letare filia	Zech. 2:10	
12r	R. Iuraui dicit dominus	Isa. 54:9–10	7045(47)
	V. Iuxta est salus	Isa. 56:1	
	*V. Non transibunt per Hierusalem	Joel 3:17–18	
12r	R. Non discedimus	Ps. 79:19–20	7227(48)
	V. Domine deus uirtutum	Ps. 79:20	
	V. Memento nostri domine	Ps. 105:4	
	*V. Intuere et respice	Lam. 5:1, Mark 9:21	
Third Nocturn			
12r	R. Intuemini	Heb. 7:4	6983(49)
	V. Et dominabitur a mari	Ps. 71:8	
	V. Precursor pro nobis	Heb. 6:20	
12r	R. Modo ueniet	Mal. 3:1, Isa. 7:14	7172(53)
	V. Orietur in diebus	Ps. 71:7	
	*V. Appropinquabit enim salus	Rom. 11:11	
12r–v	R. Adnunciatum est	—	6103(93)
	*V. Suscepit infirma nostri corporis	—	
	*V. Missus ab arce patris	—	
12v	R. Nascetur nobis	Isa. 9:6–7	7195(91)
	*V. Adueniet nobis angelus	—	
	V. In ipso benedicentur omnes	Ps. 71:17	

Notes

Part of this chapter was delivered at the annual meeting of the American Musicological Society in Montréal, 7 November 1993. I thank Margot E. Fassler for her thoughtful response. This study is part of a project to edit the complete works of Adémar de Chabannes for the Corpus Christianorum Continuatio Mediaevalis, directed by Richard Landes of Boston University. I am grateful to the Principal's Development Fund and the Advisory Research Committee, both of Queen's University, the Social Sciences and Humanities Research Council of Canada, and the A. Whitney Griswold Faculty Research Grant and the John F. Enders Research Assistance Grant, both of Yale University, for a series of grants that enabled research trips to Paris and Limoges during the period 1989–97. I am also very grateful to M. François Avril and Mme Contamine of the Section Latine, Institut de Recherche et d'Histoire des Textes, for their many kindnesses.

1. On the history of the Abbey, see Lasteyrie (1901), Aubrun (1981), Sohn (1989), and Landes (1995).

2. On the musical culture of the Abbey, see Chailley (1960) and Evans, *The Early Trope.*

3. On the manuscripts and library of Saint-Martial, see Delisle, *Le Cabinet,* 1:387–97, 452–54, 2:493–504; id. (1895); Chailley (1957); id. (1960), 73–119; and Gaborit-Chopin (1969). On the sale of the library, see Grier (1990), 7–8, where further bibliography is cited.

4. For a highly speculative biography of Roger and his role in this codification, see Grier (1995).

5. On the possibility that Roger is the scribe of Paris lat. 1085, see Grier (1995), 82. The brief antiphoner in Paris, BNF lat. 1240, fols. 66r–78v (also from Saint-Martial), predates Paris lat. 1085; see Emerson (1993), esp. 206–8. The only monastic chant books for the Office of comparable age cited by Hiley (1993), 304–5, are the Hartker Antiphoner (St. Gall, SB 390–91; facsimile reproduction in PM [1900]) and the Mont-Renaud manuscript (private collection [hereafter MR]; facsimile reproduction in PM [1955]); on these manuscripts, see Franca (1977), 38–55; Beyssac (1957); Huglo (1971), 91–102, 233–40; and Robertson (1991a), 425–34. See also the list of Office manuscripts in *CAO* 5:5–18. Paris, BNF lat. 17436, the ninth-century manuscript from the Abbey of Saint-Corneille in Compiègne, follows the secular or Roman cursus; see *CAO* 1, pp. xvii–xix; and Franca (1977), 29–37. See also chapter 6 in this volume.

6. On Paris lat. 1834, see Emerson (1962). On the palimpsest in Paris lat. 1085 and its relationship with Paris lat. 1834, see Grier (1995), 70–82.

7. [Adémar de Chabannes], *Commemoratio,* in Duplès-Agier, ed., *Chroniques,* 4–5; Bernard Itier, *Chronicon,* ibid., 42–43.

8. On Adémar's relationship with his uncle and teacher Roger de Chabannes, and his knowledge of contemporary musical notation, see Grier (1995), 62–68.

9. Benedict of Nursia, *Regula,* 9.6, 11.3; ed. Vogüé and Neufville (1971–77), 2:510, 514.

10. *Ordo romanus* XVI, 15, ed. Andrieu, *OR* 3:148–49 and n. 15 (Hiley 1993, 74, incorrectly identifies this text as *Ordo romanus* VI); Amalarius of Metz, *Liber de ordine antiphonarii,* 18.6–7, ed. Hanssens, 3:55; and Walafrid Strabo, *Libellus de exordiis et incrementis quarundam in obseruationibus ecclesasticis rerum,* 26, ed. Boretius and Krause, MGH Leges 2:507. The unanimity of these sources allows us to dismiss Pierre Salmon's assertion that Amalarius was referring only to the last responsory of each nocturn, in accord with St. Benedict: Salmon (1967), 34. See also the twelfth-century ordo written for Cardinal Guido of Castille before he became Pope Celestine II (and therefore before September 1143), published as *Ordo romanus* XI, 3, PL 78, cols. 1026–27 (not edited by Andrieu; see *OR* 1:309–11). For commentary, see Wagner (1911), 133–37; Hucke (1973), 160–62; and Crocker (1990b), 126–28.

11. The tonary of Paris lat. 909, also from Saint-Martial, and written 1028–29 with musical notation and corrections to the literary text by Adémar de Chabannes, gives responsorial tones that include the full text of the lesser Doxology, fols. 251r–54v; see Grier (1995), 65–66, and id. (1997), 239–40.

12. Amalarius, *Liber de ordine antiphonarii,* 18.6, ed. Hanssens, 3:55; and *Ordo romanus* XI, 3, PL 78, col. 1027. See also Wagner (1911), 136; Apel (1958), 182; A. Hughes, *Medieval Manuscripts,* 29, 301; and Hiley (1993), 70.

13. Amalarius, *Liber de ordine antiphonarii,* 18.6, ed. Hanssens, 3:55; and *Ordo romanus* XI, 3, PL 78, cols. 1026–27.

14. See, for example, the tenth-century customary from Einsiedeln, *Consuetudines einsidlenses,* in Albers, *Consuetudines monasticae,* 5:77–80; and the eleventh-century customary of Cluny, *Liber tramitis aeui Odilonis abbatis,* 2.26, ed. Dinter, p. 238. See also Fassler (1985), 39–51. Emerson (1993), 207, reaches the same conclusion about Paris lat. 1085.

15. Amalarius, *Prologus de ordine antiphonarii*, 12, and *Liber de ordine antiphonarii*, 18.6–8, ed. Hanssens, 1:362 and 3:55, respectively. But *Ordo romanus* XI, 3, PL 78, cols. 1026–27, shows that the repetendum after each verse is shortened, as in the Frankish practice, but that the final repetendum, after the lesser Doxology, is complete.

16. Paris, BNF lat. 17296 (Hesbert's MS D) places *Cantabant* in Lauds; see *CAO* 2, no. 22, where the contents of all six manuscripts are listed synoptically for this feast.

17. *Vidi turbam magnam* in Benevento, BC V-21 (Hesbert's MS L); *Hi sunt qui* in Zurich, Zentralbibl. Rh. 28 (R); and *Hi empti sunt* in London, BL Add. 30850 (S).

18. *CAO* 4, no. 7879 in Paris, BNF lat. 12584 (Hesbert's MS F); and *CAO* 4, no. 7880 in L.

19. I am very grateful to Professor Ruth Steiner, founding Director of CANTUS, for supplying me with the inventory of this codex.

20. Frere, ed., *Antiphonale Sarisburiense*, 3–5; Wagner (1921), 188–216; Ferretti (1935), 265–83; Apel (1958), 234–41; and Hiley (1993), 65–66.

21. Hesbert (*CAO* 5:5–18) lists the manuscripts consulted. He did not consider Paris lat. 1085.

22. In appendix B, numbers in brackets give the numerical codes Hesbert assigned to the Advent responsories; see Hesbert, *CAO* 5:32–33. An asterisk denotes a verse unique to Paris lat. 1085. For the biblical sources, cf. the identifications in Alfonzo (1936), 136–58.

23. Complete lists of responsories for each of the three Sundays are given in *CAO* 5:62–68, 86–92, 108–14, respectively. Monastic manuscripts bear sigla starting from 601. Hesbert analyzes the groups of monastic manuscripts for these three feasts in *CAO* 5:84–85, 106–7, 129–30, respectively.

24. List of responsories, *CAO* 5:35–41; groupings of monastic manuscripts, ibid., 5:60–61.

25. For the manuscripts that agree on each of the Sundays in Advent, see ibid., 5:57–59, 82–85, 104–7, 128–29, respectively.

26. Hesbert (*CAO* 1, no. 22) presents synoptically the contents of all six secular manuscripts for this feast.

27. *CAO* 6:2–3; Hesbert gives the complete listing of verses for the Advent responsories in all 800 sources ibid., 6:56–78.

28. Wagner (1911), 137–38. See also Hucke (1973), 159–60, and Hiley (1993), 70.

29. Amalarius, *Liber de ordine antiphonarii*, Prologue 1–2, ed. Hanssens, 3:13.

30. Episcopal liturgy, Paris lat. 1085, fols. 76v–77r; apostolic, Paris lat. 909, fols. 62v–74v.

31. Cybard, Paris lat. 1978, fol. 102r–v (see Delisle 1896, 351–52); Valery and Austriclinian, Paris lat. 909, fols. 78r–81v and 81v–85v, respectively (see Emerson 1965, 43–46).

32. Hesbert (*CAO* 6:7–55) gives the complete list of verses.

33. The scriptural origins of the texts are indicated in appendix B. A dash denotes a nonscriptural text.

34. For an example from the Sanctorale, see Steiner (1984). On Matins for Christmas, see Crocker (1990b), 125–26.

35. It occurs in all but 18 of Hesbert's sources: *CAO* 6:25. Below I give the text of *CAO* because Paris lat. 1085 provides the incipit only.

36. Levy (1984). See also Wagner (1911), 322–43; Pietschmann (1932), esp. 114–30; and Hucke (1970).

37. *CAO* 6:20–21, 33–34. The sigla for St. Gall, SB 390–91 and MR are 500 and 728, respectively; see *CAO* 5:11, 16. Alfonzo (1936), 37–39.

38. On the presence of Gallican items in Aquitanian manuscripts, especially Paris, BNF lat. 776, see Gastoué (1937–39) 41:132–33; Huglo (1955), 361–83; and Cullin (1982), 287–96.

39. Wagner (1911), 133; Apel (1958), 180–85; A. Hughes, *Medieval Manuscripts,* 26–30 and fig. 2.2, p. 33. On the Eastern origin of solo psalmody, see Dyer (1989); and on its introduction to the west, Jeffery (1984).

40. Most of the pertinent texts are collected and translated in *MECL;* see especially passages from Tertullian (no. 78, p. 44), Athanasius (no. 102, p. 54), Basil the Great (no. 139, pp. 68–69), John Chrysostom (nos. 178, 184, pp. 84, 86), Eusebius of Caesarea (no. 208, p. 98), Sozomen (no. 221, p. 103), Egeria (no. 253, p. 117), Ambrose (nos. 276, 289, pp. 126–27, 130), Augustine (nos. 364, 374, pp. 159, 162), and Gennadius (no. 398, p. 170). See also Leeb (1967), 17–18, 31, 53–80; and Hucke (1973), 150–55.

41. Augustine of Hippo, *Enarrationes in Psalmos,* ad 46.1, 119.1. CCSL 1:529, 3:1776.

42. Gregory of Tours, *Historia francorum,* 8.3, in *Libri historiarum X,* ed. Krusch and Levison, 372–73.

43. Isidore of Seville, *De ecclesiasticis officiis,* 1.8, ed. Lawson, p. 8; see also *Etymologiae,* 6.19.8, ed. Lindsay, without pagination.

44. Batiffol (1894). On the early state of the texts, see pp. 223–24, citing correspondence from a M. Berger (Samuel Berger, according to Alfonzo); M[orin] (1890), 321; and Alfonzo (1936), 46–47.

45. Batiffol (1911), 121–22. See also Hucke (1973), 157–59.

46. Paris lat. 1085 (see appendix B): Responsory *Audite verbum* (first Sunday of Advent, second nocturn), and Responsory *Ecce dominus veniet* (second Sunday of Advent, first nocturn). *CAO* 6:7–55.

47. Hesbert (*CAO* 6:1–282) considers this issue with the aim of attempting to establish an "archetypal" list of verses for the Advent responsories. See also Alfonzo (1936), 42–45.

48. *CAO* 6:15–16. In Paris lat. 1085, it falls in the second nocturn of the first Sunday of Advent; see appendix B.

49. The respond is taken from *CAO* 4, no. 7562, because Paris lat. 1085 gives only the incipit. The verses are taken from Paris lat. 1085, fol. 4r, as are the cues for the repetenda.

50. Amalarius, *Prologus de ordine antiphonarii,* 12–13, and *Liber de ordine antiphonarii,* 18.6–8, ed. Hanssens, 1:362–63 and 3:55. See also Crocker (1990b), 126–27.

51. See the diploma copied into Paris, BNF lat. 5^2, fol. 221v; printed in Guibert, *Documents,* no. 123, pp. 111–12; and Lasteyrie (1901), pièce justificative 2, pp. 420–21. See also Adémar de Chabannes, *Chronicon,* 3.16, ed. Chavanon, p. 131; Lair (1899), 105; and Sermon 22 of Adémar de Chabannes, Paris, BNF lat. 2469, fol. 68v (Lasteyrie 1901, 45, n. 2 also cites a sermon on fol. 78v, but neither Sermon 25 nor 26, both of which appear on this page, refers to the Abbey's imperial patron). On the falsehood of this claim, see Lasteyrie (1901), 41–50.

52. The chief narrative source is a note in Paris, BNF lat. 11019, pp. 165–69; printed in Champeval, ed., "Chroniques," no. XV, pp. 322–24; and Lasteyrie (1901), pièce justificative 7, pp. 427–29. Another copy occurs in Limoges, AdH-V 3 H 6 (3). See also Peter Damian, *De gallica Petri Damiani profectione et eius ultramontano itinere,* 14–15, ed. Schwarz and Hofmeister in Hofmeister, *Supplementum,* 1043–44; and Geoffrey of Vigeois, *Chronica,* 14, in Labbé, ed., *Noua,* 287–88. For commentary see Lasteyrie (1901), 83–86; and Sohn (1989), 46–78.

53. Hesbert's sigla for Paris lat. 743 and 1088: 781 and 784; see *CAO* 5:13. For their concurrence with the Cluniac sources, see 5:407–44, esp. 411, 424–25, 429–33, 443.

The Cluniac Processional of Solesmes

Bibliothèque de l'Abbaye, Réserve 28

MICHEL HUGLO

The processional is a portable book in small format containing the chants for processions (Purification on 2 February, Palm Sunday, and Rogations), as well as processional chant for Sundays and feast days.[1] The processional, unlike the gradual and antiphoner, is not an official book, but a practical book created by singers to help them to retain the melodies of long processional antiphons. The processional is therefore more recent than these notated liturgical books, because it originated from the gradual of the Mass: from the ninth century on, the oldest graduals without notation include a long list of processional antiphons for the Greater Litanies of 25 April and also for Lesser Litanies sung during the processions of Rogations on the three days preceding Thursday of the Ascension.

The transfer of such antiphons from the gradual into a small portable book, which was soon called *Liber processionarius* or *Processionale,* is observed first in three manuscripts from the Palatinate: Vatican, BAV Pal. 489, provenance Hornbach, 145 × 123 mm.; Vatican, BAV Pal. 490, provenance Lorsch, 173 × 128 mm.; and Vienna, ÖNB 1888, provenance St. Alban of Mainz, 203 × 155 mm. All include the antiphons of the Greater Litanies, which are preceded in the manuscripts from Lorsch and Mainz by the ritual antiphons of Purification, Ash Wednesday, and Palm Sunday, which are also found in many early graduals.

The processional of Lorsch observes: "Major letania unius diei a beato Gregorio, minor vero trium dierum a beato Mamerto" ("The Greater Litany, which lasts only one day, was established by St. Gregory the Great; the Lesser Litany, which lasts three days, however, was established by St. Mamertus" [bishop of Vienne in France]). Even though these two processions have different origins, they use the same Romano-Frankish antiphons, to which the Lorsch manuscript adds processional litanies from St. Gall: *Ardua spes mundi, Humili prece, Rex sanctorum angelorum,* etc. (*AH* 50:237, 242, 253, and *passim*), whereas the manuscript from Mainz and others from southern France add the litany-like *preces* from the Gallican liturgy (De Clerck, *La "Prière"*).

A similar portable book for Rogations was written in Metz somewhat later: Metz, MM 329, which was burned in 1944 but is described in its entirety by Mgr. Jean-Baptiste Pelt in his *Études sur la cathédrale de Metz* (Metz, 1935), with a facsimile of the Messine neumes in support of his arguments. This small book of 52 folios contained only the neumed antiphons for the three days of Rogations, with rubrics indicating the itinerary to follow to arrive at the stations in the churches and monasteries of the city of Metz. A second processional written in Metz in the eleventh and twelfth centuries has Lorraine neumes on a staff of four black lines (Verdun, BM 139: 125 × 105 mm.). This manuscript includes only processional antiphons for Rogations, Proper chants addressing the patron saints of the stational churches visited during these processions, and the above-mentioned litanies from St. Gall.

In the thirteenth century and even afterwards, many churches, such as the cathedrals of Piacenza, Cambrai, and Chartres, maintained this type of processional for Rogations, with rubrics of special interest to archeologists. Other attempts were made to create a processional for Sundays and feast days, which includes chant for the procession between Terce and High Mass. This latter type of processional probably originated as a supplement to the processional of the Ritual, which only contains the antiphons prescribed by the Ordines Romani and the Roman missal for the processions following the blessing of the candles on 2 February, the blessing of palms on Palm Sunday, and the procession to the cemetery during funerals. Notice in passing that the Greco-Latin antiphons of the *Ypapanthe* (Purification) on 2 February are of Roman origin, whereas the long processional antiphons for Palm Sunday are admirable vestiges of Gallican chant.

The Gallican antiphons for Easter Sunday conserved in the oldest graduals (*Antiphonale missarum sextuplex,* no. 214) remained in use for a long time in the processional, sometimes until the sixteenth century. French processionals, especially those from the south, also kept a good number of processional antiphons, such as *Venite omnes exultemus, Cum sederit Filius hominis,* and *Oremus dilectissimi nobis,* which disappeared little by little before office responsories invaded the processional, beginning in the thirteenth century.

The "processional-responsorial" is the most widely known type of processional: the manuscripts, for the most part posterior to 1500, are the most numerous among surviving processionals. Nevertheless, there is no longer unity in these processional repertories, but a great variety, due to the expansion of local repertories.

Faced with an earlier proliferation of responsories, antiphons, versus, and litanies in the processional, the Cistercians reacted severely by limiting their processions to those on 2 February and Palm Sunday. They were strongly criticized by Abelard for this suppression of a universal monastic usage.[2] Consequently, around 1150, they added a procession for the Ascension, then, between 1202 and 1225, processions for the Assumption of the Virgin and for the feast of St. Bernard (20 Aug.), and, finally, after 1289, a procession for 8 September, the feast of the Nativity of the Virgin.

Processionals fall into three broad categories: (1) secular processionals for cathedral uses, (2) processionals of the Benedictines, and (3) processionals of the different religious orders that were established in the twelfth and thirteenth centuries: the Cistercians, Premonstratensians, Dominicans, and Franciscans. Of these, those in the third group are the most rigorously standardized, because each order imposed a processional of its own, propagated through manuscripts and, subsequently, in printed editions. The processionals of most of the orders remained identical with their prototype throughout the history of each order.

For example, in Paris, in 1254, Humbert of Romans, Master General of the Dominican Order, reorganized its liturgy and introduced a short processional-responsorial for eight feasts of the year and the end of Holy Week, followed by the ritual of extreme unction and burial. This Dominican processional in square notation was disseminated throughout Europe and always kept its original notation, even in the regions of central Europe where Germanic notation was customary. About 130 Dominican manuscript processionals remain, that is, about 14 percent of all known surviving manuscript processionals.

The Franciscans used a processional limited to the processions of 2 February and Palm Sunday as well as funerals. Unlike the missal and breviary of the Curia, however, this processional was not officially elevated to the rank of *Processionale Romanum,* even though several sixteenth-century imprints are entitled *Liber processionum secundum usum Romanum et potissime secundum usum fratrum minorum,* etc.

The preceding historical observations have determined a classification of the over 1,000 manuscript processionals that survive today. They fall easily into the following nine categories:

1. "Roman" processionals for the Greater Litanies
2. "Romano-Frankish" processionals for Rogations
3. processionals with long antiphons
4. processional-responsorials
5. Cistercian processionals (mid-twelfth century)
6. Sarum processionals (after 1200)
7. the Dominican processional (after 1254)
8. the Romano-Franciscan processional (thirteenth century)
9. the Augustinian and Premonstratensian processional

There is evidence that the Benedictines of Cluny had adopted, at least by the eleventh century, a standard processional, which is therefore exceptional among Benedictine processionals. The earliest known witness to this book is Paris, BNF lat. 12584, an eleventh-century source that contains a complete processional notated in French neumes between an antiphoner and a gradual.[3] Another early Cluniac processional is Brussels, BR II 3823 (Fétis 1172), an early twelfth-century gradual from the priory of Sauxillanges in Auvergne, which contains processional antiphons in Aquitanian notation (*Le Graduel romain,* 38).

A third early Cluniac processional is Solesmes, Bibliothèque de l'Abbaye, Réserve 28, which comes from a small monastery in southern France affiliated with Cluny. This manuscript is of particular importance because it is a copy of an intermediary source transcribed from a model from the mother house of Cluny.[4] The plainchant tradition of Cluny has been very carefully studied by Ruth Steiner in several articles, in which she sought to understand the extent to which the liturgical practices and the chant of Cluny were imposed upon the hundreds of houses reformed by monks from this order of Benedictines between the tenth and the thirteenth century (Steiner 1987 and 1993).

The Solesmes manuscript, although from the fifteenth century, is a useful witness to the early tradition of processions at Cluny and in its subordinate houses. Comparison with the other two early Cluniac processionals reveals striking uniformity in the selection and ordering of its chant, which provides evidence for the existence of a single Cluniac processional early on. Thus, even though Solesmes 28 is incomplete in several sections, its lacunae can be reconstructed with confidence from Paris, BNF lat. 12584 (= F in *CAO* 2, no. 147) and Brussels, BR II 3823. Some comparisons with F are made in the inventory of Solesmes 28 below.

The Cluniac processional contains a few more variants than the Cistercian as it appears in different regions and times, but the chronological range of sources postdating the three cited above as well as their consistency argues in favor of a single Cluniac processional. We can cite three processionals from the important Cluniac priory Saint-Martin-des-Champs in Paris: Paris, BNF lat. 1124 (dated 1554), lat. 13256 (1544), and lat. 18050 (1630), and also lat. 9467 (eighteenth century) from Cluny itself.

The description and inventory of Solesmes 28, which follows below, presents for the first time the eleventh-century state of the Cluniac processional. As a type of processional, it belongs to category 3 listed above, transmitting long processional antiphons, not only for Rogations, but also for all of the feasts of the liturgical year. Nevertheless, it is evident that most of the chant in Solesmes 28 is borrowed from the Office, and I have supplied the references to *CAO* accordingly.

Because of its rubrics in accordance with the Cluniac customary and its notated chants, the processional of Solesmes, despite its lacunae, is a valuable witness to liturgical life at Cluny and its sister houses throughout five centuries of the Middle Ages. Scholars and musicians will find here the texts and chant for the most important processions of medieval Cluniac monasteries.

Inventory of Solesmes, Bibliothèque de l'Abbaye, Réserve 28

Physical Description

128 folios, 130 × 85 mm. Leather binding. Unfortunately, many leaves are missing: the first leaf with the title before the actual first folio, and one or more leaves after fols. 7v, 23v, 32v, 81v, 83v, 89v, 112v, 120v, 126v.

Decoration: Red and black initials, and after fol. 11, flourished initials with violet filigree: the large initials V (from *Vidi aquam,* fol. 52) and M (from *Mirabile,* fol. 97) have been cut out.

Script: Thick southern French minuscule of the fifteenth century. The chants are notated in square Aquitanian notation with the characteristic podatus consisting of punctum and virga written separately to the right over the podatus.

Staff: Six staves per page of four red lines, with clefs at the beginning and *custodes* at the end (the *custos* appears frequently in southern French notated manuscripts).

Origin

The calendar and rubrics of this manuscript show that its model was surely a processional from the Abbey of Cluny in Burgundy: it mentions the feasts of St. Odo (18 Nov.), the second abbot of Cluny; St. Maieul (11 May), the third; and St. Hugh (29 Apr.), the fifth; but not the feast of St. Odilo (2 Jan.), the fourth Abbot of Cluny, perhaps because of one missing page between fols. 14 and 15. Nevertheless, on the second day of Rogations, the station must be "in the church of St. Odilo" (fol. 79). The mention on fol. 58v of the General Chapter ("Dominica in Capitulo generali"), the second Sunday after Easter, is the best indication of the Cluniac origin of the exemplar.

Liturgical Content

For every Sunday and feast day of the liturgical year, some long antiphons without psalmody are provided for the procession "per claustrum" (through the cloister) and one for the station before the Cross affixed above the place of access to the choir. For many feasts, generally in the Sanctorale, some responsories are borrowed from the Office antiphoner: we will cite only those of unusual interest.

Advent: The first antiphon for the first Sunday of Advent (in F, no. 147a): {A. *Missus est angelus* (*CAO* 3, 3792)} is missing. The processional begins at fol. 1r with the V. *Dabit ei dominus* from the R. *Ecce radix Jesse* (*CAO* 4, 6606). Then six antiphons (as in F, no. 147a): A. *Venite omnes exultemus* (*CAO* 3, 5354), *O beata infantia* (*CAO* 3, 3994), *O virgo super virgines* (*CAO* 3, 4090), *O quam casta mater et virgo* (*CAO* 3, 4060), *O quam casta mater que nullam* (*CAO* 3, 4061), and *O beatum ventrem Mariae* (*CAO* 3, 4004). Next, "ad ingressum chori" (while entering the choir): A. *Jerusalem civitas sancta* (*CAO* 3, 3477).

Christmas: fol. 9 (after one missing leaf), the end of the A. *O beata infantia* (*CAO* 3, 3994); fol. 9v A. *O Maria Jesse virga* (*CAO* 3, 4036); fol. 11 "Ad stationem" (during the station before the Holy Cross) A. *Hodie Christus natus est* (*CAO* 3093); fol. 11v R. *Descendit de caelis* (*CAO* 4, 6410).[5]

Septuagesima Sunday: fol. 15v A. *Cum sederit filius hominis* (*CAO* 3, 2032).

Ash Wednesday: fol. 17 A. *Exurge Domine* (*CAO* 3, 2822), A. *Immutemur* (*CAO* 3, 3193), then rubrics, versicle, and collect; fol. 20v "In capella beatae Mariae" (in the chapel of the Virgin Mary) A. *Sancta Maria succurre miseris* (*CAO* 3, 4703). F adds the A. *Cum sederit Filius hominis* (*CAO* 3, 2032).

First Sunday of Lent: fol. 22v "eundo ad sanctam Mariam" (going to the church of St. Mary) A. *Christe pater misericordiarum* (*CAO* 3, 1784 F). Unfortunately, the other Sundays of Lent are missing because one gathering is lost.

Palm Sunday: fol. 25 after lacuna A. *Pueri Hebreorum* (*CAO* 3, 4416), A. *Cum adpropinquaret* (*CAO* 3, 1976), A. *Cum audisset populus* (*CAO* 3, 1983); fol. 28v R. *Contumelias et terrores* (*CAO* 4, 6335) and the rubric "alia responsoria quantum necesse fuerit" (other responsories as needed [from the night office of this Sunday]); fol. 31v "Ad ingressum ecclesiae sancti Maioli" (while entering the church of St. Maieul) R. *Sancte Maiole, Christi confessor* [from the common office for Confessors]. "Ad stationem adorando sanctam crucem" (At the station for adoring the Holy Cross); A. *Ave rex noster* (*CAO* 3, 1543); fol. 33 "Praefati VI cantores, terne divisi in utroque choro alternatim cantent hos versus" (the above-mentioned six singers, now divided into two groups of three on each side of the choir, should sing these verses in alternation) H. *Gloria laus* (*CAO* 4, 8310; *AH* 50:160). After each strophe the refrain must be sung by the cantor together with the monks ("Cantor cum conventu cantant: *Gloria laus*").

Maundy Thursday: fol. 35v "Ad Mandatum quod fit post mixtum, primo incipiente cantore omnes petunt veniam" (At the Mandatum celebrated after the dipping [of the bread in the wine] all prostrate themselves when the cantor begins the antiphon) A. *Dominus Jesus postquam* (*CAO* 3, 2413), A. *Mandatum novum* (*CAO* 3, 3688), etc. Cf. F in *CAO* 2, 147b.

Good Friday: fols. 45–51v V. *Popule meus* (*CAO* 3, 4312). "Cantor cum conventu" (Cantor with the monks) *Sanctus deus*. "Illi qui sunt ante armario reliquiarum" (Those who are before the chest of relics) *Agios o theos* etc. as in the gradual.

Easter: fol. 53 A. [*V*]*idi aquam* (*CAO* 3, 5403). "Eundo ad sanctam Mariam" (going to the church of St. Mary) A. *Tota pulchra es* (*CAO* 3, 5162; Steiner 1993, 196, 199–200); fol. 53v A. *In die resurrectionis meae* (*CAO* 3, 3222), fol. 55v "In Galilaeam adorando crucem dicitur haec antiphona" (In the aisle of the cloister next to the church, this antiphon is sung during the Adoration of the Cross) A. *Christus resurgens* (*CAO* 3, 1796).

First Sunday after Easter: fol. 57v A. *Locutus est ad me* (not in *CAO*).

Second Sunday after Easter: fol. 58v "Dominica in Capitulo generali" (The Sunday of the General Chapter [Sunday of the Good Shepherd]) R. *Veniens a Libano* V. *Favus distillans* (*CAO* 4, 7829).[6]

Rogations: fol. 59 the Monday of Rogations, after the Hour of Sext (after noon): A. *Exurge domine* (*CAO* 3, 2822). "Eundo ad Sanctum Marcellum" (going to the chapel of St. Marcel, for the Mass): the series of long antiphons without psalmody (almost the same series as in F: *CAO* 2, 148): A. *De Jerusalem exeunt* (*CAO* 3, 2109), A. *Cum jocunditate* (2015), A. *Ecce populus* (2534), A. *Custodit dominus* (2084), A. *In sanctis gloriosus* (3284), A. *Annuntiate inter gentes* (1427), A. *Plateae Iherusalem* (4299), A. *Propitius esto* (4393), A. *Ego sum deus* (2591), A. *Populus Syon* (4314), A. *Domine deus noster* (2336), A. *Confitemini domino* (1879), A. *Exclamemus omnes* (2780), A. *Parce domine, parce populo* (4219), A. *Iniquitates nostrae* (3346), A. *Domine imminuti sumus* (2347), A. *Domine non est alius* (2360), A. *Exaudi domine deprecationem* (2766), A. *Miserere domine plebi* (3772), A. *Dimitte domine peccata tua* (2237), A. *Exaudi deus deprecationem* (2765), A. *Deprecamur te domine* (2151), A.

Inclina domine (3315), A. *Multa sunt* (3829), A. *Domine miserere nostri* (2359), A. *Peccavimus domine* (4257), A. *Invocantes dominum* (3400), A. *Non in justificationibus* (3917), A. *Convertere domine* (1919), A. *Libera domine populum tuum* (3615); fol. 77 Missa: [Introit] *Exaudivit* (*AMS* 94).

Tuesday of Rogations: fol. 79 A. *De Iherusalem* (*CAO* 3, 2109).

Wednesday of Rogations: fol. 79v the same antiphon and then, fol. 80 Missa *Omnes gentes* (*AMS* 101bis).

Ascension: three responsories (Pentecost is missing).

Corpus Christi (this feast was introduced to Cluny in 1315): after a small lacuna, R. *Unus panis*, V. *Parasti*.

First Sunday after Trinity: fol. 84v A. *Asperges me* (*CAO* 3, 1494); fol. 85v A. *Omnipotens deus* (*CAO* 3, 4143); fol. 87v A. *Cum venerimus* (*CAO* 3, 2042); fol. 89 A. *Oremus dilectissimi nobis* (*CAO* 3, 4190), then the incomplete sequence of responsories *De Trinitate* (Auda 1923; Huglo 1993b, 56). The last responsory (fol. 95v), *Deus majestatis* V. *Gloriam psallat* (*CAO* 4, 6426), with V. *Benedictio et claritas*, is not present in F.

Sanctorale (*Sequitur Sanctuarium* [*sic*]), from Epiphany (6 Jan.) on, with A. *[M]irabile mysterium* (*CAO* 3, 3768, from Vespers). Purification (fol. 99) A. *Lumen* (*CAO* 3, 3645); R. *Gaude Maria virgo* V. *Gabrielem* (*CAO* 4, 6759) with the prosula (MS *Prosellum!*) *Inviolata*. St. Benedict, 21 March (fol. 106v) R. *Sanctus Benedictus* (*CAO* 4, 7609). St. Hugh of Cluny, 29 April: R. *Sanctus Hugo digne in memoriam:* the melody of this responsory is taken from that of the R. *Iste sanctus* (*CAO* 4, 7609): the copyist has written this incipit in the body of the initial letter S. Then fol. 110 R. *Agmina sacra* (*CAO* 4, 6063): cf. Brou 1961, 26 and 32); A. *Confessor domini Hugo adstantem plebem* (*CAO* 3, 1868). St. Maieul, 11 May (fols. 111–112v) A. *Sanctissime confessor Christi Maiole*, A. *O beati viri Mayoli sancta praeconia*, A. *Exultet omnium turba fidelium:* these antiphons are adapted from those for the feast of St. Benedict.[7] The Mass follows, but the beginning is missing: at fol. 113, there is the end of the sequence: *...chie subjici. Illic patres dispositi* etc. (perhaps the end of the sequence *Maiolus perhumilis*, RH 11044, after the *Missale Cluniacense* of 1717); then (fol. 114) the OF. *Repleti sumus* and the COM *Laetabitur justus.*

St. John the Baptist, 24 June (fol. 115) The R.R. *CAO* 4, 7420 and 7791. St. Peter and Paul, 29 June (fol. 117v) R. *Quem dicunt* (*CAO* 4, 7467). Transfiguration of Jesus, 6 August (fol. 121; the beginning is missing) R. *[Coram tribus]* V. *Ut in ore* (*CAO* 4, 6338), A. *Hodie ad patris vocem;* fol. 121v R. *Primogenitus prodii* V. *Quae est ista* (*CAO* 4, 7432). These chants are taken from the Office *In Transfiguratione domini* composed by Peter the Venerable, Abbot of Cluny (1122–56) and edited in J. Leclercq (1946), 384, after Paris, BNF lat. 17716 from the Cluniac priory of Saint-Martin-des-Champs now in Paris.

Assumption of the Virgin Mary, 15 August (fol. 123) and her Nativity, 8 September (fol. 124v) R.R. only.

"Ad pluviam postulandam" (to obtain rain) (fol. 127) A. *Domine rex deus* (*CAO* 3 2376), A. *Numquid est in idolys* (*CAO* 3, 3971); fol. 128 A. *Exaudi domine populum tuum* (*CAO* 3, 2768). The series is comparable to F in *CAO* 2, 148b. The end of this processional is missing.

Translated by Susan Boynton and Barbara Haggh

Notes

1. Bibliography on the processional may be found in Huglo (1980c), 281; (1996), 1435–36; and in Huglo (1999).

2. "Epistola X ad sanctum Bernardum," in Abelard, *Epistolae,* 335–40. Cf. Waddell (1973).

3. *CAO* 2, p. xvii (= F) and plate X, for the neumatic notation; p. 781, no. 147a: *Dominica prima de Adventu Domini, Ad processionem.*

4. See Hourlier (1951), 233, and the inventory below, under Origin.

5. Text corrected according to the Cluniac tradition: see Huglo (1979).

6. Cf. Charvin (1965–79), covering the period from 1290 until 1746.

7. These chant compositions are not taken from the monastic office of St. Martial (Paris, BNF lat. 5611, fols. 104–8, in Aquitanian notation). The *Hymnus de sancto Maiolo, Christe cunctorum pariter tuorum* (fol. 102v), composed by St. Odilo (*AH* 50:300), is notated in French (perhaps Cluniac) neumes.

Taking the Rough with the Smooth

Melodic Versions and Manuscript Status

SUSAN RANKIN

Let the paschal feasts be celebrated   with a diastematic harmony of voice!
New songs should now be modulated   *in melic, rhythmic, metrical music!*
On the feast of feasts the holy of holies has arisen.
Eya, eya, eya!
Let the faithful people shout: let the church rejoice!

The song *Diastematica vocis armonia* belongs to an extensive repertory of songs
with which, from the late eleventh century on, clerics in the north and south of
France and related areas were accustomed to celebrate the highest feasts of the
church year.[1] Questions about how and when such songs were actually sung rarely
find precise answers in the repertorial collections that constitute the main means
of their preservation. Yet their content, language (textual and musical), and associations all suggest that many of these monophonic Latin songs belong close to the
circumstances of performance of the liturgy. Indeed, one of the main focuses of
their interest was the Christmas season, and in this respect their connection with
the Office is of primary importance. Thirteenth-century books from Laon, Beauvais, and Sens that contain detailed local liturgies for the celebration of the Circumcision feast reveal an officially sanctioned practice of infusing the night and
day Offices with such songs.[2]

    The existence of such collections gives physical expression to an awareness that,
in the Middle Ages, the Divine Office could represent a more substantial and col-
ored celebration than the regulated collections of texts and melodies in Office antiphoners and breviaries might imply. In many regions the Divine Office celebrated
on major feast days would have been made more elaborate through the singing of
such songs, especially in those parts of the liturgy that involved the movement of
clergy from one part of the church to another.[3]

    Yet, even if sung by clerics and, at times, within the confines of liturgical Offices,
these songs belong to a more fluid, less fixed dimension of musical expression

than the central chant repertories of the Mass and Office. Not only are the songs themselves to be distinguished from the Office chants, but also their modes of dissemination and their sources. That indications of their use should appear so rarely is no coincidence: books made for the celebration of the liturgy would tend to neglect such ephemeral material, while the primary interest of the large repertorial collections of verse songs was in form and content rather than possibilities of use. The existence of these songs on the margins of the liturgy therefore led to a variety of types and qualities of source much broader than that of contemporary chant books. The interest of this study is in the space between established approaches to the written recording of music and ways in which these songs were actually written down. To bring the Divine Office—especially as it was celebrated in the later Middle Ages—to life again, we must therefore allow not only the well-presented but also the sometimes careless collections of songs a place beside the more standardized materials presented in antiphoners.

Diastematica vocis armonia survives as one of a small collection of songs gathered in the shabbiest, worst copied, most unfinished, and generally least attractive book of music that anyone could imagine. This is Cambridge, UL Ff.1.17(1) (henceforth Ff.1.17), named by Otto Schumann "Die jüngere Cambridger Liedersammlung." The tiny libellus came to the University in 1664 from the library of Richard Holdsworth, Master of Emmanuel College.[4] Not considered of interest in itself, the libellus at that time formed the front and back flyleaves for a *Summa* on the vices and virtues, now Cambridge, UL Ff.1.17(2); of the provenance of the libellus before 1664 nothing is known. It is but small compensation to one's aesthetic sensibilities to know that the four bifolia of Ff.1.17 have themselves remained relatively complete, in contrast to the more famous and older collection of songs in Cambridge, UL Gg.v.35, which had the misfortune to lose various folios, including that with most musical notation—now happily restored to the manuscript.[5] The obstacles to survival met by Ff.1.17 were of a different kind: its contents having apparently lost value, it was used as binding material, possibly as early as the end of the thirteenth or beginning of the fourteenth century (the date of copying of the *Summa*). Damage of various kinds resulting from this binding (cutting, folding, gluing) combined with large water stains renders this little book of songs even more visually obscure than when first compiled in the late twelfth or early thirteenth century.

Yet the intrinsic interest of Ff.1.17 is considerable: it contains 34 songs, 13 in more than one part (including one of the earliest extant three-part pieces, *Verbum patris humanatur*), and has concordances with a variety of earlier and later sources of diverse provenance. Moreover, as if in contradiction of these indices of textual value, Ff.1.17 provides evidence of the written circulation of music in a state not often accessible to modern scholars—because of the shabbiness of its presentation and consequent lack of value to any but the thoroughly initiated. It is a simple libellus, apparently complete in itself, made up of the worst quality of parchment I have ever seen used for the recording of text. This is rough, and was already full of holes before it was written on; there is no evidence of pricking, and very little of any kind of ruling for text, although in some places there are traces of lead pencil. For those who wrote on this material (and there were several scribes for both text and music),[6] red ink and a rastrum were only available up to the time of preparation of the fifth recto folio (now fol. 300r). From this point on, staves had to be ruled using the same ink as that for text and music notation and in many cases freehand. The general impression is one of material poverty. Whatever kind of community lies behind this heterogeneous song collection, it appears to have lacked either the means (material and financial) and skills (of writing and presenting)—or, simply, the desire—to give this song collection any greater physical significance.

It may be that the collection was produced, literally, "on the margins" of working time in a scriptorium, belonging to what was left over of energy, parchment, and ink. As a community effort, it was most likely copied by those who were responsible for and involved in performances of the songs. In this sense, Ff.1.17 could be seen as something sanctioned by and simultaneously marginalized (as insignificant or improper) by the clerical establishment under whose auspices it was made.

Paradoxically, this very distance from the norms of French and English written musical artifacts of the high Middle Ages (such as chant books) may have ensured the preservation of an unusually rich store of musical information. A modest example of this is the notational sign written as a squiggle on one pitch, differing from an ordinary single note—notated as a virga with a square head:

As a single note, or as part of a longer neume, this sign can be found on many pages throughout the libellus, but I know of no equivalent in other contemporary sources or in later square notations. It may denote simple lengthening or some more expressive treatment of a note, perhaps even a way of expressing musical sound used in these particular pieces and not in the singing of chant. Whatever its meaning, the presence of the sign indicates an attempt to differentiate between two ways of singing a single pitch.

It is perhaps the book's lack of self-importance—its messy state, and total lack of names, dates, and places which could help towards a neater pigeonholing—that has allowed some musicologists to dismiss or ignore the richness of information conveyed in the song notations. The comparison of a published version of *Diastematica vocis armonia* (example 9.1*a*) with a transcription made from the manuscript (example 9.1*b*) demonstrates one aspect of this dismissal.[7] There are no concordances, either textual or musical, for this song. In example 9.1*a* the melodies for text lines 1 and 3 adopt the manuscript's version for line 3, ignoring the rather more decorated melodic version for the parallel text in line 1. The relation of the transcription of lines 2 and 4 to the manuscript version is less clear: what is published represents a hybrid between the two melodies offered by the manuscript, and thus neither line is exactly reproduced. Later, the three *Eya* exclamations have lost the liquescences indicated in the source. But so what? Maybe this published version contains errors resulting from the state of the source and its less than perfect legibility (in photographs at least). Such an apologia would miss the point, however: the alignment of two text lines under one melody indicates a specific approach to how this music *should* be presented, an approach that rides roughshod

Example 9.1 *Diastematica vocis armonia*, Cambridge, UL Ff.1.17(1), fol. 1v: (a, *this page*) transcribed by Hans Schmid; (b, *facing page*) transcribed from manuscript

Di - a - ste - ma - ti - ca vo - cis ar - mo - ni - a
Mu - si - ca me - li - ca, rit - mi - ca, me - tri - ca

fes - ta pas - ca - - li - a ce - le - - - bren - - - - tur!
iam no - va can - ti - ca mo - du - - len - - - - tur!

Refr. Sanctus sancto - rum ! fes - ta fes - to - rum!

re - - sur re - - - - - - - - - xit!

E - y - a, e - y - a, e - y - a!

Plebs fi - de - - lis ju - - bi - let,

gaude - at Ec - cle - - - - - - - - - - - si - a!

over the quite different attitude and procedures followed in the original source. The implied ideal is that for text lines similarly formed and linked with similar melodic ideas, the manuscript ought to show an identical notation for each, the fact that it does not representing some level of scribal failure.

Such streamlining is characteristic of the melodies in that rather more famous source of conductus songs, Florence, Laurenziana, Plut. 29.1 (henceforth F).[8] Comparison between various aspects of the notations preserved in F and Ff.1.17 will help to elucidate more directly the nature of each source. The notation for one strophic song in Ff.1.17 presented more than one way of expressing a repeated mel-

Example 9.1   (*continued*)

1. Di - a - ste - ma - ti - ca   vo - cis ar - mo - ni - ca

2. fe - sta   pa-sca - li - a   ce - le - bren - tur.

3. Mu-si - ca me - li - ca   rid - mi - ca   me - tri-ca

4. iam no-va can - ti - ca   mo-du - len - tur.

[Refrain:]

San-ctus san-cto-rum   fe-sta fe - sto-rum re-sur- re - xit.

e - y- a, e - y- a, e - y- a,

plebs fi de lis iu-bi-let gau-de-at ec - cle - si - (*) a.

* Text scribe wrote syllable "-si-" here; amended by music scribe.

ody; the treatment of melodic repeats in a series of monophonic and polyphonic songs in F will now be examined, drawing on both page layout and musical notation as evidence. As a representative example of monophonic strophic song in this source, the first strophe of Philip the Chancellor's *Dum medium silentium* is transcribed in example 9.2. The song has a melodic structure of X X Y_1 Y_2, followed by a refrain that takes up the Y intonation in its second half (*processit sol iusticie*). In this source, the first musical phrase (X) is repeated without alteration for the second text line (from *et littere*), and the second musical phrase (Y) is sung to both

Example 9.2   Philip the Chancellor, *Dum medium silentium* (first strophe), F, fol. 422v

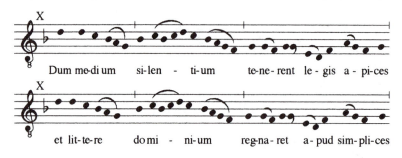

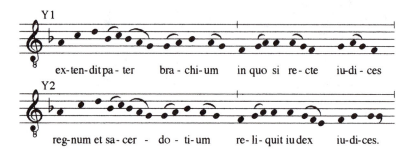

the third and fourth text lines, altered only for the last five syllables of the fourth
(*iudex iudices*), and then, it seems, in order to create a different tonal structure.

In the first melodic phrase (X), the half line closes on *f* (*silentium*) and the full
line on *g* (*apices*). In the second melodic phrase (Y_1), this pattern is reversed, the
half line closing on *g* (*brachium*) and the full line on *f* (*iudices*). The end of Y_1 is
thus tonally open; in addition, the beginning of Y_2 flows on directly, the closing *f*
of Y_1 forming the base of a chain of thirds (*f a c'*). The structural caesura between
the end of Y_1 and the beginning of Y_2 is thus musically bridged, a link that corresponds to the textual syntax. In contrast, at the end of Y_2 the melody returns firmly
to *g* (on the last two syllables, rather than just one, as in X). That tonal close on *g*,
preceding the refrain, is then followed by a liquescence that allows the singer to
join the end of the strophe to the refrain. The tonal close and "joining" liquescence
do not act in opposition but underline the same phenomenon: the main structural
division within the strophe. The portion of the refrain that takes up the Y melody
(*processit sol iu-*) again presents an identical reading.

There are many such examples of exact identity in the song repertories collected
in F; these examples include not only monophonic songs, but polyphonic also.

Example 9.3   Conductus *O vera, o pia* (beginning), F, fol. 242v

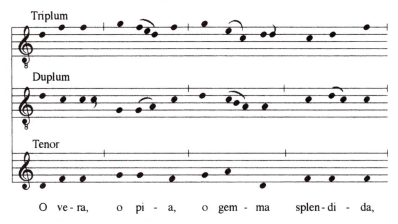

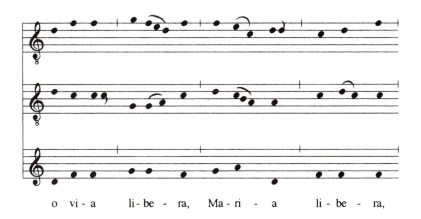

Example 9.3 shows the first two phrases of the three-part conductus *O vera, o pia.* The whole piece has the musical form V V X X Y Y Z (of which the V phrases appear in example 9.3), the repetitions followed through with exactness in each of the three phrases V, X, and Y. Of course, in a polyphonic situation other structural solutions can be applied to a single line that includes repeats. In Peter of Blois's *Vite perdite* (example 9.4), the monophonic version has the form X X Y_1 Y_2 (thus including a considerable amount of repetition), while the combination of two parts in which this acts as a lower line has the form V X Y Z, without repeats in the new upper voice.[9] But here we are faced with an upper line that deliberately presents different solutions to ways of singing against the lower voice, cadencing first in unisons, then in 3rds and 5ths, and finally again with a unison—rather than variations of the same.

One of the most striking examples of melodic identity in F is Philip the Chancellor's much-admired lai, *Veritas, equitas, largitas.* By far the longest among the

Example 9.4   Conductus *Vite perdite*, F, fol. 356

83 conductus of F's tenth fascicle,[10] this is formally elaborate while retaining a fairly consistent syllabic relationship between words and melody. The repetition structure of text and music combined may be expressed as:

AAA BBB CCC′ D EEE F GGG HHH JJJ KKK LL MMM′ N O P Q R.[11]

In the first gathering of this tenth fascicle (fols. 415–30), the text for the second part of a double versicle or for extra strophes of a song was always added, thus forcing a revised and individual layout for each successive page. In contrast, the practice in the second and third gatherings of the fascicle (fols. 431–45, 446–62) was *not* to include text sung to the same melodies, whether for double versicles or extra strophes. Thus, the layout has an entirely different aspect, with staves ruled consistently across the pages, from top to bottom. In many cases longer and more complete texts for these songs can be recovered through concordances, but there are many single-verse unica, possibly representing the torsos of longer compositions. The procedure of not copying text for repeated music was broken only three times in the second and third gatherings of the fascicle; on all three occasions, the layout chosen was not that of the first gathering, but the repeated notation of the music. These three exceptions include *O mens cogita* (fols. 438v–439r), *Veritas, equitas, largitas* (fols. 440v–442v), and *Ave gloriosa virginum* (fols. 447r–448r).[12] As a consequence of the sheer size of *Veritas, equitas, largitas,* its copying with melodic repeats takes up a record four and a half pages. Why the scribe of F decided on this particular course of action for the copying of the lai can only be guessed at: possibly its structure was too complicated to allow of any solution that omitted text. But there can be no doubt that the procedure was not the result of a desire to record varied melodic lines. For whole passages no musical variation, even at the level of liquescence, is apparent. In fact, the copy of the whole lai in F has only five instances of variation between linked parts of the melody (two of these caused by a different syllable count), and these are themselves minimal.[13] Even the closing line repeats the melody of the first precisely (followed by a melismatic setting of the final word).

The varied notation of similar melodic lines in Ff.1.17—where it is more exceptional to find identical notations than not—thus contrasts with a clear pattern in the F notations of precise repetition. This qualitative difference has formed a point of departure for consideration of the relation of these written sources to the musical culture that produced them. Provoked by the description of one of the Ff.1.17 songs as "an unusually full, written-out version of a virtuoso performance,"[14] I wondered just what the notes on the page really meant, how they related to the central musical act of performance, and how interpreters of a different age might learn to understand them. For some of the musical repertories of this era, the need to accept written sources as existing in the context of a predominantly oral musical culture is more critical than for others. In the twelfth and thirteenth centuries, when the physical materials and the skills necessary to make books were more and more widely available, the singing of conductus songs is likely to have involved written sources in a quite different way from, for example, the liturgical chant— the official and regulated body of church music. But I do not want to argue that written and oral practices can be disassociated as if they divided into black and white. On the contrary, I would suggest that we should exercise great caution in putting individual melodic versions down to individual performances, and in differentiating between scribes and performers.

The difficulty in making a separation between scribal (editorial) techniques and performance practice can be illustrated with an example central to the Notre Dame conductus repertory, a setting of another of Philip the Chancellor's poems, *Crux de te volo conqueri.* Composed in the form of a sequence, this consists of a complaint addressed to the Cross by the Virgin Mary, followed by the reply of the Cross, each section in several strophes. The song survives as text only in numerous sources.[15] With its melody it appears in the tenth fascicle of F (fol. 439r–v) and in a Parisian

Example 9.5   Philip the Chancellor, *Crux de te volo conqueri*

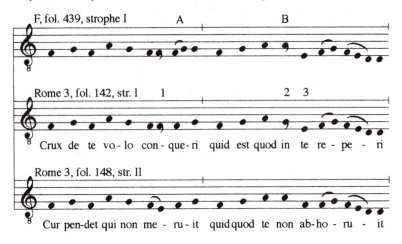

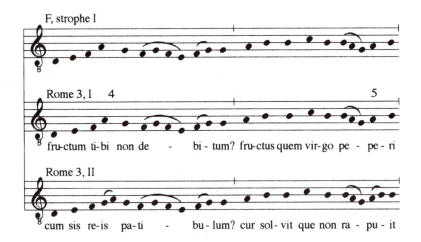

manuscript of the mid-thirteenth century: Rome, Santa Sabina XIV L 3 (hence-forth Rome 3).[16] As usual, the version in F sets out only the first of each double versicle, thus notating the melody once only. But in Rome 3 the whole text is writ-ten out, with the melody notated twice, thus offering the chance for a melodic comparison in a manuscript more closely related to the Parisian situation than Ff.1.17. Example 9.5 shows a transcription of the first four strophes of this song, the melodies and texts for the parallel strophes I and II, III and IV laid out to-gether.[17] The melodic versions in F and in Rome 3 are, by any assessment, very close; the first Rome 3 notation could almost have been copied directly from F. However, it is not primarily the differences between what is transmitted in the two manuscripts that is of interest here, but the differences between the two Rome 3

Example 9.5   (*continued*)

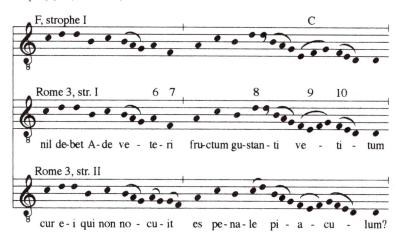

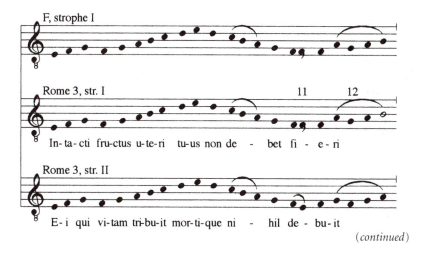

(*continued*)

notations. The numbers 1–29 placed above the staves indicate where these differ, the letters A–I those places where F and the first Rome 3 notation differ.

In this example, differences between the F melody and the first Rome 3 melody appear much less often (nine times) than differences between the two Rome 3 melodies (29 times), and on eight out of the nine occasions where the F and the first Rome 3 notations differ, the two Rome 3 notations also differ. This implies that certain points in the combined structure of text and music were not as exactly fixed as others in the transmission. The idea that the principle of variation is linked with structure is further strengthened by the evidence that a large majority of these "points of variation" occur toward the end of a melodic unit corresponding to a text line. Moreover, many variants between the two Rome 3 notations are evidently

Example 9.5   (*continued*)

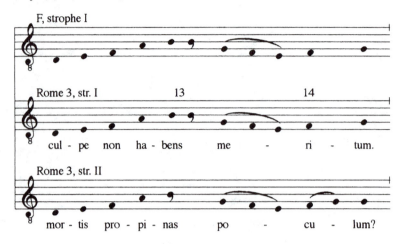

F, strophe I

Rome 3, str. I   13   14

cul - pe   non   ha - bens   me   -   ri   -   tum.

Rome 3, str. II

mor - tis   pro - pi - nas   po   -   cu   -   lum?

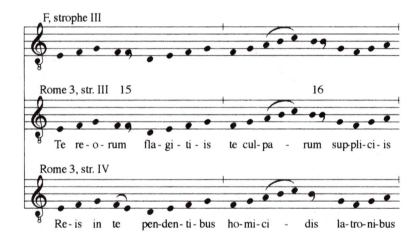

F, strophe III

Rome 3, str. III   15   16

Te   re - o - rum   fla - gi - ti - is   te cul - pa - rum sup-pli-ci- is

Rome 3, str. IV

Re - is   in   te   pen-den- ti- bus ho- mi - ci - dis   la- tro- ni- bus

the result of a need to formulate the melody in relation to different textual patterns, as, for example, at numbers 8 and 23. At 8, the first Rome 3 melody makes a plicated join between the repeated *d*s and the falling figure *bag,* so that the last two syllables of the word *gustanti* are smoothly linked, the melodic shape described by the word being an arch. In the second Rome 3 notation, the division between words comes between the arrival at *d'* and the falling figure *bag;* here the rise to the *d'* is empha- sized by the inclusion of the passing note *c* beforehand, and the jump from *d'* to *b* is left bare. Here the scribe-editor has paid attention to the melodic shape for *poenale,* an inverted arch. At 23, the procedure appears even more transparent. The word division changes position, that is, instead of 4 + 4 syllables, the second stro- phe has 3 + 5 (*sociavit nequitia* replaced by *debetur benedictio*). On the second singing the melody respects the new word division by abandoning the *e'* cadence,

Example 9.5 (*continued*)

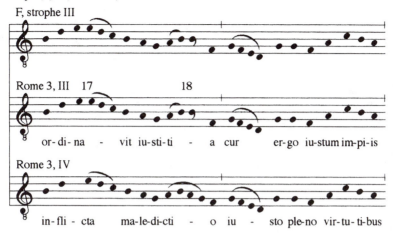

F, strophe III

Rome 3, III 17   18

or- di- na - vit iu-sti-ti - a cur er-go iu-stum im-pi-is

Rome 3, IV

in- fli - cta ma-le-di-cti - o iu - sto ple-no vir-tu- ti-bus

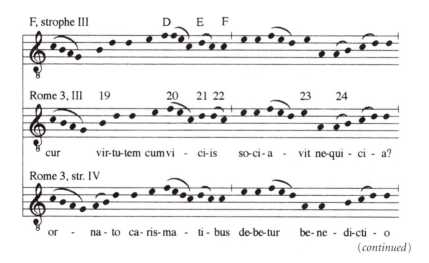

F, strophe III   D   E   F

Rome 3, III   19   20   21 22   23   24

cur   vir-tu-tem cum vi - ci-is   so-ci-a - vit ne-qui - ci - a?

Rome 3, str. IV

or - na - to ca- ris-ma - ti- bus de-be-tur   be- ne - di-cti - o

(*continued*)

and beginning the new pattern on *a* a fifth below one syllable earlier, thereby co-inciding with the beginning of the second word (*benedictio*).

The variants found in these Rome 3 notations are simple, repetitive, and relatively mechanical. There is no quality of variance here that could be imagined to stem directly from a performance of the song rather than from the work of a cautious but well-trained scribe. Indeed the very uniformity of the variants actually suggests the latter. Moreover, the variation displayed here can be seen to be motivated not only by a desire for variety but also by care for a suitable relation between text and music, arguably as important in a "good" performance of the song as any more superficial (ornamental) aspect of virtuosity. In other words, a scribe acting as editor may proceed with artifice as impressive as that of an expert performer. Variation between the two notations of *Diastematica vocis armonia* in Ff.1.17 might

Example 9.5   (*continued*)

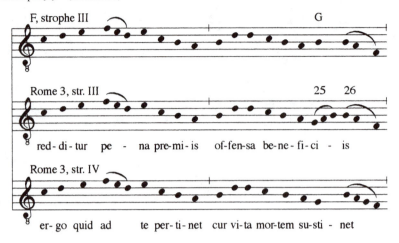

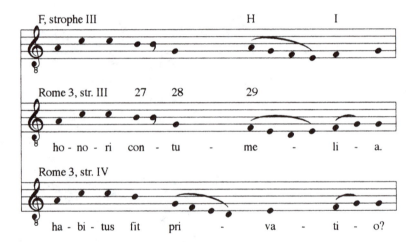

actually represent how scribes imagined—or remembered—a performance, rather than a transcription made directly at the time of a performance.

It is thus the mutuality of the acts of writing down and performing a song that render differentiation between "written" and "performance" versions redundant. Commenting on the comparison of Aquitanian trope melodies, Treitler stated: "the most we can say about writing down here is that it is a way of exemplifying the piece, just as performing it was a way of exemplifying it" (Treitler 1981, 209). For every way in which one can imagine a performer treating a song, one can imagine a scribe with the same inclinations, whether it be a question of tonal organization, melismatic expression, or text/music relations. The reality of our modern situation, cut off from actual performances, is that the written versions of songs can only reflect *rather than represent* actual performances.

Example 9.6   *In hoc ortus occidente*

F, fol. 417v, Strophe I

Hu, fol. 167

Ff.1.17, fol. 298v

In hoc or - tus oc- ci-den - te sol e- mer-gens   de tor-ren - te

F

Hu

Ff.1.17

te- ne-bras il - lu - mi - nat no - stre sor- tis um-bra te - ctus

(*continued*)

With this in mind, the last part of this study will further explore the relation of
Ff.1.17 and F through the comparison of their settings of the song *In hoc ortus
occidente*. This has the sequential form X X Y Y Z Z. In example 9.6, the first pair
of versicles is transcribed from each of F (fols. 417r–418r) and Ff.1.17 (fols. 298v–
299r); the third version is that transmitted in Burgos, Monasterio de Las Huelgas,
cod. 9 (fol. 167r–v).[18] This last source has music for the first strophe only. In their
degree of prolixity, the Ff.1.17 and F versions for the first pair of versicles are
roughly comparable. But from the beginning of the second pair on, and particularly in the closing melisma of this, the F melody is conspicuously more extrava-
gant than that notated in Ff.1.17. It seems to be one of the rules of the way the *In
hoc ortus occidente* melodies are made that there should be considerable musical
ornamentation of the last three syllables of each text versicle. A comparison of each
of the versions with each other and of the melodies for each successive pair of
versicles shows that each part of the melody has been formulated with a clear
procedure in mind. Each closing melisma begins from d', or somewhere close to
it (the important thing here is that the melismas do not begin from the final g),

Example 9.6   (*continued*)

Example 9.6 (*continued*)

sal - vo   ta   -   men   pu - do - ris   sig - na - cu -

lo   pa - rit na - ta   ge - ni - to - rem fa - ctor

se - cli   su - pra   mo   -   rem   fa - ctus est in

- cu -

se -

(*continued*)

Example 9.6   (*continued*)

Strophe V

cu — lo. Qui dum re-um sol-vit gra - tis

ob-vi-a- trix ve - ri - ta - tis   fit mi-se-ri-cor - di - a

et de lu - to   pax   e - re - xit   et de ce-lo

—a.

rises by step to g', falls to g, and soon cadences on g. Those are the basic rules. Taking each melisma in turn, that at the end of the first versicle (*ter-mi-*nat) is the shortest of the three. It has a direct and symmetrical shape with the rising fourth d' to g' balanced by a falling fourth c' to g. The scalic rise to g' and fall to d' has already been heard several times, most recently with the words *fert languores et defectus*. There the rise to g' and immediate fall is followed by the fall c' to g, leading here not to g but to f. The melodic endings of these two text lines are therefore arranged in the relation ouvert/clos. In the F and Las Huelgas melodies, these patterns are formed in simple scalic gestures, whereas the Ff.1.17 version has its own micro-pattern, the falling fourth each time missing one note, $a'g'e'$, $g'f'd'$, $c'ag$.

In the next versicle a contrast between long- and short-term planning in the F and Ff.1.17 versions is again apparent. On "*matri*," both melodic versions have a melisma, both substantially falling, and succeeded by the note c'. Here, the F melody returns directly to the pattern of the melisma heard twice in the first versicle, using a stepwise rise to g' and fall to a'. The Ff.1.17 melody has no rising element, but begins with the ornamental motif $e'd'e'd'$, taken up from the immediately preceding syllable (obumbra*vit*). For the second text line (*que concepit salvo tamen*), the Ff.1.17 melody includes two similar four-note motives ($d'e'd'c'$, $bc'ba$), each sung to the third of four text syllables. F, on the other hand, has an altogether more complex line for *salvo tamen*, contriving thereby to introduce a falling pattern from b to f, which later forms a basic constituent of the melisma at the end of the third line (*pudoris signaculo*) in both versions.

Finally, at the end of this second strophe, both versions include sequential patterns: in Ff.1.17 on $e'd'e'd'c'$, $d'c'd'c'ba$, in F on the higher pitches $a'b'a'g'f'$, $g'a'g'f'e'$, $f'g'f'e'd'$. Such motivic sequences are a standard way of building up ornamental gestures. After this both versions have the scale falling from g' to g. Characteristically, F repeats this in the exact form of the first strophe (moving from d' up to g' before falling to g), and also adds an anticipation of this, left incomplete on b.

The melodic versions of *In hoc ortus occidente* in F and Ff.1.17 are thus extremely close, the differences between them a matter of surface detail. Nevertheless, their comparison highlights some specific behaviors of their respective scribe-editors. Long melismatic elaborations in the F melodies suggest an emphasis of rhetorical elements of musical presentation. In this respect the Ff.1.17 version of *In hoc ortus occidente* is less elaborate (or "virtuoso"), its "high style" less developed. Equally, the F melodies indicate an interest in long-term organization and uniformity, set against the working out of localized patterns in the Ff.1.17 versions. This movement toward integration of musical behavior in different melodic passages appears consistent with that other characteristic of the F song melodies pointed out above, that is, their repetition of melodic passages in identical (as opposed to varied) form.

It is an outstanding characteristic of the two major sources of Parisian polyphony actually copied in Paris (F, and Wolfenbüttel, Herzog-August-Bibliothek, Helmstedt 1099), that they represent written artifacts of a high grade. In F, the quality of parchment, regularity of text and music scripts, care in layout, and presence of fine illuminations match a concern to provide music for all the texts copied. The significance of this meticulousness is all the more clear when the numerous thirteenth-century sources that transmit texts of conductus songs only, without any interest in the transmission of musical settings, are brought into consideration.

While F exemplifies the highest grade of book ever prepared for music—a grade rarely found among notated liturgical books (with the rare exception of a few pontificals), Ff.1.17 stands just as far away from the average notated liturgical book in an opposite sense. Subject to frequent omissions of music, irregularly and untidily written and notated, messy in all aspects of presentation, and not thoroughly planned—in all senses, a less sophisticated physical object than F—the little libellus must have occupied an entirely different kind of role in relation to the recording and transmission of conductus songs. In its numerous gaps and general roughness, Ff.1.17 appears to place less emphasis on the fact of writing music down, to be less conscious of this as an act in its own terms and with its own ramifications; in consequence, the libellus might be considered to represent a document with a more immediate relation to an oral situation than F, and to reflect something less distant from actual moments of performance of the music. As a beautiful and highly organized written artifact, F displays a new level of engagement with the potential offered by written transmission, showing a concern with the quality of its musical texts and with their status as written "things." Crucially, that concern appears to have had a direct effect on how the detail of specific melodic structures was recorded.

In the fifty or so years that separate the making of Ff.1.17 and F, attitudes to the written transmission not only of music, but many other kinds of texts also, as well as ownership of books and perceptions of their status, had begun to alter, above all in Paris and the Île-de-France.[19] Of course, that is far from enough to explain the differences between the two sources—for which specific scribal intentions and localized resources must provide much of the answer. But perceptions of the songs that make up most of the content of Ff.1.17, and a distinct portion of F, must have played some part in shaping scribal intentions. Created, enjoyed—indulged in—on the margins of the liturgy in the eleventh and twelfth centuries, those conductus songs had become by the mid-thirteenth century an officially supported (and thus controllable) part of the performance of the Divine Office in many parts of France. So much is clear both from the highly organized Circumcision Offices produced in this period, and from the inclusion of such songs in a codex as deliberately polished as F. Seen from this perspective, it is the very marginality of Ff.1.17 that determines its high historical interest, its roughness and immediacy suggesting enthusiastic cultivation by those who made the libellus—in the face of mere tolerance by those who controlled the situation in which it was made—of these unchantlike songs.

Notes

1. For the Latin text of *Diastematica vocis armonia* and its musical setting see example 9.1; for this translation I am indebted to David Howlett. Two further strophes

are reproduced in Schumann (1943–50), 64–65; the use in the song of vocabulary associated with contemporary music theory was the subject of Schmid (1971).

2. The Circumcision Offices of Laon, Beauvais, and Sens transmit a large number of non-chant songs. On these see especially Arlt (1970) and Fassler (1992). To the three thirteenth-century Offices may be added a further example from Le Puy, recorded in two later medieval books; on this see Arlt (1992) and this volume, chap. 14.

3. On possible interpretations of the name "conductus," a term sometimes used in relation to this material, see Reckow (1973).

4. The manuscript is reproduced in facsimile in Bryan Gillingham, *Cambridge.* See also Schumann (1943–50), Reaney, *Manuscripts,* 485–86, and Stevens (1982).

5. On the restoration to Cambridge Gg.v.35 of a missing folio see Gibson, Lapidge, and Page (1983).

6. That a multiplicity of scribes worked on these pages is beyond doubt; on the basis of paleographical observations Schumann suggested a division of the copying into 11 stints (1943–50, 51).

7. Example 9.1*a* is reproduced from Schmid (1971), 396; fol. 1v of Ff.1.17, containing *Diastematica vocis armonia,* is reproduced in Stevens (1982), 42, as well as in Gillingham, *Cambridge,* 4.

8. The manuscript is reproduced in facsimile in Luther Dittmer, *Firenze;* for a recent discussion of the source with further bibliography, see Roesner, *Le Magnus liber,* lxx–lxxiii.

9. The song was transmitted in both versions, in F for two voices and in Munich, BS lat. 4880 (fol. 4r) for one.

10. On the songs in this fascicle of F see especially Steiner (1963) and (1966); the songs are edited (in a mensural interpretation) in Anderson, "1 pt Conductus."

11. C′ has one less syllable than C, M′ one more than M. R is the same as A, with a closing extension.

12. For this last, the scribe entered the full text, and in this sense declared an intention that musical repeats be written out, but no notation was ever entered for the portions of the song on fols. 447v–448r.

13. Just four instances of variation are not provoked by different numbers of text syllables: these include (a) two falling notes replaced by a single liquescent note, (b) a single note placed on a different pitch, (c) a rising liquescence replaced by two rising notes, and (d) two falling notes replaced by a single note.

14. Thus Stevens (1986), 70 ff., on the song *Argumentur falluntur.*

15. Listed in Anderson, "1 pt Conductus," 145.

16. For a discussion of this source see Husmann (1967).

17. The comparison of strophes V and VI does not alter the results won from examination of the first four; they are omitted here only for reasons of space.

18. A black and white facsimile of the manuscript was published by Anglès in 1931 (*El còdex*); a colour facsimile has recently been published by the Patrimonio Nacional of Spain (*Códice*).

19. The literature on books and book ownership in this period is too immense to list; a recent study that confronts changing attitudes to the collecting of music and poetry in books is Huot (1987).

IV ✦ REGIONAL DEVELOPMENTS

The Carolingian Period to the Later Middle Ages

Office Compositions from St. Gall

Saints Gallus and Otmar

HARTMUT MÖLLER

The name Saint Gall is inextricably linked to the monastery of the same name and its influence, which spanned several centuries. Founded in the seventh century by the wandering Irish monk Gallus, this one-time hermit's cell rapidly developed in the Carolingian period into a magnificent monastic complex, which for the most part corresponds to the sketch of the much-studied ground plan from around 820. The position of this monastery politically, intellectually, and linguistically parallels its multifaceted and extensive contributions to liturgy and music, broadly documented in a large number of extant sources. From St. Gall there are classic manuscripts representing the *Ordines Romani,* pontificals, early lectionaries as well as numerous evangeliaries, calendars, sacramentaries (among them the well-known younger Gelasian sacramentary), martyrologies, psalters, sequence books (Notker's *Liber hymnorum*), hymnals, graduals, and antiphoners (see introduction in Auf der Maur 1990).

Early examples of important types of chant books from St. Gall are central sources in the field: the St. Gall cantatorium (a source containing solo Mass chants) from the early tenth century and the antiphoner of the monk Hartker, which dates from around the year 1000 and is one of the earliest fully notated sources for the Office, have been used as the primary sources for many studies; both are printed in facsimile in the series Paléographie musicale. St. Gall has earned its leading position in chant studies not only through its wealth of sources, but also through the innovative leaders who, in some cases, actually produced these books: Notker, Tuotilo, and others who with their specific contributions to the new genres of chants from the ninth century onward ornamented and supplemented the standard Gregorian repertory: tropes, sequences, and versus. The oldest written chant texts for the Office may very well originate from St. Gall: the Winithar fragment from around 770, which documents a pre-Carolingian arrangement of chants through its antiphons and responsories for the Purification of Mary (2 February) and for one of the Sundays in Lent (see Dold 1940). Unfortunately, subsequent sources for Office chants from St. Gall, either texts or music, are extremely rare in both the ninth and tenth centuries. There are, however, two precious manuscripts in which Office chants for the local saints Gallus and Otmar have been recorded, together with *vitae* and other related texts for these saints. These unique sources provide the keys for understanding the development of cult at St. Gall; the newly created Office chants allow a glimpse into the creation of Offices in tenth-century St. Gall, helping to shape a picture of this particular process in its formative period. If, as Walter Berschin has stressed, "music and poetry of the Latin Middle Ages are so closely connected that it is practically impossible to understand the one without the other" (Berschin 1981, 21), then the musical realization of the poetry of antiphons and responsories requires close attention. What exactly did a St. Gall monk of the tenth century do when, according to the testimony of Ekkehart IV (*Casus S. Galli*, p. 238), he *fecit* or *scripsit* or *dictavit* a particular Office? What—as Ekkehart said in the case of responsories for the feast of Gallus and the antiphons for the feast of Otmar—determines the "delicate" element of these chants: the sparse formulations? the dramaturgy of the entire Office? or the melodies themselves? Did the creator of the new Offices restrict himself to the combining of texts and "to a rhythmic and occasionally rhyming rounding off of the texts, what might be called a 'musical preparation' of the texts?" (Berschin 1981, 22–23). But then who took on the musical creation once the texts were so "prepared"? Or did the musical formulation belong to the author himself, the one who "created," or "wrote," or "dictated" an Office? As the following study will show, there are strong indications that the study of Office poetry from tenth-century St. Gall requires simultaneous reflection on the musical composition as well.[1] The work was a collaborative one between composer and poet, and in this chapter I will demonstrate how we know this, and how this knowledge affects our understanding of not only texts and music, but also the process by which they were created.

What appears to be the oldest source of the two manuscripts containing chants for the two primary local saints is an exquisitely written codex on fine parchment, Wolfenbüttel, HAB Guelf. 17.5. Aug. 4° (= *W*). Based on the so-called "Initialenzeile" of the marking system, Walter Berschin has dated this manuscript to the epoch of Abbot-Bishop Salomo III (890–920).[2] The Office for St. Gallus is on fols. 87v–91v, between Walafrid Strabo's *vitae* for Gallus and for Otmar; Otmar's Office itself is at the end of the manuscript, following Iso's *Miracula S. Otmari* on fol. 140r. The less magnificent, but still deluxe, London, BL Add. 21170 (= *L*), dated by Berschin to around 920 (the end of the Salomonic epoch), has the Gallus Office in a similar location, on fols. 95r–99r. The Offices of both saints were also copied around the year 1000 in the Antiphoner of Hartker (= *H*), St. Gall, SB 390/91. Other early sources of the Offices from the tenth or early eleventh centuries are the Brussels manuscript, BR 8860–8867 (= *B*), on fols. 74v–76r, and the introductory bifolio of St. Gall, SB 211 (= *S*).[3]

In the two oldest St. Gall "Codices domestici" *W* and *L* as well as in the Hartker Codex, the Gallus Office consists of 22 antiphons and 12 responsories for First and Second Vespers, Matins, and Lauds. Thirty-two of these 34 text units have Walafrid Strabo's *Vita S. Galli* as their source; the other two texts are praise formulations extracted from the common Office for a Confessor, and serve both as the twelfth responsory and as the Magnificat antiphon.[4] The contents are as follows:[5]

Liturgical position	Chant
First Vespers	
Magnificat ant.	Venerabilis Gallus
First Nocturn	
Ant. 1	Parentes vero + Ps. 1
Ant. 2	Cumque bone indolis vir + Ps. 2
Ant. 3	Cum proficiscendi tempus + Ps. 3
Ant. 4	Pedibus vero sui + Ps. 4
Ant. 5	O febrem omni laude colendam + Ps. 5
Ant. 6	Pro nobis Gallus doluit + Ps. 8
Resp. 1	Parentes vero V. Erant enim religiosi
Resp. 2	Beatus Gallus zelo V. In conspectu omnium
Resp. 3	Columbanus itaque V. Cum ad horam orationis
Resp. 4	Athleta dei Gallus V. In oratione quoque
Second Nocturn	
Ant. 7	Inter prandendum + Ps. 10
Ant. 8	Videntibus qui aderant + Ps. 14
Ant. 9	Coeperunt omnes clerici + Ps. 20
Ant. 10	Sanctus pater respondit + Ps. 23
Ant. 11	Ecclesiae pastores + Ps. 64
Ant. 12	Cum artifices + Ps. 91
Resp. 5	Beatus Gallus cum orandi V. Hoc videns diaconus
Resp. 6	Domine Iesu Christe V. Qui de virgine nasci
Resp. 7	Electus dei Gallus V. Prepara in hoc loco
Resp. 8	Vir deo plenus V. Pro eius ergo requie
Third Nocturn	
Canticle ant.	Gallus dei famulus
Resp. 9	Pater sanctus V. Expletis nonaginta V. Cum iam bonorum
Resp. 10	Deus pro cuius amore V. Qui per tue
Resp. 11	Quidem mendicus V. Et exiliens gratias
Resp. 12	Iste sanctus digne V. Vinculis carnis
Lauds	
Ant. 1	Habuit vir dei capsellam
Ant. 2	Huius ipse clavem
Ant. 3	De hac vero vita
Ant. 4	Corpus autem
Ant. 5	De vulneribus
Benedictus ant.	Superposito
Second Vespers	
Magnificat ant.	Iste sanctus digne

The Otmar Office exists in more than one version, and in part these versions reflect the changing nature of the saint's stature. Originally the *Vita S. Otmari* by Walafrid, with its 17 chapters, had been conceived merely as a "continuation" of the monumental Gallus *vita*, with 80 chapters. However, in connection with the two translations of Otmar's relics in 864 and 867, the Otmar *Memoria* acquired greater significance. The results of this augmentation of his cult were, among other things, the two books of *Miracula* by Iso of St. Gall, a figure famous also as the teacher of Notker. "In the period of 35 years . . . consistently increasing the work of biographical house literature" (Berschin 1981, 328), these local saints obtained three fixed and interrelated bodies of materials: Walafrid's *Vita S. Galli* and *Vita S. Otmari* plus Iso's *Miracula S. Otmari*. The most truncated version of Otmar's Office is that found in *W* and *B*, which consists of the following antiphons:

Liturgical position	Chant
First Vespers	
Magnificat ant.	Mendaces ostendit
Lauds	
Ant. 1	Beatus Otmarus abba
Ant. 2	Sepultus ergo decem annos
Ant. 3	Post decem vero annos
Ant. 4	Cumque navi sanctum corpus
Ant. 5	Fratribus autem ad refectionem
Benedictus ant.	Beati ergo corpus Otmari
Second Vespers	
Magnificat ant.	In vinculis non dereliquit

In his antiphoner Hartker took over these older Lauds antiphons in their entirety from earlier sources, but then expanded the two Vesper antiphons and inserted a series of antiphons for the Night Office (*CAO* 2, no. 117[5], p. 618). Yet more materials are found on the younger bifolio *S*, which contains twelve responsories written by a clearly defined hand of the eleventh century—a hand that, according to Walter Berschin, displays a remarkable likeness to that of Ekkehart IV (d. around 1060). Noticeable, too, are the numerous corrections made by the first hand.

Liturgical position	Chant
First Nocturn	
Resp. 1	Sanctus confessor domini V. Domino initiatus
Resp. 2	Pontificali manu benedictus V. Scale Iacob somnii
Resp. 3	Virtutum operibus Otmarus V. A quo ecclesiam sancti florini
Resp. 4	Dilectus deo et hominibus V. Ipsum deduxit dominus
Second Nocturn	
Resp. 5	Quidam vir nobilis de suevos V. Et gloriosissimi regis
Resp. 6	Summe fame pastore gratantes V. Quoniam illic mandavit
Resp. 7	Vir deo plenus monasterio V. Studiis et sumptu locum
Resp. 8	Sanctus Otmarus pater pauperum V. Ieiuniis atque vigiliis
Third Nocturn	
Resp. 9	Cum decreivisset dominus dilectum V. Ibi diem obiens
Resp. 10	Descendit dominus cum sancto Otmaro V. Donec afferet illi
Resp. 11	Sancte deo dilecte confessor V. Sancte et gloriose certator Christi
Resp. 12	Mendaces ostendit dominus V. Candelabrum ponite tante lucerne

Through these twelve responsories, the series of Matins antiphons in the Hartker Codex was supplemented to create the Office; the texts show numerous verbatim overlappings with the antiphons. In the opinion of Walter Berschin "the series of responsories has the appearance of a 'rival' to the series of antiphons, rather than a mere supplement to them."[6] If this is correct, then the twelve responsories arranged on an inserted bifolio of *H* may be an attempt to supplement the earlier antiphons with corresponding responsories for a complete Night Office.

Liturgical position	Chant
First Nocturn	
Resp. 1	Sanctus confessor V. Saluti hominum
Resp. 2	Hic ut in virile robur V. Omni laudabilis vite
Resp. 3	Vir dei Otmarus celle beati Galli V. Vere fidelis et prudens
Resp. 4	Quodam tempore sanctus pater V. Paternis visceribus inopie
Second Nocturn	
Resp. 5	Igitur pater venerandus V. Nam lupis ovile domini
Resp. 6	Iudices vero iniqui tecnis V. Sed nimiis doloribus
Resp. 7	Beatus confessor Christi Otmarus V. Iussu tyrannorum carcere
Resp. 8	Cum autem creator agonum certamine V. Dilectus deo et hominibus
Third Nocturn	
Resp. 9	Preciosissimo corporis almi V. Ut tante claritas
Resp. 10	Quidam vero de tecto basilice V. Non sine ammiratione
Resp. 11	Sanctimonialis quedam utrisque V. Auditis de eo tantis
Resp. 12	Inclite confessor fratrumque fidelis V. Virtutum radiis qui clarus

The following investigation traces the musical creation of both Offices, but with varying emphases, depending upon the nature of the materials. With the Gallus Office questions regarding the stability and variation of the transmission of syllabic and melismatic sections as well as issues concerning detailed melodic shaping of the antiphons stand in the foreground. With the Otmar Office, however, I will be dealing with observations on the relationship of transmission routes and the musical classification of the Brussels manuscript (*B*) as well as the modal ordering of the various responsory series. Finally, the music-historical consequences will be considered, especially as these relate to the dating of the oldest Otmar antiphons. With valuable and unique sources such as these, we are able to glimpse at first hand the ways in which music and texts for new offices were created in the tenth and eleventh centuries, examining the adaptation of older materials to new circumstances, and the rich textures of the final products themselves.

The Chants of the Gallus Office

The manuscripts Wolfenbüttel (= *W*) and London (= *L*) predate the notated antiphoner of Hartker (= *H*) and are the oldest extant sources for the chants of the Gallus Office. Text and neumes—as both a collective impression and comparison of individual signs show—are by different hands. Both copies of the *Historia* in *W* and *L* were planned from the start for neumation. This is demonstrated first by the common decrease in the script size for the chant texts, as is observable at the transition from the Gallus hymn to the Office in both manuscripts (*W*, fol. 87v, *L*, fol. 95r). Second, the syllable division with respect to the extended melismas attests to a planned notation, especially obvious, for example, in the responsory *Beatus Gallus cum orandi* at *seculum* (*W*, fol. 89r, *L*, fol. 97v). In two places syllables added in the margin indicate that these emendations were planned in connection with the neumation; thus the neumator was active as redactor along with the person editing the text. In the responsory *Iste sanctus* in *L* (fol. 98r) the *pat(ria)* that belongs between *aeterna* and *conversatus* was entered in the margin; in the antiphon *Superposito* in *W* (fol. 91r) the word *itere* has been corrected to *itinere* through an added syllable in the margin. In *L* the neume grouping tractulus-virga-clivis-tractulus stands over the four-syllable word *itinere;* in *W* the *-re* was added with the tractulus in the margin, and although the erroneously written *itere* was not actually corrected, still, in connection with the syllable *-re* (added in the margin), it clearly should be read as *itinere:*

$$\text{-}\ /\ \Lambda\ \text{-} \qquad \text{-}\ /\ \Lambda \qquad \text{-}$$
$$\text{i-ti-ne-re} \qquad \text{i-te-re} \qquad \text{re}$$

The paleographic closeness of text hand and neume hand to the main contents indicates that text scribe and neumator worked around the same time; that is, in *W* and *L* the texts of the Gallus chants were provided with neumes soon after they were copied.

Stability and variation

With respect to the transmission of musical notation, a comparison of the sources reveals that none of the three versions (*W, L,* and *H*) was directly copied from another: all three versions are independent, and represent clarified reworkings of the sung sequence of pitches. Thus we can tell that neumation existed alongside the oral transmission of the melodies, serving to jog the memory of the initiated singer and deriving their meanings primarily from the remembered sung melodies of the tenth century. What took place was an associative and interactive process dependent upon both memory and neumation, which we can no longer recover, the oral tradition being lost to us. Certainly comparison of older neumed sections with the versions in Karlsruhe, Landesbibl. Aug. LX (twelfth or thirteenth century) brings us astonishingly close to the lost melismas of the tenth century.[7] But select examples reveal very different situations regarding the predominantly syllabic antiphons, on the one hand, and the melismatic passages in the responsories on the other.

As the antiphon *Parentes vero* demonstrates (example 10.1), among the three manuscripts with adiastematic (unheightened) neumes there are a series of differences—in the areas of agogic and articulating distinctions through the episema—and in the case of the Hartker antiphoner through the *litterae significativae.* The two variants in the number of tones (clivis + virga strata or clivis + oriscus at "gal*li*" as well as clivis and torculus, respectively, at "ma*gis*terio") are, if one compares the neumation of all Gallus chants with one another, more the exception than the rule. In addition, with respect to the number of individual pitches in the compound neumes, no other variants can be discerned between *W* and *L*. In comparison with the more recent version in Karlsruhe Aug. LX we find only three places in this antiphon with neumatic variants (see neumes in the example). This evidence corresponds to that of the other five antiphons of the first mode.

Example 10.1   Antiphon *Parentes vero beati Galli*

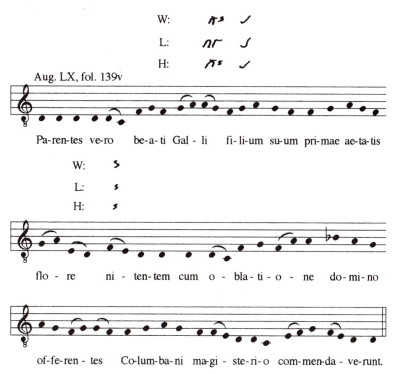

The transmission of melismatic excerpts is also remarkably consistent in the three neumed manuscripts: in the first and fourth responsories of the third nocturn, melismas stand above one syllable at the close of the responsory, unquestionably for the embellishment of each responsory with its final repetition at the doxology (example 10.2). There are early examples of *neumata* in the Office responsories, resembling the types of phrases described by the liturgist Amalarius of Metz in the first half of the ninth century, and exemplified by the famous and later widely disseminated *neuma triplex* (see T. Kelly 1988, 1–30). And just as this triple melismatic interpolation occurs in the first mode, so too, as can be seen at the psalmodic formula of the verse, are the two *neumata* of the Gallus responsories in mode 1.

In both melismas the neume groupings are repeated, and through their repetition structure they share a similar musically autonomous syntactic course. The *neuma* for *Pater sanctus* has the form aa bb c, that for *Iste sanctus* aa bb cc'. Hartker divides the individual members through the added letters of *x* (= *expectare*) (Froger 1962). His attentiveness to details within each repeated section, including the signifying letters, shows his efforts at an especially precise transcription and performance of a melisma not bound to language, which indeed, according to the famous testimony of Notker in his *Liber ymnorum*, adheres less well in the memory than when the notes move syllabically. Still, *W* and *L*—apart from the two minimal and semiologically irrelevant differences in the neumation—are completely in

Example 10.2　Responsory *neumata* in the first tone

W

H

Con- ver-sa- - - tus est

W

L

H

P_{ER} -en-ni--bus

agreement with one another as far as the apparent pitches are concerned. However, as the example demonstrates, the repetition structures in the melismas of *W* and *L* are not standardized in the manner of writing. As can be seen in the comparison of those places marked (3) and (1), the neumation is varied. In *W* the clivis is modified by episema only the first time; in *L* the clivis and pressus are written separately the second time. The neumation of the sources suggests remarkable uniformity of practice within particular codices, but variation in the use of the neumation and its purposes between individual sources themselves.

Formulaic composition

In the texts of the Office of St. Gall, as Peter Ochsenbein has shown, "the heritage of Walafrid . . . is preserved in almost all of the 32 texts, even down to matters of diction, and adapted only to the extent that, although no longer precisely part of the narrative, still the *Memoria Sancti Galli* can be sensed throughout" (Berschin, Ochsenbein, and Möller 1991, 22). As far as music is concerned, it is precisely in the Office antiphons that the somewhat varied musical forms present a more colorful, varied picture than, for instance, do the melodies of the Mass propers or Office responsories for the feast. Therefore, using select antiphon melodies as examples, we will investigate the relationship between the musical formulation of the newly composed songs and the received repertory of antiphon melodies. Are we looking at a simple adaptation to existing melodic models, or do we see traces of artistic transformation of the traditional forms and formulas? What were the attitudes of composers for the Office toward the inherited practice, especially as regards antiphon formulas and melody types?

Six of the St. Gall Office antiphons are in the first mode and are assigned to psalmodic cadences identified with tonal letters in the margins of Hartker's Antiphoner.[8] In the chanting of psalms and antiphons, there are always two major musical events taking place. First of all, each psalm was sung to one of the eight tones, and each of these tones has a range of possible termination formulas, or

Example 10.3   First-mode psalm endings and antiphons for St. Gallus

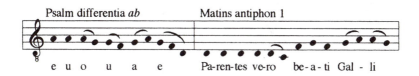

"differentiae" (see Berschin, Ochsenbein, and Möller 1991, 22, and example 10.3). But not only were the verses of every psalm sung using the tones; in addition, each of these was prefaced and closed by the singing of an antiphon, and the melodies of many antiphons are formulaic. One of the questions music historians are concerned with is the relationship between the actual music of the antiphons and the formulaic types of these melodies; the nature of these musical relationships helps explain how the music developed and how the tonal systems supporting the chanting of the psalms both evolved and were defined. The openings of antiphons seemingly belonging to a particular group are compared in example 10.3; three antiphons belong to a group using differentia *a*, one antiphon uses differentia *ab*, and one antiphon is realized by differentia *ag*.

As can be observed from comparing their opening phrases, the first four of these antiphons do in fact begin with a common melodic formula, one found in over 100 antiphons in the modern antiphoner. As these antiphons continue, however, they cease to follow any common base melody. (The fifth antiphon, *Iste sanctus*, follows the typical incipit of antiphons belonging to the tonal letter *ag*.) At the root of the first four antiphons lies a common melodic contour comprised of four

Example 10.4   Antiphon *Ecclesiae pastores*

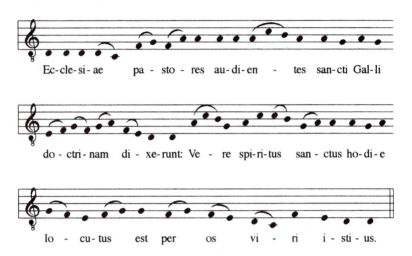

parts, with several formulas belonging to the section of melody that follows the first statement (see Schmidt 1980). The fact that in the Hartker Antiphoner and in the more recent Alemannic tradition these four antiphons are classified with two different differentiae (or cadential formulas), *a* and *b*, despite their common melodic incipit, does not agree with Ephrem Omlin's general observation that the melodic framework of an antiphon's opening is the determining factor in assigning a piece to a specific tonal letter (Omlin 1934, 90). In principle the first and second members of this type of antiphon are related to each other as question and answer; comparison of the two antiphon melodies *Parentes vero beati Galli* (example 10.1) and *Ecclesiae pastores* (example 10.4) shows that the initial rise from *dcd* to *a* is answered by the descent to *d*. The two antiphons use different formulaic paths to accomplish this tonal journey from an ornamented *d* up to *a*, and back again to *d*.

But what is the relationship between these particular formulations of the descent from *a* to *d* in these two St. Gall antiphons and the usual melodic formulas of first-mode antiphons? As can be seen in example 10.5, the formulaic descent from *a* to *d* in *Ecclesiae pastores* corresponds to the use of this formula in older mode 1 antiphons. In fact, the section in the antiphon *Ecclesiae pastores* expands one of these formulas by the addition of a recitative-like oscillation on *a*.

What does the neumation of this passage reveal? The juxtaposition of comparable passages from older antiphons shows that the neume on "audi*e*ntes" is not particularly significant; it merely includes the upper third that is so characteristic of the mode. Moreover, the use of a torculus in the predominant alternation of individual tones and two-tone groups is rare but not unknown.[9] A noteworthy aspect of this figure is its appearance on a stressed syllable, "audi*e*ntes", so that the "hearing" is emphasized in a particular way, and moreover that this figure corresponds to the setting of the word *Vere* at the beginning of the third line of text, which introduces the reaction of the *pastores ecclesiae*, quoted verbatim from the message of Gallus: their witness is legitimized by the fact that they have *heard*

Example 10.5   Mode 1 antiphon formulas of the descent from *a* to *d*

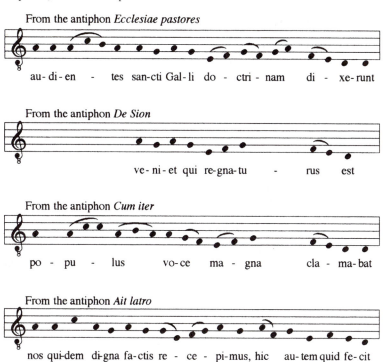

From the antiphon *Ecclesiae pastores*

au- di- en - tes san-cti Gal- li do - ctri - nam   di - xe-runt

From the antiphon *De Sion*

ve- ni- et qui re-gna-tu   -   rus   est

From the antiphon *Cum iter*

po - pu - lus   vo- ce   ma - gna   cla - ma-bat

From the antiphon *Ait latro*

nos qui-dem di-gna fa-ctis re - ce - pi-mus, hic   au- tem quid fe- cit

Gallus with their own ears and acknowledged this by the musical character of their reply (see example 10.4).

Another fascinating permutation of formula types is found in the second section of these mode 1 antiphons, as exemplified by the music of the antiphon *Parentes* (see example 10.6). Normally the opening of the formula *fga* emphasizes the *g*. But in *Parentes* the initial *f* is accentually superordinate to the *a*. The series of tones on *filium suum* is repeated exactly in the adjacent *primae aetatis*. The word *flore* receives the second accent of the normal formula on *g*. The sequence of the pes *ga* plus clivis *ed* gives the contrasting third *ge* its own weight, whereby the "flower of youth" in which the young Gallus abounds is given expression. In this antiphon, the corresponding text of the *vita* has been shortened to four lines, which would have made a musical setting following the model of a four-part melody very possible, even obvious. And yet at *cum oblatione* the antiphon begins again with the familiar initial formula of the beginning: the unity of the antiphon text contrasts with the two-part nature of the music, in which the initial and final formulas correspond. This two-part character is, moreover, prepared by a connection of the two first sections at the genitive "beati Gal*li*" by means of the clivis *ag* instead of the usual *a* (see example 10.1).

These repetitions and correspondences, and others that can be observed in the new St. Gall antiphoner of the tenth century, are in a remarkable state of tension with the general melodic style of the antiphon repertory. Richard Crocker convinc-

Example 10.6   Antiphon formula

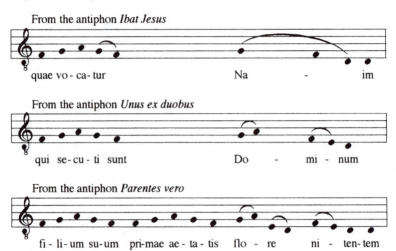

From the antiphon *Ibat Jesus*

quae vo - ca- tur   Na   -   im

From the antiphon *Unus ex duobus*

qui se- cu- ti sunt   Do   -   mi - num

From the antiphon *Parentes vero*

fi - li- um su-um pri-mae ae - ta - tis flo - re   ni - ten- tem

ingly described this relationship in negative terms as a "tendency to avoid repetition" on the different levels of configuration of melodic detail (Crocker 1986). In the play with correspondences and possibilities of shaping, as described here, we see the beginnings of a sovereign self-awareness in the composer's handling of the traditional formulaic material—something that would certainly warrant further study.

An instructive comparison can be made between the St. Gall antiphons and the antiphon ascribed to Ekkehart I (d. 973), *Cum pervenisset beatus Andreas.* There is a question whether this antiphon, together with the two antiphons *Ambulans Hiesus* and *Adoremus gloriosissimum*, ascribed to Ekkehart I by his namesake Ekkehart IV in his *Casus S. Galli*, should be extended to the attribution of the entire Office to Ekkehart I, as is sometimes done (Berschin 1981, 15). Arguing against attribution of the whole Office is the fact that almost all of the texts for these Offices can already be found in the oldest preserved sources of the Office of the ninth century, namely the antiphoner of Compiègne and the tonary of Metz (*CAO* 1:340–44; Lipphardt 1965, 170–72). It should be noted that precisely the two chants cited by Ekkehart IV, as well as the canticle antiphon *Cum pervenisset* for Second Vespers, are the ones missing in the oldest chant books of the ninth century. Thus it seems more likely that Ekkehart IV had only these chants in mind, and not the whole Office, as being the work of his namesake. In any case, one can also be observe in the antiphon *Cum pervenisset beatus Andreas* that the play with musical correspondences has a part in forming the text and makes the textual correspondences considerably more apparent:

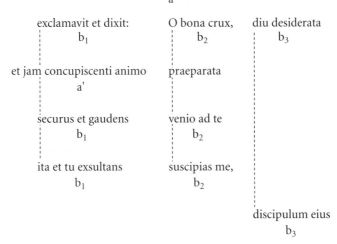

Cum pervenisset beatus Andreas ad locum ubi crux parata erat
a

exclamavit et dixit: O bona crux,   diu desiderata
b₁   b₂   b₃

et jam concupiscenti animo   praeparata
a'

securus et gaudens   venio ad te
b₁   b₂

ita et tu exsultans   suscipias me,
b₁   b₂

                                              discipulum eius
                                              b₃

qui perpendit in te.
c

The concentrated repetition of the a section coincides with the exact repetition from the *vita* of the expression of Andrew's mystical relation to the Cross. The rhyming correspondence and internal construction of these words is brought out by the repetition of the musical sections b¹ and b² *securus et gaudens / venio ad te* and *ita et tu exsultans / suscipias me* (see example 10.7).[10]

Even though verses for the Office such as this one, as Walter Berschin has shown, are impressive poetic settings of the veneration of the Cross, typical of the piety of the tenth century, as texts these verses are completely devoid of originality: the Office of Andrew is almost entirely centonized from biblical sources and the apocryphal *Passio Andreae* (Berschin 1981, 21–23; see also above, chapter 6). From a musical point of view, however, various compositional devices observed in this antiphon and in the first-mode St. Gall antiphons considered above bear witness

Example 10.7   From the antiphon *Cum pervenisset*

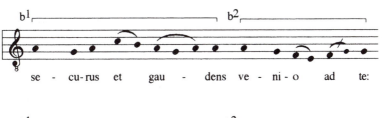

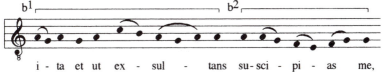

to a supreme ease in dealing with the varied forms and formulas of the antiphon repertory and the accommodation of the music to the text. We have already been able to show from the few examples analyzed that the musical formulation in some instances clearly stresses the meanings of the texts and stems from a knowledge of form.

The Chants of the Otmar Office

When Ekkehart IV spoke about the liturgical and literary activity of Notker II (d. 975; called Notker Peppercorn because of his strictness in maintaining the culture of the cloister), he mentioned "those delicate antiphons on Otmar" (*Casus S. Galli*, 399). Ekkehart must have assumed that the chants he referred to were perfectly well known to his contemporaries. And it is likely that he had no idea what a great service he would have done for our research today if he had spoken in more detail of "those delicate *Lauds* antiphons" or "those delicate *Magnificat* antiphons." Or if, following the example of Stephen of Liège, the first named poet of an office and author of the Prologue to Lambertus, he had written of the artful arrangement of the Matins antiphons in which "the order of the psalm tones and antiphons corresponds to the numerical sequence of the ecclesiastical modes, to the extent that their number extends to this analogy."[11] But instead we have only the ambiguous reference mentioned above, and must ourselves try to understand what it means.

There are two main strands of transmission of the Office of Otmar in the sources of the tenth and eleventh centuries. One is a short version, consisting of Lauds antiphons arranged by mode with one or two framing Magnificat antiphons, a series also attested to outside St. Gall at the turn of the millennium (Brussels, BR 8860–8867, fols. 74v–76) and which later circulated even more widely. Another tradition has Hartker's Antiphoner as an early witness, and adds to the Lauds antiphons mentioned above a series of Matins antiphons, also arranged by mode, and antiphons for the hours of the day. The group of chants for St. Otmar found in Harker was expanded in the eleventh century with the addition of some responsories, arranged by mode, which were later integrated into the existing Office in the younger St. Gall antiphoner, SB 388. The subject of our investigation is the manner in which this complete Office for the feast of St. Otmar, seen in St. Gall 388 as a coherent whole for the first time, "developed" into this collection. Can we speak of a linear, chronological expansion or not?

The relationship between the branches of the tradition

Already in the oldest St. Gall source from the early tenth century (*W*) there exists a series of seven antiphons also found with the addition of one or two other antiphons in the above-mentioned sources *W, B,* and *Z* as well as in the younger antiphoners Karlsruhe Aug. perg. LX from Zwiefalten, the Rheinau Liber Ordinarius, and the Bamberg Antiphoner, Bamberg, Staatsbibl. lit. 23 (Ed. V.6). The existence of proper Offices in this form, that is consisting of Lauds and expansions, or some-

Table 10.1 Magnificat and Benedictus antiphons for the Office of Otmar

W, B	H, SG 387, SG 388	Aug. LX (Zwiefalten)	Z (Rheinau)
IN I. VESPERIS			
Mendaces ostendit	(4) og *Descendit*	(4) *Descendit*	(7) *Mendaces*
	SUPER III CANTICA		
	(7) yb *Mendaces ostendit*	(7) *Mendaces*	
			AD HORAS. IX
			(8) w *In vinculis*
IN II. VESPERIS			
In vinculis	(8) w *Beatus Otmarus athl.*	(8) *In vinculis*	(4) og *Descendit*

times only canticle antiphons, is well documented also in Hartker's Antiphoner and in the Quedlinburg Antiphoner (as representative of the tradition in the German-speaking realm around the turn of the millennium). For example, in the Quedlinburg Antiphoner (see Möller, *Das Quedlinburger Antiphonar*) there are only Lauds antiphons for the feasts of Alexander and his Companions, Brice, Matthew, Holy Virgins, and Scholastica; in addition, for Hippolytus and for Lucy there are also a Magnificat antiphon and from one to three responsories.

The collection of Lauds antiphons for the Office of Otmar in the sources of the two traditions mentioned above agree, but there are differences in the Magnificat antiphons. It is natural that these differences should be the starting point for an inquiry into the relationship between the two traditions of this Office. I have placed side by side the incipits of the Magnificat and Benedictus antiphons from the two traditions as they are found in the sources studied here (see table 10.1). (Modes in parentheses. In addition, for the St. Gall antiphoners *H*, 387, and 388, and the Rheinau Antiphoner *Z* [Zürich, Zentralbibl. Rh. 28] the tonal letters from the manuscripts are given as well.)

As this arrangement shows, there are four antiphon texts in all that are used in the individual source groupings as Magnificat or canticle antiphons for the feast of Otmar. Correspondence in usage is shown in the St. Gall antiphoners and only the two early sources *W* and *B*. These four antiphons, differing in the extent of their texts, and with melodies in different modes, are all textually based on the same biblical verses, Wisd. of Sol. 10:13–14: "Descendit cum illo in foveam et in vinculis non dereliquit illum, donec adferret illi sceptrum regni et potentiam adversus eos, qui eum deprimebant, et mendaces ostendit, qui maculaverunt ipsum, et dedit illi claritatem aeternam." (The Magnificat antiphon in *H* for Second Vespers contains in addition the verse 2 Tim. 4:7 "Bonum certamen certavi, cursum consummavi, fidem servavi.") Obviously the intention in composing and shaping the Office was to relate the fate of Otmar to the passage in Wisdom: "God did not leave him while he was in chains, until he brought him the scepter of the kingdom and the power against those who oppressed him, and showed his detractors to be liars." Chapter 5 of the *vita* recounts that "the lying knave Lantpert" (*falsitatis minister*), after accusing Otmar of the crime of rape, was punished by God in the following way:

Therefore, the vengeance of God seized Lantpert, so that all would understand that Otmar's purity had been falsely impugned. For he was tormented
with feverish trembling, the strength of his limbs grew ever weaker, and
he finally became a cripple. And as, in this way, all his limbs lost their
straightness and natural form, and his head was bent to the ground in the
manner of a four-footed animal, he bore witness constantly, not only with
his terrifying appearance, but also with a loud voice, that he had sinned
against God (Duft 1959, 33).

The four Magnificat antiphons from Offices I and II are very close to the verse in
Wisdom. In the following excerpt, the expansions that do *not* come from the scriptural text are italicized. The verse in Wisdom underscores the point made in the
vita that Otmar was protected by God from those who slandered his name.

I (beginning)	Mendaces ostendit dominus qui maculauerunt *beatum OTMARUM* et dedit illi claritatem aeternam *alleluia al-leluia*
I (ending)	In vinculis non dereliquit eum dominus donec afferet illi sceptrum regni · et potentiam aduersus eos qui eum depri-mebant
II (beginning)	Descendit *dominus* cum *sancto OTMARO* in foueam et in uinculis non dereliquit illum donec afferet illi sceptrum regni et potentiam aduersus eos qui eum deprimebant · Mendaces ostendens qui maculauerunt illum
II (ending)	*Beatus Otmarus athleta dei electus* Bonum certamen certauit cursum consummauit fidem seruauit [Tim. 4:7] *Quapropter* non dereliquit *eum dominus* donec afferet illi sceptrum regni et potentiam aduersus eos qui eum depri-mebant

Although the texts of the antiphons demonstrate that the compilers were sensitive to the events of the saint's *vita*, they reveal little about historical development
and chronology; it cannot be discerned from this evidence which came first, the
short version of the Office or the longer, and which was derived from which. In
fact, since all the antiphons are based on the same verse of Scripture, there are no
clues to either development or chronology in these series of texts. It is at least clear,
however, that both antiphons of the short Office (I), which are already found in
the oldest sources *W* and *B*, are *not* abbreviated forms of texts found in Hartker,
just as, conversely, a text like *Descendit dominus* found in Hartker is not merely an
"expansion" of the shorter texts. In favor of a composition where text and music
are independent is the evidence that the antiphons are not all in the same mode,
but that they contain different melodies in the fourth, seventh, and eighth modes.

Musical assessment of the Brussels manuscript

The neumes of the Otmar antiphons in the Brussels codex *B* differ from the overall
picture of these chants in other sources, particularly for the form of the angular

pes and cephalicus, and also because of the complete absence of episemata and additional letters in the Wolfenbüttel codex *W* and in Hartker (*H*). A comparison of the seven antiphons common to these three sources from the point of view of variations in text and neumes shows a broad agreement between the two St. Gall manuscripts (with the usual additional differentiations based on notation, that is, the use of episemata and additional letters in Hartker.) The marginal notations in the Brussels codex, on the other hand, show some limited textual deviations;[12] moreover, in several places there are variant neumes, usually the substitution of two-note groups for single notes in the St. Gall *W* and *H* manuscripts. In these deviations, *B* always agrees with Karlsruhe Aug. LX from Zwiefalten, third quarter of the twelfth century. In contrast, the thirteenth-century Rheinau antiphoner *Z* follows the readings of the two St. Gall manuscripts of the tenth century in four or five instances. Individually these pieces contain the following variant neume readings:

Mendaces ostendit
    *de*dit Clivis *WHZ*] Virga *B*

Beatus Otmarus
    in insulam Virga *WHZ*] Pes *B Aug*
    mi*gra*vit Oriscus *WH*] Clivis *B Aug*

Cumque navi
    na*vi* Virga *WHZ*] Virga strata *B*] Clivis *Aug*
    im*posui*ssent Virga+Virga *WH*] Pes+Clivis *B Aug*
    se*ui*uit Virga *WHZ*] Pes *B Aug*
    *pe*lago Virga *WH*] Clivis *B Aug Z*

The Otmar antiphons in the Brussels codex, as can be seen, form an independent early branch of the tradition.

The status of composition in the responsory series

The 12 responsories on the bifolio inserted into the Hartker Antiphoner, as well as their copy in the St. Gall antiphoner (SB 388, p. 341 ff.), clearly follow the numerically ascending order of the eight-mode system,[13] but the 12 responsories from the first half of the eleventh century on the bifolio *S* of St. Gall, SB 211 are not composed and arranged this way. I have arrived at this observation by studying the responsory verses traditionally sung in the individual modes in typical, formulaic recitative manner where particular formulas, especially initium and final cadence, are connected by recitative sections. In addition, the individual formulas as found in the older manuscripts with adiastematic neumes permit an unambiguous determination of the mode of the responsories.[14] In the case of the Otmar responsories found in *S,* these observations are relevant for individual verse melodies. For example, the comparison of initial and final cadence formulas in the second responsory verse *Scale Iacob* (in the responsory *Pontificali manu benedictus*) with the *Gloria patri* responsory verse written in neumes shows that the initium consisting of

Example 10.8   Initial and final cadences of the first two responsory verses of *S* compared with the responsorial doxology

R. Sanctus confessor

V. Domino   [. . .]   -eris im-bu- tus   est

R. Pontificali manu benedictus

V. Scale Iacob   [. . .]   filius am- ple-   cten-   dus

Glo- ri-   a   Pa- tri et Fi- li-   o   et Spi- ri-

tu- i   San-   cto.

a single pitch or pitches plus two clivis plus pressus (written connected in *Scale Iacob*) as well as the final cadence of five syllables are undoubtedly in the first mode. It is not quite so clear in the case of the first verse in the responsory *Sanctus confessor domini:* it is true that the initium corresponds to that of the second verse (written in the same connected style), which, taken alone, would seem to indicate the first mode. But the final formula does not follow the expected final cadence. All in all, it is not an unambiguous first mode. (See example 10.8.)

The third responsory verse, on the other hand, can be unambiguously classified in the eighth mode. Without going into further detail here, it is already clear that only the first three of these responsories are not in the mode that corresponds to their position. Overall, the following modes can be determined:

1.	I?	7.	II
2.	I	8.	VIII?
3.	VIII	9.	(?)
4.	(?)	10.	II
5.	II?	11.	VIII?
6.	(?)	12.	(?)

From the point of view of mode, this series of responsories corresponds to the older layer of Gregorian music that is characterized by an unsystematic multiplicity in the choice of melodic types and modes. Thus, it does not follow the compositional principle established at the beginning of the tenth century of the so-called numerical Office, in which the modal and musical order of the Divine Office corresponds to the ideal unity of content. This was the "règle quasi-absolue" (Michel Huglo) until some time in the Renaissance. It is for this reason that the series of responsories that can be ascribed to Ekkehart IV or members of his circle may indeed be a completion of the Office in Hartker's antiphoner from the formal textual point of view. From the musical-modal point of view, however, these responsories do not attain the level of Hartker's numerical Office. Only the responsories in rhymed prose, entered on a bifolio in Hartker's codex, achieve this correspondence. The tradition of the responsories for Otmar in modal order, then, begins with their insertion into Hartker's antiphoner.

Liège or St. Gall?

What music-historical conclusions can be drawn from the dating and study of the Otmar antiphons? Long before the beginning of the written tradition of chants for the feast of St. Otmar, his feast was celebrated with a Vigil and Mass on the day after the translation of his remains from the St. Peter Chapel at St. Gall and his subsequent canonization in 864. Ute Schwab has asked how the *memoria* of St. Otmar was celebrated: "One could imagine that, at the commemoration, there was a reading from the first Vita [written in 834/838]. But in what form? Already antiphonally and like our short Office or at least similar to it?" (Schwab 1993, 85). Any answer to this question must necessarily remain hypothetical. In the St. Gall calendars, the feast of Otmar is relatively late, beginning with a calendar from the period between 926 and 950 (Turic. 176).[15] As has been said, the oldest known source today for the Otmar antiphons is the Wolfenbüttel MS *W*. The *terminus ante quem* for the composition of the Otmar antiphons (Short Office I) is thus connected to the dating of MS *W*, placed currently during the reign of Abbot-Bishop Salomo III (890–920) (see n. 4). If it is correct that the antiphons together with the whole manuscript were really composed before 920, that would be an explosive discovery for musicology. It would mean that the idea of modal ordering for chants (first antiphon in the first mode, second antiphon in second mode, etc.) is documented at St. Gall at the same time as at Liège, where Stephen, who was famous in this regard, was bishop from 901 to 920. This would mean as well that more thought has to be given to the point of origin of tonally ordered antiphons and responsories. It would also suggest that the poet-composer of St. Gall who created the oldest Otmar antiphons might compete with Stephen of Liège for the honor of the first known poet to create tonally ordered chants. One more conclusion must be drawn from an early dating of the oldest source *W* for the Otmar Office: since Notker II, who died in 975, can hardly be considered as author of the short Office for the feast of Otmar, the "delicate antiphons on Otmar" ascribed to him by Ekkehart IV must refer to the Matins antiphons as they are documented in the antiphoner of Hartker.

On the subject of possible relations between Liège and St. Gall, Susan Rankin has pointed out briefly the simultaneous theological and political significance of the Trinitarian opening formula, found only in a St. Gall source from around 900, the oldest source for the famous *Liber ymnorum* of Notker I (*In nomine sanctae trinitatis*).[16] Using this as grounds for concluding that there was an early Trinity

Office at St. Gall (from which the anonymous composer of the oldest Otmar Office could have gotten the idea of tonal ordering) would remain merely speculative. And the indication that the Trinity Office was obviously placed after the Ferial Office in the model for Hartker's antiphoner, that is, that possibly it was added later, is not helpful in determining whether there is a possible link between St. Gall and Liège. Thus, if we accept the above-mentioned *terminus ante quem* of the manuscript *W,* the question of where the principle of tonally ordered Office songs originated is one of the many open questions that arises in working with early medieval texts and songs—always a challenge to our ideas and an invitation to further research.

Notes

1. In this respect see the following related contributions: Berschin, Ochsenbein, and Möller (1991) and Berschin, Ochsenbein, and Möller (1999).

2. Berschin's evidence is based on the styles of decorating deluxe editions in Salomo's reign. It should be pointed out, however, that Hartmut Hoffmann, without giving reasons, has observed that the codex "was created in the second half of the tenth century." Hoffmann (1986), 397.

3. With respect to the sources, see Berschin, Ochsenbein, and Möller (1991), 11–12, as well as supplemental details in Berschin, Ochsenbein, and Möller (1999), 1–11.

4. See Peter Ochsenbein's thorough analysis of the contents in Berschin, Ochsenbein, and Möller (1991), 18–28.

5. Edition ibid., 13–17.

6. See Berschin in Berschin, Ochsenbein, and Möller (1999), p. 16.

7. Karlsruhe, Badische Landesbibliothek, Aug. perg. LX, Zwiefalten, 12th century (= *Aug*); see the CANTUS Index by Möller and Steiner (1996).

8. For an edition of *seculorum amen* formulas on staff see Omlin (1934), 202 ff.; see also "Differentiae of the Zwiefaltener antiphoner" in Möller (1996), pp. xlv ff. The vowels *euouae* correspond to the sounds *in sEcUlOrUm AmEn,* the final phrase of the doxology sung at the close of each psalm. Thus the notes set to *euouae* presented in the example are the differentiae, or termination formulas, for that particular rendering of the psalm.

9. Transcription of *Aug* and examples of comparisons from Schmidt (1980), 36. The following examples are taken from the same source, 40.

10. *CAO* 4, no. 2024; *Antiphonarium monasticum secundum traditionem Helveticae Congregationis Benedictinae* (Engelberg, 1943), 2:768.

11. Following the translation of the Lambert prologue by Berschin; see Berschin (1991), 425.

12. With respect to the text variants in this group of antiphons, the younger antiphonaries *Ba*(mberg), *Z,* and *Aug* do not demonstrate any clear relationships: *CAO* 1653 *Beatus Othmarus* abba *WHAugZ]* abba *Ba;* insulam *WHBa]* insula *ZAug; CAO* 2067 *Cumque navi* nulli eis *WHBaAug]* nulli eius *Z; CAO* 1579 *Beati ergo corpus* clarificatum *WH]* glorificatum *BaZ]* glorificandum *Aug.*

13. *Sanctus confessor Dei* = mode 1, etc. to *Beatus confessor Christi* = mode 7, *Cum autem creator* = mode 8 (?), *Preciosissimo corporis* = mode 4, *Quidam vero* = mode 3, *Sanctimonialis quaedam* = mode 5 (?), *Inclite confessor* = mode 1.

14. See the introduction to J. Froger's new edition of the Hartker Antiphoner.

15. Regarding 15/16 November, see the edition by Munding (1951), 19.

16. Rankin (1991), 218–20 with table 1, "Incipit notices in sources of the 'Liber ymnorum.'"

The Development and Chronology of the Ambrosian Sanctorale

The Evidence of the Antiphon Texts

TERENCE BAILEY

O f all the churches in medieval Europe, only Milan's was able to preserve suc-
cessfully its own liturgical and musical traditions against the centuries-long
assault of the Roman-Frankish chant and liturgy, first launched in Charlemagne's
time, and triumphing almost everywhere by the early twelfth century. But although
the Milanese Church is ancient, and its liturgical practice unique, its independence
must not lead us to assume that the Ambrosian liturgy and chant (misleadingly
but commonly named after Ambrose, the revered bishop of the fourth century)
are entirely indigenous and uniformly old. In the more than 800 years between the
city's first bishop, ca. 200, and the earliest books to detail its Offices, the long and
complex history of the Milanese liturgy is shadowy at best. This chapter will focus
on the Ambrosian Offices for the saints, especially Vespers and the characteristic
stational Vigils, which followed Vespers and were extraordinarily well developed
in Milan. An examination of the texts of the antiphons sung in these Offices reveals
distinct layers and suggests a chronology for the development of the Sanctorale
and the enrichment of the public veneration of the saints in the course of these
centuries.

The saints had a place in the Milanese Mass liturgy from at least the fifth century. Ambrosian Mass prefaces, the introductions to the great eucharistic prayer,
date from at least this period, if not earlier. Specific saints are mentioned in the
earliest surviving Milanese witness to these prayers, the sacramentary from Bergamo (Paredi, *Sacramentarium*), which is probably not earlier than the third quarter of the ninth century.[1] But even if these prefaces were written, as tradition and
some modern scholars would have it, by Eusebius, bishop of Milan from 451 to
462, there is no indication that there were any *chants* proper to the saints in the
middle of the fifth century. Such evidence is very much later. Introits, respond-
graduals, and other *Mass* chants of the saints are documented first in Gregorian
books written about the year 800, proper *Office* chants only at the end of the ninth
century. In the earliest Gregorian service books—as in the oldest Ambrosian ex-

amples written a century or so later—the list of saints with proper Mass and Office chants is already extensive. But this is by no means proof that such chants were ancient; an extrapolation from the rapid increase in the number of saints with proper Offices in the first centuries of the written tradition would rather suggest the opposite.

The Offices of the Saints in the Ambrosian Liturgy

In the Roman-Gregorian liturgy of the Middle Ages, the festivals of saints and the special liturgies commemorating the events of Jesus' life regularly displaced the ordinary observances of the day. Occasions "of the Lord" were treated similarly in the medieval Ambrosian liturgy, but the saints' feasts were not so assertive. On six days of the week—including Saturday, which in Milan was not treated as an ordinary feria—the ongoing rota of psalms and canticles and the neutral ferial antiphons assigned to them were displaced by others that were particularly appropriate to the occasion. But not so on Sunday. Moreover, the Milanese ferial liturgy did not give way to the saints in *all* of the Offices. The lesser Hours of Prime, Terce, Sext, None, and Compline were unaffected by the yearly commemorations.[2] Similarly, in the Ambrosian night Office, the sequential series of psalms and their usual antiphon refrains were usually undisturbed: the psalms sung in the first part of Matins on saints' feasts were those normally allotted to Monday, Tuesday, or whatever the day happened to be. The only exceptions were the four feasts of Stephen, John the Evangelist, Holy Innocents, and James—the saints of Christmas Week. In the morning Office, that is, in the second part of the Ambrosian Matins, the part that corresponded to the Gregorian Lauds, the psalmody was invariable—the same on saints' feasts as on regular Sundays. In the medieval books, some of the antiphons for the fixed psalms and canticles at Matins do refer to the occasion, but there is ample evidence that these refrains *de sanctis*—virtually all of them borrowed from other occasions[3]—were a late development.

Although a student of the Sanctorale of the Roman-Gregorian rite must look primarily at Matins and only secondarily at Vespers, the opposite is true for the Ambrosian liturgy. There, the principal Office of the saints—and the earliest—was Vespers. In the Middle Ages, on saints' feasts, the five psalms of the Vespers sequential series and their neutral refrains were replaced by two specially chosen psalms[4] whose antiphons, and usually the antiphon sung with the invariable Magnificat canticle, were topical—appropriate to the particular day. The Ambrosians had an additional, idiosyncratic, Office that was exclusively *de sanctis*. Vespers on the eve of a saint's day marked the beginning of the festival (just as the Jewish Sabbath is reckoned from sundown on Friday). On most such feasts, Vespers was followed by Vigils (the Latin term is *Vigiliae*), an Office that began in the cathedral but—after remarkably protracted observations at various stations in the city—concluded in another church that was considered especially sacred to the cult of the particular saint. Although Vigils is an impressive Office that was peculiar to saints' festivals, the psalms, antiphons, and other chants assigned to it show that it was a secondary development of the Ambrosian liturgy—a later elaboration rather than an essential and primary element of the liturgy.[5]

Support for some of these assertions, and answers to some of the primary questions about the development of the Ambrosian Sanctorale, emerge from an analysis of the liturgical assignments, and the classification of the antiphons according to specific textual criteria.

The Text Classes

The largest group of antiphons in the Ambrosian Office[6]—those I will refer to as Class 1—have texts cited directly from the psalms or canticles they are sung with.[7] Normally, such citatations are verbatim, but slight departures from Scripture are sometimes encountered: for example, the reordering of words (*Anima mea magnificat* for *Magnificat anima mea*); the appending of the phrase "saith the Lord"; the substitution of "we" or "us" for "I" or "me" (appropriate, obviously, in a choral refrain); a change of tense from from oblique to direct.[8] Some of the alterations appear casual; but others seem to have been made deliberately—in order to provide a distinctive text when the same psalm citation was employed in another liturgical chant (see Bailey 1994, 176–78, 257–58). It is worth keeping in mind that such slight departures from the exact text of Scripture may all be the result of later revision.

The antiphons forming the second-largest group are taken from Scripture outside the psalms and canticles they are sung with. Thus, a refrain that is an exact citation from a psalm, but not the psalm it was sung with, belongs to Class 2, not Class 1. The great majority of Class 2 refrains have texts selected from the New Testament, and all but a few of these are from the Gospels. Generally speaking, such scriptural excerpts are treated more freely than those from the Psalter: far fewer are verbatim citations. For the present purposes there seems to be no advantage in distinguishing between exact citations of Scripture and paraphrases, but I have assigned no antiphon to Class 2 whose direct source is not a passage from Scripture. All nonbiblical refrains have been assigned to Class 3, even those that feature—in a different context—words and phrases whose source in the Bible is readily identified. (The Bible, it need hardly be said, remained the most important influence in the composition of free refrains.)

Although it is obviously pointless to multiply categories where the assignments become increasingly arbitrary, there is one subclass that should be identified. A considerable number of antiphons that—according to the criteria given earlier—belong squarely in Class 3, might rather be assigned to a Class 1A.[9] These refrains are pastiches made up of phrases taken from the psalm or canticle they accompany.

These three or four categories of antiphon represent at least two historical strata in the development of the Office, and probably three. But while this hypothesis of a correspondence between class and stratum seems to hold true generally, the idea must still admit individual exceptions. It is easy to imagine circumstances that would explain the ancient assignment of an exceptional nonscriptural antiphon,[10] just as it is conceivable that a refrain might still be selected from the psalms at a much later time, after freely composed, topical antiphons had become the fashion.[11]

The Antiphons Assigned to the Proper Psalms at Vespers: The Earliest Stratum

In the Manuale (ed. Magistretti, *Manuale*), which is the earliest document to provide details of the Ambrosian Office, and in the earliest antiphoners—that is, in the period from the eleventh to the thirteenth century—there were 40 Vespers Offices *de sanctis*. In 23 of these Offices, antiphons of Class 1 are assigned to both psalms. The actual preponderance of Class 1 antiphons in the Sanctorale is greater than these numbers might suggest, for the figure 23 includes all six Offices of the *commune sanctorum*,[12] which served for the rest of the more than 100 saints of the medieval Milanese calendar.[13] The plurality of Class 1 refrains is general in the Ambrosian liturgy: not only in the proper psalmody at Vespers *de sanctis,* but also in all of the ferial Offices and in all of the Offices of the Temporale, a clear majority of the refrains—those that belong to the oldest layer—are drawn from the poems they were sung with.

All but two of the saints' feasts with Class 1 antiphons for both psalms at Vespers are attested in the Bergamo sacramentary.[14] St. Martin is not,[15] but he was one of the first holy men, not martyrs, to be publicly venerated; and since he was brought up in Ambrosian territory (in Pavia), it is all the more likely that his feast would have been celebrated early in the local liturgy. The evangeliary of Busto Arsizio, whose exemplar is said to date from the eighth century, does include St. Martin (see Borella 1934, 212). The other exception is not significant: the Feast of St. Babylas and the Three Boys is mentioned in none of the Milanese formularies before the eleventh century (see the chart given in Frei 1974, 90), but its antiphons and psalms are simply borrowed from the ancient Feast of the Holy Innocents. The age of the *commune sanctorum* is not as easy to establish. It may perhaps be taken for granted that these Offices are not as old as those of some of the proper Offices of the saints, but the evidence of the earliest Mass books does suggest that an Ambrosian *commune sanctorum* was pre-Carolingian.[16]

For most of the saints' festivals, only Class 1 antiphons are assigned for the Vespers psalms. There are, however, six occasions[17] when one of the Vespers psalms was sung with an antiphon of Class 1 and the other with an antiphon of Class 2 or 3, and a further thirteen festivals[18] at which both the antiphons assigned to the Vespers psalms belong to Class 2 or Class 3.

Feasts with an Antiphon of Class 2 or Class 3 for One of the Proper Psalms at Vespers

The six feasts with a single Class 1 antiphon (the other being of Class 2 or 3) are all attested by ancient prefaces. I hope, in what now follows, to show that these six

Offices have been revised—that the medieval books do not contain the original assignments. If my arguments are correct, then at least 29 of the 40 Vespers *de sanctis* found in medieval books had, originally, Class 1 antiphons for both psalms. The explanation for the Offices that employ only antiphons of Class 2 or Class 3 is not as simple: some of the festivals are are obviously post-Carolingian, but eight are unquestionably ancient. This matter will be taken up later, but first I will consider the question of the six ancient Offices that have only one refrain of Class 1, the other being of Class 2 or Class 3. In every case, there are indications suggesting that both psalms were originally sung with antiphons of Class 1.

The Feast of St. Andrew

On the feast of St. Andrew, the Second Vespers psalm is assigned the refrain *Unus ex duobus,* which is taken from the Gospel (John 1:40). At Vigils, however, *Unxit te deus* is sung with the third psalm, the refrain taken from verse 8. *Unxit te* is assigned on no other occasion in the Ambrosian liturgy; it is, in fact, the only antiphon of Class 1 whose sole assignment is in the supernumerary Office of Vigils. The obvious explanation is that Ps. 44 and the Class 1 antiphon at Vigils actually belong at Vespers; and the Class 3 chant (*Unus ex duobus*) and Ps. 138—which is one of the Vigils psalms of the Common of Apostles—was originally intended for that Office. This kind of mistake—*Unus* for *Unxit*—is encountered a number of times in the Ambrosian liturgy, and gives support to the notion (generally accepted, in any case) that before the compilation of the Manuale and the other medieval service books, the cantor had to rely on simple lists of incipits in determining the content of the Offices.

The Feast of the Decollation of St. John the Baptist

The circumstances are similar for the feast of the Decollation of St. John the Baptist and the feast of St. James. At Vespers on the first occasion, a Class 3 antiphon was assigned for Ps. 35. It was a normal Ambrosian practice to repeat the Vespers psalms and their antiphons at Vigils. In the case of the Decollation of St. John the Baptist, the two psalms and *one* of the antiphons are in fact repeated; but at *Vigils,* Ps. 35 has a Class 1 antiphon (*Verba oris eius*), and it seems likely that this had formerly been sung at Vespers, that is, that there had originally been two Class 1 refrains.

The replacement of *Verba oris eius* at Vespers was perhaps intended to correct a mistake made by the compilers of the Manuale. The antiphon (with its psalm) was also sung at Matins on the Thursday in Holy Week, where the refrain seems to belong. On that occasion the text ("The words of his mouth are iniquity and deceit; he hath left off to be wise and to do good") is obviously appropriate, and refers to the betrayal of Judas. For a feast of the Baptist, Ps. 35 is certainly apt (cf. v. 9, "For with thee is the fountain of life"), but the antiphon is not.

The Feast of St. James

The assignment of *Iacob puer meus,* the Class 3 antiphon for Ps. 45 at Vespers on the feast of St. James, was probably another mistake on the part of the compilers of the Manuale. This feast was one of the four within the octave of Christmas that have proper psalms at Matins. Vigils are not specified for St. James, but the two Vespers psalms on this occasion are assigned also at Matins—as would be expected.[19] At Matins and Vespers, Ps. 46 is sung with the same Class 1 antiphon; but for Ps. 45, the Matins antiphon was *Dominus virtutum nobiscum,* taken from v. 8. This, presumably, was the intended assignment at Vespers.[20]

The Feast of St. Stephen

The argument is slightly different in the case of the feast of St. Stephen, although the the same kind of mistake seems to have been involved. *Coronavit te dominus,* the Class 3 refrain assigned in the medieval books for Ps. 114 at Vespers, is repeated, not once, but twice on the same feast: at Vigils the same evening, and again the next morning at Matins. But in both of the latter Offices the antiphon is sung, not with Ps. 114, but with 111, for which, as a v. 9 makes clear, the refrain was actually intended.[21] The first antiphon at Vespers is thus doubly anomalous: a Class 3 chant for an ancient feast, and associated with the wrong psalm.

It is conceivable that Ps. 114 was the intended psalm at Vespers (although it is only generally appropriate)[22] and that the original, Class 1 antiphon has somehow been lost.[23] But there is another, perhaps better, explanation. Among the Matins assignments on the day are Ps. 102 and its refrain from v. 4, *Qui coronat te.* To confuse *Qui coronat te* and *Coronavit te* would certainly be easy—especially if the confusion dates from a time when assignments were determined from bare lists of incipits. The suggestion is that the correct assignment at Vespers was Ps. 102 and *Qui coronat te,* its Class 1 antiphon. *Coronavit te* is probably a mistake at Vespers, and Ps. 114 was probably assigned in an attempt to repair a gap in the assignments[24]—a late attempt, if the mismatch of psalm and antiphon is any indication.

The Feast of St. John the Evangelist

Next, the feast of St. John the Evangelist. The first two psalms at Matins, numbers 118 (beginning at v. 153) and 55, were chosen because they contain—as epitomized in their antiphons taken from verses 153 and 11, respectively—plausible references to the Gospel of John: the first refrain, *Principium verborum tuorum,* is meant, unmistakably, as a reference to the opening words of the fourth Gospel, "In principium erat verbum"; the second antiphon, *In deo laudabo verbum,* was obviously chosen with a similar intention ("In God will I praise his word: in the Lord will I praise his word"). The principal theme of the day's liturgy is John as Gospel writer—a theme that is reinforced by most of the other assignments at Matins.[25] The first of the Matins psalms and its antiphon is assigned also at Vespers; but the other Vespers assignment is Ps. 114—here too, only generally[26] appropriate—with the Class 3 refrain, *Hic est discipulus qui.* It seems likely that *Hic est discipulus qui*[27] and Ps. 114 replace at Vespers one of the other psalms and its Class 1 antiphon assigned at Matins, probably Ps. 55 and the refrain *In deo laudabo,* which contains the most explicit reference to the Gospel.

The Feast of St. Sisinius

Of the six ancient Offices with one antiphon of Class 1 and the other of Class 2 or 3, only that of St Sisinius remains to be examined.[28] The explanation in this case is fairly obvious. All of the psalms for the feast of St Sisinius, and all but two of the refrains sung at Vespers, Vigils, and in the Morning Office are from the *commune sanctorum. Nolite timere pusillus grex* at Vespers and *Sint lumbi vestri* at Vigils are late substitutions—taken, very likely, from Gregorian books (I will have more to say later about such borrowings).

Ancient Feasts with Antiphons of Class 2 or 3 for Both Proper Psalms at Vespers

At least seven of the thirteen saints' feasts with Class 2 or Class 3 antiphons for both psalms at Vespers are ancient,[29] that is, these festivals are attested by authentic Ambrosian prefaces in the Bergamo sacramentary or by genuine Ambrosian hymns.[30] It is certainly conceivable that Ambrosian commemorations of the saints were at first confined to Mass,[31] but it is more difficult to explain why the seven ancient festivals for which there are no refrains of the primary type would have remained at this primitive stage long after *proper* Offices were developed for the others. As the arrangements for St Sisinius suggest, it is more than likely that chants *de sanctis* for Vespers, Vigils, and Matins were—until proper chants became available—provided from the *commune sanctorum.* Later, I will give evidence in support of this hypothesis.

There is no obvious alternative to believing that the ancient feasts that did receive proper, Class 1, chants *de sanctis* (whenever that occurred) were those considered at the time to be the most important—those, perhaps, with important local or regional churches dedicated to their cult. But rank cannot have been the deciding factor for the seven ancient feasts whose proper psalms were all sung with refrains of Class 2 or Class 3. How would we account for the case of St. Thecla, who was revered by St. Ambrose, who was included in all of the ancient formularies (see Frei 1974, 93), and who—in the Middle Ages at least[32]—was the patron saint of the Summer Cathedral of Milan? Her Offices, even in the latest books, were provided for entirely from the *commune virginum.* These circumstances allow some inferences: (1) that the proper Offices of ancient feasts not at first provided with topical refrains for the Vespers psalms date from a time when antiphons of the old type were no longer fashionable, and (2) from a time, when—as would appear from the case of St. Thecla—new chants could no longer be produced locally. The suggestion is that proper Offices were added only when and where ready-made chants were available.

Late Feasts

Six of the feasts with no Class 1 antiphons for the Vespers psalms—namely those of the Chair of Peter, St. Bartholomew, the Discovery of the Cross, and the three[33] Marian festivals of Annunciation, Purification, and Nativity—seem to have been added to the Ambrosian calendar significantly later than the others.

The earliest mention of the feasts of Purification and Annunciation in Ambrosian territory is in marginal additions dated ca. 700 that mark the Mass pericopes in an ancient Gospel book of northern Italy.[34] But there is some question whether this document represents the official Ambrosian liturgy. Only the first of these feasts is included in the evangeliary of Busto Arsizio,[35] whose exemplar may date from the eighth century.[36] Both Annunciation and Purification are found in an evangeliary[37] dating from the end of the ninth century (Ghiglione 1984, 224) and used by the cathedral clergy of Milan. (This evidence, it must be repeated, relates only to commemorations at Mass—not to any special Offices.) The Nativity of the Blessed Virgin seems not have been introduced until much later. In a Milanese calendar dating from the eleventh century[38] the feast is noted as being specially observed in Foligno[39]—with the implication, perhaps, that it was not yet observed in Milan. In the Manuale, a book intended for the archiepiscopal liturgy, there is no trace of the festival in copies written before the thirteenth century,[40] although there seems to be some evidence that Nativity was introduced before the end of the eleventh (see Magistretti, *Beroldus,* 140–41, n. 46).

Vespers on the feasts of Annunciation and Purification are irregular, the irregularity established by the circumstances of Annunciation, which—as will be apparent in a moment—was the first of the Marian feasts to be assigned proper psalmody in the evening Office. The ancient date of Annunciation was 25 March.[41] The festival is entered for this day in the Milanese calendar referred to just above, but already in the oldest copy of the Manuale, the celebration has been transferred to the last Sunday of Advent (presumably to remove it from Lent[42]), and in this new position[43] its Vespers[44] were constituted, not like those of the other saints' feasts, but like an important occasion of the Temporale: only one psalm is assigned. This has been chosen with reference to the Virgin and sung with the (borrowed)[45] refrain, *Ave virgo Maria* (Hail, virgin Mary, full of grace, the Lord is with thee), the Angel's greeting on the occasion commemorated in the feast. The irregularity can be explained if we assume that the single psalm[46] and antiphon *de Maria* have simply been substituted for the single psalm and antiphon *de tempore* that would be expected at Vespers on an important Saturday.[47]

Although the feast of 2 February is generally regarded as the earliest of the great Marian feasts, and was certainly known in Milan by the ninth century, the Ambrosians simply repeated Annunciation chants for Purification. This is an unsatisfactory expedient, since the antiphon for the single Vespers psalm and the three refrains sung at Vigils[48] all refer to the Angel's announcement, and are not really appropriate in their second assignment.[49] For the feast of the Nativity of the Virgin, the *Vigils* chants are once again those of Annunciation—no more appropriate on this third occasion than on Purification. At *Vespers* on the feast of the Nativity, topical, Class 3 antiphons are assigned to the *two* proper psalms, but these antiphons, like *Ave virgo* on Annunciation, are obviously late borrowings. Such *ad hoc* arrangements suggest that the proper Offices for these three feasts of the Virgin were among the last to be added. For Assumption, the psalms and their antiphons at Vespers were simply taken from the *Commune virginum*.[50]

Although Ambrose spoke of the discovery of the Cross (*De obitu Theodosii* 46; PL 16, col. 1399), neither the festival that commemorated this event nor the other feast of the Cross, the Exaltation, is mentioned in Ambrosian documents until the tenth century.[51] But these documents relate only to the Mass; special *Offices* seem to be later still—even in the twelfth and thirteenth century, the feasts of the Cross are not fully integrated into the service books.[52] In the earliest copies of the Manuale and antiphoner, no proper psalms or antiphons are specified at Vespers of the Discovery—although these books do include the antiphon for the Magnificat.[53] The only items found in the Manuale for the feast of the Exaltation on 14 September are three prayers;[54] in the earliest antiphoners nothing at all is entered for this occasion. It may be presumed that the Discovery chants were meant to be repeated for the Exaltation—as they are in Gregorian books.[55] The two refrains assigned in antiphoners of the thirteenth century and later[56] for the Vespers psalms on the feast of the Discovery are nonspecific, and could serve for either feast.[57] The same can be said of the chants assigned at Mass.[58] But the Magnificat antiphon, *Orabat Iudas deus,* is appropriate only for the Discovery: the Judas in this refrain is the Jew (later christened as Quiriacus) who is said to have aided the empress Helen in her search for the True Cross.[59] This is the same kind of anomaly encountered in two of the Marian feasts; such carelessness is characteristic of the latest revisions to the liturgy, whether Ambrosian or Gregorian.[60]

Of the late feasts there remain two to be discussed: that of St. Bartholomew and the feast of the Chair of Peter. These are absent in Mass books earlier than the eleventh century.[61] In the case of the latter feast, the evidence for the Office is in keeping with the contents of the Mass books: the Chair of Peter is not mentioned in the earliest copies of the Manuale, nor, indeed, in the earliest antiphoners. Only in the thirteenth century[62] is an Office provided, but then the chants needed at Vespers and Matins (no Vigils are indicated) were simply borrowed from the feast of SS. Peter and Paul. The proper Offices of St. Bartholomew are probably older, since they are constituted in the usual way in the oldest copy of the Manuale, albeit with lurid, Class 3 antiphons.

In both cases, for St Bartholomew and the Chair of Peter, the psalms chosen are numbers 46 and 138. These are not *proper* psalms at all, but rather the Vespers psalms of the Common Office of Apostles. The antiphons assigned to the latter feast, *Tu es pastor* and *Petre amas me,* contain no reference to the psalms they accompany: indeed, these refrains are multipurpose; *Tu es pastor* is repeated at Matins the following morning with the Benedictus canticle, and is assigned to Ps. 18 at Vespers on the Feast of SS. Peter and Paul, when *Petre amas me* also doubles as the antiphon for the Benedicite canticle. The two Class 3 antiphons for St. Bartholomew are also without any obvious reference to their psalms. These circumstances make it likely that on these occasions the free antiphons were late substitutions for the Class 1 chants that usually accompany Pss. 46 and 138 in the Common Office of Apostles—in other words, the Office of Vespers on these occasions had earlier been taken from the *commune*. The Vespers psalms on feast of St. Maurice and his Fellow Soldiers and on the feast of SS. Peter and Paul are also shared: in this case the numbers are 32 and 127. These are the psalms assigned to the *commune plurium sanctorum* at Vigils. The arrangements are similar in the case of St. George: the Class 3 antiphons that are assigned are sung with Pss. 20 and 63, the usual Vespers psalms of the *commune martyrum*. So also for the feasts of St. Agnes, St. Agatha, St. Apollinaris (all three share Pss. 114 and 115) and the Nativity of St. John the Baptist (the psalms are numbers 127 and 115).

It emerges that for the seven feasts known to have been adopted in post-Carolingian times, psalms from the *commune* are assigned in nearly every instance.[63] The only exception—an obvious one, since it is not the feast of a saint—is the Discovery of the Cross.[64] It may seem that I have given more examples than necessary, but I have multiplied them in order to show that *commune* psalms are also assigned for all seven of the *ancient* feasts whose Vespers psalms were sung only with antiphons of Class 2 and Class 3. This is the evidence I promised earlier in support of the hypothesis that ancient feasts not assigned Class 1 refrains were originally provided for from the *commune sanctorum*. Of course, these offices were only partly transformed—from common to semi-proper (so to speak): the psalms were not specially chosen, only the antiphons. And I want to repeat my suggestion that these changes were made only where appropriate, ready-made refrains happened to be available. Other important festivals, for example, those of St. Matthew, St. Mark, St. Luke, St. Barnabas, the Assumption of the Virgin—and, of course, the feast of St. Thecla—were never revised.

The Magnificat Antiphons

At Ambrosian Vespers, the last of the items sung in the choir[65] was the New Testament canticle of Mary. This was a fixed assignment[66] in the ferial liturgy, in the Temporale and in the Sanctorale. The canticle was invariable, but on important occasions it was sung with refrains that were appropriate to the day or to the season. Magnificat antiphons *de sanctis* were among the latest developments of the Sanctorale. This is shown most obviously by the character of the texts employed as refrains.

To begin with, no Class 1 antiphons are assigned, except in the *commune sanctorum,* and even there the two[67] exceptions are probably *commune* chants appropriated from the Temporale.[68] The first of these two Magnificat antiphons, *Fecit mihi magna dominus qui potens est et sanctum nomen eius,* is an almost exact citation from the canticle (the *dominus* is added). This refrain ("The Lord that is mighty hath done to me great things; and holy is his name") contains no obvious reference that would account for its assignment in the Sanctorale,[69] but there is no doubt that *Fecit mihi magna* did come to have a special connection with the liturgy of the saints: its text is also employed (internally) in one of the processional antiphons of the *commune sanctorum.*[70] The appropriation to the Sanctorale of *Fecit mihi magna,* the seemingly neutral Magnificat refrain, is perhaps explained through its association with *Qui fecisti magnalia*[71] (a psallenda sung in Ambrosian penitential processions) and *Loquebantur variis linguis apostoli magnalia dei* (cf. Acts 2:11), the antiphon for the *Laudate* psalms at Matins on Pentecost. If my hypothesis is correct, this latter text provided the the direct source of the assignment of *Fecit mihi magna* to the Common of Apostles.

The other Class 1 Magnificat refrain of the *commune sanctorum* is very similar. Like *Fecit mihi magna, Quia respexit humilitatem dominus ancillae suae,* for the Common of Virgins, is an exact scriptural citation with the addition of the word *dominus.* This text ("For the Lord hath regarded the low estate of his handmaiden") is appropriate enough for the occasion, but the same could be said for most or all of the Magnificat antiphons collected in the *commune* for Sundays and the other days of the week. *Quia respexit* would not be out of place among the Sunday chants, but in the Common of Virgins the neutral character of refrain antiphon is placed in relief by the surrounding liturgical forms. The *commune in natali virginum* was intended for a virgin *martyr,* and in the successive texts of the Vespers hymn, the *responsorium post hymnum,* and the four Vespers prayers—that is to say in all of the free texts of this Office—we hear of "wounds," of the "spilling of blood," of the "victory of the martyr," of the "anniversary of the virgin martyr," the "blessed martyr," and so on (Magistretti, *Manuale,* pt. 2, 395–96). Obviously, other similar (neutral) Class 1 antiphons from the *commune dominicarum et feriarum* could easily have been seconded to the Offices of Apostles, Martyrs, and Confessors; in the medieval books, however, antiphons of Class 2 and Class 3 have been assigned (*Euge serve bone* and *Per os apostoli*). The inconsistency suggests that the *commune* did not originally include Magnificat refrains *de sanctis*—that these chants belong to a later stage.

The argument *ex discrepantia* also applies in general. Outside the *commune sanctorum,* only refrains of Class 2 and Class 3 have been assigned to the Magnificat—even in those Offices where both Vespers psalms are sung with antiphons of Class 1. This is an even clearer indication that Magnificat refrains *de sanctis* are a tertiary development. Some signs of the stages in that development are in fact visible, and most obviously in the disagreement in the service books of the eleventh, twelfth, and thirteenth centuries. Some copies of the Manuale and the antiphoners assign a refrain from the *commune* where others provide a chant that is appropriate to the day.[72] In some instances, *three* chants are variously assigned.[73] For certain important festivals with indigenous, Class 1 antiphons for the Vespers psalms, the refrain for the Magnificat was taken from the *commune sanctorum,*[74] or borrowed from another occasion.[75] Yet a number of saints whose provisions are otherwise entirely from the commune were assigned Magnificat antiphons appropriate to the particular festival.[76]

General Remarks Concerning the Evolution
of the Repertory of Refrains

I conclude with some remarks on the stages in the evolution of refrains for the psalmody of the Sanctorale, and some comments concerning the origins of the antiphons added at the end of that development. In the oldest stage of the Ambrosian Office that is represented by service books,[77] the integrity of the psalmody was obviously an imperative: the refrains were invariably taken from the poems themselves. In the earliest liturgy, when the weekly, Sabbath cycle was dominant, when each Sunday was a commemoration of Easter and the series of annual commemorations was still rudimentary, the topicality of refrains could not have been an issue. But with the development of the Temporale and Sanctorale, it became increasingly important to employ liturgical forms that made reference to the events of the particular day or season. The psalms sung in the liturgy *de sanctis* were chosen because they were seen to contain a reference (the antitype) that was especially appropriate to the saint (the type) whose feast it was. Usually this reference involved a single phrase, which would then be employed as the refrain. In such circumstances it is, in fact, the text of the antiphon that explains the choice of psalm.

With the entire Psalter to choose from, a psalm could usually be found that would provide an appropriate reference: for example, at Vespers of the ancient Feast of St. Romanus,[78] a fourth-century martyr who had his tongue torn from his mouth, Pss. 48 and 70 have been chosen because of verses 4 and 24 respectively ("*Os* meum loquetur"; "*Lingua* mea meditabitur"), the texts that were selected as refrains. The Magnificat was not specially chosen at Vespers; it was an invariable assignment, and the canticle does not provide the same opportunities for appropriate references.[79] As long as Class 1 refrains were mandated, a special repertory of Magnificat antiphons *de sanctis* could hardly develop. But it would appear that the fashion for topical refrains eventually overcame earlier concern that an antiphon should at least contain a reference to its psalm.

The Magnificat antiphon for St. Romanus, *Si linguae membrum* ("If your tongue be cut away, God will hear its silence"), is a free text, like so many of the refrains sung with the Vespers canticle in the Sanctorale. But it may be supposed that before such free texts became acceptable, efforts were made to find topical refrains that were less radically different from those of antiquity. The first may have been the refrains I have called Class 1A—those whose texts are pastiches of phrases from the psalms or canticles they accompany. The Magnificat antiphon of the Common of Martyrs, *Respexit dominus ad humilitatem sanctorum suorum,* is not an authentic scriptural verse (the canticle reads "quia respexit ad humilitatem *ancillae suae*"), but its assignment was doubtless more acceptable because something of the original connection between psalmody and refrain was maintained.

The next step in the evolution, and it is a small one, is seen in the Office of a saint that must have been one of the first to be provided with a proper liturgy in Milan. The Magnificat refrain for the Ordination of St. Ambrose is from verse 20 of Ps. 88: *Posui adiutorium super potentem, et exaltavi eum, dicit dominus.* This text, "I have laid help upon one who is mighty; I have exalted him, saith the Lord," provides a remarkably fortuitous reference to the elevation of Ambrose, formerly the Roman governor of the province, to the post of bishop of Milan. More than that, the words *posui, potentem,* and *exaltavi* are, no less fortuitously, echoes of words in the seventh verse of the canticle: "*Deposuit potentes* de sede et *exaltavit* humiles." In this case, the text of the refrain is not taken from the psalmody it accompanies, but the essential connection between refrain and psalmody is maintained.

It may be supposed that the first *free* texts were also expected to preserve this kind of connection. The feast of St. Andrew, from all apearances,[80] was one of the most important saints' festivals in the Ambrosian calendar, and more likely, therefore, to be assigned earlier than later a proper refrain for the Magnificat. The refrain assigned is *Suscipe beata crux humilem propter deum, suscipe discipulum eius qui pependit in te,* a Class 3 chant, whose text refers to the apostle's martyrdom on the cross ("Uphold this humble man, O Blessed Cross, for God's sake; uphold his disciple who hangs upon thee"). The text is a free composition, but *suscipe . . . humilem* and *suscipe discipulum eius* are meant to echo the *exaltavit humiles* and *suscepit . . . puerum suum* of the seventh and ninth verse of the Canticle. This antiphon too, preserves a specific connection with its psalmody.[81]

Both *Posui adiutorium* and *Suscipe beata crux* preserve the relationship between refrain and psalmody that is characteristic of the oldest stratum of Ambrosian liturgy. Such antiphons[82] may be authentically Ambrosian,[83] but most of the refrains of Class 2 and Class 3 lack this connection with their psalmody, and it seems likely that these are either authentic chants displaced from their original Ambrosian assignments or foreign borrowings. I have already suggested that two of the so-called proper antiphons of the *commune sanctorum* were not originally intended for the Sanctorale. There is another interesting example. The feast of St. Genesius is ancient, and Class 1 antiphons are provided for both Vespers psalms. The refrain for the Magnificat belongs to Class 2: it is an exact quotation from Scripture, but from Ps. 50, not from the Vespers canticle. The fiftieth psalm, the *Miserere,* was sung in the Ambrosian morning Office on ordinary weekdays and—no doubt because it was sung so often—is provided with a large repertory of antiphons: 35 are included in the medieval books—all of Class 1 or Class 1A. The Magnificat antiphon for St. Genesius is *Incerta et occulta.* Its seemingly neutral text, *Incerta et occulta sapientiae tuae, domine, manifestasti mihi* ("What is hidden and obscure in thy wisdom, O Lord, thou has made plain to me") would serve equally for any of the ordinary occurrences of Ps. 50. But for St. Genesius, who as legend has it was an actor suddenly converted while playing the part of a candidate for baptism in a satirical play performed before the emperor Diocletian, the text has a fortuitous relevance, and I want to suggest that this chant was originally a thirty-sixth *antiphona in quinquagesimo,* seconded to the feast of St. Genesius at a time when cantors were looking around for topical refrains. This hypothesis is strenthened by the close melodic similarity of *Incerta et occulta* and other antiphons for the Ambrosian *Miserere.*[84]

The inexorable development of the liturgy was away from the weekly Sabbath cycle. The annual commemorations and topical liturgical forms became the focus of change, and eventually all but overwhelmed the ferial cycle and its neutral chants. By the Middle Ages, except only in Lent (whose penitential character restrained the development of festivals), there was not a single week in the year when the psalms of the sequential series and the other regular fixed assignments of Sunday, Monday, or whatever day were not at least once displaced by the specially chosen psalms and liturgical forms of the growing Temporale and Sanctorale. At some point in this development, the original relationship of refrain and psalmody ceased to be an issue and the topicality of the refrain text became the *only* concern.

This new attitude allowed for assignments that would not previously have been acceptable. In later times, as we have seen, the same refrain could be assigned to two and even three psalms or canticles, in different Offices. More striking (even shocking) is the interchangeability of Mass and Office chants, several examples of which are offered by the medieval Ambrosian service books, for example, all three of the Vespers antiphons for the Nativity of the Virgin[85] and two of the three on the feast of St. James.[86] This unconcern for proper forms speaks to the decay of the Ambrosian tradition in the late medieval period.

The Sources of the Latest Antiphons of the Ambrosian Sanctorale

None of the festivals known to have been added to the Ambrosian Sanctorale after the Carolingian conquest had proper antiphons of Class 1 for the Vespers psalms. However (if the arguments I presented earlier are acceptable), *all* of the unquestionably ancient feasts did have such refrains, and from these circumstances it seems to follow (1) that Vespers antiphons *de sanctis* are authentically Ambrosian, and (2) that Class 1 antiphons fell out of fashion. In fact, circumstances allow us to say more: they suggest that after the conquest of Milan by Charlemagne (in 773), the Ambrosians found it difficult or impossible to produce antiphons of any kind. Purification was certainly known in Milan in the ninth century, but for this feast, only borrowed refrains were assigned at Vespers and at Vigils. The Vespers and Vigils antiphons for Assumption, which seems to have been introduced about the same time,[87] were all taken from the *commune,* as were those for All Saints. Although their status in the Ambrosian Office is equivocal, these were universal feasts of the first rank—elsewhere among the most important in the calendar. The circumstances are similar for important local feasts: for St. Babylas, the patron of one of Milan's most impressive medieval churches, borrowed chants were used; for St. Thecla, the patroness of the Summer Cathedral, chants from the *commune.* The obvious question is, if proper refrains of Class 2 and 3 were assigned for saints of lesser importance (as for St. Agnes and St. Thomas), why were such refrains not assigned to all the others, or at least to the more important?

Before I try to answer this question I want to bring the proper antiphons for the Magnificat into the discussion. All proper refrains for the evening canticle on saints' feasts—even those that are unquestionably ancient—belong to Class 2 or Class 3. Proper Magnificat antiphons were obviously wanted: they are provided in the medieval books even where the antiphons for the Vespers psalms were taken from the *commune.* But circumstances suggest that the Ambrosians were unable to provide enough of these refrains. Antiphons from the *commune sanctorum* are employed for the feasts of some of the greatest saints of the Ambrosian calendar, that of Nazarius, for example, and for the feast of Nabor and Felix—saints for whom proper antiphons of Class 1 are assigned to the Vespers psalms. On the other hand, some relatively unimportant saints otherwise provided for from the *commune* (St. Domninus, St. Euphemia, St. Quiricus) are seen to have proper Magnificat antiphons that mention them by name. How are we to explain these circumstances? I raised earlier the possibility that Ambrosians were unable to produce new antiphons after the encirclement of the archdiocese by the Gregorian rite in the wake of the Carolingian conquests. I have also suggested that nearly all of the newer refrains of the Sanctorale were borrowed. But we must add to this the notion that ready-made chants were not available in every case. Nothing else explains why proper refrains are distributed so unsystematically in the Ambrosian Sanctorale.

It is impossible to make precise determinations, but some general observations are enough to suggest the main sources of the borrowed refrains of the Ambrosian Sanctorale. Even though Class 1 refrains were usually taken verbatim from the psalms, the Gregorian and Ambrosian antiphons for the ferial cursus and even the Gregorian and Ambrosian antiphons for the substantial number of psalms that happen to have been selected for the same occasions in both liturgies are overwhelmingly independent. For refrains of other kinds, the facts are different. Sixty-seven antiphons of Class 2 and Class 3 are assigned in the Ambrosian Sanctorale for the Vespers psalms or the Magnificat.[88] It must be remembered that only a very few of these refrains are exact citations from Scripture; the rest are free compositions or paraphrases, and this is to say that a correspondence between Gregorian and Ambrosian texts is almost bound to be significant. Fully two-thirds of these 67 refrain texts are found easily in Gregorian books, and it seems likely that concordances for some of the remaining third will be discovered.

Of course, this is not to suggest that Ambrosian borrowings were all from Gregorian books: *Responsum accepit Symeon, Rubum quem viderat Moyses,* and several other less familiar antiphons are known to be Byzantine in origin, even though they may have been brought to Milan via Rome. And although the primary assignment cannot in every case be determined, there can be no doubt that some of the topical antiphons of the saints' Offices were simply borrowed from elsewhere in the Ambrosian liturgy. Mention has been made of chants seconded from the *commune* and even borrowed from Mass. It seems likely that a substantial number of the borrowed Vespers refrains were originally processional chants. The Ambrosian repertory of processional antiphons is very large: well over 700 are assigned for processions; and more than 500 of these have no other assignment. It is probably significant, therefore, that all of the 18 Vespers refrains of Class 2 and Class 3 that I have *not* found in Gregorian books (or have not otherwise explained) do double duty as processional antiphons.

Several of the refrains given proper assignments in the Ambrosian Office were employed in the Gregorian *commune sanctorum.* If the Ambrosians were content to take over such unspecific antiphons for specific occasions, why were *all* Ambrosian saints not provided with proper Magnificat antiphons? The Gregorian antiphoners contain many suitable refrains that were not taken over, but the fact is, antiphons known to us were not necessarily known to the Ambrosians. The written tradition of their chant is remarkably simple—so simple that it seems likely that all known copies of the antiphoner descend from a single exemplar compiled for the cathedral. The same can be said of the Manuale. The Ambrosian codification—perhaps prompted by the alarming encroachment of Roman-Frankish usages—

made official a liturgy that contains obvious mistakes, inconsistencies, and lacunae, a liturgy that was in the process of change, but was frozen before some of the developments were thoroughly carried out. Those who set down the official form of the Ambrosian chant were limited by their own experience: they provided antiphons of the new topical kind whenever suitable chants were known to them; but where such refrains were not available, the *commune* continued to serve.

Notes

1. For the dating of the Bergamo sacramentary, see Heiming, *Das ambrosianische Sakramentar*, part 1, p. xlvi.

2. In the Ambrosian rite all of these lesser hours were very simple and sung without antiphons.

3. For an analysis of the antiphon assignments in the Ambrosian Office see Bailey and Merkley (1989).

4. At Second Vespers of the Feast of St Lawrence only one psalm and antiphon are assigned. The editors of the modern Ambrosian books (see Suñol, *Liber*, 708–9) have supplied a second psalm and antiphon (actually, a psallenda) treating the anomaly as a simple mistake. The special circumstances of Annunciation and Purification will be discussed below. There is little doubt that Second Vespers were a late development of the Ambrosian Sanctorale (see Bailey 1994, 293–94).

5. Almost all of the chants assigned at Vigils are borrowed from elsewhere in the liturgy. See Bailey and Merkley (1989), *passim*.

6. I have excluded the processional antiphons (psallendae) from this discussion; these chants accompanied actions that took place outside the choir.

7. Frequently, as in the Matins ferial cursus, two or more psalms are sung under a single antiphon. I have assigned such antiphons to Class 1 if their text is taken from one of these psalms.

8. As, for example, in the case of the Magnificat antiphon *Sic eum volo manere donec venio* (properly, *veniam*; see John 21:22).

9. The subclass under discussion is also found in the Temporale, especially among the antiphons for the Benedicite (the Sunday Matins canticle) and the Magnificat.

10. Very brief, nonscriptural refrains ("Save us, Lord," "Glory to you, O God," etc.) were used for the distributed Psalter and the canticles in the Byzantine cathedral Office. For a list of these refrains, see Strunk (1977), 140–41.

11. The *antiphonae duplae* are certainly among the latest authentic Ambrosian antiphons (see Bailey 1995); several of them are exact citations from a psalm or canticle. None of these impressive antiphons is assigned at Vespers.

12. The medieval books contain what might seem to be an exception. The antiphon for the first psalm at the common Vespers of a Virgin is *Ego autem sicut*, taken verbatim from verse 10 of Ps. 51. Although the psalm and refrain ("I am like a green olive tree in the house of God") are obviously suitable, the Manuale assigns Ps. 53. This seems to be a simple mistake. In the modern Ambrosian books Ps. 51 is assigned (see Suñol, *Liber*, 492).

13. The saints' feasts with Class 1 antiphons for both Vespers psalms were those of St. Martin, St. Romanus, St. Ambrose, Holy Innocents, St. Vincent, St. Babylas and the Three Boys, St. Victor ad Ulmum, St. Nazarius, the Translation of Victor with Felix and Fortunatus (one antiphon on this occasion is from the *commune martyris*), SS. Protasius and Gervasius, SS. Nabor and Felix, SS. Nazarius and Celsus, St. Sixtus, St. Lawrence, SS. Mamas and Agapitus, St. Genesius, and St. Michael in Monte Gargano. The medieval categories of the *commune* were: (1) for a single Apostle, (2) for plural Apos-

tles, (3) for a single martyr, (4) for plural martyrs, (5) for a Confessor and (6) for a Virgin (martyr). Some chants were shared, and the circumstances suggest that the earliest *commune* was more loosely structured.

14. Paredi, *Sacramentarium,* xxv–xxvi; see also Pietro Borella in Paredi (1937), 56.

15. This is one of the indications that the document represents a much earlier period than the time of its earliest copy.

16. Frei (1974), 158–61. She suggests that the Ambrosian redactor compiled the *commune sanctorum* along Roman-Gregorian lines.

17. The feasts of St. Andrew, St. Stephen, St. John the Evangelist, St. James, the Translation of St. Sisinius (with the Passion of SS. Felix and Fortunatus), and the Decollation of St. John the Baptist.

18. Namely, Annunciation, St. Agnes, Purification, St. Agatha, the Chair of Peter, St. George, the Invention of the Cross, the Nativity of St. John the Baptist, SS. Peter and Paul, St. Apollinaris, St. Bartholomew, the Nativity of Mary, and the feast of St. Maurice and his Fellow Soldiers.

19. Six of the eight Vespers psalms assigned on the four saints' feasts with proper psalms and antiphons at Matins are repeated in the morning Office. Although these numbers alone are perhaps too small to establish what was normal, the similar borrowing between Vespers and Vigils (throughout the Sanctorale) adds considerable weight to the presumption.

20. The two Vespers psalms on the feast of the Holy Innocents are repeated at Matins with the same antiphons.

21. The antiphon reads: "Coronavit te dominus *corona iustitiae* et *dedit* tibi nomen sanctum *gloriae.*" Cf. Ps. 111:9: "dispersit *dedit* pauperibus *iustitia;* eius manet in saeculum saeculi; *cornu* [i.e., of a head-dress] eius exaltabitur in *gloria.*" There is no obvious connection between *Coronavit te* and Ps. 114.

22. It was regularly assigned in the *commune confessorum.*

23. It is curious that although Ps. 114 was assigned as a proper psalm 14 times for saints' feasts, some of which were certainly ancient, no Ambrosian Class 1 antiphon survives.

24. It may be presumed that the psalms were not specified in the primitive lists. At a time when Class 1 refrains were normal, their bare incipits would suffice to identify the psalms they were sung with. The incipit of a Class 2 or Class 3 refrain, unless it contained an obvious reference to a psalm, would give no such indication.

25. The fourth and fifth psalms contain general references to St. John as evangelist (*Dominus dabit verbum:* "The Lord gave the word: great was the company of those that published it"; *Diffusa est gratia:* "Grace is poured into thy lips" [i.e., the lips that proclaim the Gospel]). The third psalm and the verse chosen as its refain (*Vox tonitrui tui:* "The voice of the thunder was in the heaven") are meant as a references to John as one of the "sons of thunder" (cf. Mark 3:17).

26. It has already been shown that the other psalms for this feast were chosen for very clear references to the Evangelist.

27. This Class 3 antiphon stands apart from the other Ambrosian refrains: it is not set to one of the standard melodies. See Bailey and Merkley (1990), 208. There can be little doubt that *Hic est discipulus* is a Gregorian borrowing.

28. The feast was multipurpose: The Translation of SS. Sisinius, Martyrus, and Alexander and the Deposition of St. Simplicianus.

29. Namely, the feasts of St. Agnes, St. Agatha, St. George, the Nativity of St. John the Baptist, SS. Peter and Paul, St. Apollinaris, St. Maurice and his Fellow Soldiers.

30. Concerning the authentic Ambrosian hymns see Borella (1934), 64.

31. Or, in any case, confined to prayers. References will be made below to two instances (Annunciation on 25 March and the Feast of the Exaltation of the Cross) where

prayers—some of them certainly for Vespers—are the only items entered in the Manuale for feasts of the Sanctorale.

32. That the feast of St. Thecla was not provided with proper Offices may be an indication that the dedication to her of the Summer Cathedral was not ancient.

33. For Assumption, the psalms and antiphons are simply taken from the *commune virginum*.

34. The manuscript is Milan, Ambrosiana SP 45 (*olim* C 39 inf). The marginalia were edited by Morin (1903), 375–89; see p. 378: "in sanctae Mariae" (the pericope indicated is the one assigned in the Manuale for Annunciation); "in sanctae Mariae in februario" (the feast of the Purification, certainly, but whether 2 or 14 February is not clear).

35. Borella (1934), 212; Frei (1974), 91. Frei's chart indicates that Annunciation is missing in the Busto manuscript on 25 March; but the Gospel reading "ad sanctam mariam" for the sixth Sunday of Advent (the medieval date for the Ambrosian feast) is "Missus est angelus."

36. See Borella (1934), 221. The manuscript itself (Busto Arsizio, BC di S. Giovanni M. I. 14) is probably from the third quarter of the ninth century; see Ghiglione (1984), 222.

37. Milan, Ambrosiana A 28 inf. See Frei (1974), 91.

38. Muratori, *Rerum*, vol. 2/2, 1021, dated the calendar to the year 1000; Magistretti, who included it in his edition of Beroldus' ordinal (*Beroldus*, xv), refers to parts that he believed to be from the tenth century. Inserted in the calendar are records of important incidents. Some of the entries seem to belong to the oldest stratum of this complex document; they record very early events imprecisely, for example, the date of the discovery of the Cross is given as 233, although St. Helen was born ca. 255, and the date of the entombment of St. Ambrose is given as as 381, although he died in 397 (see Magistretti, *Beroldus*, 4, 5). But records of a series of more recent local events (fires, earthquakes, etc.) are also inserted; the earliest of these have dates in the eleventh century.

39. "Nativitas s. Mariae Fulcuini" (Magistretti 1894, 10).

40. Cf. Magistretti, *Manuale*, pt. 2, 348. It should be noted, however, that the eleventh-century copy from Brezzo di Bedero (Milan, BC D.2.30) does include Assumption.

41. In the the Biasca manuscript (Milan, Ambrosiana A 24 bis inf.) and in the other ancient Ambrosian sacramentaries, the feast is assigned to 25 March (Frei 1974, 91; Magistretti, *Beroldus*, 4).

42. The Council of Toledo in 656 ordered that Annunciation should be kept on the octave before Christmas day. This is not exactly the practice in Ambrosian regions, where the feast was always celebrated on the *Sunday* prior to 25 December.

43. In the Manuale, Annunciation is actually entered twice: for the Last Sunday of Advent and also for 25 March—where, however, only prayers are given.

44. I.e., Vespers on Saturday, the eve of the feast. Advent was the theme of Vespers on Sunday: the single proper antiphon (for Ps. 113) was *Ecce dominus sedet* (cf. Isa. 19:1).

45. The antiphon was assigned to the Benedicite canticle at Matins on the previous Sunday (the fifth Sunday of Advent). The appropriateness of *Ave virgo Maria* for this canticle—called the "Benedictio," i.e., "the blessing," by St. Benedict and others—is explained by the very next phrase of the scriptural passage cited in the antiphon: "blessed art thou among women" (cf. Luke 1:28). *Ave virgo Maria* belongs to one of the standard Ambrosian melody families, but is particularly related to that of *Anania Azaria et Misael*, the *antiphona in Benedicite* for the Sunday *de Samaritana*. See Bailey and Merkley (1990), 435, 632.

46. Number 114. Here again, the assignment seems unspecific. It may be that the

psalm's prominent references to "trouble and sorrow" are intended to refer to Mary's later sufferings, but that suggests late-medieval thinking.

47. On the Saturday *in traditione Symboli* (but cf. Bailey and Merkley 1989, 41), and the Saturday *ante dominicam I de adventu,* analogous occasions of the Temporale (i.e., occasions important enough to have proper psalmody), a single psalm is similarly assigned. Cf. the arrangements for the Vigil of Christmas. The Ambrosian service books assume the day will be a Saturday: the Cantemus canticle is assigned at Matins (which are designated alternately as *die sabbati* and *In vigiliis nativitatis domini*). As might be expected on such an important occasion, a single psalm (number 84) is assigned at Vespers. In the service books, this psalm, short as it is, has been divided into two, each part provided with an antiphon, but the division is probably a later development. See Magistretti, *Manuale,* pt. 2, 170, 53, 55–56.

48. *Ave Maria gratia plena, Beatus ille venter, Magnificamus te dei genetrix quia ex te natus est.*

49. In this respect, the circumstances are similar to those of the two Feasts of the Cross (see below).

50. The ancient Ambrosian festival of SS. Sisinius, Alexander, and Simplicianus also fell on 15 August. This feast, for which there were proper chants and prayers in the Office, was evidently the more important. In one of the manuscripts of the Manuale there is a note: "After Mass all of the priests, cardinal deacons, subdeacons . . . [here follows a detailed list of those who were involved in the celebration] are to dine magnificently in the monastery of San Simpliciano" (Magistretti, *Manuale,* pt. 2, 338, note to line 23).

51. The first Ambrosian document to include them is the Biasca sacramentary (see Frei 1974, 91, 93). For the dating of this document, see Heiming, *Das ambrosianische Sakramentar,* xxxv–xliii.

52. This seems to be evidence that Mass commemorations sufficed for some feasts.

53. Bedero di Val Travaglia, S. Vittore B and Milan, Ambrosiana M 99 sup. do not mention Vespers psalms or antiphons, although these antiphoners do specify the Magnificat refrain. Slightly later manuscripts, for example, Vimercate, S. Stefano C and D, agree on *Laudamus te Christe* and *Adoramus crucem tuam.* The modern books (cf. Suñol, *Liber,* 354–55) assign *Crucem tuam adoramus* and *Adoramus crucem tuam.*

54. Only the first of these refers specifically to the Exaltation (Magistretti, *Manuale,* pt. 2, 350). The fact that prayers alone are entered for certain feasts (the case of Annunciation on 25 March has already been mentioned) makes it clear that a sacramentary was one of the sources for the compilation of the Manuale. Among the other sources would have been the lists of chant incipits postulated above.

55. The modern Ambrosian books assign the same antiphons for the Vespers psalms on the feast of the Discovery and the feast of the Exaltation, but *Crucem tuam adoramus* is put in place of *Laudamus te Christe* (Suñol, *Liber,* 354, 411).

56. As in Vimercate D, fol. 67r–v.

57. The melodies of *Laudamus te Christe* and *Adoramus crucem tuam* are significantly related (cf. Bailey and Merkley 1990, 212, 207). Both have other assignments in the Ambrosian liturgy. *Laudamus te* is assigned at Mass as the Confractorium and at Matins as the antiphon to the *Laudate* psalms. The Matins assignment was doubtless suggested by the first word (*Laudamus*), but an equally plausible assignment would have been to the Benedicite canticle, to which the antiphon is obviously related (cf. "Laudamus te, Christe; et *hymnum dicimus* tibi, quia per crucem redemisti mundum" and the last verse of the canticle as it was sung at Matins: "*Hymnum dicamus* et superexaltemus eum in saecula"). The antiphon for the second psalm at Vespers ("Adoramus crucem tuam, et signum de cruce tua, et qui crucifixus est virtute") was assigned also to the Benedicite canticle at Matins.

58. It is probably significant in this respect that the Byzantine Church did not have a separate feast for the Exaltation and the Discovery, but commemorated both events on the same occasion (on 14 Sept.).

59. In the modern Ambrosian books, the (Gregorian) antiphon *Nos autem gloriari* is substituted on the feast of 3 May (see Suñol, *Liber*, 357).

60. In the ordinal of Beroldus, compiled shortly after 1126, there is notice of a special celebration of the Exaltation of the Cross on the first Sunday of October, this occasion instituted by a certain Tado or Tadelbertus "for the relief of his soul" (see Magistretti, *Beroldus*, 125–26 and 228, n. 265). On this occasion the two psalms of First Vespers (i.e., on Saturday) are the same as for the Discovery, but the antiphons are *Crucem tuam adoramus* and *Adoramus crucem tuam;* the Magnificat antiphon is *Laudamus te Christe.*

61. The feast of St. Bartholomew appears first in Milan, Ambrosiana A 24 inf., the Lodrino sacramentary (source D in Heiming, *Das ambrosianische Sakramentar,* pt. 1, xxxix); the Chair of Peter, in Milan, Ambrosiana T 120 sup. (see Frei 1974, 91). For the dating of these manuscripts, see Heiming, xxxix.

62. For example, in Milan, BC D.2.28 (MS M in Magistretti, *Manuale,* pt. 1, 17; pt. 2, 115).

63. For Annunciation and Purification, the single psalm is 114 (*commune virginum*); for the Nativity of the Virgin, the psalms are numbers 66 (*commune apostolorum*[!]) and 44 (*commune virginum*). As mentioned earlier, the psalms (and refrains) for Assumption are taken from the Common of a Virgin.

64. For the Discovery, proper psalms were assigned, the first is number 66, chosen, certainly, for verse 3 ("ut cognoscamus in terra uiam tuam in omnibus gentibus salutare tuum"), which can, in this context, be understood to mean "that we may discover, in the earth, thy salvation." The second psalm is 118; the portion allocated (v. 25 and following) begins with a reference to the *pavement* (*pavimento*) under which the Cross was discovered.

65. On most occasions of the Temporale, the Office concluded (with additional psalms, prayers, etc.) in the baptistery.

66. The Magnificat was, however, omitted on Fridays in Lent and in Holy Week.

67. It might seem there is a third exception, but *Respexit dominus ad humilitatem sanctorum suorum,* the Magnificat antiphon for plural saints, must be assigned to Class 1A. The citation has been significantly altered to make it appropriate: the canticle verse reads "quia respexit ad humilitatem *ancillae suae.*" The alteration might, of course, be a late revision.

68. In the *Manuale* and in the antiphoners, 19 refrains (four of them exact citations, but most, close paraphrases of verses from the canticle, i.e., antiphons of Class 1A) are collected in a *commune* for the Magnificat on Sundays and the other days of the week.

69. It is assigned to the Common of Apostles and to the Common of Martyrs. In later times, the text was used as a Gregorian Magnificat refrain on the feast of the Holy Name.

70. "Anima mea, magnifica deum, qui *fecit mihi magna, qui potens est; et sanctum nomen eius.*" The text notwithstanding, this antiphon was never assigned as a Magnificat antiphon, but used only as a processional.

71. The full text is: "Qui fecisti magnalia in Aegypto, mirabilia in terra Cham, terribilia in mare rubro, non tradas nos in manus gentium, nec dominentur nobis, qui oderunt nos."

72. The feasts of St. Quiricus and of SS. Cosmas and Damian.

73. The feasts of St. James and of St. Vincent.

74. The feasts of Martin, James, the Translation of Nazarius, Protasius, and Gervasius, Nabor and Felix, Quiricus, Sisinius et al., Mamas and Agapitus.

75. The feasts of Vincent, Lawrence, Genesius, and the Nativity of the Baptist.

76. Clement; Thomas; Philip and James; Alexander; Cosmas and Damian; Quiricus; Nazarius and Celsus (ad S. Celsum); Euphemia; Domninus; Simon, Jude and Fidelis; Hippolytus and Cassianus; All Saints.

77. Evidence of an earlier stage, i.e., psalmody without antiphons, may survive in the Paschal cursus (see Bailey 1993).

78. Romanus is one of the saints with authentic Ambrosian prefaces in the earliest sacramentaries.

79. The same is true, of course, of the fixed assignments in the second part of Matins.

80. Vigils are doubled on the Feast of St. Andrew: the first Office begins in the (winter) Cathedral, the second "ad sanctam Andream" (Magistretti, *Manuale*, pt. 1, 13). This is the only Ambrosian feast so distinguished.

81. In *Sub clamide terreni*, the Magnificat antiphon for St. Victor, the last word, *potuit*, may similarly be meant as a reference to the *potens, potentiam* and *potentes* of the canticle.

82. *Errant iusti*, the Vespers antiphon for the Nativity of St. John the Baptist, may also be purposefully connected with Ps. 127. A striking series of Class 2 and Class 3 antiphons connected with their psalmody is found outside the Sanctorale at Matins in Holy Week (see Bailey 1994, 322–35).

83. The melody is a close adaptation of a standard Ambrosian type-melody, as is *Suscipe beata crux* (Bailey and Merkley 1990, 305, 620–21; 279, 605). The Gregorian *Posui adiutorium super potentem*, from the Common of Confessors, is a responsory.

84. Cf. *Miserere mei quia peccavi, Averte faciem tuam*, and *Asperges me domine*. The relationship between these *antiphonae in quinquagesimo* and the antiphon for St. Genesius is at least as close as the relationship between *Occulta* and the other Magnificat antiphons that develop the same type-melody (see Bailey and Merkley 1990, 295, 464–65).

85. *Beata progenies unde* and *Rubum quem viderat* (the Magnificat antiphon) are also assigned as the confractorium and the antiphona post evangelium, respectively, at the Mass of the day. *De radice Iesse* can be found in some books as the confractorium for the late feast of the Presentation of the Virgin on 21 November (cf. Suñol, *Antiphonale*, 390).

86. *Iacob puer meus* was sung as the confractorium (see Magistretti, *Manuale*, pt. 2, 76–77) and *Audi me Iacob* (the Magnificat antiphon) is also sung as the antiphona post evangelium on the feast of St. James. *Audi me* is not assigned to Vespers in the *Manuale*, but this assignment *is* found in certain antiphoners, for example, Vimercate, S. Stefano B, fol. 80r.

87. Mass prayers are found in the Biasca sacramentary (see Frei 1974, 93).

88. This figure is slightly higher if refrains that have been adapted for different feasts (such as *Sancte Georgi [Fidelis] martyr Christi fiduciam habens intercede pro nobis*) are counted separately.

Performing Latin Verse

Text and Music in Early Medieval Versified Offices

GUNILLA BJÖRKVALL & ANDREAS HAUG

Among Offices created during the early Middle Ages some contain antiphons and responsories written in verse form. "Versified Offices," as these are commonly termed, have many features in common with Offices composed in prose from the same period. What distinguishes them from the latter is the verse form of some or all of their texts. However, they have been little studied, and the portion of the entire corpus consisting of texts in verse form has not yet been determined.[1] Even if they should turn out to be a *quantité negligéable,* peripheral in the panorama of the Latin Office, their historical significance is not in doubt. Versified Offices are symptomatic of a central aspect of Office composition during the late Carolingian period, epitomizing an interactive dynamic between an earlier layer of liturgical chant on its way to becoming standardized, and the manifold attempts at its completion, amplification, and adornment.

In this chapter we consider whether and to what extent the distinctive textual form of versified Offices has a bearing on the melodies composed for their performance. Are there ways in which aspects of the verse form were rendered by the music and thus made perceptible to those singing and listening to the Office?[2] This question is crucial not only for an understanding of the genre and its place in the history of medieval Office composition, but also, more generally, for an assessment of the aesthetic prestige of verse in early medieval liturgy, and attitudes towards its use for Latin liturgical chants. Choosing an interdisciplinary approach, we intend to analyze the intricate relationship between the different verse forms appearing in select early medieval Office texts and the melodies to which they were sung.[3]

The very earliest examples of the versified Office as a genre with a recognizable profile date from the tenth century. Dating these early works is possible either by the attribution of the Office to a known author or through its appearance in a datable manuscript. The Office of the Trinity and the Office of St. Lambert are attributed to Stephen of Liège (d. 920);[4] moreover, the earliest records of the Trinity Office date from the tenth century,[5] and the earliest record of the Lambert Office is even dated to the time of Stephen's episcopate (901–20).[6] Another early versified Office is that of St. Fuscianus, written by an unknown author and contained in the Mont-Renaud manuscript, the text of which was copied during the late tenth century; the notation was added later, at the beginning of the eleventh century.[7]

As to the history of the genre, the basic question is whether the ninth- and tenth-century Offices "plus ou moins versifiés," as Ritva Jonsson (Jacobsson) has preferred to call them (Jonsson 1968, 19), should actually be seen "only as an antecedent to the later repertory" of the "fully metrical and rhymed office," which "emerged in the late eleventh or early twelfth century," as Andrew Hughes stated (Hughes 1988b, 371–72). Since his article is the most recent comprehensive discussion of the topic, we want to illustrate the historiographical problems involved by quoting in full the sole example from an early versified Office analyzed by Hughes, namely the first antiphon of First Vespers of the Trinity Office by Stephen of Liège (Hughes 1988b, 374) (see example 12.1).

> *Gloria tibi Trinitas equalis una deitas* divides most naturally in syntax and meaning into three phrases of two words each. But splitting it after *Trinitas* creates poetry of the modern kind, with a minor amount of syntactical and semantic difficulty. The consequences of dividing the chant into two phrases rather than three are almost as significant musically (Hughes 1988b, 371).

Hughes's second comment concerns the music:

> If divided at (1), mandated by a rendition of the text divided into three sections, marked by commas in parentheses, the phrase conforms entirely to a standard melodic motive in mode 1 with the reciting note extended by ornament; if divided at (2), by a "modern" rendition, the whole nature of the melody is changed. The phrase is divided into balanced sections, the first of which conforms to a standard phrase in mode 1, and the second takes on the character of a triadic phrase more like mode 5. This division is emphasized by the rhyme, and by the presence of the musical rhyme GAA at the end of each section; this figure is the most common cadence in the other most prominent new musical style of the time, the sequence. There can be little doubt that the increase in regularity of meter and rhyme forces balanced phrases, each articulated by cadencelike figures, onto the melodies. Thus, the older plainsong style, notable for its fluidity, even unpredictability, had changed into one of careful and deliberate architecture. If the poem, as

Example 12.1 Antiphon *Gloria tibi trinitas* (after Hughes)

is usually the case, has four lines, the new chant style will resemble a hymn, and choirs, especially if untrained, will inevitably perform in such a way as to emphasize the phrasing (Hughes 1988b, 374).

Hughes does not consider that the text quite simply is verse, nor even that it is borrowed from a hymn. In fact, it is a wandering doxological strophe that can be found since the ninth century as an ending for several different hymns (cf. Jonsson 1968, 221). The verse form is iambic dimeter. The division after *trinitas* rather than after *tibi* and *aequalis*, then, is not a mere option, but the end of the first verse line, and it does not "create poetry of the modern kind," but corresponds to the traditional form of the most common hymn stanza. The "minor amount of syntactical and semantic difficulty" is of the sort one meets wherever a line of verse in a hymn continues into the subsequent line without a grammatical break, thus causing an enjambment. Hughes's analysis of the melodic structure is sensitive to the ambiguity of the relation between text and music. The question is, however, whether the ambiguity is due to a "rudimentary" stage of stylistic development or to an ambivalent attitude toward the verse form. Also, Hughes's notion that the perception of form can be affected by the manner of performance, since performance can either emphasize melodic caesuras or weaken them, points to an important aspect of the problem. Indeed, the evidence of conventions of performance provided by early neumatic notation takes this notion beyond the realm of mere speculation. As we will show below, the notation of the Trinity Office in its earliest sources suggests that the phrasing marked by melodic cadences that underscores the verse form of the antiphon was differentiated, modified, or even suspended by performance strategies.

We can describe Hughes's example in different and simpler terms, based on example 12.2:[8]

> Glory be to you, equal
> trinity, one deity,
> before all time,
> and now, and in eternity.

The verse form of the antiphon *Gloria tibi, trinitas* is iambic dimeter, built according to rhythmical rather than metrical principles, that is, built on syllable count and regular accent pattern at the end of lines rather than on syllable quantity. The form of the strophe can be described as $4 \times 8pp$: four lines with eight syllables, each line ending on a proparoxytone, that is, a word stressed on the antepenultimate syllable (Norberg 1958, 106 f.). If one accepts the punctuation suggested by Hughes, the divisions of syntax and meaning are not congruent with the divisions of verse in lines 1 and 2.[9] The boundaries between syntactic groups and sense units (|) are as follows:

> Gloria tibi, | trinitas aequalis, | una deitas

The division of the verse line falls after *trinitas*, in the middle of the second sense unit, between a noun and its attribute, thus causing an enjambment. This enjambment would be even more forceful if the endings of the nouns *trinitas* and

Example 12.2   Antiphon *Gloria tibi, trinitas* for Trinity Vespers (from Vienna, ÖNB
1888, fol. 197)

deitas were heard as a rhyme. The hymnlike melody underscores the verse structure
rather than the sense units: identical cadence figures appear at the end of *trinitas*
and *deitas*. They not only reinforce the proparoxytone verse endings, but also the
rhyme of the nouns. In the original setting of the text as a hymn strophe, this
would not be remarkable: in a hymn, the melodic lines must render the verse lines
throughout, without regard for the individual syntax of a single strophe; in an
antiphon, it would have been possible to create a melody, or adapt the text to a
melody, in which a cadence did not cut the sense unit in half. It seems that either
the melody of the antiphon is borrowed from an existing hymn just as the text is
(although, to our knowledge, no melodic concordance has been identified within
the hymn repertory), or the setting deliberately imitates the melodic idiom of
hymns, through phrasing that renders the verse division.

Example 12.3   Beginning of antiphon *Gloria tibi, trinitas* (Hartker Codex, St. Gall 390, fol. 101)

That the antiphon might actually have been performed "in such a way as to emphasize the phrasing" can be verified by a look at the neumatic notation in the Hartker codex, St. Gall, SB 390–91 (p. 101) shown in example 12.3.[10] The slowing and pausing effect of the melodic cadences at the end of verse lines 1 and 2 has been modified as intimated by the nuances of the notation: there is an episema—a horizontal stroke at the upper end of the neumatic sign indicating a prolongation of the note—only at the final virga of verse line 2 (c), which coincides with the end of a sense unit, but not at the end of verse 1 (b), which cuts the sense unit "trinitas aequalis." Furthermore, there is the angular instead of the round form of the pes at the last syllable of *tibi* (a), indicating a retardation at the end of the sense unit. Thus, at least at the monastery of St. Gall around the year 1000, the antiphon was not performed in the manner Hughes proposed: the perceptibility of syntax and meaning was subordinated, but not sacrificed, to that of the verse structure.

As Ritva Jonsson (Jacobsson) has shown, the early medieval versified Office did not develop gradually from Offices in prose, but had its origin in the more or less sporadic transfer of existing verses from other genres. Such a transfer might not have been primarily motivated by a genuine interest in verse form, but rather by a need for texts with specific contents. This seems to be true for new saints' Offices, where the chant texts are drawn from poems dedicated to the saint in question, as well as for the Trinity Office, where the frequent use of doxological hymn strophes meets the requirement of trinitarian formulations. The formal qualities of verse may well have been esteemed, but this esteem was not the determining criterion for the compilation of the texts (Jonsson 1968, 166–83).

Hughes interprets the antiphon *Gloria tibi, trinitas* in terms of a gradually emerging "new style," already different from what he calls the "older plainsong style," but still an antecedent to the new style of twelfth-century chant. What he describes in terms of stylistic evolution might be better understood in terms of different idioms appropriate to various liturgical genres, in terms of differing attitudes toward the presence of verse in liturgy, and in terms of different ways in which music might "respond to" the complex structure of versified texts, ranging from total indifference toward verse to a nuanced mediation between the demands of verse form on the one hand, and syntax and meaning on the other. The situation is much more complex, then, than it might initially seem.

In order to pursue this point, we will first compare the setting of another antiphon belonging to the same Office but rendered in a different verse form. Secondly, we will compare the melody of that antiphon with a hymn melody used for hymn texts of the same verse form.

The text of the third antiphon of the Trinity Office, *Gloria laudis resonet in ore*, borrows the doxology strophe of Alcuin's hymn for St. Vedast *Christe salvator hominis*.[11]

> Gloria laudis resonet in ore
> omnium patris genitaeque prolis,
> spiritus sancti pariter resultet
> laude perenni.
>
> May glory and praise of the Father and of his begotten Son
> resound in the mouth of everyone
> and equally let that of the Holy Spirit
> leap up in eternal praising.

The form is a metric Sapphic stanza, built of three Sapphic verses (eleven syllables each) plus one adonius (five syllables). An enjambment in the second line allows us to examine whether the melody corresponds to syntax or to verse. Syntax and meaning divide as follows:

> Gloria laudis resonet in ore / omnium | patris genitaeque proli,

However, the end of the verse line (/) falls after *ore*, between a noun and its qualification in the genitive.

A cursory glance at the music, as presented in example 12.4, reveals that the demarcation between the first two verse lines after *ore* is not marked by a melodic cadence.[12] A control test at the division between sense units substantiates the observation that the setting renders a reading of the verses as a text in prose: the melodic figures at *omnium* and *pariter* can be perceived if not as cadential, at least as cadence-like. A closer look at the music shows a clear-cut melodic parallelism: the section from *Gloria* to *omnium* is, to a large extent, identical with the section from *patris* to *pariter*. The parallel sections in the melody correspond to main sense units in the poetry, but totally fracture the verse structure.

The text/music relationship can once again be evaluated by consultation of the notation of this chant as recorded at St. Gall. Example 12.5 shows the relevant section in the Hartker codex (St. Gall 390–91, p. 101). Two significant details (marked by circles) can be observed. First, the scribe writes the letter *c*—meaning *celeriter*—above the neumatic sign at *ore*, presumably in order to prevent a slowing down or a pause at the end of the verse line. Secondly, he writes the word *patris* with a capital letter, a capitalization that does not occur elsewhere in the antiphons of this Office, presumably in order to advise the singer to make a pause after *om-*

Example 12.4   Trinity antiphon *Gloria laudis resonet in ore* (from Vienna, ÖNB 1888, fol. 197)

nium (the end of the sense unit) rather than after *ore* (the end of the verse line). This would mean that the scribe was as aware of the text as versified as of the convention of performing it as prose.

Gloria laudis resonet in ore resembles many other mode 3 antiphons, sharing the melodic features typical of this class of chants. It is most unlikely, then, that the antiphon melody is borrowed from the repertory of hymn melodies. In any case, the antiphon melody would poorly serve the text of Alcuin's Vedast hymn: in the first stanza, the melodic cadence in the second verse would cut through a word: "Christe salvator hominis ab ore / Hostis anti——qui . . ."[13]

To review then: the two antiphons *Gloria tibi, trinitas* and *Gloria laudis resonet in ore* display different strategies of setting music to verse. Whatever the explanation for these different, even contradictory, strategies may be, the differences cannot simply be ascribed to historical change of style since both antiphons belong to the same Office.

Example 12.5   Trinity antiphon *Gloria laudis resonet in ore* (Hartker Codex, St. Gall 390–91, p. 101)

in ore omnium Patri geniteque proli

The basic difference between a musical setting treating the Sapphic stanza as prose (as with *Gloria laudis resonet in ore*) and a musical setting actually rendering the strophe form (as with *Gloria tibi, trinitas*) becomes evident with analysis of a melody frequently used for hymns in the same meter. Example 12.6 shows the first two stanzas of *Virginis proles opifexque matris:*[14]

> Son of the virgin and creator of your mother,
> whom the virgin carried and brought forth . . .
>
> This virgin, having a twofold blessed
> destiny, since she desired eagerly to subdue her fragile (sex . . .)

Here, too, we encounter two identical melodic sections, but they correspond to the first two verse lines. Wherever an enjambment appears, the melodic division will unavoidably come into conflict with syntax and sense. This happens in the second strophe, where the music causes the inevitably nonsensical reading *duplici beata | sorte, dum gestit* ("twofold blessed | destiny, since she eagerly desired") instead of *duplici beata sorte, | dum gestit* ("twofold blessed destiny, | since she eagerly desired").

Thus, at the very beginning of the history of the versified Office there are chants with texts in perfectly regular verse form, and, as we have seen, this verse form is underscored by the music to varying degrees. The strategies of rendering may be so subtle as to be grasped only by close examination of both the textual and melodic parameters as well as of the details of notation. But it is exactly these subtle strate-

Example 12.6   Hymn *Virginis proles opifexque matris*

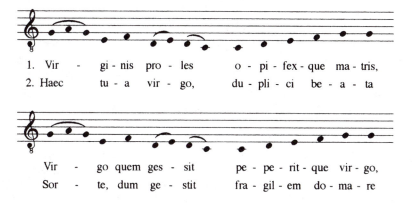

gies that require our attention and careful consideration if we are to appreciate the earliest versified Offices as cases of artful interaction between text and music.

The examples from the Trinity Office contain iambic dimeter and Sapphic stanza, forms common in hymns. Office items having these forms have been described here in terms of a resemblance to the formal aspects of hymnody (Jammers 1929, 205). In order to include other verse forms in our study, we will now analyze examples in hexameters and elegiac distichs, beginning with some settings of hexameters in the Lambert Office by Stephen of Liège.

The famous early tenth-century Brussels manuscript (BR 14650–59) of the Lambert Office contains not only the Office itself under the rubric "ANTIPHONAE ET RESPONSORIA" (copied on fols. 37–39 by several different hands), but, among other related hagiographical texts, also the *Vita et passio beati Landberti episcopi* as well as the metrical *Carmen de sancto Landberto,* which are the literary sources for the Office texts. Most of the responsories are taken from the *Vita et passio;*[15] they are prose (usually rhymed prose), whereas most of the antiphons are taken from the metrical *Carmen.*[16] Thus these latter are verse, mostly pairs of hexameters, sometimes groups of three or four hexameter lines.

The visual layout in the Brussels manuscript calls attention to verse form: the texts of the antiphons are written out as verse lines, each beginning with a capital letter. This layout and emphasis through capitalization is not common in liturgical chant books and may be due to the special character of this manuscript. In any case, it is evidence for a genuine interest in the verse form.

The Latin hexameter is based on the quantities of the individual syllables (long or short). It consists of six dactylic feet (long–short–short), of which the first four may be substituted by spondaic feet (long–long); the last one is catalectic (incomplete). Due to the different combinations of dactylic and spondaic feet the number of syllables may vary from 13 to 17. The verse line can be structured by internal caesuras, that is divisions of words within a foot. The main and predominant caesura (pentemimeresis) falls after the fifth half-foot. Further subordinated caesuras are possible after the third (trihemimeresis) and after the seventh (heptemimeresis) half-foot. How and to what extent these formal qualities of the verse were perceptible in the oral delivery of the text has been a matter for discussion among Latinists: whether the different quantities were perceived as different durations of the syllables, whether the caesura was perceived as a pause, and whether the verse was scanned, i.e. the verse ictus was enhanced by stressing the first syllable in each foot of the hexameter, are unanswered questions (Norberg 1988, 13–16, Klopsch 1991, 95–106). Therefore, analyses of musical settings of metrical verse must not be founded on unverified assumptions about how the verse was read. On the contrary, the nature of the melodies to which the verse was sung might provide evidence concerning conventions of reading.

Example 12.7 presents three antiphons from the last nocturn BR 14650–59:

> Worried about the people, he went through countries and cities
> and strengthened the faith that is born from the name of the Trinity,
> so that everyone who loves the divine power of the Father and the Son
> together with the Holy Spirit believes that it is one God.

He remained constantly under God's law,
and no sin came close to his body.
Because the last day always stood before his eyes,
whence he maintained the good course in his struggle.

Decades ago Antoine Auda, in his study on Stephen of Liège, observed the melodic correspondences between these three chants. He interpreted the similar endings of the verse lines of different antiphons as melodic "rhymes," connecting all the antiphons of one nocturn (Auda 1923, 178–80). Most of the verse lines end with a recurrent cadential figure, slightly varied only when the cadence occurs on *g* instead of *d* at the end of the first antiphon.

The one-verse caesura that all these hexameter lines have in common is the central caesura after the fifth half-foot. In almost all lines, melodic cadences mark these caesuras; indeed, the cadence of the second-line caesura of *Sollicitus plebis* uses the same cadence employed for the final verse of the antiphon.

Nothing indicates that the melodies render the quantities of the syllables in any way: neither is the setting sufficiently syllabic to allow for long- and short-note durations representing long and short syllables, nor is there any tendency to place more notes on long syllables than on short. Actually, half of the syllables sung on two notes are short, and only one of those sung on three notes is long.

As to the question whether the verse was scanned or read with prose accent, nothing speaks in favor of the former. In the case of the hexameter, scansion would imply a verse accent, a so-called ictus, on the first syllable of each foot. Thus, a reading of the opening lines of the first and second antiphon enhancing verse ictus would have been like this:

> Sóllicitús plebís patriás lustrávit et úrbes
> Híc indéficiéns dominí sub lége manébat

whereas a reading of these two lines with prose accent would be as follows:

> Sollícitus plébis pátrias lustrávit et úrbes
> Híc indefíciens dómini sub lége manébat

If one perceives the ascent from the *g* to the upper *c* in these seventh- and eighth-mode antiphons as a melodic accentuation, such accents as at *Sollícitus, indefíciens, dómini,* and *astábat* all coincide with prose accents, only the one at *astábat* at the same time with the ictus. The ascent to the upper *c* at the beginning of *contagio* (in the second antiphon) renders neither the prose accent nor the ictus. (It might perhaps be interpreted as a rhetorical emphasis on an important word, "sin," "pollution"). The remaining hexameter texts found in the Lambert Office are consonant with these observations, although they are less convenient for demonstration since the melodic phrases are less clearly demarcated.

Thus, neither quantity nor ictus is rendered by the settings. But by consistently marking both the end of the verse lines and the internal caesuras through cadential figures, the music makes features of the meter perceptible to singer and listener. Nonetheless, performed with prose accent, the specific structure of the hexameter

Example 12.7   Three Matins antiphons from the St. Lambert Office (Brussels, BR 14650–59, fol. 38)

stands out less distinctly in delivery: the strongest perception, perhaps, is of lines (13–17 syllables each) divided into two sections of roughly 5–7 and 8–10 syllables respectively. This is not dissimilar to the length and inner proportions of the trochaic septenarius: 8 + 7 = 15 syllables.[17] As a cursory comparison of the hexameter settings examined with that of the only trochaic septenarius setting in the Lambert Office will show, the music enhances the shape and the proportions of the bipartite form common to both meters more than emphasizing the distinctive and defining traits of the respective meters.

> The voice resounding with loud praise
> is fitting to you in every respect;

Example 12.7   (*continued*)

(2) Hic in-de-fi - ci-ens   do - mi-ni sub le-ge   ma - ne-bat,

Cui-us nul-la me-ans   sub-er-at con   -   ta-gi-o   car-ni.

(3) Ul - ti-ma nam-que* di - es   a - sta-bat sem-per   o - cel-lis

Il-li-us,   un-de bo-num   fe-cit cer-ta-mi   -   ne   cur-sum.

* MS: nanque

Enriched by such a dignified member
the troop of heavens takes delight in you.
The world applauds and rejoices
worthy of such a great bishop.
O holy martyr, Lambert!
Receive our prayers.

As can be seen in example 12.8, the Magnificat antiphon *Magna vox laude sonora* is in the second mode.[18] There are cadences on the finalis *d* at the end of each verse line. Furthermore, the first three half-verses are marked off by "rhyming" melodic figures, ending on *d* or *A*. The balance between the melodic phrases within the

Example 12.8   Lambert Magnificat antiphon *Magna vox laude sonora* (Utrecht 406, fol. 167r–v)

lines and the discrete parallelism between them will not be described in detail here. While in the first three lines the melody stays within the regular melodic range of the mode, this range is drastically exceeded at the beginning of the final line, where Lambert is addressed directly: the exclamatory *O* is sung on a melisma ascending to *c′*—a third above the upper limit of the melodic range of the mode. That this is an original feature of the melody is evident from the Brussels manuscript, where the extreme pitch is indicated by the additional letter *a*, here obviously signifying *altius* ("higher"). There are two more melismas in the supplication concluding the antiphon, emphasizing the saint's name, and the word *vota* ("prayers") in the petition formula.

For isolated verses it may be difficult to decide whether the verse is built on metrical or rhythmical principles. As for *Magna vox laude sonora*, a text perhaps taken from an existing (though unknown) longer poem, it seems to be a rhythmic

imitation of the trochaic septenarius. The form of this verse can be described as
8p+7pp: the first half-verse comprising eight syllables ending with a paroxytone
word (a word stressed on the penultimate syllable), the second comprising seven
syllables ending with a proparoxytone word (as mentioned earlier, a word stressed
on the antepenultimate syllable). These closing stresses of the half-verses are
emphasized by the musical setting: melismas occur both on the penultima of the
first half-verse and the antepenultima of the second.

Let us now return to the antiphons of the third nocturn in example 12.7. Only
two lines are not closed by the recurrent cadential figure. One of them is the opening line of the third antiphon, *Ultima namque dies*. Here the ending of one verse
line and the beginning of the next separate the noun *ocellis* from its qualification
in genitive *illius*. The melody, however, veils rather than highlights the enjambment: by omitting the cadential figure, the melody "slips" discretely over the
boundary between these verse lines. The music upholds the sense units in two
other examples of this nocturn. Among the internal cadential figures in the first
antiphon, the one at *nati* in line 3 is clearly the less distinct. And the only division
between verse units in the second antiphon not marked by a cadence on the finalis
g is at *means*. Here, too, a marking off of verse units by more distinct melodic
cadences would have interrupted sense units.

A general characteristic of hexameters is an intricately woven word order, as
with the second antiphon *Hic indeficiens*. Instead of a more straightforward "Cuius
carni nulla contagio means suberat," the complicated yet elegant word arrangement of the second line of this antiphon reads "Cuius nulla means suberat contagio
carni"—a word order not easily divided into comprehensible units at any point.
Syntactical units that belong together are separated and distributed over the two
halves of the verse. No matter where the placement of the cadence might occur, it
would interfere with syntax and sense. We will return to this particular especially
intricate issue of setting metrical verse later in the chapter.

A regard for syntax and meaning similar to that found in the antiphons of the
third nocturn can be observed in the antiphon *Fortis in adversis* in the second
nocturn. Again, the hexameter lines have the main caesura after the fifth half-foot.
The final syllable of the verse lines rhymes with the syllable before the main caesura. This so-called Leonine rhyme was not a device used in the antiphons of the
third nocturn.

> Fortis in adversis, humilis per prospera pacis,
> Nec terrore teri potuit, nec munere frangi.

> Strong in misfortunes, humble in prosperous times of peace,
> He could neither be crushed by fear, nor broken by duties.

Both verse lines consist of two membra each, parallel in form and meaning. This
parallelism is further underscored by rhymes relating the beginnings of the membra: *Fortis—humilis, Nec terrore—nec munere*.

As can be seen in the second verse from example 12.9, the cadence does not
occur at the pentemimeresis, where it would have split the sense unit, but instead
at the heptemimeresis, where it corresponds with a punctuation mark between the
parallel text units (Utrecht, Rijksuniversiteit 406, fol. 163). Paul Klopsch describes

Example 12.9   Matins antiphon *Fortis in adversis* for St. Lambert (Utrecht 406, fol. 163)

For — tis in ad - ver - sis, hu-mi-lis per   pro-spe-ra pa-cis,

Nec ter - ro - re   te - ri   po - tu - it,   nec mu - ne - re fran-gi.

the rhyme in hexameter poems as a means of marking the division of the verse in minor units; this is the effect of Leonine rhymes. Another function of the rhyme is the creation of a stanzalike form by joining two hexameters; this form is obtained through rhymes at the end of the verse lines (Klopsch 1972, 76). The antiphons of the third nocturn of the Lambert Office, as we have seen, have no textual rhymes, but melodic cadences consistently subdivide the verse after the fifth half-foot, and melodic endrhymes relate the verses to one another.

What makes this observation relevant to the history of Latin verse is that the subdivison of the verse by melodic means seems to serve the same purpose that the Leonine rhyme does: it makes the hexameter appear as a bipartite form. The melodic endrhymes, too, take over a function proper to textual rhymes: they underscore the joining together of two hexameters and its resulting stanza-like composite form.

The verse form that answers to the striving for self-contained couplets in the best way possible is of course the distich, consisting of a dactylic hexameter followed by a dactylic pentameter (the latter can be described as a hexameter in which the unaccented parts of the third and sixth feet have been dropped). And, in fact, within early medieval Office composition, there are not only examples of the use of elegiac distichs for antiphon texts, but also cases where hexameter pairs have been reworked into distichs. The Office for St. Fuscianus is such a case (textual edition in Jonsson 1968, 187–94). This Office is contained in the Mont-Renaud manuscript, and thus is datable to no later than the tenth century. The responsories are drawn from the *Passio sanctorum Fusciani et Victorici*, while the antiphons for the most part are from the *Carmen de sancto Quintino* and the *Carmen de sancta Benedicta*, hexameter poems describing the lives and passions of these saints.[19] However, several of the hexameter lines from the *Carmen de sancto Quintino* used as antiphon texts have been transformed into elegiacs.

A demonstration of how two chant texts adapted their literary model will show whether the transformation might have been realized in order to modify the contents or to change the meter. Verses 150–55 of the *Carmen de sancto Quintino* read as follows (textual edition in Winterfeld, ed., *Poetae*, 197–208):

> Regia martirii redimitum munere celi
> Sed iam Quintinum posuit super astra polorum.
> Cumque Somanobrium gressus tetigisset eorum,
> Nobilitate cluens quibus obvius ecce viator
> Gentianus adest, procurvus temporis aevo,
> Iam senior, sed cruda illi viridisque senectus.

> But the kingdom of heaven had already placed Quentin, who was
> crowned with the gift of martyrdom, above the stars of heaven.
> When their steps had reached Somanobrium,
> see, Gentianus, famous for his nobility, presents himself to them
> as traveler, bent through old age,
> already an old man, but his old age is healthy and vigorous.

Two antiphons for the second nocturn have been drawn out of this passage (Jonsson 1968, 190):

> Regia martyrii redimitum munere celi
>   sed iam Quintinum sumpserat emeritum.

> Nobilitate cluens quibus obvius ecce viator
>   Gentianus adest, inclitus atque senex.

> But the kingdom of heaven had already received Quentin, who
> now had finished serving and was crowned with the gift of martyrdom.

> See, Gentianus, famous for his nobility and old age,
> presents himself to them as traveler.

The modifications somewhat simplify and condense the text, but no change in the contents is significant enough to motivate the rephrasing. Thus, the intention must have been to change the meter. This, again, points clearly to a genuine interest in verse.

The setting of *Regia martyrii* had to deal with an extremely syntactically complicated text. A straightforward word order not constrained by demands of meter and artful diction might be as follows:

> Sed iam regia celi Quintinum emeritum munere martyrii redimitum sumpserat.

In the versified text almost all words belonging together are separated and distanced from each other; in other words: successive words hardly ever belong together. The consequences of this for music has been discussed at length by Ritva Jonsson and Leo Treitler in connection with an analysis of a trope in hexameter form. They describe the problem as follows (Jonsson and Treitler 1983, 16):

> To make a melody continuous over successive words that do not belong
> together semantically would obscure the sense of the text. The response of
> the trope-melody's creator to the virtually atomic word-sequence of the

trope verses was, therefore, to establish a melodic phrase-boundary wherever there was no continuity in the sense of the words, and to reinforce through melodic associations the syntactical links across the line. By these means, the stylistic factor of text segmentation was translated into melody as the articulation and structure of phrases.

The creator of the antiphon *Regia martyrii* (see example 12.10) formulated a fifth-mode melody that is in certain respects "fragmented" like the text and yet possesses coherence and continuity (MS Mont-Renaud, fol. 113). Practically every single word is set to a self-contained melodic unit ending with a descent to either the finalis *f* or its upper fifth *c'*, and on one occasion with a descent to *a*. All the endings of these melodic units have a more or less distinctive cadential character. Thus, they clearly do "establish a melodic phrase-boundary wherever there was no continuity in the sense of the words." Actually, one could just as well sing the melodic segments following the straightforward word order proposed above. On the other hand, the sequence of melodic segments is not without direction. It forms a double melodic arch rising from and returning to the finalis: the first arch, reaching its peak at *f'*, comprises the hexameter, the second, with its peak on *d'*, comprises the pentameter. Thus, the length of the verse lines is related to the height of the melodic arch. In the hexameter, syntactically linked words symmetrically placed on both sides of the central verb form *redimitum* are in the same melodic register. Since both verse lines end on the finalis, and the central caesuras of the hexameter and the pentameter are marked by identical melodic figures, the form of the elegiac distich is strongly brought forward by the music. What the listener perceives is a composition that is elegantly shaped and well balanced on both the textual and the melodic level—textual and melodic lines that resemble one another without being related.

Example 12.10   Matins antiphon *Regia martyrii* for St. Fuscianus (Antiphoner of Mont-Renaud, fol. 113)

Re- gi- a mar- ty- ri - i   re- di - mi- tum mu   -   ne - re   ce-li

sed   iam   Quin- ti - num   sum- pse- rat   e - me- ri - tum.

The Fuscianus Office displays a plurality of verse forms (see Jonsson 1968, 96–104). Besides hexameters and elegiac distichs, we find examples of rhythmic trochaic septenarius, hybrids consisting of elegiacs with hypermetrical additions (additional lines of either eight or six syllables), and a form, uncommon during the Middle Ages, but which has been used in classical Latin poetry, and may have been known to the composer of the Office through examples from Boethius and Martianus Capella.[20] This form is encountered in the Benedictus antiphon *Membra beata forent* and consists of an alternation between hexameter and iambic dimeter. If one interprets the iambic dimeter as rhythmic rather than metrical verse, the antiphon displays contrast not only between dactylic and iambic measures, but also between metrical and rhythmic verse (Jonsson 1968, 192):

Membra beata forent cum vitae munere cassa,
    sanctis paratur gloria.
Contigua lux missa polo loca forte venustans
    dignos fuisse indicat,
Quo caeli penetraret eorum spiritus aulam
    Christi favente gratia.

When the holy limbs were to be deprived of the duty of life,
the glory is being prepared for the saints.
A light chancing to come from the sky beautifying
the adjoining lands indicates that they are worthy,
that their spirit may enter the palace of heaven
with Christ's favorable grace.

This text has been obtained from hexameter lines in the *Carmen de sancto Quintino,* and thus is the result of a deliberate change of the verse form. The first two lines of the antiphon are drawn from lines 365–66 of the *Carmen,* a passage too seriously damaged to be restored. The remaining lines are drawn from lines 283–86 (letters restored by the editor are in italics; Winterfeld, ed., *Poetae,* 206–7):

*Eff*ulget lux *clara* polo loca forte ve*n*ustans,
Indicat *e*mer*i*tos nimiumque fuisse pe*remp*t*os,
Quo celi pen*e*tra*r*et eo*ru*m spiritus aulam
*Pr*eveniente deo, qu*i iu*re triumph*a*t ab alto.

A bright light chances to come from the sky, shines and beautifies the lands,
it indicates that the killed ones deserve
that their spirit may enter the palace of heaven
God having gone before, who justly exults in heaven.

If one compares the antiphon line "dignos fuisse indicat" with line 284 of the metrical poem, one realizes that two words are kept unaltered (*indicat* and *fuisse*), the four-syllable word *emeritos* has been substituted by the shorter synonym *dignos,* and that the remaining two words have been omitted. Likewise, the antiphon line "Christi favente gratia" is a condensed version of line 286 of the poem. The *Carmen* has sporadic Leonine rhymes, as with the passage under discussion *emeritos—*

peremptos and *deo—alto* in lines 284 and 286 respectively. Since these lines are transformed to iambic dimeter, the rhymes disappear. Instead we find new assonances on *a* at the end of every single line, creating coherence between them.

As for the music, presented in example 12.11 (MS Mont-Renaud, fol. 114), there are unambiguous cadences on the finalis *g* or on *d* at the end of each verse line; the only clear melodic incision within a verse occurs in the first line after *forent*. The cadence on the finalis there is identical with the cadence at the end of the second verse. This is the only hexameter in that antiphon having a caesura after its fifth half-foot, the pentemimeresis. The cadence at *forent* cannot be explained as a melodic marking of the end of a sense unit: the word order in this verse is entangled, be it for metrical or for rhetorical reasons, and at any place a melodic cadence would interrupt the meaning:

> Membra beata forent cum vitae munere cassa

A more straightforward order would be:

> Cum membra beata cassa vitae munere forent

Basic features of the textual form are reflected in the melody: the endings of both the dactylic and the iambic verses as well as the only pentemimeresis are marked off by cadences either on the finalis *g* or on *d*, underscoring the alternation of lines of different length. That the first and the last hexameter end on *d,* and all three iambic dimeters on the finalis, can be understood as a means of grouping the lines into couplets. Still, nothing indicates that the setting aims at contrasting the two measures, and even less at contrasting metrical and rhythmical verse (Jonsson 1968, 102–3). As can be seen from example 12.11, the closing phrases of the iambic lines 2 and 4, the dactylic line 3, and the first five half-feet before the caesura in line 1 resemble each other to a degree that speaks against any basic difference in the oral delivery of the lines, and instead in favor of a declamation of both meters based on prose accents that will neutralize the contrast between dactylic and iambic measure.

We have examined melodic settings of the verse forms most frequently employed in early medieval versified Offices. As became obvious, no clear-cut understanding of how these versified items were sung emerges, and so the problem regarding general modes of performance for Latin verse during the early Middle Ages remains unresolved. We are confronted with strikingly different, and even contradicting, strategies of setting verse. The variation should come as no surprise, and the search for established rules seems to be in vain. There were as many ways to set verses of a given form as there were ways of writing them. The constraints of the verse form imposed upon the poets and the composers certain recurrent problems, without preventing them from finding a multiplicity of individual solutions.

Seemingly, there was an ambivalent attitude toward verse within the Office during the early Middle Ages: although there was apparent appreciation for the song-like sound of sung verse, still the perceptibility of verse structure should not fracture syntax and meaning. In other words, the form should not obscure the content. A compromise had to be found by the composer in each individual case.

.

Example 12.11   Benedictus antiphon *Membra beata forent* for St. Fuscianus
(Antiphoner of Mont-Renaud, fol. 114)

Mem - bra be - a - ta   fo - rent cum vi-tae mu - ne - re   cas-sa,

san - ctis   pa - ra - tur   glo - ri - a.

Con - ti - gu - a lux mis-sa   po - lo lo-ca   for - te ve - nu-stans

di - gnos fu-is - se   in - di - cat,

Quo   cae - li pe-ne-tra-ret e - o - rum spi - ri - tus au - lam

Chri- sti fa - ven - te   gra-ti - a.

Certainly the differences in the musical settings cannot simply be ascribed to different approaches to verse employed at different places and different times, since they also occur in examples from Offices by the same composer. A basic criterion for how verse was performed seems to be the chant genre in question: the features of a hymn are more likely to be adopted by the melody of an antiphon than by the more elaborate melody of a responsory. With few exceptions, the responsories in the Offices examined are not even versified. And a hymn strophe, a pair of hexameters, or an elegiac distich have just about the length customarily required for an antiphon text. On the other hand, in the case of the antiphon, the stylistic contrast between a hymnlike frame chant and the psalmody had to be appreciated or at least accepted, if a hymnlike setting was chosen.

Another criterion might have been the verse form itself. There is some evidence that different verse forms called for different settings: the examples of antiphon texts in iambic dimeter were set like hymn strophes; the antiphon texts in Sapphic stanzas received a proselike musical treatment; and the hexameters examined were clearly set like verse, but only as far as syntax and sense would not be obscured. The iambic dimeter, as the most common textual form for hymns, was more likely than any other verse form to attract a hymnlike melody.

The early Latin versified Office results from an encounter between a melodic idiom emerging from the setting of the biblical prose of the liturgy and the more refined and intricate diction of classical Latin verse. Another obvious factor was the model provided by the Latin hymn: indeed, one might expect a transferral of the features of Latin verse to music to have taken place. But the fact that, as we have seen, versified Office items did not simply adopt the melodic features of a hymn strophe shows that resemblance to a hymn—"Annäherung an den Hymnus" as Ewald Jammers (1930, 205) put it—cannot have been the primary goal. The earliest layer of versified Offices comprises settings of verse texts characterized by a tension between different and partly contradicting principles. These settings appear as individual experiments and cannot be described in terms of linear transition from prose setting to verse setting. With respect to subtlety and differentiation they are in no way inferior to the rhymed Office of the twelfth century with its more unambiguous, but at the same time one-dimensional, relation between words and music.

Notes

1. Our understanding of the early medieval versified Office is still limited and superficial. Unfortunately, no counterpart to Ewald Jammers's study of later rhymed Offices in a regional repertory (a study that comprises a discussion of the relation between text and music) exists for the early layer of versified Offices (Jammers 1929–30). The work already done by philologists has not been utilized by musicologists. A case in point is the lack of attention paid to Ritva Jonsson's (Jacobsson's) fundamental study of Office texts and the origin of the genre (Jonsson 1968). Auda (1923) in his book on Stephen of Liège deals with some of the earliest materials without giving much thought to questions of this sort. For an overview of the topic see Irtenkauf (1963), 172–76; Hughes (1988b), 366–77; Hiley (1993), 273–79; and Haug and Jacobsson (forthcoming).

2. The problem has been touched upon by David Hiley in his introduction in *Western Plainchant* (Hiley 1993, 274); he queries "to what extent the music of these early offices [with verse texts] differs from that of the rest of the repertory [with prose texts]."

3. There is, of course, a wide range of problems regarding the relationship between Latin verse, music, and notation during the early Middle Ages that lie outside the scope of a study on versified Offices. See our forthcoming book *Lateinischer Vers, Musik und Notation im frühen Mittelalter*. Some studies on the topic undertaken by the two present authors are Björkvall and Haug (1992), (1996), (1999a), and (1999b). For a discussion of how Latin verse was read during the Middle Ages, see Norberg (1958), 136–60, Norberg (1988), 131–14, Klopsch (1991), 95–106, esp. 104–6; and Björkvall and Haug (1992), esp. 71–74, (1996), esp. 169–75 and 198–203.

4. Cf. Auda (1923), 35–37, 96–198; Jonsson (1968), 115–83; and Berschin (1991), 3:421–29.

5. Vienna, ÖNB 1888, fols. 197–203v, and Vienna, ÖNB 515, fol. 5v.

6. Brussels, BR 14650–59, fols. 37–39; facs. ed. by François Masai and Léon Gilissen, *Lectionarium*.

7. Antiphonary of Mont-Renaud, facs. ed. in PM 14; edition of the text in Jonsson (1968), 187–98, as well as a facsimile of the MS Paris, BNF lat. 1258, fols. 336v–341v.

8. *CAO* 2948; Vienna 1888, fol. 197; Bamberg, Staatsbibl. lit. 25, fol. 71, a 13th-century antiphonary from Bamberg (see *CAO* 5:5).

9. The punctuation with a comma after *aequalis* (this adjective being interpreted as attributive of *trinitas*) is also found in Auda (1923), 113, Jonsson (1968), 221, and Blaise (1966), 354: "Gloria tibi, trinitas aequalis, una deitas. 'Gloire à vous, Trinité dans l'égalité, divinité une.'"

10. *Saint Gall, Stiftsbibliothek, Codex 390–391;* facs. ed. in PM 2/I.

11. Edition of the hymn for St. Vedast, *Christe salvator hominis*, in Dümmler, ed., *Poetae*, 313; antiphon no. 2947 in *CAO*. The antiphon text has the readings *patri, proli,* and *spiritui sancto.*

12. Vienna 1888, fol. 197, and Cividale, Museo Archeologico Nazionale 44, fol. 128v, an antiphonary from Cividale dating from the 14th/15th century; see Raffaella Camilot-Oswald (1997), 13–17.

13. Dümmler, ed., *Poetae*, 313. To our knowledge a melody for Alcuin's hymn *Christe salvator* no longer survives.

14. Text in *AH* 51, no. 121, and melody no. 107 in MMMA 1:55.

15. Textual edition in Krusch and Levison, eds., *Passiones*, 353–84.

16. Textual edition in Winterfeld, ed., *Poetae*, 141–57.

17. Norberg (1958), 112–17 and (1988), 84 ff., Klopsch (1972), 16–19.

18. Utrecht, Rijksuniversiteit, 406, fol. 167r–v, a 12th-century antiphonary from Utrecht (see Hofmann-Brandt 1971, 187).

19. *Passio SS. Fusciani et Victorici, BHL* 3226; *Carmen de S. Quintino, BHL* 7010; *Carmen de S. Benedicta, BHL* 1088.

20. A dactylic hexameter alternating with the iambic dimeter or the iambic trimeter is used e.g. by Horace in Epodes 15 and 16, Boethius in *Consolatio philosophiae*, iii. 3 and 4, and Martianus Capella in *De nuptiis philologiae et Mercurii*, iv. 704 ff. and ix. 902 ff.

From Office to Mass

The Antiphons of Vespers and Lauds and the
Antiphons before the Gospel in Northern France

ANNE WALTERS ROBERTSON

The new cathedral at Chartres was the scene of many splendid celebrations in the thirteenth century. Mass on Pentecost Sunday was no exception, with special chants resounding throughout the sacred spaces.[1] These melodies included an introit trope (*Fomes sensificans*), which told of the burning love of the Holy Spirit that ignites the hearts of the faithful. Later on, the royal acclamations (*laudes regiae*) were chanted prior to the Alleluia in honor of the bishop who attended services on that day. During the sequence that followed, flowers cascaded down from the heights of the church to reenact the Spirit's fiery descent upon the disciples. And just before the Gospel reading the choir chanted the Pentecost antiphon *Cum venerit paraclitus*. The introit trope, *laudes,* Alleluia, and sequence are all familiar parts of the Mass, but the antiphon is unexpected. Why was a chant typically associated with the *opus dei* sung in this service?

Amédée Gastoué, a pioneer in the study of medieval music, suggested an answer earlier in this century, when he drew attention to antiphons from the Office that returned in the Mass. Noting the use of these antiphons at the Parisian abbey of Saint-Denis, he hinted tantalizingly that the practice had taken root in other French churches as well (Gastoué 1937–39, 42:11–12, 57–58; also published in Gastoué 1939, 25–30). Since Gastoué's time, a handful of studies have treated antiphons before the Gospel,[2] yet many fundamental questions remain to be asked, and these are the focus of this chapter. What are the beginnings of this curious use in northern France? Which houses cultivated it? And how can we interpret this custom?

Although these antiphons make their surprising appearance at Mass, it is within the Divine Office that they originate as accompaniment to the canticles of Vespers and Lauds. Thus the nature of the connection between the canticles and the Gospel, a topic discussed at length by medieval commentators on the divine rite, will be explored. These authors' understanding of the parallels between canticle and Gospel offers a rationale for the analogous movement of the antiphons from Office to Mass. But if the migration of the antiphons into Mass can be explained in this way, the reason that a number of churches adopted the ritual raises a different issue. As we will see, the striking new architecture that swept northern France in the twelfth and thirteenth centuries appears to have inspired a novel liturgical practice.

Medieval interpretations of the canticles and Gospel form only a small part of the extensive body of writings that attempted to uncover the inner workings of the Divine Service. Some treatises on the liturgy had enormous influence, being re-stated with only minor reshufflings by subsequent authors. But while the level of interrelatedness might be quite high, each new work imparted some unique perspective that in turn affected the style and substance of later writings. A brief and highly selective summary of the commentaries that figure in this study follows.[3]

Authors from the patristic period set the stage for their medieval counterparts through their choice of topics. These early writers generally write descriptively, explaining in detail the objects and actions of sacred rites: baptism, prayer, fasting, and the like. By contrast, a pointedly interpretive approach was taken in the East in the late fifth century in such works as Pseudo-Dionysius' *De ecclesiastica hierarchia,* a treatise that focused on the symbolism and mysticism of cultic acts. Although the Dionysian corpus did not immediately penetrate the West, it enjoyed important revivals there in the ninth and twelfth centuries (see Robertson 1991a, 38–40). In his *Etymologiae* from the seventh century, Isidore of Seville likewise offered a semi-allegorical exegesis of liturgical themes, framed in an encyclopedic and historical exposition.

If style was paramount in these early medieval works, didacticism came to the fore two centuries later, when Charlemagne and his descendants tried repeatedly to impose a single, unified liturgy on the Frankish kingdom. For these rulers, it was essential that clerics should thoroughly understand the significance of ritual.[4] In keeping with this goal, Amalarius of Metz's voluminous *Liber officialis* established a new standard for discussions of the Mass and Offices. Owing perhaps to the long shadow cast by Amalarius, the art of liturgical commentary experienced a decline immediately following his death. His influence was still evident in the eleventh century, however, in works like the widely circulated *Liber quare,* a tract in dialogue form. Although not a liturgical commentary, the *Expositio in Matheo* of Paschasius Radbertus (d. ca. 860) does mention the Vespers canticle (Magnificat) in its discussion of the Virgin Mary. This treatise likewise stands as one of the monuments of Carolingian theology, drawing both on church fathers and on patristic writers (Augustine, Ambrose, Origen, and others).

The next great age of reflection on the Divine Service came in the twelfth and thirteenth centuries. Honorius of Autun's *Gemma animae,* written probably in Augsburg (see Flint 1982), is one of the most intriguing manuals from this period, analyzing the basic components of the liturgy in part through analogy to events in Christ's life. The work served as model for Parisian Johannes Beleth's popular *Summa de ecclesiasticis officiis,* which also owes a debt to Amalarius. The contemporaneous *Speculum ecclesiae,* falsely attributed to Hugh of Saint-Victor, likewise harked back to Amalarius and a number of other authors. If these twelfth-century authors reached a new plateau in the craft of liturgical commentary, the tour de force of the thirteenth century and beyond was Guillelmus Durandus' *Rationale divinorum officiorum.* Copied and quoted endlessly, the *Rationale* was one of the first printed books, published originally in 1459. Of all the commentators, Durandus alone documents the use of the antiphon before the Gospel. But the roots of the custom come to light only through a study of the earlier liturgists, who offer interpretations of the parts of the Office and Mass that contain these pieces.

We have already mentioned that the antiphons which move from Office to Mass are typically those associated with the Magnificat and Benedictus, the canticles of Vespers and Lauds. This group of antiphons is sometimes called the "Gospel canticle group,"[5] because the texts of the Magnificat and the Benedictus are taken directly from the Gospel (Magnificat: Luke 1:46–55; Benedictus: Luke 1:68–79). Medieval commentators clearly have this connection between Gospel and canticles in mind. Amalarius, for instance, dubs the Magnificat the "evangelic hymn" (*Opera*, 3:34, cap. 6), and Johannes Beleth links the canticles to the Gospel when he says: "Likewise in all Gospel texts we should make the sign of the cross, for example, at the end of the Pater noster and Gloria in excelsis deo and Benedictus and Magnificat and Nunc dimittis, and just as in the Gospel [at Mass], we ought to stand while hearing these."[6] Beleth also perceives the affinity between Vespers and Mass when he compares this Canonical Hour with the Last Supper, the prototype for the eucharistic ceremony: "At Vespers [Christ] was taken down from the cross. At the same hour He dined with His disciples and handed down to them the sacrament of his body and blood" (Beleth, *Summa*, cap. 29, p. 57). As these examples illustrate, medieval authors viewed the canticles and Gospel as parallel texts in both a practical and a historical sense. The antiphon that accompanies the canticles serves then to foreshadow the *evangelia* or "good news" to come in the Magnificat or Benedictus.

Although the antiphon before the Gospel may hail either from Vespers or from Lauds, it is the Magnificat at Second Vespers that most often serves as the source for these chants (see table 13.1 below). The song sung by Mary upon learning she would be the Mother of Christ, the Magnificat was hallowed through the centuries as a key text on the Incarnation.[7] The piece was popular in part because it was set in the first person ("Magnificat anima *mea*"), a feature that gave the faithful a very personal way to experience the joy of promises soon to be fulfilled.[8] Commentators discuss the theological import of the key word "Magnificat" at some length: "Hence also the Virgin Mary with thankful heart sings 'My soul doth magnify the Lord,' not because the great and lofty Lord who has no end can be greater or smaller, but because when we believe in Him, it is as if He is magnified in us."[9] Other writings go further to suggest not only why the canticle was sung, but also how it functions at Vespers:

> Why is the Magnificat sung daily? So that the oft-repeated remembrance of the incarnation of the Lord might set the souls of the faithful on fire for the work of God and for the teaching of those training themselves for devotion to the work that has begun. . . . Why is the Magnificat sung at Vespers? So that if our mind, fatigued during the day by diverse thoughts, has taken in something superfluous and harmful in its diurnal wanderings, we might recall the words of the Mother of God in a restful moment of quiet and might cleanse everything with prayers and tears through her intercession. . . . Just as the five psalms wash away daily the [offenses] which the five

senses of the body have committed, so at the beginning of the night the Magnificat corrects those thoughts that torment us in the fullness of the day. . . . The hymn of Saint Mary, that is the Magnificat, is begun with its antiphon. In this example of humility and obedience we are strengthened and the memory of the incarnation of the Lord, thus restored, excites the devotion of our faith.[10]

These and other explanations portray Vespers as a time of introspection and restoration of the soul (see also Taft 1986, 355–56). Small wonder that the Magnificat, vividly recalling the central message of the Gospel, was reserved for an hour such as this, when the canticle could perhaps penetrate the soul most effectively. And it is easy to understand why the antiphons composed for this chant even include some texts drawn from the Magnificat itself (see Udovich 1980).

Just as the Magnificat and its antiphon occur at a climactic point near the end of Vespers, so the antiphon before the Gospel stands in a crucial spot within the Mass. The Gospel occurs in the first half of the service, called the Mass of the Catechumens, in the final section known as the Service of Readings.[11] The fusion of the Mass of the Catechumens with the eucharistic celebration was an especially fortuitous combination in the days of the first Christians, who held that the Word of God, revealed in the lessons, should be absorbed before the mystery of the sacrifice in the Eucharist could be fully appreciated. By the Middle Ages, the Service of Readings consisted of the epistle, gradual, Alleluia or tract, sequence, and finally the Gospel. The reading of the Gospel was thus the culmination of the first half of the Mass, the moment at which "the 'Word of the Lord' finds its consummation in the 'Word made Flesh'" (Dix 1945, 39).

Emphasis on the Gospel reading was apparent at every turn in the Mass. Manuscripts containing Gospel texts were among the most luxurious that have come down to us (for some examples, see Mütherich and Gaehde 1976), and the Gospel book was generally the only item allowed to sit upon the altar, apart from the Eucharist. The person assigned to read the Gospel was high-ranking, usually a deacon but sometimes even the bishop himself. Durandus stresses the preeminence of the Gospel through analogy to the human body: "You should know that just as the head is in charge of the other parts of the body, and just as the other parts serve the head, so the Gospel is the chief of all that is said in the Office of Mass and rules over the entire Office of Mass."[12] For him the very movements of the person who reads the text are meaningful. In detailing these actions, he offers one of many medieval explanations of the concept and place that we sometimes call the "Gospel side" of the church: "After the sequence is sung, the priest rises and goes to the left side of the altar, where he reads the Gospel. This signifies that Christ is not come to call the righteous, but sinners . . . for the right side symbolizes the just, and the left the sinners."[13]

The ancient Ambrosian and Gallican rites, moreover, featured a procession before the Gospel, and this ceremony symbolized the arrival of Christ Himself in the church.[14] Other rituals saw Christ as manifest in the lights that guided the person carrying the Gospel book.[15] While it might seem that the purpose of the candles was to illuminate both the way and the text, descriptions of the actual ceremony contradict a solely practical interpretation, for the cerifers generally did not climb the steps with the reader to the lectern. Instead, the candles functioned as part of the messianic allegory, recalling both the prophecies about Christ ("The people who have walked in darkness have seen a great light"; Isa. 9:2) and the testimony of the Gospels ("In him was life; and the life was the light of men"; John 1:4).[16] Medieval liturgists echo these biblical authors: "Why on Holy Saturday before Easter is a light not carried in front of the Gospel? Here is the reason. The light before the Gospel is a manifestation of the good news which has not yet been made."[17]

Given the prominence of the ritual surrounding the Gospel reading, the enhancement of this text with an antiphon is certainly appropriate. And in this sense, the antiphon before the Gospel serves alongside the sequence as an enrichment to the Gospel rite (Fassler 1993a, 30). But unlike the sequence, the antiphon reinforces the features of the Office that Joseph Jungmann notes within the Service of Readings: "The arrangement [of the Service of Readings is] the same that is still in use in the Roman Breviary as the second part of every canonical hour" (Jungmann 1951, 1:393). That is, the Service of Readings, consisting as it does of lessons and responsorial singing, has many points of contact with a typical Office. And the use of an antiphon at Mass bolsters the illusion of an "Office within the Mass."

Apart from their awareness of the structural similarities between the Service of Readings at Mass and the Office of Vespers, the medieval liturgists also perceive the dramatic and mystical qualities of the Gospel. The notion of drama within the Mass is commonplace, of course, and it is certainly no accident that the deacon who reads the Gospel traditionally had a prominent role in the liturgical plays that were extremely popular in the Middle Ages (Young, *The Drama*, 2:246; Robertson 1995, 284). But for Durandus and others, drama can be seen every day in the Mass, as the deacon is transformed during the reading of the Gospel:

> Indeed, the nature of the deacon [who reads the Gospel] is changed: whereas earlier [at the beginning of Mass] he represented a prophet, now he represents John the Evangelist, since the law and the prophets [extend] up to [the time of] John, and through him the Kingdom of Heaven is evangelized. Therefore the Gospel is read so that, as Christ preached from his own mouth after the law, the prophets, and the psalms [were handed down], so his preaching to the people might be announced through the Gospel after the epistle, responsory, and Alleluia.[18]

Here Durandus identifies the Gospel reader with St. John; Honorius of Autun, on the other hand, equates him with another New Testament figure: "the deacon who reads is Peter, who answers for all the people."[19] From these various witnesses, it is clear that medieval commentators worked to develop a potent, multilayered symbolism for the Gospel rite, just as they did for the Magnificat at Vespers. And the evangelic origin of both of these parts of the Divine Service, in addition to the symbolism they shared, explains how the same chant might serve as accompaniment to both.

These examples of medieval representations of the Magnificat and the Gospel lead us into the actual repertories of antiphons before the Gospel in medieval France. As we have mentioned, Durandus was the first to discuss these antiphons for Mass: "In certain churches on the highest festivals the deacon who wants to go read the Gospel intones an antiphon."[20] By identifying Durandus' "certain churches," we find that the actual custom of singing antiphons prior to the Gospel was more prevalent in northern France than has been previously known. In addition to the uses at Saint-Denis and Amiens noted in recent scholarship,[21] the practices in three other northern French churches, the cathedrals of Bayeux and Chartres, and the abbey of Saint-Corneille of Compiègne, have until now gone unrecognized.

Table 13.1 shows the distribution of antiphons in these houses along with the location of the music for each chant in a related antiphoner or breviary. The appendix lists the entire repertory of antiphons alphabetically. The name of the Office from which each antiphon is borrowed and the function of the chant in that service are also given in table 13.1. In all cases, the feasts enhanced by the antiphon number among the most august ceremonies of the year: Christmas, Easter, and other solemn festivals of the Proper of the Time, the major Marian festivals, and the celebrations of saints whose relics were housed in the various churches. For reasons to be explored further on, the monks of Saint-Denis even included the anniversaries of two kings, the legendary Merovingian founder of the monastery King Dagobert (19 Jan.), and a royal personage of more recent memory, King Philip Augustus (14 July).

The number of antiphons before the Gospel in each place varies from only a handful at Amiens and Compiègne to the larger repertories of 18 and upwards at Bayeux, Chartres, and Saint-Denis. The disparity may indicate that the antiphons before the Gospel were preserved in part as an unwritten tradition, and their scant notation in the sources supports this theory, as we will see in a moment. But if the actual references to antiphons before the Gospel are a fairly accurate indication, the most vibrant practice of all was that of Bayeux, where an antiphon before the Gospel was sung some 31 times annually. Here the practice was more inclusive than elsewhere, embracing the major duplex feasts as well as celebrations of higher rank. The usage at Saint-Corneille of Compiègne, on the other hand, was less lively and not particularly distinct from that of Saint-Denis, no doubt because the ritual of Saint-Corneille largely copied that of the royal abbey in the twelfth century.[22] Compiègne nonetheless made its own choice of antiphon on a few occasions (table 13.1).

Given the relatively small number of congregations in medieval France that sang antiphons at Mass,[23] we might wonder how Durandus knew about the custom. Two plausible answers come to mind: either he spotted them in the numerous liturgical books he must have surveyed while composing his *Rationale,* or he experienced them in actual practice, perhaps even at Chartres.[24] Today ordinals and customaries are virtually the only witnesses to the usage. This comes as no surprise, for the chant was not new, but borrowed from one of the Offices. Ordinals and customaries that tell how to conduct services simply note the presence of an antiphon within the instructions for Mass. The mention is normally quite brief, consisting only of a textual incipit, although sometimes the entire Gospel procession is spelled out in detail. Only at Saint-Denis is the chant recorded differently: besides the references in ordinals and customaries, two notated missals from the abbey also include the music of five antiphons (table 13.1 and figure 13.1*b*). In these manuscripts, the chant appears in the sequentiary alongside the sequence that

Table 13.1 Repertory of antiphons before the Gospel in northern France, listed calendrically

Abbreviations:

A1 = Amiens ordinal (ed. Durand)
A2 = Amiens breviary (Amiens, BM 112; summer only, 13th c.)
B1 = Bayeux ordinal (ed. Chevalier)
B2 = Caen breviary (Paris, Bibl. de l'Arsenal 279; 13th c.)[a]
Ch1 = Chartres ordinal (ed. Delaporte)
Ch2 = Chartres breviary (Vatican, BAV Vat. lat. 4756; 13th c.)
Co = Compiègne ordinals (Paris, BNF lat. 18044, lat. 18045, lat. 18046; 13th c.)[b]
D1 = Saint-Denis ordinals (Paris, Mazarine 526; BNF lat. 976, 13th c.); Paris, AN L863, No. 10 (18th-c. copy of 14th-c. MS); see Walters [Robertson] (1985)
D2 = Saint-Denis antiphoner (Paris, BNF lat. 17296; copied between 1140 and 1150)
D3 = Saint-Denis missal (Paris, BNF lat. 1107; copied between 1259 and 1275)
D4 = Saint-Denis missal (London, V&A 1346–1891; copied 1350)

Date	Feast or anniversary (A)	Antiphon	Reference to antiphon at Mass in ordinals					Location of music of antiphon						Office of origin of antiphon	Place of antiphon in Office
			A1	B1	Ch1	Co	D1	A2	B2	Ch2	D2	D3	D4		
Proper of the Time															
25 Dec.	Christmas	Ecce annuntio	x		x									2nd Vespers	Magnificat
		Hodie christus		x					88v		25v		373v	2nd Vespers	Magnificat
		Verbum caro				x	x								
26 Dec.	Stephen	Beatus es		x					94v					2nd Vespers	Magnificat
27 Dec.	John	Ecce ego Johannes	x	x			x				268v			1st Vespers	Magnificat
28 Dec.	Innocents	O quam gloriosum		x					103					Lauds	Benedictus
1 Jan.	Circumcision	Magnum hereditatis		x					109v					2nd Vespers	Magnificat

Date	Feast	Chant					fol.	fol.	fol.	fol.	Position	Genre
6 Jan.	Epiphany	Ab oriente		x			116v				2nd Vespers	Magnificat
		Hodie celesti sponso			x				48		Lauds	Benedictus
		Tribus miraculis			x			118v			2nd Vespers	Magnificat
	Easter	Christus resurgens		x			200				1st Vespers	Magnificat
		Crucem sanctam		x	x	x			155	376	Lauds	psalmodic
		Ego sum alpha		x	x			195				processional
	Easter Monday[c]	Ite nuntiate		x								
	Easter Tuesday[d]	Surrexit dominus		x								
	Easter Wednesday[e]	Crucem sanctam		x								
	Ascension	O rex glorie		x	x		233v	234	159v		2nd Vespers	Magnificat
	Pentecost	Cum venerit paraclitus		x	x			236v			2nd Vespers	Magnificat
		Hodie completi sunt		x	x		240	164			2nd Vespers	Magnificat
	Trinity	Gratias tibi		x			246				1st Vespers	Magnificat
		Te deum patrem		x			251v			379v	2nd Vespers	Magnificat
Proper of the Saints												
13 Jan.	Inv. of Firminus	Letetur clerus	x									
19 Jan.	King Dagobert (A)	Salvator omnium deus			x			330	348v		Lauds	Benedictus
2 Feb.	Purification	Homo erat in Jerusalem		x	x		365v				2nd Vespers	Magnificat
		Responsum accepit		x				317		69v	Lauds	psalmodic
												processional
24 Feb.	Ded. St. Denis	O beate Dyonisi			x				232v	419	2nd Vespers	Magnificat
25 Mar.	Annunciation	Gaude dei genetrix			x			14				
		O virgo virginum		x	x		385v				2nd Vespers	Magnificat
22 Apr.	Invention of Denis	O beate Dyonisi		x	x		232v				2nd Vespers	O-antiphon
16 May	Renobert	Filie Jerusalem		x							2nd Vespers	Magnificat
		Gloriosus		x								

(continued)

Table 13.1 (continued)

Date	Feast or anniversary (A)	Antiphon	A1	B1	Ch1	Co	D1	A2	B2	Ch2	D2	D3	D4	Office of origin of antiphon	Place of antiphon in Office
24 June	John Baptist	Inter natos		x					406					2nd Vespers	Magnificat
		Perpetuis nos domine			x									2nd Vespers	Magnificat
29 June	Peter, Paul	Hodie illuxit nobis		x							180			2nd Vespers	Magnificat
		Quodcumque					x		414v					Lauds	Benedictus
1 July	Invention of Relics	O virgo virginum		x					419					2nd Vespers	Magnificat
14 July	King Philip Aug. (A)	Salvator omnium deus					x				330	348v		Lauds	Benedictus
22 July	Mary Magdalene	Hodie de presenti			x									2nd Vespers	Magnificat
26 July	Anne	Felix Anna			x									2nd Vespers	Magnificat
10 Aug.	Lawrence	Beatus es o inclite		x					445v					2nd Vespers	Magnificat
15 Aug.	Assumption	Anima mea		x	x									Compline	Nunc Dimittis
		Ascendit Christus		x					453					2nd Vespers	Magnificat
		Hodie Maria virgo				x	x			207v				2nd Vespers	Magnificat
3 Sept.	Trans. of Renobert	Gloriosus		x											
8 Sept.	Mary Nativity	Nativitas tua		x	x		x		470v		213			2nd Vespers	Magnificat
		Nativitatem				x					213			Lauds	Benedictus
16 Sept.	Trans. of Lubin	Iam super astra			x										
25 Sept.	Firminus	Resp. Laudemus	x					268v						1st Vespers	Magnificat
29 Sept.	Michael	In civitate		x					487v					2nd Vespers	Magnificat
1 Oct.	Piat	O gloriose			x									2nd Vespers	Magnificat

Date	Feast	Antiphon			Folio	Folio	Service	Chant
9 Oct.	Denis	O beate Dyonisi	x	x	495	232v	2nd Vespers	Magnificat
14 Oct.	Ded. Amiens	Filie Syon		x				Magnificat
16 Oct.	Octave of Denis	O beate Dyonisi	x			232v	2nd Vespers	Magnificat
17 Oct.	Ded. Chartres	Pax eterna	x				processional	
	Mem. of Ded.	Ibo mihi	x				2nd Vespers	Magnificat
1 Nov.	All Saints	Beati estis sancti	x		504		2nd Vespers	Magnificat
		Laudem dicite		x		243	Lauds	Benedictus
		Salvator mundi salva nos		x		234v	2nd Vespers	Magnificat
		Te gloriosus	x				Lauds	Benedictus
		O quam gloriosum		x		240v	Matins	psalmodic
3 Nov.	Vigor	Gloriosus	x					
11 Nov.	Martin	Media nocte	x				Matins	psalmodic
		O beatum virum	x	x	515v		2nd Vespers	Magnificat
25 Nov.	Catherine	Simile est regnum	x					
28 Nov.	Ded. Bayeux	Pax eterna	x		560v		2nd Vespers	Magnificat
30 Nov.	Andrew	Ambulans Jesus	x		328v		Lauds	Benedictus
6 Dec.	Nicholas	O Christi pietas	x	x	334v		1st, 2nd Vespers	Magnificat
11 Dec.	Fuscian	Speciosus		x			2nd Vespers	Magnificat

a. Although this manuscript is from Saint-Sépulcre of Caen, it is compatible with the liturgy of Bayeux, for which no antiphoner or breviary survives.

b. Since the Saint-Denis antiphoner Paris, BNF lat. 17296 was later used at Saint-Corneille, it is treated as belonging to both monasteries in the present study.

c. Mass sung at the neighboring church of Saint-Martin in Chartres.

d. Mass sung at the neighboring church of Saint-Père in Chartres.

e. Mass sung at the neighboring church of Saint-Jean-en-Vallée in Chartres.

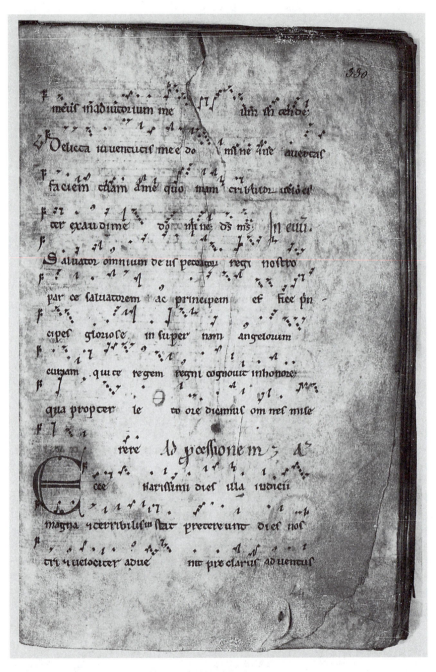

Figure 13.1 The antiphon *Salvator omnium deus* for King Dagobert from the abbey of Saint-Denis: (a, *this page*) Paris, BNF lat. 17296; (b, *facing page*) Paris, BNF lat. 1107

Figure 13.1 *(continued)*

precedes it in the Mass. In general, however, the antiphons are not written out in books for the Mass, owing no doubt to the fact that the music was already available in breviaries and antiphoners (figure 13.1a).

Since the first witness to these pieces comes in the thirteenth century, we might assume that the practice originated at this time. Indeed, there is little trace of it in earlier sources, hence we can surmise that it either began or increased dramatically during this period. In fact, it is difficult to know to what extent the five churches surveyed here may have employed the antiphon before the Gospel, if at all, in earlier eras. As we have noted, there is precedent for such a practice in the ancient Ambrosian and Gallican liturgies, which favored the use of chants prior to the readings of Mass. But the task of establishing which of these chants may be Merovingian in origin is rendered nearly impossible due to the difficulty in distinguishing what is "Gallican" in this music. The abbey of Saint-Denis, which made pointed efforts to maintain many of its ancient customs, may indeed have preserved some of its pre-Carolingian antiphons before the Gospel. This is suggested both by the styles of certain chants and by the scattered traces found in eleventh-century sources (Walters [Robertson] 1985, 205–29; Robertson 1991a, 261–71). But elsewhere, if the custom flourished in times past, it may have remained dormant from the ninth through twelfth centuries.

The texts of these pieces seem to fall into one of three different types: (1) those taken directly from the Gospel for the day, (2) those that summarize the significance of the feast, and (3) those that extol the Virgin Mary or another saint. The first two kinds appear most commonly during the Proper of the Time, when feasts celebrating the life of Christ abound; the third type fills the summer months (table 13.1). Antiphons closely related to the Gospel for the day are the kind we might expect to find most often. The Christmas antiphon *Verbum caro factum est* at Saint-Denis exemplifies this type:

> Verbum caro factum est et habitavit in nobis, et vidimus gloriam eius, gloriam quasi Unigeniti a Patre, plenum gratiae et veritatis, alleluia alleluia alleluia. (Paris, BNF lat. 17296, fol. 25v; see also *CAO* 3, no. 5363)

> And the Word was made flesh, and dwelt among us, (and we beheld his glory, the glory as of the only-begotten of the Father,) full of grace and truth (John 1:14).

The corresponding Gospel for Christmas, preserved in a thirteenth-century missal from Saint-Denis (Paris, BNF lat. 1107, fol. 20v), matches this text precisely, and the identity between antiphon and Gospel ensures that the announcement of Christ's birth received added emphasis at this climactic moment in the Mass. The chant quite literally anticipates the Gospel, reinforcing it as if through *Vorimitation*. In its later appearance at Second Vespers, the antiphon serves as a last reminder of this message at the end of the day. Curiously, only a few antiphons before the Gospel exhibit this close relationship with the Gospel. Instead, the other two types are more numerous.

The second kind of antiphon sums up the importance of the celebration. These chants are best represented by the so-called "Hodie" antiphons (table 13.1 and appendix), a special type that appears most often at Second Vespers (see Huglo 1980a, 478). *Hodie Christus natus est* for Christmas from Bayeux Cathedral is an example:

> Hodie Christus natus est; hodie salvator apparuit; hodie in terra canunt angeli, laetantur archangeli; hodie exsultent justi, dicentes: Gloria in excelsis Deo, alleluia. (Paris, Bibl. de l'Arsenal 279, fol. 88v; *CAO* 3, no. 3093)

> Today Christ is born. Today a Saviour has appeared. Today angels sing on earth, and archangels rejoice. Today the just exult, saying "Glory in the highest to God." Alleluia.

It is easy to see how the "Hodie" antiphons earned their place in the liturgy of Second Vespers. In the final hours of the feast day, these pieces rehearsed the importance of the festival in succinct, memorable phrases, punctuated through repeated use of the word "Hodie." In this respect, they stand in stark contrast to the tropes and sequences that typically offered protracted exegesis on the theological significance of the celebration. That is, if the sequence preceding the antiphon served to elaborate, the "Hodie" antiphon offered concise recapitulation.

The third type of antiphon includes those that render praise to Mary or some other saint. The preferred chant for the Nativity of Mary (8 Sept.) represents this class:

> Nativitas tua dei genetrix virgo, gaudium annuntiavit universo mundo; ex te enim ortus est sol justitie, Christus Deus noster, qui solvens maledictionem dedit benedictionem, et confundens mortem donavit nobis vitam sempiternam. (Paris, Bibl. de l'Arsenal 279, fol. 470v; *CAO* 3, no. 3852)

> Your birth, Virgin Mother of God, has proclaimed joy to the entire world, for from you the sun of justice is risen, Christ our God, who has ended cursing and given blessing, confounded death and given us eternal life.

Here the exaltation of Mary seems at odds with the symbolism of the Gospel: the Gospel signifies the preaching of Christ, and yet the text of the antiphon focuses on the Virgin or, even more remotely, on a saint. The sense of competition is illusory, however, for to couple the Gospel with an antiphon for a saint was simply to give Christ a companion at the moment when word of Him made its way into the church through the reading. At the same time, this pairing obviously benefited the saint in question. In some cases, this was undoubtedly the primary goal, especially when the saint was the patron of the church. The antiphon *O beate Dyonisi* for the Feast of St. Denis aptly illustrates this point:

> O beate Dyonisi magna est fides tua, intercede pro nobis ad dominum deum nostrum ut qui caritate tibi sumus dissimiles sua gracia largiente faciat esse consortes. (Paris lat. 17296, fols. 232v, 240; *CAO* 3, no. 3999)

> O blessed Dionysius, great is your faith. Intercede on our behalf with the Lord our God so that those of us who are unlike you in love might be made partakers when he bestows His grace.

The prominent display of this chant at the first high point of the Mass gave St. Denis pride of place at the right hand of Christ Himself. At the same time, it stressed the saint's intercessory role as the means through which both the community of monks and the kings who favored this church might approach Christ.[25] When this type of antiphon followed a proper sequence for the saint, as it almost invariably did, the emphasis on the martyr was redoubled.

In addition to the five churches that adopted the custom of singing an antiphon before the Gospel, later records indicate that a few other houses also nurtured the practice, although it is difficult to know precisely when they cultivated it. An eighteenth-century ceremonial from the cathedral of Auxerre shows that the antiphons at Mass existed there, and this same book likewise mentions that the chants were heard in the church of Angers.[26] Extant medieval sources from these places, however, do not record the use. Undoubtedly other churches from which medieval records are even more sparse sang antiphons at Mass.[27]

On the other hand, some churches that might have been candidates for antiphons at Mass evidently never adopted them. There is no trace of these chants in the liturgy of Notre-Dame of Paris, for instance. One reason may be that Notre-Dame had a strong tradition of polyphonic performance of the Alleluia on high feasts in the twelfth and thirteenth centuries (Wright 1989). And there may also have been other polyphonic accretions, namely a conductus or motet, that might have been sung prior to the Gospel. Many of the motet texts in the Notre Dame corpus comment on the occasion in precisely the same way as the words of the Gospel antiphon.[28] At the very least, the mere existence of antiphons before the Gospel in several places northern France suggests a use for some of the repertory of polyphonic votive antiphons that proliferated in northern Europe in the late Middle Ages, the liturgical placement of which is in many cases is still in doubt.

If Notre-Dame did not cultivate this rite, we must ask why the five churches discussed here did. There are undoubtedly several reasons for this, one of which goes hand-in-glove with our discussion above of the symbolism of the parts of the Office and Mass that pertain to the usage. Two houses that employed antiphons before the Gospel, the abbey of Saint-Denis and the cathedral of Chartres, are well known for their philosophical and/or exegetical traditions. As a result of their scholarly interests, the communities in each of these churches actively displayed theological symbols in their liturgies. The monks of Saint-Denis, for example, found it politically expedient to maximize their connection with the writings of the aforementioned Pseudo-Dionysius and with the Pauline apostle Dionysius the Areopagite, figures they erroneously believed to be identical with the true namesake of the monastery, the third-century apostle to Gaul, St. Denis. Their unique relationship with the crown depended on this mistaken identity, for kings of France revered this conflated saint and adopted him as their patron. And the congregation went to great lengths to emphasize this association through their liturgy: to this end they incorporated numerous chants and services whose texts openly promoted the St. Denis/Pseudo-Dionysius/Dionysius the Areopagite connection (Robertson 1991a). Likewise the cathedral of Chartres boasted a long line of scholars from the eleventh to thirteenth centuries, including Bishop Fulbert, Ivo of Chartres, and possibly even Guillelmus Durandus, who discussed topics ranging from canon law to the liturgy. As Margot Fassler has shown, both Ivo and Durandus portray the entrance ceremony of the Mass at Chartres in terms of "the voice of the prophets foretelling the coming of the Christian Messiah," and the introit tropes found in Chartrain manuscripts underscore these themes (Fassler 1993b, quotation from p. 503). These multifaceted uses of the liturgy help explain why Saint-Denis and Chartres would have been attracted to the symbolically charged Gospel antiphons as political and didactic vehicles.

A second and more general explanation for the adoption and sudden growth of this usage is found in the expansion in the number of Gothic cathedrals in the twelfth and thirteenth centuries. Four of the five churches that cultivated antiphons before the Gospel were renovated or rebuilt in the Gothic style: Chartres and Amiens were reconstructed in the thirteenth century after devastating fires,[29] Abbot Suger's twelfth-century church at Saint-Denis was rebuilt between 1231 and 1281 (Bruzelius 1985), and the cathedral of Bayeux was likewise refashioned in the thirteenth century (see Vallery-Radot 1958). Along with these reconstructions came heightenings of the liturgies that accentuated the grandeur and pointed out the significance of these novel structures. New liturgical books containing added feasts, processions, sequences, and, in some places, polyphony record these liturgical accoutrements to the architecture. The antiphon before the Gospel is yet another witness to the increase in the level of the divine cult in these churches.

One important aspect of the typical rebuilding scheme calls for specific comment in this regard. In many Gothic churches, including those treated here, we can document the presence of a choir screen or *jubé* that was intended to separate the choir from the rest of the nave.[30] Atop this structure stood the pulpit from which the Gospel was read, and to this exalted spot the deacon traveled to perform his task. As the distance from the main altar or sacristy to the *jubé* increased as a result of the reconstruction,[31] the silence between the end of the sequence and the beginning of the Gospel reading grew proportionally. It is probably no accident, therefore, that one does not find antiphons before the Gospel in the ordinals of smaller churches. For our handful of French cathedrals, however, the antiphon offered a smooth transition from sequence to Gospel, in which capacity it functioned as a processional piece, one that turned the attention of the congregation to the imminent reading of the Gospel.

In this regard, the relationship between the antiphon and the sequence takes on added depth. As recent studies have illustrated, many of the new sequences composed in the twelfth and thirteenth centuries appeared simultaneously with the new side chapels that housed the saints' relics in the great Gothic cathedrals (Robertson 1991a, 276–85; Fassler 1993a). In similar fashion, the custom of singing an antiphon before the Gospel grew as *jubés* were built in these great churches—indeed, in our five French cathedrals, the antiphon effectively became the song of the *jubé*.

Whereas commentators prior to the thirteenth century rarely mention the pulpit or lectern by name, they unanimously assign the Gospel to be read from a high place. Certainly this concern about height was a decisive factor in the construction of the *jubé*, for the liturgists are at pains to establish the priority of the Gospel over all other readings at Mass. Pseudo-Hugh of Saint-Victor states: "The Gospel is read on a higher step than the epistle, because the teaching of Christ greatly surpasses the teaching of the apostles."[32] And Honorius of Autun likewise reports: "The Gospel is read from a high place, because Christ is said to have preached from the mountain. The Gospel is read on high therefore because the evangelic precepts through which the heights of Heaven are reached are sublime."[33] The precedence of the Gospel could only be enhanced through use of an antiphon that prepared listeners to hear these "evangelic precepts."

Despite the existence of the *jubé* in many of the churches that employed antiphons before the Gospel, the actual performance of these pieces in Mass and Office differed substantially from place to place. We noted at the outset that a shower of flowers ushered in the singing of the antiphon on Pentecost at Chartres. In addition, on the three days following Easter, the antiphons were chanted at three neighboring churches in the town (table 13.1). And finally, on the feast of St. Theodore (9 Nov.), a procession to the precious relic of the saint took place prior to the Gospel. No antiphon is mentioned in this ceremony, however (Delaporte, ed., *L'Ordinaire*, 63, 187).

The procession that accompanied the Gospel ritual likewise varied in detail from one church to another. Christmas Mass at Bayeux Cathedral demonstrates how elaborate the ceremony might be. During the singing of the Sequence *Christi hodierna,*

> the *major archichorus* goes up to the cantor to find out from him which antiphon should be chanted before the Gospel. He himself conveys this information to the deacon, who then rises. Once the sequence is finished and after the deacon has done all he has to do in the interim, as mentioned earlier, he should go to the left corner of the altar and, turning toward the choir, intone the Ant. *Hodie Christus natus est.* When [the singing] has begun, he should immediately seek the blessing, take the Gospel text, and go to the pulpit to read it after the antiphon is finished. The cross precedes him both going and coming back.[34]

Undoubtedly the choice of antiphon was left to the cantor because he was the person who had an antiphoner or ordinal at hand, perhaps the only copies of such books in the choir. With the assistance of these texts, he could if necessary locate the antiphon that would be performed. It was probably also the cantor who gave the opening pitch of the chant to the *archichorus,* just as the *archichorus* was charged "by order of the cantor" to intone the antiphon to the canticle at Vespers and Lauds.[35] At these times, in fact, the antiphon was sung thrice: after the versicle that precedes the canticle, at the end of the canticle, and following the lesser doxology (Gloria patri). One further aspect of performance of the antiphons at Vespers and Lauds on duplex feasts emerges from the Bayeux ordinal. Here the antiphons were embellished with "neumas," melismas added to the ends of the chants (on neumas, see Hiley 1980; Robertson 1991a, 133–35). The intonation of the canticle that followed was the job of the cantor, and at this moment, he removed his cap "out of reverence for the Gospel."[36] Once again the analogy between the canticles of Vespers and Lauds and the Gospel at Mass is apparent.

At Saint-Denis, the singing of the antiphon before the Gospel likewise involves the cantor, who gives the pitch to the soloist and sometimes even reminds him to "sing well."[37] The intonation of this same antiphon, when it introduces the canticles, is likewise the responsibility of the cantor, the abbot, or the *hebdomadarius* (weekly cantor), depending on the level of the celebration (Robertson 1991a, 307, 309). And as at Bayeux, the antiphon was chanted three times at Vespers and Lauds on the highest celebrations.

A detailed description of the Gospel procession at Amiens demonstrates how the event was conducted in this northern church. After the sequence, the precentor ruling the choir steps in front of the deacon, who follows along with his ministers. They all stop in the middle of the sanctuary to intone the antiphon. While the choir continues the chant, the precentor accompanies the deacon to the base of the *jubé,* and the deacon then climbs up to chant the Gospel.[38] The temporary halt of the procession for the beginning of the antiphon places the chant all the more in the limelight. In some instances, the antiphon was intoned in the sacristy, whence the precentor and deacon emerged with Gospel book in hand. And on the feast of St. Fuscian the chant was sung twice, once by each side of the choir. These and other rubrics for antiphons before the Gospel at Amiens are explicit about the processional function of these pieces, stating that the chant was sung "at the leading of the Gospel" (*ad conducendum evangelium*).[39]

Paradoxically, despite the processional nature of the antiphon before the Gospel, very few of these chants come from the *fonds* of great processional antiphons (table 13.1). The only exceptions appear to be *Ego sum alpha* and *Responsum accepit Simeon* for Easter and Purification, respectively, at Bayeux, and *Pax eterna* for the Dedication of Chartres. The remainder of the repertory nevertheless function like processional pieces. And this similarity between antiphons before the Gospel and the great processional antiphons has another dimension as well. In addition to the mutation of the Office antiphon into an independent, processional antiphon at Mass that we have just noted, the liturgists recognize two other metamorphoses in the ritual: the transformation of the deacon who reads the Gospel into a saint, usually John or Peter; and the reading of the Gospel as the turning point between the prophecies and teachings about Christ and the moment of his metaphorical arrival in the Eucharist of the Mass. These mystical changes, intermingled with the equally symbolic movements of the Gospel procession itself, heighten the experience of the final moments of the Service of Readings, drawing the observer inexorably into the eucharistic portion of the Mass.

In a few churches, pieces other than antiphons were infrequently sung prior to the Gospel. A troper from St. Gall includes an item rubricated "ante evangelium" (St. Gall, SB 382, fol. 24). The chant, *Letitie studeat,* contains four strophes, each of which ends with a refrain. The text of the final strophe tellingly begins with the words "Textus evangelicus." In addition, the Circumcision Office composed by Pierre de Corbeil and preserved in a thirteenth-century manuscript from Sens records a *conductus ad evangelium.* The piece, entitled *Quanto decet honore,* consists of two rhymed verses set to the same music.[40] This conductus evidently enjoyed some currency in France, for it is also found in the Feast of Fools ceremony at Beauvais, prior to the sixth responsory at Matins.[41] The use of a conductus before the Gospel is certainly appropriate for the procession that preceded the Gospel reading, described literally in the aforementioned rubric from Amiens (*ad conducendum evangelium*). These and undoubtedly many other houses that did not adopt the custom of singing antiphons before the Gospel nonetheless show an appreciation of the Gospel ceremony, as well as an occasional desire to elevate the moment with special music.

Quanto decet honore from Sens, moreover, demonstrates that the chant prior to the Gospel could in fact be something other than an antiphon. Indeed, within the French tradition this is also true, for in one instance the piece was not an antiphon at all, but a responsory. The exceptional feast is the celebration of the patron of Amiens, Saint Firminus (25 Sept.), a day on which the "Resp. *Laudemus* without its verse" was sung prior to the Gospel (table 13.1) (Durand, ed., *Ordinaire*, 465). The rubrics give only this brief incipit, but the responsory at First Vespers is *Laudemus dominum*, a chant with a generic text from the Common of Saints that could be adapted for any number of saints simply by inserting a different name (see *CAO* 4, no. 7082). No doubt the verse was omitted because soloistic music, normally reserved for stational moments, was not usually performed in processions.

These examples of miscellaneous Gospel pieces mirror the more fully developed practice whose traces have come down to us from Amiens, Bayeux, Chartres, Saint-Corneille, and Saint-Denis. One final characteristic of these antiphons ties them to the broader repertory of late medieval chant. This trait bears directly on their double use in Office and Mass. Beginning in the thirteenth century, a marked tendency toward standardization and shrinkage of the liturgy arose on many fronts, even as new chants appeared. Certain proper Offices vanished, their unique chants being replaced by ones from the Common of Saints (Robertson 1991a, 442). In similar fashion, music for the concluding versicles for the Office and Mass, Benedicamus domino and Ite missa est, was increasingly based on a single melisma drawn from a responsory or Alleluia (Robertson 1988). This recycled music ensured that the same melody might be heard three or four times in one day, both in the Offices and at Mass. In addition, many of the sequences and alleluias composed in the late Middle Ages were new in text only, their melodies being contrafacts or reworkings of older chants (Fassler 1993a, 161–81). Even some of the polyphony written for a place like Notre-Dame of Paris was specifically designed to be reused for saints of equal stature (Wright 1989, 262–63).

This emphasis on economy of music and text in a culture increasingly dependent on the written word clears the way for the emergence (or reemergence) of the antiphon before the Gospel in at least five preeminent churches in thirteenth-century France. The presence of this chant both in the Offices and at Mass parallels the repetition of musical and liturgical material in other areas of the ritual. At the same time, the antiphon serves as aural analogue to the visually towering *jubés* from which the Gospel was proclaimed in the magnificent new cathedrals of France. As such, it heralds Christ's symbolic arrival in the Mass, permeating Office and Mass alike with its eloquent expression of the significance of the day.

Appendix: Repertory of antiphons before the Gospel in northern France, listed alphabetically

Abbreviations (see table 13.1 for details):
A1 = Amiens   Co = Compiègne
B1 = Bayeux   D1 = Saint-Denis
Ch1 = Chartres

Antiphon	Feast or anniversary (A)	Date	Church where antiphon was sung				
			A1	B1	Ch1	Co	D1
Ab oriente	Epiphany	6 Jan.		x			
Ambulans Jesus	Andrew	30 Nov.		x			
Anima mea	Assumption	15 Aug.			x		
Ascendit Christus	Assumption	15 Aug.		x			
Beati estis sancti	All Saints	1 Nov.		x			
Beatus es o inclite L.	Lawrence	10 Aug.		x			
Beatus es	Stephen	26 Dec.		x			
Christus resurgens	Easter			x			
Crucem sanctam	Easter					x	x
Crucem sanctam	Easter Wednesday				x		
Cum venerit paraclitus	Pentecost				x		
Ecce annuntio	Christmas	25 Dec.	x		x		
Ecce ego Johannes	John	27 Dec.	x	x			x
Ego sum alpha	Easter				x		
Felix Anna	Anne	26 July			x		
Filie Jerusalem	Renobert	16 May		x			
Filie Syon	Dedication, Amiens	14 Oct.	x				
Gaude dei genitrix	Annunciation	25 Mar.			x		
Gloriosus	Renobert	16 May		x			
Gloriosus	Trans. of Renobert	3 Sep.		x			
Gloriosus	Vigor	3 Nov.		x			
Gratias tibi	Trinity			x			
Hodie celesti sponso	Epiphany	6 Dec.					x
Hodie Christus	Christmas	25 Dec.		x			
Hodie completi sunt	Pentecost			x		x	x
Hodie de presenti	Mary Magdalene	22 July			x		
Hodie illuxit nobis	Peter, Paul	29 June					x
Hodie Maria virgo	Assumption	15 Aug.				x	x
Homo erat in Jerusalem	Purification	2 Feb.		x			x
Ibi mihi	Mem. of Dedication, Chartres	18? Oct.			x		
In civitate	Michael	29 Sep.	x				
Inter natos	John Baptist	24 June	x				
Ite nuntiate	Easter Monday				x		
Iam super astra	Trans. of Lubin	16 Sep.			x		
Letetur clerus	Inv. of Firminus	13 Jan.	x				
Laudem dicite	All Saints	1 Nov.			x		
Resp. Laudemus	Firminus	25 Sept.	x				
Magnum hereditatis	Circumcision	1 Jan.		x			
Media nocte	Martin	11 Nov.			x		
Nativitas tua	Mary Nativity	8 Sep.	x	x			x
Nativitatem	Mary Nativity	8 Sep.			x		
O beate Dyonisi	Dedication, St-Denis	24 Feb.					x

(continued)

Appendix (*continued*)

Antiphon	Feast or anniversary (A)	Date	Church where antiphon was sung				
			A1	B1	Ch1	Co	D1
O beate Dyonisi	Denis	9 Oct.	x				x
O beate Dyonisi	Invention of Denis	22 Apr.					x
O beate Dyonisi	Octave of Denis	16 Oct.					x
O beatum virum	Martin	11 Nov.	x	x			
O Christi pietas	Nicholas	6 Dec.	x	x			
O gloriose	Piat	1 Oct.		x			
O quam gloriosum	All Saints	1 Nov.				x	
O quam gloriosum	Innocents	28 Dec.	x				
O rex glorie	Ascension		x	x			x
O virgo virginum	Annunciation	25 Mar.	x				x
O virgo virginum	Invention of Relics	1 July	x				
Pax eterna	Dedication, Chartres	17 Oct.			x		
Pax eterna	Dedication, Bayeux	28 Nov.	x				
Perpetuis nos domine	John Baptist	24 June			x		
Quodcumque	Peter, Paul	29 June	x				
Responsum accepit	Purification	2 Feb.			x		
Salvator mundi salva nos	All Saints	1 Nov.					x
Salvator omnium deus	King Dagobert (A)	19 Jan.					x
Salvator omnium deus	King Philip Aug. (A)	14 July					x
Simile est regnum	Catherine	25 Nov.	x				
Speciosus	Fuscian	11 Dec.	x				
Surrexit dominus	Easter Tuesday				x		
Te deum patrem	Trinity		x				
Te gloriosus	All Saints	1 Nov.			x		
Tribus miraculis	Epiphany	6 Jan.			x		
Verbum caro	Christmas	25 Dec.				x	x

Notes

1. The directions for this service are found in Delaporte, *L'Ordinaire*, 130: "Missa *Spiritus domini*, ps. *Exurgat* ultimum tropus *Fomes sensificans*. Regie laudes, *Alleluia* v. *Emitte, Alleluia* v. *Veni sancte spiritus,* sequentia *Fulgens preclara*. Interim de celo ecclesie dimittantur flores arborum in chorum. Ante evangelium ant. *Cum venerit para[clitus]*."

2. See Walters [Robertson] (1985), 205–29 and Robertson (1991a), 267–69 for the practice at Saint-Denis; Johnson (1991), 188–90 for Amiens; and Borders (1988) for northern Italy, and his n. 4 for other mentions of the usage there.

3. For brief summaries of these and other medieval liturgical treatises, see Reynolds (1986); Kaske (1988), 64–77; and Macy (1997). The works named in the three following paragraphs are listed in the Bibliography (Primary Sources).

4. For a discussion of the aims and methods of Carolingian exegesis, see Mayeski (1997), esp. pp. 70–72.

5. This designation is used in Crocker (1990a), 161. See other discussions of this repertory in Huglo (1980a), 478; Steiner (1980c), 495; Udovich (1980); Hiley (1993), 96–98; Apel (1958), 393.

6. Beleth, *Summa,* cap. 40, 74–75: "Similiter et in omnibus uerbis euangelicis debet fieri signum crucis ut in fine Pater noster et Gloria in excelsis Deo et Benedictus et

Magnificat et Nunc dimittis, et sicut euangelium, ita et hec debemus audire stando." Jocqué and Milis, eds., *Liber,* cap. 39, p. 187, requires further that the people stand during the antiphon preceding the Magnificat.

7. The other texts include, of course, the story of Gabriel's visit to Mary, which begins "Missus est angelus Gabriel," and includes the famous "Ave Maria." For a summary of the Annunciation theme in medieval culture, see Robertson (1995).

8. *DS* 10:416–17. In his discussion of the Magnificat, Farris (1985), 126, writes: "The Magnificat declares with exultant joy that God the Saviour has acted decisively for Israel. This decisive help is best explained as the coming of Jesus Christ and, more specifically, his death and resurrection. This is an event which, from the viewpoint of the poet, is one which has already occurred, but it is also one which has future, indeed eternal, consequences. The hymn uses motifs familiar from frequent use in the OT to describe the present salvation. It is also strongly emphasized that this present and future salvation is firmly rooted in Israel's past. The present salvation, with all its future consequences, is a fulfillment of God's past promises to his people"; ibid., 126.

9. Paschasius Radbertus, *Expositio,* lib. 4, p. 383: "Hinc quoque virgo Maria gratanti animo canit: *Magnificat anima mea Dominum* non quod magnus et excelsus Dominus nullam habens consummationem maior minorve esse possit sed quia dum nos in eo crescimus ille in nobis quasi magnificatur."

10. Götz, ed., *Liber Quare,* quaestio 181, p. 72: "Quare Magnificat cotidie canitur? Ideo ut frequentior dominicae incarnationis memoria animos fidelium in opere Dei et in doctrina se exercentium ad deuotionem incepti operis accendat." Ibid., quaestio 182, p. 73: "Quare Magnificat canitur ad vesperum? Ideo ut mens nostra fatigata per diem diversis cogitationibus incumbente tempore quietis recolendo dicta Dei genetricis quicquid superfluum vel nocium diurna vagatione contraxerat, totum hoc precibus et lacrimis ea intercedente mundet." Ibid., appendix I, quaestio 182, p. 126: "Sicut cotidie diluunt quinque psalmi, quicquid delinquunt quinque sensus corporis, ita Magnificat in initio noctis castigat, quicquid cogitationum in prosperitate diei se iactat." Ibid., appendix II, additio 21, p. 150: ". . . hymnus sanctae Mariae id est Magnificat cum antiphona incipitur, in quo humilitatis et oboedientiae exemplo roboramur et incarnationis dominicae memoria ad excitandam nostrae fidei devotionem reducitur."

11. On the early history of the Mass, see Jungmann (1951) 1:391–455.

12. Durandus of Mende, *Rationale,* 341 (bk. 4, chap. 24): "Et est sciendum, quod sicut caput praeeminet caeteris corporis membris, et illi cetera membra seruiunt: sic et euangelium principale est omnium que ad officium missae dicuntur, et toti praeeminet officio misse."

13. Durandus, *Rationale,* 339 (bk. 4, chap. 23): "Post dictam ergo sequentiam, surgens sacerdos, et ad sinistram partem altaris accedens, pronunciat euangelium, significans quod Christus non venit vocare iustos, sed peccatores . . . per dextram enim iusti, per sinistram vero peccatores significantur."

14. Ratcliff, ed., *Expositio,* 7; Gamber, ed., *Ordo,* 18; Levy (1990), 71; Hiley (1993), 500–1.

15. See, for example, Isidore of Seville, *Etymologiarum,* 7.12.29–30.

16. Dix (1945), 418. See also the first Ordo Romanus, ed. Andrieu, *Les Ordines,* 2:87–88.

17. Götz, ed., *Liber quare,* appendix I, quaestio 59, additio 4, p. 113; and appendix II, additio 79, p. 225: "Quare in sabbato sancto ante pascha non portetur lumen ante evangelium? Haec est ratio. Lumen ante evangelium est manifestatio evangelii, quae nondum facta erat."

18. Durandus of Mende, *Rationale,* 341 (bk. 4, chap. 24): "Sane iam figura mutatur, nam diaconus, qui prius representabat prophetam, nunc representat euangelistam— quid nisi lex et prophete usque ad Joannem—et ex eo regnum celorum euangelizatur.

Ideo autem euangelium legitur ut, uelut Christus, post legem, prophetas et psalmos, ore suo praedicauit: ita, post epistolam, responsorium et alleluia, per illud populo predicatio eius annuntietur."

19. Honorius of Autun, *Gemma,* col. 550: "Diaconus qui legit est Petrus qui pro omnibus respondet."

20. Durandus of Mende, *Rationale,* 340–41 (bk. 4, chap. 24): ". . . in quibusdam ecclesiis, in praecipuis festiuitatibus, dyaconus proficisci volens ad legendum euangelium incipit antiphonam."

21. See n. 2 above.

22. Robertson (1990); Robertson (1991a), 48 and *passim.* In 1252 Abbot John of Saint-Corneille arranged for the repair of a Gospel book that had been given to the abbey by Charles the Bald; *GC* 9, col. 438.

23. My search for antiphons before the Gospel in France included all published ordinals and customaries, along with most of the manuscript ordinals listed in *GR* 2.

24. For a summary of the indications of Durandus' presence at Chartres, see Fassler (1993b), 502.

25. On the importance of the saint in the liturgy of the abbey, see Robertson (1991a).

26. *Eclaircissemens sur quelques rits particuliers à l'église d'Auxerre en réponse aux questions d'un pieux laïc, par un chanoine de la Cathédrale d'Auxerre,* pp. 13–22. I am grateful to Craig Wright for pointing out this source to me.

27. Edmund Martène, *De antiquis,* 4:104, mentions having heard them at Senlis, Tours, Langres, and Bayonne, but it is unclear whether he is speaking of the Middle Ages or a later period.

28. For some suggestions for the liturgical placement of motets in the Notre Dame repertory, see Baltzer (1985) and (1990).

29. On Chartres, see Branner (1969); and on Amiens, see Durand (1901).

30. For the *jubé* at Amiens, see Durand, ed., *Ordinaire,* plate 1 (letter A); for Saint-Denis (15th c.), see Robertson (1991a), 303; for Chartres, see Delaporte, ed., *L'Ordinaire,* 23 and floor plan at the end of the text. The *pulpitum* (*jubé*) in Bayeux Cathedral is mentioned frequently in Chevalier, ed., *Ordinaire.*

31. In the older churches the Gospel was often read at the main altar or at an eagle lectern in the middle of the choir (see, for example, n. 13 above).

32. Pseudo-Hugh of Saint-Victor, *Speculum,* col. 361: "In altiori gradu legitur Evangelium quam Epistola, quia doctrina Christi longe excellit doctrinam apostolorum."

33. Honorius of Autun, *Gemma,* col. 551: "Evangelium in alto loco legitur, quia Christus in monte praedicasse perhibetur. Ideo et in sublimi legitur, quia sublimia sunt evangelica praecepta per quae altitudo coelorum scanditur."

34. Chevalier, ed., *Ordinaire,* 62–63: ". . . major archichorus accedit ad cantorem querens ab eo antiphonam que debet cantari ante evangelium, quam acceptam defert ipse diacono sibi assurgenti; tunc diaconus, percantata sequentia, et factis hiis que ipse interim habet facere, ut predixi, eat ipse ad cornu altaris sinistrum et conversus ad chorum incipiat ant. *Hodie Xpistus natus est;* qua incepta, statim petat benedictionem sumens textum euvangeliorum et eat in pulpitum ad legendum, antiphona finaliter decantata, cruce ipsum in eundo et redeundo ante omnia precedente."

35. Chevalier, ed. *Ordinaire,* 4: "Item in omni festo duplici in quo episcopus exequitur officium sacerdotis . . ., inchoat ipse ter ex precepto cantoris antiphonas super psalmos *Magnificat* et *Benedictus,* (primo) scilicet post versiculum, secundo in fine psalmi, tercio post *Gloria Patri.*"

36. Chevalier, ed., *Ordinaire,* 5: "Et cantor, dum intonat psalmos eosdem, debet ob reverentiam evangelii suum piliolum amovere."

37. "Ad finem cuius [sequentiae] transmittat cantor quemdam bene cantantem in capicio ante martyres qui honeste ante evangelium intonet antiphonam *Crucem sanc-*

tam subiit"; Paris, Bibl. Mazarine, MS 526, fol. 57v; Paris, BNF lat. 976, fol. 30v, as cited in Walters [Robertson] (1985), 231.

38. Ceremony summarized in Durand, ed., *Ordinaire,* xlix, from a seventeenth-or eighteenth-century document (Archives de la Somme, IV G 3027).

39. Durand, ed., *Ordinaire,* 48, 80, 85, 465, 554, 569.

40. Villetard, *Office,* 171. The manuscript is Sens, BM 1033, and the conductus appears on fols. 19v–20 (published in *AH* 20:226). See also the discussion of the piece ibid., 113–14.

41. Arlt (1970) 1:97, 2:60–61. The manuscript is London, BL Egerton 2615, fol. 26r–v. Seven of the other eight responsories in the Office are similarly introduced by conductus.

14

The Office for the Feast of the Circumcision from Le Puy

WULF ARLT

Acquérir un livre longtemps désiré! Posséder un document laborieusement cherché! C'est le comble du bonheur rêvé par les amateurs et les bibliophiles. Ce bonheur est le nôtre, car un exemplaire du livre de proses ou *Prosolaire* de Notre-Dame du Puy est maintenant en notre possession (Payrard 1885, 152).

The Sources: Recovering a Tradition

The enthusiasm with which the Abbé Payrard reported "his" discovery in 1885 is understandable: before him lay a unique codex from his very church—a festival book specific to the Feast of the Circumcision. We now know that the Abbé was poring over a book measuring 22.5 × 16.5 cm., and that it contained over 300 pages of chants, monophonic songs, and texts of various types—in short, all the materials necessary for the celebration of this extraordinary Office by the clerics of Le Puy, a feast lasting from First Vespers of 31 December through Compline of New Year's Day. It has taken nearly a century for scholars to "rediscover" the book, and to locate the materials necessary to support its study.

Although the manuscript itself dates from the sixteenth century, Jean-Baptiste Payrard was certain for two reasons that the extensive Circumcision Office it contains had to be much older. First of all, he had compared the contents with information about a *Prosolarium* found in two of the church's early ordinals, and found close correspondences. Secondly, he ascertained from Gaspar Chabron's unpublished *Histoire de la maison de Polignac* that a canon by the name of Guilhaume de Chalencon from the church of Le Puy had been supporting the celebration of this special Office with an endowment as early as 1327, and that the word "prose" had provided the service with its name. The endowment was, as he read in Chabron's *Histoire*:

20 sous annually to the canons and the clerics of the church who will take part in the Office celebrated annually on the first day of each year and the feast of the Circumcision [a service] which in the language of its region is called *lo Prosolari,* generally corrupted to *lo Bosolari,* an Office that lasts twenty-four hours, in which night and day without interruption are sung beautiful prayers, lessons, and proses.[1]

After the death of Payrard (1892), Ulysse Chevalier published the texts of the manuscript Payrard had described, but he provided no indication of the location of this precious source (Chevalier, *Prosolarium*). Thus, as far as scholars were concerned, the manuscript was lost and the historical significance of the Office it recorded remained in question. Although the only extant source known to have survived from Le Puy was this sixteenth-century copy, there were tantalizing hints that the Office it contained might well date back to some time before the fourteenth century. And at least the texts as copied in the sixteenth century had been transcribed and published by Chevalier. Using Chevalier's transcription, Hans Spanke was able to identify 17 concordances between Le Puy and southern French manuscripts dating from the end of the eleventh through the early thirteenth century (Spanke 1931, 387–88). His findings further served to stimulate interest in the special Office of Le Puy and to provoke scholars to wonder how far back into the dark "night of the Middle Ages" its practice might actually be traced.[2]

Chevalier mentioned a second manuscript of this Circumcision Office at the Grand-Séminaire of Le Puy, but added that he had not been able to see it, only knowing of its existence through another person (Chevalier, *Prosolarium,* 59). Leo Treitler, however, did use this second and more recent source in the preparation of his doctoral dissertation in 1967 (Treitler 1967). Still located in Le Puy, the paper manuscript is comprised of 136 leaves and measures 27 × 19 cm., a somewhat larger book than its older cousin, the *Bozolari* described above. It contains—with minor deviations—the same monophonic repertory, but has as well an appendix of no fewer than 19 of the same chants in four-voice settings with peculiar archaic features (Arlt 1978).

In 1981, the older manuscript that had been the basis for Chevalier's edition was rediscovered. In fact, it had been shipped along with the rest of Chevalier's books and papers to the Bibliothèque Municipale in Grenoble in 1939. Over 40 years after its arrival, Robert Amiet identified it as the long-missing book from Le Puy (Amiet 1982, 112). Thus the Office of Le Puy is now available in two notated sources, both copied in the sixteenth century:

A   Grenoble, Bibliothèque Municipale, MS 4413
B   Le Puy, Bibliothèque du Grand Séminaire, A V 7 009.[3]

In addition, one of the ordinals referred to by Payrard has also been discovered. According to a note in this manuscript, the book was apparently in Payrard's possession, and later became part of the holdings of a bibliophile merchant from Le Puy, whose large collection is today preserved as Fonds Léon Cortial at the Bibliothèque Municipale in Le Puy, where the ordinal bears the signature 152 [hereafter

C]. Like A and B, this source is also from the sixteenth century, and can be dated to around 1580 from its script and watermarks. However, an entry on its cover— today only partially legible ("Copie de l'ancien cérémonial du Puy"), but already reported by Payrard—permits its identification as the book he knew. The ordinal contains yet another witness to the Office on fols. 19r (beginning with the entry "Incipit bozolarium") through fol. 22r, but with only the text incipits of the chants and readings, though some of them have extensive rubrics.[4]

Both notated sources offer further useful information, including numerous additions, and names and dates; Chevalier included in his edition much of such material found in A. But comparison of the wealth of materials in all three written records allows us to reconstruct the more recent history of this Office at Le Puy. Findings of this sort are well supplemented by other types of related evidence, including accounts of those clerics of the cathedral named in the codices as scribes or as owners. Older sources of the Office are attested to in a 1432 inventory of the sacristry, with information that relates to the repertory of the surviving manuscripts. Even the previously mentioned endowment in the testament from 1327 is found verbatim in a copy with a vidimus from 21 September 1331.[5] Gathering all this information together, it is now possible to explore the history and meaning of the Le Puy Office with greater precision, and to use the Office as a key to understanding the nature of elaborate festive celebrations in the Middle Ages.

Festive Clerical Offices: The Context of the Le Puy Circumcision Office

The celebration contained in the sources studied here belongs to a lively and important layer of medieval song and ceremony, designed for the celebration of clerical orders during the Octave of Christmas, and sometimes extending through Epiphany. These joyful commemorations of priests, deacons, subdeacons, and acolytes are documented from the tenth century, with a growing body of evidence in subsequent centuries. Thus liturgists from the eleventh and twelfth centuries forward supplied ever more detailed instructions as to how the deacons, priests, and acolytes were to celebrate each of "their" feasts on the three days after Christmas: "omnes enim isti quam sollemnius possunt festa sua celebrant," as stated in the ample instructions concerning this usage in a thirteenth-century ordinal from Bayeux.[6] The deacons claimed St. Stephen's day, 26 December; the priests, the Feast of John the Evangelist, 27 December; and the acolytes or *pueri*, the Feast of Holy Innocents, 28 December. But the subdeacons, who evolved into a raucous group in some towns, usually had their celebration on 1 January, the Octave of Christmas, the Feast of the Circumcision, a day that came to be known in some regions as the Feast of Fools.

Although the celebrations of these special and elaborate clerics' Offices are widely attested, the only surviving examples of the actual services originate from a handful of northern French cathedrals—Beauvais, Sens, and Laon—and date from the twelfth and thirteen centuries.[7] Those from Beauvais and Sens were specifically composed for the Feast of the Circumcision, and they have much in common regarding both the nature of their repertories and modes of organization. Although the earliest attestation (albeit indirect) of the repertory to be studied here is from Beauvais, and dates from around 1160, the two manuscripts from Beauvais and Sens containing the actual Circumcision liturgy from First Vespers to second Compline date from the thirteenth century. The source from Laon is very different in character from those of Sens and Beauvais, containing materials for a greater number of feasts, but without the ample details found in the other two sources. Under the rubric "Christi natalis I est prima dies specialis, I ordine scribuntur I que maxima festa sequntur" there are indications for the elaboration of the liturgy of the Mass and Office for Christmas and other feasts of the Lord, as well as those for the four feasts of Stephen, John the Evangelist, Holy Innocents, and Epiphany, the date on which the subdeacons celebrated their special feast.

Both the sources described above offer the liturgy of this one feast day from First Vespers to second Compline, including numerous processions and several songs that function outside the liturgical celebration, which indicate the ways in which the liturgy of this special Office was connected to the festive lives of the communities themselves (see also Kindermann 1991). At Sens, for example, there is a special song to process to the drinking cup—a "conductus ad poculum"—and a song to go to the meal—a "versus ad prandium." Indeed, many extraliturgical details were associated with the election of a *baculifer* or minister of the feast, from whom gifts were expected. The elected official had to be fetched, and the participants entered the church with him. And, most importantly for the musical aspects of the feast, there were ample opportunities on each of these occasions for song. A rubric at the end of the Laon festival of the subdeacons, for example, demonstrates the manner in which pure joy in singing and dancing at the conclusion could lead to the performance of more and more songs: "Tot Benedicamus I quot novit quisque canamus."[8] The nonliturgical aspects of the feast gave rise to abuse, as is apparent in the condemnations and bans from the end of the twelfth century on, and corroborated in the later Middle Ages in more detailed accounts.[9] The expressions "festum stultorum" and "fête des fous" for the celebration of the subdeacons correspond to the broader frame of the feast and have attracted the interest of historians since the mid-eighteenth century. Occasionally even today, the clerics' feasts and the "feasts of fools" have been regarded as synonymous.[10]

The relationship between liturgy and secular celebration and the apparent excesses in connection with clerics' feasts, especially from the thirteenth century on, must be clarified through study of chronological and regional distinctions. In fact, the blurred line between what is "liturgical," narrowly defined, and what is outside of the liturgy should spur the researcher to a more profound understanding of how these materials were understood by those who conceived and organized them. The festival books are part of a larger context, as is clearly shown by the general rubrics and the treatment of the other feast days at Laon, linking song and ceremony to liturgy. The broader context depicted in these sources is also witnessed to by materials from the St. James liturgy in the late twelfth-century "Codex Calixtinus." In this liturgy one can find connections with comparable collections in Aquitanian and Norman-Sicilian sources, but, in this case, drawn into the festive celebration of the patron saint.[11]

The Age and Significance of the Texts
and Music from Le Puy

In order to evaluate the importance of the materials contained in the sources from
Le Puy, the kind of work initiated by Hans Spanke can be carried further, with
comparisons of the various layers of the Le Puy repertory to extant sources from
the eleventh through the thirteenth centuries. A good place to begin is with the
relevant materials in the oldest parts of the Aquitanian collections, Paris, BNF lat.
3719 and particularly lat. 1139[12] and in the Norman-Sicilian sources Madrid, BN
288, 289, and 19421.[13] More than half of the approximately 60 songs found in Le Puy
sources occur in these older manuscripts.[14] A detailed study of the concordances as
well as philological study of individual song texts make the connections with the
older sources all the more apparent.[15] The Circumcision Office from Le Puy agrees
with the oldest documents from the Norman-Sicilian region in an understanding
of the genre of Benedicamus chant as a two-section form with parallel structure:
the salutation and the rejoinder "Deo gratias."[16] For two other groups of songs,
the "constellation" of concordances with Paris lat. 1139 is concentrated in a sort of
net of transmission ("Überlieferungsnest")—so much so that one might conclude
that groups of these songs were transmitted in circulating libelli.[17]

Pertaining to one of these concordances, Hans Spanke judged that the Circumcision Office from Le Puy offers "a much better text" (Spanke 1931, 291). Other
songs demonstrate similar findings as well. A part of the celebration after Sext—
"ad prandium," "iuxta portem refectorii," and "ad crucem"—which appears in the
ordinal [C] but not in the notated sources—may be used as a test case (fol. 21r–v).
As many as four of the seven pieces (identified by their rubrics as songs) are found
in the twelfth-century sources, and of these, three occur in Paris lat. 1139, including one with the garbled annotation "B[e]n[edicamus] *Stirpsesse* et dicitur cum
orgue," which indicates polyphonic performance of this rare and consequently significant organum trope *Stirps Iesse*.[18]

These various types of evidence suggest that the contents of the Le Puy Office
as expressed in these late sources—the Ordinal and the copies of the service—are,
in fact, contemporary with the contents of the other major festival books not only
in terms of its songs, but also in terms of the essential character of the structure of
the service itself. The fact that 26 of the 60 songs in the Le Puy repertory are
otherwise unknown need not speak against this argument for an early date: the
percentage of unica in the other festal Offices is also high.[19] In addition to preserving contents that date to a great degree from the twelfth and thirteenth centuries,
the sixteenth-century Le Puy sources witness not only to the service as performed
in the central Middle Ages, but also to its unbroken continuation in later periods.
At the end of the Office on fol. 154r of A, the main scribe identifies himself and
dates his work: "Pigeri 1552." A certain Jacques Pigier, who in 1550 can be demonstrated to have been one of four clerics from the "Université de Saint-Mayol"
among the members of the chapter of the cathedral (Rivet 1988, 190), died, according to another note in the manuscript, in 1553. And the second manuscript [B]
is perhaps even 30 years younger than manuscript A.[20] Both books, as numerous

and frequently datable owners' entries show, were passed among the various clerics of the cathedral to the beginning of the eighteenth century. In addition, entries preceding and following the primary contents, later redactions, and not least of all general traces of handling and wear indicate that the sources were used at least up to the seventeenth century, and therefore indicate as well that there was an ongoing concern with and interest in this repertory. Therefore it is possible that some material found in our sources stems from the long period of time between a first redaction of the Office and the later extant documents. Only further study will reveal which features belong to the earliest layers of repertory, and which may date from the fourteenth, fifteenth, and early sixteenth centuries. At least it can now be claimed that the tradition was alive and well throughout this period.

The contents of the song repertories are of special interest, especially given that the Le Puy sources contain a significant number of polyphonic settings. It seems symptomatic that precisely those few songs belonging to the general repertory but missing in the "Copie de l'ancien cérémonial du Puy" [C], are, for the most part, present in the older festal Offices. So too the other way around: the abovementioned longer part of the ordinal after Sext, which is lacking in the notated sources, clearly points to twelfth- and thirteenth-century manuscripts through their concordances. Both phenomena speak in favor of a later abbreviation of contents rather than an expansion. It is also instructive that melodic divergences (found between the sources as well as within the notation of multiple strophes of a song in the same source) seem to stem from later polyphonic reworkings of earlier materials.[21]

Polyphony can be found on four levels:[22] (1) "successively" notated polyphony; (2) rubrics in the ordinal; (3) the later addition of voices to the basic repertory (which expanded a monophonic melody to the simplest polyphony); and (4) the four-voice compositions of the appendix of manuscript B. In the simple progression of the "setting" and in the different possibilities of a polyphonic expansion of the same melody, the added voices indicate the presence of an ad hoc practice of polyphonic performance that must still have been present in this cathedral up through the second half of the sixteenth century. The five "cum orgue" cues found in the ordinal, obviously a substitute for the "cum organo" of the exemplar, might well be referring to this unwritten practice. These pieces correspond only in two cases with the 19 four-voice pieces of the more recent manuscript B. This difference is underscored through the fact that the monophonic version of the first conductus of Matins, *Revirescit et florescit*—which also has a corresponding four-voice setting in the appendix—is preceded by a rubric calling for a performance by "duo cantores" without any further reference to polyphony (Le Puy-en-Velay, BM Cortial 152, fol. 20r). Even in some of the four-voice pieces we find clear indications of an origin within the practice of three- and four-voice polyphonic renderings of melody according to the formulaic rules documented in the fifteenth century. On the other hand, the listing of a "liber organorum" in the sacristy inventory of 1432 mentioned above indicates that written polyphony was present at the cathedral, although the specifics of this particular collection have been lost. However, this and several other observations indicate that the festive Office—even before the

date of the extant sources—was not undergoing major alterations in its basic contents, and that additions and corrections were of the minor sort, tending toward
further truncation rather than greater elaboration.

The Performance of the Festive Office
in the Middle Ages

A primary reason for close study of the *Bozolari* and the other festive Offices is
that they contain detailed information of the sort not usually provided for the
study of the medieval Office: complete instructions for the performance of the
Office, including its chants, prayers, and readings, plus examples demonstrating
the means of amplifying the standard materials of the Office on a singular and very
important occasion. In addition, the wealth of material is gathered in single, well-
coordinated sources, and this is very different from the situation with liturgical
materials for the Office in the earlier Middle Ages, which were collected by genre
in a variety of books.[23] During the tenth century, the trend continued with the
independent tropers for the Mass liturgy, and from the end of the eleventh century
is exemplified in the more diverse collections containing new monophonic and
polyphonic songs, works labeled either "versus" because of their form, or "conductus" and "Benedicamus" because of their function. The comparatively rare expansion of responsories of the Office through "prosulae" are found rather sporadically,
however, and notated along with the base chants themselves.

There is a large variety of indications as to which tropes were sung during the
Mass at specific places and on specific feast days: through the redaction of local
tropers, by their integration into graduals from the eleventh century on, and occasionally through ordinals, which survive for cathedral use in most of Western Europe from the twelfth century forward. But the evidence regarding the expansion
of the Office is much rarer, in part because it grew through the addition of new
chants and texts of local interest, rather than through expansion of and elaboration
upon fixed components, as was the case with the Mass liturgy. The transformation
of the Office from the late eleventh century through the addition of new Latin
songs for festive occasions is much more difficult to document, and one relies
upon rare special collections, such as that described by Susan Rankin in this volume, and the extant notated festal Offices of the type described in this chapter.

With this background in mind, the Office from the cathedral at Le Puy is of
special significance. It provides an explicit clerics' feast for the Circumcision, and
as far as methods of expansion and materials are concerned, it belongs to the
sphere of festival books. But it is not a feast of a definite rank, that is, for one
clearly defined class of clerics (such as St. Stephen for the deacons); rather it is a
feast for all of the orders. This is clearly indicated in the rubrics: from the singing
of the very first piece by four canons (stated in the ordinal as "a iiij[or] Canonicis";
C, fol. 19r) to the dance of the "clericuli" at the close of the feast. It might be noted
that the Circumcision was celebrated especially solemnly in Le Puy because the
cathedral had a corresponding relic in its possession.

An examination of these late sources and their various repertories, then, provides a kind of blueprint for how the Office was rendered and understood, and although the festive Offices described above have much in common, there are differences as well, not only in their overall scope and size, and in their choice of individual chants, but also and most importantly with regard to which genres and liturgical structures dominate; each of the redactions reveals different interests and priorities. As concerns function and structure, the *Bozolari* is certainly the most extensive of the festival books. The Laon source, for example, deals only with the pre-Mass procession and Mass on Christmas, and primarily with Matins, Lauds, and Mass on the following three days; only on the Feast of the Subdeacon for Epiphany, however, does the Laon source deal with a larger part of the feast day: Prime of Vigil, First Vespers, then Matins, Lauds, Prime, Mass, Second Vespers, and an extremely elaborate "completorium infinitum." The Offices of Sens and Beauvais offer much richer elaborations for the Mass and each of the Office Hours—though the sources differ from one another in their particulars: Beauvais with processions, Sens with an appendix of chants for eating and drinking as well as a "conductus ad bacularium" or to the master of the feast, and farsed lessons for Stephen, John the Evangelist, and Holy Innocents.

Only in the *Bozolari*, however, do we find the following:

a. Between First Vespers and the procession "ad chorum sancte crucis" there are detailed segments "ad lectionem in capitulo," "ad cenam" in the refectory, and "in aula capituli."
b. In addition to High Mass, there is a first Mass "ad Sanctum Iohannem."
c. Before Prime, a song "ad Breviatorium" and a station in front of a picture.
d. After Prime, a section in the chapter hall and another station: "in gradibus coram transfiguracione domini" and "coram ymagine beate Mariae," that is, in front of the fresco at the entrance after the long ascending stairs to the cathedral.
e. Again after Second Vespers chants for the meal in the refectory as well as for the procession.
f. An expansion at the close of Compline, again with a procession and immediately thereafter three chants for the dance of the youngest among the clerics ("clericuli tripudiant").

In addition to these only the ordinal contains the aforementioned section for the meal after Sext and "ad crucem."

It is through the festive Offices that the liturgical function of the most recent layer of sung poetry in the liturgy can be clarified. The growth of this repertory is apparent in the number of new liturgical songs evident since the end of the eleventh century.[24] The sources, however, offer different information. In the festal Office of Laon, as a rule only the liturgical place of a song is precisely stated. We find only the particular *Alto consilio* for Epiphany, and at the close of Compline *Nos respectu gratie*, a song that was sung by all the subdeacons "in medio choro."[25] The Office from Sens contains 16 such songs (including those in the appendix), that from Beauvais has 22 songs, one of which is given only as an incipit; lost part of the manuscript may very well have contained others. In the notated *Bozolari*, however, there are no fewer than 59 such songs, with seven additional ones in a section of the ordinal [C] not (or no longer) copied into the notated sources.

This difference in information relates to the methods of expansion used in each of the sources, which include the following possibilities: (1) the integration of sequences and textings of short, independent melismas into the Hours; (2) the further development of the great responsories; (3) the "farsing" of lessons, the Pater noster, and other chants; (4) those chants accompanying change of place within or outside of the church ("conductus"), as well as (5) the substitution at the conclusion of the Hour of the *Benedicamus domino* and respond *Deo gratias* with a strophic song that either incorporates the call literally or invokes its sense and which was rubricated as "Benedicamus." The presence of numbers 2–4 demonstrate that a primary purpose of these expansions related to the rendering of the lessons for which the invitation to the Benediction and the Benediction itself could be more precisely stated through the use of particular songs. Less important in the comparison of these Offices is the use of specific chants such as as the distinctive opening *Deus in adiutorium | intende laborantium*, which is already found in the compilation of relevant materials of Paris lat. 1139, for First Vespers at Sens and Laon (the latter for the feast of Epiphany), for Second Vespers at Beauvais, as well as for Prime and second Compline at Le Puy; this is to say nothing of the larger historical context of this text as a polyphonic opening of the large motet sources and in its reworking as a Benedicamus (see Arlt 1970, 2:252). This is similar to the presence of older methods of expansion in troped Ordinary chants or to the introductions to the proper chants of the Mass, as with the early offertory trope *Regnorum domino regi regumque potenti eia* for Epiphany in the Laon source, and *Hodie cantandus est* in Le Puy, the only southern French witness of Tuotilo's trope.[26]

In the Laon manuscript the first two procedures, that is, the integration of sequences and the expansion of the *responsoria prolixa*, are particularly conspicuous. Both methods are carried further than in the other festal Offices. The sequences (rubricated *prosa*) not only occur in place of hymns but are interpolated into the structure of the Hours in other ways as well. Sequences are especially important at Second Vespers and the *completorium infinitum* of Epiphany, which has a sequence after each psalm, and indeed even after the singing of the hymn! Moreover, the elaboration of the greater responsories is found not only in the widespread melismas and their textings (see Hofmann-Brandt 1971 and T. Kelly 1977), but also—as Jacques Handschin was the first to recognize—in the integration of long sequence melodies, in part labeled explicitly by their titles.[27] Furthermore, we find notated in detail in the Laon codex farsed lessons of the Mass and versicles in the Hours, and in the great *completorium infinitum* numerous other chants that have been elaborated in special ways.[28] It is all the more striking that there was less emphasis upon new songs in the redaction of these Offices: indeed conductus are provided for the readings of the Mass and Benedicamus at the conclusion of the Hours, but normally only rubricated *quale volueris!*

In the Office from Sens the use of sequences is confined to that of the function of hymns, though—as in Beauvais—with one such "hymn" for each of the three nocturns, each of which always opens with an invitatory. Regarding the responsories of Matins, only the sixth and ninth are expanded by a melisma for the repetition after the verse. The individual responsories of both Vespers are broadly elaborated: *Descendit de celis* (First Vespers) through its three prosulas for the *Fabrice mundi* melismas (for these see Kelly 1988) and *Gaude Maria virgo* (Second Vespers) through the texting of *Inviolata, intacta et casta,* which is also used as an independent *prosa* (see Arlt 1970, 2:203 f.), though it should be noted that in this particular Hour, the unique expansion of Vespers can be found through a *responsorium prolixum* after each of the psalms. In contrast to Laon, however, the Benedicamus chants are more exactly defined in Sens, as are the conductus, which are specified for the readings of the Mass as well as for the accompanying of special features and actions—including a conductus *ad ludos* before the Te deum at the conclusion of Matins.

This broad interest in and commitment to new songs at Beauvais is attested to by a twelfth-century version of the Office, whose source is only indirectly documented and which has the "Conductus of the Ass," *Orientis partibus,* as a processional song for the festal master as well as some chants at Matins (see Arlt 1970, 1:30–31). Moreover, the extant version of the Office from the thirteenth century demonstrates each of the five methods of expansion of the basic repertory mentioned earlier, with sequences as "hymns" as well as an augmentation of each of the readings at Matins with a conductus, a benediction, and numerous extensions of the responsories (for details see Arlt 1970, 1:95–141).

Of all the Offices, the use of strophic songs is nowhere more widely represented than in the repertory from Le Puy. Here the expansion of responsories is omitted, but all other previous possibilities concerning the use of songs can be discerned. In addition, a new structure for the integration of song, the "farsumen," amplifies the lessons. The fact that the repertory of the *Bozolari* has—in addition to the numerous conductus and Benedicamus for the processions—more than 20 such elaborations contributes to the high percentage of songs in the Office from Le Puy.

Farsed Lessons in the Le Puy Sources

Like the term *tropus,* the Latin and vernacular word formations (*farcimen, farcitus, farcitura,* and *farsa, farce,* etc.—which go back to the Latin *farcire* and the vernacular *farcir* respectively) were also used since the twelfth century as terms for the most varied expansions of preexisting material.[29] The farsed chants and lessons of the liturgy were to a great extent (and apparently increasingly so) centonized expansions made up of fragments from preexisting chants.[30] This is also the case for various chants of the festal Offices, which are not explicitly labeled as "farsed" and correspond to a tendency in late tropes (see Asketorp 1992).

In fact, however, the farses proper differed from older tropes through their reliance on preexisting chants, although not through the interaction between base chants and expansion, but rather by taking over wholesale various snippets of the chants themselves. As long as the compiler chose the expansions from appropriate places, it was possible to retain a subtle connection between the expanded and the inserted sections. This changed when a lesson—as in the nine farses of Matins—

was expanded by several preset strophes and in most cases by entire songs. And this is true aside from the number of times the parts of songs and lessons alternated: as a rule farsed lessons begin with a part of the song, continue with brief sections of the lesson between strophes 1–3, and end again with a part of the song. In the alternation of individual sections the connection of larger units inevitably requires flexibility when compared with the tighter and more complex interaction between base chants and the interpolated elements found within older trope repertories as well as within the farses proper.

Characteristic for Le Puy is the expansion of the first lesson, which can be seen in the following example, where the refrain has been emphasized throughout in italics and the parts of the lessons through indentation:[31]

Adam pomo
primus homo
   male gustans vetito,
excecavit
et dampnavit
   orbem secum subito.

Orbis inde doleat

     Postquam consummati sunt dies octo, ut circumcideretur puer,
     vocatum est nomen eius Iesus, quod vocatum est ab angelo
     priusquam in utero conciperetur.

Mortem pavit,
ut gustavit,
   quod deus vetuerat.
Per hoc crimen
exit limen
   ubi prius fuerat.

Orbis inde doleat

     Ritus et religio circumcisionis a beato Abraham patriarcha
     sumpsit exordium.

Fit deceptus
vir ineptus
   ductus ad illicita,
exsequatur
et dampnatur
   gustans sibi vetita.

Orbis inde doleat

The song treats the fall of man: in concrete terms, Adam, through his consumption of the fruit of the forbidden tree, brings ruin not only upon himself but upon all the world. The lesson consists of the opening of the Gospel text of Luke 2:21, followed by exegetical treatment of the text.

At first glance, the chant and the lesson seem to have little to do with one another. Certainly the musical setting underscores the distance between the two:

the lesson is sung to a tone for the purpose of recitation, while the song, as demonstrated in the first strophe, is highly melismatic (see example 14.1).[32] Upon closer inspection, however, especially if one looks at the totality of the new readings and the songs that expand them, in these farses the older interaction between trope and base text is taken up at a far more general level and realized in a new way.

This is already indicated by the excerpts from the lesson. They follow a widely attested tradition that goes back to Bede's exposition: either simply the text at 2.21 from the *Expositio* of St Luke's Gospel or for the last three lessons also Homily 1.11 for this day. The former is attested for Le Puy by a fifteenth-century breviary (Paris, BNF lat. 1304, fols. 46v–47v). However, the editors of the *Bozolari*, after the usual insertion, began the exposition with their own choice of text passages.

The particular lessons and their song commentaries require study of the entirety and its significance, and not just of individual sections. The farses relate to the Gospel of the day from Luke 2, the story of the Circumcision, to Bede's *Expositio* of the Gospel of Luke 2:21, and to the last three lessons, taken from Bede's Homily I.11 for this day;[33] the former of these texts by Bede is witnessed to by a

Example 14.1 Matins for feast of the Circumcision: farsed lesson 1

breviary of the fifteenth century from Le Puy (Paris, BNF lat. 1304, fols. 46v–47v). After a typical beginning, the redactors of the *Bozolari* came up with their own choice of text passages. And these apparently were associated with the choice of chants and point to a typological connection, made also in other sermons for the feast of the Circumcision.[34]

The interaction between song and lesson begins with the juxtaposition of Adam and Christ. In its essence, atonement for the Fall and Adam's actions have been made through the Incarnation and the sacrifice of Christ (Rom. 5:12–21). In addition, Christ, through *circumcisio,* enters into the covenant symbolized by the Father's command for this ritual (Gen. 17:7–14). Circumcision represents fulfillment, and is related in time to Christmas, having occurred eight days after the event of birth. And just as Abraham's trust in the righteousness of God is confirmed in Circumcision, so then the acceptance of the birth of Christ—as written in Luke 2:21—opens the way to salvation. The chants are a celebratory response to the lessons, linking their meanings to the present liturgical action.

This context becomes clearer as the lessons unfold. In the second farse before the text of the lesson (which takes up the ending of the first with the words "Qui cum adhuc positus in preputio perfecte credidisset deo reputatumque ei ad iusticiam") the song *Congaudeat ecclesia* | *per hec sacra solempnia* enjoins the celebrating throng to rejoice over the birth of the Son of God, the significance and consequence of which is then addressed in the following *Humanatur verbum patris.* The third farse illuminates this aspect with the first part of the magnificent *Alto consilio,* which is also known as the entrance song of Ecclesia in the play of the Antichrist (A, fols. 31v–33r; B, fols. 18v–19v).

> Alto consilio
> divina ratio
>   restaurat hominem:
> immittit celitus
> vim sancti spiritus
>   qua replet virginem.
>
> Pectus virgineum
> celo capacius
>   totum et integrum
> claudit interius
> illum qui deus est
>   et dei filius.
>
> Visitatur sede de supera
> Babilonis filia misera,
> persona filii missa, non altera,
> nostre carnis sumit mortalia.
>
> Moratus est fletus ad vesperum,
> matutinum ante luciferum,
> castitatis egressus uterum
> venit Ihesus nostra leticia.

The fourth farse, in the sections of the readings, presents an explicit reference to the diverse typological senses of the Circumcision as well as to the message of the faith of Abraham and his line, and bears in the song the reference to the prophetic announcement of the birth (A, fols. 36r–37r; B, fol. 21r–v):

> Res nova, principium
> facti subit seriem:
> rerum factor omnium
> novam sumit speciem
> *in virgine,*
> *Miranda comercia,*
> *que sic naturalia*
> *frangit iura.*

Erat autem circumcisionis typus ac figura multiformis.

> Est inregressibilis
> lex fatalis ordinis,
> sed fit regressibilis
> sumpta forma hominis
> *in virgine* . . .

Nam et signaculum, ut dictum est, iusticie fidei Abrahe et semini eius

> Ut propheta docuit,
> virga Iesse floruit.
> Verbo sic innotuit
> quod fieri potuit
> *in virgine* . . .

And thus the commentary proceeds in this way from lesson to lesson, with the songs providing steady reflection on the larger meaning of the lesson and its connection with the feast.

Such an extensive composition was possible precisely because the majority of new liturgical songs treat Christmas themes, and because they repeatedly illuminate this event in continually varying ways. Of course, some of the songs might have originated expressly for farsing. Thus, the first one, *Adam pomo*, only appears as a *farsumen*. Its strophic structure is the same as that of the preceding conductus *Revirescit et florescit*, which itself can be traced back to the thirteenth century in a source from the German-speaking realm (though this source contains French repertory to a large extent; Stuttgart, Landesbibl. HB I 95, fols. 79v–80r). The connection of the two poems is further underscored in that the conductus here contains only the first four strophes of the eight making up the piece in the Stuttgart manuscript—that is to say, those concerned with the serpent and Eve.[35] The *Bozolari* closes with a formulaic strophe leading into the Benediction:

> Eia, rector,
> dicat lector:
>   Iube benedicere,
> nos queamus

redemptori
laudes cuncti reddere.

In the other strophes of the Stuttgart version, Adam is the subject, as in the *farsumen* of the *Bozolari*. Just as the farse can be read as a continuation of the conductus, so too the texts of other conductus indicate that a well-planned elaboration of the parts of the readings also included the song preceding the lesson, thereby implying that the ideas and broad outline determined the composition of the entire Office. The connections between conductus and other song repertories and the lessons of the day call for further exploration.

At Matins only one form of farsing is present in the *Bozolari*. The other can be found in the farses as they were sung in the chapter hall or also at the common supper. These are defined even more strongly by the new Latin song since here the text of the "lesson" is also taken from the existing song, which, as in the following example, is preceded explicitly by the rubric "lege" (A, fols. 36r–37r; B, fols. 73r–74r):

Humanatur deitas
carnis tecto pallio,
gaudeat humanitas
de tali consortio.

Felix hec coniunctio
miro fit commercio,
cum in dei filio
nostra fit redemptio.

Reformavit novitas appetitum baculi.

Reformavit novitas
appetitum baculi,
gaudet hec sollempnitas
honore munusculi.

Excitentur singuli
et sint novi moduli,
sit in ore populi
omnis amor tituli.

Radix Iesse, castitatis lilium, nova stella novum profert radium.

Radix Iesse,
castitatis lilium,
nova stella
novum profert radium:
rosa mitis
et conculcans solium.

. . .

The farse underscores the connection between the parts of the entire complex of the lesson since it begins—after the invitation "Iube [domne, benedicere]"—with the strophe of a song that is also found in the Circumcision Office from Beauvais, the beginning of which, *Dies ista celebris,* precedes the *farsumen* as a conductus at Le Puy.[36] The first "lesson" takes up the beginning of a strophe (likewise preserved in the Beauvais source), the second the beginning of a long song already known in the oldest of the Aquitanian collections containing songs.[37] In both cases—as also with the other examples of this type of farse—the openings that are performed as lessons can be separated as a statement that is then illuminated in the song. One point concerning this farse, which is sung after Second Vespers and before the common meal in the chapter hall, is that it joins both aspects of farsing found in the most elaborated festal Offices: in the first "lesson" the reference to the "feast of baculum" is found with the cue word for the master of ceremonies as *baculus,* with the allusion to the little "gift" and finally with the naming of new songs, as they originated for this occasion; the second "lesson" is about the events of Christmas and contains a point of reference to the liturgical celebration.

In this form of the farses, the traditional interaction between old and new is, in fact, structurally retained, whereas the basic liturgical repertory is wholly discarded in favor of the new songs. In comparison with the older forms of expansion found in the tropes as well as in actual farses, this is certainly a later phenomenon. And this may suggest that the redaction of the Le Puy Circumcision Office as contained in sixteenth-century sources is indeed younger than that of all the other festival books.

Conclusion

The *Bozolari* determined the framework and the course of a feast of the clerics at the cathedral in the Massif central from well before the sixteenth century and beyond. Its history is documented for the late period in more detail than that of all the other festal Offices. It seems all the more remarkable that aspects of the celebration of a secular New Year are only mentioned in passing and without compromising the liturgical framework. This is the case, for example, for the final entry of the *Bozolari* after a procession following second Compline and significantly in front of a chapel. There the succentor sings for the end of the long festival (more than twenty-four hours and practically uninterrupted) with a raised voice ("alta voce") "Hoc in anno" three times (according to A, fol. 154r) (see example 14.2). The summons is taken up in a repeated syllabic melody, which is notated in the later manuscript rhythmically (see example 14.3).[38]

At the same time the youngest dance vigorously, as a rubric in the older source A—though added later in the margin—notes: "Clericuli tripudiant firmiter." New

Example 14.2 Exclamation of the succentor at the end of the office in MS A

Hoc in an - no, hoc in an - no, hoc in an - no.

Example 14.3   Answer to the succentor in MS B

Hoc   in   hoc,   hoc   in   hoc,   hoc   in   hoc,   hoc   in   hoc,

hoc in hoc,   in hoc,   in hoc,   hoc in an   -   no.

Years' wishes have existed previously in the liturgy, as with the recasting of the
bishop's lauds before the dismissal formula of the mass at Beauvais (see Arlt 1970,
1:145–46). Dance has also had its history in the context of the liturgy. At best,
criticism seems to emerge in Le Puy indirectly in the ordinal where a general indication "Et nota quod istud festum est festum de clargastres" has a word for the
celebrating that, according to evidence from a wider context in the thirteenth century, was used with negative connotations.[39]

The fact that a medieval clerics' feast was practiced for so long, and that in the
sixteenth century it was still being adapted for the redaction of four-voice settings,
is due not only to the special relic of the cathedral mentioned earlier, but also
points to increasing shifts in the composition of new repertory for the liturgy. The
heyday of such compositions was during the late eleventh, twelfth, and thirteenth
centuries, when songs of this type were transmitted in great quantities. These elaborations of the Office through song parallel the ways in which—as a consequence
of the Carolingian reception of the Roman liturgy and its chant—the earlier layer
of chant was expanded from the ninth century on through new genres of chants:
tropes, sequences, versus, and new Offices. The redaction of the festal Offices of
the twelfth and thirteenth centuries occurred in a period during which a second
far-reaching shift was taking place through the addition of great numbers of new
types of rhythmical Latin songs, from the new style of sequences, to conductus,
greater quantities of versus, and the increasing numbers of rhymed Offices.

The integration of new possibilities of composition and an unfolding of the
musical language caused major changes within the Office, and not just during the
Christmas Octave, although this is by far the most important liturgical position
for such works. With the new compositions, especially as polyphonic compositions
became prominent among them, a new aspect came into the foreground: "music
within the liturgy," compared to the earlier concept of "music for the liturgy." This
shift is apparent in the special form of the farse in the "late" Office from Le Puy.
Here, the integration of the new artforms occurs where an older reading is ex-

panded in a troped manner and integrated within a broader framework of typological interpretation and presentation. The Office of Le Puy offers not only a powerful sense of older, festive repertories; it also points to a time when freely composed polyphonic pieces dominated the liturgies of both the Mass and the Office. Positioned as they are in time, the sources of the Le Puy festive Office look both forward and back, and suggest the many ways that earlier repertories survived long after the Middle Ages had come to a close, and indeed thrived with transforming additions that continued the process of change.

Translated by Lori Kruckenberg,
Kelly Landerkin, and Margot Fassler

Notes

1. The text of Chabron, as reported by Payrard (1885), 147: "20 sols annuels aux chanoines et clercs de l'Eglise Nostre Dame qui assisteront à l'office qui se faict annuellement le premier jour de chascune année et feste de la Circoncision appelée en langage du pays *lo Prosolari* et par corruption communément *lo Bosolari,* office qui dure vingt-quatre heures et pendant lesquelles incessamment, tant la nuit que le jour, l'on change de belles oraisons, leçons et proses. De ce dernier mot de prose l'office a pris le nom de *Prosolari.*"

2. To paraphrase Chevalier, *Prosolarium,* 1, who wrote "Je n'oserai dire qu'elle se perd dans la nuit du moyen âge."

3. This is the location; the manuscript itself bears no siglum.

4. For the sake of simplicity, all foliations of the ordinal and the noted sources are rendered here in arabic numerals.

5. Detailed evidence is offered in my annotated edition of the Office with observations on its transmission and survival; the edition, now being prepared for publication, will be titled: *Lo Bozolari. Ein Klerikerfest des Mittelalters aus Le Puy, Lieder des 12. Jahrhunderts und Mehrstimmiges aus der Kathedrale des 16. Jahrhunderts.* Parts of the edition have been realized in performance on a CD: *Le Manuscrit du Puy* (1992): Virgin Classics, London 1992, VC 7 59238 2. The Provençal word "Bozolari," which derives from the word "Prosa," is attested to in this form from the fourteenth century in various sources demonstrably from Le Puy.

6. Chevalier, ed., *Ordinaire,* 59–72 with quotation on p. 65; concerning the entire subject see Arlt (1970), 1:38–51, and Fassler (1992).

7. Editions and studies with detailed bibliographies can be found as follows: for Beauvais (London, BL Egerton 2615): Arlt (1970) and D. Hughes (1985); for Sens (Sens, BM 46 A): Villetard (1907); and for Laon (Laon, BM 263): Arlt (1970), 1:218–28, and D. Hughes (1972).

8. Laon 263, fol. 141v; for general information, see Arlt (1968), esp. 375–82.

9. For an explanation of the feast and the play of Daniel as attempts to contain and "purify" abuse, see Fassler (1992).

10. As is the case with Heers (1983), with a generous "harmonization" of the various kinds of information from different feasts and places.

11. Santiago de Compostela, Catedral s.s.; for editions and studies see especially Wagner (1931), Whitehill et al., *Liber,* and López-Calo (1982), 36–54 and 136–67; regarding contacts with French repertories, see Hohler (1972) and Arlt (1970), 1:219.

12. Regarding the stratification of these sources, see Fuller (1979).

13. For general information concerning these see Hiley (1981) and (1983) and for the song repertory see Arlt (1970), 1:175–90 and 206–17.

14. See Arlt (1978), 13–25, with a compilation of concordances known at that time on 16–22.

15. For one song, see most recently Treitler (1992), and for the complete repertory see the pertinent chapters in my forthcoming *Lo Bozolari*.

16. For this and the other situation in the Aquitanian sources, see Arlt (1970), 1:160–206.

17. The groups of songs mentioned here will be described in greater detail in the edition of the Le Puy sources.

18. Regarding this, see Fuller (1971), esp. 181–83; Arlt (1986), 53–60 with further literature; Plocek (1985), 1:145–49 as well as 2:72–73; Rothe (1988), 194, and the sound recording *Nova Cantica: Latin Songs of the High Middle Ages* (Freiburg, 1990) in the series Schola Cantorum Basiliensis Documenta (deutsche Harmonia Mundi RD 77196).

19. For example, in the festival book from Beauvais, six of the 13 conductus and three of the nine Benedicamus chants are unica.

20. The watermark corresponds to Briquet 13148, "Raisin," with evidence from 1588 and Le Puy.

21. See, for example, the observations in Arlt (1978), 25–28.

22. For more on this, though before knowledge of [A], see Arlt (1978), 25–26 and 33–46.

23. See chapter 1. For general information on the following topic consult Huglo (1988) and Hiley (1993), the latter with a detailed bibliography.

24. For general information see Arlt (1990a).

25. Concerning the transmission of these songs see Arlt (1970), 2.261 and 1:226, n. 6 respectively.

26. CT 1: Epiph off 22 and Nat III intr 25, respectively.

27. See Handschin (1954), 149, and especially the detailed study of responsories for St. Stephen's Day in D. Hughes (1972).

28. See also the observations by Ruth Steiner (1980b), 598 f.

29. A comprehensive terminological study investigating this semantic field and related words in Latin and the vernacular is, as far as I can see, still wanting. An introduction to the sources and literature can be found in lexica of the respective disciplines.

30. See as a paradigm the analyses and observations in Villetard (1907), 197–215, as well as in Hiley (1993), 233–38, with references to further literature.

31. The orthography follows the manuscripts: A, fols. 25v–26v and B, fols. 14v–15v.

32. According to B; A differs only in the use of some ligatures and in the downward movement *gffe* instead of *gfe* over *orbem*.

33. For decisive information regarding the choice of lessons and sermons, I am grateful to David Chad of the University of Norfolk and Martin Steinmann of the Universität Basel. For Bede's commentary, see Hurst's editions in CCSL 120, 56–61 and CCSL 122, 73–79 respectively.

34. Thus in the sermon I.15 of Heiric of Auxerre, which is even more closely affiliated with Bede's interpretation than can be seen in the index to Quadri's edition, CCCM 116, 127–31; generally for this ninth-century collection of sermons, see Barré (1962).

35. The text from the Stuttgart manuscript is available in *AH* 20:99.

36. Arlt (1970), 2. 156 f.; cf. 1:157–59. Contrary to my original presumption (2:260), the philological analysis supports the idea that the use as Benedicamus with a corresponding conclusion in the Office from Beauvais represents a secondary reworking.

37. Paris lat. 1139, fol. 46r; see also Treitler (1992) for an edition of both melodic versions: p. 11 following the Parisian manuscript and p. 12 for the Le Puy version.

38. Fol. 94r–v; for the pragmatic aspect of the rhythmically clearer notation in this manuscript, see the provisional remarks in Arlt (1978), 33–37, as well as more general comments in Arlt (1990b).

39. C, fol. 19v. For the information about the semantic field of "clargastres" I am grateful to my colleague Germán Colón of the Department of Romance Languages, Universität Basel.

The Palm Sunday Procession in Medieval Chartres

CRAIG WRIGHT

Students of the liturgy are accustomed to think of the Divine Office as the total-ity of the Canonical Hours and high Mass of the day. These services were cele-brated, whether in monastery or cathedral, in the sanctuary and chancel of the church, in what architectural historians refer to broadly as the "choir." But there were many other liturgical ceremonies belonging to the *Opus dei* that were not part of the Canonical Hours or Mass and which transpired outside of the physical confines of the choir. The centrality of these other ritual acts to the theological subject of the liturgy suggests that they were in no way "extra-liturgical" or of secondary importance. If these acts transpired beyond the choir walls, it was only because some aspect of an "outside" location made it possible to commemorate the events of the Christian story of that day in a way that was more individual, intense, and, sometimes, dramatic. A sepulchre play at a "tomb" in the nave of the monastery early on Easter morning,[1] the Washing of the Feet within the chapter house on Maundy Thursday,[2] the Expulsion of the Penitents from the west door of the cathedral on Ash Wednesday:[3] these are a few of the liturgical acts in which an outside venue suggests not merely a commemoration, but a reenactment of a religious event.

Processions were the most numerous of these extramural services. Each Sunday (except during Lent) the monastic or cathedral clergy departed from their choir stalls and processed to the rood screen before the west choir door, where a com-memoration of the Resurrection was offered immediately prior to the celebration of Terce and high Mass. On Sundays, Mondays, Wednesdays, and Fridays during Lent the procession went farther afield, progressing each day to a different stational church in and near the town, thereby demonstrating a unity of the Christian com-munity traditionally associated with the Lenten season. Similarly, on the feasts of saints of local importance, the clergy would visit a nearby church or chapel dedi-cated to that saint and celebrate there either First Vespers or, the next day, Mass of the day, or, if two processions to that church were effected on successive days, both

Vespers and Mass. Naturally, the day, duration, and route of the procession varied from town to town, depending upon local geography and the saintly relics to be venerated in the various churches of the area. On four special feasts of the liturgical year—the Rogation Days, Purification (or Candlemas), Corpus Christi (a late medieval feast), and Palm Sunday—the clergy of other churches and the laity of the town joined with the chaplains, canons, and bishop of the cathedral in a great general procession.[4] Of these lay–clerical processions, the one for Palm Sunday was, if not always the longest, certainly the most dramatic.[5]

The origin of the Palm Sunday procession in the Latin West can be traced back to Jerusalem and the scriptural account of Christ's triumphant entry into the Holy City as a prelude to His final great work of Redemption. The joyful scene, described in varying degrees of detail in the four Gospels,[6] naturally lent itself to vivid re-creation. As early as the late fourth century the nun Egeria, a pilgrim to the Holy Lands from Spain or southern France, observed the people of Jerusalem reenacting the entry of the conquering Christ.[7] From the top of the Mount of Olives they led their bishop back to the celestial City,[8] the children running before him shouting "Blessed is he who comes in the name of the Lord." From Jerusalem the Palm Sunday ceremony moved westward, to the lands of the Gallican rite, undoubtedly carried by pilgrims such as Egeria and by later monastic refugees fleeing the Holy Lands.[9] The Bobbio Missal, a Gallican source of the early eighth century, contains a blessing of the palms ("Benedictio palme et olivae super altario"), which implies that a procession followed thereafter (Hermann Graef 1959, 11; and Tyrer 1932, 50). And although there are suggestions that a procession was known in Spain by this time,[10] documents of the ninth century originating in northern France are the first to prove incontrovertibly its existence.[11] Most important among these is the statement by Amalarius of Metz indicating that the tradition of a Palm Sunday procession was already widespread.[12] Later, the custom was carried into Italy, though apparently not until the twelfth century was it officially adopted in Rome.[13]

Thus, invoking Amalarius as the witness, we can say with confidence that the clergy of the principal monasteries and cathedrals of the Carolingian Empire were accustomed to celebrate Palm Sunday with an appropriate procession by the ninth century. But although the principal churches in northern France and surrounding territories had such a ceremony, the particulars of the procession varied from one institution to the next. As the centuries passed, these local practices became more idiosyncratic. By the thirteenth century the cathedrals of Paris, Cambrai, Reims, Rouen, Amiens, Bayeux, Laon, Sens, Metz, and Chartres, for example, all enjoyed a Palm Sunday ritual that included a procession, a blessing of the palms, a reading of the Gospel, a sermon, visits to stational churches, and a ceremonial entrance into the city. Nevertheless, the order in which these events occurred and the selection of chants to accompany them varied greatly from cathedral to cathedral. Among these churches the cathedral of Chartres offers the most rewarding study, for not only is Chartres the most thoroughly preserved of the great French cathedrals, but the sources regarding the Chartrain Palm Sunday survive in unusually large number.

The pageant of Palm Sunday at Chartres is transmitted in three main manuscripts.[14] The oldest is the *Ordo veridicus,* an ordinal compiled at the cathedral during the first half of the twelfth century. As is true of every ordinal, the *Ordo veridicus* contains a list of the constituent parts of the liturgy, but no music. For much of the music of the Palm Sunday procession we must rely on Chartres, BM 520, a notated missal of cathedral usage copied perhaps as late as 1230 but representing a state of liturgical affairs that existed about 1190.[15] A description of the Palm Sunday procession at Chartres as preserved in MS 520 is given in appendix A. Finally, Chartres, BM 1058 offers a thirteenth-century expansion of the twelfth-century *Ordo veridicus;*[16] rather than suggesting major changes to the ceremony, it provides details not contained in the earlier, twelfth-century ordinal. Though it is a source copied about 1230, MS 1058, like MS 520, records liturgical practices as they existed at Chartres in the late twelfth century. Consequently, saints' feasts inaugurated in the thirteenth century are wholly lacking as well as any notice of the monumental architectural changes being wrought upon the cathedral during the years 1194–1233.[17] Taken in sum, these three primary sources allow us to extrapolate the essence of the Palm Sunday procession as it existed at Chartres around 1190, give or take a year or so in either direction. The stage for the ceremony described below, therefore, was at first the Romanesque church of Bishops Fulbertus (episcopal dates 1006–25) and Yvo (1090–1115).[18] Most of this early cathedral was destroyed by fire in 1194 and rebuilt in the Gothic style during the first half of the thirteenth century. Only later, during the thirteenth, fourteenth, and fifteenth centuries, was the point of departure and return for the procession the thirteenth-century Gothic edifice that we see today. Let us follow the liturgy of Palm Sunday as it unfolded in and around the cathedral in late twelfth-century Chartres.

Called to the cathedral by two great tollings of the bells (*duo signa magna*), the chaplains, canons, and dignitaries of the cathedral, as well as members of the clergy from other nearby churches, assembled in the choir of the cathedral. To the sounds of now a great general pealing, they exited through the royal west door,[19] preceded by crosses, Gospel books for the clergy of each church, and feretories bearing the relics of saints.[20] The succentor[21] soon sang forth the incipit of the first of the *responsoria de historia,* the succession of nine great responsories that tell the story of Christ's triumphant entry into Jerusalem. This cycle had already been sung at the cathedral earlier that morning at Matins and now was chanted again as the procession made its way through the streets of Chartres.[22] Moving toward the east, the assembly passed beyond the walls of the city and to the first station, a cemetery outside the priory of Saint-Barthélemy[23] (see figure 15.1), where it was joined by processions coming from other churches.[24] The route of the procession had obviously been chosen so as to traverse a topography reminiscent of that of ancient Jerusalem.[25] The cemetery at Saint-Barthélemy corresponds to Golgotha, the site of Christ's crucifixion to the east and beyond the walls of Jerusalem. From there the procession of Chartres ascended a hill to the abbey church of Saint-Cheron.[26] Again, the topography was perfectly chosen. Saint-Cheron, then as now, sits atop a hill, a substitute Mount of Olives, whence one can see the celestial Jerusalem of Chartres with its cathedral some four kilometers distant to the west.

Upon entering the church of Saint-Cheron, the assembled clergy commenced

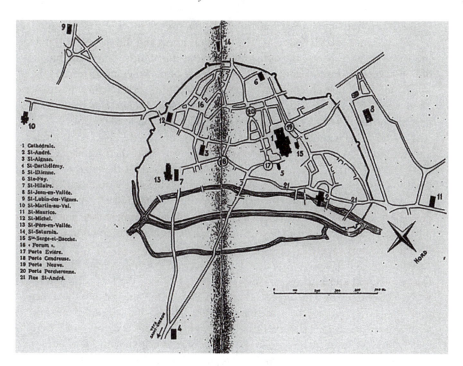

Figure 15.1 A map of medieval Chartres as drawn by Yves Delaporte

to sing antiphons in honor of that Chartrain saint.[27] The monks of Saint-Cheron and the canons and choirboys of the cathedral then proceeded to celebrate the office of Terce, at the end of which was read Matthew's account of Christ's entry into Jerusalem ("Cum appropinquasset . . ."; 21:1–9).[28] Immediately thereafter the bishop of Chartres blessed the palms and boxwood,[29] and the sacristan of the cathedral and the prior of the monastery distributed them to the faithful. Now the assembly departed from Saint-Cheron.[30] The cantor or succentor having intoned the ancient and exquisitely beautiful antiphon *Collegerunt pontifices,* clergy and laity descended the road back to Chartres, heading once again to the cemetery adjacent to Saint-Barthélemy.

At the great cross in the cemetery the clergy and populace stopped in station and divided themselves into two distinct performing groups. The bishop, cantor, priests, and deacons, and the multitude of townsfolk (*populus multus*) remained on the east side of the cross looking west. The succentor, subdeacons, and choirboys, all in a prearranged order, moved to their customary place (*consuetus locus*) on the west side and faced the other group to the east. With the choirboys singing the verses and the bishop's group and the succentor's group alternating with the refrain, they chanted the ninth-century processional hymn *Gloria laus et honor.*[31] This antiphonal singing of the *Gloria laus* was a musical and dramatic high point of the ceremony.

But it was not all that occurred at this station, for the ritual of the Adoration of the Cross immediately followed. The bishop's chorus and the succentor's choir proceeded in turn to sing the antiphon *Occurrunt turbe* three times, alternating bishop–succentor–bishop, and each time when one or the other group reached the words "filio dei," that ensemble prostrated itself on the ground before the cross. Then, while all the clergy chanted together the antiphon *Turba multa,* the bishop, or someone deputized by him, prepared to deliver a sermon to the people.

Yvo, the influential early twelfth-century bishop of Chartres, has left us a sermon for just this occasion. It concludes with an exhortation to the faithful of Chartres to allow the remembrance of the blood Christ spilled on the cross to incite them to greater fervor (PL 161:586–88). Perhaps in accordance with this theme, a separation of the unbelievers (or malefactors) from the faithful of Chartres was now effected: "If there is to be made a complaint of injury against the church, let it be made; and if anyone is to be excommunicated, let him be excommunicated," declare the sources.[32]

With the church now purified of miscreants, the assembly began the ascent back up the hill and into the city of Chartres. It followed the Rue Saint-Pierre, which led from the Benedictine house of Saint-Père up the hill and into the upper town (*haute ville*). Along the route the succentor intoned and the multitude sang after him a succession of antiphons and responsories, the texts of which were mainly reworkings of the four evangelists' accounts of Christ's entry into Jerusalem: A. *Ceperunt omnes,* A. *Cum audisset populus,* A. *Ante sex dies,* R. *Cum audisset turba,* R. *Dominus Jhesus ante sex dies,* and R. *Ingrediente domino.* At the Porte Cendreuse,[33] one of the half-dozen gates leading through the old walls into the upper town of Chartres, the clergy sang this last responsory, *Ingrediente domino.*[34] This chant, a Matins responsory on Palm Sunday at Chartres and elsewhere, was reserved for this special moment of "entry into Jerusalem" here in Chartres and in most of the other dioceses in northern France (see appendix B). Finally, as the procession passed through the west door of the cathedral of Notre-Dame, the spiritual theme, as communicated in the text of the plainsong, switched from one extolling Christ's triumph to one honoring the Virgin Mary (A. *Letare virgo* v. *Post partum virgo*).

Although this was a standard liturgical practice—to change to chants honoring the patron of the church at the moment of entry—the transition from chants for Palm Sunday to one for the Virgin is of interest here, for it occurred beneath a similar thematic transition represented in sculpture and glass. The tympanum of the west side of the famous royal portal, as is well known, is constructed around an imposing sculpture of Christ in Majesty surrounded by four apocalyptic animals symbolizing the four evangelists. Those in the procession celebrating the First Coming of Christ looked up to a vision of the ultimate prophecy, the majestic Second Coming of Christ, when He would judge the quick and the dead.

Passing through the portal and into the church, the sudden darkness brought to light, then as now, three of the finest examples of stained glass ever created, the dazzling twelfth-century lancet windows immediately below the great west rose. The largest and most central of these lancet windows, the one directly above the royal portal, is the Incarnation Window, which recounts the story of the principal events in the life of Christ up to, but not including, His passion and resurrection.[35] At the top of the central Incarnation Window are three panels depicting Christ's entry into Jerusalem on Palm Sunday (see figure 15.2). The telling in glass of the story of Palm Sunday concludes the history of His earthly life. Accordingly, these panels are then immediately surmounted by a great crowned Virgin and Child in Glory, a fitting capstone to the theme of the Word made flesh. Thus, just as the processional chants proceed from a theme commemorating Christ's final triumphant arrival to one honoring the Virgin, so the sculpture and stained glass directly above the heads of the clergy and laity of Chartres depict the same subjects. At this moment musical and visual arts stood in perfect harmony.

As the faithful reentered the cathedral the bells of the church rang again. Inside a candelabrum holding seven candles was illuminated, and the crosses and relics were left uncovered for the remainder of the day. Having entered the chancel and

Figure 15.2 Christ's entry into Jerusalem depicted in the Incarnation Window in the cathedral of Chartres

mounted to their choir stalls, the canons and chaplains of the cathedral again celebrated the office of Terce, just as they had earlier that morning at Saint-Cheron.[36]
High Mass then immediately followed. Briefly stated, these were the main features
of the Palm Sunday procession as it was celebrated at the cathedral of Chartres in
the late twelfth century.

Were this the extent of the information surviving from Notre-Dame of Chartres, the documentation describing this ceremony would be in no way exceptional.
What makes the case at Chartres unusual, perhaps unique, is that this entire Palm
Sunday procession is described by clerics having a second vantage point, namely
by the Canons Regular living at the nearby monastery of Saint-Jean-en-Vallée. Because the history of this Augustinian house is tightly bound to that of the cathedral
of Chartres, a brief discussion of the founding and development of this institution
is warranted.

Situated in a valley just a kilometer to the north of the cathedral, the ancient
collegiate church of Saint-Vincent was refounded in honor of St. John the Baptist
in 1099 by Bishop Yvo of Chartres, who commanded the resident clergy to adopt
a life according to the rule of St. Augustine.[37] In the succeeding decades of the
twelfth century two other churches near Chartres, La Madeleine at Châteaudun
and Notre-Dame at Gâtines, also came under Augustinian rule (Delaporte, *L'Ordinaire*, 11). Thus, by the middle of the twelfth century, there were no fewer than
four churches in the Augustinian nexus in proximity to Chartres: Saint-Jean-en-
Vallée and Saint-Cheron, both just outside the city walls, and, far more distant, La
Madeleine at Châteaudun and Notre-Dame at Gâtines. Because these houses had
been refounded by bishops of Chartres, their liturgies were virtually identical, at
least at the outset of the reform of these institutions, with that at the cathedral.[38]
For this reason, information preserved in their liturgical books is often relevant to
ceremonies practiced at the cathedral, and this is especially true for the procession
of Palm Sunday. Two manuscripts, an ordinal from the mid-twelfth century (Paris
lat. 1794) and a notated missal from the thirteenth (Chartres, BM 529), reveal how
clerics from a filial church participated in the great general procession.[39] (The Latin
account of MS 529 follows that of MS 520 in appendix A.)

Preceded by copies of the Gospel and by crosses, the Augustinian canons of
Saint-Jean-en-Vallée departed from their monastery and headed east up the hill to
the cathedral. They passed through the Porte de Saint-Jean and into the close of
the canons, finally entering the church itself by means of the north door. En route
they chanted the same set of responsories (*responsoria de historia*), beginning with
In die qua invocavi te, which earlier they had sung at Matins and which they would
soon sing again when the general procession left the mother church. Once inside
the chancel of the cathedral, the canons of Saint-Jean arranged themselves two by
two, faced the high altar, and chanted the antiphon *Aula Maria dei* in honor of the
Virgin. Because descriptions of how the Divine Office unfolded around the high
altar of Chartres are rare in the extreme, the subsequent actions of the Augustinians deserve to be quoted in full:

> Next, once both sides of [our chorus], joined two by two, have passed
> through the chancel, they humbly bow toward the altar at the point at which

they reach the left corner of the altar; and thus, having progressed behind the altar and genuflected at the altar of the Holy Trinity, they say the Lord's Prayer and salutation of the Blessed Virgin Mary [the *Ave Maria*]. And they should sit there in order without talking until the time of moving forth shall come.

When the time for beginning the procession shall arrive and all Gospels and crosses have been arranged in the middle of the chancel, the processions move forward, preceded by banners, a dragon, crosses, and the Gospel books, in which assembly next walk the priests of the parish churches, next the canons of Saint-Cheron, next we canons of Saint-Jean, and finally the canons of the mother church. At the threshold of the chancel, the cantor or the succentor of Chartres begins the responsory *In die qua invocavit* with the verse and the repetendum [a repeat of the end of the respond]. When that responsory has been sung, however, we canons of Saint-Jean-en-Vallée re-commence that responsory with its verse and repetendum, and so with each of the other responsories which the canons of Chartres will sing up to the church of Saint-Barthélemy.

A number of points beg attention here. Obviously both the chancel and the sanctuary, including the high altar and the altar of the Trinity immediately behind it, are utilized as staging areas for the clergy while the full general procession takes shape. Undoubtedly the canons of Saint-Jean moved into the area of the sanctuary so as to make room for the processional groups from other churches gathering before them in the chancel.

As with all medieval clerical processions, there was at Chartres a protocol that reflected the status of the participating churches. The clergy of institutions of lesser rank preceded those of greater importance. Here on Palm Sunday the order of the march was priests of the parish churches, canons of Saint-Cheron, canons of Saint-Jean, and finally, canons of the cathedral. Invariably, the bishop of the diocese came last. Clerics from other churches and lay persons undoubtedly joined the procession as it passed through the streets; the *Ordo veridicus,* for example, mentions that the monks from Saint-Martin-au-Val entered the line of march at the priory of Saint-Barthélemy. No hint, however, is found of any participation by the Benedictines of the powerful house of Saint-Père situated between the cathedral and the church of Saint-Barthélemy.[40] As at Paris at this time, the cloistered monks seem not to have been part of the urban Palm Sunday procession. This ceremony was mainly an affair of the clergy of "this world," of the secular canons and parish priests.

Toward the head of the general procession went a mock dragon, a creature which undoubtedly did much to excite the imagination of the populace. The dragon of Chartres was no mere banner with a painted emblem, but an effigy probably made of wood and straw manipulated by an employee of the cathedral (called the *dragonarius*).[41] As such, he was a regular participant in liturgical ceremonies at the church. He appeared at processions on the feast of St. Mark, on Ascension, and on the Rogation Days when the clergy went to the nearby collegiate church Saint-Aignan.[42] In this folkloric practice Chartres was not alone, for many cities in medieval France—Paris, Rouen, Orléans, Laon, Bayeux, Metz, Tarascon, and Provins among them—had their mythical dragon, serpent, lizard, or *gargouille*.[43] If the Gospel book, or the Host, or a carved Christ seated on a donkey represented the presence of the Lord in the midst of the Palm Sunday procession,[44] the dragon embodied the spirit of evil, a malevolent force that Christ would vanquish by means of His passion and Ascension. The early thirteenth-century Parisian theologian Praepositinus Cremonensis mentions a widespread tradition in which the dragon departs from the church with a long tail and returns with short one, thereby signifying Christ's victory over the forces of evil.[45] At Chartres, the *trumeau* of the south porch represents an enormous Christ whose intentionally enlarged feet press down upon a lion and a serpent-dragon, thereby revealing as truth the prophecy of Ps. 91 (Vulgate 90) in which it is foretold that the Lord will trample these two animals, symbols of the Antichrist and the Devil, respectively.[46]

As the general procession set forth from the cathedral the *responsoria de historia*—the plainsong accompaniment for the journey to Saint-Barthélemy—were sung not once, but at least twice. The canons of the cathedral chanted each one first, and then the canons of Saint-Jean repeated that same plainsong in its entirety with the identical mode of execution (respond–verse–repetendum). Since the clergy of other churches were also present, it is even possible that these responsories were sung more than twice. The canons of Saint-Cheron, for example, may have taken their turn, perhaps thereby assuring that chant would be heard throughout the duration of the lengthy journey.[47]

Once the general procession from the cathedral of Chartres reached its first station in the cemetery of Saint-Barthélemy, the clergy rearranged itself. As we have seen, the main march, including the monks of Saint-Martin-au-Val who had come over from their priory, continued on up the hill to Saint-Cheron. But now the canons of Saint-Jean stayed behind and entered the priory of Saint-Barthélemy. There they celebrated Terce, read Matthew's account of Christ's entry into Jerusalem, and blessed and distributed the palms to the faithful. In sum, they did precisely what the main procession would do when it entered Saint-Cheron. Then, when the principal group had returned from Saint-Cheron to the cemetery outside Saint-Barthélemy's, the canons of Saint-Jean went outside to rejoin them. Presumably these clerics of Saint-Jean were excused from marching up the hill to Saint-Cheron because they had already come a considerable distance, from the valley of Saint-Jean up the hill to the cathedral and down the other side to the priory of Saint-Barthélemy—and they would have to retrace their steps returning home.

The entry of the general procession into Chartres, as previously mentioned, was accomplished to the sounds of a collection of antiphons and responsories, the texts of which were mainly drawn from the evangelists' accounts of Christ's triumphant arrival: *Ceperunt omnes, Cum audisset populus, Ante sex dies, Cum audisset turba, Dominus Jhesus ante sex dies,* and *Ingrediente domino.* But during this chanting the canons of Saint-Jean were silent. For a reason that will soon become apparent, they neither sang with the canons of the cathedral nor repeated these chants after them. Once the general procession reentered the cathedral, the clerical groups of the participating churches began to disengage themselves so as to return to their particular churches. While the canons of Notre-Dame entered the chancel singing an antiphon to the Virgin (*Letare virgo*), those of Saint-Jean passed through the cathedral now chanting *Ceperunt omnes* and *Collegerunt pontifices* quietly, presumably so as not to disturb the service of the cathedral canons inside the chancel. Here is yet further proof that in large churches in the Middle Ages various liturgical rites were performed simultaneously. In this case the canons of Chartres sang and offered prayers to the Virgin inside the chancel while their Augustinian counterparts chanted a commemoration of Christ's entry into Jerusalem outside the chancel walls.

With the lengthy *Collegerunt pontifices* providing musical inspiration along the route, the canons of Saint-Jean-en-Vallée left the cathedral and returned to their monastery. As they passed through the gate of their compound they began the responsory *Ingrediente domino,* which they had refrained from singing with the general procession during the entrance into the city at the Porte Cendreuse. Then, exiting immediately from the choir of their church, the canons made a circuit of their cloister. They passed before the infirmary, where either the hebdomadary priest or the master of ceremonies said a blessing, and, finally, reentered the chancel of their abbey, where they then sang the office of Terce. As often happened when a clergy left its choir stalls to go forth in procession, a "double office" resulted.[48] In Chartres the canons of the cathedral said Terce twice (first at Saint-Cheron and then again at the cathedral), as did those of Saint-Jean (first at Saint-Barthélemy and then again back home at Saint-Jean-en-Vallée).

Was the procession for Palm Sunday in medieval Chartres in any way distinctive or unusual? Certainly the plainsong sung by the clergy in procession was in no way exceptional: that is to say, not one of the processional and stational chants sung here was unique to Chartres. Many of them, including the antiphons *Ante sex dies, Ceperunt omnes, Cum audisset populus,* and *Occurrunt turbe,* as well as the responsories *Ingrediente domino, Circumdederunt me,* and *Collegerunt pontifices,* are preserved in literally hundreds of medieval liturgical sources throughout Europe.[49] Others, namely the responsories *Dominus Jhesus ante sex dies* and *Cum audisset turba,* were somewhat less widespread but nonetheless were known as far north as England, in the case of the former, and as far south as Spain, in the instance of the latter.[50] The history of *Cum audisset turba,* which is found in the earliest source of the Mozarabic rite, points up the fact that many chants for the Palm Sunday procession are of great antiquity. It, like the equally venerable *Collegerunt pontifices* and *Cum audisset populus,* originated in the Gallican rite, the liturgical usage indigenous to Gaul prior to the imposition of Roman practices there in the eighth and ninth centuries (Huglo 1980b, 115 and 117). While many Gallican chants were suppressed during this Carolingian reform, other melodies found a new liturgical home in portions of the Christian service for which nothing was prescribed in the Roman books (Huglo 1980c, 280–81). Since by the ninth century a procession for Palm Sunday was well established in Gaul, but not in Rome, Gallican chants continued to be used on this day in the Caroligian Empire, to fill a gap in the imported Roman service. This was as true in Paris, Metz, and Reims as it was in Chartres. Likewise during the ninth century, these Carolingian churches augmented the supply of musical material for Palm Sunday by embracing several newly created Frankish pieces, most notably the enormously popular processional hymn *Gloria laus et honor* written by Theodulf of Orléans about 830 (See n. 31 above).

Gloria laus et honor, as we have seen, began the dramatic station at the cross in the cemetery next to the church of Saint-Barthélemy. Similarly, nearly all other cathedrals in the northwest of Europe made use of this chant at some point in the rites for Palm Sunday, and almost invariably it was performed with the adults chanting the refrain and the choirboys singing the verses. But although *Gloria laus et honor* was ubiquitous, nonetheless each institution had its own particular tradition for the melody of the refrain as well for the reciting tone of the verses. The comparison offered in example 15.1 reveals in what ways the Chartrain version of the refrain differed from those of nearby and more distant liturgical usages. In this respect *Gloria laus* is typical of the Palm Sunday melodies: although the churches drew from a common fund of plainsong, local variants for each and every chant existed in all dioceses.

But if all institutions drew upon the same pool of chants, accommodating local variants in the melodies as shown in example 15.1, what then was distinctive about Palm Sunday at Chartres? Certainly the selection of chants and the order in which they came was unique. Yet this same unique quality obtained within each and every diocese: no two northern cathedral churches sang the same chants in the same order. What is more, there appears not to have been a prescribed order for the various parts of the ceremony (see appendix B). The procession might come after rather than before Terce. The palms might be blessed in the cathedral church and before the procession started, or they might be blessed at a stational church. The sermon might come before or after the blessing of the palms.

Discounting, therefore, local melodic variants as well as the peculiarities that occurred everywhere due to local autonomy in arranging the particulars of the ceremony, the distinctive qualities of the Palm Sunday procession at Chartres appear to have been the following. First, the general procession to the church where the palms were blessed, Saint-Cheron, was a sung procession: specifically, the responsories of Matins of that day accompanied the marchers. In most usages the procession to the stational church for the blessing of the palms was done silently: the thirteenth-century ordinal of Metz, for example, explicitly states that the canons of the cathedral made their way to the church of Saint-Symphorien "nihil cantando",[51] whereas the ordinal of Bayeux declares, in regard to the procession to the stational church of Saint-Vigor, "nihil dicitur in eundo" ("nothing is said en route").[52] Of the more than twenty French secular and monastic usages surveyed, only one other, that of the cathedral of Soissons, prescribed a procession with music to the stational church (Paris, BNF lat. 8898, fol. 45). In truth, the silent procession to the stational church makes more sense for a historical reenactment of the events of Palm Sunday, for it was only Christ's one-way entry into Jerusalem that the clergy celebrated.

The Chartrain practice of singing the *Gloria laus* in the cemetery of Saint-Barthélemy, and thus far removed from the town, was likewise unusual. Most churches reserved the processional hymn *Gloria laus* until the moment of return to a gate guarding the city at which the voices of a group of soloists, usually choir-

Example 15.1   Hymn *Gloria laus et honor* (refrain)

(*continued*)

boys, singing from inside the gate alternated with a larger choir still outside. In medieval Paris the choirboys were placed within the Châtelet that guarded the entry to the Île de la Cité from the south; they sang out to the larger choir that stood on the Petit Pont bridging the Seine (Wright 1989, 189). At Salisbury cathedral the *Gloria laus* was delayed even further; it was sung only at the moment of entry into the mother church, the choirboys singing down antiphonally from an interior gallery and sounding for all the world like the angels of God (see Blum 1986, 145–50).

Finally, although a fully sung Palm Sunday procession and a distant *Gloria laus* were exceptional, the distinction "unique to Chartres" rests with the ceremony of excommunication that occurred shortly after the singing of the *Gloria laus*. Whether an opportunity to remove publicly from the Christian community those malefactors who had done injury to the church (or, rightly said, to the clergy of

Example 15.1   (*continued*)

Chartres), or whether a vestige of an ancient Gallican practice of expelling temporarily those who had not yet been welcomed into the church as communicants, this
was a singular ritual. Judging from the surviving ordinals, it was without parallel in
the Palm Sunday rites of all other French churches.

The Palm Sunday procession at Chartres, including the ceremony of the excommunication, continued on without fundamental change for centuries. Sometime
toward the end of the fifteenth century the dramatic *Attollite portas* ritual was
added to the ceremony at the moment the general procession returned to the cathedral.[53] Here the bishop would strike the closed royal portal three times with the
base of the cross and then sing out: "Open your doors and raise the eternal gates,
and the King of glory will enter." To this an ensemble of choirboys inside the
church responded: "Who is this king of glory?" And to this the bishop in turn
replied: "A strong and powerful Lord, mighty in his battle; open your doors and

Example 15.1   (*continued*)

raise the eternal gates, and the King of glory will enter."[54] And so the question and respond continued *alternatim* for several verses, and ultimately the great door swung open and the procession entered the church now chanting the responsory *Ingrediente domino.*

In this more dramatic fashion the Palm Sunday service was celebrated at Chartres until sometime during the late seventeenth century, when a wholesale revision of the music occurred. The ancient *responsoria de historia* as well as the lengthy and equally ancient processional antiphons were replaced by simple antiphons and psalms. Undoubtedly this reflected a diminished reliance on aural memory and oral tradition for the learning and performance of chant. Certainly all of the music for the procession of Palm Sunday at Chartres prior to the late seventeenth century was sung by memory.[55] Aside from the fact that books are particularly awkward to use during a processional march, the capitular acts of the cathedral had long decreed that not only the antiphons and psalms of the ferial psalter, but also the *responsoria de historia* be committed to memory as a condition of employment in the choir of the church.[56] Evidently, by the late seventeenth century the singing men at Chartres no longer had these old lengthy and difficult chants in their ears and had begun to rely more and more on music chanted to simple, repetitive psalm tones. This sign that the clergy of Chartres had lessened its reliance on oral practices only in the seventeenth century bespeaks a very belated transition from the ancient to the modern musical world. Indeed, the deeply rooted medieval tradition of the Palm Sunday procession was slow to lose its hold on the spiritual imagination of the churchmen at Chartres. As late as 1783 the clergy were still making the trek out to Saint-Cheron on that day, though presumably with far fewer faithful than had participated in the Middle Ages.[57] Then in 1784, in an apparent recognition of diminished popular fervor, the bishop and canons decided to process henceforth only to the nearby Franciscan monastery for the blessing of the psalms.[58] Finally, with Revolutionary sentiments of secular humanism sweeping down from Paris, the ceremony was suppressed in its entirety in 1790 (Clerval 1899, 273). At Chartres the colorful tradition of a great medieval pageant had come to an end.

Appendix A: The Palm Sunday procession at Chartres

Chartres, BM 520 (Cathedral of Chartres; early thirteenth century

[Fol. 128] Dominica in ramis palmarum. Antequam ordinetur processio sonent diu duo signa magna et exeunte processione fiat classicum. Processio cum textis et crucibus et capsa sine cereis eat. Qua ordinata incipit succentor responsoria de historia per ordinem, reservato *Ingrediente domino* et R. *Insurrexerunt* [fol. 128v] usque ad reditum ante portam civitatis. Ubi vero conveniunt simul processiones cum nostra incipit cantor [MS 1058: Et quando conveniunt processiones in cymiterium sancti Bartholomei incipit cantor vel succentor summa voce] R. *Circumdederunt* cum versu et regressu et aliud R. *Insurrexerunt* cum versu et regressu donec veniant ad ecclesiam sancti Caruanni [*sic*].

Illis intrantibus incipit cantor R. [*sic*] *O beate* vel R. [*sic*] *O quantus es* V. *Gloria et honore;* sequitur oratio. [1058: A. *O beate athleta* vel *O quam gloriosus* V. *Gloria et honore* et oratio de sancto.] Qua finita dicunt terciam: hymnus *Nunc sancte nobis spiritus* A. *Pueri hebreorum* [*tollentes ramos*]. In fine non dicitur pneuma [1058: in fine antiphone] nec capitulum. Duo clerici R. *Osanna* V. *Pueri hebreorum* sine *Gloria* et ab eisdem repetatur R. *Osanna*, V. *De ore leonis* [1058: Duo canonici de v. statu cantent R. *Osanna* in medio choro cum versu sine *Gloria*, rursum incipiunt responsorium illi qui cantaverunt. Duo pueri dicant V. *De ore leonis*]. Sequitur oratio [1058: Sequitur oratio *Omnipotens sempiterne deus da nobis*]. Post orationem legitur evangelium *Cum appropinquasset* [Matt. 21:1–9]. Deinde benedicuntur omni palmarum et aliarum arborum frondes. Capicerius dividat palmas et abbas

sancti Carauni dividat buxum. [1058: Dum tercia benedicuntur flores arborum et
capicerius noster dat palmas et prepositus sancti Carauni dat buxum, postea si
episcopus voluerit facit sermonem in ipsa ecclesia, vel ad crucem.] Postea pergant
ad crucem. [fol. 129]

Egressa processione de ecclesia [1058: Carauni] cantor vel succentor incipit A.
Collegerunt cum versu quod sufficit usque ad crucem. Episcopo autem remanente
[1058: ex parte orientis] cum capsis et crucibus et cantore, sacerdotibus et diaconi-
bus et populo multo, succentor transgreditur crucem usque ad consuetum locum
cum subdiaconibus et iuvenibus et pueris albis indutis, prius statutis diligenter per
ordinem. Incipiunt pueri *Gloria laus et honor** [* = complete music given]. Quo
finito incipiat episcopus aut cantor ex illa parte iterum *Gloria laus* post pueri aliud
V. *Israel es tu rex;* succentor cum choro iterum [fol. 129v] *Gloria laus;* pueri V. *Cetus
in excelsis;* episcopus aut cantor *Gloria laus;* pueri *Plebs hebrea;* et succentor cum
choro *Gloria laus.* Pueri eant.

Episcopus aut cantor incipiat A. *Occurrunt turbe,* cum dixerint "filio dei," pro-
sternant se ad terram; iterum succentor incipiat ex parte sua A. *Occurrunt turbe;*
episcopus aut cantor incipit A. *Occurrunt turbe* et fit genuflexio de parte episcopi
ijᵃ et de parte succentoris una tantum. Tunc episcopus aut cantor A. *Turbea [sic]
multa,* postea veniant ad crucem cum textis et crucibus. Deinde faciat episcopus
sermonem ad populum aut aliquis cui iusserit; et querelam iniurrariarum [fol.
130] ecclesie si quis excommunicaturus est excommunicetur. Postea episcopus
faciat benedictionem.

Illis redeuntibus [1058: Redeunte processione et transito sancto Bartholomeo]
incipit cantor A. *Ceperunt omnes* A. *Cum audisset populus** [fol. 130v]. Sequitur
alia antiphona: *Ante sex dies sollempnitatis** R. *Cum audisset turba* [fol. 131] V. *Et
cum appropinquasset. Cum ramis.** R. *Dominus Ihesus* V. *Convenerunt. Quem sus.**

Illis intrantibus [Paris, BNF lat. 1265: Cum ramis] in portam civitatis incipit
cantor R. *Ingrediente domino* V. *Cum audisset.* Quo finito A. *Letare virgo.* V. *Post
partum virgo.* Oratio *Famulorum tuorum* vel de sancto cuius est ecclesia. Videndum
est ut cum regressa fuerit processio [fol. 131v] ascensi septem cerei [1058: et sonetur
classicum] et altaria sint discoperta et capsae, et sic permaneant tota die [1058: et
nocte] cum textis et crucibus. Tunc dicitur tercia: hymnus *Nunc sancte nobis* A.
Pueri hebreorum cum pneuma sine capitulo R. *Fratres mei* V. *Amici mei* V. *De ore
leonis.*

Dominica in ramis palmarum ad missam *Domine ne longe.* . . .

Chartres, BM 529 (Abbey of Saint-Jean-en-Vallée; thirteenth century)

[Fol. 58v] Dominica in ramis palmarum. Matutina missa non dicitur nisi forte
continguat quod processio ad sanctam Karaunum non eat, et tunc missa erit de
Trinitate. Antequam ordinetur processio sonantur diu duo magna signa. Parata
processione cum textu et crucibus precedentibus vexillis, exeunte processione de
choro, incipit cantor R. *In die qua invocavi te* cum versu et regressu et sic cetera
responsoria de hystoria sicut sunt in ordinem excepto R. *Ingrediente domino* usque

ad ecclesiam Beate Marie. Ministri vero qui portant textum et cruces induantur capis rubicundis; subdiaconus vero ebdomadarius debet portare textum et debet esse rasus de novo.

Intrante itaque processione magnam ecclesiam Beate Marie, ordinamus nos in medio ecclesie secundum ordinem chori nostri hinc et inde versis vultibus ad altare Beate Marie. Ministri portantes textum et cruces sint in medio secundum suum ordinem sic versis vultibus ad altare, et tunc cantor noster incipit antiphonam de Beata Maria A. *Aula Maria dei.* Finita antiphona cantor V. *Post partum inviolata permansisti,* sacerdos ebdomadarius collecta *Famulorum tuorum* que finitur "per eundem dominum amen benedicamus domino." Deinde uterque chorus simul iuncti bini et bini humiliter chorum transeuntes. Cum per sinistrum cornu altaris transierint humiliter se inclinant ad altare; et sic, retro altare ingressi flexis genibus circa altare Sancte Trinitatis, dicent orationem dominicam et salutationem Beate Marie Virginis; et sedeant ibi ordinate sine fabulationibus usque quo tempus progrediendi adveniat.

Cum vero tempus progrediendi advenerit, textis et crucibus omnibus in medio chori ordinatis, progrediuntur processiones, in quo processu, precedentibus vexillis, dracone, crucibus et textis, progrediuntur deinde presbiteri parrochiales, post canonici Sancti Karauni, deinde nos canonici Sancti Johannis, de hinc canonici matris ecclesie. In ipso autem limine chori cantor carnotensis aut succentor incipit R. *In die qua invocavit* cum versu et regressu. Finito responsorio nos vero canonici de Valleia reincipimus eundem responsorium cum versu et regressu, et sic cetera responsoria quod canonici carnotensis cantabunt usque ad ecclesiam beati Bartholomei. Processiones vero transeunt per ante ecclesiam beati Bartholomei et vadunt ad sanctum Karaunum et ministri nostri portantes cruces et textum in ordine suo vadunt cum illis. Nos vero canonici Valleia intramus ecclesiam beati Bartholomei et ibi sumus usque dum redeant processiones de sancto Karauno.

Intrante processione nostra in ecclesiam beati Bartholomei cantor incipit antiphonam *Vos estis qui permansistis,* cantor vero V. *In omnem terram* V. *Nimis honorati* sacerdos ebdomadarius collecta *Quesumus omnipotens ut benedic,* que finitur "per dominum." Hora tercia ibi dicatur. Incipitur ex altera parte ex qua non est septimana *Deus in adjutorium,* hymnus *Nunc sancte,* antiphona *Pueri hebreorum,* post *Legem pone.* In fine antiphone non dicitur neupma nec dicitur capitulum. Duo canonici electi ad voluntatem cantoris R. *Osanna* V. *Pueri hebreorum* sine *Gloria* ab eisdem qui cantant, repetitur responsorium *Osanna.* Juvenis canonicus ex parte illius septimane V. *De ore leonis,* sequitur oratio *Omnipotens da nobis* ita dominice passionis, que finitur "per dominum benedicamus domino." Finita tercia a diacono pallij capa induto legatur evangelium *Cum appropinquassent* et a sacerdote ebdomadario benedicuntur rami palmarum et alia arborum flores et dividantur singulis a capicerio.

Redeunte ad crucem processione Beate Marie cum ceteris processionibus, egreditur processio nostra de ecclesia beati Bartholomei obviam eis. Succentor vero carnotensis cum suo choro ex occidentali parte stationem facit. Nos vero iuxta illos sumus. Tunc unus de pueris ex parte succentoris alta voce incipit v. *Gloria laus.* Nos vero stantes iuxta illos cum illis cantamus. Finito v. *Gloria laus* incipit episcopus aut cantor ex alia parte V. *Gloria laus.* Post pueri alium V. *Israel es tu* et succentor cum choro iterum V. *Gloria laus,* pueri V. *Cetus in excelsis.* Episcopus aut cantor V. *Gloria laus,* pueri V. *Plebs hebrea* et succentor cum choro V. *Gloria laus.* Episcopus aut cantor A. *Occurrunt turbe* et cum dixerunt "filio dei" prosternunt se ad terram episcopus cum suo choro tantum. Qua finita incipiat succentor cum suo choro A. *Occurrunt turbe* et prosternunt se ad terram similiter. Episcopus aut cantor A. *Occurrunt turbe* et prosternunt se ad terram iterum. Deinde succentor A. *Turba multa* continuo conveniunt ad crucem.

Hiis omnibus adimpletis benedictione facta ab episcopo processionibus redeuntibus, incipit cantor carnotensis A. *Ceperunt omnes turbe* A. *Cum audisset populus.* Nos vero canonici de Valleia in reditu illo post illos nichil cantamus.

Intrantibus illis in civitatem incipit cantor illorum R. *Ingrediente.* Cum vero perventum fuerit ad ecclesiam Beate Marie, processione ejusdem ecclesie chorum intrante, nos canonici de Valleia per eandem ecclesiam transeuntes, in eodem ingressu incipit cantor noster A. *Ceperunt omnes;* deinde incipit submissa voce A. *Collegerunt* posteaque finitur ad portam abbatie nostre.

In introitu porte abbatie nostre incipit cantor R. *Ingrediente domino.* De hinc fratres exeuntes de choro transeunt per claustrum et vadunt ante infirmaria et ibi ab ebdomadario vel a magistro ordinis dicitur *Benedicite.* Statim pulsatur ad terciam. Tunc redeuntes omnes in chorum ab ebdomadario incipitur tercia.

Appendix B: A summary comparison of the Palm Sunday procession at Chartres with those at ten other northern French cathedrals

Chartres (Chartres, BM 520, fol. 128)

1. Prime at cathedral
2. *responsoria de historia* en route to priory of Saint-Barthélemy
3. *Circumdederunt* en route to abbey of Saint-Cheron
4. Terce at Saint-Cheron
5. reading of Gospel
6. blessing of the palms
7. *Collegerunt* en route to crucifix in cemetery outside Saint-Barthélemy
8. *Gloria laus* and *Occurrunt turbe* at station before the cross
9. ceremony of excommunication
10. procession with antiphons to Porte Cendreuse
11. *Ingrediente* entering the upper city
12. *Letare virgo* entering the cathedral
13. Terce again at cathedral

Amiens (Durand, Ordinaire, 217–19)

1. Prime at cathedral
2. blessing of palms at cathedral
3. *Pueri hebreorum* and other chants by divided (left and right) choirs

4. procession around town if weather favorable, within the cathedral if not
5. *Adoremus crucis signaculum* sung in station
6. reading of the Gospel
7. sermon
8. *Gloria laus* at city gate (within cathedral if raining)
9. *Ingrediente* entering cathedral
10. *Collegerunt* in choir of cathedral
11. Terce at cathedral

Bayeux (Chevalier, Ordinaire, *118–20)*

1. Prime at cathedral
2. silent procession to church of Saint-Vigor
3. Terce at Saint-Vigor
4. blessing of palms
5. procession "ad locum eminentem"
6. reading of the Gospel at the station
7. sermon at the station
8. procession "ad crucem consuetam"
9. procession with antiphons to gates of city
10. *Gloria laus* at gate
11. *Ingrediente* entering the city and entering the cathedral
12. *Collegerunt* inside cathedral
13. Sext at cathedral

Laon (Chevalier, Ordinaires . . . Laon, *104–5)*

1. Prime at cathedral
2. silent procession to abbey of Saint-Martin
3. (no office at Saint-Martin)
4. blessing of palms
5. reading of Gospel
6. *Gloria laus* still at Saint-Martin
7. sermon
8. procession with antiphons from Saint-Martin to gates of the city
9. *Ingrediente* at gate
10. *Collegerunt* entering the cathedral
11. Terce at cathedral

Metz (Paris, BNF lat. 990, fol. 43v)

1. bishop and his attendants go to church of Saint-Arnoul Saturday evening
2. bishop blesses palms at Saint-Arnoul Sunday morning after Prime
3. reading of the Gospel
4. canons of cathedral process silently to Saint-Symphorien
5. blessing of palms by the dean

6. reading of the Gospel
7. *Occurrunt turbe* as palms are distributed
8. bishop and his clergy and canons join in a field before a cross
9. sermon
10. procession with antiphons to the Gate of the Serpent
11. *Collegerunt* and *Gloria laus* before the gate
12. stations at several churches as procession moves to the cathedral
13. *Pueri hebreorum tollentes* entering the cathedral
14. Terce at cathedral

Paris (Brussels, BR 1799, fol. 31)

1. Prime at cathedral
2. silent procession to abbey of Sainte-Geneviève
3. blessing of palms
4. reading of the Gospel
5. sermon
6. *Circumdederunt* at "station on the road"
7. *Gloria laus* at gate of the city
8. *Ingrediente* entering the city
9. *Tota pulchra es* entering the cathedral
10. Terce at cathedral

Reims (Chevalier, Sacramentaire, 118–20)

1. Prime at cathedral
2. silent procession to abbey Saint-Pierre-lès-Dames
3. blessing of palms by archbishop
4. *Collegerunt* exiting Saint-Pierre-lès-Dames
5. station before the cross at Saint-Maurice
6. reading of the Gospel
7. sermon
8. *Magno salutis gaudio* en route to abbey of Saint-Denis
9. *Gloria laus* with choirboys in "old tower" of Saint-Denis
10. *Ingrediente* entering the city
11. *Gloria laus* and *Ingrediente* again at entry to cathedral
12. procession around cloister, *Ingrediente* when reentering cathedral
13. Terce at cathedral

Rouen (Ordinario ms. ad usum ejusdem ecclesiae = PL 147:117–19)

1. Terce at cathedral
2. blessing of palms at cathedral
3. procession with antiphons around the cathedral
4. Gospel read in pulpit of cathedral
5. procession with antiphons to station "ad locum determinatum"

6. sermon, then antiphonal singing of *Salve, quem Jesum*
7. procession with antiphons to doors of the city
8. *Gloria laus* before the gate, six boys sing from the tower
9. *Ingrediente* entering the city
10. *Collegerunt* entering the cathedral
11. *Circumdederunt* by four from pulpit at the rood screen
12. Mass at cathedral

Sens (Paris, BNF lat. 1206, fol. 55)

1. Prime at cathedral
2. [silent procession to unnamed stational church]
3. blessing of palms
4. *Occurrunt turbe, Pueri hebreorum,* and *Pueri hebreorum* [*tollentes?*] sung during distribution of the palms
5. sermon
6. procession returns to the city singing antiphons
7. *Gloria laus* at the city gate
8. *Ingrediente* entering city
9. *Ave rex* and other antiphons en route to the cathedral
10. *Collegerunt* entering the cathedral
11. Terce at cathedral

Soissons (Paris, BNF lat. 8898, fol. 45)

1. Prime at cathedral
2. procession exits singing *Magno salutis gaudio* en route to Saint-Pierre
3. Terce at Saint-Pierre
4. *Pueri hebreorum tollentes* during blessing of the palms
5. procession to Notre-Dame with antiphons
6. reading of the Gospel
7. *Gloria laus* at return to the cathedral
8. *Ingrediente* entering cathedral
9. Mass at cathedral

Notes

I wish to thank Abbé Pierre Bizeau, director of the Archives du diocèse de Chartres, for numerous kindnesses extended during sojourns in that city in March 1992 and July 1994, as well as Professor Margot Fassler, who generously shared both ideas and her personal copies of microfilms of Chartrain sources not available in Chartres or Paris.

1. Such a liturgical drama took place in the nave at the monastery at Speyer and at the nunnery of Origny-Saint-Benoît near Saint-Quentin, for example. Numerous examples of this sort are cited in Young, *The Drama,* 1, chap. 13.

2. The pediluvium at most cathedrals and collegiate churches usually transpired in the chapter house. For details with regard to this ceremony at Notre-Dame of Paris, see

Wright (1989), 53–54. At Notre-Dame of Chartres it seems as if the Washing of the Feet took place in the nave of the cathedral (Chartres, AdE-L G 504, liasse, no folio).

3. It was traditional for the penitents to be sent forth by the bishop from the west door of the nave, historically the people's end of the church. For the tradition at Notre-Dame of Chartres, see Delaporte, *L'Ordinaire*, 97, and Orléans, BM 144, fol. 105v; for Notre-Dame of Paris, see Paris, BNF lat. 961, fol. 113.

4. In the late Middle Ages a procession in which the different clergies of the city participated was by definition a "general" procession (Delaporte 1922, 207). Bailey (1971) is the only work that approximates a general history of the music and liturgy of ecclesiastical processions in the West. Also useful is Huglo (1980c).

5. For general discussions of Palm Sunday and its procession, see "Palm Sunday," *CE* 11:432–33; "Palm Sunday," *NCE* 10:934–45; "Palme," *DACL* 13/1:954–57; and "Karwoche," *LThK* (1961) 6:4–5.

6. Matt. 21:1–11; Mark 11:1–11; Luke 19:29–38; and John 12:12–15.

7. The most accessible edition of Egeria's account of the events she witnessed on Palm Sunday is that of Paul Geyer, *Itinera*, 39:83–84.

8. The bishop served as the *figura* of Christ in this reenactment ("et sic deducetur episcopus in eo typo quo tunc Dominus deductus est"; "and so the bishop was led in a manner in which the Lord then was led"), ed. Geyer, 84.

9. Hermann Graef (1959) offers an exhaustive documentary study of the development of the ritual of Palm Sunday, from its very beginnings to its ultimate adoption in Rome, while Bailey (1971), 115–17, provides a concise synopsis of what is generally the same material. A general discussion, along with extensive bibliography, of the migration of liturgical practices from Jerusalem to the West is found in Jeffery (1994).

10. Isidore mentions a "dies palmarum" in his *De ecclesiasticis officiis* (PL 83:763) and in his *Etymologiae*, 6.18.13, but without a specific reference either to the blessing of the palms or to a procession. Also, the León Antiphoner (León, Catedral 8; facs. ed. in Brou and Vives) contains seven chants for the Palm Sunday procession. Although this Mozarabic source dates from the tenth century, it is apparently a faithful copy of an eighth-century exemplar (Brou 1950, 3–10).

11. The earliest of these, which dates not much after 800, is an *ordo* written by Abbot Angilbert for the Benedictine house of Saint-Riquier just outside Abbéville. It describes a modest procession with several stations *in via* (Bishop 1918a, 320–22).

12. *De officiis*, 1:10 (Amalarius, *Opera*, 2:58): "In memoriam illius rei nos per ecclesias nostras solemus portare ramos et clamare Hosanna" ("In memory of that event we traditionally carry palms through our church and cry out 'Hosanna'").

13. Hermann Graef (1959), 137–42; Bailey (1971), 116; and *NCE* 10:934.

14. The following sources are listed in Delaporte, *L'Ordinaire*, 203–13, and discussed more fully in Fassler (1993a), 87–89. Following Delaporte and Fassler it was possible to consult more than 20 other manuscripts of Chartrain usage relevant to this study that corroborate and occasionally add to the information contained in the three primary sources. These corroborative manuscripts appear in Fassler's list as numbers 4–8, 11–12, 14, 16, 18, 19, 22–26, 31–32, 34–36.

15. Facsimile edition now available in Hiley, *Missale*. Hiley's assessment of the date of MS 520 concludes that it was copied between 1225 and 1250 (pp. 7–8). However, his dating is based, in part, on a confusion of the date of the *natale* and canonization of St. Thomas of Canterbury (1173) with the date of that saint's *translatio* (1220). There is, in fact, no celebration in the Sanctorale of the manuscript that commemorates a ceremony inaugurated after 1173. This oversight in no way diminishes the value of Hiley's exceptional edition.

16. MS 1058 was destroyed, along with MSS 520 and 529 (see below) and most of the medieval library at Chartres, in the horrible, inadvertent bombing of the Bibliothèque

municipale on 26 May 1944. (The American army air force was attempting to cut the main railroad line from Paris into Brittany in preparation for D-Day; the French had stored the major treasures of the library in the château de Villebon outside Chartres, but the Germans ordered that they be brought back; the mayor of Chartres, a resistance leader, had stored a secret cache of petrol next to the library–and so acts of human heroism and folly were compounded disastrously; Delaporte, *Fragments*, 13–14; and verbal account told to the present writer in 1992 by Abbé Pierre Bizeau, Delaporte's associate and de facto literary executor.)

Fortunately, canon Yves Delaporte had made a copy of the *Ordo veridicus,* which is today preserved among his papers in the Archives du diocèse, as well as of MS 1058, which he subsequently published (Delaporte, *L'Ordinaire*). Microfilms of MSS 520 and 529 had been made before the war and may be consulted at the Bibliothèque municipale (microfiche number 26 and 25, respectively).

17. MS 1058 records the procession on the feast of St. Thomas of Canterbury as still proceeding to the crypt, where his relics were kept in the late twelfth and early thirteenth centuries. It makes no mention of the fact that, apparently upon completion of the St. Thomas of Canterbury window in the confessors chapel of the upper church (1220), this procession henceforth proceeded to this new monument in stained glass (Delaporte 1930, 221).

18. The early architectural history of the cathedral is discussed, among other places, in Hilberry (1959) and Branner (1969). A complete list of architectural studies done prior to the late 1980s can be found in Meulen (1989).

19. On days of inclement weather or when the streets were deemed not safe, the processions at Chartres remained within the cathedral (Delaporte, *L'Ordinaire*, 136; and AdE-L, supplément à la série G, MS 169, p. 7). The same was true at the cathedral of Amiens (Durand, *L'Ordinaire*, 217–18) and at other churches.

20. The prominence of the Gospel book is significant because it symbolized the presence of the body of Christ. Churches in other regions would later carry the Host to symbolize the presence of Christ (Normandy and England; see Bailey 1971, 116–17) or pull a statue of Christ seated on a wooden donkey (Germanic countries; see Young, *The Drama,* 1:93) to symbolize the presence of Christ.

21. The position of succentor (subcantor) at northern French cathedrals in the Middle Ages was tantamount to musical director of the choir. Although the cantor was nominally in charge of liturgical song, in point of fact his position was as much ceremonial as it was functional. By 1200 many of the most important duties of beginning and leading the plainsong fell to his subordinate, the succentor (see Wright 1989, 291).

22. The text and music of these prolix responsories may be found in Vatican, BAV Vat. lat. 4756, a mid-thirteenth-century notated breviary of Chartrain usage (on this source see chap. 1 in this volume). The sixth and ninth responsories, *Ingrediente domino* and *Insurrexerunt,* which speak specifically of Christ entering the gates of the Holy City, were not sung at this time, but held in reserve until a later moment in the ceremony when the procession reentered the city of Chartres. The use of the responsories of Matins as the chants initiating a procession may be a peculiarity of the liturgy of Chartres. The same practice can be observed there beginning in the fourteenth century with the instauration of the feast and procession of Corpus Christi (Delaporte 1922, 199). At Paris the first three responsories of Matins on Maundy Thursday were sung again in the procession to the washing of the altars (Baltzer 1992, 49–53 and 61–62).

23. The Benedictine priory of Saint-Barthélemy, of which nothing survives today except a street name, was founded in 1077 and converted to a parish church in 1553. It was destroyed during the siege of the Huguenots in 1568 but rebuilt, surviving into the nineteenth century. Already by 1080 the important cross in the cemetery of the church was well known, enjoying "grande vénération dans le peuple" (Lépinois 1854, 1:266, n.

2). The site of the cemetery outside Saint-Barthélemy is adjacent to what was to become and is today the principal cemetery of the town of Chartres. On the history of this church, see Buisson and Bellier (1896), 134; Lépinois (1854) 1:265–66; Delaporte, *L'Ordinaire*, 29; and especially Lacour (1985), 144.

24. Although MS 520 makes no mention of the cemetery at Saint-Barthélemy's at this point, MS 1058 does so explicitly ("Quando conveniunt processiones in cymiterium sancti bartholomei . . . ;" Delaporte, *L'Ordinaire*, 104). The *Ordo veridicus* (p. 28 of Delaporte's copy) states that the monks of Saint-Martin-au-Val were among the clerics who joined at that point.

25. Notre-Dame of Chartres, with a valley and a gracefully rising hill to the east, was often viewed as the heavenly Jerusalem (Prache 1993, 6–13). The Benedictine monastery of Josaphat founded in 1117 to the northeast of the cathedral, in the valley of the Eure and Loir, was so named because of the topographical parallel to the valley of Josaphat to the east of Jerusalem (Lépinois 1854, 1:289).

26. The priory of Saint-Cheron, supposedly built on the burial site of the saint of that name, traces its history back to the late sixth century. It was reformed under the Augustinian order in the mid-twelfth century and thereafter had close liturgical ties to both the cathedral and the Augustinian house of Saint-Jean-en-Vallée. Like Saint-Barthélemy, it was destroyed by the Huguenots in 1568 and subsequently rebuilt. The monastic community having been suppressed during the Revolution, the buildings served as home to a seminary during the nineteenth century and, more recently, as a public high school. The present chapel dates only from 1859. The history of this institution is recorded in *GC* (1744), 8:1305; Lépinois (1854) 1:284–86; Buisson and Bellier (1896), 145; Delaporte (1951); and Lacour (1985), 43–46.

27. The story of the fantastic life of St. Cheron (Latin Caraunus) merits a separate study. The *vita* of this "sixth-century saint" is a wholesale fabrication arising from an etymological confusion and the zeal of later medieval hagiographers eager to create heroes for the local church (Villette 1975, and Oury and Viguerie 1983, 39–40). The legend of St. Cheron has its origin in the Celtic word "Car" or "Ker" meaning "a pile of stones." At one time such a "car" marked a Roman or Druidic ossuary three kilometers east of Chartres. In time "car" phonetically became "Caraunus," soon to be personified as Sanctus Caraunus, and on this site a church was constructed in honor of this spurious saint. By the ninth century the necessary *vita* began to emerge. The fully formed version preserved in later breviaries describes him as a son of a noble Roman family, a diligent student of the seven liberal arts, an early apostle to Gaul slain on the route from Chartres to Paris, but, like his northern model St. Denis, still able to progress some distance head in hand (*AASS*, May VI, 752). In the early eleventh century Bishop Fulbertus composed a hymn for this bogus hero (PL 141:349) and, in the next century, an anonymous cleric at the monastery of Saint-Cheron composed a lengthy sequence in his honor in which the music of the popular melody *Laudes crucis attolamus* is reworked (Delaporte 1931). A full proper office was entered into the liturgical books of the cathedral (see, for example, the breviaries: Vatican 4756, fol. 342; Paris, BNF lat. 1053, fol. 290v; and Paris, BNF lat. 13240, fol. 372). In the archivolts of the south porch of the cathedral the beheading of St. Cheron was sculpted in a cycle devoted to the martyrs important to Chartres. Having been adopted as the patron saint of the stonemasons of the town, St. Cheron became the beneficiary of a stunning stained-glass window placed by this guild in the cathedral's northeast Chapel of the Martyrs, where it may still be seen today (Delaporte 1926, 1:337–44; and Manhès-Deremble 1993, 108–10 and 322–23).

28. The ordinal printed by Delaporte (MS 1058) adds two points of interest to the history of performance practice. First, the antiphon *Pueri hebreorum*, which surrounds the psalms of the office of Terce, is sung without a "neuma," a proscription that implies

that vocalises of some kind were on occasion appended to antiphons. Second, that the responsory of Terce was sung in the middle of the choir by two canons of high standing (of the fifth of six degrees of rank among the canons of Chartres). The respond of the responsory was repeated, but no "Gloria patri" was sung. This mode of execution—a small number of soloists intoning the opening of the respond and singing the verse from the middle of the choir—was the norm for responsorial chant on high feasts not only for monophonic chant but polyphony as well (see Wright 1989, 239–41, and Roesner, *Le Magnus,* xcvi).

29. Presumably boxwood or yew was used in France as a less expensive substitute for the exotic palm, although these had no symbolic associations. A pontifical blessing of the palms is preserved in the twelfth-century Chartrain pontifical Paris, BNF lat. 945, fol. 16.

30. This was not the only time the clergy of the cathedral processed to Saint-Cheron: it did so twice in connection with his feast day (28 May), first at Vespers and then again the next day for Mass, as well as for Mass on Friday in the second week of Lent, on Thursday of Easter week, and on Tuesday of the three Rogation Days. On each of these other visits the monks of Saint-Cheron were required by custom to provide the men of the cathedral with bread, pork, and wine of Chartres. The boys of the choir received collectively six deniers. In 1241 these meals were converted into payments of coin amounting to an annual sum of approximately ten livres (Lépinois and Merlet, *Cartulaire,* 2:131).

31. *Gloria laus et honor* was composed ca. 820 by Theodulf of Orléans and from its conception seems to have been viewed as an appropriate chant for Palm Sunday (on its history, see Szövérffy, *Die Annalen,* 202–3, and Messenger 1949). In its complete form, the hymn contains 38 two-line strophes (*AH* 50:160), but it is by no means certain that all of these were always sung. Most ordinals simply list the first few stanzas, invariably assigning these to choirboys. From this we may infer that the cantor or succentor determined the precise number of verses the boys were to sing, basing his decision on the exigencies of the moment.

32. "Quaerelam iniurrariarum [*sic*] ecclesie. Si quis excommunicaturus est excommunicetur." Chartres 1058 reads: "Quo finito, si querela est, fiat; si aliquis excommunicandus est, excommunicetur" ("That finished, if there is a complaint, let it be made; if anyone should be excommunicated, let him be excommunicated"). Paris, BNF lat. 1794, fol. 91, has: "Querelam de iniuriis ecclesie; si quis excomunicandum est ibi excommunicetur" ("Complaint of injury against the church; if anyone is to be excommunicated, let him be excommunicated there"). What is the meaning of this ceremony of excommunication? At face value it appears to have been the moment in the liturgical year for the public hearing of complaint and excommunication of those who had done injury to the church. The bishop, and later the chapter, had the right to effect such excommunications (Lépinois and Merlet, *Cartulaire,* 2:226–27): "Quod iniuriatores notorios et manifestos possit Capitulum libere excomunicare." It may also be possible to see this ceremony of excommunication in the midst of the Palm Sunday as a vestige of an ancient Gallican act belonging to the *Missa in traditione symboli.* In Gaul and Spain, as well as in Milan, Holy Week was traditionally the time during which the secrets of the Symbolum (the Creed) were imparted to the "competentes" and the uninitiated separated from the faithful (Tyrer 1932, 45). Although this dismissal of the uninitiated eventually came to be part of the service of the Saturday before Palm Sunday in Milan and of Holy Saturday at Benevento, its original position in the influential Ambrosian rite was on Palm Sunday. In all of these usages the expulsion of those unworthy began "Si quis"—"Si quis cathechuminus est procedat, Si quis iudeus est procedat, Si quis hereticus est procedat, etc." On this point, see PM 6:262; Borella (1939), 101–10; Hesbert

(1947), 197–202; and T. Kelly (1989), 290. On excommunication generally in the Middle Ages, see Vodola (1986), and in relation to penance, see Mansfield (1995), 122–24.

33. Souchet (1868), 1:17; and Delaporte, *L'Ordinaire*, 45. On the etymology of the name Porte Cendreuse and the liturgical rites associated with that gate, see Delaporte (1923), 93–96.

34. Two processioners dating from about 1475 (Chartres 538 and 539) but destroyed in the bombing of May 1944 contained the following rubric relevant to this point in the ceremony: "Provideatur quod ante portam civitatis que dicitur Porte Cendreuse iuxta Sanctum Vincentium incipiatur R. *Ingrediente Domino*" ("See to it that the responsory *Ingrediente Domino* is begun in front of the gate of the city which is called the Porte Cendreuse, near Saint-Vincent") (Delaporte 1923, 94).

35. The Palm Sunday panels of the Incarnation Window are discussed in Delaporte (1926), 153, and Manhès-Deremble (1993), 376–77.

36. The only change evident in the repeat of the office of Terce is that a "neuma" now was appended to the antiphon *Pueri hebreorum tollentes* (see above, n. 28; and Delaporte, *L'Ordinaire*, 105).

37. Augustine himself, unlike St. Benedict, did not write a rule. But during the eleventh century, more than six hundred years after his death, a group of reform-minded theologians extracted from his writings on the nature of the Christian life a set of principles for guiding a community of monks. For a history of the Augustinians at Saint-Jean-en-Vallée in particular, see Merlet, *Cartulaire, passim;* Cottineau, *Répertoire*, 1: 744–45; *DHGE* 12:560; and Fassler (1993a), 88–94. An English translation of the rule can be found in Augustine of Hippo, *Regula.*

38. Delaporte, *L'Ordinaire*, 18. The events that unfolded at Chartres are not dissimilar to those that developed only slightly later in Paris: an urban bishop and an urban archdeacon (Yvo at Chartres, William of Champeaux at Paris) reformed a church situated outside the walls of the city so as to provide a more spiritually pure retreat for the clergy of the cathedral (Saint-Jean at Chartres, Saint-Victor at Paris). These two dignitaries, and many canons of these two cathedrals, were ultimately buried in the comparative quiet of their respective suburban monasteries. For histories of Saint-Victor of Paris, see, among other sources, Bonnard (1904), 1, chapters 1–3; Wilesme (1977); and Fassler (1993a), 197–206.

39. The description that follows is drawn from Chartres 529, fols. 58v–59.

40. Evidence to the effect that the Benedictines of Saint-Père did not participate in the city-wide procession is found in the cartulary of that church (Powell 1988, 31, n. 47).

41. Mentions of the *dragonarius* of Chartres can be found in extracts from capitular acts of the 1360s now preserved in AdE-L G 504, liasse, no folio. Clerval (1899), 185, discusses the dragon in connection with the sometimes riotous ceremonies at the cathedral during Vespers and Compline of Easter, but the source that he cites, Chartres, BM 1093, was destroyed in 1944, and his account cannot be verified. Delaporte (1924, 109–13) discounts the myth created by Lépinois (1854, 1:549) that the dragon was some sort of fire-breathing monster. He does not, however, discredit Clerval on this issue.

42. Clerval (1899), 185; and Delaporte, *L'Ordinaire*, 123 and 127.

43. Jean Beleth (*Summa,* CCCM 41a:233 = PL 202:128) and Guillaume Durandus (*Rationale,* Liber VI, cap. CII), both with ties to Chartres, offer explanations of the symbolism of the dragon in processions. An extensive discussion of the meaning of the dragon in medieval life generally is offered in Le Goff (1980), 159–88, where further bibliographical citations may be found. For more on this subject, see also Bailey (1971), 115; and Delaporte (1924), 111.

44. Bailey (1971), 116; and Young, *The Drama,* 1:93.

45. "In quibusdam autem ecclesiis maius representamus mysterium, nam in tribus

precedentibus diebus precedit draco vexilla qui habet caudam plenam vento in signum quod in illis temporibus diabolus habuit potestatem in hominibus, qui erant quasi ventus, quia movebantur quolibet vento doctrine, et ipsum diabolum in idolis adorabant. Postremo sequitur draco, acuta cauda, in signum quod diabolus per passionem Domini et ascensionem potestatem suam amisit." ("Moreover, in certain important churches we dramatize the great mystery, for during the three preceding days a dragon's standard leads the way, which has a long tail blowing in the wind, a sign that in these times the Devil had power over mankind, who were moved about like the wind because they were swayed by any old doctrine, and they worshipped the image of the Devil. Afterward the dragon follows, now with shortened tail, as a sign that the Devil, because of the power of the Lord's passion and His Ascension, lost his power.") (Praepositinus, *Tractatus,* 198.) Jacobus de Voragine mentions that "in some churches and especially in France, the custom obtains of carrying a dragon with a long tail stuffed with straw . . . on the first two days it is carried in front of the cross and the third day, with the tail empty, behind the cross" (*The Golden Legend,* 1:288).

46. Katzenellenbogen (1959), 87. Katzenellenbogen quotes the following two important commentaries on this passage from Ps. 91:13: "Leo aperte saevit; draco occulte insidiatur: utramque vim et potestatem habet diabolus" ("The lion rages openly; the dragon secretly is insinuated: and the Devil has the force and power of both"); Augustine, *Enarratio in Psalmum XC,* in PL 37:1168; and "Sed in adventu Domini pedibus ejus, id est, a sanctis, omnia haec nocumenta prostrata sunt" ("But with the coming of the Lord through his feet, that is, holy actions, all noxious things were laid prostrate"); Peter Lombard, *Commentaria in Psalmos,* in PL 191:853. For other sculptural representations of this theme, see Mâle (1972), 43–44.

47. The destruction of the ordinal of Saint-Cheron (Chartres 81) in the infamous fire of May 1944, however, reduces such a postulation to mere speculation.

48. On the concept of a double office, see Amalarius of Metz, ed. Hanssens.

49. For an introduction to the sources for these chants, see Bailey (1971), 167. I am indebted to Mr. Finn Gundersen of Yale University for compiling a more complete list of concordances for these chants than the preliminary accounting given by Bailey.

50. *Dominus Jhesus ante sex dies* is found, among other places, in Worcester, Cathedral Library, F 160, fol. 112; and London, BL Add. 12194, fol. 83. *Cum audisset turba* also appears in Worcester, MS F.160, fol. 112; and León 8, fol. 153. Both melodies are also found in sources coming from Rouen (PL 147:117–19).

51. Paris, BNF lat. 990, fol. 43: "Canonicj vero majoris ecclesie et sancti Salvatoris post primam cantatam et tertiam pulsatam indutis superpelliciis albis faciendo processionem nihilque cantando debent similiter ire ad sanctum Symphorianum" ("However, the canons of the cathedral church and Saint-Sauveur, after Prime has been sung and Terce rung, dressed in white surplices and proceeding processionally, but singing nothing, should similarly go to Saint-Symphorien"). At Notre-Dame of Paris, the canons went their way up the hill to the Augustinian monastery of Sainte-Geneviève in a similar fashion: Brussels, BR 1799, fol. 31r–v: "Dominica in ramis palmarum cum congregatis processionalibus conventualibus in ecclesia Beate Marie capicerijs portantibus capsam et tribus clericis in albis paratis tres textus exitur de ecclesia nichil cantando et sic eundum est usque ad ecclesiam sancte Genovese de monte" ("On Palm Sunday, when the monastic groups have gathered processionally in the church of the Blessed Virgin Mary, with the relic-bearers carrying the relic and three clerics dressed in white [surplices] bearing three Gospels, the church is exited singing nothing; and so it should go until the church of Sainte-Geneviève on the Mountain").

52. Chevalier (*Ordinaire*), 118: "Apparatis igitur capsis et vexillis, et processione ordinata, cruce majoris ecclesie omnes alias ultima subsequente (subdiacono), itur ad Sanctum Vigorem magnum, et nichil dicitur in eundo" ("Therefore, when the relics

and standards and the order of the procession have been put in place, the cross of the cathedral church being last and subsequent to all others, the procession should go to Saint-Vigor the Great, and nothing is said en route").

53. This ritual is lacking in the printed missal of Chartres published in 1482 (Langois 1914, 32), but is prescribed in the following sources: *Manuale continens ecclesie sacramenta et modum administrandi ea, secundum usum diocesis Carnotensis* (Paris: Johannes Higman, 1492), fol. 56; *Rituale Carnotense* (Paris: Johannes Higman, 1500), fol. 27; and *Processionale Carnotense juxta ritum et formam missalis et breviarii Carnotensis restitutum* (Chartres: Louis Sevestre, 1674), 48.

54. The ritual *Attollite portas* was drawn from the ceremony for the dedication of a church at the moment when the bishop makes his ceremonial entry. Such a moment at the cathedral of Chartres is described in the twelfth-century pontifical Paris lat. 945, fol. 47.

55. This was also true at Notre-Dame of Paris (Wright 1989, 327–29).

56. AdE-L G 504, liasse, no folio, chapter acts of 1305 and 1548. The *responsoria de historia* in this case referred not only to those of Palm Sunday but to the larger collection of responsories sung during the months between Pentecost and Advent.

57. *Processional à l'usage de l'église cathédrale de Chartres suivant le nouveau bréviaire* (Chartres: Michel Deshayes, 1783), 38.

58. Clerval (1899), 138; and *Processional à l'usage de l'église de Chartres suivant le nouveau bréviaire* (Chartres: François Labalte, 1788), 56.

Nonconformity in the Use
of Cambrai Cathedral

Guillaume Du Fay's Foundations

BARBARA HAGGH

Many studies confirm that Western plainchant embraces distinct repertories
particular to regions, dioceses, religious orders, or churches, and that an
understanding of their composition can help to situate plainchant and even polyphony in time and place.[1] Service books have provided the primary evidence for
such repertories, since they are generally thought to represent actual practices and
contain distinct "uses," an impression given by inscriptions on the title pages of
imprints, such as *ad usum cameracensis* or *ad usum sarisburiensis*.[2] The underlying
premises are that only one set of texts and chants was used at a given establishment
at a particular time, and that the leaders of that establishment prescribed the use,
seeking conformity if not imposing it.

When the testimony of the archives is added to that of surviving service books
from Cambrai Cathedral, it proves that such premises, which reflect post-
Tridentine and post-Vatican II thinking, are misleading and wrong. Many individual foundations shaped the history of this cathedral's use: foundations for chapels,
for musicians' stipends, for chant for the Mass, Office, and processions, and for
different genres of sacred polyphony. (See Haggh 1992 and 1996a.) The founders
prescribed the ceremony, which was controlled by the dignitaries and chapter only
in some instances.[3] As a result, rituals were used in at least one cathedral chapel
that were not present in the use of the choir.

The final foundations made by Guillaume Du Fay (ca. 1398–1474), the leading
composer in Cambrai and one of the major composers of his time, and the manuscript sources that document them, demonstrate that music, texts, and devotions
not conforming to the use of the choir of Cambrai Cathedral were introduced by
Du Fay. They not only reveal the devotional priorities of the composer and prove
that the late medieval cathedral's "use" was less unified than has been assumed,
but also elucidate the origin and ritual context of some of his most important
sacred polyphony: his Masses for St. Anthony of Padua and St. Anthony Abbot,
his Office for the Dead, and his Mass on the antiphon *Ave regina celorum*.

Du Fay's foundations intended for the chapel of St. Stephen do not follow the calendar of the choir of Cambrai Cathedral, as two contemporaneous obituaries show. Lille, AdN 4 G 2009 appears to be a single obituary reconstructed from separate leaves, but these are in fact from different obituaries. Only a few folios remain from an obituary destined for the chapel of St. Stephen; more are from another used in the main choir, the latter a counterpart to Cambrai, MM 39, a complete choir obituary.[4] The two choir obituaries of like appearance share second folios beginning *A O*[bitus] *Osto Miles,* thus matching exactly the description of two choir obituaries listed in the inventory of cathedral books of 1461.[5]

The calendars of the obituary leaves from the choir and of the other obituary leaves differ. Among the feasts appearing only in the latter are several founded by Du Fay when he died, including an obit on his death day, evidence that these leaves were for the St. Stephen chapel, where Du Fay was buried:[6]

3 Feb.   Translation of St. Waudru, with Mass for the saint *sub discantu.*

10 Feb.   Feast of St. William (= William of Maleval, d. 1157), with Mass for the saint *in discantu.*[7]

13 June   Feast of St. Anthony of Padua, with Mass for the saint performed by *grandes vicaires* and altarboys "as is described at length at the end of the manuscript" (now missing).[8]

27 Nov.   Du Fay's obit, held on his death date because his tomb was in the chapel. (The obit held in the choir for Du Fay was on 5 August.)

None of these Masses was ever celebrated in the choir except the Requiem. St. Waudru, who stands behind Du Fay on his funeral monument, was accorded a feast of six lessons in the choir, a rank not requiring discant, which was reserved for duplex feasts of nine lessons.[9] Du Fay's will prescribes that three candles should burn in the chapel of St. Stephen "in all Hours and Masses" (*in omnibus horis et missis*) of the feasts of SS. Waudru and William, confirming that there the two feasts had full and not incomplete Offices.[10]

St. William never graced the Cambrai Cathedral calendar throughout the Middle Ages, nor did St. Anthony of Padua.[11] Both were well established in the Roman calendar, but it had little influence on the cathedral calendar in the Middle Ages, to judge from surviving service books and foundation documents. It is true that Cambrai, MM 164, among the oldest manuscripts from the cathedral, may be a direct copy of Hadrian's sacramentary, which was sent from Rome at Charlemagne's request. Yet the church of Cambrai suppressed the devotions to Roman saints in favor of their northern saints soon thereafter and only adopted the Roman breviary in the eighteenth century.[12]

Thus, Du Fay founded discant Masses in the St. Stephen chapel for saints not recognized in the choir, Anthony of Padua and William, and requested more extensive Office chant and polyphony for St. Waudru than she received in the choir. That one of the three discant Masses honored a saint having the same name as the composer is in keeping with similar earlier foundations by cathedral canons.[13]

Du Fay not only selected the saints' days, but also requested or composed the music, according to his will of July 1474, his executors' account, and their inventory of his possessions.[14] The documents prescribe that every year on the feasts of St. Waudru and St. William, the *grandes vicaires* and "others" (the *petits vicaires,* singing master, and choirboys, if they were available), were to sing a high Mass in discant that would be followed by a memorial for the deceased. The composer of these two discant Masses is not named, and was probably not Du Fay, because the same documents clearly ascribe the polyphony for St. Anthony of Padua to the composer. No Masses in polyphony for St. Waudru and St. William are known to survive.

The ceremonies for St. Anthony of Padua, depicted near Du Fay's funeral monument in the chapel, are prescribed in the greatest detail in the composer's will.[15] After Compline on the Vigil of the feast, six boys were to sing the responsory *Si quereris miracula* with verse *Gloria patri,* and the motet *O sydus Hispanie,* all surviving compositions by Du Fay.[16]

A Mass probably by Du Fay for the saint's day had already been celebrated for "a long time," a point that has not been emphasized before but is made in the executors' accounts.[17] According to the will and account, the composer's Mass for St. Anthony of Padua was to be "chanted and discanted" (*ditte et descantee*) after his death, with three *grandes vicaires* serving as priest, deacon, and subdeacon, as many able singers among the *grandes* and *petits vicaires* as were available, the *maître de chant,* and the choirboys.[18] According to the obituary of the St. Stephen chapel, six choirboys were to sing the *Et in terra* of the Mass.[19]

Du Fay donated a parchment manuscript with several Masses for St. Anthony of Padua (*les messes de St. Anthoine de Pade*), listed in the inventory of his possessions, to the St. Stephen chapel, which makes it possible that he intended several different Masses for his foundation, and not necessarily the one Spataro cited. Two other entries refer to only one Mass, however.[20] The will states that at the end of the Mass, choirboys will recite the antiphon *De profundis,* just as the priest begins Mass in the Trinity chapel.[21] The others present will respond with the collects *Inclina* and *Fidelium* (Lille, AdN 1313, p. 73). After Compline, those who have sung the Mass will come to the St. Stephen chapel and sing the antiphon *O proles Hispanie* "on the plainchant" (*super cantu plano*), probably meaning singing on the book.[22] Then they will recite (*dicant*) the verse and the celebrant will recite the collect. Finally the boys will recite (*dicant*) the motet *O lumen ecclesie* or another motet, at the discretion of their *maître de chant.*[23] Surely it is this material sung after Compline by those who had sung Mass that comprised the "many other antiphons in black notation" that were copied after the Masses for the saint in the parchment manuscript.[24]

Du Fay's obit in the choir and in the St. Stephen chapel, where his funeral was held, probably included his polyphonic Requiem Mass and his Office for the Dead, the latter not mentioned in his will but in an account of the 1501 meeting of the Order of the Golden Fleece in Brussels.[25] According to the will, the Requiem Mass was to be sung for the first time on the day after his funeral by twelve of the most capable *grandes* and *petits vicaires.* The will assigns a sequence to follow the Mass, but Du Fay's executors' account only mentions antiphons and does not name them. The will also prescribes for this location the antiphon *De profundis* and the collects *Inclina* and *Fidelium,* probably the first of the "antiphons" cited in the executor's account.[26]

Du Fay also willed to the St. Stephen chapel a large paper manuscript containing his Mass for St. Anthony Abbot (*natalis* 17 Jan.) and Requiem, but, curiously, he did not make a foundation for this saint in the choir or in any chapel of the Cathedral, as far as we know.[27] In 1404, before his death, canon Guillaume de Loghenaer founded the feast of St. Anthony Abbot in the choir at greater duplex rank, but this saint is absent from the surviving January page of the obituary of the St. Stephen chapel.[28]

If there was no mid-fifteenth-century foundation for St. Anthony Abbot at Cambrai Cathedral, then why was Du Fay's Mass for the saint willed to the chapel, and why do two different sets of Mass proper texts for the saint first appear in mid-fifteenth-century service books?[29] Planchart asked whether Du Fay might not have introduced the second, later, set of propers.

Both sets are intermingled in Cambrai, MM 233 on fol. 460r–v: introit *Os justi, aliud Scitote quoniam;* gradual *Os justi, aliud Thronus eius;* Alleluia verse (which remains the same) *Vox de celis;* offertory *Veritas mea, aliud Inclito Anthonio;* communion *Beatus servus, aliud Orabat Dei famulus;* but Cambrai, MM 184 only has the second set.[30] A *missale parvum* printed for Cambrai Cathedral in 1507 contains both sets as well, and clarifies the mystery.[31] The "earlier" propers, derived from the Common of Confessors, constitute the Mass for St. Anthony Abbot's day, 17 January.[32] The "later" propers appear in the supplement to the print as the votive Mass for the saint, which could be celebrated at any time of year.

It seems unlikely that this widely known votive Mass for St. Anthony Abbot was composed initially by Du Fay, but it is indeed possible that he was responsible for introducing its propers at the Cathedral, not for use in the main choir, but in the St. Stephen chapel, and not by foundation, but by accident.[33] Three missals from after 1458 including the votive Mass for St. Anthony Abbot and singled out by Planchart all contain anomalies suggesting that they could have found use in the St. Stephen chapel.

The earliest of the three, Cambrai 233, a fifteenth-century missal, includes both sets of propers for St. Anthony Abbot among additions at the end. The main part of Cambrai 233 is from the abbey of St. Aubert in Cambrai, as is evident from the inclusion of the feast of the saint's translation and date of the Dedication.[34] This part of the manuscript also has three large illuminations, and the last depicts the martyrdom of St. Stephen, which might explain how the missal reached the cathedral and why it would have been appropriated for the chapel of St. Stephen. That the missal came to the St. Stephen chapel of the cathedral is suggested by its last folios, which were copied after 1450 (Planchart 1988, 147). They contain, in order, the Mass for St. Anthony Abbot, a sequence for St. Sebastian, whose feast came a few days after St. Anthony Abbot's, and a Mass for St. William, followed by a sequence for St. Vedast, whose feast was celebrated a few days after St. William's. St. William was not recognized in the cathedral, but he was precisely the saint for whom Du Fay founded a polyphonic Mass. Moreover, in the added sequentiary copied by yet another scribe, there is a sequence for St. Stephen, *Cordis et vo*[cis], not assigned to the saint in cathedral manuscripts or in the 1527 printed missal of the Use of Cambrai, which has *Alleluia unus amator,* also in cathedral manuscripts of the eleventh century onwards (Cambrai, MM 60, 151, and 185). Finally, Cambrai 233 has a second sequence for St. Stephen, *Prothomartir et levita clarus,* added toward the very end of the manuscript, evidence of an unusual need for sequences for St. Stephen.[35] Thus, it seems possible that the additions to Cambrai 233 reflect rituals celebrated in the St. Stephen chapel. If the additions were made at the cathedral, then they probably date from the end of Du Fay's life, since they include a Mass for St. Quintin, whose feast was founded at duplex rank for the choir of Cambrai Cathedral in 1466 and celebrated by 1472/3, but there are no Masses for feasts founded later.[36]

In a second, even later missal, Cambrai, MM 152, a fifteenth-century scribe added the feast of St. Anthony of Padua to the calendar in a cursive script, suggesting that this manuscript might have found use in the St. Stephen chapel as well. Cambrai 152 also contains both St. Anthony Abbot Masses.

Finally, Cambrai 184, written throughout by a single scribe, is identified by Molinier as following a vaguely defined "usage of Cambrai," but the feasts represented do indeed correspond to foundations that were made in the cathedral in the 1470s and earlier, the most recent being St. Augustine (1470/1), the Translation of St. Nicholas (1473/4), and St. Amatus (1475/6) (cf. Haggh 1992, 555–62). The manuscript may have been destined for the St. Stephen chapel, because it lacks the propers used elsewhere for St. Anthony Abbot's feast day and appropriates the votive Mass propers instead, the only missal surviving from Cambrai to do so. It also includes a Mass for St. Waudru, for whom Du Fay founded a polyphonic Mass, and a sequence for St. Anthony Abbot, *Anthonius humilis sanctitate nobilis,* which is added at the back and found only in this manuscript. There is no Mass for St. William, however.

Cambrai 184 is the earliest surviving manuscript from Cambrai to give the text of the unusual offertory *Regina celi letare,* assigned here to the votive Mass of the Virgin from Easter to Pentecost (cf. the discussion in Planchart 1988, 141–42). This offertory may have been used in the St. Stephen chapel as well. One of the seventeen Masses founded by Du Fay in the St. Stephen chapel was a low Mass to be held in the morning on Easter Sunday, and Du Fay requested specifically that it was to be modeled after a similar Mass that had been founded in 1417 by Egidius de Bosco to be celebrated on the first Sunday in Advent. De Bosco's foundation included a Mass at the Holy Cross altar, but does not specify the kind of Mass it was supposed to be. Might it have been a Marian votive Mass? (See Haggh 1992, 556.) Now *Regina celi letare* is the text of the Marian antiphon for Paschaltide, and in 1438 De Bosco made a different foundation specifically for Easter and the six following Sundays, in which he requested the singing of the antiphon *Regina celi letare,* versicle, and collect *Interveniat* in the nave in front of the crucifix after Compline (see Cambrai 200, fol. 63v, and Haggh 1992, 557). It seems at least possible that both of De Bosco's foundations encouraged Du Fay to use the offertory *Regina celi letare* as part of a low Easter morning votive Mass. In Cambrai 184, this offertory is without music.

The 17 January St. Anthony Abbot Mass is given in the missal of 1507 and in another printed in 1527, so the other votive formulary did not replace this one, but coexisted with it. And since the three missals with the votive Mass formulary may have been used at the St. Stephen chapel, there is the possibility that the votive Mass was introduced precisely in that chapel.

Du Fay's polyphonic Mass Ordinary for St. Anthony Abbot has not been identified with certainty, nor have Mass propers, but Planchart credits him with the apparently unique plainsong cantus firmus of a polyphonic introit, *Scitote quoniam . . . stolam glorie,* in an anonymous plenary Mass for St. Anthony Abbot, that is, a Mass including settings of the Ordinary and Proper. This introit, in Trent, CBC 89, is the introit for the votive Mass. Planchart attributes this work to Du Fay since it has a text variant and mode 3 melody found in the cathedral missals but not elsewhere, and suggests that this is Du Fay's lost Mass.[37] Comparison of the introit melody with Du Fay's *Recollectio* chant is inconclusive.[38]

Why did the manuscript willed to the St. Stephen chapel include Du Fay's Mass for St. Anthony Abbot and Requiem side by side, since a Mass for St. Anthony Abbot was not among his last foundations? An explanation may be found in one devotion introduced in Brussels for Duke Charles the Bold. At least from the time of Duke Philip the Bold (d. 1404), who took St. Anthony Abbot as his patron saint, the dukes of Burgundy had venerated the saint,[39] but after Duke Charles's death in 1477, an unusually splendid obit was celebrated for him, on St. Anthony Abbot's feast day precisely, in the collegiate church of St. Gudula in Brussels, the leading secular church in this principal residence of the court of Burgundy.[40] Votive Masses were celebrated along with Requiems at funerals and obits, and also at the meetings of the Order of the Golden Fleece, and Du Fay's Requiem was adopted by the Order. A polyphonic Mass for St. Anthony Abbot and Requiem, both by Du Fay, could have been appropriated if not requested for this obit of a former duke and sovereign of that same Order.[41] Indeed, the obit in St. Gudula could well have included polyphony. The *cotidiane* was functioning as such in 1474 and officially established in 1477, with the requirement that its singers be able to sing polyphony; in payments for the obit celebrated after 1477, the performers were singers (*sangers*), not canons, vicars, or chaplains, and it was a full obit with a vigil and nine lessons (Cf. n. 40 above and Haggh 1995b, 335).

The obit was first performed after Charles the Bold's death in 1477 and after Du Fay's death in 1474, but the Masses could have been commissioned earlier, since the initial foundation for the obit was made at Charles the Bold's birth. At this time, since two earlier children had died, his parents, Philip the Good and Isabella of Portugal, consecrated him to the miraculous bleeding Host at St. Gudula, where a Mass was founded for Charles to be held yearly on 8 November (Octave of All Saints' Day) as long as he lived, but on 17 January after he died. The miraculous bleeding Host had a special meaning for Charles's father, Philip the Good, founder of the Order of the Golden Fleece, since a miraculous bleeding Host was the principal relic of the chapel of the Order, the Sainte-Chapelle in Dijon. An allusion to the relic is made in the sequence of the new Marian Office commissioned by the Order and approved in 1458, *Lauda Sion roris vellus,* a parody of the famous Corpus Christi sequence, *Lauda Sion salvatorem.*[42]

Therefore it seems likely that Du Fay composed his Mass for St. Anthony Abbot specifically for Duke Charles, but then willed the paper manuscript copy with the Requiem to the St. Stephen chapel, because the Requiem was needed for his obit. Eventually, the St. Anthony Abbot votive Mass was sung in the chapel as well. It may also be more than coincidence that the paper manuscript, even if destined for the St. Stephen chapel, immediately precedes the six music manuscripts that Du Fay willed to Duke Charles in the list of his books.[43]

An Office for the Dead as well as the Requiem Mass are ascribed to Du Fay in a letter discovered by William Prizer, in which Nicolas Frigio describes the ceremony accompanying the meeting of the Order of the Golden Fleece held on 15 January 1501 at the Coudenberg palace in Brussels:[44]

> The Office of the Dead was sung in the following manner. A canon of Cambrai being the most renowned musician to be found in that area, and having composed this Office of the dead and a Mass for three voices, mournful, sad, and very exquisite, he did not let it out during his lifetime but left in his testament that they should be sung after his death for his soul, but the Order took them for its own use (Prizer 1985, 133–34).

Frigio's letter raises many questions. Did the Office include three-voice polyphony like the Mass, which would be exceptional since no three-voice settings of that Office survive from the time? Or was it entirely newly-composed plainchant, and if so, what was "composed" and what did its composition entail? A more basic question concerns the meaning of the word "Office" (*officium*). Rubrics and archival sources make it clear that an *officium mortuorum* consisted of Vespers, Matins, and Lauds, but could refer to the Mass as well, or to the entire burial or commemorative ritual. A manuscript associated with the Order of the Golden Fleece and the archives and service books of the cathedral confirm that no plainchant by Du Fay for the Office of the Dead survives, and that his Office must have been a polyphonic setting. The cathedral sources also reveal the existence of two different musical settings for the cathedral's unique texts for the Office of the Dead, another example of diversity in that use.

Dufay's Office of the Dead was undeniably used by the Order of the Golden Fleece after 1501, so an especially intriguing document is Brussels, Archives générales du Royaume, Church Archives of Brabant, Archives of St. Gudula, 7834, a ritual for the dead used prior to the Council of Trent at the collegiate church of St. Gudula, where Philippe Nigri, chancellor of the Order of the Golden Fleece from 1531 to 1562, was dean. (Nigri himself donated the manuscript to the church in 1557.) The manuscript is incomplete and lacks the Office, however, and there are no unique melodies among the supplements it contains.[45]

There is no evidence that proves that Cambrai Cathedral adopted Du Fay's Office of the Dead intended for the Order, but if Du Fay composed chant of this kind, one would expect it to survive in sources from the cathedral postdating the composer's death. It is therefore worth checking to see whether significant changes in the cathedral's Office of the Dead occurred in the 1470s or 80s. Moreover, since the Office of the Dead was celebrated in the chapels and choir of the cathedral, comparison of the chant readings can test the uniformity of the music in use.

The Cambrai Office of the Dead, which was the same for the cathedral, the collegiate church of St. Géry, and the subordinate secular churches, survives in nineteen manuscripts and prints prepared for different owners and occasions: in Cambrai as elsewhere it was celebrated not only at burial, but on the first, third, seventh, and thirtieth days thereafter and then every year on the anniversary of the day of death. It was also used for All Souls' Day (2 Nov.) and on Mondays as part of weekly cycles of votive Offices. Consequently, the Office may be found in the Sanctorale, in a separate section of a manuscript, or as a separate libellus (see table 16.1).

The Office of the Dead of Cambrai Cathedral used the same series of responsories from the twelfth to the seventeenth century, with few exceptions: (1) *Credo, quod,* (2) *Heu mihi,* (3) *Qui Lazarum,* (4) *Domine, quando veneris,* (5) *Peccante me,* (6) *Libera me, domine, de viis,* (7) *Si facta mea recompensare,* (8) *Memento mei, deus,* (9) *Libera me, domine, de morte.*[46] Since the order of Matins responsories and of the versicles for the *Libera me* responsory varied from church to church, this order distinguishes the Cambrai rite.

Only two manuscripts from the late thirteenth or early fourteenth centuries exchange the second and third responsories of Matins, the only significant structural variants in any source. Cambrai, MM 38 was prepared for a dean, Ubald de Sart, between 1286 and 1298, but has material added in the early fifteenth century and was still kept in the vestry along with other books for use in the choir in 1461.[47] The Office of the Dead in the Sanctorale of the original layer of the manuscript gives as second and third responsories *Qui Lazarum* and *Heu michi,* with no indications to suggest that their order was ever to be changed. The fourteenth-century Office of the Dead in Cambrai, MM 29 also uses these disordered responsories,

Table 16.1 The Office of the Dead of Cambrai Cathedral: notated sources

---

1. Cambrai, MM 193, fols. 84v ff., separate (1130–80)
2. Cambrai, MM 46, fols. 237r ff., separate (1200–20)
3. Cambrai, MM 38, fols. 356r ff., All Souls (1286–98, with early 15th–c. additions)
4. Cambrai, MM 29, fols. 162r ff., separate (1300–20)
5. Cambrai, MM 106, (1300–1400)[a]
6. Cambrai, MM 55, fols. 143r ff., separate (before 1405/6)
7. Cambrai, MM 51, fols. 53v ff., *post missam defunctorum* (1455–57), processional chants
8. Cambrai, MM 62, fols. 12r ff., All Souls (1475–84), invitatory only
9. Cambrai, MM 63, fols. 12r ff., All Souls (1475–84), invitatory only
10. Cambrai, MM XVI C 4, fols. 188v ff., All Souls (ca. 1508–18)
11. Cambrai, MM R IMP F B 6, pp. 71 ff., separate (1562)
12. Brussels, BR LP II 17171 1, pp. 71 ff., separate (1562)
13. Cambrai, MM 70, fols. 113r ff., All Souls (16th c.), processional chants
14. Cambrai, MM 71, fols. 83r ff., All Souls (16th c.), processional chants
15. Cambrai, MM 79, fols. 163v ff., *post missam defunctorum* (16th c.), processional chants
16. Cambrai, MM Impr. De. l. 153, fols. 31v ff., separate, n.d. (16th c.)
17. Cambrai, MM 124, fols. 127r ff., All Souls (17th c.), processional chants
18. Brussels, Bibliothèque des Bollandistes, 1018 V and 1018 VI, pp. 172 ff., separate (1659)
19. Brussels, Bibliothèque des Bollandistes, 1016 IV, pp. 255 ff., separate (1779)

---

[a] I was unable to consult this source.

but they were copied with evident confusion: the scribe wrote the first two responsories in the order of Cambrai 38, but then rushed to begin the first antiphon of
the second nocturn. Recognizing the error, he went back to copy the third responsory *Heu michi,* also third in Cambrai 38, and finally continued with the rest of the
second nocturn. The scribe may have followed the order of initial responsories in
other, more common, series, but the remaining responsories of the Cambrai series
find no counterparts elsewhere.[48]

The confusion could have resulted from the texts themselves. Ottosen points
out that the first nocturn that appears in the sources predating and following Cambrai 29 and 38 produces contradictions in the text, since the second responsory in
the Cathedral series, *Heu mihi,* confesses that the departed has sinned, contrary to
the assertion of the preceding lesson.[49] Thus, the erroneous order of Cambrai 29
and 38 is actually a correction.

The anomalies in the texts of Cambrai 29 and 38 find no counterpart in the
music. The chant for the Cambrai Office of the Dead was remarkably stable for
500 years; variants in the antiphons and responsories are only local nuances of
pitch. Cambrai 29 follows most of the sources, and even Cambrai 38 shows only
small melodic variants.

Yet different plainchant sets the Cambrai texts in Cambrai, MM 55, a collection
of prayers, readings, and Offices in small format, probably intended for private
use.[50] Only the Office of the Dead is notated. Its chant appears to be derived from
the chant of the other sources, but also gives evidence of deliberate recomposition.

The distinctive melodies of Cambrai 55 begin with the second antiphon of First
Vespers, which terminates differently at *prolongatus est* (see example 16.1), although
this could be a misreading or misremembering. There is an artful symmetry in the
counterbalancing of the two *clivis*es (neumes for descent) on *Heu* and the last
syllable of *incolatus* with the later *pes* (neume for ascent) on the penultimate syllable of *prolongatus* not found in the other versions, which gives evidence of composition. The restricted range of the chant and the placement of the notation in
Cambrai 55 also show greater sensitivity to the text.

The fourth antiphon of First Vespers is the same in every source but Cambrai
55, where the repetition of *domine* is emphasized (example 16.2). Cambrai 55 also
transposes the setting of the second *domine,* an evident correction of the more
widely used melody.

In the fifth antiphon (example 16.3), the three earlier sources share the outline
of the melody but place the text differently. Cambrai 55 shares the two phrase
beginnings but not the cadences of the common melody. Cambrai 38 has the same
beginning and final cadence, but variants occur in the middle of the antiphon.

Example 16.4 shows the invitatory *Circumdederunt.* In Cambrai 55 the entire
chant is moved up a fourth, mitigating the *dolores inferni,* and contains many variants. Its version is closest to that in Cambrai 38.

The substantial variants in Cambrai 55 may result from its being a private
manuscript.[51] Chronology cannot be held accountable, because earlier and later
sources share melodies and texts. In any case, the Office of the Dead in Cambrai
55 is evidence that different melodies were composed to the same texts and that
they coexisted.[52]

Example 16.1 First Vespers, second antiphon

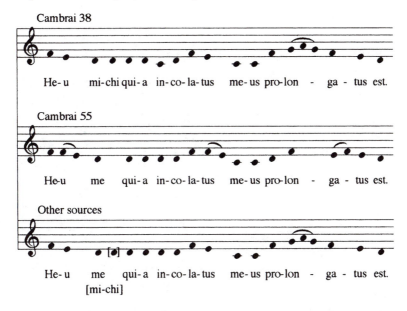

To the cluster of "nonconformist" rituals described above we may add another of Du Fay's last foundations. Du Fay established an obit to be celebrated in the choir of Cambrai Cathedral on 5 August, the feast of Mary of the Snows, so-named in an entry of ca. 1473 in the obituary Cambrai 39.[53] That this feast should be named is exceptional, because it was only established at the cathedral by foundation in 1566.[54] Indeed, when the early seventeenth-century chronicler Julien de Lingne described a celebration of the feast of Mary of Snows in 1529 by bishop Robert of Croy, he considered it unusual because the yearly celebration of the feast had not been founded.[55] That Du Fay requested the celebration of this feast, which was in the Roman calendar (as was the feast of St. William discussed above) but not in the calendar of Cambrai Cathedral, suggests that the Roman rite had personal meaning for Du Fay, who did indeed own a Roman missal and breviary when he

Example 16.2 First Vespers, fourth antiphon

Example 16.3   First Vespers, fifth antiphon

died.[56] It is also worth noting that the miracle celebrated on the feast of Mary of Snows, a miraculous snowfall marking the place where the church of Santa Maria Maggiore would be built in Rome, parallels another miracle known to Du Fay, that of the miraculous dew moistening the fleece of Gideon (see Haggh 1995a, 17, 20).

Reinhard Strohm, Rob C. Wegman, and I have each argued independently that Du Fay's *Missa Ave regina celorum* was sung on if not composed for this occasion, because the entry in the obituary Cambrai 39 prescribes a Marian Mass for Du Fay for 5 August.[57] The description of the Marian Mass is crossed out. The celebration was probably discontinued when Du Fay died, because the Mass is mentioned in the Fabric accounts of the cathedral only from 1471/2 until 1473/4, but not afterwards.[58] Du Fay may have given the copy of the Mass to Charles the Bold because it was no longer needed at the cathedral.

New evidence explains why Du Fay would have considered a Mass on the Marian antiphon *Ave regina celorum* appropriate for the services later replaced by his obit. A series of Marian antiphons assigned to the seven days of the week appears in Cambrai 55 (see table 16.2). All of the antiphon texts are followed by a versicle and collect, suggesting use at foundations, devotions after Compline, or at processional stations. This series provides a clue to the origin of Cambrai 55, because it is also found in an ordinal of the Sainte-Chapelle of Paris (Paris, Bibl. de l'Arsenal 114), where Pierre d'Ailly, bishop of Cambrai from 1396 to 1411, had held the highest

Example 16.4 Matins, invitatory antiphon

Table 16.2 Weekly cycles of Marian antiphons in the fifteenth century

Day	Cambrai Cathedral	Senlis	Aix-en-Provence	La Chaise-Dieu	Sélestat
Sun.	Alma redemptoris	?	Alma redemptoris	Quam dilecta	Ave regina caelorum
Mon.	Ave regina caelorum	Alma redemptoris	Mater patris	Gaude virgo	Nigra sum
Tues.	Beata dei genitrix	Sub tuum	Ave regina caelorum	Ave regina caelorum	Ista est
Wed.	Vidi speciosam	Haec est	Ave virgo sanctissima	Ave stella	Tota pulchra
Thurs.	Tota pulcra es	Tota pulchra	Ave regina . . . mater	Gaude dei genitrix	Descendi
Fri.	Anima mea	Ave regina caelorum	Ave virgo sanctissima	Speciosa	Alma redemptoris
Sat.	Salve regina	Salve regina	Salve or Regina caeli	Salve or Regina	Salve or Regina

Sources: Cambrai, MM 55, fol. 22v; Michel Huglo (1980a), 480.

rank of treasurer beginning in 1399.[59] Cambrai 55's main layer dates from approximately the time of d'Ailly's tenure as bishop of Cambrai, and it contains some of his writings. If this was not his personal book, it may well reflect his personal devotions. Moreover, the bishop of Cambrai had an oratory in his residence that was separate from the cathedral, a possible explanation for the variant Office of the Dead.

Du Fay was greatly influenced by d'Ailly's writings, according to Planchart.[60] He may well have been aware of d'Ailly's devotions, since the antiphon in the series of the Sainte-Chapelle and Cambrai 55 that was assigned to Monday, the day customarily assigned to the Office of the Dead in the weekly round of votive Offices, is none other than *Ave regina celorum,* which was also known more widely as the Marian antiphon for the penitential season of Lent, and was, as we know, the antiphon selected by Du Fay for his supplicatory motet and great cantus-firmus Mass. Moreover, *Ave regina celorum* was sung in Cambrai Cathedral in conjunction with at least one funeral, since the account of the executors of canon Gilles d'Inchy (Lille, AdN 1375) lists a payment for two *Regina celorum*s to be sung in the choir of the church, but not specifying the precise occasion. This evidence does suggest why Du Fay chose this antiphon rather than another Marian antiphon for his supplicatory motet and for the cantus firmus of his Mass. It is also worth mentioning that the antiphon would have been especially appropriate for a Mass sung on 5 August, in the period just preceding the 15 August feast of Mary's Assumption into heaven.

Planchart credits Du Fay with the introduction to the cathedral use of a new plainchant melody for *Ave regina celorum,* basing his hypothesis on a comparison of the melody of *Ave regina celorum* as found in several fifteenth-century processionals with musical notation, and the melody as conflated from the sources for Du Fay's motet and Mass based on *Ave regina celorum* (see example 16.5).[61] Closer scrutiny of these sources shows that Du Fay could have recomposed only one pitch. Vertical rectangles surround the places where the melody of Du Fay's Mass differs from the chant in other cathedral sources, differences consisting mostly of repeated or passing notes that do not affect the structure of the melody. Two significant differences can be seen in rectangles 1 and 3, however. The pitch *b* appears only in the later chants, that is in Du Fay's model, in the early sixteenth-century printed antiphoner, Cambrai, MM XVI C 4, and in the late fifteenth-century processional, Cambrai, MM 131. It is not in the earlier processional, Cambrai, MM 77, or in the two thirteenth-century sources. Du Fay's model also uses a similar figure elsewhere in the chant, which does not appear in the other Cathedral manuscripts: see rectangle 10 at *orta* (top left of rectangle), and 14 at *speciosa* (bottom left of rectangle). The change is only ornamental, however. Thus, only the *b* seems important enough to represent a conscious change, although comparison of this example with other versions of the *Ave regina celorum* in regional sources will be necessary to confirm an attribution of any adjustment to Du Fay. It is important, however, that slightly different versions of *Ave regina celorum* appear in Cambrai Cathedral sources, and that scribes made mistakes copying other Marian antiphons there.[62] Two of these, *Alma redemptoris mater* and *Salve regina,* were painted on the walls of chapels in Cambrai Cathedral, perhaps to remind singers of the correct melody.[63] It

Example 16.5   Versions of the antiphon *Ave regina celorum*

seems entirely possible that several versions of these antiphons were in use at the same time, in the choir and chapels.

The nonconformity described above includes different melodies for the Office of the Dead and Marian antiphons, and celebrations introduced by Du Fay that followed the Roman Use and not that of the Cathedral's main choir. Taken together with evidence that foundations could introduce the same music to churches in very different locations, as was true of Walter Henrici's foundations of the Marian feast of the *Recollectio* (see Haggh 1990a, 1990b), it reveals that uniformity and variety in plainchant and ritual were not necessarily determined by location or by local practices, but by the wishes of individual founders.

Indeed, no mention is made of a Use of the diocese of Cambrai in any of the service books of the cathedral before the sixteenth century. Earlier manuscripts do

Example 16.5　(*continued*)

(*continued*)

refer to the Use of the church of Cambrai, which—given what we have discussed above—should be taken to mean the main choir. We do have some discussions of diocesan Use in the sixteenth-century *Regulae generales breviarii* at the back of Cambrai, MM 231. Important is tradition, and feast days for saints venerated in other parish churches of the diocese for a long time, even if they were not recognized by the cathedral, could still be celebrated. But other churches were encouraged to conform, and were required to celebrate the Dedication of the cathedral especially. It is interesting that the first sources to refer to a diocesan Use of Cambrai are printed ones. No doubt such printed books were the primary vehicle for unification of ritual within a diocese, even before the reforms of Trent.[64] Thus a uniform Use became possible just when the proliferation of foundations had produced the greatest diversity.

　　The past twenty years have seen the publication of much new historical scholarship on the late Middle Ages. A thread running through all of it is recognition of

Example 16.5   (*continued*)

the importance of the private or lay underpinning of ecclesiastical wealth (see, e.g., Oakley 1979). Canons founded most of the celebrations introduced at Cambrai Cathedral, but it is their individual foundations and varied prescriptions that help us to interpret the late medieval service books and the additions made to them. Indeed, once foundations established chapels as part of the architecture of churches in thirteenth-century Cambrai and introduced chaplains to perform the founded celebrations, diversity had to follow.[65] It is certain that an increase in foundations for services of personal preference necessitated greater tolerance for different kinds of worship just when sacred polyphony was gaining widespread acceptance. Future research must address the implications of this diversity, and of the foundations that produced it, for the history of plainchant and of sacred polyphony.

Example 16.5   (*continued*)

(*continued*)

Example 16.5   (*continued*)

Example 16.5   (*continued*)

Notes

Earlier versions of this paper were presented at the annual conference on Medieval and Renaissance Music, Reading, in 1989, and at the 56th annual meeting of the American Musicological Society, Oakland, 1990. I am grateful to the University of Maryland, Baltimore County, for funding my research.

1. Molinier, *Catalogue,* describes briefly the manuscripts in the Médiathèque Municipale of Cambrai that are discussed here. Piétresson de Saint-Aubin (1968) inventories the archives of Cambrai Cathedral. See Bloxam (1987), 59–66, on Cambrai, and Robertson (1991b), a case study of Machaut's Mass.

2. RELICS at the University of Michigan is a comprehensive on-line database listing service books printed to 1600, compiled under the direction of David Crawford and James Borders (WWW address: http://www.umich.edu/~davidcr).

3. The *acta capituli* of the cathedral (Cambrai, MM 1055–62, covering the years 1395–1494) rarely regulate the divine service or approve foundations.

4. Lille, AdN 2009, fol. [1] is an older obituary. The fifteenth-century obituary, which must be of the chapel of St. Stephen because of the date assigned to Du Fay's obit (cf. n. 6 below) and the frequent mention of the *grandes vicaires,* who used that chapel, is on fols. [2–12], numbered 1–11. The fifteenth-century obituary for the choir of Cambrai Cathedral is on fols. [13] ff.

5. "Item ung obituaire commenchans ou second foeillet du kalendier A o osto miles" (left choir, inventories of 1461 and 1519); "Item ung aultre tout pareil" (right choir, ibid.). See Lille, AdN 4554, 18 March–6 May 1461, "Inventoire des Relicques, Joyaulx, capes, draps, livres, et aultres choses et biens, estans, tant en le Tresorie de leglise de Cambray, comme ou Reliquiaire du cuer dicelle," which is not published in Houdoy (1880; cf. 350, n. 1), and Lille, AdN 4555, 1519 [n.d.], also unpublished. The earlier entries in both obituaries predate 1461. The additions at the back of Cambrai 39 were made through 1473 inclusive, to judge from the dates of the foundations. Cf. Strohm (1993), 285–87. On the dates of the foundations, see Haggh (1992). On the inventories, see Haggh (1995d).

6. Lille, AdN 2009, with February feasts on fol. [3r], 13 June on fol. [7r], and 27 November on fol. [12v]. This is not the circular argument it would appear to be, because obits were held on death dates only at the location of the tomb, and Du Fay's tomb was in the St. Stephen chapel.

7. Maleval founded the Hermits of St. William or Williamites. Cambrai, MM 1277 and 1284, sixteenth- and fifteenth-century antiphoners of the Williamite monastery of the village of Walincourt near Cambrai, contain the plainchant for the office of St. William. No Cambrai gradual with the Mass survives. On William of Maleval, see Mottirani (1966). His feast was introduced to the Roman Use by Pope Alexander III.

8. Lille, AdN 2009, fol. [7r]: "Anthonij de padua. Habemus missam de beato Anthonio in capellaniam fundatam per magistrum G. du Fay ubi sunt revestiti et capellani de communitate. Ibi conveniunt cum pueris altaris sicut ad longum declaratus in fine huius libri." [Anthony of Padua. We have the Mass of St. Anthony in the chapel founded by Master G. du Fay where the newly invested [priests] and chaplains of the community are. There they meet with the altarboys as is declared at length at the end of this book.] (Other documents stating that Du Fay founded the chapel of St. Stephen are not known, but the history of the chapel remains to be written, and indeed the charters of the cathedral have yet to be searched. It may be significant that Gregory Nicolay, procurator for Du Fay in 1427, according to Planchart 1993, 342, founded his obit in the same chapel. See Haggh 1992, 557.) It cannot be coincidental that the obit Regis founded at the collegiate church of St. Vincent in Soignies for Du Fay was to be celebrated on 12 June, the vigil of the feast of St Anthony of Padua; cf. Fallows (1989), 150.

9. See the calendar in Cambrai, MM XVI C 4. Older calendars show St. Waudru sharing the day with St. Brice. On Du Fay's funeral monument, see Fallows (1987), 82–83 and ills. 1–2. On duplex feasts and discant, see Wright (1978), 298. All foundations for polyphony listed in Haggh (1992) introduced feasts of duplex or higher rank only.

10. A full secular office included two Vespers, Compline, Matins with nine lessons and responsories, Lauds, Prime, Terce, Sext, and None. See Harper (1991), chap. 6, "The Divine Office."

11. St. Anthony of Padua is not represented in the Sanctorale of any surviving missal from the cathedral.

12. On the adoption of the Roman breviary, see Hautcoeur (1881).

13. Before Du Fay's foundation, Fursy de Bruille founded the feast of St. Fursy (16 Jan.) at greater duplex rank in 1449; Gregory Nicolay founded the feast of St. Gregory (12 Mar.) at duplex rank in 1449 and raised it to greater duplex rank in 1462; Gilles Carlier raised the feast of St. Giles (1 Sept.) from semiduplex to duplex rank in 1450 and to greater duplex rank in 1465; and Michael de Beringhen founded a procession for St. Michael (29 Sept.) in 1457. See Haggh (1992) and Cambrai, MM 200.

14. The will, executors' account, and inventory of possessions are in Lille, AdN 1313. Houdoy (1880) transcribes the entire will, 409–14, and excerpts from the inventory, 267–69. Fallows (1987), 79–82, discusses these documents. Du Fay founded seventeen Masses along with his obit, all in the St. Stephen chapel, but Strohm (1993), 286, counts only sixteen and thinks that one foundation was made earlier. The sixteen Masses are three for SS. Waudru, William, and Anthony of Padua each, with each held on the second day of every month in the manner of the foundation of Gregory Nicolay (not studied), and a low Mass held on Easter Sunday in the manner of the 1417 Advent foundation of Egidius de Bosco (cf. Haggh 1992, 556). The seventeenth Mass is the obit for Du Fay's parents, which followed his own obit.

15. Lille, AdN 1313, p. 70: "Item volo exequias funeris mei fieri honeste In ecclesia Cameracensis cum pulsatione toto luminari et accensione quatuor cereorum ante ymaginem sancti Anthonii de padua et epithaphium meum in dicta capella sancti stephani . . ." [Item I wish the exequies of my funeral to be done honestly in the church of Cambrai with bell-ringing, full lighting, and the burning of four candles before the image of St. Anthony of Padua and my epitaph in the said chapel of St. Stephen.]

16. See Fallows (1987), 190–91, on Du Fay's polyphonic setting of this responsory and motet.

17. We are not told when the Mass was first performed: Lille, AdN 1313, p. 23: "Item pour le messe de St. Anthoine avoir fait celebree ceste annee ainsy que ledit deffunct la ordonne et avoit grant temps devant son trespas entretenue . . ." [Item for the Mass of St. Anthony celebrated this year as the deceased ordered and had maintained for a long time before his death]; p. 30: "Item pour les despens fais par les dessusdits executeurs et aultres quilz appellerent au disner le jour St. Anthoine de pade apres le messe ditte et descantee en le Capelle dessusdicte de St. Estienne comme avoit acoustume de faire chacun an ledict deffunct—4 L. 2 s. 6 d." [Item for the expenses of the above-mentioned executors and others who were called to dinner on the day of St. Anthony of Padua after the Mass said and discanted in the above-mentioned chapel of St. Stephen as he [Du Fay] had customarily done every year—4 livres, 2 sous, 6 deniers.]

18. See the preceding note. According to the will and account, Lille, AdN 1313, p. 30, Du Fay does not specify the number of singers, but Fallows argues convincingly that the Mass was to be performed by nine adults, after taking the amount Du Fay assigned for payment of the *grandes vicaires* singing the Mass in his will, 30 s., and dividing it by the amount specified for each singer, 3 s. 4 d. (Fallows 1987, 66–67). Fallows argues for a distribution of 5/2/2 to all adults, but thinks that the duos were performed by soloists (Fallows 1983, 117–20).

19. This is curious statement, because the Gloria of the Mass that Spataro and Fallows have attributed to Du Fay is generally low in pitch. See Fallows (1987), chap. 14, on the Mass, which he dates ca. 1450, and pp. 185–87, on the challenges it poses to singers. Fallows (1983), 119, points out that the entire 14-note range of the discantus is used in the Credo and Agnus Dei of the Mass; the entire 13-note range of the contratenor is used in the Agnus Dei as well. The Mass is edited in Dufay, *Opera omnia*, ii, no. 3, where it is called "Missa sancti antonii viennensis"; manuscripts do not provide a title for the mass (see Fallows 1987).

20. The entries are in Lille, AdN 1313, p. 6: "Item pour 1 livre en grant volume en parchemin contenant *les messes* de Saint Anthoine de pade aveuc pluiseurs aultres anchiennes en noire note"; p. 20: ". . . et lautre en parchemin contenant *le messe* Saint Anthoine de pade pro se 40 s. ensemble"; p. 65: "Item 1 livre en grant volume en parchemin contenant *les messes* de saint Anthoine de pade avec pluiseurs aultres anthienes en noire note—40 s."; p. 71: "Item lego capelle sancti stephani unacum libro in quo continetur *missa* sancti Anthonij de padua in pergameno . . ." (emphases mine).

21. The documentation for the daily Mass in plainchant held after Matins with all *petits vicaires* and choirboys, cited in Wright (1978), 301, postdates Du Fay.

22. On *cantare super librum*, see Bent (1983).

23. On *O proles Hispanie*, see Fallows (1987), 62, 128–29, 191. On *O lumen ecclesie*, see ibid., 191.

24. On the "many other antiphons" see n. 28 below. For a different interpretation, see Fallows (1987), 190–91, and Planchart (1988), 145. Planchart thinks that they included Mass propers (and a memorial) for St. Francis as well as Mass propers for St. Anthony of Padua. Introits, offertories, and communions are antiphonal chants.

25. On Du Fay's funeral and obit, see Wright (1975), 219–20. On his Office of the Dead, Requiem, and obit, see Planchart (1988), 117–22. On the Requiem, see Fallows (1987), vii–viii, 55, 78–79, 82, 85, 191, 309. Du Fay's Office of the Dead and the Order of the Golden Fleece are discussed at length below.

26. Lille, AdN 1313, p. 22: "Item aux 11 [*sic*, actually 12, see immediately below] des plus souffissans tans grans comme petis vicaires qui dirent landemain des exeques en le capelle St. Estienne le messe de Requiem qui fist ledit deffunct en son vivant aveuc certaine anthiennes de profundis et les colectes Inclina et fidelium comme il avoit ordonne par son testament avoit fait legat—4 L." [Item to [12] of the most sufficient, both *grands* and *petits vicaires* who will recite the next day the exequies, and, in the chapel of St. Stephen, the Requiem Mass made by the said deceased while he was living with certain antiphons *De profundis* and the collects *Inclina* and *Fidelium* as he had ordered in his will—4 livres]; p. 70: "ad missam [of the funeral] cantetur sequentiam dies illa" [the *Dies irae* after the intonation; on the *Dies irae*, see Vellekoop 1978); p. 72 [cf. Houdoy 1880, 412]: "Item volo quod xii de sufficientioribus sive sunt magni sive parvi vicarii in crastinum exequiarum decantent missam meam de requiem in capella sancti Stephani et fine misse post requiescant in pace dicant unam de sequentiis aliis quam voluerint, deinde de profundis cum collectam Inclina et fidelium . . ." [Item I wish 12 of the most sufficient, either *grands* or *petits vicaires*, on the day after the exequies to chant my Requiem Mass in the chapel of St. Stephen, and at the end of the Mass, after the *Requiescant in pace*, to recite one or another of the sequences as they wish, then the *De profundis* with collects *Inclina* and *Fidelium*.]

27. Lille, AdN 1313, p. 7: "Item pour 1 livre de le messe de St. Anthoine de vienne et de Requiem—15 s."; p. 20: "Item a le Capelle St. Estienne ont este legates 2 livres lun en grant volume de papier contenant le messe St. Anthoine de vienne et le messe de Requiem composee par ledit deffunct pour se 15 s. et lautre en parchemin contenant le messe St. Anthoine de pade pour se 40 s. ensamble."; p. 66: "Item le livre de le messe de St. Anthoine de vienne et de Requiem—15 s."

28. Loghenaer had an image of St Anthony Abbot placed in the nave of the church (Lille, AdN 200, fol. 4r).

29. Planchart argues that Du Fay introduced new propers for St. Anthony Abbot as part of reforms of the cathedral's chant that he supervised, reforms suggested by the recopying of the cathedral's antiphoners in the mid-fifteenth century. On the St. Anthony propers, see Planchart (1988), 146–49. On the copying of the antiphoners, see Curtis (1991), 158–63; the documents are transcribed on pp. 229–43. I see no evidence of reform, only of recopying, and this in response to the proliferation of foundations earlier in the century, in Haggh (1992).

30. The Masses and their sources are presented in a table in Planchart (1988), 147–48.

31. *Missale parvum secundum usum venerabilis ecclesie Cameracensis, solerti et recognitione impressum. In quo annexe sunt misse infrascripte: que in magno missali nequaque sunt inserte. Missa compassionis beate Marie. Missa ad beatam virginem pro mulieribus pregnantibus. Missa Sancti Rochi. Missa Sancti Claudii. Missa Sancti Sebastiani. Missa Sancti Anthonii. . . .* [Paris], 30 September 1507. 8° A full list of surviving copies is available from RELICS (see n. 2).

32. Cambrai, MM 185, cited by Planchart as containing the earlier Mass propers for St. Anthony Abbot, is not from the cathedral but from the nearby collegiate church of St. Géry: it contains a full formulary for the octave of the feast of St. Géry not found in cathedral missals. (The feast of St. Géry had only semiduplex rank at the cathedral: cf. Cambrai 200, fol. 31v.) The post-Pentecostal Alleluia verses that usually distinguish the missals of individual churches are known to have been the same at the cathedral and at St. Géry, no doubt the reason behind the misidentification. The Mass propers in this manuscript are also not for St. Anthony Abbot alone. The introit *Os justi* is for the saint, but the remainder of the Mass here is comprised of propers for SS. Sulpicius, Speusippus, and other martyrs, who were venerated on the same day. The "gradual" incipit cited by Planchart, *Deus qui nos concedes,* is actually the incipit of the prayer preceding the gradual. Such a formulary, a conflation of the Masses for two feasts, was used when neither feast was especially prominent. It would not have found use at the cathedral in the fifteenth century, because St. Anthony Abbot's day was celebrated at greater duplex rank, and he was thus unchallenged by other saints.

33. I am most grateful to Jeremy Noble for making his copious notes on the Offices and Masses for St. Anthony Abbot available to me.

34. Molinier writes that the missal is from the cathedral, no doubt because of the later additions.

35. Cambrai 233, fols. 266–72, dating from the fifteenth century; fols. 434–77, also from the fifteenth century, contain sequences copied by different scribes. The added sequence is on fol. 468v.

36. On using dates of foundations to date service books, see Haggh (1992).

37. Planchart (1988), 146–49. *Scitote quoniam* is in Trent, CBC 88, fols. 176v–177r, and in Trent 89, fols. 59v–60r, but only the latter has the unique third-mode melody. Both melodies are published in Fallows (1984), 76. Fallows suggests that Du Fay composed a plenary Mass for this feast but does not believe that it has been identified (1987, 191–92, 310).

38. The intonation of the chant for *Scitote quoniam* is predictably similar to those of mode 3 chants composed by Du Fay in 1457 or 1458 for the Marian feast of the *Recollectio festorum beate Marie virginis.* But *Scitote quoniam* extends a third below the final, has long series of stepwise descents, and incorporates phrases not clearly in either species, all three features absent from the *Recollectio* chant. Yet since *Scitote quoniam* cannot be compared with another introit composed by Du Fay, given that the *Recollectio* introit was borrowed, the evidence remains inconclusive (cf. Haggh 1990a, 1990b, and Forthcoming [b]).

39. On Offices for St. Anthony Abbot in the Burgundian library, see Wright (1979), 141, 144, 147.

40. This collective obit benefited the souls of Philip the Good and later Mary of Burgundy as well. See Haggh (1988), 371–73.

41. Du Fay was present for Charles the Bold's formal investment as a knight of the Order. See Haggh (1995a), 36, 43.

42. On the Order, the Sainte-Chapelle in Dijon, its miraculous bleeding Host, and the Marian Office, see Haggh (1995a, 1996b, and 1997a). On the Burgundian and Habsburg rulers' devotion to the Eucharist, see Tanner (1993), chap. 9, 207–22.

43. Lille, AdN 1313, p. 6. Since it was a paper manuscript, it was unsuitable for the duke—he would have had the lavish original.

44. Du Fay had one and perhaps two copies of an Office of the Dead among his possessions when he died. The inventory of his books includes one paper book of Vigils and a small book with black binding and a silver-plated boss, beginning on the second folio with the end of a text and the word *Opera*. The latter may have been a copy of the Office of the Dead, since the fourth antiphon of First Vespers begins *Opera manuum.* Lille, AdN 1313, p. 6: "Recepte pour Livres . . . Item pour 1 petit livret couvert de Noir a 1 bouton de fil dargent—15 s. Item pour 1 vigile en papier—50 s."; pp. 64–65: "Livres . . . Item 1. petit livret couuert de noir a ung bouton de fil dargent commenchant au second feuillet etc. opera—15 s. . . . Item 1 virgille [sic] en papier—50 s."

45. The first gathering contains the litany and psalmody performed at the bedside of the dying as well as the rite of extreme unction. After a blank folio, the next gathering, beginning with a stub, includes the chant accompanying the body to the grave and texts to be read at the grave. Commemorations and collects end the main part of the manuscript. Office antiphons were added much later, in the seventeenth or eighteenth century, but these are simplified to the point of being completely syllabic and are surely not from the fifteenth century. The seven notated chants in the main part of the manuscript, the responsories *Paucitas dierum, Induta est caro mea, Libera me,* and their verses, as well as the antiphon *Domine suscipe me,* have the standard melodies.

46. See Ottosen, *The Responsories,* esp. 211–16, and Haggh (1989).

47. This is the manuscript listed in the inventories of 1461 and 1519: "Item ung antiphonier commenchant ou second foeillet aprez les venite .dicite nuntia nobis." (See n. 6 above.) Ottosen calls it MS CAMBR 37, dates it 1200–50, and signals that it gives the correct order of the responsories, all erroneous statements. For a published index of the manuscript, see Haggh (1995c). Also see Haggh (1995d), *Two Offices,* and Haggh (forthcoming (a)).

48. There *are* other manuscripts in the Cambrai Médiathèque Municipale *not* from the cathedral that do have the first two responsories in the order of Cambrai 29 and 38, so it is possible that the scribe began with an exemplar from another church. Indeed, this "wrong" series for the first nocturn was quite common—it is in sources from Angers, Chartres, Senlis, Sens, Soissons, Tournai, and elsewhere. See Ottosen, *The Responsories,* 98, 153–58, and 300–6.

49. Ottosen, *The Responsories,* 211–12. He notes on 211 that the combination *Credo quod* and *Heu mihi* in the first nocturn is found only in Cambrai (sources listed, 99–100).

50. Cambrai 55 in its earliest layer contains Hours of the Virgin and Passion, a psalter, and writings of Pierre d'Ailly. This layer probably predates 1405/6 or shortly thereafter, because a longer addition at the back of the manuscript, immediately following the Office of the Dead, includes Offices that were introduced at the cathedral in the thirteenth, fourteenth, and early fifteenth centuries, the most recent being the Transfiguration Office founded by canon Ponce Boerii by 1405/6 (see Haggh 1992, 555). For further on Cambrai 55, see the discussion in the text corresponding to nn. 59–60 below.

51. Explained in the paragraph following n. 58 in the text.

52. Compare the comments made by Jean Le Munerat in the 1490s on the recomposition of chant in the dioceses of Sens, Bourges, and Paris, in Harrán (1989), 44.

53. Transcribed in Planchart (1988), 122, n. 23, and discussed 122–23.

54. Jean Happé founded the feast at greater duplex rank by 1566 (Cambrai 200, fol. 29v).

55. On 5 August 1529, "Pax facta Cameraci Robertus de Croy episcopus 70 suas primitias celebravit in choro et predictum magnum S. Maria ad Nives fecit celebrari. Sed fundatum non fuit."

56. See Lille, AdN 1313, p. 6: "Recepte pour Livres. Item pour 1. messel en 2 volumes a lusaige de Rome—20 L. . . . Item pour 1. grant breviaire a lusaige de Rome a 4 afficques dargent et 2 dorees—20 L."; p. 64: "Item ung messel en deux volumes a lusage de Romme commenchant celuy et ladvent au second feuillet apres le kalendier arbores, et au penultime sedes ad Et le second au second feuillet est Christus alleluia et au penultime perpetui ignibus—20 L. . . . Item 1 grant breviaire a lusage de Rome et 4 afficques dargent et 2 dores commenchant au second feuillet secula Amen et au penultime ige consurge—20 L."

57. On the *Missa Ave regina celorum,* see Fallows (1987), 78–79, 209–14, Haggh (1987), Strohm (1993), 284–87, 432, 472 n., 486; Wegman (1995), and Planchart (1995); and on the motet or antiphon, Strohm (1993) and Wegman (1995), 280, 284, 432, 436, 481. Planchart's original hypothesis, that the Mass was for the Dedication of Cambrai Cathedral in 1472, is in Planchart (1972), but see Fallows (1987), 289, who suggests that the Mass was composed by 1468. Planchart (1995), 71, writes that the Mass was not released by the composer until 1473 and heard only in 1473 and 1474.

58. The obituary entry is transcribed and discussed in Strohm (1993), 283–87, "The functions of chapel music, and Dufay's last works." Strohm, 169, argues that verses of the text of Du Fay's motet *Nuper rosarum flores* allude to the foundation legend of the Roman basilica of Santa Maria del Fiore, commemorated with the feast of Mary of Snows. On the obit in the main choir, see Lille, AdN 1313, p. 29: "Item le 5 daoust an dessusdit 75 fu celebree pour le premier fois lobit solennel dicelluy deffunct en ceste eglise de Cambray. Se furent donnees aux petis vicaires pour boirre ensemble affin quilz prient pour ledit deffunct 50 s." [Item on 5 August 1475 was celebrated for the first time the solemn obit of the deceased in this church of Cambrai. A gratuity was given to the *petits vicaires* so that they would pray for the deceased—50 sous.]

59. See Piétresson (1968), xxviii on d'Ailly, and see Haggh (1997b) on the ordinal. D'Ailly is listed twice as treasurer in a fifteenth-century obituary of the Sainte-Chapelle, Paris, BNF lat. 17741, on 25v (obit with procession on the feast of SS. Peter and Paul, 29 June) and on 31r (duplex obits on the feasts of SS. Justin, 1 August, and Ciriacus, 8 August).

60. Planchart (1988), 120–21, and (1995), 342.

61. See Planchart 1988, 140–41, who provides no transcription of his evidence.

62. Curtis (1991), 242, cites a payment made to Simon Mellet in 1456/7: "Et ossy pour noter deux antiphonez de Alma en deux livrez et les degratter pour pluseurs faultez qui y estoient." [and also for notating two antiphons of the *Alma* in two books and for scraping them for several mistakes that were there.]

63. See Wright (1978), 304–5, on the *Salve regina,* which was in the Trinity chapel, and on the *Alma,* copied on the wall of the chapel of Notre Dame *la flamenghe.* The *Salve regina* melody is not included in the thirteenth-century antiphoner, Cambrai 38, but is given as one of the Marian antiphons for Compline in Cambrai, MM, Impr. XVI C 4, fol. 227v.

64. Discussed further in Haggh (forthcoming (a)).

65. Cf. Cambrai, MM 1302, a chronological list of the chapels and chaplains of Cambrai Cathedral.

V ★ HAGIOGRAPHY

Transforming a Viking into a Saint

The Divine Office of St. Olav

GUNILLA IVERSEN

This Caesar was a tyrant.
                              Nay, that's certain:
We are blessed that Rome is rid of him.
Peace! let us hear what Antony can say.

· · · · · · · · · · · · · · · · · · ·

Most noble Caesar! We'll revenge his death.
O royal Caesar!
                              Shakespeare,
                    Julius Caesar, act 3, scene 1

The Norwegian Viking Olav Haraldson was reevaluated by his countrymen very soon after he had been killed, and he was even celebrated as a saint, the patron saint of Norway. That a man who had obviously been feared and controversial in his lifetime so quickly could become established as a venerated saint is certainly a fascinating, if not unique, phenomenon and raises many questions. In this chapter we will concentrate on the liturgical texts of the Divine Office in its early and later forms, used as the means of transforming King Olav, the Viking, into a saint and a Christian symbol.

Olav in History

Olav was born in 995, of the lineage of Harald Hårfagre (Fairhair), son of Harald Grenske by Asta of the Uplands. According to the Sagas he was brought up in the family of his stepfather Sigurd Syr in the south of Norway. At the age of 12 he took part in his first Viking expedition. Before long he was harrying the coasts of Norway, Sweden, Denmark, Flanders, and France. He was called Olav Digre (which means "thickset and stocky," but also "proud," "haughty," or "full of self-esteem"). In *Heimskringla*, Olav is described as having "a bright and red face with good eyes, beautiful and sharp, but horrible to look into when he was angry," as "bold and wise of speech, and at an early age he was developed in both strength of body and mind. All his kinsmen and friends thought well of him. He wished to be the leader in all games and would always be before all others, as it ought to be because of his rank and birth."[1]

Soon we find him in England as the active adherent of the unfortunate Ethelred against the usurping Danes under King Cnut, who had also invaded the kingdom of his father in Norway. With his men he conquered and burned Canterbury, and among other victorious battles related in the Saga he tore down London Bridge at Southwark, which was then held by the Danes, with the result that Ethelred was restored to the throne. In *Heimskringla*, Snorri quotes Ottar the Black, one of King Olav's scalds:

> Thus says Ottar the Black:
> Yet didst thou break, warrior chief,
> The bridge in London, with boldness
> (Thou hadst luck with thee
> To win gold in battle);
> The hard-pounded shields
> Rang out, when the battle waved,
> And the iron rings sprang asunder
> In the old brynies.
>   And thereto he said this:
> Land-warder. Thou camest into the land
> And didst set Ethelred therein;
> Thou hast might, and therof
> The friend of men got heed.
> The passage was hard, when thou
> Didst bring Edmund's heir
> To this own now peaceful land,
> At one time ruled by his kin. (chap. 13; Monson, 131.)

For several years Olav stayed with Ethelred with his army of Norsemen and his ships. In England Olav must have met several impressive Christian personalities among the bishops and clerics around Ethelred and his sons, who might have influenced him and made him fight also for Christianity.[2] He was baptized in Notre-Dame in Rouen in 1012.[3] In 1016, when Erik the Jarl followed King Cnut to England and left his young son to defend Norway, Olav returned to Norway in order to restore the royal power to his own family, that of Harald Hårfagre. He came back bringing an enormous booty, after having also plundered and laid waste to north-western France, and in that same year, at the age of 21, Olav became the King of Norway. He built himself a palace at Nidaros (Trondheim), surrounded himself with all the pomp that became a king, and married Astrid, the daughter of the Swedish king Olov. He had also brought to Norway a number of English priests and bishops, among them Grimkell, who became bishop of Nidaros. Now he set-tled new laws according to the advice of Bishop Grimkell and other learned clerks, uprooting heathenism and propagating Christianity in his country (*Heimskringla*, chaps. 53–58). It seems that Olav Haraldson used the same violent methods he had used as a Viking when he now became a warrior against paganism. But, on the other hand, he might also have been a thoughtful legislator and mild ruler filled with new Christian ideals. We are left with literary sources written for different purposes. Even if we might never come to know the truth about the real person of King Olav in all the different stories told about him, we can at least study the remaining texts, saga-texts and liturgical texts, as means of creating a specific pic-ture of Olav's person, a picture that varies distinctly according the interests of the propagators.

What we know is that Olav was not the first to try to Christianize the Norwe-gians. Already King Hakan the Good, who had been raised at the court of King Athelstan, had tried in vain to impose Christianity in Norway. Though loved by his subjects, he was not successful in persuading them to adopt Christianity. After his death in 960, his scald ignored Hakan's Christian inclinations and made the heathen gods receive him in Valhalla (see, e.g., Gjerløw, ed., *Ordo Nidrosiensis Ec-clesia*, 124). More successful was King Olav Tryggvason, the most outstanding Vik-ing chief of his times, who during the short span of five years, 995–1000, by dint of tremendous energy managed to introduce Christianity as the "state religion" of Norway. He also prevailed upon the Icelanders to follow suit. In the year 999 the Althing, the Parliament of Iceland, after having deferred the question to one of their old wise men, also adopted the new religion "officially"—if not in practice.

Olav Haraldson obviously managed to do what his namesake could not. Al-though Olav strengthened the position of the peasants, the bonders, at the same time diminishing the power of the nobles, he must have been more objectionable than Olav Tryggvason and must have more openly threatened their old beliefs and traditions. Clearly, the harshness of his methods provoked fierce resistance from his subjects, and in 1028 the nobles, who had rallied round King Cnut, forced him to leave Norway and live in exile at the court of his relative Queen Ingegerd and King Jaroslav in Russia at Kiev. There he stayed until 1030, when he returned via Sweden to Norway to meet his countrymen and enemies and fight his last battle. At Stiklestad, not far from Nidaros, he was killed by his kinsmen on 29 July 1030 at the age of 35.

However, the noblemen who had put their confidence in King Cnut, hoping to get back what they had lost under Olav, soon realized that they had not gained anything by killing him, since King Cnut chose to put his own son Swein on the throne instead of restoring their power. Obviously the nobles very soon found it more profitable to restore the honor of the late king. They brought back Olav's son Magnus from Russia to inherit the throne of his father and they named Olav "eter-nal king of Norway" (*rex perpetuus Norvegiae*). Possibly they had also come to realize that King Olav with his new laws and Christianity represented a new age. A most efficient medium in the process of restoring Olav was then to canonize the late king and celebrate him as a martyr saint. Sigurd, loyal to King Cnut and at that time bishop of Nidaros, was expelled by Olav's men and replaced by Bishop Grimkell, and one year after Olav's death, in 1031 on 3 August, his body, which had been secretly saved by his men, was transferred by Bishop Grimkell to the high altar of the church of St. Clement in Nidaros.

This event was evidently celebrated as a proper translation, and from then on Olav must have been venerated as a holy man and a saint. His feast came to be celebrated from 29 July, the day of his passion, through its octave on 5 August.

What textual components were used to celebrate the feast of this new saint? How is the transformation of Olav from Viking into saint carried through in the texts? To what extent are texts from legend, homilies, and saga and the poems of the scalds used as liturgical texts in the Divine Office and Mass of St. Olav?

The wide span from glorious Viking king to holy saint is reflected in the wide span covered by the textual genres relating to Olav: there is the early Icelandic Saga material; there are the poems by Sigvat scald and other scalds quoted in the Saga, as well as different earlier versions of the Olav Saga used by Snorri when he formed his outstanding literary version of the Saga in *Heimskringla*.[4] There are further poems by scalds, such as *Geisli* (The Sunbeam) by Einar Skulason, which was written in connection with the inauguration of the new cathedral of Nidaros in 1152/53.[5]

There is also a large body of Latin material concerning Olav, such as the historical chronicles by Adam of Bremen from around 1070 and by Saxo Grammaticus from the twelfth century, and there are the different legendary versions, the *Passio et miracula*, from 1180, and the *Acta sancti Olavi regis et martyris* from 1190–1200. Further, there are liturgical texts in the form of litanies, prayers and lessons, antiphons, responsories, hymns, and sequences used in the different versions of Olav's Office and Mass.

But in spite of the exhaustive inventories of the liturgical material from Nidaros provided by the learned Norwegian scholars Helge Fehn and Lilli Gjerløw, who have made indispensable studies of fragments of manuscripts used in Norway and of the Nidaros Ordo, and in spite of an overwhelmingly large literature on the sagas and legends, the relations between these and the liturgical texts still remain to be analyzed.[6] In the following pages we will make a few preliminary observations, trying to distinguish some of the steps in the process of establishing the Viking King Olav as a saint, and at the same time we will try to trace passages from the Saga dealing with the Viking and that are used in the liturgical texts.

Traces of an Early Cult

In Nidaros there are no substantial remains from the very earliest decades. According to tradition, St. Olav was first celebrated in the church of St. Clement, a wooden church, whereas a stone church was commenced in 1070 at the site of the place where Olav was originally buried. Still according to tradition, the high altar of Nidaros Cathedral was situated over his burial place.

There are some early traces of a cult of St. Olav in England. For instance, there seems to have been a church at York dedicated to St. Olav by the middle of the eleventh century. In the reign of William the Conqueror, Alan, Earl of Brittany, gave "a certain church of St. Olav at York with four acres of land to some monks from Whitby."[7] According to *Acta sanctorum* this church was built by Siward, the Danish earl of Northumberland who died in 1055.[8] In a letter dating from 1050–60, a certain countess donates her land in Scireford to the church of St. Olav ("concedo ecclesie sancti Olavi regis et martyris terram meam de Scireford").[9]

The Earliest Mass of St. Olav

The earliest Latin liturgical material concerning St. Olav that remains today is English. There is no complete Norwegian manuscript preserved, but only a few loose leaves.[10] A votive Mass for St. Olav found in an English missal from Sherborne, the "Red Book of Derby" (or Darley) from 1061, has until now been considered to be the earliest material (Warren, ed., *The Red Book of Derby*, 271–75). The high status of this book is shown by an indication in the colophon on the last page revealing that it was used, as if a Bible, for swearing oaths: "the rede boke of darbye in the peake of darbyshire. This booke was sumtime had in such reverence in darbieshire that it was comonlie beleved that whosoever should sweare untrulie uppon this book should run mad" (Dewick and Frere, eds., *The Leofric Collectar,* 271). According to its modern editor Warren, the manuscript, written in some monastery in the diocese of Winchester, can be localized to the province of Canterbury.[11] The Mass of St. Olav contains the following three Mass prayers:[12]

> [Collect:] God, Crown of kings and Victory of the martyrs, let us experience the pious protection of *Olav, the holy king and martyr,* that through your magnificence which we glorify in his passion we may receive the crown of eternal life which is promised to those who love you.

> [Secret:] Trembling in front of the inscrutable power of your mystery, we implore you, Almighty Father, that you may sanctify these creatures chosen for the holy sacrifice to the flesh and blood of Christ in heaven, and that you may let *Olav, the holy king and martyr,* intervene for us, that we may reach salvation of life and soul.

> [Postcommunion:] Revived by the delights of the lifegiving sacrifice, the Word made flesh, we beseech you, Almighty God, that our sins may be reconciled through him and *through the intervention of Olav, the most holy king and Your martyr,* that we may be worthy of enjoying the fruits of the present life and of participating in eternal life.

These are all prayers used for the Common of Martyrs and in particular for an English king and martyr. It is notable that these prayers, in which St. Olav is called by his name and as king and martyr, are retained in the 1519 printed Missal of Nidaros (Gjerløw, ed., *Ordo,* 124).

St. Olav in Litanies

St. Olav also occurs in some early litanies in English sources. The earliest example has long been considered to be the litany of the so-called "Leofric Psalter" donated to Exeter Cathedral by Bishop Leofric (1050–72).[13] The company of martyrs into which St. Olav is inserted in this litany is interesting. He stands here together with a number of English martyrs as the last in their line: St. Alban, the protomartyr of Britain, whose relics were translated to Ely under Abbot Frederick in the eleventh century; St. Oswald, king of Northumbria (d. 642); St. Edmund, king of East Anglia (841–69); St. Edward the Martyr, king of England (962–79); St. Kenelm, prince of Mercia buried in Winchcombe (d. 812 or 821); St. Frederick, abbot of Ely (11th century); St. Ermengild, queen of Mercia and abbess of Ely (d. ca. 700); St. Alphege, archbishop of Canterbury (ca. 953–1012); St. Ethelbert, king of East Anglia (d. 794); and St. Ethelreda, queen, foundress, and abbess of Ely (d. 679). It is notable that most of these English saints had been persons in a royal position and were either newly established as saints in the eleventh century or reestablished in connection with translations during this period. This litany, as noted above, has been regarded as the earliest liturgical source mentioning St. Olav.

But there is in fact an even earlier source, namely, a litany found in a pontifical now kept in the British Library (Cotton Vitellius A VII, fol. 18; ed. in Lapidge, *Anglo-Saxon,* 73–74). There we find Olav's name at the very end of the litany. According to Michael Lapidge, who edited the text, this litany was made for Exeter or Ramsey and dates from the first half of the eleventh century (Lapidge, 73). If this is true, we are confronted here with the earliest known occurrence of St. Olav in the liturgy. The fragment, now very torn, was originally written in a fine hand and includes red, blue, and green initials. It is the litany for the Dedication of a Church.

Another litany including Olav is found in a manuscript of similar size and form with similar red, blue, and green initials—a pontifical written at Exeter in the second half of the eleventh century (London, BL Add. 28188, fol. 3; Lapidge, *Anglo-Saxon,* 67, 133). Once again it is the litany for the Dedication of a Church. But here Olav is not the last but the penultimate martyr, followed by St. Pancras. Both St. Pancras and St. Olav had a church at Exeter.

The Early Divine Office of St. Olav

The oldest known Divine Office for St. Olav is that found in the so-called Leofric Collectar, another of the books donated to Exeter Cathedral by Bishop Leofric and written in the years 1050–60, possibly in Winchester (London, BL Harley 2961; Dewick and Frere, eds., *The Leofric Collectar, I,* cols. 209–14). As the name indicates, it contains all the collect prayers used in the Office, and, as is usual with ancient Office books, it includes collects for all hours except Prime and Compline. Since the prayer for First Vespers is, as expected, the same as the collect for the Mass in the Red Book of Derby from the Canterbury–Winchester diocese (already quoted above), we begin with the collect for Matins.[14]

Collects

[Matins:] Almighty eternal God, strength of the warriors and victory of the martyrs, look gracefully upon the solemn feast of this day and let your Church rejoice in a solemnity without end, and with the intercession of *Saint Olav, king and martyr,* make perfect the prayers of all your faithful ones.

[Terce:] Almighty eternal God, who has sanctified the blessed and happy joy of this day when we celebrate *your holy servant Olav,* fill our hearts with your love and care, so that we may celebrate the shedding of his holy blood on earth and through his merits perceive his patronage in heaven.

[Sext:] God of ineffable compassion, who allowed *the holy king Olav* to conquer the enemy in dying for the sake of your name, mercifully grant to your servants that with his intervention, in your name they might deserve to overcome and extinguish the temptations of the ancient enemy.

[None:] God, who through the passion of *Saint Olav, king and martyr,* consecrated this day, we pray you, that through this same intervention, may flourish in our actions that which will be rewarded by heavenly prize.

[Second Vespers:] Almighty God, we pray you, grant that just as we praise the divine miracles in the passion of *the holy king Olav,* so also through his pious prayers may we attain your indulgence.

The collect at Terce is borrowed from the Office of St. Oswald, and the one used at Sext is taken from the Office of St. Edmund, king and martyr, celebrated on 20 November in English uses and in Rouen.

All of these collects, like those in the Red Book of Derby, refer to Olav as the blessed and holy king and martyr in expressions such as "beati Olavi regis et martyris," "sancti servi tui Olavi," "beatum Olavum regem," "beati Olavi regis et martyris," "sancti Olavi regis." And notably, these collects, like the prayers of the Mass in the Leofric Missal, were not replaced by new texts in the later Office but were retained in the *Breviarium Nidrosiense.*

Capitula

The capitula (or chapters), the short and generally biblical texts read in the Office, are not all taken from the Common of Martyrs, as one might well have expected. In fact, only the first one is, and this text does not have a close biblical reference. The other capitular texts, however, are all biblical; in particular they are taken from the praises of Moses, Josias, and Elias in Sirach (Ecclesiasticus)—that is, they are texts praising God's chosen prophets and strong leaders of his people:

[First Vespers:] Blessed is the man whose head the Lord has crowned and surrounded with the wall of salvation, armed with the shield and the sword of faith, for conquering the people and all enemies.[15]

[Matins:] The Lord conducted the just man through the right ways. His memory is in benediction. At his word the wind is still, and with his thought he appeases the deep, and the Lord Jesus has planted him.[16]

[Terce:] In the goodness and readiness of his soul the just man appeased God for Israel. He implored the almighty Lord. And God granted to him, the man strong in battle, to sit on his right side and to exalt the horn of his people.[17]

[Sext:] In his days the just man feared not the prince, and no man was more powerful than he. No word could overcome him, and after death his body prophesied.[18]

[None:] In his life the holy man did wonders, and in death he wrought miracles. His remembrance shall be sweet as honey in every mouth, and as music in a banquet of wine.[19]

[Second Vespers:] The just man was directed by God unto the repentence of the nation, and he took away the abominations of wickedness. He directed his heart toward the Lord, and in the days of sinners he strengthened godliness. And his bones were visited, and after death they prophesied.[20]

The antiphons of First Vespers

Most of the antiphons are taken from the Common of Martyrs. But the texts of the second and fourth antiphons of First Vespers in the Leofric Collectar have not been traced in other sources, whereas the fifth antiphon appears in the Common of more recent English sources as well as in Nidaros (Gjerløw, ed., *Antiphonarium*, 182–86).

Ant. 1: Hic est qui non est derelictus a deo in die certaminis sui et ipse conculcavit caput serpentis antiqui modo coronatur quia fideliter vicit in mandatis domini. Alleluia.[21] (This is the man who on the day of his struggle was not abandoned by God, and he who trod down the head of the old serpent will soon be crowned, for he was victorious following the commands of the Lord. Alleluia.)

Ant. 2: Beatus vir qui suffert temptationem quoniam cum probatus fuerit accipiet coronam vite quam repromisit deus diligentibus se. (Blessed is the man who endures temptation, for since he has been tested, he will receive the crown of eternal life, which God has promised to those who love him.)

Ant. 3: Iste sanctus pro lege dei sui certavit usque ad mortem et a verbis impiorum non timuit fundatus enim erat supra firmam petram (Gjerløw, ed., *Antiphonarium*, 137; *CAO* 3, 3434). (This holy man fought unto death for the law of his God and did not fear the words of the wicked, for he was founded on the firm rock.)

Ant. 4: Iste est vir misericordiæ cuius oblivionem non acceperunt iustitiæ cum semine eius perseverant bona et memoria eius non derelinquetur in secula; gratiam et misericordiam a domino eius nobis optineat intercessio. (This is the man of mercy; those who steadfastly follow him on his way of justice are not forgotten and the memory of him will never leave the world; may his intercession bring us grace and mercy from the Lord.)

Ant. 5: Beatus vir qui inventus est sine macula qui post aurum non abiit nec speravit in thesauris peccuniæ quis est hic et laudabimus eum fecit enim mirabilia in vita sua. Alleluia (Gjerløw, ed., *Antiphonarium*, 139; cf. *CAO* 4, 6230). (Blessed is the man who is found without stain, who did not leave the right way for the sake of gold nor set his hope in treasures of wealth. This is that man and we will praise him, for he made miracles in his life. Alleluia.)

None of these texts mentions Olav's name but simply refers to the protagonist of the feast as "This is the man" (*hic est vir, iste est vir*), "blessed is the man" (*beatus vir*), "that holy man" (*iste sanctus*). These are texts perfectly fitting for the Common of any martyr, but they are far distant from the descriptions of the Viking hero that we meet in the poems of the scalds and in the Sagas. Especially the last of these antiphons—the only one kept in the new Office in Nidaros—which tells about Olav as free from interest in worldly riches, depicts a person who seems to be unlike the young hero described in the Saga. We remember the description in the song of Ottar the Black quoted above: "Thou hadst luck with thee to win gold in battle."

The Vesper responsory after the first capitulum, *Beatus vir cuius capiti*, in this early Office is indicated by the words "Sanctus Olavus" and "r"—probably "r" for *require*, suggests the editor, adding that such a text is not found elsewhere in the manuscript.[22] But this "r" might perhaps rather be read as for *rex*, "King." The manuscript here presents another, alternative responsory, *O sancte Olave concivis gloriose martyrum* (O Saint Olav, glorious fellow citizen of the martyrs), a responsory that is also used for the Common of a Martyr in Worcester "in the case of a king" (*si tabula fuerit de rege*) (Gjerløw, ed., *Antiphonarium*, 172).

Gospel antiphons

The first Gospel antiphon, *Iste est qui pro lege* (This is he who abandoned himself unto death for the sake of God's law), is also found with the indication that it should be used for the feast of any martyr not a bishop or priest (*In natale unius martyris qui non fuit pontifex vel sacerdos*).[23] However, this antiphon is also followed by an alternative antiphon, *Exultemus omnes*, which actually refers to Olav by name:

Exultemus omnes in deo, salutari nostro, qui recordatus misericordie sue suscepit *sanctum regem Olavum* in collegio martyrum, quem rogemus omnes ut pro nobis ipsum regem regum semper adoret Ihesum Christum.[24] (Let us all exult in God, our salvation, who, remembering his mercy, received *the holy king Olav* into the company of his martyrs. Let us all pray that for our sake he may always adore the King of kings himself, Jesus Christ.)

At Matins also the alternative Gospel antiphon *Sit semper summa laus* ends in a specific reference to the Norwegian king:

> Sit semper summa laus deo patri per quem triumphant sancti quique ordi-
> nes angelicos victorioso hodie cumulavit colono et mortales glorioso fovit
> *patrono, cuius nunc membra felix amplectitur Norvegia* animam habet celestis
> regia in qua cum Christo nunc regnat pro nobis, precamur, semper in-
> tercedat.[25] (Glory be forever to God the Father through whom triumph the
> holy and who today has placed the angelic orders on the highest column
> and given to the mortals a glorious *patron. May he whose limbs are now em-
> braced by fortunate Norway* and whose soul belongs to the heavenly king-
> dom, where he now reigns together with Christ, always intervene for us,
> we pray.)

Likewise the other Gospel antiphon at Terce, *Auctor iustitie legis divine,* which re-mains untraced in other textual sources, specifically refers to Olav in an image that became of special importance in the iconography of the Olav cult:[26]

> Auctor iustitie legis divine plantavit *regem Olavum* tanquam lignum fructif-
> erum prosperantem permansurum in via iustorum. (The Author of the jus-
> tice of divine law planted *King Olav* like a prosperous tree, abounding in
> fruit and everlasting in the path of the righteous.)

The Gospel antiphon in Second Vespers, *Corde et ore,* refers to Olav as a crowned king and saint:

> Corde et ore laudemus pariter sanctorum sanctificatorem dominum qui in
> sanctis suis semper est mirabilis quique *sanctum regem olauum martyrem*
> uenerandum gloria et honore coronatum de terris transtulit per martyrium
> ad celestis regni palatium cuius anima uictorissima in celis sublimiter coro-
> nata nobis optata quesumus amplificet suffragia. (With heart and mouth
> together, let us praise the Lord who makes the saints holy, who is forever
> marvelous in his saints, who transferred from earth *the holy king and venera-
> ble martyr Olav,* crowned through martyrdom with glory and honor, to the
> royal palace of the celestial kingdom. May his most victorious soul, exalted
> and crowned in heaven, we pray, reinforce our humble prayers.)

It is notable but not surprising that all three alternative Gospel antiphons, *Exul-temus omnes, Sit semper summa laus,* and *Corde et ore,* which are proper to this early Office and which all specially mention St. Olav by name, are retained in the later liturgy of Nidaros, as we shall see below (Gjerløw, ed., *Antiphonarium,* 182).

Like many of the other texts used in the early Office, the short hymn *Martyr dei qui unicum* also belongs to that generally used for the Common of Martyrs, and is only indicated by incipit.[27]

In all these liturgical texts found in the earliest Divine Office for St. Olav, there is not yet any legendary material. In collects, alternative Gospel antiphons, and responsories containing Olav's name, he is above all defined as a holy king (*sanctus, beatus rex*). It seems that in this first step, universal material for a martyr, and in particular that used for English martyr kings, was chosen in order to create and establish the feast of King Olav as a regular feast. Both the first capitular text and the biblical texts in the capitula that are proper to St. Olav seem to be well chosen for this purpose.

From the manuscript sources of litanies and of Mass and Office texts it seems that not only York but also liturgical centers in the southern regions, such as Winchester, Canterbury, London, and Exeter, might be of special interest for the location of the earliest cult of St. Olav in England in the eleventh century. The early Office might perhaps also be seen as a memorial of the Anglo-Saxon missions to Norway. Some historians have considered the missionary bishop Grimkell, belonging to King Olav's household, as the most likely author of this Office. If so, then he was the same bishop who acted in the translation of St. Olav in 1031, and who has also been identified with the English bishop Grimkillus or Grimcytel, who died in 1047 as bishop of Selsey (Johnsen 1975; Gjerløw, ed., *Antiphonarium*, 182, n. 1).

We do not know for how long and to what extent this type of liturgical text was used. But as the cult of Olav grew stronger, there must have been an increasing need for an Office composed entirely for St. Olav. It seems possible that the writing of a proper Office started already in the decade following his death, at a time when Olav was being praised in the poetry of the scalds. Although there are no such sources preserved, it seems possible that parts of such an Office might have been incorporated into the new Office. Moreover, most of the general material, such as that found in the Leofric Collectar, was swept away when the new text by the archbishop of Nidaros Augustin or Eystein Erlandson (d. 1188) was being promoted around the middle of the following century.

The *Passio et miracula* and the New Divine Office for St. Olav

The new Office for St. Olav by Archbishop Eystein, which opens with the responsory *In regali fastigio*, belongs to the twelfth century, contemporary with the new cathedral of Nidaros inaugurated in 1152/3. Most of the texts in this Office were taken from a new source of legendary material, namely the *Passio et miracula Beati Olavi*. This text exists in two versions, one longer and one shorter, principally differing from each other only in the number of miracles. For long its existence was unknown to scholars investigating the legendary material on St. Olav. Thus it did not come to the attention of the Norwegian historian Gustav Storm, who in 1880 published all material known to him and who tried to reconstruct the Latin legend in *Monumenta historica Norwegiae latine conscripta*. Storm used as his main source a text found in a fifteenth-century manuscript that had belonged to the Augustinian abbey of Böddeken in Paderborn and which had been edited by the Bollandists in *Acta sanctorum* before it disappeared. In his 1880 study Storm also edited the Latin legend in a version from Leuven from 1485.[28]

In 1881, a year after Storm's impressive work had appeared, the English scholar Frederick Metcalfe published a new hitherto-unknown Latin text of an Olav legend written down in the 1180s and belonging to Fountains Abbey in Yorkshire.[29] In fact, it is in this manuscript that the archbishop of Nidaros, Eystein (or Augustine)

Erlandsson, is indicated as its author or compilor. Eystein, who was in exile in England between 1180 and 1183 and was entertained at Bury St. Edmunds from August 1181 to February 1182, may have been working to promote the cult of Olav there during these years and may have carried a copy of the legend with him, or sent it, on his return, to St. Edmund's monastery and that of Fountains, as Metcalfe suggests (*Passio et miracula*, 5).

The text of this manuscript not only contains the miracles related in the Old Norse Homily book (from after 1153) but also thirty new miracles: a second series of miracles and then a third series of miracles that had taken place in Eystein's own time.[30] This is the text that now is called the longer version of the *Passio et miracula*.

But Metcalfe, who believed that he had presented "a complete history of the miracles of the Saint," turned out to be wrong. In 1901 the Bollandists published one version of the legend, the *Passio beati Olavi gloriosi regis et martyris* found in a manuscript of around 1200 from the Benedictine abbey of Anchin near Arras.[31] They also presented another manuscript from the beginning of the thirteenth century from a Cistercian abbey in York[shire?], Oxford, Bodleian Rawlinson C 440. This manuscript contains all the miracles in the one from Arras but also the miracle *Miles quidem de Britania*, "A certain knight of Britain." On folio 193v it also has an epilogue opening with the words "Let us end the page" (*Finem imponamus paginae*), which seems to be parallel to the epilogue found in the Old Norse Homily Book: "Nu skulum vér luca pesse rødo" (Indebrø, ed., *Gammel*, 168; Storm, *Monumenta*, 125–32). On the following folio this manuscript also contains an Olav Mass with the collect *Deus qui beatum Olavum*, the secret *Suscipe clementissime*, and the postcommunion *Sancti martiris tui Olavi*.

In the manuscript from Fountains Abbey edited by Metcalfe, we read the confusing statement that Olav was killed not on 29 July but on 28 September (*4 kal. Octobris*, evidently a mistake for August). It is notable that the same error is found in the other manuscript from the region of York, and this points to a connection between the two manuscripts as witnessing to a common source.

When Storm edited all the different versions of the Latin legend known to him, he presented the Office in the Swedish *Breviarium Nidrosiense* as well as in the *Breviarium Lincopense* and in a number of other breviaries.[32] The two mentioned are of special interest for the present study as witnesses to new versions of the Olav Office, the former since it represents the established liturgy in Olav's own church and the latter because it reflects influences from the Icelandic Saga.

The new Divine Office for St. Olav in Nidaros

According to Lilli Gjerløw, the formation of the new Office liturgy for St. Olav to be used in the new Nidaros Cathedral culminated during the reign of King Sverre (1177–1202) with Archbishop Eystein, the second metropolitan of Nidaros (1161–88), and his successor Eirik (1189–1205).[33] The texts of the printed *Breviarium Nidrosiense* from 1519 that were edited by Storm in 1880 represent a further step in the history of the Nidaros liturgy. Since the manuscript material is full of lacunae, there are of course parts of the repertory where we cannot identify the twelfth-century liturgy from the printed breviary. (See the appendix for one MS source representing a state between the new Office and the later printed one.)

But let us try to see what is retained from the old liturgical texts from the manuscripts from the Winchester–Canterbury tradition in the books of the Exeter Bishop Leofric studied above, and what is new.

Collects

First, we can state that the collects presented in the *Breviarium Nidrosiense* are the same as those used in the early Office in sources from the first decades of the cult (Gjerløw, ed., *Ordo*, 125). Thus we recognize the collect *Deus (qui est) regum corona* from the early Office; it is used at First Vespers, Lauds, and Second Vespers (Storm, *Monumenta*, 237, 238), as well as in the Mass. We recognize the collect used at Matins in a slightly varied form: *Omnipotens sempiterne . . . intercessor sit ipse perpetuus.*[34] Likewise we recognize the prayer at Terce, *Omnipotens sempiterne deus . . . sentiamus,* as well as the collect for Sext, *Deus ineffabilis misericordie.* The oratio for None, *Deus qui hunc diem beati Olavi regis . . . celestibus,* is used as the collect of St. Pantaleon (28 July) in English sources. Finally the collect of Second Vespers, *Presta, quesumus . . . assequamur,* is the same as that in the old Office. As we noted above, the title "King" (*rex*) has an important place in these prayers, and perhaps that was one reason to retain them in the new Office for the martyr king.[35]

Capitula, lessons, and responsories

Of the Capitula texts, only the first of them, *Beatus vir cuius capiti,* quoted above, which was used for the Common of Martyrs, seems to be retained from the early Office as presented in the Leofric Collectar. In the new Office of St. Olav in Nidaros, Matins is expanded to nine lessons, which, together with their responsories and verses, are all taken from the *Passio et miracula,* and replace the shorter old Office texts with their biblical lessons.

Thus the first lesson and its reponsory and verse describe Olav's conversion, his baptism in Rouen, and his missionary work, presenting him as poor in spirit, turned from the world, and constantly meditating over celestial things. The new Office is often called *In regali fastigio* from the opening words of the first responsory, whose text is taken from the *Passio et miracula* (Reiss, *Musiken,* 77; Storm, *Monumenta,* 233). *In regali fastigio* is essential also for later compositions in the Olav liturgy, as we shall see below. In the illuminated initial "I" in a choir antiphoner written for Nidaros Cathedral in the thirteenth century, King Olav is shown sitting on his throne holding his axe "placed in his royal position."[36]

R. 1. In regali fastigio constitutus spiritu pauper erat rex Olavus. Ac licet regni negotiis implicatus mentis devote libera contemplatione meditabatur celestia. V. Sordebat ei omnis vana spes et terreni regni gloria ac voluptas vilescebat. (Placed in his royal position, King Olav was poor in spirit. Although he was involved in the governmental duties of his royal power, his open mind was constantly meditating over celestial things. V. All wordly vanity bored him, and the glory and pleasure of his worldly kingdom seemed vile to him.)

The second lesson describes Olav as a successful Christian preacher, and this theme is continued in the responsory repeated from Vespers:[37]

R. 2. O quantus fidei fervor inuictissimi martyris pectus accenderat qui in medio gentium eferrarum constitutus. Non cessabat tamen salutis verbum cunctis predicare. V. Multos habebat aduersarios qui vias domini rectas conabantur euertere. (O such a great fervor of faith that had inflamed the heart of the most unvanquished martyr who was placed in the midst of savage peoples. But he never ceased to preach to all the word of salvation. V. He had many enemies who tried to convert the right ways of the Lord.)

The third lesson presents Olav as indefatigable preacher of the evangelic message (*indefessus evangelii predicator*) and as a wise legislator.[38] The responsory describes him as a fearless lion, a follower of Job (Job 31:34) who feared neither the multitude opposing him nor the contempt of his kinsmen, and who willingly offered himself to perils:

R. 3. Iustus vero ut leo confidens absque terrore et iuxta exemplum sancti Iob, non expavescebat ad multitudinem nimiam: nec desectio propinquorum terrebat eum. V. Offerebat se sponte periculis: martyrium suscipere non recusans (cf. *Passio et miracula,* 69, 72). (Righteous as a lion, full of confidence and without fear, and following the example of Job, he was not afraid of the multitude nor feared the contempt of his own kinsmen. V. He offered himself to perils and did not refuse to accept martyrdom.)

The fourth lesson presents Olav as a follower of the first missionary martyrs preaching about Christ. The responsory takes up the line in describing Olav with words from Paul's letter to the Ephesians (6:13–17).[39]

R. 4. Itaque devotissime perficiens officium euangeliste: indutur lorica fidei et galea salutis. Circuibat civitates, vicos et villas: salutarem doctrinam ubique disseminans. V. Iesu bone quantos labores sustinuit antequam populum incredulum convertere posset (cf. *Passio et miracula,* 69, 72). (And thus faithfully fulfilling the office of an evangelist, he fastens on the armor of faith and the helmet of salvation. He went around to towns, villages, and country houses, everywhere spreading the doctrine of salvation. V. Such great labors for good Jesus sustained him before he could convert the unbelieving people.)

The fifth lesson says that "it is impossible to mention all the blessed martyr's benefits toward his people" and—with a slight exaggeration?—that "through his honorable way of life (*honestam vite formam*) he left to the inhabitants a celebrated memorial of his religion."[40] The responsory mentions the name of his country and alludes at the same time to the Psalter (Ps. 106:42):

R. 5. Confluebant ad baptisma certatim populi: et in multis Norvegie partibus. Propter fidelium multitudinem omnis iniquitatis opilabat os suum. V. Confusi erat confidentes in scultili et numerus credentium augebatur in dies

(*Passio et miracula,* 70). (The people eagerly gathered to be baptized also in many parts of Norway. Because of the multitude of the faithful, iniquity held its mouth closed. V. Those who trusted in idols were confused, but the number of believers increased from day to day.)

The sixth lesson describes Olav's eagerness and zeal in propagating Christianity, but also how he was pressed by many enemies, and his return to his own country via Sweden from exile in Russia.[41] The responsory and its verse praise his zeal in inspiring his people and building churches:

R. 6. Florebat fides et ubertim germinabat verbi dei nova plantatio. Fabricandis ecclesiis offerebant dona populi devoti et alacres. V. Exaltabat rex plus quam credi potest iam laboris sui suavissimos fructus pregustatus (*Passio et miracula,* 70). (Faith flowered, and the new plant of the word of God blossomed copiously. Devout and cheerful people offered gifts for the building of churches. V. The king extolled more than can be believed the sweetest rewards of his labor already tasted.)

Thus, we see how all six lessons of the first two nocturns describe Olav as a glorious king, a wise legislator, and a successful missionary, persecuted and exiled but faithfully fulfilling his evangelic office, fighting for Christ.

The third nocturn: Olav's death at Stiklestad

The lessons of the third nocturn all deal with Olav's passion. The texts present Olav as Christ's faithful follower. This is underlined through the biblical passage (Luke 9:23) that opens the seventh lesson: "If any man will come after me, let him deny himself and take up his cross daily, and follow me." The long lesson continues with a passage from the *Passio et miracula* describing the opening of Olav's last struggle against his enemies at Stiklestad:

Lesson 7: . . . Some of his enemies, corrupted through bribes from King Cnut to hate the faithful and blessed martyr, and others who by the impulse of their wickedness rejected the new religion, which was against the laws of their fathers, formed an army to fight against the king. But the glorious martyr, although entirely intent on celestial things, collected an army as great as he could in a such short time, in order to fight for faith and justice, and went against his enemies. There he was blessedly (*feliciter*) killed on the fourth day before the Kalends of August on the fourth day of the week in the one thousand and twenty-eighth year from the Incarnation of the Lord. He moved from the camp to the royal palace of the heavenly King, from war to a peace which surpasses all understanding.[42]

R. 7. Devenerat martyr Christi in locum ubi corpus eius sanctissimum modo requiescit, huius loci incole obstinati in malicia veritatis hostes erant inexorabiles. V. Hi ergo collecto exercitu convenerunt in unum adversus dominum et adversus Christum eius. [Acts 4:26] (*Passio et miracula,* 72). (Christ's martyr had come to the place where his most holy body recently rested, where the cruel inhabitants of this place were stubborn in their ill-will and enemies to the truth. V. They collected an army and came together against the Lord and against his Christ.)

The eighth lesson recalls the vision described in the *Passio et miracula* where Olav in a visionary dream the night before the battle sees Christ—and like Jacob in his vision in the desert, sees a ladder to heaven—and Christ tells him that he will ascend to heaven after a glorious martyrdom.[43] This scene is depicted on the famous altar frontal of St. Olav from the fourteenth century in the Cathedral of Nidaros.

Lesson 8: The night before the day on which the glorious martyr suffered his death, the Lord Jesus appeared before him and conforted him with sweet words, words of consolation. "Come to me," he said, "my beloved. It is time for you to pick the sweet fruits of your labors, to enjoy our company in eternal joy and to receive the crown of eternal glory." Fully comforted by this dream and rejoicing beyond measure over the ineffable delight that had filled him, he gladly abandoned himself to his passion, since he already miraculously recognized the ladder which he had just seen erected to heaven in his dream, and on which he would happily ascend to the sweetness he had tasted.

R. 8. Egregius martyr Olavus nocte precedente diem sue passionis splendore amictum contemplatur Iesum astantem sibi ac dicentem: "Veni chare meus, tempus est ut laborum tuorum dulcissimos percipias fructus." V. In admiratione aspectus illius attonitus celeste percepit oraculum (cf. Ecclus. 50:12; *Passio et miracula*, 74). (The night before the day of his passion the honorable martyr Olav saw Jesus dressed in a splendid garment standing before him and saying to him: "Come, my beloved, it is time for you to pick the sweet fruits of your labors." V. Wondering over this sight and seized with inspiration, he received the divine prophecy.)

Finally, the ninth lesson recounts the first of the miracles that took place after Olav's death in the *Passio et miracula*. It tells about the blind man who could see again after having touched his eyes with water mixed with the blood of the martyr.[44] The responsory recalls the effusion of the blood of Olav himself in his own passion:

R. 9. Rex inclytus Olavus martyr Domini preciosus claritate confortatus divine visionis exultans accessit ad locum passionis. V. Et per effusionem sanguinis pervenit ad palmam eterne iocunditatis (*Passio et miracula*, 74). (The glorious King Olav, the Lord's precious martyr, was strengthened by the divine vision and came exulting to the place of his passion. V. And through effusion of his blood he achieved the palm of eternal joy.)

The Battle of Stiklestad in Lesson Seven
of the *Breviarium Lincopense*

Comparing the seventh lesson of this version of the Office of St. Olav with one of the lessons found in the Swedish *Breviarium Lincopense*, we find an interesting variation in the description of the battle of Stiklestad and Olav's death. The *Lincopense* lesson starts with a passage from the *Passio et miracula* that is closely related to the one used in the seventh lesson in Nidaros:

> Exercitu itaque in breui prout potuit congregato obuiat inimicis (*Breviarium Lincopense,* 728; cf. *Passio et miracula,* 73). (He brought together an army as large as he could within such a short time and went against the enemies.)

This statement corresponds to what is told in Olav's saga in *Heimskringla,* chapter 224, where Snorri relates:

> It is said that the bonders had no fewer than a hundred hundred men,
>
>> but thus quoth Sigvat:
>> Sore is my sorrow that the king,
>> Who swung the gold-decked
>> Sword handle, brought
>> Little gathering from the east.
>> Therefore the bonders won;
>> They were double as many;
>> It was to Olav's scathe.
>> I charge no man with cowardice.[45]

Then follows in the Office text another passage that is different from that in the *Breviarium Nidrosiense,* but still taken from the *Passio et miracula:*

> Porro dominus qui martyri suo mercedem pro quo tot agones pertulerat reddere decreuerat: ut gloriosius eum coronaret: iniquorum iaculis gloriosum martyrem occumbere permisit (*Breviarium Lincopense,* 728; cf. Metcalfe, ed., *Passio,* 73). (Moreover the Lord had decided to give to his martyr his reward for all the many struggles he had endured. In order to crown the glorious martyr even more honorably, he sent him out to die through the javelins of the enemies.)

After this, the Breviary expands the lesson, recalling the dramatic scene in the Saga:

> Legitur enim in chronicis islandie:
> quod Thorirus Hundir pupungit sanctum Olauum in pectore
>
> Torstanus Knarra Smidher secuit eum in genu
> et Kalffwer Arnasson secuit eundem in collo
> in sua sanctissima passione (*Breviarium Lincopense,* 728).
>
> (For it is read in the Icelandic chronicle
> that Thorir the Hound pierced Saint Olav in his breast,
> Thorstein Knarra Smidher [the Shipwright] cut his knee
> and Kalffwer Arnason cut him in his neck
> in his holy passion.)

The same passage reads in the Saga:

> Thorstein the Shipwright struck with his axe at King Olav and the blow fell on his left leg above the knee. Finn Arneson straightaway slew Thorstein.

But after that wound, the king leaned against a stone, cast away his sword, and bade God help him. Then Tore the Hound struck at him with his spear and the thrust went under the brynie up to his maw. Kalv then struck him and the blow fell on the left side of his neck, though men are not agreed which Kalv it was that wounded the king. These three wounds brought about King Olav's fall. And after his death most of the followers fell who had gone forth with the king (*Heimskringla*, chap. 218; Monson, *From the Sagas*, 281).

The final expression of the liturgical lesson, "in his most holy passion" (*in sua sanctissima passione*), changes the meaning of the scene at Stiklestad, transferring it into its theological and liturgical context and transforming it into a description of the death of a martyr. Thus, the lesson in this Office combines the passion of a saint and the saga of a Viking hero. In chapters 226–28 of the Saga, describing the battle at Stiklestad, both sides have right on their side. Snorri quotes Sigvat scald, who says:

> I think the men were frightened
> when they met in the battle
> the sharp fierce eyes
> of Olav, the warrior.
> The men from Trond
> lacked the courage
> to meet his eyes,
> hard as eyes of a serpent.
> Horrible seemed the king.

And Snorri quotes another scald, Bjarne Gullbrascald, who "quoth like this on Kalv Arnesson":

> Fight-bold, you
> defended the land against Olav.
> I heard that you waged war on the king.
> At Stiklestad you stood forth
> proud before the sign.
> You fought with great courage,
> stood fast till the king had fallen (ibid.).

Here it is clearly not Olav who has all the sympathy, and he is definitely not treated as a saint, so it seems rather strange to see passages from these texts used in the Divine Office. It is even more dramatic when we consider the context in the Saga, recalling, for instance, the speech that Snorri puts in the mouth of the Danish Bishop Sigurd in Nidaros before the battle. There Olav and his men are described as evildoers by King Cnut's loyal bishop:

From his youth he was wont to rob and slay folk, and for that he went far about the lands . . . ye know well how he bore himself towards the landed men; the best are slain and many have fled the land because of him. He has also gone far about the land with his bands of robbers, has burnt the lord-ships and slain and robbed folk. Who is there here amongst the great men who has not good reason to take vengeance on him? . . . let no man be so bold as to move them to churches, for they are all Vikings and evildoers (ibid.).

The Five Antiphons at Lauds

Turning back to the Office of St. Olav in Nidaros, we find that the five antiphons at Lauds, which follow the final lessons of the nocturn about Olav's miraculous vision, are all taken from the *Passio et miracula* and describe the first five miracles after Olav's death.

Ant. 1: Post mortem martyris aqua mixta sanguine qui de vulneribus fluxerat lavans cecus oculos lumen recipit (Storm, ed., *Monumenta*, 237; Metcalfe, ed., *Passio*, 74–75). (After the martyr's death, a blind man who touched his eyes with water mixed with the martyr's blood regained his sight.)

Ant. 2: Implorata ope martiris dux Guthormus cum parva manu ingentem fudit exercitum (*Monumenta*, 237; *Passio*, 75–76). (Having implored the martyr's help, Duke Guttorm scattered a large army with a handful of men.)

Ant. 3: Ad sepulcrum sancti martiris pernoctans enormiter contracta mulier integre reddita sanitati et leto vultu alacri animo ad propria remeavit (*Monumenta*, 237; *Passio*, 87–89). (A woman with a grievously shrunken body who spent a night at the holy martyr's tomb could return home fully recovered, with joyful face and happy soul.)

Ant. 4: Adolescens qui lingua precisa loquendi officium ammiserat ad sepulcrum martiris adiens recepto usu lingue recessit cum gaudio (*Monumenta*, 237; *Passio*, 74–75). (A young man who could not speak after his tongue had been cut through visited the martyr's tomb and went away full of joy, having regained the use of his tongue.)

Ant. 5: Quidam sacerdos truncatis membris exanimis imploravit opem gloriosi martiris. moxque sanctus in sompnis ei apparuit et subito plene sanitati restituit (*Monumenta*, 237; *Passio*, 80–82). (A certain priest, at the end of his strength and with mutilated limbs, implored the glorious martyr for help, and soon the saint appeared to him in his sleep and at once restored him to full health.)

Versified Songs in the New Office

In the new Olav Office toward the end of the twelfth century there are new versified compositions; one is the hymn *Rex Olavus gloriosus*.[46] The first six strophes are sung at Vespers. They describe Olav as a successful propagator of Christian faith and report his death as a martyr, that is, they follow the line of the lessons and responsories, whereas strophes six to twelve, which are sung at Lauds, narrate the

same miracles as do the antiphons at Lauds, but in versified form (*AH* 11:208–9, no. 383):

1. Rex Olavus gloriosus,	Glorious King Olav,
sanctus martyr domini	holy martyr of the Lord,
agonista pretiosus	precious warrior and fighter,
dat honorem numini,	gives his praise to God;
spe constanti copiosus	full of everlasting hope,
offertur certamini.	he offers himself to the struggle,
. . . .	. . . .
7. Multitudo adunatur	Many men are brought together
et bellum indicitur	and war is declared,
iniquitas dominatur	injustice becomes the ruler
in regem erigitur,	and rises against the King;
leo fortis victimatur	the strong lion is sacrificed
et iustus conteritur.	and the just man is punished.
8. Christiani mox caeduntur,	The Christians are soon vanquished;
rex truncatur gladio.	the King is cut with a sword.
Quorum animae creduntur	Their souls are shining forth,
clariores radio,	more brilliant than the sun;
sede sacra disponuntur	in the celestial battle-place
victores in stadio.	the victors are placed on the holy throne.
9. Caecus lapsus casu bono	A blind man happened luckily
aqua tangit pupillam,	to touch his eye with water;
visum capit aquae dono,	by this water his sight was restored,
visus perdit maculam,	and his sight was without fault;
Christum laudat dulci sono	he praises Christ in lovely song
lucis videns faculam.	when he sees the flame of light.
10. Lingua cuidam amputatur	The tongue of a man is cut off,
et mutus efficitur.	and he becomes a mute.
Opem sancti deprecatur,	He implores the saint to help him.
martyr prece flecitur,	The martyr listens to his prayer.
usus linguae reformatur,	Use of the tongue is restored,
adolescens loquitur.	and the young man speaks again.
11. Sacerdotis detruncati	A priest with limbs
membris truncus vehitur	badly truncated is taken
regis aram ad beati	to the altar of the holy King
et ibidem ponitur,	and laid upon the altar.
restauratur sanitati	He is restored to health
et sospes regreditur.	and leaves it safe and sound.

In its versification this poem is closely related to that which was frequently used for hymns and sequences by the end of the twelfth century in northern France and England, with each stanza regularly containing lines of 8p + 8p + 7pp,[47] that is, a rhythmic trochaic septenarius (the so-called "*Stabat Mater* verse"). In the text we can see more or less clear references to the *Passio et miracula* (and to the Saga). Thus we recognize the king filled with hope and inspired by his visionary dream before the battle. We recognize him as a valuable warrior (*agonista pretiosus*), which is of course a usual description for many martyrs fighting for their faith. He goes out into a battle against a much larger army, and he is cut down with a sword, just as is told in the *Passio et miracula* and in the Saga. Likewise the miracles about the blind man, the mute, and the priest with truncated limbs correspond to passages of the *Passio et miracula* that are also used in the antiphons at Lauds, as we have seen. This new hymn replaces the old hymn *Martyr dei qui unicum* that we met in the old Office.

We find, however, this old hymn *Martyr dei qui unicum* for the Common of Martyrs together with the new antiphons in a fragment of an English manuscript (London, BL Add. 34888, no. 24; see appendix and figure 17.1). This is only one example of that stage in the history of the Olav Office in which new Office texts, lessons, antiphons, and responsories from the *Passio et miracula* were combined with older material from the early Office (Gjerløw, ed., *Ordo*, 186).

In the new Office attributed to Bishop Eystein, Olav is presented as a king and martyr, a righteous man, humble and wise (*vir iustus, humilis, sapiens*), according to the normal pattern of the Church (Büttner 1983). The same ideal as that expressed in Eystein's Office is found in a letter of privilege to the archbishop by Magnus Erlingsson, Olav's vassal. Magnus promises to be Olav's follower in virtue (*virtutum imitator*), and to strive "for the protection of law and justice" (*pro lege et iusticia tuenda*). This ideal of *rex iustus* can even be seen as the basis for the law of 1163 concerning the "suitability" (*idoneitas*) of a king-to-be (see Tobiassen, 1956–78; see also Gunnes 1996).

Conclusion

St. Olav might be seen as a good example of a patriot who met a violent death being accorded the title of martyr, even in the Roman Martyrology. As in the case of English kings such as Edward, Oswald, and Edmund, dynastic and patriotic considerations greatly helped the establishment of his cult and made him the patron saint of Norway.

In the first step of establishing the king as a saint, it seems clear that the most important issue was not to write new texts, but rather to make the right choice of texts previously used for the celebration of well-established and prestigious royal saints. Evidently not until a century later, when St. Olav himself had won an indisputable position as a saint and his cult had become an important factor for the new cathedral of Nidaros as a pilgrimage site, was it essential to have a special Office with new proper texts for the saint, the *Passio et miracula*, and to retain only those texts from the early Office which mentioned Olav by name.

Different kinds of texts describe the hero. On the one hand, the liturgical texts in prayers, lessons, and chants, with many biblical allusions, place St. Olav among the Old Testament leaders of the people, such as Moses or Jacob, and also allude

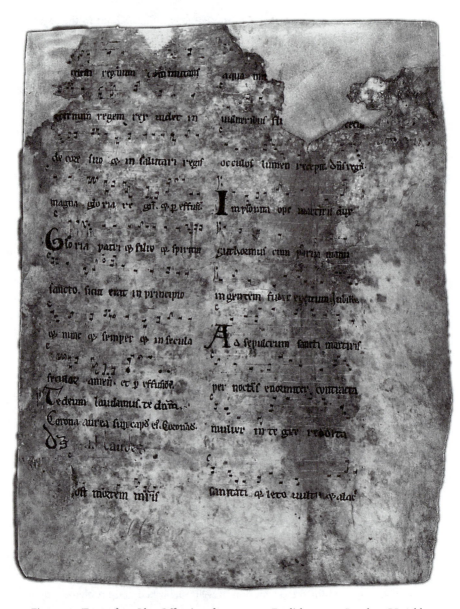

Figure 17.1 Texts of an Olav Office in a fragmentary English source. London, BL Add. MS 34888, no. 24: (a, *this page*) recto; (b, *facing page*) verso

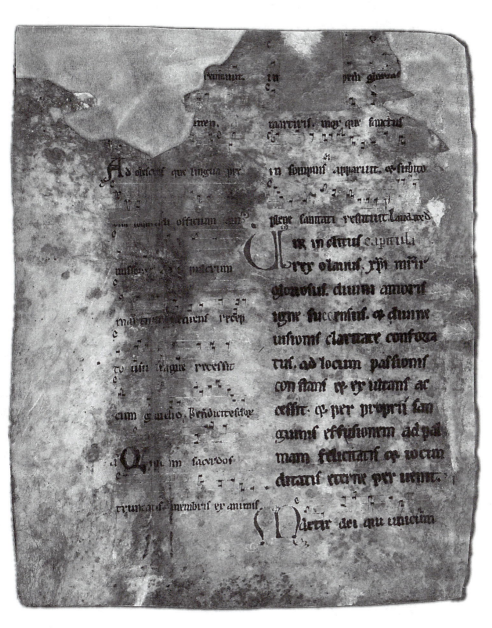

Figure 17.1 (*continued*)

to texts used for the dedication of a new holy place. Likewise, many of the Common liturgical texts present King Olav as one among the martyr kings, as a brave fighter for Christ. On the other hand, the songs of the scalds and the Sagas place him among the old Viking heroes. These different texts seem to express different ideals in presenting the hero.

So, we might ask, was Olav good or bad—or both? His real person we will never know; we can only follow him as he is depicted in these different texts. But we can conclude that when he was killed, happily dying (*feliciter occumbens*) at Stiklestad in 1030, he was evidently in the right place at the right moment to become a Christian symbol representing a new era in Nordic history. The solemn and prestigious liturgical texts of his Divine Office were used in parts of England and Norway as efficient means of presenting Olav Haraldson as a high Christian model. And for long, Olav the Viking came to be the most celebrated Nordic saint.

Appendix: A Fragmentary St. Olav Office

Liturgical position	Text
[Matins:]	
[Last resp.:]	\<Felici commercio pro\> celesti regnum commutans eternum [sc. terrenum] regem rex videt in decore suo et in salutari regis magna gloria regis Et per effusionem \<sanguinis pervenit ad palmam eterne iocunditatis\> Gloria patri et filio et spiritui sancto sicut erat in principio et nunc et semper et in secula seculorum Amen. Et per effusionem \<sanguinis pervenit ad palmam eterne iocunditatis\> Te Deum laudamus. Te dominum. Corona aurea super capitem eius.
AD LAUDES	
Ant. 1:	Post mortem martyris aqua mi\<xta sanguine qui de\> vulneribus fl\<uxerat lavans\> cecus occulos lumen recipit.
[Psalm:]	Dominus regnavit \<decorem indutus est\>
Ant. 2:	Implorata ope martiris dux Guthormus cum parva manu ingentem fudit exercitum.
[Psalm:]	Iubilate \<Deo omnis terra, psalmum dicite nomini eius\>.
Ant. 3:	Ad sepulcrum sancti martiris pernoctans enormiter contracta mulier integre reddita sanitati et leto vultu alacri \<animo ad propria\> remeavit. \< . . . \> Amen.
Ant. 4:	Adolescens qui lingua precisa loquendi officium ammiserat ad sepulcrum martiris adiens recepto usu lingue recessit cum gaudio
[Psalm:]	Benedicte \<dominum omnes angeli eius\> . . . seculorum.
Ant. 5:	Quidam sacerdos truncatis membris exanimis im\<ploravit o\>pem glorios\<i\> martiris. moxque sanctus in sompnis ei apparuit et subito plene sanitati restituit.
[Psalm:]	Laudate Dominum.
[Capitulum:]	Vir inclitus rex Olavus Christi martir gloriosus divini amoris igne succensus et divine visionis claritate confortatus ad locum passionis constans et exultans accessit et per proprium sanguinis effusionem ad palmam felicitatis et iocunditatis eterne pervenit.
[Hymn:]	Martir dei qui unicum //

Source: London, BL Add. 34888, no. 24 (see figures 17.1 and 17.2).

Notes

1. *Heimskringla,* chaps. 1–3; Olason, ed., *Heimskringla;* English translation by Monson, *From the Sagas,* p. 127. For other English translations see Laing, *Heimskringle;* Hollander (1987). For further bibliographic references in the vast literature concerning the Saga material, see, e.g., Clover and Lindow (1985), G. Weber (1988), Whakey (1991), Foote (1993), and Hallberg (1993).

2. The events in England are told by Snorri in wrong sequence (see Monson, 132, n. 1). It seems that Olav first attacked Canterbury, then proceeded to the Isle of Wight, and then landed in Hampshire. King Ethelred collected an army against which they did not seek battle, but instead turned back to Kent and from there to the Thames and London. In 1011, King Ethelred sued for peace, but it was not secured till Canterbury was again sacked and the Archbishop Alphege killed, because he would not make terms with the Norsemen. Elmar, the abbot of Augustine's monastery, was, however, given his freedom. The peace between King Ethelred and Olav was made in 1012. In the following year Swein Forkbeard landed in England, conquered Oxford and Winchester, and attacked London, whereupon the whole of the North of England submitted to him. In the battle of London Swein was repulsed by Ethelred, assisted by Olav and Thorkel— and these are the events related by Snorri in chaps. 12 and 13.

3. Snorri specifically states that he was in Normandy in the autumn of 1013, where he remained until the spring of 1014, when he returned to England with Ethelred's sons. In chap. 20: "King Olav had been on this raid to the west of France for two summers and one winter. Thirteen years had then passed since the fall of Olav Tryggvason. There were in France two jarls, William and Robert; their father was Richard (II 996–1026), Jarl of Ruda (Rouen), and they ruled over Normandy. Their sister was Emma, whom Ethelred, King of England, had married, and their sons were Edmund and Edward the Good, Edwig and Edgar." Emma subsequently married King Cnut; cf. Monson, *From the Sagas,* 133. On Olav's stay with Robert in Rouen, see *Historiae Northmannorum libri octo* by the monk from Jumièges, Willemus Calculus, PL 149:830. See also Barlow (1979).

4. There are also the poems *Glølungskvida* from 1032 by Thoraren Lovtunga and *Arvedrapa* from 1040. See Andersson (1964).

5. Gjerløw, ed., *Ordo Nidrosiensis Ecclesiae,* 124; from the time after 1153 we also know the Old Norse Homily Book, Indebrø, ed., *Gammel norsk homiliebok* (Copenhagen, KB Codex Arn. Magn, 619 Q. V). A thorough comparative study of this text and all the liturgical texts still remains to be done. A doctoral dissertation containing an investigation of a large number of remaining Nordic fragments of varying versions of later Office material for St. Olav is currently under preparation by the musicologist Eyolf Østrem at Uppsala, with the title "The St. Olav Office: Liturgy for a Patron Saint in the Periphery of Europe." Cf. also Østrem (1998).

6. Concerning texts used in the Olav liturgy in Nidaros, Føhn and Gjerløw have made available basic material in their studies and modern editions of the *Antiphonarium Nidrosiensis Ecclesiae, Missale Nidrosiensis Ecclesiae, Manuale Norwegicum,* and *Ordo Nidrosiensis Ecclesiae.* The 1519 prints of the *Breviarium Nidrosiense* and *Missale Nidrosiense* are available in facsimile editions. Concerning Olav in the Saga literature, see n. 1 above. For a musical edition of material from the office, see Reiss, *Musiken.*

7. Metcalfe, ed., *Passio et miracula Beati Olaui,* 34; see also Dickins (1940) and Rumar (1997).

8. *AASS* 7/29, Chron. D; *Passio et miracula Beati Olaui,* 34.

9. Kemble, ed., *Chartae Anglosaxonicae* DCCCCXXVI (926). See also Østrem (1998).

10. See n. 6 above on the Norwegian sources.

11. Warren also writes (p. 274): "The following two Masses have been transcribed, because the saints named in the body of the Collects, St. Alphege, St. Dunstan, St.

Swithun, assist in localizing the MS to the province of Canterbury and the diocese of Winchester."

12. Ibid., 271–75, p. 274: [Collect:] Deus, regum corona et martirum victoria, annue nos *beati Olavi regis et martiris* apud te pia experiri patrocinia, ut per tuam quam in eius glorificamus passione magnificentiam coronam uite diligentibus te percipiamus repromissam. Per.

[Secret:] Inscrutabilem secreti tui virtutem trepitidi imploramus, omnipotens pater, has electas ad sanctam sacrificium creaturas in corpus et sanguinem Christi tui de celo sanctifices, et interventum *sancti Olavi regis et martiris* nobis in salutem vite et anime provenire concedas. Per.

[Postcommunion:] Vitalis hostie verbi caro facti delicta refocillati per ipsum, et per suffragia *sanctissimi Olavi regis et martiris tui,* omnipotentie deus, obsecramus reconciliari, ut presentis vite commoda prefrui, et eterne digni abeamus participari. Per.

13. London, BL Harley 863, fol. 109v. See Lapidge, *Anglo-Saxon,* 74 and 196. The litany is reproduced in facsimile in Dewick and Frere, eds., *The Leofric Collectar, II,* plates XII–XVIII, pp. 435–43.

14. [Matins:] Omnipotens sempiterne deus fortitudo certantium et martyrum palma sollemnitatem hodierne diei propitius intuere, et ecclesiam tuam continua fac celebritate letari et intercessione *beati Olavi regis et martiris* omnium in te credentium vota perficias. Per.

[Terce:] Omnipotens sempiterne deus qui huius diei iocundam beatamque leticiam in *sancti servi tui Olavi* sollemnitate consecrasti, da cordibus nostris tui amoris caritatisque augmentum, ut cuius in terris sancti sanguinis effusionem celebramus, illius in celo collata patrocinia meritis sentiamus. Per.

[Sext:] Deus ineffabilis misericordie qui *beatum Olauum regem* tribuisti pro tuo nomine inimicum moriendo vincere, concede propitius familie tue, ut eo interveniente mereatur in te antiqui hostis incitamenta superando extinguere. Per.

[None:] Deus qui hunc diem *beati Olavi regis et martyris* passione consecrasti presta quesumus ut ipsius interventu hoc in nostris floreat actibus quod premiis remuneretur celestibus. Per.

[Second Vespers:] Presta, quesumus omnipotens deus ut sicut divina laudamus in *sancti Olavi regis* passione magnalia sic indulgentiam tuam piis eius precibus assequamur. Per.

15. [First Vespers:] Beatus vir, cuius capiti dominus coronam imposuit, muro salutis circumdedit, scuto fidei et gladio munivit, ad expugnandas gentes et omnes inimicos. [Cf. Isa. 59:17–18; Ecclus. 45:9.]

16. [Matins:] Iustum deduxit dominus per viam rectam, cuius memoria in benedictione est in sermone eius siluit ventus et cogitatione sua placavit [MS: placuit] abissum et plantavit eum dominus Ihesus. [Cf. Wisd. of Sol. 10:10; Ecclus. 45:1 and 43:25.]

17. [Terce:] In bonitate benignitatis et alacritate anime sue placuit iustus deo Israhel, invocavit dominum omnipotentem et dedit in dextera eius tolerare hominem fortem in bello et exaltare cornu gentis sue. [Ecclus. 45:29; cf. 1 Sam. (1 Kings) 2:1.]

18. [Sext:] In diebus suis non pertimuit iustus principem et in potentia nemo vicit illum nec superavit illum verbum aliquod et mortuum prophetavit corpus eius. [Ecclus. 48:13–14.]

19. [None:] In vita sua fecit sanctus monstra et in morte operatus est mirabilia in omni ore quasi mel indulcabitur eius memoria et ut musica in convivio vini. [Cf. Ecclus. 48:15, 49:2.]

20. [Second Vespers:] Iustus directus est divinitus in poenitentia gentis et tulit abhominationes impietatis et gubernat ad dominum cor ipsius et in diebus peccatorum corroboravit pietatem et ossa ipsius visitata sunt et post mortem prophetaverunt. [Ecclus. 49:3–4, 49:18.]

21. *CAO* 3, 3058. The words describing the hero as the one "who trod down the head of the old serpent" evidently influenced the iconography of St. Olav; see Lidén (1999).

22. MS Harley 2961, fol. 123v; Dewick and Frere, eds., *The Leofric Collectar, I*, col. 210.

23. MS Harley 2961, fol. 123v; Dewick and Frere, eds., *The Leofric Collectar, II*, col. 210.

24. Ibid.

25. Ibid.

26. Gjerløw, ed., *Antiphonarium*, 182; on St. Olav in the Carrow Psalter and the Tree of Jesse, see Lidén (1992), and Lidén (1999).

27. For an edition of the text, see *AH* 51, no. 113, pp. 129–30.

28. Storm, *Monumenta*, 125–32. Later he also published another Latin legend written in 1460 by the priest Mathias in Ribe in Denmark; see Storm (1885). This source, Copenhagen, KB n. saml. 123, is a Latin legend that includes a number of biblical references, together with passages from ballads and from the *Passio et miracula*. The Latin text with Swedish translation is published in Lidén (1999).

29. Metcalfe, ed., *Passio;* the text is contained in a miscellany in Oxford, Corpus Christi College 209, fols. 57–90.

30. *AASS* 7/29, pp. 113–16, reprinted in *Monumenta*, 125–44). See Maliniemi (1920) (including an edition of "Miles quidem de Britania"), and also Hagland (1990).

31. Douai, BM 295, fols. 94–108 ("Membraneus exaratus variis manibus saec. XII–XIII. Passio beati Olavi gloriosi regis et martyris"); published in *Analecta Bollandiana* 20; Storm, *Monumenta*, 258–59.

32. Storm, *Monumenta*, 229–65. Among these are *Breviarium Arhusiense* (1519), *Breviarium Scarense* (1498), with variants from *Breviarium Arosiense* (1517), *Strengnense* (1495), *Upsaliense* (1496), *Otthoniense* (1483), *Roschildense* (1517), and *Lundense* (1517).

33. *Breviarium Nidrosiense* (facs., 1964); Storm, *Monumenta*, 229–38; Gjerløw, ed., *Ordo*, 30.

34. Storm, *Monumenta*, 239; "Omnipotens sempiterne deus maiestatem tuam suppliciter exoramus, ut sicut beatus Olavus tua providentia rex extitit catholocus, ita apud tuam in celis misericordiam pro nobis intercessor sit ipse perpetuus." According to Gjerløw the collect prayer used at Matins is also used for Priscus martyr (1 Sept.); "Omnipotens sempiterne deus fortitudo . . . intercessione beati Olavi regis et martiris . . . vota perficias."

35. We may also note, as mentioned above, that the three alternative Gospel antiphons found in the Leofric Collectar—*Exultemus omnes, Sit semper summa laus,* and *Corde et ore*—are retained in the Nidaros breviary (the last for the octave of the feast of St. Olav).

36. Copenhagen, KB Add. 47, fol. 4v; "probably written in the third quarter of the thirteenth century"; see Gjerløw, ed., *Antiphonarium*, 230–31, and plates 34–35.

37. Lectio II: Confluebant ad baptisma certatim populi . . . mugire non audens omnis iniquitas opilabat os suum . . .; cf. Metcalfe, ed., *Passio*, 70.

38. Lectio III: Non cessabat autem indefessus evangelii predicator nunc obstinatos evincere . . . leges divinas et humanas multa plenas sapientia et mira compositas discretione scripsit et promulgavit; cf. *Passio et miracula*, 70.

39. Lectio IIII: In dictis namque legibus suum cuique conditioni ius assignavit . . . quam benignus erga proximum rex gloriosus extiterit. Cf. *Passio et miracula*, 71.

40. Lectio V: Explicari minime vero potest quanta beneficia beatus martyr populis contulit . . . per honestam vite formam etiam sue religionis celebre monimentum incolis reliquit. Cf. *Passio et miracula*, 71.

41. Lectio VI: Denique decoctus igne persecutionis: divino inspiratus instinctu: per Suecia ad propria remeavit. Indutus igitur lorica fidei: et armatus galea salutis obiciebat

sponte periculis . . . erat namque eius doctrina operibus eorum valde contraria. *Passio et miracula,* 72.

42. Lectio VII: In illo tempore. Dicebat Iesus ad omnes. Si quis vult post me venire abneget semetipsum et tollat crucem suam quodie [= quotidie] et sequatur me. Et reliqua. In odium igitur fidei et beati martyris quidam adversarii eius cuiusdam Chanuti muneribus corrupti. quidam vero malicie sue instinctu novam religionem paternis scilicet legibus contrariam recusantes exercitu ordinato bello regem excipiunt. verum illustrissimus martyr totus suspensus in celestia pro fide et iustitia pugnaturus exercitu quantum in brevi potuit collecto obviat inimicis. ibidem filiciter occumbens quarto kalendas augusti feria quarta millesimo vicesimo octavo anno ab incarnatione Domini. de castris ad regni regis palacia de bello migravit ad pacem que exupat omnem sensum. *Passio et miracula,* 73.

43. Lectio VIII: Nocte vero precedente diem qua martyr inclitus passus est apparuit ei Dominus Iesus . . . iam divinitus scalam sperans quam in somnis nuper ad celos erectam viderat per quam ad dulcedinem quam gustaverat feliciter erat ascensus. Cf. *Passio et miracula,* 74.

44. Lectio IX: Evoluto itaque passionis illius tempore cum corpus regales lavissent ministri proiecta ante ostium aqua mixta sanguine . . . omnes audientes miraculum divinam pietatem et martyris meritum dignis extulere preconiis. Cf. *Passio et miracula,* 74.

45. Monson, *From the Sagas,* 278; "a hundred hundred" is 120 × 120, i.e., 14,400 men.

46. Other versified poems used for St. Olav are the hymns *Procul pulso* in Storm, *Monumenta,* 261; *AH* 11:207, no. 381; *Pange lingua gloriosi | Caput tuum* in Storm, *Monumenta,* 260; *AH* 11:206, no. 380; and *Polum pingit iam aurora* (*AH* 11:207–8, no. 382); the antiphon *Adest dies laetitiae* in a version unique for St. Olav; and the sequence *Postquam calix Babylonis* in Reiss, *Musiken,* 57–58, as well as *Lux illuxit,* for which see below. A further investigation of relations between the motifs in these texts and the iconography of Olav in paintings and sculptures promises to be rewarding. See Lidén (1992) and (1999).

47. 8p + 8p = two lines, each of eight syllables with the accent on the penultimate syllable (paroxytone); 7pp = one line of seven syllables with accent on the antepenultimate syllable (propaproxytone). See Norberg (1958), 117 and 173–74. Cf. Iversen (1990), 49–50.

On the Prose *Historia* of St. Augustine

JANKA SZENDREI

It is surprising to note that although Augustine, the theologian and philosopher, bishop and saint, enjoyed a high reputation, he was little venerated liturgically within the territory of the Roman rite (or to be more precise, the Frankish-Roman rite) during Christianity's first thousand years. Nor was his feast celebrated widely (on 28 August for a long time the veneration of the early Roman martyr Hermes enjoyed preference in many places), and wherever it was, it had no proper Mass or Office items. It is true that few saints enjoyed universal liturgical veneration in the beginning. Yet compared with Augustine's universal recognition, the absence of his feast is all the more striking.

The liturgical veneration of Augustine developed at the turn of the eleventh and twelfth centuries and culminated in the emergence of the saint's complete proper Office, or *historia*. As we shall see, a wide circle of liturgical institutions accepted the Office—but not all of them. This fact, as well as the interpretation of the Office, shows that it is not simply a matter of the steadily increasing cult of a saint, but rather a trend or tendency displays its ideals in the cult. As is well known, there came into being at this time a number of religious orders or similiar communities that placed themselves under Augustine's protection—Premonstratensians, Augustinian Canons, and diocesan cathedral and collegiate chapters that received legal status on the basis of their Augustinian rules.

The fundamental contradiction of the chiefly political and disciplinary church reforms associated with the name of Pope Gregory VII—reforms that exerted an influence on other fields of church life as well—is that they were prompted by *monastic* (Benedictine) communities, yet they aimed at renewing the life of *priests* as a first priority. It was very difficult to carry out the task of improving the morals of the clergy (a kind of "conversion")—refusing worldliness and reviving the spiritual scholarship and piety of the priests that had become "worldly" in a pejorative sense—in a social group whose members as clerics had a fairly safe existence and were more or less separated even from each other. The key to the reform was thus to integrate these clergy into communities and, through the community, make them institutionally "available" for the reform. While the reform was relatively easier to execute in the Benedictine monasteries and associations of monasteries, the diocesan clergy could be persuaded to accept reformist ideas primarily through the various movements that aimed at communal life.

This is why it became topical—particularly in the period of Benedictine influence—to revaluate the ideal of the priests' life and to establish, in association with it, the various institutions of the *monasterium clericorum*—that is, to sum up the virtues regarded as highly important (purity, conversion, poverty, pious scholarship, pastoral industriousness) within the concept of the *vita apostolica*. Just as Benedict was considered the father of all monastic orders, so this movement of priests could hardly have any other patron than Augustine. (The word "movement" is used deliberately because the new institutions were founded as communities of the clergy, rather than as monastic orders in the earlier sense.) Thus the reverence for and the Office of Augustine have not only cultic meaning but ideological content as well, in cultic forms.

Like other prominent historical figures, Augustine exerted a continuous influence on intellectual life for centuries. But at the same time, each epoch selected a different trait of his personality for emphasis, thus reflecting by the element selected the spirituality of the time. Limitations of reinterpretation are the objective facts of his biography and lifework, as well as the general outlines of the description of sanctity. In the case of the Augustinian Office, this means, in addition, the raw material with which the redactor had to work. Nevertheless, the redactor's choice of motifs from the hagiographic materials and their placement in the foreground were anything but haphazard. The hagiographic patterns themselves received a new meaning through the context, the interrelationship of the motifs, and the wording on a high literary level.

The first such motif is the variety of terms for conversion. Augustine is called by grace from the captivity in Babylon (*de servitute Babylonis:* V1-a1),[1] a land far from God; from the realm of alienation (*in regione dissimilitudinis:* R1); from the darkness of the pagans (*de tenebris gentium:* Inv.); to save not only him alone, but to make him a light of the Church (*lumen ecclesiae suae vocavit:* Inv.).

Thus his outstanding virtue is repentance, or contrition. He himself had been born spiritually of his mother's tears (*mater . . . quem carne prius peperat mundo . . . postmodum multo semine lacrimarum genuit Christo:* V1-a2) and answered the call with his tears (*flebat autem uberrime:* a7). This is more than the individual contrition that appears in numerous *vitae*. It has to do with the church community: *Flebat . . . in hymnis et canticis, suave sonantis Ecclesiae vocibus vehementer affectus* (He wept . . . in hymns and canticles, profoundly moved by the sweetly sounding voices of the Church: a7).

Conversion is followed by accepting the vocation of a priest, and the Office here accordingly underlines the dignity of the priesthood. The Church gained "a sedulous steward" in Augustine (*dispensatorem strenuum:* V1-a1). On recognizing his suitability, Valerius, bishop of Hippo, ordained Augustine a priest almost against his own will (*et licet invitum presbyterum ordinavit:* L-a2). Monica speaks to her son as follows: "I do not look for pleasures in life any more, since I can see you, despising earthly happiness, as a servant of God" (*cum te, contempta felicitate terrena, videam servum Dei*: R8). Although all of these motifs have biographical relevance, they also serve the aim of the Office to make the clergy conscious, through this model, of the greatness of their vocation.

Augustine represents an ideal of a specific way of clerical life, that is, a community of priests. His fate is closely connected with that of his companions on the path to God, although people walk by different routes (*ad ambulandum in via dei in qua alius sic, alius sic ibat*: R6). At important stages of his conversion, the influence of friends, visits, discussions, community experiences, and models can be seen (*et exempla servorum dei, quos de mortuis vivos fecerat tamquam carbonas vastatores;* and the example of the servants of God, whom he raised from death to life, were as consuming coals—R7). At a moment of doubt, God instilled into his mind the fortuitous plan to go to Simplicianus, who he knew was a good servant of God—which indeed he was (*misit ergo Dominus in mentem ejus . . . pergere ad Simplicianum, qui ei bonus apparebat servus Dei . . . et vere sic erat*: R5). After his conversion he immediately set out in search of companions (*adjunctus inde Nebridio et Evodio . . . quaerens quis eos ad bene vivendum locus haberet utilius;* accompanied by Nebridius and Evodius . . . seeking a more suitable place to live devoutly—a9). And to crown it all, he instituted a monastery of clergy living together right after his ordination—perhaps the most important sentence of the Office: *Factus ergo presbyter monasterium clericorum mox instituit . . .* (When he became a priest, he soon founded a monastery of clergy: L-a3).[2] The life of this community of priests is under Augustine's rule, as the words of the hymn explain:

> Tu de vita clericorum sanctam scribis regulam,
> quam qui amant et sequuntur viam tenent regiam.
>
> (You wrote on the life of clerics a holy rule
> that all who love and follow will keep to the kingly road.)

Augustine's conversion and way of life become consummate, according to the hymn, in the ideal of the *monasterium clericorum* (L-a3) and not in his individual sanctity. This is why "our mother Jerusalem" (*mater nostra Jerusalem*: V1-a1) should rejoice at this turn of events.

The *monasterium clericorum* is not only a location but a way of life—the new ideal of clerical life. But in fact it is not new; it is the very way of life of the Apostles: *et coepit vivere secundum regulam a sanctis apostolis constitutam* (and he began to live according to the rule given by the holy Apostles: L-a3). Its first rule is poverty. In the hymn *Magne Pater Augustine* the followers of poverty praise Augustine as a lover of poverty (*amatorem paupertatis te collaudant pauperes*). This is the reason that the compiler of the Office (and the trend supporting it) gave such emphasis to a sentence from Possidius' biography: Augustine did not make a testament because Christ's poor had nothing to bequeath in a will (*testamentum nullum fecit quia unde faceret, pauper Christi non habuit*: R9).

In this spirituality, certain Christian values and virtues were given particular emphasis, such as the appreciation of liturgy and liturgical chant, which is, of course, expressed in the context of the biography and the poetic style of the Office. Augustine ascends from the valley of tears singing "the pilgrims' song" or song of the steps (the gradual hymn): *ascendenti a convalle plorationis et cantanti canticum graduum:* R7. For him the beauty of God's house comes before everything else (*displicebat enim ei quidquid agebat in saeculo prae dulcedine dei et decore domus ejus quam dilexit;* he disliked everything he had done in the world, compared with the sweetness of God and the splendor of his house that he loved most—R6). Because of it this world is imbued with an extremely emotional, festive, "sweet" atmosphere, in spite of the spirit of repentance. His heart had been wounded by the arrow of Christ's love (*vulneraverat caritas Christi cor ejus . . . :* R7). From the womb of her love, his mother had already brought him to new life, through the seed of her tears (*caritatis visceribus postmodum multo semine lacrimarum genuit Christo:* V1-a2). Love forms his intellectual world as well (*non secum ferebat nisi amantem memoriam;* he brought with him nothing but a loving memory—R3), and conversion helps people to gain real maturity. Christ himself is the adult's food, and people must grow up to him (*tamquam audiret vocem dei de excelso: Cibus sum grandium, cresce, et manducabis me, nec tu me mutabis in te, sicut cibum carnis tuae, sed tu mutaberis in me;* as if from on high he heard the voice of God: I am the food of adults; grow, and you shall eat me, and you will not change me within you, as with the food of your flesh, but you will be changed in me—R1).

The eminent role of the intellect forms an important part of the Augustinian ideal. By refusing worldly wisdom, the pious intellect comes to the light of truth. Augustine had earlier postponed baptism, *tumens inani philosophia* (puffed up with empty philosophy: V1-a3). In vain had he tried to reach, through intellectual efforts, what he could have grasped by the vivid force of faith (*volebat humana ratione comprehendere quod pia mens vivacitate fidei nititur apprehendere;* he wished to understand by human reason what the pious mind strives to grasp by a lively faith—V1-a3). First, he found the Bible rough and not understandable (*primam hujus lectionem non intelligens, totumque tale arbitrans:* a4). Truth initially offended him, as food hurts the ailing palate, or light annoys sick eyes (*palato non sano poena est panis qui sano est suavis, et oculis aegris odiosa est lux quae puris est amabilis:* R2). But as soon as the soul carries out the conversion, previous darkness disappears (*et statim quasi infusa luce securitatis, ab eo omnes dubitationis tenebrae diffugerunt;* and immediately, as if infused by the light of security, all the shadows of doubt fled from him—a1), and the apparent contradictions of the Bible are resolved (*perierunt illae quaestiones; apparuit ei una facies eloquiorum castorum;* all those controversies vanished; there appeared to him the one face of the eloquent words [of the Bible]—R4). Intelligence penetrates into truths it had been unable to grasp before (*aciem figere non valuit:* R3). This is not the accomplishment of reason, but of grace and pious faith exclusively.

This twelfth-century Office seems to proclaim the fifteenth-century ideal of the *devotio moderna,* also rooted in Augustinian spirituality, but in fact the negation is counterbalanced by the command to search for and teach the truth through which the intellect regains its dignity. He discusses the truth diligently with "the watchmen of the town," that is, his companions ahead of him (*diligenter pertractata cum illis veritate:* V1-a5). Books play an important role in his conversion as well as in establishing his lifestyle (*insinuavit ergo per litteras sancto viro Ambrosio praesens votum suum . . . quid sibi de libris sanctus legendum esset;* he told of his vow to the holy man Ambrose through a letter asking him for advice, . . . which of the holy books he should read—a2). In Isaiah he recognized the forerunner of the call of the Gospel—and of his own call (*evangelii vocationis gentium praenuntiator:* a3). Therefore the bishop ordaining him rejoices at having found a man capable of sound teaching (*hominem sibi talem datum . . . qui in doctrina sana aedificare Ecclesiam esset idoneus;* for such a man has been given him . . . who by sound learning is suitable to build the Church—L-a4). And indeed, Augustine preached the Gospel with a sound mind to his last day (*Verbum dei . . . sane mente sanoque consilio in sancta Ecclesia praedicavit:* R9). He used all his intellectual capacity to defeat heresy (*in conventu omnium disputans publice superavit;* disputing publically in a meeting [with heretics], he prevailed—L-a5). To the faithful, he disclosed the most secret teachings of the Apostles: *quorum plenus spiritu, quae praedixerunt mystica, fecit nobis pervia* (filled with their spirit, he explained to us the mysteries they foretold—V1-AM); or, in the words of the hymn, *quae obscura prius erant nobis plana faciens, tu de verbis Salvatoris dulcem panem conficis;* what was previously obscure, you made plain to us; you prepare a sweet bread from the Savior's words).

Conversion, repentance, the dignity of the diocesan clergy's life, the community of priests, the apostolic way of life, poverty, liturgy, devotion, the combination of refusing human reasoning with strong intellectual pretensions—all these are not simply Augustine's characteristic traits; they are the reform program of the eleventh- and twelfth-century generation of non-monastic clergy, described here in a liturgical text. While the influence of a text presented as a kind of ideology is doubtful, the ideas included in a regular prayer of the Office are repeatedly evoked by the reader and legitimated by the dignity of the liturgy. As death crowns Augustine's work, so to speak, his decease that takes place amidst his brothers stands for the apotheosis of the clergy's Augustinian reform (V2-AM):

> Hodie gloriosus pater Augustinus, dissoluta hujus habitationis domo, domum non manufactam accepit in coelis, quam sibi, cooperante dei gratia, manu, lingua fabrefecit in terris: ubi jam, quod sitivit internum, gustat aeternum, decoratus una stola, securusque de reliqua.

> (Today the glorious father Augustine, his house of earthly life having been dissolved, received a house in Heaven not made by hands—which, in cooperation with the grace of God, with hands and tongue he had already built on earth: where already what he thirsted for internally, he tastes forever, adorned by a stole[3] and free of all cares.)

The Office of St. Augustine is a homogeneous, coherent composition. The entire history appeared completed and in full in the twelfth-century liturgical books of the communities accepting the cult of St. Augustine. The first recorded versions already contain each constituent of the Office. The text of the *historia* is based partly on Possidius' biography, from which sections are taken word for word,[4] and it constitutes a poetic work of unknown origin, which stresses the mystic associations, the spiritual message of the saint's life so timely in the twelfth century. There is a possibility that the text was written by Abbot Rupert of Deutz (d. 1135), who, as a member of the Benedictine Laurentiuskloster of Liège, reworked Augustine's earlier biography in "splendid style" to make it suitable for monastic and liturgical use (Manser 1930, 388–89). The readings in the Office are taken from his biography—*ex legenda eius sumantur,* as the Augustinian Ordinary of Salzburg Cathedral indicates.[5] The majority of the chant texts, the Matins and Lauds antiphons as well as the responsories, were written in prose, but the antiphons of First Vespers are in rhymed prose. From a stylistic point of view, moreover, with regard to content (see the references to the Song of Songs), a separate genesis of the material of First Vespers can be postulated. The variability in liturgical use of these rhymed items seemingly supports this hypothesis. In fact, their relative independence within the entire composition may have a different explanation. The liturgical position of First Vespers may justify the more festive, hymnic wording; the alternation of arrangement may be the result of the variable liturgical rank of the feast. At present, the idea that the antiphons of First Vespers originated later or in a different community is not supported by any historical evidence.

The Office melodies were written in homogeneous musical style and, moreover, in one single compositional process, except for some supplementary items. This appears from such external evidence as the *series tonorum* arrangement[6] of the antiphons, which the twelfth-century Ordinary and other early liturgical books also indicate, placing the tone numbers at the side of the items.[7]

The Office of St. Augustine was composed with the secular arrangement of the Office in mind. This is clearly shown by the tone system of the antiphons, which converges with the structure of the secular Office (see table 18.1). The antiphons of First Vespers move from the first to the fifth tone; the great antiphon (for the Magnificat) is in the first tone. Matins starts in the first tone again and proceeds to the eighth tone, whereas the ninth antiphon is again in the first tone. By starting in the second tone, Lauds seems to be a mechanical continuation of Matins. However, after this organically joined beginning, the author switches to another system. First, the antiphons run through the even-numbered tones in ascending order (2, 4, 6, 8); then, moving backwards, the odd-numbered ones (7, 5, 3, 1). Thus the last antiphon of Lauds is in the seventh tone, the Benedictus antiphon is in the fifth tone, the Magnificat antiphon of Second Vespers receives the third tone, while the Magnificat antiphon for the octave uses the first tone. This arrangement seems to be exceptional among the *series tonorum* Offices.[8]

Compared with the secular Office of St. Augustine, the arrangement (redaction) of the monastic Office is secondary. Its major characteristics include the heterogeneous division of the tones of the Matins antiphons so that they do not tally with the liturgical units (see table 18.1). The monastic Office lists the items of the composition as almost identical to the secular one; however, almost every item has another function. The antiphon in the first tone at the beginning of secular Matins is, for example, the fifth antiphon of the first nocturn in the monastic arrangement. Here the coherent tone series and the liturgical series do not coincide.

In the monastic arrangement the first antiphon of the *historia* (*Laetare mater*) is applied as *antiphona sola* at First Vespers, followed by the great antiphon for the Magnificat identical with the one of the secular cursus (*Adest dies*). This arrangement is known in some secular churches, too, but they simply omit all the other antiphons of First Vespers. On the other hand, the monastic cursus continues the series of these antiphons in Matins. The first nocturn consequently begins with an

Table 18.1 Chants in the Office of St. Augustine

Office	Cursus saecularis			Cursus monasticus		
	Genre	Tone	Incipit	Genre	Tone	Incipit
I Vespers	a1	1	Laetare mater nostra	a	1	Laetare mater nostra
	a2	2	Hujus mater			
	a3	3	Distulit tamen			
	a4	4	Surgens autem			
	a5	5	Inventus igitur			
	AM	1	Adest dies celebris	AM	1	Adest dies celebris
Vigils	Inv.	2	Magnus Dominus	Inv.	2	Magnus Dominus
	a1	1	Aperuit Augustinus	a1	2	Cujus (!) mater
	a2	2	Insinuavit ergo	a2	3	Distulit tamen
	a3	3	At ille jussit	a3	4	Surgens autem
				a4	5	Inventus igitur
				a5	1	Aperuit Augustinus
				a6	2	Insinuavit ergo
	R1	1	Invenit se Augustinus	R1	1	Invenit se Augustinus
	R2	2	Sensit igitur	R2	2	Sensit igitur
				R3		Juravit (vel: Vir Israelita)
	R3	3	Tunc vero invisibilia	R4	3	Dum (!) vero invisibilia
	a4	4	Verumtamen primam	a7	3	At ille jussit
	a5	5	Inde ubi tempus	a8	4	Verumtamen primam
	a6	6	Nec satiabatur	a9	5	Inde ubi tempus
				a10	6	Nec satiabatur
				a11	7	Flebat autem uberrime
				a12	8	Voces igitur ille
	R4	4	Itaque avidissime	R5	4	Itaque avidissime
	R5	5	Misit ergo Dominus	R6	5	Misit ergo Dominus
				R7		Amavit eum
	R6	6	Volebat enim	R8	6	Volebat enim
	a7	7	Flebat autem uberrime	a13	1	Adjunctus inde
	a8	8	Voces igitur ille			
	a9	1	Adjunctus inde			
	R7	7	Vulneraverat caritas	R9	7	Vulneraverat caritas
	R8	8	Accepta baptismi	R10	8	Accepta baptismi
				R11		Justum deduxit
	R9	1	Verbum Dei usque	R12	1	Verbum Dei usque
Lauds	a1	2	Post mortem matris	a1	2	Post mortem matris
	a2	4	Comperta autem	a2	4	Comperta autem
	a3	6	Factus ergo presbyter	a3	6	Factus ergo presbyter
	a4	8	Sanctus autem	a4	6	Sanctus autem
	a5	7	Eodem tempore	a5	7	Eodem tempore
	AB	5	In diebus ejus obsessa	AB	5	In diebus ejus obsessa
II Vespers	aa		de laudibus	aa		de laudibus
	AM	3	Hodie gloriosus pater	AM	3	Hodie gloriosus pater
(Octave	AM	1	O Rex altissime)			—

antiphon in the second tone. The four unused antiphons of First Vespers then come to the first nocturn, followed by the items beginning Matins according to the secular order (*Aperuit* and *Insinuavit,* in the first and second tones). The order of tones in the monastic first nocturn is thus: 2, 3, 4, 5, 1, 2. The second nocturn is more regular. In it the tones follow in succession from 3 to 8; then comes the third nocturn, which has only one antiphon (*Adjunctus,* in the first tone). But from Lauds onward, the tonal order of the two Office structures, secular and monastic, coincides.

The repertory of responsories is more revealing of the secondary character of the monastic arrangement. The original composer provided only nine responsories (in tones 1–8, then tone 1 again), because he evidently had a secular cursus in mind. In the monastic cursus this could not be helped by rearranging the items; the monastic ordinary was compelled to insert a responsory from the Common into each nocturn to reach the appropriate number of items. The addition was made at the *third* responsory (R3, R7, R11) in order to avoid distorting the usual festive closing of each nocturn. The fourth responsory of each nocturn (R4, R8, R12) is taken from the *historia,* supplemented by the doxology.

The spread of this artistically formulated Office coincided with the acceptance of the Augustinian reforms. Hence, its acceptance was extremely uneven with regard both to institutions and age and spread out across the centuries. In the twelfth century only those institutions whose central, foundational ideal was the intellectual content represented by the personality of Augustine gave the feast a high rank and adopted the entire Office. First were the communities of canons that came into being under the inspiration of the Gregorian reforms, the Augustinians and the Premonstratensians. The origin of these orders coincides almost exactly with the emergence of St. Augustine's Office. 28 August is one of their major festivals, although they also celebrate the saint's translation, 11 October.[9] In the monastic environment the existence of the feast, and even more the use of the full Office, was a rare exception (but see Prague VI E 13, and a variant with music in University Library, XIII C 7). The Benedictine nunnery of St. George in the castle of Prague, as an important intellectual supporter of the political power, was more than a monastic community. It represented the church reform trends of that period on a high level, being familiar with the other reform monastery in the immediate vicinity, that is, the Strahov Premonstratensians.

In the thirteenth century the clergy of several dioceses adopted the Augustinian Office.[10] In certain regions it thus reached the canons of cathedrals and collegiate chapters and the diocesan clergy ministering to the faithful in parishes as well. Since in most cases Augustine's feast did not receive the same liturgical rank in the dioceses as it had in the orders that followed Augustine's rules, simplified variants of the Office emerged. There were places, for example, where an *antiphona sola* was used with ferial psalms instead of the five-antiphon form of First Vespers provided with the *quinque* series of *Laudate* psalms. Elsewhere items from the Common were substituted for proper Matins material.[11] The emergence of the reduced form of the Office, with the variation in function of its items, seems to be a secondary phenomenon, the result of adaptation to different liturgical customs.

Example 18.1   Office of St. Augustine, antiphon 5 for First Vespers: (a) Paris, BNF lat. 9425, fol. 121; (b) Klosterneuburg Ccl 1012, fol. 53; (c) Prague, Universitní Knihovna XIII C 7, sine fol.; (d) Esztergom, Főszékesegyházi Könyvtár I.3, fol. 20v; (e) Zagreb, Metropolitanska Knjižnica MR 8, p. 639

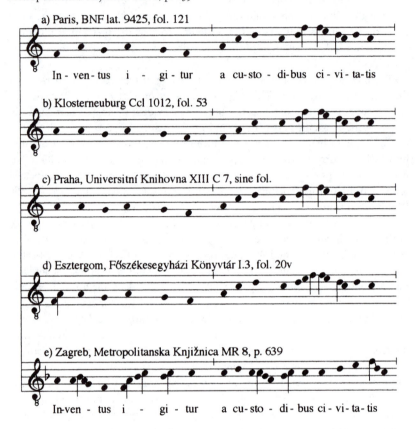

A further expansion in the diffusion of the Office was brought about by certain orders that were being formed in the thirteenth century. St. Augustine's cult was accepted by the Dominicans and Augustinian hermits as well as the Hermits of St. Paul in Hungary, an order following the Augustinian Rule. These orders incorporated the *historia* of Augustine into their liturgical books: the Dominicans with an octave but with *antiphona sola* at First Vespers, the Augustinian hermits with First Vespers of five antiphons but with only eight responsories at Matins, due to the curial structure of their office; the Hermits of St. Paul adopted it in its full form.[12] The Office of St. Augustine sung by the Hermits of St. Paul, however, was special. To my knowledge, this is the only version that contains unaltered text with substantial musical differences, compared with the widespread tradition of Europe. Four of the five antiphons of First Vespers, the second to fifth, have radically different melodies, though they retain the original order of tones. This suggests that the Paulines, on accepting the Office, did not have a fully notated version at

Example 18.1   (*continued*)

(*continued*)

their disposal. Thus they were forced to compose items, since they insisted on using the entire *historia*. (For a comparison of melodies for the fifth antiphon, see example 18.1, where the Pauline melody is version e.)

The Hermits of St. Paul, who honor the blessed Eusebius, canon of Esztergom, as their founding father, formed their liturgy from the beginning (1225) according to the rite of Esztergom (Török 1977). In the latter there was a variant of the *historia* in the thirteenth century in which only the very first item was prescribed at First Vespers as *antiphona sola*.[13] Consequently, even if they came into possession of the text of the other antiphons from elsewhere, it seems that they had to provide for the melody themselves. As a matter of fact, they contributed to the celebration of the saint, whom they held in very high esteem, not only by this creative work. They even wrote a separate hymn for the Office of St. Augustine, *Flos cleri, norma praesulum* (*AH* 43:86). By the end of the Middle Ages the first five antiphons of the Office of St. Augustine can be found with music both in the sources of Esztergom and in other Hungarian diocesan sources.[14] The melodies agree with the tunes known throughout Europe. The Paulines did not carry out further changes at that time; instead they adhered to the state which had been established in the thirteenth

Example 18.1   (*continued*)

century, transmitting their own St. Augustine melodies into the eighteenth century.

By the mid-fourteenth century the boundaries were, by and large, firmly established. Following that period, the Augustinian *historia* gained ground in some diocesan regions, yet a conscious programmatic use was no longer characteristic. It is striking to observe how many institutions did *not* accept the Office. The Benedictine monasteries celebrated Augustine with items from the Common, while the Carthusians, Cistercians, and certain chivalric orders had no feast whatsoever. Several dioceses refrained from it; Bamberg, Passau, and Kraków[15] did not take up the *historia* for the public, common Office until the late Middle Ages. If a reliable, detailed map could ever be drawn indicating how far the Office for St. Augustine actually spread, it would be of great benefit not only for liturgy, but for music history as well, and would contribute much toward a better knowledge of trends within the history of ideas in the Middle Ages.

Example 18.1 (*continued*)

Notes

1. The texts of chants from the Office are identified by the following abbreviations: V1, First Vespers; V2, Second Vespers; L, Lauds; V1-a1 (etc.), first antiphon of First Vespers; a1 (alone), first antiphon of Matins (Vigils); Inv., invitatory antiphon; AM, Magnificat antiphon; AB, Benedictus antiphon; R1 (etc.), first responsory (of Matins). See also table 18.1.

2. This antiphon plays an eminent role in the liturgy of the Premonstratensians and the Augustinian Canons as an ordinary *suffragium*. Its isolated position accounts for the text variant; it begins *Factus Augustinus presbyter* instead of *Factus ergo presbyter*. See the twelfth-century Premonstratensian antiphoner Paris, BNF lat. 9425, fol. 115 (cf. *Antiphonarium . . . Praemonstratensis*, 79), and the antiphoner of the Augustinian Canons, Vorau, SB 287, fol. 164.

3. Indicative of priestly authority.

4. Possidius, *Sancti;* cf. pp. 44, 48, 140, 142.

5. Salzburg, UB II. 6., fol. 92.

6. In numerical order according to tone or mode; see table 18.1.

7. The Augustinian Ordinary book (after 1164) for Salzburg Cathedral (Salzburg II. 6.); a twelfth-century Benedictine breviary for the monastery of St. George in Prague (Prague, Knihovna Národního Muzea VI E 13); a thirteenth-century Ordinary book for Prague Cathedral (Prague, Universitní Knihovna IV D 9).

8. For Offices composed this way, see Crocker (1986), with further bibliography. Cf. also A. Hughes (1993).

9. Augustinian antiphoner, saec. XII (1st half): Klosterneuburg, Augustiner-Chorherrenstift Ccl 1012, fol. 52v; *translatio Augustini*, fol. 83v. Cf. two fifteenth-century Premonstratensian antiphoners: Wrocław, BU F 396, and Budapest, Egyetemi Könyvtár 67.

10. Among others, Frere, ed., *Antiphonale Sarisburiense* (13th c.), 502; breviary of Esztergom: Zagreb, Metropoliotanska Knjižnica, today in the University Library, MR 67; antiphoner of Beauvais (13th c.): Paris, Bibl. Ste.-Geneviève 117; Ordinary of Prague (13th c.): Prague, Universitní Knihovna IV D 9; antiphoner of Cambrai (13th–14th c.): Cambrai, MM 38; antiphoner of Freising (13th–14th c.): Munich, BS clm. 6423; antiphoner of 1347: Sion/Sitten, Arch. du Chapitre 2.

11. *Antiphona sola, psalmi feriales:* antiphoner of 1412: Prague, Knihovna Národního Muzea XIII A 7; antiphoner of 1426: Wrocław, BU R 503. The same method is followed, but the remaining antiphons are distributed during the octave in Frere, ed., *Antiphonale Sarisburiense*, 502. *Antiphona sola, quinque Laudate:* antiphoner (Intonarium) (15th c.), for Zagreb Cathedral: Zagreb, Metropolitanska Knjižnica, today in the University Library, MR 10; and similarly in the Office of the Dominican order. *Five antiphons, psalmi feriales:* antiphoner of Wrocław (14th c. saec. XIV (1st h.): Wrocław, Arch. Archidiecezjalne 52n; breviary of Trier (14th c.): Trier, Stadtbibl. 387/1151. *Five antiphons, quinque Laudate:* antiphoner of Várad (15th c.): Győr, Szemináriumi Könyvtár, sine signatura; antiphoner of Esztergom (15th c.): Bratislava, Archív Mesta, EC Lad 3; noted breviary of Olomouc (14th c.): Brno, Universitní Knihovna R 626. *First Vespers lacks proper chants* (the *historia* begins with Vigils): antiphoner of the Wrocław diocese, collegiate chapter of Glogau (15th–16th c.): Wrocław, BU I Q 219. *Antiphona sola* in First Vespers, "*psalmi de die*," Invitatorium and after then: "*alia omnia de simplici confessore*"): antiphoner of 1426: Wrocław, BU R 505. *Five antiphons in First Vespers, proper in the first nocturn, commune in the second and third nocturns:* antiphoner of Płock (15th c.): Płock, Biblioteca Seminarium duchownego, Cz II.

12. Cf. the Antiphonarium ad usum eremitarum S. Augustini (14th c., 1st h.: Budapest, Egyetemi Könyvtár, Cod. 120, fol. 202; Breviarium OP (Venice, 1477 or 1478), fol.

366v; Antiphonarium ad usum eremitarum S. Pauli (15th c.): Zagreb, Metropolitanska Knjižnica, today in the University Library, MR 8, p. 639.

13. Breviary of Esztergom (13th c.): Zagreb 67, fol. 233v.

14. Antiphoner of Várad (15th c.): Győr, Szemináriumi Könyvtár, sine signatura; antiphoner of Esztergom (15th c., 1st h.: Bratislava EC. Lad. 3, fol. 128 (etc.).

15. The first printed breviary of the Kraków diocese (*Breviarium Cracoviense,* 1508, fol. 354) contains the Office, but adds the following rubric: *Augustini episcopi et confessoris in vesperis in matutinis et in horis ecclesia tenet omnia de confessore et pontifice in communi. Historia sequens in beneplacito orantis ponitur.* (For Augustine, bishop and confessor, in Vespers, Matins, and in the Hours, the church keeps everything in the Common for a confessor bishop. The *historia* following is included at the discretion of the one who prays.)

The *Historia* of St. Julian of Le Mans by Létald of Micy

Some Comments and Questions about a North French Office of the Early Eleventh Century

DAVID HILEY

In recent years much fine work on the chants of the liturgical office has been accomplished, building on the foundations laid by Walter Howard Frere a century ago. In the introduction to *Antiphonale Sarisburiense* Frere supplied an alphabetical index and also provided a wealth of musical information, and his discussion of typical melodies among the responsories, invitatories, and antiphons remains the single best guide of its type. The biggest step forward in indexing sources, incorporating the best elements of Frere's method but extending it in a variety of most valuable ways, has of course been the work masterminded by Ruth Steiner. This chapter is intended to raise questions about the other aspect of Frere's achievement, that is, his identification of typical melodies and phrases (particularly at cadences) across the Office repertory. My intention is by no means to query the identifications. Rather I simply wish to ask how we are to deal with the other musical material, that is, the chants that do *not* employ those stock turns of phrase.

> Sane responsoriorum et antiphonarum, ut petistis, digessimus ordinem; in quibus pro vitando fastidio de unoquoque modo singula compegimus corpora: neque omnino alienari volumus a similitudine veteris cantus, ne barbaram aut inexpertam, uti perhibetur, melodiam fingeremus. Non enim mihi placet quorumdam musicorum novitas, qui tanta dissimilitudine utuntur, ut veteres sequi omnino dedignentur auctores: nam hi qui conjugiis vacant, malunt liberos hominibus similes gignere, quam alicujus invisi monstri effigiem procreare (PL 137:784B, after *AASS* Jan II).

We arranged the order of the responsories and antiphons in a rational way, as you required; in which [chants] we constructed their individual substances each from one mode in order to avoid [reactions of] repugnance. We did not want to distance ourselves in any way from the likeness of old chant, so that we should not form a barbarous or, as one says, untried melody. For the novelty of certain musicians, who practice so many inconsistencies that they have utterly disdained to follow the old composers, does not please me: for those who are devoted to their consorts prefer to engender offspring similar to men rather than to procreate the image of some odious monster.

Sane carries the implication not simply of soundness, being well-disposed, but also of rational order. This appears to reflect the probable meaning in this passage of *modus* as mode in the music-theoretical sense, rather than the more vague "manner" or "way."[1] It presumably refers to the way in which successive chants are set in different modes, in ascending numerical order. The author sets up a contrast between pieces that are meant to be similar to old chant and the "dissimilarities" (I have used "inconsistencies") perpetrated by certain presumably more modern composers.

These sentences are taken from the *Epistola dedicatoria* with which the monk Létald of Micy (Lethaldus Miciacensis) prefaced his *Vita* of St Julian of Le Mans. Bishop Avesgaud of Le Mans (d. 1036) had commissioned Létald to compose the *Historia* of the saint, and the *Epistola* speaks of the literary sources and, in the above brief passage, about the melodies. Although it tells us no more than we would expect to find by looking at the music itself, such instances of a composer's explaining his musical intentions are rare. In what follows I shall describe briefly the music of the office and test it against Létald's observations. I shall present some chants in transcription and try to identify elements in them that may described as traditional or new. The older elements naturally relate Létald's compositions to established practice, but the nontraditional or nonstandard turns of phrase pose the problem of how we are to find our bearings in the very large body of such music that has come down to us not only from Létald's time but also from before and after.

The Sources

In 1963 Michel Huglo gave almost the only information about this office that has so far appeared in the musicological literature, mentioning all the earliest sources at present known (Huglo 1963, 75–76 and nn. 110–14). One of the oldest surviving copies, unfortunately incomplete, is closely connected with Le Mans: this is the Le Mans evangeliary Paris, BNF lat. 261, where the office is notated in French neumes. Since only the Magnificat antiphon of First Vespers and three antiphons and one responsory for the first nocturn of the Night Office survive, the manuscript is of limited value in reconstructing the office. The principal early manuscript sources are Madrid, BN 288, and Oxford, Bodleian Bodley 596. Part of the office also survives as a flyleaf of Paris, BNF lat. 2142 (Huglo 1963, 74). A facsimile from Paris lat. 261 was published by Hourlier,[2] from Bodley 596 by Frere.[3]

Madrid 288, Bodley 596, and Paris lat. 261 are all notated in staffless neumes, and it is fortunate that one more manuscript copy of the office survives with staff notation. This is Vendôme, BM 17E, a breviary of the thirteenth century from La Trinité, Vendôme, copied by an accomplished scribe in double columns after the

Table 19.1 The Office of St. Julian of Le Mans

Genre	Incipit	Madrid	Oxford	Vendôme	Mode
First Vespers					
Mag. A.	Urbs provecta Cenomannis	x	x	x	8
Night Office					
Inv.	Corde puro	x	x	x	3
First Nocturn					
A.	Ad collocandum	x	x	x	1
A.	Primus igitur	x	x	x	2
A.	Signum apostolatus	x	x	x	3
A.	Hic itaque Julianus		x	x	4
A.	Vir domini Julianus		x	x	5
A.	Novitas sancte		x	x	6
R.	Sicut complacidas V. Ad Christi sequenda	x	x	x	1
R.	Primus igitur V. Ad Christi veritatem	x	x	x	2
R.	Sancte Ju . . . (inc.)		x		
R.	Ecce vere . . . (inc.)			x	
R.	Signum apostolatus V. Area tu paterni	x	x	x	3
Second Nocturn					
A.	Hic itaque Iulianus	x			4
A.	Vir domini Julianus	x			5
A.	Novitas sancte	x			6
A.	Miraculorum potentia		x	x	7
A.	Per manus reverendi		x	x	8
A.	Cum ad eum multi		x	x	1
A.	Sacerdos et pontifex	x			
A.	Dum eveneret(?) summus . . . (inc.)			x	
A.	Sancti dei dilecti		x		
A.	Celica iam meritas		x		
R.	Hic itaque Jul. V. Primus urbi	x	x	x	4
R.	Per manus Jul. V. O gloriosum	x	x	x	5
R.	Miles Christi . . . V. Ut celestis (inc.)		x		
R.	Ecce vir prudens . . . (inc.)			x	
R.	O gloriosum V. Eum semper	x	x	x	6
	Prosa O Juliane		x		
Third Nocturn					
A.	Miraculorum potentia	x			7
A.	Per manus reverendi	x			8
A.	Cum ad eum multi	x			1
R.	Urbs provecta V. Cuius vera	x	x	x	7
R.	Splendens Lucifer V. Sendentem in tenebris	x	x	x	8
R.	O quam admirabilis V. Laudibus (no music)		x		
R.	Iste sanctus . . . (inc.)			x	

Table 19.1 (*continued*)

Genre	Incipit	Madrid	Oxford	Vendôme	Mode
R.	Beatissimus Jul. V. Immortalis palme	x	x	x	1
	Prosa Semper tibi	x	x	x	
Lauds					
A.	Julianus Cenomanensium	x	x	x	1
A.	Immortalis palme	x	x	x	2
A.	Ad Christi veritatem	x	x	x	3
A.	Domine Hiesu Christe	x	x	x	4
A.	Mox quasi a somno	x	x	x	5
Ben. A.	At vero cunctorum	x	x	x	6
Second Vespers					
Mag. A.	Sacerdotum diadema	x	x	x	1

Parisian fashion. The office appears on folios 344r–349r, with chants notated in full, lessons (mostly very short), and some prayers.

Finally, the office is also to be found in the printed *Antiphonarium Cenomannense* of 1529.[4]

If it were composed for the cathedral liturgy of Le Mans, the office was presumably set out by Létald according to the secular cursus. This is the form in which it is transmitted in Madrid 288 (compiled, I believe, around 1100 for the chapel of the Norman rulers of south Italy and Sicily), in as much as remains of Paris lat. 261, and in the *Antiphonarium Cenomannense*. Bodley 596 and Vendôme 17E, on the other hand, have a monastic version of the office. Table 19.1 lists the chants preserved in the three principal manuscript sources. The chants in Madrid 288 are those shared by the monastic sources. Furthermore, it is these chants that are composed in the well-known fashion according to the numerical order of the modes. All this indicates that the secular form of the office is the original one, while the monastic cursus is adapted from it, supplementing it with chants drawn from the Common of Saints.

We may now turn to some selected musical items from the office and try to see how they have been put together. (There is clearly no space to discuss more than a few pieces. A forthcoming edition of the office[5] will enable the reader to inspect the chants not given here in full.)

Responsory Verses

Since Létald's texts are written for the most part in prose (albeit often rhymed), the textual constraints upon his adapting traditional melodies to them would have been negligible. His verses could be treated like those of a psalm or most of the other texts for traditional responsories or antiphons. Létald's most obvious adaptations of old melodic formulas are to be found in the verses for responsories, where at least a half of the material is drawn from the traditional tones:[6]

Verse	For Respond	Tone
Ad Christi sequenda	Sicut complacidas	1 traditional
Ad Christi veritatem	Primus igitur	2 new
Area tu paterni	Signum apostolatus	3 traditional
Primus urbi	Hic itaque Jul.	4 traditional
O gloriosum	Per manus Jul.	5 mostly traditional
Eum semper	O gloriosum	6 traditional
Cuius vera	Urbs provecta	7 new
Sedentem in tenebris	Splendens Lucifer	8 mostly traditional
Immortalis palme	Beatissimus Jul.	1 new

The designation "new" in this list needs a gentle qualification, for in no case is the melody at all adventurously different from the standard manner. That is, it retains the range and melodic behavior of a traditional verse. Example 19.1 gives the verse *O gloriosum*, marking those sections that draw upon the usual formula. (All examples are transcribed from the Vendôme manuscript.)

The verse in mode 8, *Sedentem in tenebris* (example 19.2), uses the second tone traditional for this mode, which was relatively infrequently deployed.[7] But the descent to *c* during *preco veritatis* does not belong to the formula.

Responds

In analyzing the musical makeup of the melodies for the first section of the responsories, the respond, one can again refer to the cadences and other formulas given by Frere (*Antiphonale*). There are nevertheless a number of difficulties in assessing the composer's debt to tradition. For a start, there is often a certain ambi-

Example 19.1   Responsory verse *O gloriosum*

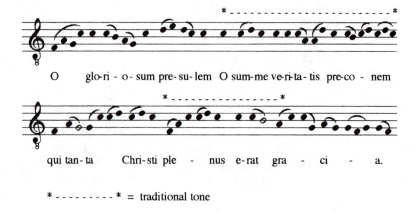

O   glo-ri - o- sum pre-su-lem O sum-me ve-ri-ta- tis pre-co - nem

qui tan-ta   Chri-sti ple - nus e-rat gra - ci - a.

* - - - - - - - - - * = traditional tone

Example 19.2   Responsory verse *Sedentibus in tenebris*

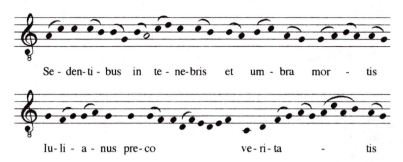

Se - den- ti - bus in te - ne- bris   et   um - bra   mor -   tis

Iu- li - a - nus pre- co   ve- ri- ta   -   tis

guity about the division of a chant into phrases, although in most cases the literary text and musical cadences suggest the same breaks. More problematic is the handling of stock turns of phrase. A cadential ending may be used in more than one mode, and it may not be restricted to responsories. The same is true of some opening gestures. Such recourse to the "common coin" of Gregorian chant is of a different dimension than the adaptation of a whole phrase from the responsory stock. Thirdly, we are still heavily dependent on Frere's analysis for our identification of standard phrases. Comparative analyses of other antiphoners, from other European traditions, would help make our descriptions of individual chants considerably more secure.

Even given these reservations, it quickly becomes evident that the composer of the Julian office has not restricted himself to the most common musical phrases for each mode. Sometimes he has taken a cadence used more frequently in another mode (a phenomenon already noted by Frere), sometimes he has fallen back on only the very last notes of a common cadence; only rarely has he used a whole phrase from the common stock. We may look first at the three responds in D mode, that is the first, second, and ninth.

The first responsory, *Sicut complacidas*, is transcribed in example 19.3, where those phrases traceable elsewhere are bracketed and labeled according to Frere's formulas. (For ease of reference I give in parentheses the page reference for the phrases cited by Frere.) It begins with a common opening, that given by Frere in his group I^a (17) for this mode, but also to be found in responsories of mode 2 (13). After the first word *Sicut*, however, the phrase continues with the music of Frere's formula f^1, rather than O^a (20). The next, *verni clementia*, proceeds independently of the idiomatic phrases cited by Frere; *temperat auras* resembles Frere's D^8 (20, 24; this cadence also occurs in mode 2); *redolentes arbusta* is again individual. For *prorumpunt in flores* the composer uses a phrase that starts and ends like the fifth example of Frere's Δ^{11} (25), though the middle is different. Yet this ending, if we look at the last seven notes alone, is a very common one, found in all of Frere's Δ^{7-11} here, but also in mode 2 (14–15). And, as we know for example from Homan's table of common cadences (Homan 1964, examples on p. 76), it is not restricted to responsories, or to the note D.

The divisions for the next phrases are not very clear, but at *ecclesie* there is a cadence common in responsories of modes 5 and 6 (39), while *restituta* uses phrase

Example 19.3   Respond *Sicut complacidas*

C[1] (22–23). For *effulsere viri* the music of *temperat auras* is taken up again, and a similar procedure occurs with the next phrase, *Fidei fulgore insignes,* where the music is similar to *redolentes arbusta.* The relative independence from traditional formulas seems to be epitomized in the final phrase, which is independent right up to the last seven notes, the cadence already discussed for *prorumpunt in flores.*

The second respond, *Primus igitur* (example 19.4), again ventures beyond the stock phrases for the most part, always excepting common cadences. Both halves of the respond use the same common opening (p. 13 in Frere), the start of the piece continuing with another common phrase, K[2]. The opening *cdf* at *non tantum presul* is of course very common, but not significant in a larger context. The respond ends with cadence D[8] again (20, 24), also found in the first respond.

Example 19.3   (*continued*)

The ninth respond, *Beatissimus Iulianus* (example 19.5), is a wide-ranging piece, a fitting climax to the series, which correspondingly moves well beyond the old conventions. The low opening for *Beatissimus* is typical for mode 2 pieces, not mode 1 (opening O, Frere, pp. 6–8); the setting of this word ends somewhat similarly to k² (17), with a cadence actually used one octave higher in mode 7 (C¹, p. 44). The subtonal cadence for *Iulianus*, on the other hand, is untraditional. (Such a cadence, usually found on D, E, G, and A, is sometimes referred to as "Gallican," on no good historical grounds.)

For these three responds, therefore, Létald has made use of a few common cadences, sometimes choosing the same ones in all three pieces rather than exploiting the considerable variety available even within the same mode. The investigation

Example 19.4   Respond *Primus igitur*

Example 19.5   Respond *Beatissimus Iulianus*

(*continued*)

Example 19.5   (*continued*)

tri - um - pha - ta.

Ho - di - e fe - lix et vi - ctor

reg - na su - bi - it

sem - pi - ter - na.

need not be repeated in this fashion for all nine responds. Let it suffice to point out that instances where the composer uses a complete phrase from the traditional stock are very rare indeed, and even there internal extensions of the phrase are to be found.

Beatissimus Iulianus

If Létald does not rely on traditional formulas very much, what does he do? A few further remarks about *Beatissimus Iulianus* may focus attention on some significant points.

The wide range of the piece was already noticed. The low tessitura of the opening, which inhabits the tetrachord A–d, does not recur, though phrases in the next available tetrachord, c–f, with cadences on c, are quite frequent. The melody also moves beyond the conventional range at the top end, with one phrase in the tetrachord c′–f′, already introduced by a phrase cadencing on d′. Nearly every phrase can be assigned unambiguously to a particular tetrachord (a trichord in the case of f–a), or at least a linked pair of tetrachords, in this way, for the composer seems to have conceived his melody very much in melodic units, which we can define by range and cadence. Many of these phrases set no more than one word of text, four to six syllables. (Cadence notes are given in parentheses, the principal cadences with an asterisk; neighbor notes extending the basic tetrachord are given in superscript.)

Text	Tetrachord	Cadence note
Beatissimus	A–d (d), c–f	(c)
Iulianus,	f–a'	(a*)
Cenomannensiumat	at first a–c' or g–c', then ^{e}f–a	(g)
pontifex primus,	c–f with a brief excursion into f–a	(d*)
virtutum	c–f^g	(c)
fulgore	f–a^{b,}	(a)
clarissimus,	c–f^g	(d*)
antiqui hostis	f–a (f), then c–f (c), rising back to f^g	(f)
superbia	f–a	(a)
triumphata.	^{c}d–f^g	(d*)
Hodie felix	a–d', rising, falling back and rising again	(d')
et	c'–f'	(d')
victor	a–d'	(a*)
regna	f–a, then c–f	(c)
subiit	c–f^g	(f)
sempiterna.	f–a, then d–f or d–g	(d*)

These tetrachordal units, although clear in themselves, coalesce smoothly in wide-ranging phrases that on occasion can span a whole octave or more. Thus the opening section, *Beatissimus Iulianus,* rises steadily from A to a, even touching c' so that the cadence on a will sound more natural; *Cenomannensium pontifex primus,* with the total range c–c', progresses equally steadily back to the tonic note; *virtutum fulgore clarissimus* moves up to a again, but instead of progressing further returns to d. The fourth phrase moves in the same range, with principal notes in the order a–d–a–d–f–d. The second section of the respond begins by reaching up boldly for the higher octave, before subsiding on a (*Hodie felix et victor*). The final phrase, *regna subiit sempiterna,* resembles the fourth.

Casting an eye over the examples of mode 1 responsories in Frere, one does not gain quite the same impression of clear-cut small units and wide-ranging larger units. The direction is not as clear, the motion not as sweeping, the range not as wide. It is significant that in the Julian respond the main cadences are limited to d and a, and the only other note where another tonal permanent center seems briefly to be about to establish itself is the upper octave d'.

Add a few other nontraditional details such as the chains of thirds in sequence at *fulgore, triumphata,* and *sempiterna,* the oscillations at *Cenomannensium* (g–a and f–g), and the subtonal cadences at *Iulianus* and *felix* (almost repeated at *victor*), and we have a fairly complete picture of the eleventh-century composer's response to the demands of ending his series of responsories in a fitting manner.

The actual climax comes in the prosula *Semper tibi* (example 19.6), an insertion at the end of the respond, where *sempiterna* would normally be sung. This is characterized by those features that seem least traditional in the respond, that is, it emphasizes all that is new in Létald's music. Like contemporary sequences, it is built in pairs of verses, and like them it uses the subtonal cadence on the tonic, d, and the upper fifth, a. There is free and rapid movement between these poles. At one point the melody swings up to the top octave, something again typical of

Example 19.6   Prosula *Semper tibi*

1a Sem-per ti-bi rex O Chri-ste glo-ri - a laus ho-nor vir-tus de-cus at-que.
1b Ec - ce ho-di-e vo-ti - va perfun-dis nos lu-ce Iu - li - a - ne lau-de.

2a Ce - li   lu - ci - fer splen-di-dus no-ctis um-bras fu-gat so-le
2b In fun-da-men-to hunc tu - e col-lo-ca-sti ec-cle-si-e

2b: D C

sic quo-que Iu-li-a-nus ra-di-at tu-o nos-met o-vans ful-go-re.
post pru-nos col-lo-ca-re quos ti-bi pla-cu-it ar-chi-te-cte sum-me.

3a: B

3a Nunc i-gitur con-ci-nat in-cre-pans psallans hec mune-ra tu-e graci-e.
3b Iu - li-a-ni qui mundum ra-di-at me-ri-tis et virtutum—lampa de.

4a O   bo-ne__ O   pi-e rex vo-ta no-stra li-bens su-sci-pe
4b Tu - que mag-ne Iu - li-a-ne hu-ic a-de-sto fa-mi-li-e

(4b) me-ri-tis et o-pe. Sem - pi - ter - na.

sequences, but all of a piece with the phrase *Hodie felix* in the respond. Not surprisingly, since the setting of *sempiterna* is its starting point, it makes much of the
chains of thirds.

Invitatory

The invitatory *Corde puro* (for a Venite tone corresponding to 4. d. in the Solesmes
Liber responsorialis) relies to some extent on the melody classified as IV² by Frere,
though it is considerably longer than Frere's example (*Adoremus regem apostolorum* for John the Evangelist, facs., p. 62).

Antiphons for the Psalms

The classic investigations of antiphons, by Gevaert, Frere, and Hucke, have concentrated largely or even exclusively on the simpler antiphons—psalter or ferial antiphons, antiphons for the psalms on feast days—which are very simple, or relatively so, and can often be assigned to melodic families. More ornate melodies, such as are commonly provided for the Magnificat and Nunc dimittis on feast days, have usually resisted such classification. Most of the antiphons in the Julian office are of the more ornate type, and it is consequently difficult to relate them to previous classifications. In fact, apart from some typical openings and cadences, very little strikes the eye immediately as traditional.

I give here three examples, the first of which employs traditional material, while the second is more independent and the third is markedly original. The first antiphon of the Night Office, *Ad collocandum* (example 19.7), in mode 1, coincides for the greater part with Frere's melody type protus/a (pp. 65–66; Gevaert 6). The first phrase, *Ad collocandum in Galliis,* is the same as in all the examples that Frere gives, while the next phrase, *nove fidei fundamentum,* resembles nos. 2 and 4 in Frere's group. Thereafter the resemblances are less close.

The fourth antiphon of Lauds, *Domine Ihesu Christe* (example 19.8), in mode 4, is a long piece ending with a prayer formula. At first sight the text may seem unusual, but in fact we have here one of many references or actual extracts from the *Vita* of St. Julian. Such narratives frequently feature the saint invoking the Lord's aid in a time of supreme need. In the second chapter of this *Vita* Julian raises no fewer than three persons from the dead, and the antiphon *Domine Ihesu Christe* paraphrases sentences from the first of the three episodes, where Julian calls upon Christ to help him bring back to life the son of the nobleman Anastasius. The antiphon text omits the references in the *Vita* to Christ's raising of the widow's son and Lazarus from the dead and expands the formal ending:

Example 19.7   Antiphon *Ad collocandum*

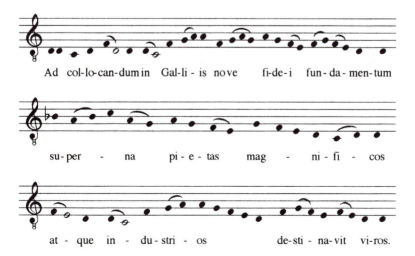

Ad col-lo-can-dum in Gal-li - is no ve   fi-de-i fun - da - men-tum

su- per - na   pi - e - tas   mag - ni - fi - cos

at - que in - du - stri - os   de-sti - na-vit vi-ros.

Example 19.8   Antiphon *Domine Ihesu Christe*

Do - mi - ne Ihe-su Chri - ste   iu - be   ut   re - sur - gat

a - do - le-scens   i-ste   ut   tan - ti   fa - cti   po - ten - ti - a

et   fi - des   cre - den - ti-um   in   te ro - bo - re-tur

et   non cre-den - ci - um   cor - da sub - dan - tur   per   te

u- ni - ge-ni-tum   de - i   vi-vi   quem cum   pa - tre et

spi-ri-tu   san - cto   reg - nan -   tem et do-mi-nan - tem

con - fi - te - mur   in   se-cu - la   se-cu - lo-rum   a - men.

Vita	Historia
Domine Jesu Christe, qui viduae filium	Domine Iesu Christe,
extra portam elatum multis astantibus	
suscitasti, et quatriduanum Lazarum	
jamque foetentem verbo potentiae tuae	
a mortuis revocasti;	
tu praecipe ut suscitetur puer iste,	iube ut resurgat adolescens iste,
quatenus isto resuscitato in corpore,	ut tanti facti potentia et fides credentium
multi per tuam fidem resurgant in anima,	in te roboretur et non credentium
praesentesque cognoscant,	corda subdantur,
quia tu es Christus filius Dei vivi,	per te unigenitum dei vivi,
qui praecepto Patris mundum salvasti,	quem cum patre et spiritu sancto
cui per te condignas gratias referimus	regnantem et dominantem confitemur,
per infinita saeculorum saecula.	in secula seculorum, amen.

The music for this long text is relatively simple and unadventurous. Most phrases move within the pentachord *c–g*, circling round and cadencing on *e* with the subtonal cadence. There is an excursion into a higher region at *quem cum patre*, using the leap *d–a* to gain the necessary height for a cadence on *a;* the next phrase begins in the tetrachord *g–c*, but subsides onto low *c*. After that comes the expected cadence on *e*. Such music is fairly typical of the longer traditional mode 4 antiphons for Magnificat and Benedictus, though it is easier to speak of "characteristic movement" than of clear-cut melodic formulas shared between chants. Here the composer seems to be occupying the middle ground between tradition and innovation.

For the Magnificat and Benedictus antiphons of his own office, Létald goes a good step further. The first item in the *Historia*, the Magnificat antiphon *Urbs provecta Cenomannis* in mode 8, is given as example 19.9. The principal cadences are all the non-Gregorian subtonal *f–g–g*. The upper fifth, *d'*, is highlighted very prominently at the start of the phrase *ut quo duce*, but otherwise it is the series of thirds *d–f–a–c'* (in the first and last phrases) or *f–a–c'–e'* (in the middle two phrases) that constitute the framework supporting the finalis. Such melodic material is not unique to this office, as a cursory inspection of other compositions of the tenth and eleventh centuries will show. But it can by no means be called traditional.

Some Conclusions

After this brief inspection of Létald's music it is time to draw some conclusions, about Létald's compositions and also about eleventh-century Office chants in general.

Létald says: "We did not want to distance ourselves in any way from the likeness of old chant." It is clear that he drew a certain amount from old tradition, while building upon it in a contemporary but not extravagantly adventurous way. There are no modal inconsistencies, phrases that go beyond the approved range. Perhaps Létald meant no more than that he had "kept to the rules" in respect of mode and

Example 19.9   Magnificat antiphon *Urbs provecta Cenomannis*

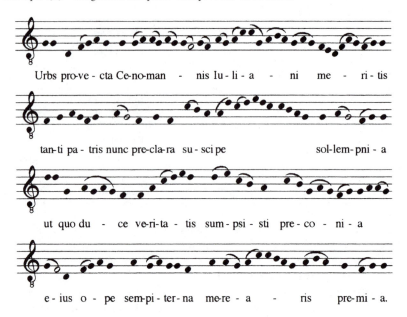

Urbs pro-ve - cta Ce-no-man - nis Iu - li - a - ni me - ri - tis

tan-ti pa - tris nunc pre-cla-ra su - sci pe   sol-lem-pni - a

ut quo du - ce ve-ri-ta - tis sum - psi - sti pre - co - ni - a

e - ius o - pe sem-pi - ter- na me-re - a - ris pre-mi - a.

range. To judge by the contents of our earliest notated antiphoners (the Mont-Renaud manuscript and Hartker's Antiphoner), which after all are only a few decades older than this Office, by Létald's time a good deal of "non-Gregorian" material (using the subtonal cadence, for example) was established in the standard Office repertory, so that stylistic features that to us seem relatively recent (say, of the tenth rather than the eighth or ninth century) may not have seemed that way to Létald and his immediate contemporaries.

There is one more possible interpretation of Létald's words. Could it be that he adapted his music from a previous Office? The music would indeed then be "tried," "like old chant," made by an "old composer." Until more exhaustive searches and comparisons have been made, the question had perhaps best be left open. Meanwhile, my own hunt through north French offices of the period has so far revealed much that is similar but nothing that is identical.

This brings us to a second conclusion of a much more general nature. As remarked at the outset, we lack the tools for assessing precisely the degree of originality or adherence to tradition in an office such as this. It is obvious that we need not only analyses of a sufficient body of the new Offices of the eleventh century and later, but also much more careful sifting of the Office repertory up to the end of the millennium, in order to uncover the various stylistic and chronological layers in our oldest notated sources. The task appears to require new techniques, unless we are fall back on such phrases as Frere was so often forced to use, for example: "[the antiphons] have a common opening, but little else in common" (p. 69; cf. the remarks on p. 73 *b*, p. 74 *f, h*, and so on); "In the [antiphons of the] Seventh Mode there is much similarity of material and method, which does not amount to a unity of theme" (p. 72). Let us remember that Frere's analysis was largely concerned with what he designated as "typical," not "original" responds. Once we have sifted out the "typical" material (Frere sometimes referred to it as "classical," belonging to a golden age, and he readily assigned chants to periods of increasing decadence: silver, bronze, and clay) we are left with the question of how to respond to the "original" compositions. Can we define their essence in a way that will both pinpoint what is "original" and help us to trace contrafacta?

It would clearly be neither feasible nor very informative to repeat the sort of comment attempted above for all of the offices that cross one's path. Rather it is likely that we shall find general agreement upon the use of a few types of phrase, whose range, tonal backbone, and cadence points are selected from a limited number of favorite models. It seems to me that, at least in northern France in the eleventh century, these are in fact the ones employed by Létald, who was trying to provide music in an accepted, orthodox manner. We could therefore replace Frere's two broad categories of "typical" and "original" by a threefold distinction:

1. Passages or complete chants that make more or less literal use of traditional, stock turns of phrase, particularly at cadences, with the minimum of adaptation necessary to accommodate varying numbers of syllables (Frere's "typical" category).
2. Passages that behave in one of a limited number of orthodox ways, according to range and associated tonal structure, without involving literal reproductions of a particular succession of notes.
3. Unorthodox or eccentric passages that do not conform to the established norm (1 or 2).

It is my impression that the definition of orthodoxy for the second category changes with time, so that second-category chants of the ninth century do not have the same melodic quality as those of the eleventh century. (It adds considerably to the interest of the investigation of these layers of musical material that manuscripts vary significantly in their transmission of melodic detail, so that older melodies were often adapted to reflect current taste.)

Since by definition there will be a high degree of similarity between chants in the second category, it will not be easy to trace contrafact compositions. We shall no doubt have to wait for many more comparable Offices to become accessible before much progress can be made in this direction.[8]

Notes

1. Odorannus of Sens, writing at roughly the same time and general area (contemporary French music-theoretical texts are otherwise rare), uses *modus* in the sense of "mode." Thus his tonary is entitled "Formae regularium modorum," though admittedly glossed "Tropi et toni et modi idem sunt"(!). See Odorannus, *Opera*, p. 156, and other references cited in the index of musical terms.

2. Hourlier (1960), plate 22, reproduces fol. 149v, giving the start of the office. No more survives.

3. Frere (1894), no. 126, p. 45. Plate 6 reproduces fol. 212v, giving the end of the Night Office and the beginning of Lauds. Frere describes the manuscript as a miscellany

from Westminster Abbey, including a form of the coronation service, Lydgate's *Life of Our Lady,* lives of St. Julian and St. Cuthbert, as well as the Office of St. Julian. Van Dijk (1957), 2:361 and 3:35, gives further concise information about the source. The part of the manuscript containing the office of St. Julian can be assigned to the late eleventh century and at one time belonged to the library of St. Augustine's, Canterbury (see fol. 175r). Van Dijk had previously published a description of the manuscript in the Bodleian Library exhibition catalogue (1952), no. 63.

4. Paris, BNF Rés. B. 1470 is an incomplete, Solesmes, Bibliothèque de l'Abbaye LLa. 7–7-2 a complete copy of this rare printed book.

5. To appear in the series "Historiae" of the I.M.S. Study Group "Cantus Planus" (see n. 8).

6. The tones are most easily accessible in Frere, *Antiphonale,* Introduction, 4.

7. Frere mentions it in a footnote on p. 60, citing pp. 171 and 174 of the facsimile (that is the verses *Cumque vidissent Ioseph* and *Merito hec patimur,* respectively), but does not give a transcription.

8. The new project "Historiae," under the aegis of the Study Group "Cantus Planus" of the International Musicological Society, has been launched to make good some of this deficit. The series editors are Ruth Steiner, Barbara Haggh, and László Dobszay.

20

The Little Office of the Virgin
and Mary's Role at Paris

REBECCA A. BALTZER

The Little Office of the Virgin, in place by the early thirteenth century at Notre-Dame, was performed on most ferial days and feasts of three lessons at the cathedral of Paris. By a considerable margin it was thus the most frequently performed Marian liturgy in a cathedral in which the Virgin was the most important saint. Beginning with the service of Matins, the Little Office included all eight Canonical Hours: Matins, Lauds, Prime, Terce, Sext, None, Vespers, and Compline. In this it contrasts with the Saturday Office of the Virgin, which typically began with First Vespers, not Matins, and included a votive Mass for the Virgin as well (see Wright 1989, 104). The Little Office of the Virgin is doubly important in that it became the Hours of the Virgin in the Book of Hours, a development in private devotion that began in the first half of the thirteenth century and resulted in a flood of devotional books through the rest of the Middle Ages.[1]

The origins of the Little Office of the Virgin seem to go back to the Carolingian period; certainly it was extant by the tenth century in various places around Europe, with sometimes substantial local variations.[2] Because liturgical books of Paris use are few and far between before the thirteenth century, we cannot trace the complete development of this Office in Paris from its beginnings; we can only look at it from the thirteenth century onward. But prior to the appearance of the first extant version of this Office in a late thirteenth-century Parisian source, rubrics in other Parisian liturgical books from the early years of the thirteenth century give us a glimpse of the presence of the Little Office of the Virgin at Notre-Dame before the year 1200.

For example, the two earliest extant liturgical books for the Office services of the church of Paris, BNF lat. 748 and 749, both contain no feast added to the Paris liturgy after 1200. Thus, though both were copied in the early thirteenth century, they represent a liturgical state prior to the year 1200. Lat. 749 is the sanctoral portion of a breviary without music, while lat. 748 is a noted summer breviary.[3] In both books, the feast for St. Quentin, martyr, on 31 October has a rank of three lessons if it falls on a weekday but nine lessons if it occurs on Sunday; hence, the Little Office of the Virgin would be performed on St. Quentin's day as long as it was not on Sunday. On the feast of St. Quentin, both books have a rubric pertaining to the Little Office of the Virgin. The rubric in lat. 748 on fol. 146r says "Non dicitur eodem die vespere beate Marie post nonam." Lat. 749, fol. 269, conveys the same idea with "Vespere beate Marie non cantantur post nonam." Thus Vespers of the Little Office of the Virgin was not to be sung after None on St. Quentin's day—for the reason (not explained in the manuscripts) that it was the eve of All Saints' Day (1 Nov.), which began with First Vespers on 31 October, short-changing both the lesser feast of St. Quentin and the Little Office of the Virgin. But such rubrics tell us that the Little Office was in use before 1200 at Notre-Dame.

Also in lat. 749, just a few folios later on 278v, comes further evidence for the presence of the Little Office. Between the feast of St. Marcel, the most important Parisian confessor bishop, celebrated on 3 November, and its octave, observed on 8 November, a rubric says, "Per oct[avam] cantantur hore beate Marie et fient mem[orie] de reliquiis et de omnibus sanctis." Thus during the octave of this feast, the Little Office was performed (the Latin word is "sung") because the days within the octave were not ranked at more than three lessons, though the feast itself had duplex rank and the octave on the 8th had nine lessons.

Several periods during the church year did *not* include the Little Office as part of the liturgy on ferial days and feasts of three lessons. With regard to the first of these, Advent, the situation seems to have changed by the latter part of the thirteenth century. Even though the liturgy of Advent was already saturated with a Marian presence, the Little Office was apparently observed on the ferial days of Advent (there being no saints' feasts of three lessons in the Paris calendar during these four weeks), at least for a time. Performance of the Little Office is specifically mentioned in the *Ordo officii* for Advent in Paris, BNF lat. 16317, a Paris ordinal from the second half of the thirteenth century. At the end of Lauds on Feria 2 after the first Sunday of Advent, the ordo states: "A memorial of the Relics and of All Saints after Lauds of the Blessed Mary ought to be done as above throughout Advent." A few lines later, it adds: "After Vespers of the Blessed Mary, a memorial of the Relics is made by means of the antiphon *Et facta est,* versicle *Letamini in domino,* and collect *Propiciare.*" This is followed by the memorial for All Saints, and then Compline begins.[4] The Little Office of the Virgin was also performed in other cathedral churches during Advent—at both Laon and Worcester, for instance—so this was not a singular practice at Notre-Dame of Paris. But by the last quarter of the thirteenth century, if not earlier, the absence of the Little Office is specifically mentioned in the Paris *Ordo officii* for Advent following Lauds on Feria 2 after the first Sunday: "et per totum adventum hore beate Marie non dicitur in choro per totum adventum."[5]

Other periods when the Little Office of the Virgin was not performed included the days from Christmas through the octave of Epiphany, the three weeks from Passion Sunday through the octave of Easter (none of which was merely "ferial"), and the period from Ascension Day through Pentecost and its octave (the feast of Trinity Sunday). This information is precisely spelled out in the earliest extant Parisian ceremonial of 1662 (p. 549), and there is no evidence that this represents any change of procedure from four and a half centuries earlier. Also, during the octaves of several other major feasts besides Christmas, Easter, and Pentecost—for example, the Assumption, the Nativity of the BVM, and St. Denis—the days within the octave were of sufficient rank that the Little Office was not observed.

Was the Little Office of the Virgin performed in choir, or was it done in some other place within the cathedral? The answer is that in cathedrals known as Notre-Dame, in which the Virgin was the most important saint, the Little Office was indeed done in choir. The Paris ordinal mentioned above, lat. 16317, makes this clear in its first mention of the Little Office in the Temporale, a rubric on Feria 2 (Monday) following the octave of Epiphany. After outlining Matins and Lauds on this feria, the next sentence states: "Hic incipiunt hore beate Marie *in choro* que cantande sunt usque ad *Isti sunt dies*."[6] Each Hour followed that of the main Office of the day on ferias and feasts of three lessons, except that Matins and Lauds of the Little Office together followed Lauds of the day. At Notre-Dame of Paris, the main altar was dedicated to the Virgin; the sanctuary surrounding it was thus *her* space, and there was nowhere else in the cathedral more appropriate for her daily Office than in the choir, with the altar of the Virgin ever before the performers. Virtually every time the clerics of the choir left their stalls as a group in liturgical procession, they returned to the choir singing a Marian antiphon, followed by a versicle with response and a collect in honor of the Virgin, no matter what the occasion in the church calendar. It was impossible to ignore or to forget that this was the Virgin's cathedral; on major feasts she was regularly commemorated at Vespers and Lauds, and on lesser days the Little Office of the Virgin "shadowed" the Office of the day. Since virtually no laity would have been present for any of the Divine Office on these lesser days, the Little Office of the Virgin was essentially a liturgy that reenforced the sense of mission and devotion of the cathedral's clerics who regularly performed it. And it is worth noting that the Little Office would have been performed many more times per year than the Psalter or the ferial Office; it was undoubtedly the most familiar Office for any member of the choir, the chapter, and the ecclesiastical hierarchy at Notre-Dame.

Versions of the Little Office of the Virgin appear in four different thirteenth-century sources that follow (to varying degrees) the liturgical use of the cathedral of Paris. The earliest of the four is Rouen, BM 3016 (Leber 6), a large psalter and hours from the second quarter of the thirteenth century.[7] Second is Cambridge, Fitzwilliam 300, the so-called Isabelle psalter and hours, from the 1260s;[8] third is Baltimore, Walters W.40, a small book of hours that is more modest in both size and decoration, also made in the third quarter of the thirteenth century.[9] Last is Paris, lat. 10482, a noted breviary from the last quarter of the thirteenth century.[10]

The Little Office of the Virgin is normally described as having only a single nocturn at Matins, since it was observed in tandem with the ferial Office or with that of lesser feast days having no more than one nocturn. However, the three earliest sources of Paris use all have a full three nocturns with nine lessons; only the late thirteenth-century breviary, lat. 10482, has a single nocturn with three lessons. Later manuscript and early printed sources from the fifteenth century offer three nocturns that are alternatives, varying according to the day of the week: one nocturn for Sundays, Mondays, and Thursdays; another for Tuesdays and Fridays;

and a third for Wednesdays and Saturdays.[11] But the three earliest thirteenth-century sources do not indicate that their three nocturns are alternatives; they are instead intended to follow each other on the same day.

All three of these books were apparently made for private individual devotion rather than institutional liturgical use, and they exemplify one change that occurred in such books during the course of the thirteenth century: the change from a preference for large, decorated psalters[12] to the combined psalter/hours and then to small, decorated books of hours without psalters. Rouen 3016 is large enough to be a lectern book (318 × 212 mm.), but with fifteen full-page miniatures and many illuminated initials, it, along with the Isabelle psalter/hours, may have been intended for a high-born layperson.[13] Further support for this idea comes from the fact that neither the psalter in Rouen 3016 nor that in Fitzwilliam 300 includes the antiphons or hymns that would be necessary for liturgical use.[14] Walters 40, whose dimensions are only 172 × 129 mm., shows that the small book of hours, without a psalter but enriched with a number of other items, was becoming the devotional book of choice. If all three books were made for a layperson's private devotions, this circumstance offers a probable reason for the full three nocturns with nine lessons at Matins that they contain: in private devotion the Little Office of the Virgin did not have to follow the regular Office of the day with its single nocturn of three lessons; it stood alone.

Lat. 10482, on the other hand, was clearly a secular cleric's liturgical book, since despite its small size (severely trimmed to 172 × 125 mm.), it is a full, notated breviary with a ferial psalter that does contain notated hymns and antiphons. As a Paris liturgical book rather than a private devotional book, it serves as the basis for the text of the Little Office of the Virgin given below in the appendix. But the differences among all four sources still require comment, for they show a fluidity of content that was only beginning to become standardized.

Most of the liturgical material in the Little Office is drawn from the major Marian feasts already established in the liturgy, particularly the feast of the Assumption of the Virgin (15 August). The psalms used in the Little Office of the Virgin are those which are "ordinary" for Marian feasts, a natural choice for compilers of the Little Office.[15] In lat. 10482, the psalms for Matins are cued by their text incipits, but specific psalms are not mentioned for the other hours except for Vespers, which has the cue "*Letatus, cum aliis*" (*Letatus,* with the others). The other three manuscripts, all for private devotion, write out the full text of each psalm. The cursus, not counting the invitatory Ps. 94 (*Venite exultemus*) that always begins Matins, is thus:

Matins: Ps. 8, *Domine dominus noster*
Ps. 18, *Celi enarrant*
Ps. 23, *Domini est terra*
Ps. 44, *Eructavit cor meum*
Ps. 45, *Deus noster refugium*
Ps. 86, *Fundamenta*
Ps. 95, *Cantate domino*
Ps. 96, *Dominus regnavit*
Ps. 97, *Cantate domino*

Lauds:	Ps. 92, *Dominus regnavit*
	Ps. 99, *Iubilate deo*
	Ps. 62, *Deus deus meus,* and Ps. 66, *Deus misereatur*
	Canticle, *Benedicite*
	Pss. 148–50, *Laudate dominum, Cantate domino, Laudate dominum*
Prime:	Ps. 1, *Beatus vir*
	Ps. 2, *Quare fremuerunt*
	Ps. 5, *Verba mea*
Terce:	Ps. 119, *Ad dominum*
	Ps. 120, *Levavi*
	Ps. 121, *Letatus sum*
Sext:	Ps. 122, *Ad te levavi*
	Ps. 123, *Nisi quia dominus*
	Ps. 124, *Qui confidunt*
None:	Ps. 125, *In convertendo*
	Ps. 126, *Nisi dominus*
	Ps. 127, *Beati omnes*
Vespers:	Ps. 121, *Letatus sum*
	Ps. 122, *Ad te levavi*
	Ps. 123, *Nisi quia dominus*
	Ps. 124, *Qui confidunt*
	Ps. 125, *In convertendo*
Compline:	Ps. 12, *Usquequo domine*
	Ps. 42, *Iudica me*
	Ps. 128, *Sepe expugnaverunt*
	Ps. 130, *Domine non est exaltatum*

While the nine psalms of Matins form a single service in Rouen 3016, Fitzwilliam 300, and Walters 40, in lat. 10482 they comprise three groups of three, for alternate days of the week (*In alia die . . .*).

As the longest service in the Canonical Hours, Matins also has the greatest variations among the four manuscript sources studied, but all agree on the first three lessons and great responsories. Interestingly, lessons 1–3 of the Paris Little Office appear also in the Little Office at Chartres and in that of the nearby Cluniac abbey of Saint-Maur-des-Fossés; it is not yet clear which way the influence went. These three lessons begin *Surge beatissima virgo Maria, Cecos cordium oculos,* and *O sacratissima virgo Maria.*[16] For the other six lessons, the three private devotional books Rouen 3016, Fitzwilliam 300, and Walters 40 agree in adopting two sets of three that were both in use elsewhere in the general area. Most notably, lessons 4–6 were the three used at the neighboring Benedictine monastic institutions of Saint-Germain-des-Prés (already in the eleventh century),[17] Saint-Denis,[18] and Saint-Maur-des-Fossés,[19] but they also appear at Saint-Martial de Limoges, at Font Avellane, at Worcester, in the thirteenth-century Sarum rite, and in the mid-thirteenth-century Dominican liturgy.[20] These lessons begin with the words *Sancta Maria, virgo virginum; Sancta Maria, piarum piissima;* and *Sancta dei genitrix, que digne.* Lessons 7–9 are found also at Chartres Cathedral, at Laon Cathedral, at Saint-

Table 20.1 Matins responsories 4–9 in the Little Office

Rouen 3016 and Fitzwilliam 300	Walters 40
4. Ecce virgo concipiet V. Tollite portas	4. Beata es . . . que dominum portasti V. Ave Maria
5. Ave Maria V. Quomodo fiet istud	5. Ad nutum V. Ut vicium
6. Solem iusticie V. Cernere	6. Missus est Gabriel V. Ave Maria
7. Styrps Iesse V. Virgo dei genitrix	7. Ave Maria V. Quomodo fiet istud
8. Super salutem V. Valde eam nos	8. Styrps Iesse V. Virgo dei genitrix
9. Ad nutum V. Ut vicium	9. Gaude Maria V. Gabrielem

Martial de Limoges (also as lessons 7–9), and in the Cistercian liturgy in the twelfth century,[21] but also in manuscripts with Compiègne and Reims connections[22] and in the twelfth-century Westminster Psalter.[23] These lessons begin *O beata Maria, quis tibi digni; Admitte, piissima dei genitrix;* and *Sancta Maria, succurre miseris.*

Responsories 1–3 of the Paris Little Office are found elsewhere in the Paris liturgy as the eighth responsory on the Assumption (*Beata es, V. Ave Maria*), the seventh responsory of Christmas (*Sancta et immaculata, V. Benedicta tu*), and the ninth responsory on both the Assumption and Nativity of the Virgin (*Felix namque, V. Ora pro populo*). These three great responsories are the only ones included in the Little Office of the Paris breviary lat. 10482, but the three devotional books each have nine responsories to follow their nine lessons. The Rouen psalter/hours and the Isabelle psalter/hours agree on the choice of responsories 4–9, but Walters 40 contains a different set, as is shown in table 20.1. Three of the six responsories—*Ave Maria, Styrps Iesse,* and *Ad nutum*—are shared by both lists, but they are not in the same position. Both groups of responsories are variously drawn from the first Sunday of Advent, Christmas, the Purification, the Annunciation, the Assumption, and the Nativity of the Virgin.[24]

Antiphons, the other major category of chants in Matins, show significantly more agreement among the three manuscripts for private devotions. The two oldest of these, Rouen 3016 and Fitzwilliam 300, since they have three nocturns with three psalms each, employ a total of nine antiphons for Matins. Rouen 3016 simply borrows the nine antiphons of Matins for the feast of the Assumption of the Virgin, omitting their special verses but retaining the order in which they occur on August 15:

1. Exaltata es sancta
2. Paradisi janue per te
3. Sicut mirra electa
4. Specie tua et pulcritudine
5. Adiuvabit eam deus
6. Sicut letantium omnium
7. Gaude Maria virgo
8. Dignare me
9. Post partum virgo

Fitzwilliam 300 shifts the third antiphon, *Sicut mirra electa*, to the ninth position, dropping *Post partum virgo* and adding *Ante thorum* (the first Matins antiphon in the Common of Virgins) as antiphon 3. The two later Paris sources, Walters 40 and lat. 10482, have only three antiphons for Matins; they take the first antiphon of each nocturn in Rouen 3016 (i.e., nos. 1, 4, and 7, *Exaltata es, Specie tua,* and *Gaude Maria*) and use each one to frame all three psalms in its nocturn.

The nine benedictions that precede each lesson of Matins also show some variation among thirteenth-century Paris sources. The Walters 40 book of hours and the lat. 10482 breviary agree on both the choice and the order of the benedictions, though lat. 10482 groups them in three sets of three each (for alternate days), since it reuses the same three lessons. In these two sources the nine benedictions are:

1. Alma virgo virginum intercedat pro nobis ad dominum
2. Beate Marie virginis filius sit nobis adiutor et propicius
3. Sancta dei genitrix sit nobis auxiliatrix
4. Sancta dei mater pro nobis iugiter oret
5. Oret voce pia pro nobis virgo Maria
6. Oret pro famulis sancta Maria suis
7. Ab hoste maligno eripiat nos dei genitrix virgo
8. In omni tribulatione et angustia succurrat nobis pia virgo Maria
9. Ad gaudia paradysi perducat nos virgo mater dei

The benedictions in Rouen 3016 agree with this set except for the last one, which in Rouen is:

9. Ad societatem civium supernorum perducat nos regina angelorum.[25]

The Isabelle psalter/hours, Fitzwilliam 300, has different texts for the fourth and sixth benedictions, which begin *Sancta Maria virgo* and *Precibus sue matris.*

Apart from the variations in Matins, the remainder of the Paris Little Office of the Virgin shows few differences (with one major exception) from one source to another. Noteworthy is the fact that in Fitzwilliam 300, Walters 40, and lat. 10482 Lauds employs the single antiphon *Benedicta tu in mulieribus* (the first antiphon at Lauds for the Annunciation) to frame all five psalms, while Rouen 3016 has a separate antiphon for each psalm, the latter four borrowed from antiphons 2–5 of Lauds on the Assumption (*Maria virgo assumpta est, In odorem unguentorum, Benedicta filia tua,* and *Pulchra es et decora*). A smaller deviation comes in the antiphon for the Nunc dimittis at Compline: the Isabelle psalter/hours uses *Ecce ancilla domini,* while the other three manuscripts all use *Cum iocunditate memoria.*

The remaining major discrepancy is the difference in commemorations following the services of Lauds, Vespers, or both.[26] Each commemoration includes an antiphon, a versicle with response, and a prayer (collect) proper to the saint or occasion being remembered. Whereas the clerical breviary lat. 10482 memorializes the cathedral's relics (which had their own feast day on 4 December) and All Saints, the Walters 40 book of hours includes memorials for St. Catherine of Alexandria and St. Mary Magdalene, who were evidently important saints for its intended owner. But Fitzwilliam 300, the royal psalter/hours, includes the truly staggering number of 23 memorials after Lauds: for the Trinity, the Holy Cross, Angels, John the Baptist, St. Peter, St. Andrew, Apostles, John the Apostle and Evangelist, all Evangelists, Holy Innocents,[27] St. Denis, St. Eustache, Several Martyrs, St. Nicholas, St. Francis, St. Benedict, Several Confessors, St. Mary Magdalene, St. Margaret, St. Catherine, Several Virgins, All Saints, and for peace (details are given in Cockerell 1905, 20–21).

Thus it can be said that the Isabelle psalter and hours, Fitzwilliam 300, shows the greatest deviations from what became the "standard" Parisian Little Office of the Virgin. In this the manuscript undoubtedly reflects its royal connections, since it was intended for an immediate female family member of King Louis IX—either his sister, his wife, or his daughter.[28] In the mid-thirteenth century, the royal court followed the use of the cathedral of Paris, but there were nonetheless distinctive variations that set the royal use apart from that of Notre-Dame.[29] In this list of memorials, for example, several saints are singled out who would not have received such recognition at the cathedral in the mid-thirteenth century: Margaret, Francis, and Eustache. In the case of St. Margaret, it is understandable that the royal family would take an interest in the saint for whom Louis' queen, Marguerite of Provence, was named. Similarly, Louis IX's great regard for the friars is well known; both the Franciscans and the Dominicans had important roles at court and in the Sainte-Chapelle, and it is natural that the royals would regularly memorialize St. Francis, who on his feast day at the cathedral received only the common Office for confessors.[30] St. Eustache, however, was not present in the cathedral calendar in the thirteenth–fifteenth centuries, though he was in the martyrology and in the calendar of Paris books of hours by the end of the Middle Ages.[31]

In sum, it is appropriate to observe that some significant aspects of the Paris Little Office of the Virgin were still in flux through most of the thirteenth century—namely, whether there were three or nine lessons at Matins; whether there were five antiphons or just one for the psalms at Lauds; the number and choice of memorials following Lauds; the order and choice of Matins antiphons, responsories, and benedictions; and the choice of the antiphon for the Nunc dimittis at Compline. But despite such variations in content—naturally more numerous in manuscripts not produced under direct control of the cathedral—the message of the Little Office was nonetheless clear.

By the time Gothic cathedrals all over northern France were being erected in honor of the Virgin in the late twelfth and thirteenth centuries, the Virgin's place in the scheme of salvation was theologically complex and multifaceted; many words of both written and spoken exegesis had poured forth from learned minds eager to share their vision of the divine economy.[32] In the shape of their liturgy and in the magnificent edifice newly built to house it, the clergy of Notre-Dame of Paris asserted a special role—one closely tied to the Virgin—for their church in their world. At the time of Notre-Dame's construction, the paramount and overriding message that the clerical hierarchy wished to communicate was the idea that the Virgin was the Mother of God, and through her, in *this* cathedral church built in her honor, salvation could best be found.

Although Mary was first and foremost the Mother of God, from this role followed her other great position, that of the Queen of Heaven, crowned and seated on the right hand of Christ. But importantly for the Little Office, Mary was also regarded as a type of the Church, as the restorer of salvation (the new Eve), as intercessor to Christ in Judgment, and as the supreme mediatrix between heaven and earth.[33] All of these roles stemmed from the fact that she was chosen to be the Virgin Mother of God; the singular precipitating event was Incarnation. To the clergy of Notre-Dame, the Virgin was, simply put, the sinner's best avenue to salvation. But she was also the Church, and it was through the Church, inside the *templum deitatis,* that she became accessible. The cathedral, like Mary herself, was meant to be the house of God and the gate of heaven.

The texts of the Little Office of the Virgin (see the appendix), which echoed so frequently in the choir of the cathedral, reminded the clergy again and again of the equation between Mary and the Church.[34] In Matins, the invitatory antiphon *Ave Maria gratia plena,* in repeating Gabriel's words to the Virgin at the Annunciation, in effect begins the Little Office with the first biblical recognition of the Virgin's exalted status. The hymn *O quam glorifica luce coruscas* in its four stanzas offers a capsule summary of Mary's role in salvation history. Its first stanza translates, "O how thou dost shimmer with glorified light, royal offspring of the stock of David; Virgin Mary, residing on high, above all heavenly peoples of the sky." Succeeding stanzas mention Mary's role in the Incarnation and then turn to the result: "Christ is God born in the flesh," adored by the whole world. Lastly, the Trinity is invoked to grant replacement of the "shadows of despair" by "the joys of [heavenly] light."

The antiphon *Exaltata es* for the psalms picks up where the invitatory antiphon left off: because Mary was chosen by God and accepted her role with great humility, "Thou art exalted, holy Mother of God, above the angelic chorus to the heavenly kingdom." Psalms 8, 18, and 23 dwell upon the glory of God and his works, both in heaven and on earth, concluding with the verses "Lift up your gates, O ye princes, and be ye lifted up, O eternal gates: and the King of Glory shall enter in. Who is this King of Glory? the Lord of Hosts, he is the King of Glory" (Ps. 23:9–10). St. Jerome and other medieval commentators regarded this as another Old Testament prophecy of the Incarnation as well as a reference to the opening of the gates of heaven through the event of Incarnation, and thought of the Virgin was never far from the idea of Incarnation.[35] In fact, the versicle and response that follow the psalms and their antiphon—"Grace is poured forth on thy lips. Therefore hath God blessed thee forever" (from Ps. 44:3)—when extracted from the rest of the psalm (as they are here), were taken to be a reference to the Annunciation to the Virgin.

The three benedictions that precede the lessons of Matins call in turn upon the Virgin, Christ, and his Mother for assistance. The three lessons themselves are really prayers invoking the Virgin's help in obtaining salvation, while the three great responsories that follow the lessons all celebrate Mary's role in the Incarnation; the first and third also contain petitions for her aid. As the third responsory praises the Virgin with its repetenda "For from thee has risen the Sun of righteousness, Christ our God," this leads very appropriately to the concluding item of Matins, the Te deum: "We praise thee, O God: we acknowledge thee to be the Lord . . ."

This, then, was the shape of Matins of the Little Office when it was performed on Sundays, Mondays, and Thursdays at Notre-Dame of Paris. On Tuesdays and Fridays, the only variations were the three psalms 44, 45, and 86 with their antiphon, the following versicle and response, and three different benedictions for the lessons of Matins, which themselves did not vary at the cathedral. The antiphon, in keeping with a venerable practice of the early Church, was a verse from the first psalm: "In thy comeliness and thy beauty, go forward, fare prosperously, and reign" (Ps. 44:5). These three psalms, in Christian interpretation, describe Christ's kingdom and the Church as his Bride, God's protection of the Church in time of trouble, and the glory of the Church. Considering Mary as a type of the Church, clerics who thought devotionally about these texts could not avoid shifting their focus repeatedly from one manifestation of the perfect spouse and mother to the other. So it is also with the following versicle and response, which applies equally to the Virgin and to the Church: "God will help her with his countenance. God is in her midst; she shall not be moved" (Ps. 45:6). The three benedictions before the lessons each seek the prayers of the Virgin on behalf of her servants.

On Wednesdays and Saturdays, Matins included Pss. 95, 96, and 97, which, in Christian interpretation, were exhortations to praise God for the coming of Christ and his kingdom; the members of his Church were called upon to thank God for his blessings. The Tuesday–Friday versicle and response were used again, and the antiphon for the psalms translates "Rejoice, O Virgin Mary; thou alone hast destroyed all heresies in the whole world." Here the Virgin is mother of Christ's mystical body, the Church, and as such, she is "the great destroyer of false doctrine" (Taunton 1903, 174). The benedictions for the lessons reflect the idea of Mary as protector of the flock of souls who comprise the Church on earth; the last benediction requests, "May the Virgin Mother of God lead us to the joys of paradise."

The psalms of Lauds[36]—indeed, virtually all the texts in Lauds—are songs of praise, blessing, and gratitude to God for his marvelous creation, whether that be the earth and its creatures, the kingdom of God and his intervention in the world, the Virgin and the Incarnation, the saints, or Christ and the Church. Following the *Benedicite* canticle that takes the position of the fourth psalm, the Old Testament texts reach a crescendo of praise with Pss. 148–50, the end of the Psalter. The focus returns specifically to the Virgin with the antiphon for the psalms, a text again taken from Gabriel's salutation at the Annunciation ("Blessed art thou among women and blessed is the fruit of thy womb"). The chapter, the hymn, the versicle and response, and the antiphon for the Benedictus then continue the Marian focus, emphasizing Mary's primary function as the Virgin Mother of God; both the hymn *Virgo dei genitrix* and the Benedictus antiphon *Hec est regina virginum* include petitions for the Virgin's intercession as well. The Benedictus antiphon is another concise summary of the Virgin's role in salvation: "This is the Queen of virgins who gave birth to the King, Virgin fair like a rose; Mother of God, through whom we gain both God and man, gracious Virgin of virgins, intercede for us to the Lord." In keeping with the idea of praise, the two collects at the end of Lauds emphasize, first, the Holy Spirit, responsible for God's presence upon earth, and secondly, the Virgin, the human partner in the enterprise of Incarnation. The two memorials that regularly follow both Lauds and Vespers at Notre-Dame acknowledge first the saints (including the Virgin) represented by relics at the cathedral, and then all saints of the Church throughout the world—the latter a remnant of what was once a votive Little Office of All Saints in centuries past (see Taunton 1903, 39–40, and Roper 1993, 57–65).

The day Hours of Prime, Terce, Sext, and None are the shortest of the Hours. All include the hymn *Veni, creator spiritus* (written out only at Prime), which requests the inspiration, grace, and understanding brought to mankind by the Holy Spirit. All include three collects, the first continuing the focus upon the Holy Spirit, the second one invoking the intercession of the Virgin, and the last one (which has the same text in all four services plus Compline) a prayer for the Church that invokes the aid of St. John the Evangelist. With regard to the choice of psalms, Terce, Sext, and None follow the ferial monastic cursus that proceeds through the so-called Gradual psalms in numerical sequence (here, the first nine, Pss. 119–27).[37] In each Hour the antiphon for the psalms, the chapter, the short responsory, and the versicle and response are all proper to the Virgin, frequently recycling texts already used in different genres (i.e., rotation of a text between a versicle/response and a short responsory) and sometimes simply reusing the same item (as in the versicle and response of Lauds and Sext). Of particular note is the fact that none of the chapters is a biblical text, though all are Marian liturgical texts found elsewhere on feasts of the Virgin in antiphons, responsories, or versicles.[38] The primary focus continues upon Mary's role in the Incarnation and the equivalence of Mary and the Church, but the chapter at Terce, *Paradisi porta*, draws the contrast between Mary and Eve: "The gate of all paradise was closed by Eve, and through the Virgin Mary was opened again."

The psalms of Vespers (nos. 121–25) have been heard earlier, spread across the day Hours; their antiphon, appropriate to Vespers of the Virgin, is a verse from the Magnificat, her own song of praise heard a few moments later in the service. In between come the chapter and the most well-known Marian hymn, *Ave maris stella*, whose seven stanzas once again sound all the Marian themes of salvation. The two collects after the Magnificat and its antiphon (a petition for the Virgin's aid) invoke again the Holy Spirit and the Virgin. The latter (*Deus qui salutis eterne*) is a well and concisely formulated theological statement: "O God, who through the fruitful virginity of blessed Mary offered to humankind the rewards of eternal salvation, grant, we beseech thee, that we may experience her intercession, through whom we were found worthy to receive among us the author of life, our Lord Jesus Christ, thy Son."

The psalms of Compline (nos. 12, 42, 128, and 130) all speak in the first person singular; their antiphon, *Sancta dei genitrix*, is a prayer that directly addresses the Virgin with a request for her intercession. Though similar in theme, the antiphon *Cum iocunditate* for the Nunc dimittis is communal: "With joy let us celebrate the remembrance of blessed Mary, that she may intercede for us with the Lord our God." Likewise, the hymn *Virgo dei genitrix*, already used in Lauds, concisely summarizes the Virgin's importance, invokes her aid, and praises the Trinity. The three collects that conclude both Compline and the entire Little Office for once nowhere mention the Virgin per se; they invoke the fire of the Holy Spirit, God's grace in man's coming to know Christ incarnate, and the guidance and protection of the Church.

The cathedral church of Paris, with its overwhelming focus upon the Mother of God, let virtually no day pass without explicit liturgical acknowledgment of her role in salvation. In the voice and ear and mind of every cleric in this cathedral, the most familiar and frequently performed Office was the one we have just examined—the Little Office of the Virgin. It had none of the stunning polyphony that adorned the highest-ranking feasts and that spread the fame of this cathedral far and wide, but it undoubtedly renewed the sense of mission and devotion of those who performed it so often. It was essentially an Office by the clerics for the clerics, without spectators, done in their private liturgical space, the choir, before the altar of the Virgin, whom they sought to praise and exalt above all other creatures. Thus spiritually fortified on a timely and regular basis, the clerics could go about their other work of spreading the Gospel and maintaining what was, in the eyes of many, for at least a few decades in the thirteenth century, the most splendid new cathedral in Christendom. It was the Church on earth, one built to honor the Virgin Mother of God, but through it and through her was the way to the Church Triumphant.

Appendix: Hore Beate Marie Virginis

from Paris, BNF lat. 10482, fols. 306–307v[39]

[MATINS]

Domine labia mea, etc.

Invitatorium: Ave Maria, etc. [Ave Maria, gratia plena, dominus tecum.]
Psalmus [94]: Venite exultemus, etc.

Hymnus: 1. O quam glorifica luce choruscas, stirpis davitice regia proles; sublimis residens, virgo Maria, super celigenas etheris omnes. 2. Tu cum virgineo mater honore, angelorum domino pectoris aulam sacris visceribus casta parasti; natus hinc deus est corpore Christus. 3. Quem cunctus venerans orbis adorat, cui nunc rite genu flectitur omne a quo nos petimus te veniente, abiectis tenebris gaudia lucis. 4. Hoc largire pater luminis omnis, natum per proprium, flamine sacro; qui tecum nitida vivit in ethera regnans, ac moderans secula cuncta. Amen.

Antiphona super tres primos psalmos: Exaltata es, sancta dei genitrix, super choros angelorum ad celestia regna.

Psalmi: [8.] Domine dominus noster. [18.] Celi enarrant. [23.] Domini est terra.

v. Diffusa est, etc. [Diffusa est gratia in labiis tuis. *r.* Propterea benedixit te deus in eternum.]

Pater noster.

Iube domne, benedicere.
[*Benedictio:*] Alma virgo virginum intercedat pro nobis ad dominum. [*r.*] Amen.

Lectio prima: Surge, beatissima virgo Maria, misericorditer actura pro nobis: surge et amplectere misericordiam redemptoris. Da preces pro nobis, quos cernis offensos ante oculos conditoris. Tu autem [domine miserere nostri. Deo gratias].

[*Rx. 1:*] Beata es, virgo Maria dei genitrix, que credidisti domino: perfecta sunt in te que dicta sunt tibi; ecce exaltata es super choros angelorum: intercede pro nobis ad dominum deum nostrum. *V.* Ave Maria, gratia plena, dominus tecum. Intercede, etc.

Iube domne.
[*Benedictio:*] Beate Marie virginis filius sit nobis adiutor et propicius. [*r.*] Amen.

Lectio secunda: Cecos cordium oculos terge atque semitas iusticie ostende. Orando, a nobis vicia subtrahe, atque sancta plantaria virtutum nobis insere: impetra cursum, quo supernum consequamur bravium. Tu autem.

[*Rx. 2:*] Sancta et immaculata virginitas, quibus te laudibus efferam nescio: Quia quem celi capere non poterant tuo gremio contulisti. *V.* Benedicta tu in mulieribus et benedictus fructus ventris tui. Quia.

Iube, etc.
[*Benedictio:*] Sancta dei genitrix sit nobis auxiliatrix. [*r.*] Amen.

Lectio III: O sacratissima virgo Maria, nos qui hoc credimus quod virgo et mater dei sis,[40] credendo sentiamus quod pro nobis deum depreceris et iuxta petencium vota, impetrata assequaris, ut qui confitemur te peperisse deum et hominem, gaudeamus per te nobis advenisse salutem. Tu autem.

[*Rx. 3:*] Felix namque es, sacra virgo Maria, et omni laude dignissima: Quia ex te ortus est sol iusticie, Christus deus noster. *V.* Ora pro populo, interveni pro clero, intercede pro devoto femineo sexu, sentiant omnes tuum iuvamen, quicumque celebrant tuam commemorationem. Quia ex te. Gloria patri. Quia ex te.

Ps. Te deum laudamus, etc.[41]

In alia die Antiphona super psalmos: Specie tua, etc. [Specie tua et pulchritudine tua intende, prospere procede et regna.]

Psalmi: [44.] Eructavit. [45.] Deus noster. [fol. 306v] [86.] Fundamenta.

v. Adiuvabit eam deus vultu suo. [*r.* Deus in medio eius, non commovebitur.]

Pater noster.

Benedictiones:
Sancta dei mater pro nobis iugiter oret. [*r.* Amen.]
Oret voce pia pro nobis virgo Maria. [*r.*] Amen.
Oret pro famulis sancta Maria suis. [*r.* Amen.]

In alia die psalmi[42] *etc.* [95.] Cantate. [96.] Dominus regnavit. [97.] Cantate.
Antiphona: Gaude Maria virgo, cunctas hereses sola interemisti in universo mundo.

v. Adiuvabit eam [deus vultu suo. *r.* Deus in medio eius, non commovebitur].

Pater noster.

Benedictiones:
Ab hoste maligno eripiat nos dei genitrix virgo. [*r.*] Amen.
In omni tribulatione et angustia succurrat nobis pia virgo Maria. [*r.* Amen.]
Ad gaudia paradysi perducat nos virgo mater dei. [*r.*] Amen.

[LAUDS]

In laudibus antiphona: Speciosa facta es et suavis in delitiis tuis, sancta dei genitrix.[43]

Deus in adiutorium, etc.

Psalmi soliciti.[44] [92. Dominus regnavit. 99. Iubilate deo. 62 and 66. Deus deus meus and Deus misereatur. Canticle: Benedicite. 148–50. Laudate dominum, Cantate domino, Laudate dominum.]

Antiphona super psalmos:[45] Benedicta tu in mulieribus et benedictus fructus ventris tui.

Capitulum: Te laudant angeli, sancta dei genitrix, que virum non cognovisti et dominum deum nostrum in tuo sancto utero baiulasti. [*r.*] Deo gratias.

Hymnus: 1. Virgo dei genitrix quem totus non capit orbis: in tua se clausit viscera factus homo. 2. Vera fides geniti purgavit crimina mundi, et tibi virginitas inviolata manet. 3. Te matrem pietatis opem te clamitat orbis: subvenias famulis, O benedicta, tuis. 4. Gloria magna patri, compar sit gloria nati, spiritui sancto gloria magna deo. Amen.

v. Elegit eam deus, etc. [et preelegit eam. *r.* Et habitare facit eam in tabernaculo suo.]

Super Benedictus antiphona: Hec est regina virginum que genuit regem, velut rosa decora virgo; dei genitrix, per quam reperimus deum et hominem, alma virgo virginum, intercede pro nobis ad dominum.[46]

Oratio: Deus qui corda. [Deus, qui corda fidelium sancti spiritus illustratione docuisti, da nobis in eodem spiritu recta sapere, et de eius semper sancta consolatione gaudere. Per dominum.]

[*Oratio:*] Deus, qui de beate Marie, etc. [Deus, qui de beate Marie, virginis utero, verbum tuum, angelo nunciante, carnem suscipere voluisti: presta supplicibus tuis; ut, qui vere eam dei genitricem credimus, eius apud te intercessionibus adiuvemur. Per eundem dominum.]

[*Memorial of the Relics:*]

Antiphona: Isti etenim maximo digni sunt honore venerari in terris, quos in celis rex regum immensa cumulavit gloria.

v. Iusti autem in perpetuum vivent. [*r.*] Et apud dominum est merces eorum.

Oratio: Propiciare, quesumus domine, nobis famulis tuis per sanctorum tuorum quorum corpora vel reliquie in nostra requiescunt ecclesia merita gloriosa. ut eorum pia intercessione semper protegamur adversis. Per dominum.

[*Memorial of All Saints:*]

Antiphona: Exaltabunt sancti in gloria; letabuntur in cubilibus suis.

v. Iustorum anime in manu dei sunt. [*r.*] Et non tanget illos tormentum malicie.

Oratio: Omnium sanctorum tuorum, quesumus domine, intercessione placatus. et veniam nobis delictorum tribue et remedia sempiterna concede. Per dominum.

[PRIME]

Ad .i. Deus in adiutorium.

Hymnus: Veni creator spiritus, etc.
[1. Veni, creator spiritus, mentes tuorum visita, imple superna gratia, que tu creasti pectora. 2. Qui paraclitus diceris, donum dei altissimi, fons vivus, ignis, caritas, et spiritalis unctio. 3. Tu septiformis munere, dextre dei tu digitus, tu rite promissum patris, sermone ditans guttura. 4. Accende lumen sensibus: infunde amorem cordibus: infirma nostri corporis virtute firmans perpeti. 5. Hostem repellus longius, pacemque dones protinus: ductore sic te previo vitemus omne noxium. 6. Per te sciamus da patrem, noscamus atque filium, te utriusque spiritum credamus omni tempore. 7. Sit laus deo patri, summo Christo decus, spiritui sancto, tribus honor unus. Amen.]

Antiphona super psalmos: Benedicta tu, etc. [Benedicta tu in mulieribus et benedictus fructus ventris tui.]

[*Psalmi:* 1. Beatus vir. 2. Quare fremuerunt. 5. Verba mea.]

Capitulum: Felix namque es, sancta virgo Maria, et enim laude dignissima quia ex te ortus est sol iusticie, Christus deus noster. [*r.*] Deo gratias.

Rx. Diffusa est gratia in labiis tuis. *V.* Propterea benedixit te deus in eterna. Diffusa. Gloria patri. [fol. 307] Diffusa.

v. Specie tua et pulchritudine tua. [*r.*] Intende, prospere procede, et regna.

[*Preces:*] Domine, exaudi orationem [meam], etc. [*r.* Et clamor meus ad te veniat.]
[*Ps.* Miserere mei deus: *totum.*]
[*V.* Gloria patri et filio et cetera].
[*v.* Dominus vobiscum. *r.* Et cum spiritu tuo.]

Oratio: Deus, qui apostolis tuis sanctum dedisti spiritum, concede plebi tue pie petitionis effectum, ut quibus dedisti fidem, largiaris et pacem. Per Christum.

Oratio: Famulorum tuorum, quesumus domine, delictis ignosce, ut qui tibi placere de actibus nostris non valemus, genitricis filii tui domini nostri Ihesu Christi intercessione salvemur. Per dominum.

Oratio: Ecclesiam tuam, quesumus domine, benignus illustra, ut beati Johannis apostoli tui et evangeliste illuminata doctrinis, a dona preveniat sempiterna, et nos famulos tuos ab omni adversitate custodi. Per Christum.

[TERCE]

Ad terciam super psalmos antiphona: Dignare me laudare te, virgo sacrata, da mihi virtutem contra hostes tuos.

[*Psalmi:* 119. Ad dominum cum tribularer. 120. Levavi oculos. 121. Letatus sum.]

Capitulum: Paradisi porta per Evam cunctis clausa est, et per Mariam virginem iterum patefacta est. [*r.*] Deo gratias.

Rx. Specie tua et pulchritudine tua. *V.* Intende, prospere procede, et regna. Et pulchritudine tua. Gloria. Specie.

v. Adiuvabit eam deus vultu suo. [*r.*] Deus in medio eius non conmovebitur.

Oratio: Assit nobis, quesumus domine, virtus sancti spiritus, que et corda nostra clementer expurget, et ab omnibus semper tueatur adversis. Per [dominum].

[*Oratio:*] Concede nos famulos, etc. [Concede nos famulos tuos, quesumus deus, perpetua mentis et corporis sanitate gaudere, et gloriosa beate Marie virginis intercessione, a presenti liberari tristitia et futura perfrui letitia. Per dominum.]

[*Oratio:*] Ecclesiam tuam, etc. [Ecclesiam tuam, quesumus domine, benignus illustra, ut beati Johannis apostoli tui et evangeliste illuminata doctrinis, a dona preveniat sempiterna, et nos famulos tuos ab omni adversitate custodi. Per Christum.]

[SEXT]

Ad sextam super psalmos antiphona: Post partum virgo inviolata permansisti: dei genitrix, intercede pro nobis.

[*Psalmi:* 122. Ad te levavi. 123. Nisi quia dominus. 124. Qui confidunt.]

Capitulum: Gaude Maria virgo, cunctas hereses sola interemisti in universo mundo. [*r.*] Deo gratias.

Rx. Adiuvabit eam [deus vultu suo], etc. [*V.* Deus in medio eius, non commovebitur.] Gloria. Adiuvabit.

v. Elegit eam deus et preelegit eam. [*r.*] Et habitare eam facit in tabernaculo suo.

Oratio: Mentes nostras, quesumus domine, spiritus paraclitus qui a te procedit, illuminet et inducat in omnem, sicut tuus filius promisit, veritatem. Per.

Oratio: Concede misericors deus fragilitati nostre presidium ut qui sancte dei genetricis et virginis Maria memoriam agimus intercessionis eius auxilio a nostris iniquitatibus resurgamus. Per.

Oratio: Ecclesiam tuam etc. [Ecclesiam tuam, quesumus domine, benignus illustra, ut beati Johannis apostoli tui et evangeliste illuminata doctrinis, a dona preveniat sempiterna, et nos famulos tuos ab omni adversitate custodi. Per Christum.]

[NONE]

Ad nonam super psalmos antiphona: Sicut lilium inter spinas sic amica mea inter filias.

[*Psalmi:* 125. In convertendo dominus. 126. Nisi dominus. 127. Beati omnes.]

Capitulum: Per te, dei genitrix, est nobis vita perdita data que de celo suscepisti prolem et mundo genuisti salvatorem. [*r.*] Deo gratias.

Rx. Elegit eam etc. [Elegit eam deus, et preelegit eam.] *V.* Et habitare [facit eam in tabernaculo suo]. Elegit. Gloria patri. Elegit.

v. Post partum virgo, etc. [Post partum virgo, inviolata permansisti. *r.* Dei genitrix, intercede pro nobis.]

Oratio: Mentibus nostris, quesumus domine, spiritum sanctum benignus infunde, cuius et sapientia conditi sumus, et providencia gubernamur. Per Christum.

Oratio: Protege famulos tuos, quesumus domine, deus subsidiis [fol. 307v] pacis; et, beate Marie virginis patrociniis confidentes, a cunctis hostibus redde securos.

Oratio: Ecclesiam tuam, etc. [Ecclesiam tuam, quesumus domine, benignus illustra, ut beati Johannis apostoli tui et evangeliste illuminata doctrinis, a dona preveniat sempiterna, et nos famulos tuos ab omni adversitate custodi. Per Christum.]

[VESPERS]

Ad vesperas super psalmos antiphona: Beatam me dicent omnes generationes, quia ancillam humilem respexit deus.

[*Psalmus* 121.] Letatus, cum aliis. [122. Ad te levavi. 123. Nisi quia dominus. 124. Qui confidunt. 125. In convertendo.]

[*Capitulum:*] Beata es, virgo Maria, que dominum portasti, creatorem mundi; genuisti qui te fecit et in eternum permanes virgo. [*r.*] Deo gratias.

Hymnus: Ave maris stella, etc.
[1. Ave maris stella, dei mater alma, atque semper virgo, felix celi porta. 2. Sumens illud ave Gabrielis ore, funda nos in pace, mutans nomen Eve. 3. Solve vincla reis, profer lumen cecis, mala nostra pelle, bona cuncta posce. 4. Monstra te esse matrem, sumat per te preces, qui pro nobis natus tulit esse tuus. 5. Virgo singularis, inter omnes mitis, nos, culpis solutos, mites fac et castos. 6. Vitam presta puram, iter para tutum, ut, videntes Ihesum, semper collectemur. 7. Sit laus deo patri, summo Christo decus, spiritui sancto, tribus honor unus. Amen.]

v. Post partum, etc. [*r.* Dei genitrix.]

Super Magnificat antiphona: Sancta Maria, succurre miseris, iuva pusillamines, refove flebiles, ora pro populo, interveni pro clero, intercede pro devoto femineo sexu.[47]

[*Magnificat* anima mea dominum.]

Oratio: Deus qui corda, etc. [Deus qui corda fidelium sancti spiritus illustratione docuisti da nobis in eodem spiritu recta sapere et de eius semper sancta consolatione gaudere.]

[*Oratio:*] Deus qui salutis eterne, etc. [Deus qui salutis eterne beate Marie virginitate fecunda humano generi premia prestitisti tribue nobis quesumus ut ipsam pro nobis intercedere sentiamus per quam meruimus auctorem vite suscipere, dominum nostrum . . . Amen.]

[*Memorial of the Relics:*]

De reliquiis ad vesperas antiphona: Et facta est comes multitudo celestis exercitus exanimi corporis beati Dyonisii, caput proprium deportantis, laudans deum et dicens: Gloria tibi domine.

v. Letamini in domino [et exaltati, iusti. *r.* Et gloriamini, omnes recti corde.]

Oratio: Propiciare quesumus domine, etc. [Propiciare, quesumus domine, nobis famulis tuis per sanctorum tuorum quorum corpora vel reliquie in nostra requiescunt ecclesia merita gloriosa, ut eorum pia intercessione semper protegamur adversis. Per dominum.]

[*Memorial of All Saints:*]

De omnibus sanctis ad vesperas antiphona: Sancti dei omnes intercedere dignemini pro nostra omniumque salute.

v. Exultent iusti, etc. [*v.* Exultent iusti in conspectu dei. *r.* Et delectentur in letitia.]

Oratio: Infirmitatem nostrum, quesumus domine, propicius respice, et mala nostra que iuste meremur omnium sanctorum tuorum intercessione averte. Per dominum.

[COMPLINE]

Ad complectorum super psalmos antiphona: Sancta dei genitrix virgo sempiterna Maria, intercede pro nobis ad dominum deum nostrum.

[*Psalmi:* 12. Usquequo domine. 42. Iudica me, deus. 128. Sepe expugnaverunt. 130. Domine non est exaltatum.]

Hymnus: Virgo dei genitrix, etc., ut supra [in laudibus].

Capitulum: Sicut synamomum et balsamum aromatizans odorem dedi: quasi mirra electa dedi suavitatem odoris. [*r.*] Deo gratias.

v. Ecce ancilla domine. *r.* Fiat mihi secundum verbum tuum.

Antiphona super Nunc dimittis: Cum iocunditate memoriam beate Marie celebremus ut ipsa pro nobis intercedat ad dominum deum nostrum.

[*Nunc dimittis*]

Oratio: Ure igne sancti spiritus renes nostros et cor nostrum domine, ut tibi casto corpore serviamus, et mundo corde placeamus. Per.

[*Oratio:*] Gratiam tuam quesumus, etc. [Gratiam tuam, quesumus domine, mentibus nostris infunde: ut qui angelo nuntiante Christi filii tui incarnationem cognovimus, per passionem eius et crucem ad resurrectionis gloriam perducamur. Per eundem.]

[*Oratio:*] Ecclesiam tuam, etc. [Ecclesiam tuam, quesumus domine, benignus illustra, ut beati Johannis apostoli tui et evangeliste illuminata doctrinis, a dona preveniat sempiterna, et nos famulos tuos ab omni adversitate custodi. Per Christum.]

Notes

1. See Wieck (1988). Adelaide Bennett is preparing a detailed study of thirteenth-century French books of hours; for much useful comparative information see Bennett (1996).

2. A partial history of the development of the Little Office can be found in J. Leclercq (1958), J. Leclercq (1960), Canal (1961), Canal (1965), and bibliography cited therein; and Roper (1993).

3. Descriptions of both manuscripts are in Leroquais (1934), 2:427–28.

4. Lat. 16317, fol. 8: "Memoria de reliquiis et omnibus sanctis post matutinum beate Marie debet fieri ut supra per totum adventum." Fol. 8v: "Post vesperas beate Marie fit memoria de reliquiis per ant. *Et facta est,* v. *Letamini in domino,* oratio *Propiciare.*" The feast of the Reception of the Relics was observed on 4 December, which always occurred during Advent.

5. Paris, BNF lat. 15181, the first volume of a Notre-Dame breviary from ca. 1300, on new fol. 7. The same rubric is found in the *Ordo officii* on fol. 298v of Paris, BNF lat. 10482, the manuscript breviary that is the source for the text of the Little Office in the appendix.

6. Lat. 16317, fol. 23 (emphasis mine): "Here begin the Hours of Blessed Mary *in choir,* which are sung until *Isti sunt dies.*" *Isti sunt dies* is the first responsory of Matins on Passion Sunday in Lent. (With regard to performance "in choro," see also the rubric from lat. 15181 and lat. 10482 quoted above.) The Paris ceremonial by Martin Sonnet (*Caeremoniale Parisiense*), p. 549, is still very explicit about performance in choir: "Officium parvum Beatae Mariae Virginis *cantatur in choro* in omnibus feriis et festis simplicibus . . ." (emphasis mine).

7. Described and illustrated in Leroquais (1940–41), 2:198–200, and plates LXXI–LXXVI. See also an illustration of part of the page beginning the Little Office in Branner (1975), 173–85, specifically, fig. 7, p. 182. I am grateful to the institutional holders of this and the three following thirteenth-century manuscripts for the opportunity to study them first-hand.

8. For the Isabelle psalter/hours, see Cockerell (1905). The manuscript was part of the library of King Charles V in the later fourteenth century.

9. The Walters MS is described in Randall (1989), 1:68–71. See also Bennett (1996), 28.

10. See Leroquais (1934), 3:197–98. On the thirteenth-century date of this MS, see Baltzer (2000, in press). In 1987 a fifth manuscript source, a Parisian psalter/hours of the 1250s, appeared only to be auctioned in Paris and returned to private ownership; see Bennett (1996), 35, n. 24.

11. As in Paris, BNF lat. 1024, fol. 112 ff., and Paris, Bibliothèque Mazarine, Inc. 663, a 1492 printed breviary, fol. 177v ff.

12. As in the psalter thought to have been made for Queen Blanche of Castile, Paris, Bibl. de l'Arsenal 1186.

13. Dimensions of the Isabelle psalter/hours are ca. 201 × 140 mm. Cockerell be-

lieved that this manuscript, a royal companion volume to the St. Louis psalter (Paris, BNF lat. 10525), was made for Louis IX's sister Isabelle (d. 1270), who founded the convent of Poor Clares at Longchamp. Branner (1977), 133, argued that it was more likely made for Louis's wife Marguerite of Provence or for their daughter Isabelle, who married Thibaut de Champagne, king of Navarre, in 1255. In this regard it is worth noting that Jean de Joinville's *Histoire de Saint Louis,* chap. 18, reports that Louis made his children learn the Hours of Our Lady.

14. Interestingly, Fitzwilliam 300 suggests an unusual devotion to the Virgin, for besides the psalter, the Hours of the Virgin, and the Office of the Dead, it includes extracts of liturgical material from the four major feasts of the Virgin—the Nativity, the Annunciation, the Purification, and the Assumption—including the Magnificat antiphon and collect of First Vespers, the lessons of Matins, and the Benedictus antiphon and collect of Lauds. See Cockerell (1905), 22–23.

15. Useful for comparison in this regard is table 3:8, Psalms for the Daily Appended Votive Office, in Roper (1993), 227–37. This table lists the psalms used for the Little Office in a variety of English medieval sources, both secular and monastic, from the eleventh to the sixteenth centuries.

16. Canal (1966), 219–20, printed Yves Delaporte's transcription of the lessons at Chartres from the twelfth-century manuscript Chartres 162, destroyed in World War II. Delaporte had sent his transcription in a letter to Canal. At Saint-Maur, the lessons appear in the mid-twelfth-century manuscript Paris, BNF lat. 12042, fol. 4 ff, where they are designated for Tuesdays, Wednesdays, Fridays, and Saturdays; the third lesson is missing. See Canal (1961), 505. On other links between the abbey of Saint-Maur and the church of Paris, see Huglo (1975).

17. See Leclercq (1958), 296–97, from Paris, BNF lat. 12405. By the early fourteenth century, however, Saint-Germain-des-Prés seems to have adopted the three lessons used at the cathedral, if the breviary Paris, BNF lat. 13239 gives an accurate representation of the Little Office then in use at Saint-Germain.

18. See the Little Office in the fourteenth-century breviary from Saint-Denis, Oxford, Bodleian, Canon. Liturg. 192, fols. 257–262v; a description of the manuscript is in Robertson (1991a), 408–9.

19. At Saint-Maur, these are the lessons for Sunday, Monday, and Thursday; see n. 16 above.

20. For the Saint-Martial Little Office, which had nine lessons, see Paris, BNF lat. 3719 (published in facsimile by Bryan Gillingham), fols. 93–100v; the text is printed in Canal (1961), 506–9. These are the first three lessons there. For Font Avellane, see PL 151, 970–74. For Worcester, see PM 12 (Worcester Cathedral, MS F 160, from ca. 1230) and Roper (1993), 260–66. The Sarum Little Office is also that included in the earliest English book of hours, that of William de Brailes from the 1240s. On the Sarum use and on this manuscript, see Donovan (1991), esp. 176–80. The Dominican Little Office is found following the psalter in Rome, Santa Sabina XIV L 1 (Humbert's Codex) and in London, BL Add. 23935, both made in Paris in the mid-thirteenth century.

21. For Chartres, see n. 16 above; these three lessons were designated *Aliae.* For Laon, see Canal (1965), 467–68. For Saint-Martial, see n. 20 above. For the Cistercians, see J. Leclercq (1958), 299–301, from Vatican, BAV Barb. lat. 523 (late 12th c.).

22. See J. Leclercq (1960), 94–101. The lessons are taken from an eighth-century sermon of Ambroise Autpert.

23. Paris, BNF lat. 10433 (end of the 12th c.), where they are the first three of nine lessons; the texts of this Little Office are printed in Canal (1961), 510–24.

24. Their occurrences in the Paris liturgy can be readily determined by searching the CANTUS database of Paris, BNF lat. 15181–82, a large two-volume choirbook breviary of ca. 1300, whose index was prepared by Susan A. Kidwell. A printed version of

this index, for which I am writing an introduction, will be published by the Institute of Mediaeval Music in Ottawa.

25. The fifteenth-century Paris breviary of Duke Philip the Good of Burgundy, Brussels, BR 9026 (the *pars aestivalis*), contains on its last written page these same ten Marian benedictions in the same order, with the tenth one labeled for feasts of the Virgin having nine lessons. For more on this breviary see Leroquais (1929).

26. In the communal liturgy of the church, such commemorations come at the end of both Lauds and Vespers on a given day, as is the case in the lat. 10482 breviary, but in the private devotions of books of hours, they are normally found only after Lauds.

27. This is the one memorial that is incomplete; it has only the collect and lacks the antiphon and versicle with response.

28. See n. 13 above.

29. I have written about some of these, with specific reference to the calendar in the Isabelle psalter/hours, in Baltzer (2000, in press). The later history of the royal use, including that of the several Saintes-Chapelles, is the subject of a forthcoming study by Barbara Haggh. See also Haggh (1997b).

30. Interestingly enough, the antiphon used to memorialize St. Francis in the Isabelle psalter/hours, *Celorum candor,* does not appear anywhere in the cathedral liturgy, according to the CANTUS index of lat. 15181–82.

31. In a mid-thirteenth-century copy of the martyrology of Usuard that belonged to Notre-Dame (Paris, BNF lat. 5185cc), Eustache is present on 2 November (fol. 121v). To the best of my knowledge, the only Paris breviary, missal, or gradual calendar to include him is that in Paris, BNF lat. 15165, a mid-thirteenth-century missal that belonged to the Sorbonne, which memorializes him on this date. According to Perdrizet (1933), 226, at some point Notre-Dame acquired relics of St. Eustache, and he appears in calendars of Paris books of hours by the fifteenth century on 24 September. I find no mention that the Sainte-Chapelle had a relic of St. Eustache.

32. A useful overview is in Hilda Graef (1985); also helpful are various essays in *De cultu Mariano saeculis XII–XV* (1980), vol. 4. See also Pelikan (1996).

33. The sculptural program of the west front of Notre-Dame of Paris depicts the Virgin in all of her roles in salvation, as does contemporaneous Parisian Latin poetry in the musical genres of sequence, conductus, and motet. All provide a direct window on the clerical understanding of the Virgin in late twelfth- and thirteenth-century Paris, about which I shall have much more to say in a forthcoming book. For much useful information, see Coathalem (1954), Thérel (1984), and Thurian (1985).

34. This point is repeatedly made by Taunton (1903) in his exegesis of the early twentieth-century version of the Little Office. In particular, Taunton follows the traditional Christian interpretation of the Psalms in the light of New Testament messianic theology.

35. See Taunton (1903), 135. As he goes on to summarize (p. 138), "In the three preceding psalms we have had suggested to us, Mary, the work of God's hands, crowned with glory and honor, sanctified as the divine tabernacle, pure and clean of heart receiving blessings from God, her salvation; or, in other words, our ever dear and blessed Lady as Daughter of God the Father, Mother of God the Son, and Spouse of the Holy Ghost."

36. Which, on all feasts of the Virgin, are those of the Sunday cursus of Lauds in secular churches.

37. On the fifteen Gradual psalms, see Roper (1993), 17, and Hiley (1993), 19.

38. This is true also of the chapters in Lauds and Vespers; only the chapter at Compline is biblical (Ecclus. 24:20).

39. The text of the Little Office is copied on these folios without music. In my transcription nearly all abbreviations have been expanded editorially, and modern punctua-

tion has been added. Texts that are only cued in the Little Office, such as prayers and versicles, but not psalms, are supplied [in brackets] from elsewhere in the Paris liturgy.

40. The MS has *scis.*

41. The Te deum was omitted in Advent and from Septuagesima to Easter.

42. The MS has *spi* instead of *psi* for *psalmi.*

43. This is said by the priest before the *Deus in adiutorium.* Cf. an example (where it is called a versus) in the twelfth-century Ordinal of Laon edited by Chevalier, *Ordinaires,* 7: "In laudibus sacerdos, antequam incipiat *Deus in adjutorium,* dicit versum *Ex Syon species decoris eius.*"

44. I.e., the usual or customary psalms. The MS again has *spi* instead of *psi* for *psalmi.*

45. The MS has *spi* for *psalmos.*

46. Rubrics elsewhere in lat. 10482 (fol. 55; also in lat. 16317, fol. 22) indicate that from the octave of Epiphany to the Purification (13 Jan. to 2 Feb.) the antiphon *O admirabile commercium* was used with the Benedictus at Lauds and the Magnificat at Vespers in the Little Office.

47. See n. 46.

The Carmelite Feast of the Presentation of the Virgin

A Study in Musical Adaptation

JAMES JOHN BOYCE, O.CARM.

Within the Carmelite liturgical tradition the feast of the Presentation of the Virgin presents a rare instance in which most of the chants for the feast are contrafacta[1] of pieces in other rhymed Offices. While recent studies have demonstrated this phenomenon within other traditions,[2] the Mainz Carmelite instance adapts chants from at least three different feasts to this new one and uses more than one style of adaptation to do so, thereby rendering it a unique example of musical adaptation. The recent publication of Owain Edwards's book on the Office of St. David (Edwards, *Matins*) provides an example of extensive adaptation against which to compare the Carmelite Presentation Office. The purpose of this chapter is to examine the Office of the Presentation in terms of the other feasts and pieces that served as models for the chants of the Office, the modal structure of the chants, and the different styles operative in adapting chants from one Office to another.

Although the origin of the Carmelite Order dates to the reception of their rule from St. Albert of Jerusalem between the years 1206 and 1214 (Clarke and Edwards, *Rule of Saint Albert*), the adoption of the common Office in choir only occurred with the revision of the rule in 1247,[3] and a uniform liturgy only came to exist with the promulgation of the Ordinal of Sibert de Beka by the General Chapter of London in 1312.[4] The establishment on Mount Carmel of an oratory dedicated to the Virgin Mary formed part of the Carmelites' identification with her as brothers and encouraged them to celebrate a large number of Marian feasts, including the Nativity, Annunciation, Assumption, and Conception.[5]

While the Ordinal of Sibert de Beka stipulated all the incipits for the chants, prayers, readings, and psalms to be used for all the Office hours, it did not deal directly with details of the text and contained no music. It nonetheless regulated the liturgical ceremonies quite carefully, although variants in textual formulas could occur from one area to another. It is not clear to what extent this textual uniformity was enforced after the promulgation of Sibert's ordinal, since no portable service books comparable to Humbert's Codex for the Dominicans were written for the Carmelites.[6]

Studies in the medieval Carmelite Office tradition have shown the fidelity with which the surviving manuscripts from this period followed the prescriptions of Sibert's ordinal and as a result the high degree of uniformity from one manuscript to another (I discuss the question of liturgical conformity to official Carmelite legislation in Boyce 1994). Thus as far as the general structure of the liturgy is concerned there is remarkable similarity between the late fourteenth-century choirbooks of the Carmine of Florence, now housed in the Carmine and in the San Marco Museum,[7] and the fifteenth-century codices of Mainz, now found in the Dom- und Diözesanmuseum of that city.[8] An early fourteenth-century pair of antiphonals from Pisa, now in the Carmine of Pisa, also follow the same liturgical prescriptions as the other two later sets.[9] Feasts that entered the Carmelite rite after the time of Sibert's ordinal were mandated by Chapter Acts to be observed in all the houses of the Order but obviously could not be included in Sibert's ordinal. If a uniform liturgy was established for such a later feast, no documents containing its format have survived. Thus considerable latitude may have prevailed in celebrating these later feasts.

The feast of the Presentation of the Virgin was introduced in the West in the Franciscan church in Avignon on 21 November 1372 in the presence of the papal court with the *Fons hortorum* Office of Philippe de Mézières.[10] The Carmelites accepted it, along with the feasts of the Visitation and Our Lady of the Snows, into their liturgy at the General Chapter of Frankfurt in 1393 (Wessels, *Acta*, 109–10), a scant twenty years after its Western introduction. Because this acceptance date virtually coincides with the time in which the Florentine Carmelite manuscripts were written, the few chants found in Florence, Museo di San Marco 575 (V)[11] are unique to that manuscript.

The complete musical portion of the Presentation Office is found in Mainz, Dom- und Diözesanmuseum D, the fourth of five antiphonals used in the Carmelite convent of Mainz, and constitutes the focus of this study. The Mainz choirbooks were written over several years, beginning in 1430.[12] The Presentation Office as contained in Codex D is unique to this source[13] and almost certainly is a product of the Mainz Carmelite scriptorium. The chants are written in the same textual and musical hands as the rest of the manuscript and feature rhymed texts that are highly original and music that was, at least for the most part, adapted from other Offices. The first antiphon of First Vespers begins with the text *Letetur ecclesia de fecundo germine* to a first-mode melody whose source has not yet been identified but which, given the preponderance of contrafacta in this manuscript, presumably was adapted from a preexisting chant.

That the Carmelites should write a rhymed Office for an important new Marian feast is significant, given the Order's standardized approach to all Marian liturgical celebrations. Sibert's ordinal prescribed the same five First Vespers antiphons, beginning with *Haec est regina*, for virtually all major feasts of Mary: the Nativity, Annunciation, Conception, Assumption, and Our Lady of the Snows.[14] The use of these five antiphons allied them with the early usage from the Holy Sepulchre of

Jerusalem, and these ties to the liturgy of the Holy Land where the Order began held sway over later temptations toward more elaborate Marian Offices.[15]

The Carmelites of Mainz chose their new Presentation Office over the well-established *Fons hortorum* Office of Philippe de Mézières, in spite of a close personal link between Philippe de Mézières and the Carmelite St. Peter Thomas as well as with the Carmelites of Paris.[16] A fifteenth-century Carmelite breviary from Mainz, now New Haven, Yale UL 41 (John Sterling 80), did in fact use the readings from the *Fons hortorum* Office in an abbreviated version, creating a liturgical problem if these were used along with the newly-composed antiphons and responsories of Codex D, since the sung chants would bear scant correlation to the Matins readings, although it may in fact have been done that way (I discussed this matter at some length in Boyce 1991).

Philippe de Mézières's celebration of the Presentation feast, now preserved in Paris, BNF lat. 17330 and its copy lat. 14454, included text and music for the Office and Mass[17] as well as the complete readings for Matins and an additional section of readings known as the *gesta,* or exploits of the Virgin.[18] The function or purpose of the *gesta* is not clear from the manuscript itself, but they provided alternate readings or reflections on the experience of the Presentation as recounted in the apocryphal Gospels of James and Pseudo-Matthew. The texts of the Carmelite Office of the Presentation seem to be loosely based on these *gesta* of the Virgin,[19] but with a proper Carmelite thrust as well. Even though the chants of Codex D do not complement the readings, at least in the Yale breviary, they do nonetheless have some internal organization as a reflection on the experience of Mary's presentation.

The main interest of the chants of this Office, however, is musical, since virtually all of them derive from other established rhymed Offices, primarily that of St. Thomas Becket. Table 21.1 gives the incipits of the chants in the Office of the Presentation, along with their sources of musical inspiration in other Offices, their liturgical function, and their mode. The table demonstrates that chants from the Offices of St. Thomas Becket, the Three Marys, and the Nativity of the Virgin Mary all served as musical inspiration for the Carmelite Presentation Office. The chant *Stirps Yesse,* composed by Fulbert of Chartres (Sainte-Beuve 1928) as a chant for the Nativity of the Virgin, was also prescribed in the Carmelite rite for the feasts of the Conception of the Virgin, Our Lady of the Snows, and St. Anne. Accordingly it occurs in four separate instances in the Mainz Carmelite manuscripts, in Codex D, fol. 73r for the Nativity, Codex E, fol. 313v for the Conception, Codex C, fol. 264r for Our Lady of the Snows, and Codex C, fol. 238r for St. Anne. The use of more than one Office as a model for the Presentation feast immediately distinguishes this Office from counterparts in the Franciscan liturgy, where the Office of St. Francis served as the direct model for those of St. Clare, St. Louis of Anjou, St. Elizabeth of Hungary, and the Trinity (cf. Edwards 1992, esp. 510–11). In these cases the texts of the later Offices were written with the same metrical pattern as that of St. Francis so that the music could readily be adapted to the earlier prototype.

Owain Edwards has established a logical association between the Offices of the Welsh St. David and the English St. Thomas Becket,[20] but the use of the St. Thomas

Table 21.1 The chants for the Mainz Carmelite Office of the Presentation of Mary with their musical counterparts in other sources

No. Chant	Presentation Office	Source[a]	Mode
First Vespers			
1. a1	Letetur ecclesia	—	1
2. a2	Per te misericordia	—	2
3. a3	Psalmus est bonus	—	3
4. a4	Suscipiens est viduam	—	4
5. a5	Divinus flavit spiritus	—	5
6. Hymn	Presens dies	—	
7. M	Pastor dives in celi	Pastor cesus (T)	1
Matins			
8. Inv	Presenti Christo	Assunt Thome (T)	2
9. Hymn	Contemplemur in confusa	—	
First nocturn			
10. a1	Annam vocatam	Summo sacerdotio (T)	1
11. a2	Auri solisque filia	Monachus sub (T)	2
12. a3	De stirpe virgo	Cultor agri (T)	3
13. R1	Germen produxit	Studens livor (T)	1
14. R2	O vite vitis	Thomas manum (T)	2
15. R3	Anna parens clausa	Hodie Marie (3 M)	1
Second nocturn			
16. a1	Anus annosa	Nec in agnos (T)	4
17. a2	Radix Yesse protulit	Exulat vir (T)	5
18. a3	Beata suxit ubera	Exulantis (T)	6T
19. R1	Ex Yoachim primam	Post sex annos (T)	1
20. R2	Puram pura paris	Iacet granum (T)	5
21. R3	Quo formosa nimis	—	3
Third nocturn			
22. a1	Scandit virgo	Sathane satellites (T)	7
23. a2	Per templi transit	Strictis Thomas (T)	8
24. a3	Anna tu felix	Hosti pandit (T)	1
25. R1	Corda velut sursum	Mundi florem (T)	7
26. R2	Amplius etherei sensit	Lapis iste (T) (N1 R3)	3
27. R3	Unam quam petii	Stirps Yesse (Nativity or Nat. BMV)	2
Lauds			
28. a1	Ab eterno presignatur	Granum cadit (T)	1
29. a2	Introivit in atria	Totis orbis (T)	2
30. a3	Fontem vite siciens	Aqua Thome (T)	4
31. a4	Virgo non minor	Ad Thome (T)	6T
32. a5	Iuvencula virginea	Tu per Thome (T)	8
33. aB	Cornu salutis	Salve Thoma (T) (M)	1
Second Vespers			
34. aM	Pandit pater potentiam	—	1

[a] T = Office of St. Thomas; 3 M = Office of the Three Marys

Office as inspiration for the Carmelite Presentation Office is far more surprising. Although the Carmelites arrived in England as early as 1242,[21] the presence of the Office of St. Thomas of Canterbury in the Carmelite Ordinal of Sibert de Beka from 1312 as well as in an earlier ordinal dating from the end of the thirteenth century[22] stems from the saint's general popularity rather than from any English hegemony within the Order. Once promulgated for universal observance, the Office of St. Thomas became part of the Carmelite liturgy and thus spread throughout the Order's convents. Thus it is present in Mainz, Dom- und Diözesan- museum A,[23] where it served as a convenient model for the Presentation Office. Unlike the Office of St. David, whose *vita* presented some parallels with the life of St. Thomas, making it a logical source for adaptation, no particular association between the feasts of the Presentation and that of St. Thomas can account for the adaptation process in the case of the Carmelites. The nature of the feast of the Presentation virtually rules out any textual similarity between the two feasts com- parable to that between two established saints such as David and Thomas, or Fran- cis and Clare, for that matter. Only the Matins and Lauds chants and the Mag- nificat chant from First Vespers of Thomas are adapted to the chants of the Presentation Office.

The two chants so far identified from Offices other than St. Thomas are *Hodie Marie* from the Florence Carmelite Office of the Three Marys found in Florence, Carmine O[24] and *Stirps Yesse* from the Office of the Nativity of the Virgin in Mainz, Dom- und Diözesanmuseum D. The inclusion of these two melodies is particularly interesting, since the Office of St. Thomas was so complete in itself that no other sources would have been necessary. More importantly, it means that the melody of this Florentine *Hodie Marie* chant was known in Mainz, either directly from Florence or through another intermediate version (cf. Boyce 1990a, 138–39, for this discussion), suggesting that the melody was held in such high esteem that it served as the model for two Carmelite chants in distinct locales, or that there was consid- erable interchange between Mainz and Florence. The use of the responsory *Stirps Yesse* is at least found within the Mainz Carmelite codices and is thus more under- standable. The feast of St. Anne is prescribed in Sibert's ordinal but with the chants from the Common of a holy woman.[25] The Carmelite Chapter of Bonn of 1411 prescribed that a memorial of St. Anne be made at Vespers and Matins throughout the Order,[26] which may have been the impetus for composing a rhymed Office for her feast,[27] which curiously also included the Marian chant *Stirps Yesse*.

The selection of a chant from the Three Marys Office and the chant *Stirps Yesse*, common to feasts of Mary and St. Anne in the Carmelite rite, establishes a musical association between the feast of the Presentation and two other significant feasts relating to the Virgin Mary. As mother of the Virgin Mary, St. Anne figures promi- nently in this feast of the Presentation and indeed draws her significance theologi- cally in terms of her relationship to Mary and by extension to the Lord himself. The legend that St. Anne's marriages to Joachim, Cleophas, and Salome brought forth one Mary from each of three husbands inspired devotion to the Three Marys in Provence as well as to St. Mary Salome in Italy, a devotion that translated into proper feasts and rhymed Offices.[28] Tradition further identified Mary of Salome as the wife of Zebedee and mother of St. James the Great, patron saint of Santiago de

Compostela, thereby linking the place of pilgrimage with two of the significant areas from which pilgrims came. The use of a chant from the Three Marys, Nativity BVM, and St. Anne Offices suggests a definite liturgical effort to associate these feasts with the closely related one of the Presentation and demonstrates the significance of theological considerations in preparing this Office.

As table 21.1 demonstrates, the five First Vespers antiphons follow a modal order, using modes 1 through 5; the Matins antiphons follow the modal order, common to a number of rhymed Offices, of modes 1 through 8 followed by mode 1 for the ninth antiphon. The question of a modal order for the responsories is a different situation, however.[29] The nine Matins responsories are in modes 1, 2, 1, 1, 5, 3, 7, 3, and 2, respectively. Numbers 1, 2, 5, and 7 conform to a predictable modal order, while the intervening ones do not. The third responsory in the St. Thomas Office, *Lapis iste,* is transferred to become the eighth responsory in this Office; thus this mode 3 responsory occurs in place of a mode 8 responsory, thereby disrupting the normal modal order of a rhymed Office. In place of the mode 3 responsory the compiler of this Office substituted the responsory *Hodie Marie* from the Florentine Carmelite Office of the Three Marys, which happens to be in mode 1, thereby further disrupting the modal scheme. The use of the mode 2 responsory *Stirps Yesse* from the Office of the Nativity of Mary as a model for the ninth responsory again disrupts the modal order. The five Lauds antiphons follow the Lauds antiphons for the St. Thomas Office, which occur in modes 1, 2, 4, 6 transposed, and 8 respectively. The Mainz Carmelite version of the Office of St. Thomas follows the cathedral rather than the monastic usage, so that the pieces had already been interpolated from an earlier monastic source and probably adopted in the newer version by the Carmelites.

Two of the responsories from the St. Thomas Office that were not included in the Presentation Office did in fact follow the predictable modal order: *Ex summa rerum,* the sixth responsory, is in mode 6, and *Christe Jesu per Thome,* the eighth responsory, is in mode 8, while the ninth responsory, *Jesus bone per Thome,* is in mode 2, the same mode but not the same melody as the model selected for the last Matins responsory in the Presentation Office. Thus while the modal order of the Carmelite St. Thomas Office already had been disrupted, it was much closer to a traditional modal order than the resulting Presentation Office. In other words, the modal order of chants was not a priority for the Carmelites who compiled the new Office of the Presentation, which parallels the situation of the St. David Office, where Owain Edwards has shown that modal considerations were not a priority either.[30]

Musically this Mainz Carmelite Presentation Office is interesting because its author used more than one method of adapting preexisting music to a new text. Example 21.1 shows the First Vespers antiphon *Pastor cesus in gregis medio* from the St. Thomas Office with its new text, *Pastor dives in celi solio,* from that of the Presentation. Benedict of Peterborough, the author of the St. Thomas Office (Edwards, *Matins,* 160–62), used a distinctive bipartite metrical pattern of 4 + 6 syllables in each line for the antiphon, which the Carmelite composer of the Presentation Office imitated as best he could:

Example 21.1 Antiphons *Pastor cesus* and *Pastor dives*

Office of St. Thomas of Canterbury

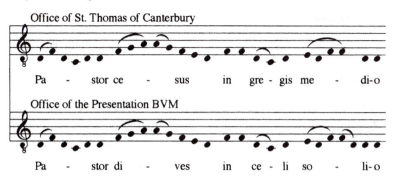

Pa - stor ce - sus in gre - gis me - di-o

Office of the Presentation BVM

Pa - stor di - ves in ce - li so - li-o

St. Thomas

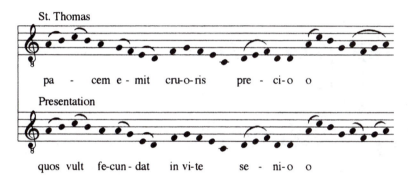

pa - cem e - mit cru-o-ris pre - ci-o o

Presentation

quos vult fe-cun - dat in vi-te se - ni-o o

St. Thomas

le-tus do - lor in tri-sti gau-di o grex re-spi-rat pa-sto - re mor-tu- o

Presentation

grex le-ta - ta ce-li de-nun-ti-o pa-stor spi-rat ros ri - gat il - li-co

(*continued*)

Example 21.1 (*continued*)

St. Thomas

plan-gens plau - dit ma - ter   in   fi- li- o qui - a   vi -

Presentation

pa-rens plau - dit fer - ti - lis   con-ci- to na - sci - tu -

St. Thomas

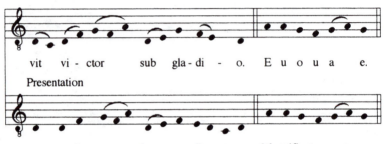

vit   vi - ctor   sub   gla- di - o.   E   u   o   u   a   e.

Presentation

ra   re-plet mun - dum   gau- di - o.   Magnificat.

Lines of antiphon text		Syllable count
Pastor cesus	in gregis medio	4 + 6
pacem emit	cruoris precio	4 + 6
o letus dolor	in tristi gaudio	5 + 6
grex respirat	pastore mortuo	4 + 6
plangens plaudit	mater in filio	4 + 6
quia vivit	victor sub gladio.	4 + 6
Pastor dives	in celi solio	4 + 6
quos vult fecundat	in vite senio	5 + 6
o grex letata	celi denuntio	5 + 6
pastor spirat	ros rigat illico	4 + 6
parens plaudit	fertiles concito	4 + 6
nascitura	replet mundum gaudio.	4 + 7

In two other cases he found it necessary to add an extra syllable of text. All the
lines of the St. Thomas piece end in "io" except for one in "uo"; the lines of the
Presentation antiphon all end in "o" but not necessarily with "i" preceding it. The
word *spirat* in the Presentation antiphon clearly is patterned on *respirat* in the
model, and the same word *plaudit* occurs in the fifth line of both texts. He con-
sciously included "o" before *grex letata*, imitating the model, which added an extra
syllable in the process. The deliberate imitation of the textual line facilitated a

musical imitation as well, with the result that the music fits each syllable of the new text in the same way that it accommodated the old. This technique is comparable to that used within the Franciscan Office tradition where, for instance, the composer clearly wrote the text for the Office of St. Clare to conform to the metrical and rhyme patterns of the Office of St. Francis.

Such a direct patterning of text on the established one of another Office proves to be the exception rather than the rule, however, and the metrical patterns of the Presentation Office tend to be *sui generis*. Example 21.2 compares the Presentation antiphon *Annam vocatam gratiam* with *Summo sacerdotio* from the Office of St. Thomas. The texts and syllable counts are as follows:

St. Thomas		Presentation	
Summo sacerdotio	7	Annam vocatam gratiam	8
Thomas sublimatus	6	grate collaudemus	6
et in virum alium	7	ut nata det audaciam	8
subito mutatus.	6	sibi nos presentemus.	7

Although *Annam vocatam* is longer than *Summo sacerdotio,* differences in length and metrical pattern between the two antiphons do not directly affect the music as such. The four phrases of *Summo sacerdotio* end on *a* at *sacerdotio, a* at *sublima-*

Example 21.2   Antiphons *Summo sacerdotio* and *Annam vocatam gratiam*

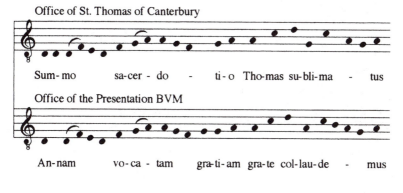

Office of St. Thomas of Canterbury

Sum-mo   sa-cer - do   -   ti-o Tho-mas su-bli-ma   -   tus

Office of the Presentation BVM

An-nam   vo-ca - tam   gra-ti-am gra-te col-lau-de   -   mus

St. Thomas

et in vi - rum a - li-um su-bi- to mu-ta - tus. P. Beatus vir.

Presentation

ut na-ta det au-da-ci - am si- bi nos pre-sen-te - mus. P. Domine dominus.

tus, c at *alium,* and *d* at *mutatus,* so that the four musical phrases conform to the four textual phrases of the antiphon. *Annam vocatam* is a direct adaptation of the melody of *Summo sacerdotio:* the phrases of this Presentation antiphon end on *a* at *gratiam, a* at *collaudemus, d* at *audaciam,* and *d* at *presentemus.* The third phrase ends on *d* rather than on *c* because of the extra syllable in the last phrase of the Presentation version: the *c* that served as the last note of the third phrase in *Summo sacerdotio* now serves as the first note of the last phrase in *Annam vocatam.* The brevity of a Matins antiphon necessarily restricts the possibilities for altering the phrase structure of a piece in the process of its adaptation. Thus in the St. Thomas example the musical phrasing conforms to the poetic meter, and the same situation predictably applies in its adaptation to this Presentation chant.

Even within the shorter chants, however, some changes may occur in the process of adaptation. Thus example 21.3 shows the text of *Auri solisque filia,* patterned on the St. Thomas chant *Monachus sub clerico.*

St. Thomas		Presentation	
Monachus sub clerico	7	Auri solisque filia	8
iam ciliciatus	6	quo virgo circundatur	7
carnis carne fortior	7	cuius parens in aurea	8
edomat conatus.	6	porta letificatur.	7

Example 21.3   Antiphons *Monachus sub clerico* and *Auri solisque filia*

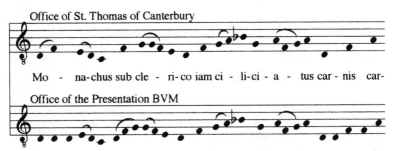

This antiphon is textually independent, with one syllable more in each line than the St. Thomas one. While the adaptor could have patterned the word *filia* to coincide with *clerico*, he chose otherwise; a similar situation occurs at the end with *aurea* and *fortior*. In both these cases the Presentation antiphon features *e* as a cadential point rather than *d* as in the model. In this case a small textual alteration in fact produces a noticeable musical change, suggesting that the composer felt obliged to follow the melodic pattern of the model but not its phrase structure.

Changes in the approach to melody become much more pronounced in the more extended antiphons, however. For instance, example 21.4 compares the Magnificat antiphon *Salve Thoma* for the Office of St. Thomas with *Cornu salutis*, the Benedictus antiphon for the feast of the Presentation. The text of these two antiphons, with the number of syllables for each phrase, is as follows:

Salve Thoma	virga iustitie	10
mundi iubar	robur ecclesie	10
plebis amor	cleri delicie	10
salve gregis	tutor egregie	10
salva tue	congaudentes glorie.	11
Cornu salutis hodie		8
dominus erexit		6
ad are cornu propere		8
Maria dum perrexit		7
ab altis venit oriens		8
qui nos visitavit		6
vitam reduxit moriens		8
quem virgo generavit.		7

Andrew Hughes has already demonstrated the stylistic similarity between *Salve Thoma virga iustitie* and *Pastor cesus in gregis medio,* the Magnificat antiphon for First Vespers (A. Hughes 1988a, 200), which is all the more interesting since the 4 + 6 syllable structure of each line precludes a sense of the two-phrase form in both pieces (ibid., 197). *Cornu salutis* is then slightly longer than its counterpart, having a total of 58 syllables as opposed to 51 in *Salve Thoma.* Moreover, the textual construction and rhyme scheme are essentially different in the two cases, since *Cornu salutis* follows a two-phrase form while *Salve Thoma* does not.

As this example illustrates, the differences in metrical structure inevitably extended to the music itself, and the adaptors either could not or did not attempt to preserve the same phrase structure in the Presentation example as had obtained in the St. Thomas chant. With the phrase endings inevitably occurring at different places in *Cornu salutis* from those in *Salve Thoma,* the musical structure of the piece is radically altered from its model. Even though the note changes, where they occur, are inconsequential as such, the termination of phrases at different cadence points radically transforms our perception of the piece. The bipartite first phrase *Salve Thoma virga iustitie* emphasizes *d* as a cadence point at *Thoma* and *iustitie,* reinforced by a *d* cadence at *iubar* and *ecclesie* of the second phrase, while its counterpart in the Presentation version highlights *a* at *hodie* and *erexit.* In *Salve Thoma*

Example 21.4 Antiphons *Salve Thomas* and *Cornu salutis*

Office of St. Thomas of Canterbury

Sal - ve Tho-ma vir - ga iu - sti - ti - e mun - di

Office of the Presentation BVM

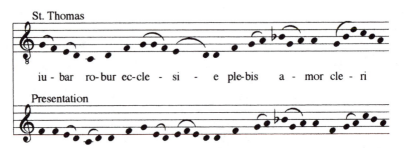

Cor - nu sa - lu-tis ho - di - e do-mi - nus e - re - xit

St. Thomas

iu - bar ro-bur ec-cle - si - e ple-bis a - mor cle - ri

Presentation

ad a-re cor - nu pro pe-re Ma - ri-a dum per - re - xit ab al - tis

St. Thomas

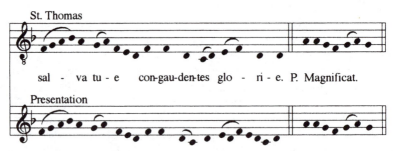

de-li - ci-e sal - ve gre-gis tu - tor e - gre - gi-e

Presentation

ve-nit o - ri-ens qui nos vi-si - ta - vit vi - tam re-du - xit

St. Thomas

sal - va tu - e con-gau-den-tes glo - ri - e. P. Magnificat.

Presentation

mo - ri-ens quem vir - go ge-ne - ra - vit. P. Benedictus.

the *ba* motive at *virga* constitutes a melodic peak but not a focal point of interest, thereby allowing the melody to continue on and terminate the phrase at *iustitie;* however, in adapting this melody to *Cornu salutis* the Carmelite redactor extended this motive to *baga,* thereby making *a* a secondary tonal center and rendering the second *a* itself a termination point of the first phrase on *hodie.* In other words, in the process of adapation he altered the melody itself in order to accommodate the conditions imposed by a new and different poetic structure.

Even in cases where the music is not deliberately changed, however, the adaptation of text to melody nonetheless influences our perception of phrase structure: thus at *salva tue* in the St. Thomas chant, the melody rises from *f* to *b* and then descends to *d,* thus yielding a self-contained phrase. In the adaptation to *Cornu salutis,* however, the syllabification is altered, forcing our perception of the phrase structure to change as well; the equivalent section, *moriens quem,* involves a phrase termination on *a* at the end of *moriens* with the return to *d* going unnoticed as the beginning of the following phrase. In other words, two words of two syllables each contrast with one word of three syllables and one word of one syllable only. Since the extra syllable of text in *moriens* necessitates the use of extra music, what accompanied the first syllable of *tue* in *Salve Thoma* now accompanies the last syllable of *moriens* in *Cornu salutis;* the word *moriens* now contains three notes on *a,* which give this pitch far more importance than it previously enjoyed, since here it becomes a termination point for the phrase *vitam reduxit moriens.* The three notes over *quem* consequently no longer serve as the termination formula of the phrase, but rather as the opening notes of the last phrase, appropriately accommodating the poetic structure of this Presentation antiphon.

Thus in the process of adapting a newer text to an established melody, the Carmelites altered our perception of the melodic structure of this antiphon; the adjustment of notes at phrase endings greatly influences this perception and strongly argues for a deliberate refashioning of the piece by those who adapted it to the newer Office antiphon.

In the case of some responsories adapted from the St. Thomas Office the rhyme scheme is more rigorously defined in the Thomas instance than in its Presentation adaptation. The textual comparison between the St. Thomas responsory *Studens livor* and the Presentation equivalent *Germen produxit,* our example 21.5, is as follows:

R.	Studens livor	Thome supplicio	4 + 6
	Thome genus	dampnat exilio	4 + 6
	Tota simul	exit cognatio.	4 + 6
V.	Ordo sexus	etas conditio	4 + 6
	nullo gaudet	hic privilegio.	4 + 6

R.	Germen produxit stirps	6
	fecundissima Yesse	7
	Quo duce nos duxit Deus	8
	ad prestantius esse.	7
V.	Quod ne destruxit quod prodi	8
	fuit ante necesse.	7

Example 21.5   Responsories *Studens livor* and *Germen produxit*

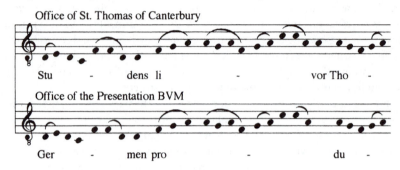

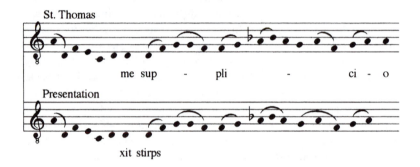

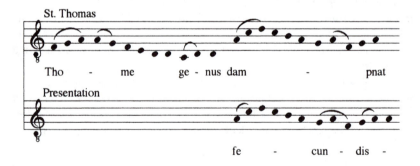

This responsory features a similar metrical pattern to *Pastor cesus,* although applied now to a responsory rather than an antiphon and with one less line of text. The clearly defined 4 + 6 pattern within each line in the Thomas Office does not extend at all to the poetry of the Presentation responsory.

Studens livor contains five lines of ten syllables each with every line subdivided into two parts of four and six syllables. *Germen produxit* contains three lines of 13, 15, and 15 syllables respectively, without a clear subdivision based on rhyme or meter such as occurs in the St. Thomas Office. Accommodating this new text to the music of the St. Thomas responsory is further complicated by the fact that *Germen produxit* is a much shorter text than *Studens livor*—41 syllables as compared with 50 in the St. Thomas example.

Example 21.5   (*continued*)

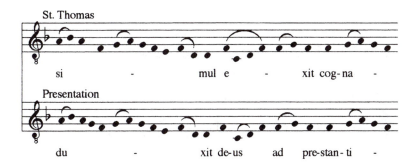

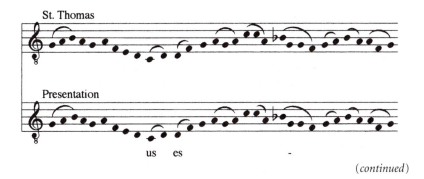

(*continued*)

As example 21.5 shows, the adaptor of this chant was careful to accommodate
the text of *Yesse* to the melodic formula of *exilio,* terminating on *d.* The other main
line endings fall on *d* at the end of the responsory and its verse, so that there was
no choice involved here. The textual midpoints of the poetic lines in *Germen produxit* are ambivalent in any case, so that potential problems of text underlay are
correspondingly diminished. Thus the word *stirps* ends on *a* to conform with *sup-
plicio,* and *duxit* conforms with *simul.* The perception of the opening phrase is
altered, since the *a* at the end of *livor* falls in the middle of *produxit;* in this case the
difference is lessened since the entire phrase *Germen produxit stirps* of six syllables
accompanies the text of the first ten-syllable line of the Thomas Office. The same

Example 21.5   (*continued*)

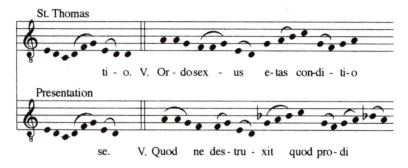

situation obtains in the first phrase of the verse, where the ending of *sexus* occurs in the middle of the word *destruxit*. The result in both cases is not that we have conflicting finals or cadence points but that we are forced to consider the entire phrase as a whole rather than in its component parts. In neither case is the structure of the melody radically affected, mainly because the less precise text of *Germen produxit* allows for this flexibility.

Example 21.6 compares the responsory *Post sex annos* from the Office of St. Thomas with *Ex Yoachim primam* from the Presentation Office. The textual comparison is as follows:

R. Post sex annos	redit vir stabilis	4 + 6
dare terre	teste vas fragilis	4 + 6
Christo vasis	thesaurum fictilis.	4 + 6
V. Ne sit lupis	preda grex humilis	4 + 6
se pro grege	dat pastor nobilis.	4 + 6

R. Ex Yoachim primam	6
felix parit Anna Maria.	9
Heeve prime ve tulit	7
et mala criminis Eve.	8
V. Que ve longeve genti dedit	9
mi proba sene.	5

Example 21.6   Responsories *Post sex annos* and *Ex Yoachim primam*

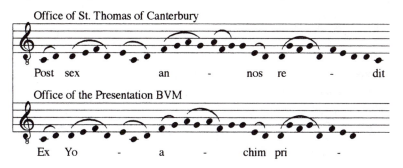

Office of St. Thomas of Canterbury

Post sex   an - nos re -   dit

Office of the Presentation BVM

Ex   Yo   -   a   -   chim pri   -

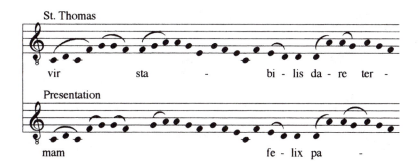

St. Thomas

vir   sta   -   bi - lis da - re ter -

Presentation

mam   fe - lix pa   -

St. Thomas

re tes - te vas   fra   -   gi - lis.

Presentation

rit An   -   na   Ma   -   ri - a.

(*continued*)

The Presentation responsory has no discernible rhymed pattern, although some
internal rhyme occurs, especially as concerns *ve* and the words that rhyme with it,
as well as *parit, tulit,* and *dedit.* Points of coincidence between rhythmic and rhyming patterns are not at all consistent, however, making it difficult to formulate any
clear pattern. Although it contains more rhyming aspects than *Unam quam petii,*
it is not fully a rhymed responsory.

  In the Thomas example the musical phrase lengths are very clear, with cadential
points on *d* at *annos, d* at *stabilis, a* at *terre,* and *d* at *fragilis,* for instance. There is
no particular attempt in the Presentation equivalent to have the new text at all

Example 21.6 (*continued*)

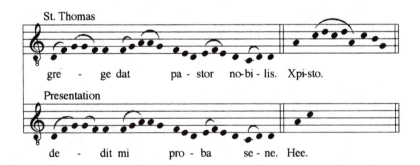

match the old placement, perhaps because of the difference in syllables and in its textual structure. The shorter text makes the melody more melismatic, since there are fewer syllables involved, and tends to unify phrases. For instance, the first phrase has ten syllables in the original and only eight in the adapted version; a melisma at the end of *primam* continues the melodic thrust to end on the final *d* at *felix*. The fact that the melody itself clearly emphasizes both final *d* and also *a* at many different points makes this quite suitable for adapting even a metrically ambivalent text.

Example 21.7 compares the responsory *Thomas manum mittit* with its Presenta-

Example 21.7   Responsories *Thomas manum* and *O vite vitis*

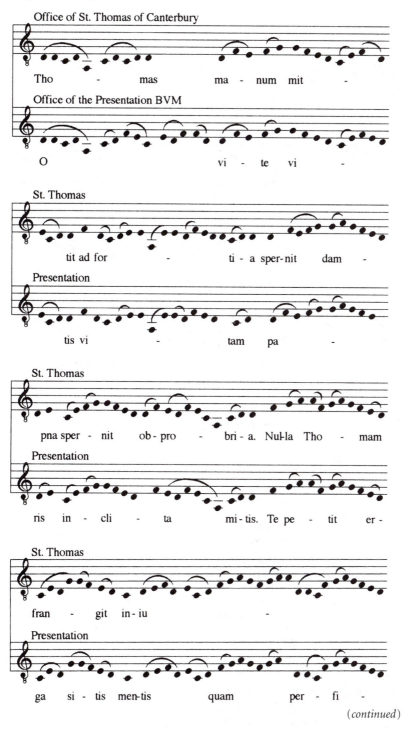

Office of St. Thomas of Canterbury

Tho - mas   ma - num mit -

Office of the Presentation BVM

O   vi - te vi -

St. Thomas

tit ad for -   ti - a sper-nit   dam -

Presentation

tis vi -   tam pa -

St. Thomas

pna sper - nit   ob - pro -   bri - a. Nul-la Tho - mam

Presentation

ris in - cli - ta   mi - tis. Te pe - tit   er -

St. Thomas

fran - git in - iu -

Presentation

ga si - tis men-tis   quam   per - fi -

(*continued*)

Example 21.7   (*continued*)

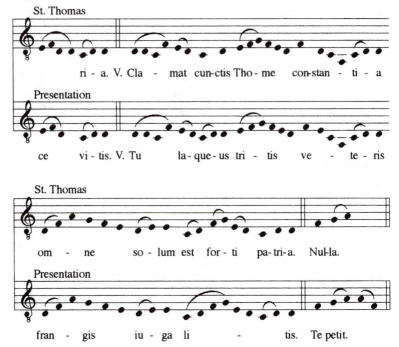

tion counterpart *O vite vitis*. The same pattern of 4 + 6 syllables in the Thomas Office obtains throughout.

R.	Thomas manum	mittit ad fortia	4 + 6
	spernit dampna	spernit obprobria.	4 + 6
	Nulla Thomam	frangit iniuria.	4 + 6
V.	Clamat cunctis	Thome constantia	4 + 6
	omne solum	est forti patria.	4 + 6

R.	O vite vitis	5
	vitam paris	4
	inclita mitis.	5
	Te petit erga sitis	7
	mentis quam perfice vitis.	8
V.	Tu laqueus tritis	6
	veteris frangis	5
	iuga litis.	4

The compressed style of poetry and considerable internal rhyme make *O vite vitis* difficult to divide metrically; its verse consists of three rhymed phrases as opposed to two in the St. Thomas example. Thus the *d* cadential point at *constantia* signals the end of the first half of the responsory verse, but in the adapted version it falls at the end of *veteris*, which must be the first word of the middle phrase, since it does not rhyme with *litis* at the end. Thus the verse structure itself is altered in the process of adaptation. A similar situation obtains in the responsory itself, where the metrical and musical lines do not really coincide in the adapted version. Thus the extended opening word *O* unites with *vite vitis* to form one unit, ending on *d* in the middle of the first St. Thomas phrase, i.e., on *mittit* rather than *fortia*. Similarly, the phrase *vitam paris* extends through the phrase ending of *fortia* in the St. Thomas equivalent. The preponderance of *d* makes this acceptable in the adapted version but quite distinct from the original model. The original 4 + 6 syllable structure of the St. Thomas exemplar also facilitates this adaptation, since the phrase structure is itself bipartite in the original example. In the Presentation case the large number of short phrases contrasts with the St. Thomas model, although the melodic structure is not radically altered, given the preponderance of *d*s available as termination points.

The Presentation responsory *Amplius etherei*, patterned on *Lapis iste* from the St. Thomas Office, is shown as our example 21.8 and demonstrates a rare instance in which a substantial portion of music from the original has been excised in the process of adaptation.

R. Lapis iste	sex annis tunditur	4 + 6
sic politur	sic quadrus redditur	4 + 6
minus cedens	quo magis ceditur.	4 + 6
V. Aurum fornax	probat nec uritur	4 + 6
domus firma	ventis non quatitur.	4 + 6

R. Amplius etherei	7
sensit per membra vigoris	8
Que nutritura fuerant	8
corpus genitoris.	6
V. Dat celi roris	5
hanc vim simul actio floris.	9

The uneven poetic structure of *Amplius etherei* creates a set of problems that make it difficult to fit the music of *Lapis iste* to the new text. The prevailing 4 + 6 syllable metrical pattern of *Lapis iste* creates a product that is structurally distinctive, with 30 syllables in the responsory and 20 in the verse. Three lines of text in the model compare with four in the product. The redactor, in seeking to align the rhymed words of *Amplius etherei* with those of *Lapis iste,* needed to consider the four lines of *Amplius etherei* as two lines of 15 and 14 syllables respectively. He therefore eliminated the music of *sic politur sic quadrus redditur* from *Lapis iste* to facilitate this alignment, despite the fact that in the process he eliminated a considerable portion of the original music.

While *vigoris* does terminate on the *e* characterizing the end of *tunditur,* the text underlay is nevertheless complicated by the fact that 29 syllables of text are now applied to music that formerly had only 20. Thus, for instance, *per membra*

Example 21.8   Responsories *Lapis iste* and *Amplius etherei*

Office of St. Thomas of Canterbury

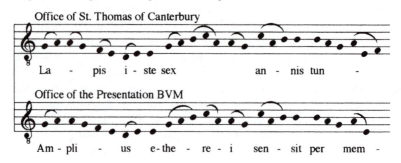

Office of the Presentation BVM

La - pis i - ste sex   an - nis tun -

Am - pli - us e - the - re - i   sen - sit per   mem -

St. Thomas

Presentation

di - tur sic po-li   -   tur

bra   vi - go - ris

St. Thomas

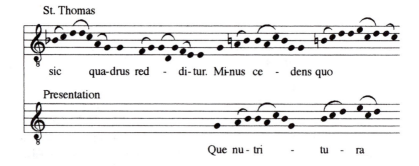

Presentation

sic   qua-drus red - di-tur. Mi-nus ce - dens quo

Que nu - tri - tu - ra

vigoris is applied to music that formerly accompanied the single word *tunditur*, and *corpus genitoris* is set to the melody that had accompanied *ceditur*, so that the impact of these two melismas in the original is lessened or lost in the adaptation. The uneven halves of the verse text yield unfortunate results in the adaptation, since the median cadence point on *b* at *uritur* is ignored by the adaptor, who placed *roris* under the *agac* figure before this cadence point. The median cadence point, which should be a significant structural entity, simply forms part of the beginning of the subsequent textual phrase. In this instance the adaptor, by eliminating a significant amount of music from the responsory and by altering the verse struc-ture, radically changes our perception of the piece itself in the process of adapta-

Example 21.8   (*continued*)

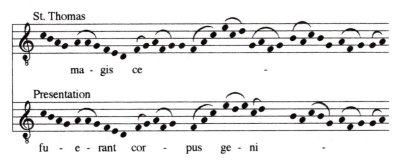

St. Thomas

ma - gis   ce   -

Presentation

fu – e - rant   cor   -   pus   ge - ni   -

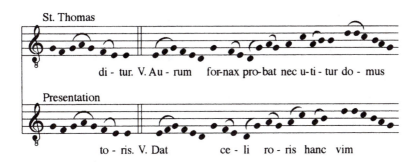

St. Thomas

di - tur. V. Au - rum   for-nax pro-bat nec u-ti - tur do - mus

Presentation

to - ris. V. Dat   ce - li   ro - ris hanc vim

St. Thomas

fir - ma   ven - tis non   qua-ti - tur.   Mi- nus   ce - dens.

Presentation

si - mul   ac - ti - o   flo   -   ris.   Que.

tion. Moreover, this changed perception occurs as a result of metrical demands imposed by a rather peculiar text.

The responsory *Unam quam petii*, example 21.9, is textually an interpolation of Ps. 26:4, "One thing I ask, this I seek, to dwell in the presence of the Lord," appropriately referring now to Mary's presence in the temple. It is also curious in that the text does not really rhyme, although its musical characteristics conform to the traits of a rhymed Office responsory. Its music is the same as that of the responsory *Stirps Yesse* from the Office of the Nativity of Mary (also used for the feast of St. Anne), also in Mainz Carmelite MS D. *Stirps Yesse* is a fairly common text, used in four of the twelve sources investigated by Hesbert in his *CAO*,[31] either for the

Example 21.9   Responsories *Stirps Yesse* and *Unam quam petii*

Example 21.9 (*continued*)

Nativity BVM

Presentation

Nativity BVM

mus.   V. Vir - go de - i ge-ni-trix vir-ga   est flos fi - li-us

Presentation

plum.   V. Sit mi - chi vel-le su-um po-te-rit   me - li - us fo-re

(*continued*)

Assumption or Nativity of the Virgin. Its text is poetic but not rhymed, which perhaps provided the reason for the Carmelites to select it for adaptation.[32] The text of *Unam quam petii* is slightly longer than that of *Stirps Yesse*, but its overall construction is different:

R. Stirps Yesse virgam produxit virgaque florem	13
et super hunc florem requiescit spiritus almus.	15
V. Virgo dei genitrix virga est flos filius eius. Et.	16
R. Unam quam petii placet	8
ut sine fine requiram	8
A domino sanctum	6
Quod sit michi mansio templum.	9
V. Sit michi velle suum poterit	10
melius fore votum. A domino.	7

The responsory *Stirps Yesse*, composed by Fulbert of Chartres, features a melody often associated with rhymed or at least metrical Offices. Textually the two parts of the verse line differ greatly in length, having ten and six syllables respectively, but they fit the melody in a manner that properly conveys the sense of the text: "The virgin mother of God is the shoot and the flower is her son."

Example 21.9   (*continued*)

Nativity BVM

Presentation

Nativity BVM

Presentation

Nativity BVM

Presentation

The text of the Presentation verse only digresses from this model by one syllable, conveniently adapted by using the words *Sit michi* to the same music as *virgo*.
The musical adaptation is changed and even flawed, however: while the original
first phrase of the verse correctly ended on the *d* final at *est,* this final *d* falls on the
first syllable of *melius* in the adapted version. In adapting this Nativity BVM chant
to the new text the redactor changed the melodic structure of the first phrase to
end on *e* at *poterit* rather than on *d* on the first syllable of *melius,* thereby altering

the structure of the verse itself. As for the responsory, the florid style of *Stirps Yesse* facilitates the accommodation of a slightly longer text to the same music, as is illustrated in the opening line of text, for example. The musical lines are changed in the adaptation because of the sense of the text, rather than for strictly metrical considerations; despite some differences in melodic contour, phrases of the new text end on *e* at *placet* and *d* at *requiram,* paralleling the *e* at *produxit* and *d* at *florem* in the original, so that there really is no great shift of tonal center that would change the structure of the responsory itself.

Example 21.10 compares the responsory *Hodie Marie Jacobi* from the Office of the Three Marys, as found in Florence, Carmine O, with the responsory *Anna parens* from the Presentation Office. The texts are as follows:

R. Hodie Marie Jacobi et Salome	13
solemnitas celebratur.	8
Quarum solemnitate	7
celum gloriatur	6
quarum patrociniis	7
terra testatur.	5
Quarum gloriosis meritis	9
ecclesia coronatur.	8
V. Ad earum igitur memoriam	11
totis viribus percurramus	9
ut ipsarum consortes	7
effici valeamus.	7
R. Anna parens clausa	6
natam parit	4
arte creatis.	5
Natam brevi pausa.	6
Natum parit	4
omnia dantis.	5
V. Corda facit	4
ausa veniam	5
rogitare beatis.	7

Not only are the metrical lines radically shorter in the Presentation text than in the Three Marys one, yielding also a much shorter textual product, but the rhyme scheme is clearly in a three-part rather than a two-part structure. Thus the textual lines of *Hodie Marie* divide into couplets while those of *Anna parens* divide into triplets. This textually different construction predictably extends to the music as well:

In the verse neither text conforms to a predictable melodic pattern, even one adapted for rhymed Office usage. In *Hodie Marie* one would expect the first phrase to end at *percurramus* on the *a* that falls on its first syllable, rather than on the *e* at the end of the word, since this *e* clearly belongs at the beginning of the second phrase of the verse. In the adaptation the repeated notes are eliminated; if the melody of the verse formula (or its substitute in the rhymed Office verse) were followed, the first phrase would end on the *a* in the middle of *veniam* rather than

Example 21.10   Responsories *Hodie Marie* and *Anna parens clausa*

Office of the Three Marys

Ho - di-e   Ma-ri-e Ia - co-bi et   Sa - lo-me so - le -

Office of the Presentation BVM

An - na   pa - rens   clau - sa na-tam

Three Marys

mni - tas ce-le-bra - tur. Qua-rum   so - lem-ni-ta - te   ce -

Presentation

pa - rit   ar   -   te cre   -   a   -

Three Marys

lum glo   -   ri - a   -   tur qua-rum pa-tro-ci - ni-is

Presentation

tis. Na-tam   bre - vi   pau - sa

on the *e* at the end of it. The brevity of *Corda facit* and *ausa veniam* allows them to be linked by the *a* that ends the first phrase and begins the second, effectively merging these two textually distinct phrases into a single musical one. A similar refashioning of musical phrases occurs within the responsory itself. While the ending on *a* at *clausa* in the Presentation case conforms to the ending of *Salome* in the Three Marys instance, the clear ending of *celebratur* on *f* in the model occurs in the middle of the word *arte* in the adaptation, whose phrase ultimately ends on *d* at the following word *creatis*, conforming to the word *celum* in the model, itself the middle of a phrase that ends on the following word *gloriatur*. Thus the divisions of

Example 21.10   (*continued*)

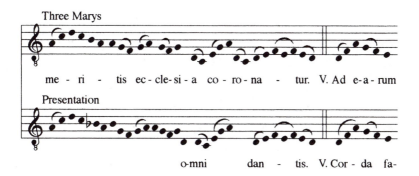

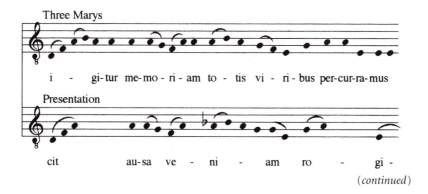

(*continued*)

musical and textual phrases become quite different between the model and its adapted version. The contours of musical phrases in the Three Marys example suggest that it may itself have been adapted from a preexisting model, since what seems to be a cadential point in this model sometimes occurs within a textual phrase.

This example of adaptation is the clearest instance of musical phrases being refashioned to accommodate a different textual situation, so that the very structure of the piece is radically altered. The use of a tripartite rhyming phrase structure

Example 21.10   (*continued*)

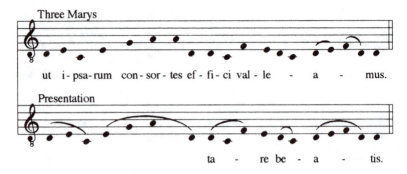

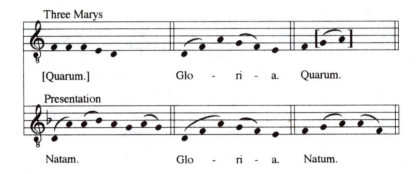

also must be accommodated to a normal two-phrase pattern, most clearly illustrated in the responsory verse but present in the responsory itself as well.

    The textual traits discussed above in a restricted number of examples give an idea of the variety of styles operative in compiling the Carmelite Office of the Presentation of Mary. The range of methods for adapting a chant from an old Office to a newer text included patterning the newer text on the old to facilitate a direct syllable-for-syllable text underlay, as in the antiphon *Pastor dives in celi solio* (example 21.1), to the case of *Annam vocatam gratiam,* where the text is different but the adaptation still parallels the music of the old antiphon (example 21.2). The use of some larger chants of the St. Thomas Office in which a 4 + 6 syllable metrical line prevailed necessitated considerable adjustment in concept, since the Presentation pieces had a totally different metrical structure. In the case of *Cornu salutis hodie* (example 21.4) a strong rhyme scheme and definite but different meter with a longer total text than that of the model required considerable alteration in the phrase structure of the music. A similar accommodation proved necessary in the responsory *Germen produxit stirps* (example 21.5) even though the rhyme scheme is much less clear than in example 21.4. In this case the imprecise rhyme in the interior sections forces us to think in terms of the larger phrase, which in fact conforms to the model from the St. Thomas Office. The responsories *Ex Yoachim primam* (example 21.6) and *O vite vitis* (example 21.7) both feature a compressed textual style, the first one not rhymed and the second one rhymed. In both cases the metrical pattern is much less defined than that of the model in the St. Thomas Office, yielding a very free accommodation of melody to new text.

The two instances of chants being adapted from Offices other than the St. Thomas one include an unrhymed model, *Stirps Yesse,* set to a melody normally characterizing a rhymed text (example 21.9) and *Hodie Marie,* the only chant used as a model identified as coming from a source outside the Mainz Carmelite manuscripts (example 21.10). In both cases the adaptation process is very free, yielding a different phrase structure in the adaptation from the model. The metrically imprecise text of *Unam quam petii* (example 21.9) minimizes the changes involved in the adaptation since neither the model nor the product is rhymed. On the other hand, in example 21.10, where both the model *Hodie Marie* and the product *Anna parens clausa* have very strong and different patterns of meter and rhyme, the changes in phrase structure from model to product become glaringly apparent. Thus the techniques used in adapting established chants to this new Office vary widely, from a literal syllable-to-syllable identification to a much more fluid approach that in the process alters our perception of the melody itself. This in turn invites further questions about the Carmelite and other approaches to these rhymed Offices.

The freedom with which these chants have been adapted into a new textual situation, one whose structure is often totally different from the original, leads further to questions about the adaptation process itself. Within the Franciscan tradition, for example, the extensive musical training and renown of the composer of the St. Francis Office, Julian of Speyer,[33] impelled the Franciscans to use his Office as a model for the subsequent ones of Sts. Clare, Louis of Anjou, Elizabeth of Hungary, and the Trinity, which they ensured by composing the texts to conform syllabically to the model. By the careful textual conformity of the adapted Office to the model they ensured that no additional musical creativity would be required. This generally holds true for at least some of the Offices within the Dominican tradition. Clearly the choice of model was significant in terms of the adaptation, where the least amount of change would ensure the preservation of the valued original musical product. Owain Edwards has established some of the alterations required in the St. David Office, whose textual lines did not particularly conform to the 4 + 6 pattern of textual lines in many pieces from the St. Thomas original.[34]

The Carmelite Presentation Office is written in the same musical and textual hands as the other Offices in the manuscript, so that, if it had not already become established in the Office repertoire of the Mainz Carmelites by the time of writing of the codex, its insertion into the manuscript would then make it an official part of their chant. The distinctive nature of the poetic text, with varying styles of rhyme and metrical patterns, clearly created some problems in adapting the music from the St. Thomas Office in terms of length of line and organization of textual units, with the result that in many instances the new chant is structurally different from the original model. The text used for the Presentation Office, while compressed in style and sometimes convoluted in approach, nonetheless reflected a contemplative approach to the event that must characterize a Carmelite approach to the feast. Clearly it was held in enough esteem that they adapted a series of chants for it. In selecting the St. Thomas Office as a model they chose a well-respected, widely disseminated, and popular series of chants as a model for their own new texts. If one may pose questions about the success of the result, one has to ask whether melodic structure and balance of phrase were inherently apparent to the performers and listeners and to what extent the close corroboration between text and music was a value for the Carmelites of the fifteenth century. Might it have sufficed to have a well-respected series of melodies and a reasonably well-regarded series of texts which, when merged, created a new and distinctively Carmelite product? Presumably had the Carmelites of Mainz been composers on the level of a Julian of Speyer they might have attempted to compose a new series of melodies for the new texts. Instead, choosing established melodies for adaptation enabled them to concentrate on theological rather than musical considerations.

The meditative quality of the texts created a sense of contemplation of the Presentation event in keeping with the general thrust of the Order's spirituality, while the assimilation of chants from more than one Office and more than one locale produced an entirely new liturgical entity. The use of source material from more than one existing Office and from two liturgical locales ensures that the Mainz Codex D Office of the Presentation is a distinctively Carmelite creation, since only they would have access to and interest in the source material. By such creativity and industry the Carmelites of Mainz not only paid fitting tribute to the Virgin Mary by their implementation of the Order's mandate to celebrate the Office of her Presentation, but in so doing they made a significant contribution to the liturgical life of the city of Mainz as well as to their own Carmelite liturgical tradition.

Notes

1. For a discussion of the term and practice, cf. Falck and Picker (1980). The term as used in this context refers simply to applying a new text to an established liturgical melody.

2. Epstein (1978) has demonstrated this for chants within the Dominican tradition. The fact that the Office of St. Francis of Assisi served as a model for later Franciscan ones is well known. Cf. Felder (1901), Wagner (1986), 269–71, and O. Edwards (1992).

3. The apostolic letter "Quae honorem Conditoris," issued by Pope Innocent IV on 1 October 1247 promulgated the revised Carmelite rule. Cf. Clarke and Edwards, *Rule of Saint Albert*, 23–24.

4. Zimmerman, *Ordinaire*. Zimmerman's edition is based on the manuscript London, Lambeth 193, which he judges (p. v) to date from around 1320. Kallenberg (1962), 104–18, also discusses the several manuscript sources for this ordinal. I discuss the Carmelite Office tradition itself in Boyce (1984 and 1990a). Sibert's ordinal is similar to an earlier English Carmelite ordinal from the end of the thirteenth century, Rushe (1912–13); once promulgated, however, Sibert's ordinal became normative for use throughout the Order, not just in one country.

5. This feast was accepted into the Carmelite rite by the General Chapter of Toulouse in 1306; see Kallenberg (1962), 25, and Forcadell (1954), 184.

6. Humbert's Codex is the compilation of liturgical service books for the Dominican rite, whose primary exemplar is Rome, Santa Sabina XIV L 1; London, BL Add. 23935 is the portable copy of this codex to be used by the Master General to correct the text and music of the local service books when he visited each convent. Cf. Bonniwell (1945), esp. pp. 85–97.

7. The Florentine Carmelite Office manuscripts are discussed in Kallenberg (1962), 247–56, and Boyce (1988a and 1986). They are included in the catalogue of manuscripts of the San Marco Museum (Chiarelli 1968). The three manuscripts from the Carmine of Florence (Florence, Carmine MSS N, O, and P) have not been catalogued.

8. The Mainz Carmelite Office manuscripts are discussed in Kallenberg (1962), 256–59, and in Boyce (1987 and 1986). Vaassen (1973) discusses them from an art-historical point of view.

9. Kallenberg (1962) mentioned these two antiphonals but doubted their Carmelite authenticity. In Boyce (1990b) I established that they are in fact genuinely Carmelite.

10. The complete texts for the inaugural celebration of the Presentation feast have been published in Coleman (1981). For a history of the feast itself cf. Pfaff (1970), esp. 103–15. Kishpaugh (1941) provides a good overview of the early history of this feast, as well as a detailed study of its literary origins. For a recent discussion of the *Fons hortorum* Office, including its relationship to that of St. Dominic, see A. Hughes (1999).

11. These chants are found on fols. 64v–66v. For a discussion of this feast in the Florentine tradition, cf. Boyce (1984), 1:160; the chants are edited in 2:260–66.

12. Thus MS B has an inscription dating the manuscript to 1432, and a single leaf, now Munich, BS clm. 29 164/13, which has been established as missing from Codex A, has the same inscription but the date of 1430; cf. Arens (1958–60), 341–45. One can presume that the set of antiphonals was composed in the years immediately following 1430.

13. The Presentation Office in Codex D is entirely distinct from Mainz diocesan usage, which used the *Fons hortorum* Office in Aschaffenburg, SB Perg. 1, fols. 199v–203v; cf. Boyce (1987), 289–90. The feast itself did not enter the Mainz diocesan liturgy until 1468, after the time of the writing of Codex D; cf. Falk (1902), 543–53.

14. For instance, the prescriptions for the feast of the Conception of the Virgin on p. 267 of Sibert's Ordinal begin thus: "In Conceptione vel potius Veneratione sanctificationis beatae Virginis, sicut totum duplex. Ad Vesperas ant. *Haec est regina.* Ps. *Laudate pueri,* et ceterae ad ceteros sicut in Annuntiatione."

15. I pointed out the significance of these standardized Marian Vespers antiphons in Boyce (1990a). Their allegiance to the rite of the Holy Sepulchre is illustrated by a transitional thirteenth-century breviary, now Paris, BNF lat. 10478, where these antiphons are used for all Marian feasts.

16. For instance, Jorga (1896), 511, n. 2, discusses the relationship between Philippe de Mézières and the Carmelites of Paris; cf. also Smet (1954).

17. These two manuscripts, described in Delisle, *Inventaire,* form the basis for William Coleman's textual edition of the ceremonies for the Western inauguration of the feast of the Presentation. I discuss the discrepancies between the versions of the Office from lat. 17330 and lat. 14454 in Boyce (1993b).

18. The *gesta* have been edited in Coleman (1981), 73–78.

19. The relationship between the chant texts of this Office and the *Gesta de presentatione sancte Marie virginis* in Philippe's Office is discussed in Boyce (1991), 241–44.

20. Edwards, *Matins* discusses the parallels; see esp. 159–66.

21. Richard De Grey of Codnor, according to his contemporary, the Franciscan Thomas of Eccleston, brought the Carmelites to England and founded the monastery of Aylesford in 1242; see Egan (1969 and 1972).

22. The liturgical prescriptions for the feast of St. Thomas of Canterbury are found in Zimmerman, *Ordinaire,* 123–24, and Rushe (1912–13), 100–1.

23. The chants are found on fols. 151v–165, and are edited in Boyce (1984), 2:1–32.

24. The complete text and music of both Mainz and Florence Carmelite versions of this Office have been published in Boyce (1989).

25. Sibert's prescription is as follows: "Sanctae Annae matris gloriosae Virginis. Fes-

tum duplex. Ad matutinum lectiones de aliqua propria legenda vel de sermone. Cetera omnia sicut in communi unius matronae." Zimmerman, *Ordinaire,* 236.

26. "Item ordinamus, quod de Beata Anna fiat per totam Ordinem memoria de B. Anna ad Vesperas et Matutinum." Wessels, *Acta,* 1:145.

27. The Office of St. Anne is found on fols. 226–239v of MS C; the chants are edited in Boyce (1984), 2:126–53.

28. The rhymed Office of St. Mary of Salome is found in Vatican City, BAV Vat. lat. 10781, a fifteenth-century antiphonary from Veroli, an Italian town located south of Rome and north of Cassino; it is edited in Boyce (1988b).

29. Andrew Hughes (1983) discusses the implications of the modal organization of antiphons and responsories.

30. Edwards, *Matins* discusses the music for the chants in chap. 3 and discusses the modal ordering of chants on pp. 94–96.

31. *CAO* 4:419. The sources are R, D, F, and L and the citation is *CAO* 7709.

32. Robertson (1988), esp. p. 11, has pointed out the significance of this responsory in terms of the application of its "Flos filius ejus" melisma to the *Benedicamus domino* chant, prescribed as early as the time of Peter the Venerable, around 1146.

33. For a discussion of the early life and musical training of Julian of Speyer, cf. Miskuly (1989), especially 93–97.

34. Of the seven responsories for the Office of St. David derived from that of St. Thomas, only one imitated the model in length and rhythmic structure; cf. Edwards (1992), esp. 511–14 for this discussion.

VI ✦ THE OFFICE AND COMPUTERS

Large Projects and Small Resources

Late Medieval Liturgical Offices

ANDREW HUGHES

A Preamble Written in 1998

In revisiting this chapter after more than five years, I was struck by how archaic even the technological events of yesterday now seem. Five years in the publishing world is an eternity in which nothing (apparently) happens. In those same years the computing world has been revolutionized. I speak of limitations in megabytes: disks now regularly hold multigigabytes. I speak of programs taking 24 hours to complete: on my newest machine, four hours is probably more realistic. ASCII encoding has now been replaced by ANSI codes, which future implementations may need to use. Filenames are no longer restricted to eight characters. Program manuals barely exist, replaced by inadequate on-line HELP screens. Software manufacturers I allude to may have gone out of business. To complement such features with up-to-date information would falsify and confuse the account. Fortunately, the results that can be obtained from the data to be described remain just as valid and potentially useful.

A scholar who has exhaustively studied and concluded a manageable piece of scholarship—say, an edition and commentary on a single Office of the late Middle Ages—usually finds it necessary to draw general conclusions. The need to relate the material to its context is natural, and perhaps irresistible. It is of course important eventually to carry out this final step. But in some cases, and the vast repertory of late medieval Offices is one, our knowledge is so slim, still so slim, that generalization must be avoided.

Of the repertory I began to investigate some decades ago, for instance, perhaps one percent has been published in satisfactory editions.[1] That repertory—the repertory of rhymed Offices[2]—is perhaps, at a guess, a third of the surviving corpus of newly-composed late medieval Offices in general. Who knows the extent of the late medieval Office corpus? I estimate that some 10,000 Office manuscripts survive. No one can with certainty make statements such as "this Office is (a)typical." Only by comparing it with what we know of the rest of the repertory and with other repertories can a scholar make such claims.

My long-term aim has always been to try to see as much as possible of the larger picture. That aim started with the rhymed repertory. Although the difference between a fully rhymed Office in regularly accentual or Classical meters and one wholly in prose may be obvious, any number of intermediate types exists (see Andrew Hughes 1995). To complicate matters, a single Office may contain items ranging from one extreme to the other. It has become clearer, as it should perhaps have been from the start, that the large picture must include the non-rhymed repertory.

If it was not clear at the beginning what should be included in the repertory as a whole, neither was it possible to predict what ought to be included in a database of late medieval liturgical Offices, other than the texts and chants themselves, nor how the material should be arranged. The incredibly varied and complex nature of the Offices and material ancillary to studying them will become apparent in the paragraphs below. The choice was between ease of use and maximal usefulness, between minimal information in a well-established format and fuller information in a necessarily compressed presentation. Naturally, as knowledge of the material accumulated and more interesting features were recognized, the tendency was to be increasingly inclusive.

Briefly, then, the project eventually encompassed, and the resulting publication incorporates in electronic form, these elements: (1) a Catalogue of some 1500 Offices; (2) the complete texts of those Offices;[3] (3) encoding of the complete chants of the Dominican Antiphonal; (4) encoding of the chants of some 100 rhymed Offices; (5) information about and inventories of some 3,000 Office manuscripts. Eventually, the collecting and organizing of all this material had to come to an end in favor of distributing it for use. For better or worse, all the available data have now been released, with comprehensive discussions of methods for working with liturgical material using the computer. I shall refer to this publication as *LMLO*.[4]

In this chapter, I have three principal purposes:

1. To outline a brief history of the project, and to explain some of its characteristics and the constraints that have shaped its progress and the results.[5] Here, I shall deal with the evolution of the database and describe some of the tools used to manage it. I shall also provide reasons for many features that appear in both the data and in the Catalogue, and take the opportunity to explain more fully the need for so many abbreviations and symbols. Even this exposition, however, cannot be comprehensive: the list of short forms in *LMLO Texts* alone runs to some 30 pages.
2. To introduce what is now available, and to show briefly how the electronic evidence may be used and applied to a range of problems and questions that will determine to some extent how a forthcoming general narrative introduction might be shaped.[6]
3. To draw some general conclusions about projects of this kind and the kinds of changes in scholarly and publishing procedures that may result from the new technologies.

Managing the Late Medieval Office Project

As a consequence of circumstances already mentioned, the history of managing the project has been one of constant change. This format or that method changed as a piece of new information or a new element or a new constraint made the existing procedure inadequate. I cite three examples:

- Methods of referring concisely to the elements of Offices proved inadequate for those of Ambrosian Offices. The latter came to my attention after many years of working with methods firmly established in an already massive database;
- the formatting of some elements of the almost complete database had to be changed globally upon discovering that the commercial software for which the data were prepared was no longer affordable and could not be distributed with the data. This was discovered just before the material was to go to press;
- an obligatory change in word-processors forced other changes in the way the data were entered.

Over the period of nearly three decades during which this project has been gathering momentum, advances in computer technology alone have necessitated similar revisions.

History

Initially, the data were entered onto 8-inch disks on a machine designed essentially for the storage and sorting of business documents. The machine had minimal editing capability. The original intention was to transfer those data to the university mainframe for indexing and other analytical procedures. Even small samples repeatedly caused the mainframe computer to crash, since it was then unable to handle the "huge" amounts of data—i.e., a half-million bytes, the size of a single large file nowadays—brought by this strange humanist. Those occurrences, and the obvious fact that my total grant would be gone after several seconds of using the facilities of the Computer Centre, drove the project onto personal machines.

Astonishing though it seems now, the first alphabetized vocabulary list, including a frequency count for each word, was produced on a homemade computer, with 64K of memory and no hard disk. That list ran to 219 pages of four neatly-formatted columns, each with 56 words: some 50,000 unique words in all. Needless to say, there was no ready-made software at the time capable of doing the job.

Need more be said to justify why many elements of the repertory were in extremely compressed form? As the simple statistic in the previous paragraph shows, about two-thirds of the present database of texts was already in machine-readable form before it was moved to a more modern system. Much could of course now be expanded and made more easy to read. Once again, however, some bald facts must be remembered. Let us take an example. The formula =WE standing for "the Magnificat antiphon for Second Vespers" occurs some 860 times. At an increase of some 40 characters for a full expansion, an extra 34,000 characters are added. This is not much, until it is multiplied by 30 for each other item of an Office, and then by six for ancillary and backup files. An extra six million characters, six megabytes, of disk space are required. Within a single Office perhaps another twenty formulas might need similar expansion. As I revised this chapter in 1999, six megabytes now seems trivial given the gargantuan size that text and database files nowadays can reach. But there is still a human limit to the size of a file that can with ease be edited repeatedly.

And with greatly expanded memory and storage capabilities has come an increase in the amount of space (exclusive of the data) that a file takes on disk and greatly expanded program size. Even now the data threaten to overwhelm quite large hard disks. And despite the great increase in processing speed of present-day personal computers, the bottleneck of loading and storing to disks alone can render editing and processing of huge files very time-consuming. To produce the comprehensive poetic analysis that accompanies every single text in the repertory, for example, most recently took some 20–24 hours of continuous processing. Later passages in this chapter will describe what files and what data are available, from which the reader can extrapolate the number and size of the files involved.

Need more be said to justify why so many elements of the data remain in highly compressed form? Perhaps not. But setting out one more reason will allow another aspect of the formatting to be explained. There are 64 files of raw textual data. Each is duplicated in a file with additional information. To expand elements of data spread over 128 files requires either extraordinarily tedious editing file by file or the ability to make global changes on multiple files while remaining certain that the changes are what was intended. In neophyte computer days, I decided to change all the Classical spellings to medieval, doing the job globally: the result included the words *Isrel, Ne* and *er.* When it is necessary to isolate all virgin saints, it is easier to search for " ,v" than for "virgin", which could find *virginibus* and similar forms. Automated global changes can be made only with data that are without question defined uniquely. Three methods may be used to achieve this end: (1) when abbreviations or formulas are used, unique characters can be attached to them; (2) the patterning within a formula can be distinctive; (3) the contextual position can be rigidly maintained. It was necessary to use all three methods in this repertory.

Ambiguity is a danger not only for global changes, but an inconvenience for the user: a distinction between V for Vespers and V for verse, for example, is necessary. Since computer searches allow lowercase letters to find both lower- and uppercase letters, it is also unfortunate if v stands for versicle. The assignation of a unique character to distinct elements of the data facilitates global editing and visual inspection of the data. For obvious reasons, such characters cannot be letters or numerals. The more esoteric symbols now available with most word-processors were not easily available when the formats were established, and are inconvenient even now. The symbols must therefore be those of the common typewriter variety, such as punctuation signs. Using punctuation for such purposes makes difficult its use in the data. But more of that later.

The evolution of a database

Careful use of unique characters also allows the user to seek specific elements without retrieving unwanted material. Such characters are sometimes known as tags. Elements uniquely defined by tags (sometimes called tagged fields) can be isolated and extracted from the data relatively easily by appropriate finding programs or even by some sophisticated word-processors.

Extracting and arranging various elements of data are functions of database programs. Many such programs operate without tagged fields, using data uncontaminated by the proprietary codes that word-processors often insert. Many excellent database programs exist. Why, then, are the Office data not organized in a conventional database? Firstly, of course, because such programs were not available, at least for personal computers, when the data were first entered. Secondly, even nowadays no database program, to my knowledge, is even remotely capable of handling the complexities and varied nature of these data. It is difficult to be certain, without great expenditure to purchase each program for experimentation. Required, at least, are the following functions: an unlimited number of fields of unlimited length; the ability to index, sort, and search on every field; the ability to use almost any symbol in any position; the ability to handle "words" with hundreds of characters and no spaces. Even the most sophisticated word-processors are hard put to manage some of these criteria. Perhaps there are now adequate word-processors and databases. But the effort of massive global transformation would be daunting, to say nothing of the huge risks of contamination and error involved in the process.

The data, then, are set out so as to be accessible by means of straightforward searching and extracting functions, perhaps enhanced by the macro abilities of most word-processors.

Here, however, there lies another difficulty. The data use only typewriter characters, spaces, and tabs. Since the meaning of ASCII or DOS as descriptors for generic text files of this kind is, in my experience, inconsistent and not widely understood, I set out in the next note some details of these terms. The importing and exporting of files by major word-processors, even in so-called DOS or ASCII format, can result in unwanted changes.[7]

To my knowledge, only one sophisticated word-processor, *Nota Bene,* handles and edits typewriter-character files so that they remain in a state that the indexing programs require. Until recently, I believe, this word-processor was maintained by a small group of programmers concerned essentially with academic and bibliographical pursuits. It is, perhaps, another example of a major project being undertaken with small resources: in the first release of version 4, *Nota Bene* had not overcome the major bugs to be expected after a major revision. Sadly, because it is full of marvelous potential for the scholar and bibliographer, I have ceased using it except to maintain the textual data. To have to abandon it completely would require a huge revision of the data. In a recent updating of version 4 of *Nota Bene* the problems seem to have corrected.

The indexing and other programs

After a brief flirtation with an indexing program called *Cocoa*, I was forced by the move to personal computers to find another indexer-concording program.

WordCruncher, associated with Brigham Young University and in version 4 released by The Electronic Text Corporation, has extraordinarily flexible indexing and viewing capabilities. It will allow exact specification of the function of 254 characters (out of 256) of the ASCII series. Thus, specified characters may turn the indexing on and off; others may serve as apostrophes or hyphens, indexed or not; some may serve as delimiters. This flexibility allows the indexing and sorting of such "words" as :F..N (for France, Normandy) or, in the music files, dominus. 123'4<%-.9>2*.3=4 where the musical pitches are specified. The user can set different sort orders, allowing for foreign letters, even such as the double-l in Spanish.

The viewing and reporting part of the program is equally flexible. It allows contextual viewing on screen of single words, of words with wildcards, of phrases, of words within specified sections of text. Statistical analyses can be carried out. Various kinds of index such as book-style and keyword in context can be saved to disk or printed. Ancillary files with other useful information may be produced.

Despite the great flexibility of its indexing routines, revising the data to meet the requirements of this program necessitated some unfortunate compromises. Some of these are described in *LMLO* and need not be repeated here. The most serious from the standpoint of the user was the inability of the program, in the version available at the time, to take formulas such as =MA3 (Matins antiphon 3) as one of the indexing levels: these had to be represented by a purely numerical code.

Unfortunately, the license under which the viewing routines could be distributed *with* the data became unaffordable, just as the electronic data were about to go to press. May one suspect again that this program, a large and complex project to maintain, and extraordinarily flexible and useful for humanists, is supported by inadequate resources?

Fortunately, however, the data can be viewed, and searched, and used in many ways without the complex and sophisticated indexing of *WordCruncher;* and alternative indexing and viewing programs are available. Two of these are free, although not without limitations to be described.

1. Word-processors. Even a word-processor can serve useful purposes, especially if it can search multiple files with a single command. Users must take care, however, not to allow such programs to corrupt the format of the data. Working with copies of the files would be the safest method.
   - *WordPerfect,* for instance, has suitable searching and indexing routines. Searching with Boolean alternatives (*and* and *or* and *but not,* for example) is somewhat limited. Its ability to produce printed results in typographically superlative manner is probably without equal.
   - *MultiEdit,* manufactured by American Cybernetics, 1830 W. University Drive, #112, Tempe, AZ 85281, can easily search multiple files, and has

the extraordinary flexibility of regular expressions to allow very complex searches. Boolean alternatives can be handled with regular expressions, but are limited practically. Its ability to produce nicely printed results is less developed.

2. Searching programs. Quite inexpensive, and in constant use for quick searches, is *The Text Collector,* manufactured by O'Neill Software, P.O. Box 26111, San Francisco, CA 94126. It is very fast, and handles multiple files easily. It has quite flexible Boolean alternatives, although limited in the practical sense by length.

3. Concordance programs.

- *KLIC.* Foreseeing difficulties with commercial programs, I wrote a concordance program specifically designed for this repertory. *KLIC* produces files with KeyLetters In Context, and has quite flexible routines tailored to allow wildcard searches. Searches may be limited by various Boolean alternatives based on the elements present in the information section that precedes the text itself. The whole keyword can be shown. Because this program does not depend on indexed files, it must search the data serially, and is thus relatively slow.

- *TACT.* The Centre for Computing and the Humanities at the University of Toronto has produced its own index-concorder, *TACT* (Text Analysis Computing Tools), now in version 2.1.[8] Developed by academics and staff of the University, all of whom have other responsibilities, it is certainly another example of a major project, full of marvelous potential, being maintained with small resources. Able to read and index various formats, fortunately including that used by *WordCruncher,*[9] it produces similar kinds of indexes, on the screen and to disk, as *WordCruncher* and with similar kinds of flexible search patterns.

  Despite some flaws, with care and experience the program is useful, and produces extremely unusual files: lists of anagrams, collocation tables, dictionaries, frequency tables, and statistical summaries. For some of these purposes alone, *TACT* is perhaps unique.

- *CHNTSRCH.* This program for SeaRCHing the ChaNT (that is, the musical pitches encoded with their texts), released with *LMLO* and named to fit the older DOS convention for filenames, is designed to allow manipulations of the files that encode the plainsongs. It will allow the extraction and concording of melodic motives and melismas according to numerous criteria such as mode, genre, feasts, season, and position in the chant. Coordinating such motives with the texts to which they are set may be more easily accomplished by using lists of chantwords and the other musical data provided in the files (see the section on *Ancillary chant information* in *LMLO: Sources & Chants,* 180–82).

Even with the programs most users will have in everyday use, the data can be searched and examined. For concording, *TACT* is free, and usable in many ways: *KLIC* and *CHNTSRCH* were made for these data, and are included for no extra charge. For more complex searching, *Text Collector* is flexible and inexpensive,

MultiEdit is even more flexible, but (since it is really a sophisticated text editor) relatively expensive. *WordCruncher* makes easy the most sophisticated and reliable searches and concordances.

Other constraints

A few other constraints may be mentioned, since in describing them other characteristics of the format are clarified.[10]

Rather than working with the files of the database proper, some of which run to 200,000 bytes, adding new data is most conveniently done in smaller files, Office by Office. To identify particular files among the many hundred that are relevant, I began to use other sets of abbreviations.

Filenames.   In DOS, Filenames are restricted to eight letters and numbers and a few symbols. The extension (maximum of three characters after a dot) that could help to distinguish groups of files carries with it risks. THOMAS.TXT and THOMAS.@ might be used for the textual and analytical data, respectively, for example. Unfortunately, editing the first will leave the original data in THOMAS.BAK: subsequent editing of the second will cause that backup text to be overwritten by the backup of the analytical data. The filename itself must carry the essential information.

The system adopted was as follows. Four characters, usually two letters followed by two numerals, identify an Office. Except when a feast was identified incorrectly (a very common occurrence with obscure saints) or "re-identified," the letters generally begin the alphabetical name of the feast. It was not possible to maintain this principle, and in retrospect a more extensible system would have been preferable. But the limit of four characters allowed qualifying symbols to be added in a visually clear way: e.g., TH21-Q@- contains an Office for Thomas of Canterbury and has the chants encoded (Q) and poetic analysis (@), but is not yet complete (-). This system was preserved only in working files and the more conventional method of distinguishing files by their extensions was used for the data issued with *LMLO*. Nevertheless, the principle of four-character identification remained.

The four-character identification for Offices was established very early in the project. One cannot continue for long to write or type Thomas of Canterbury, and the very varied length of feast names does not fit well into columnar presentation.[11] Naturally, the system became increasingly inadequate and yet increasingly hard to change, since it had filtered into hundreds of files, several computer programs, and even into print.

Placenames.   For similar reasons, a similar policy for referring to places, including the location of manuscripts, became necessary. In this case, a three-letter format representing country, city, and name-of-library formed the basis for the naming of files, and quickly became the standard method of referring to the places where manuscripts are located. These formulas, therefore, are not sigla for manuscripts, but for geographical places and features. Other systems of geographical sigla are inconvenient for computers and for sorting, and may be ambiguous amidst other similar formulations.[12]

But casual searching for ELL (England, London, Lambeth [Palace Library]) within the datafiles themselves would also find *bello* and similar words. To distinguish geographical sigla uniquely, each is preceded by a colon. For filenames, where it is illegal, the colon must be replaced by another suitable character.

Critics will say that abbreviations and formulaic representations must be unambiguous and consistent. Indeed, one critic has already noted an ambiguity (not deliberate or unwitting but unavoidable) in the publication that first set out some of the formulas that I use for liturgical reportage (Andrew Hughes, *Medieval Manuscripts*). In this repertory, especially when the musical coding is taken into account, there are not enough symbols to avoid ambiguity. Hence the need for different methods to achieve easily recognizable patterns, as outlined above. Furthermore, in the decades this project has been running, more than a score of student assistants have "assisted," often quite temporarily, yet exercising editorial initiative that was impossible completely to control because of my other university responsibilities. In this repertory, the variables are too many and too complex for firm policies regarding spelling and formatting and the like to have been established before many years of work had taken place. Even now, inadequacies sometimes require tinkering and unfortunate compromises.

Programming. To make programming and formatting simpler, formulas of a consistent length and pattern are useful. Hence, the pattern of letters and numbers to represent Offices, and of letters for geographical places. In such circumstances, it was important not to have, for example, V2A analogous to VA. Hence the adoption of W to represent Second Vespers, and strict positional patterns for Service (one letter) and Genre (one letter). Again, potential ambiguity arises. Is MA12 the twelfth antiphon of Matins, or the 12th Office for Maturinus? Hence a unique "liturgical" symbol, =, used where necessary to prevent ambiguity before or within specifications of liturgical genre: =MA12 (or, if showing that Matins has twelve antiphons, M=A12).

Printing. Printing the results of all of these decisions can itself be a nightmare. Difficulties in this process have caused other kinds of typographical and formulaic complexity. There are, I think, few serif fonts in which the numeral 1 and the lowercase l are clearly distinct, especially at the small point sizes that are sometimes necessary. O and zero may cause problems, as do 2 Z 5 S occasionally. In sans-serif fonts, the numeral 1 is usually distinct, but uppercase I and lowercase l are not. In the Catalogue of Offices in *LMLO*, printed in 8-point type for considerations of length,[13] a sans-serif font seemed most appropriate, being cleaner and less "fussy" than a serif font. Consider the formulas M=I and M=1, frequently to be found. Their contexts, it is true, clarify that the former is an I and the latter an l (for "Matins invitatory," and "the first item of Matins is a leonine hexameter"). Two solutions were available. The first involved substituting J for every I in the appropriate contexts (imagine an unsupervised global search and replace in these circumstances!). Not being used for any other genre, the J still remains as an alternative in desperate circumstances. The second alternative involved the preparation of a special font in which the lower case l was distinct. Only with computer technology would such an option be available for the ordinary author. In this process, I devised other useful characters not generally available (despite the 1,500 characters built into *WordPerfect*). Here are samples: A̷   R̷   V̷ (in both serif and sans-serif fonts) and 1 l I (in sans-serif). The differences in the latter group of characters are slight. In the 8-point type of the Catalogue 1 l and I may still be hard to distinguish. Careful inspection will be required. But the material itself of the Catalogue necessitates such inspection. No one will read the material as narrative: photocopying machines with enlarging functions are ubiquitous: trees may be endangered. And the two-volume *Oxford English Dictionary* came with a magnifying glass.

With these difficulties of precise and unconventional use of symbols, capitals, and abbreviations overcome, one encounters the copyeditor and the rules of the publishing house. . .

Summary.   As the reader who is not awash in confusion will have observed, it was not possible to maintain more than a few of these policies unmodified. Context is essential for quick and reliable identification of some formulas.

History and evolution. The end

No one could doubt, from the preceding paragraphs, that the project is extremely complex. Does this reflect the data? Is this why the Office liturgy has been less thoroughly investigated? To deal with the material adequately would, as the editor of *LMLO* cogently said, "consume all the intellectual and financial resources directed at it." To simplify the material, however, is almost as hard as to maintain it in its present state.

Fortunately, few will want or need to understand all the potential uses. I hope to have provided a tool from which scholars in many, many disciplines can learn something.

Using the Results

Let us pass to a review of what is now available in the material released with the publication of *LMLO*. I summarize the contents of the two volumes of *LMLO* so that potential users will understand the nature of the material, and need not purchase the volumes only to become frustrated with their electronic difficulties. Everything, including the texts of the volumes themselves, the Catalogue, the chant encodings, and the manuscript inventories, is provided in DOS format, so that it may be investigated without specialized proprietary software: any word-processor will be adequate. Nearly all of the electronic data are in frequent use, and various analytical procedures have been tested. I discuss some of the results.

LMLO *Texts*

The volume entitled *Texts* contains electronic editions, and a Catalogue of some 1,500 Offices. Methods of editing and presenting the texts in machine-readable form are discussed, as well as routines for indexing and producing statistical analyses and other tools.

The editions: playing with words.   Offices are provided in "generic" editions that may be manipulated for private use or, with appropriate permission and acknowledgments, be used as the basis for other kinds of published edition or analysis. They are set up, however, with the codes (in typewriter characters) that make indexing possible, and various pieces of software may be used to accomplish this process, and to produce concordances, frequency distributions, and keywords in context.

Every Office is provided with material identifying the liturgical date and the type of saint, a summary of the contents of each service and of the poetic styles of its texts, and miscellaneous other information.

Every item in every Office is identified as an antiphon or responsory, etc., and provided with a detailed analysis (produced by the computer) of the poetry, itemizing the rhyme schemes, number of syllables and words, and the number of letters, vowels, or consonants participating in the rhymes.

Using these data, and the additional information in the Catalogue (also searchable electronically), a vast range of questions may be addressed; some more easily than others.

I have, for example, discussed elsewhere the distribution in rhymed and other Offices of the topos of the wheat and the chaff (Andrew Hughes, Forthcoming (b)). It would be relatively easy to look into the association between various textual topics and specific genres. With some effort, the distribution and transmission of certain texts, or even substantial parts of Offices, could be traced.

A senior student at the Centre for Medieval Studies (University of Toronto), seeking a manageable subset of the rhymed repertory for investigation, has explored Gospel antiphons in Classical meters in Offices for confessors. Isolating this subrepertory was by no means simple. She sought to discover how the saint appears in these important items—vocatively, as in supplication to the saint, or descriptively with biographical details, or merely in a context votive in a more general way. Are the proper names in such texts accommodated to the requirements of Classical meters? Or are the meters themselves distorted? A good many commonplace liturgical phrases and terms, for instance the words *Iesu Christe,* cannot form a part of a hexameter.

The Catalogue of Offices.   The Catalogue of Offices is intended for a set of limited purposes:

1. To identify the saint or feast. Some difficulties of attribution remain, but I am satisfied that enough information is provided to facilitate further research.

2. To identify each Office clearly, using (as is usual medieval practice) the incipits of MR1 and LA1 (Matins responsory 1 and Lauds antiphon 1). The incipit of the first item is also given, as in much modern literature, although that item is so variable as to render identification of an Office by that means quite ambiguous.

3. To provide at least one source for the text. In most cases this will be *AH,* along with a summary of the medieval sources referred to in that edition. Often other editions or manuscript sources are recorded.

It is perhaps important to note that the Catalogue is not intended to be a comprehensive listing of medieval sources of an Office: the Inventory of Manuscript Sources, to be described shortly, provides a more complete method of acquiring this information.

In addition to identifying the "editions" with this basic information, the Catalogue gives the order of service and poetic summary (and, where musical transcriptions have been made, the modal organization). This information also appears before each Office in its edition. Miscellaneous other information appears— for example, about acrostics, authors, association with ecclesiastical orders, and about the relationship of the Office, as descendant or model, to other Offices.

By no means is this information intended to be comprehensive. Rather it is designed to allow the user a quick overall view of the repertory, its nature as monastic or secular, its poetic styles, its association with particular countries or eras.

LMLO Chants and Sources

This is a more complicated volume, consisting of two somewhat disparate sections: one is devoted to discussing liturgical books and the special problems of cataloging them; the second provides a basic introduction to plainchant for scholars not knowledgeable in musical matters, a description of the method by which the chants are encoded and, as with all of the elements, some discussion of methods of using the electronic data.

The manuscript inventories.[14] The manuscript inventories are not intended to be catalogs of manuscripts. They make available a selection of the extant sources for Offices in general. As with the Catalogue of Offices, they are intended rather to provide a preliminary overview of a great many Office manuscripts in a way not previously possible. Nevertheless, with care and checking, detailed work with Office books is also possible. The main emphasis, for obvious reasons, is on the Sanctorale: in the Temporale, only the most important feasts are consistently recorded.

The inventories were designed with one principal purpose: to allow a researcher to find the exact position of feasts within numerous sources. Essential, then, are only two kinds of information: the number and present location of the book, and the folio numbers of each Office within it.

Some entries are skeletal to that extent. In most cases, however, I have added information that could be gained easily without long research, trying to distinguish objective facts, observable directly in the book, from subjective conclusions, often gained only from secondary sources. Each entry, for example, normally contains various pieces of factual information: the size and number of the leaves; the method of numbering; proven or possible date, place of origin, destination, and Use; a location of a photographic reproduction; citation of explicits. In addition, each entry has a summary of the order of sections within the book. Earlier work had demonstrated that the order varies interestingly from Use to Use, and could provide assistance with determining the destination of the book.

Most of these features are indexed. But let me not mislead the reader: in far too many cases, the important facts such as date and place of use need to be confirmed. I have many times pondered the wisdom of releasing incompletely researched material: but enquiries for which the data have provided some preliminary information have been frequent enough (and the results apparently useful enough) to persuade me that others may find sufficient information here to allow at least the initial pursuit of many types of research.

Recently, for example, the data were helpful in identifying manuscripts that transmit the Office for St. Charlemagne; another colleague wanted similar facts about the Office for St. Anthony, abbot; others wanted to know about formularies for the infirm and material relating to saints celebrated in Rouen. In which books does Trinity Sunday appear at the end of the Temporale? In the books of which ecclesiastical orders are all Matins responsories and antiphons listed together in groups rather than in nocturns?

Summary. For some 3,000 Office manuscripts from across Europe and North America, a minimal checklist is printed in *LMLO: Sources & Chants* (pp. 115–37). In the electronic database, the information for about a third of the books is limited, but includes *at least* an identification of the country, city, and library, with the type of liturgical book and its current call-number. For most of the other sources, these essential elements are complemented by basic information about the book as a physical object, and by other information such as its date and the places with which it is associated (these often from secondary sources). The folio numbers of the main sections are given: for many books, a complete inventory of the Sanctorale with folio number of individual feasts is provided.

The list of indexed terms is also printed (pp. 137–58), with the number of times each term occurs in the data. Some 6,500 terms range from saints (about 1,200) and feasts to details of staves and notation: they are organized into nine major categories (including places, libraries, persons, incipits, feasts, saints, seasons, services, genres, musical matters, and Uses), each divided into numerous subcategories (e.g, digits are arranged in 10 categories).

The manuscript sources: adjusting the Kalendar. In the course of checking the information in the inventories (as far as that was possible without unlimited time and funds to revisit hundreds of European libraries), intriguing questions arose that investigation of a single book or even a few books would not bring to mind.

For example, it will be relatively easy systematically to compare a large number of Sanctorales. The initial results of a so far unsystematic comparison have, to say the least, been surprising. The order of saints within the Sanctorale, for instance, is often not what would be expected, taking the dates of their feast days from standard reference books.

A number of very good and obvious reasons may explain such discrepancies: dates differing by a single day, for example, can result from a coincidence of feasts when the newer or less important feast is moved to the adjacent day. In too many cases, even with some reasonably major saints, however, the rearrangement of order (endorsed by several books from the same area, say) can be explained only by postulating undocumented dates for feast days, or some other equally unexpected circumstance. As a result of even preliminary work on this matter, I can with some confidence state that if a user wishes to know the feast date of an unusual saint a dictionary of saints is likely to be the least trustworthy source. That difficulty should have been suspected: dictionaries concern themselves with biography, history, cult, and social matters, rather than with liturgical celebration, and their editors rarely consult liturgical books. The relevant manuscript Kalendar is the only reliable evidence.

The discrepancies in feast dates can, in fact, to some extent be discovered simply by comparing standard dictionaries of saints, but the full extent of the variability can be ascertained only by comparing a large number of Kalendars. The inventories allow that process only indirectly through a comparison of the Sanctorales, which of course reflect the Kalendar for the book.

Perhaps more than most other work in the discipline, assembling and checking the manuscript inventories has revealed the extent of difficulties with earlier liturgical research. Principal amongst these is the dating of liturgical books. It is not infrequent to discover discrepancies of several centuries. The problem can be exemplified, along with a related difficulty, by considering the Feast of the Transfiguration.

One manuscript transmitting this Office, for instance, was assigned, in a much earlier era, to the twelfth century. Several other manuscripts are clearly dated very early in the fourteenth. Many are obviously earlier than the fifteenth century (this casual assumption of "obvious" exemplifies one of the difficulties with dating). Yet a good many standard reference works allude only to the establishment of the feast in 1457.

The other inadequacy revealed here is that of many reference books. Like the dictionary of saints, an encyclopedia is likely to take the historical rather than liturgical point of view. Experience, and some knowledge of the development of the feasts of Trinity Sunday and Corpus Christi, should have suggested that other feasts, too, might have been celebrated unofficially earlier, much earlier than the date they were finally admitted to the Kalendar. In fact, a Transfiguration Office was written by Peter the Venerable in the twelfth century, and the feast was officially celebrated at least by the Carmelites from the early fourteenth.

Sadly, of course, library catalogers are rarely trained specifically in medieval liturgical studies. Nor, for that matter, are many authors of entries in encyclopedias. In fact, who is, nowadays?

To resolve such matters may take years of research. The inventory of manuscripts is merely a preliminary step to the assembly of correct data in electronic form.

Each entry in the list of manuscripts, then, usually contains a great deal of various information, available for the first time for a large selection of sources from across Europe and North America and the centuries in electronic, and thus searchable form. After many tentative experiments, I rejected any attempt to lay the entries out in a conventional manner, as though for printing: the format is oriented solely for use at the computer (although entries can of course easily be printed) and for automatic searching and indexing and categorizing of data. It thus incorporates many inelegant features.[15] The format was designed so that, within a manuscript, each feast can be described in considerable detail without running into the description for the adjacent feasts. For very few feasts has it been possible to provide more than the basic information.

As with so much of the other data, then, the setup of the manuscript inventories was mandated by electronic necessity.

The chants: variations upon themes. The chants are encoded so that they can readily be sung at sight. Each word is followed immediately by the pitches that set it, represented by numbers (1 is the final of the mode, etc.) arranged so that the syllable division is clear. I call the word with its chant a *chantword*. In order to make it possible to search for purely melodic motives within a chant, each encoded text is followed by the numerical representation of the melody alone, shorn of repeated pitches and every symbol other than pitches. With these two pieces of data, and some appropriate software to make the task easier, it is possible to analyze a good many interesting aspects of chant.

Some preliminary results of my method of encoding chants as chantwords have already been published (see Andrew Hughes 1993): the conclusions of that small piece of preliminary work have been confirmed by more recent work with different aspects of the chant data.

The Office for St. Dominic. Recently, for example, I undertook to find out how every single significant musical motive of the Office for St. Dominic was distributed within the Dominican Office chant repertory. Not enough work has been done to speak with absolute confidence but, once again, the initial results have been (to speak moderately) surprising, at least to me.

Preliminary conclusions would include the following:

1. The most unpromising musical motives, seemingly totally undistinguished or appearing to be merely conventional modal formulas, can prove significant. This confirms an earlier conclusion (in Andrew Hughes 1993): that every significant word in the (later medieval) liturgy is set to a unique musical motive unless there is some reason to set it otherwise. There are often good reasons for setting different words to the *same* motive: the use of melody types or recognized tones; the overt borrowing of whole melodies or phrases; the need for textual allusion and symbolic reference to other parts of the liturgy. The frequent appearance of unique settings may suggest deliberate compositional choice.

2. We have perhaps been misled by the conventional view that there are (to coin a quotation) "obviously recognizable motives of mode so and so,"

without taking into account that minute differences can be significant.

3. Minute differences may render tunes otherwise identical significantly different. The same principle may distinguish (and separate) tunes that are completely identical to each other from minutely different yet similar ones.

4. There is a complex and sophisticated network of allusions, references, and echoes, often involving textual relationships that enhance musical relationships that otherwise might be suspect. Such a network is difficult for us to imagine but fully in keeping with the medieval mentality.

Dominican plainsong motives: some examples. A few examples would perhaps be instructive. For the following paragraphs I use an encoding of the complete Dominican Antiphonal, transcribed directly from Humbert's Codex, and the chants of about 100 rhymed Offices. Although initial results are extremely promising, the techniques for analyzing the results are still in a preliminary stage. As the examples below show, it seemed useful to separate the results according to the origin in Temporale or Sanctorale and by genre (separating Gospel antiphons—represented by E (for *antiphona ad Evangelium*)—from psalm antiphons—A). But refinements to these categories may also be necessary: separating the Common of Saints, or Marian feasts, for example. In the examples below, too, the figures for the Common of Saints are included with those for the Sanctorale, and no allowance is made for multiple occurrences with the same chant.

An opening intonation common to many chants in mode 2 is (using letter names for pitches): *DACD*. Let us generalize this by seeking the motive anywhere in the chant and in any mode. The numerical representation, using 1 as the final, would be 1*01. How common is this, in fact? In parentheses is the tally of intonations included in the preceding figure:

Genre	Mode 2 [319 chants in all]		Mode 8 [715 chants in all]	
	Temporale	Sanctorale	Temporale	Sanctorale
R or V	16 (4)	14 (3) and 4 (1) in extended mode 1[16]	3	6 (1)
A	1	17 (4)	1	7 (4)
E	1 (1)		10 (4)	12

Surely, these tentative results are interesting. In the first place, what can we learn from the fact that there are more than twice as many chants in mode 8, yet fewer occurrences of this motive? From the distribution could one predict to some extent the genre and its place in the liturgy? Clearly in mode 2 the motive is not favored in antiphons of the Temporale, but appears heavily in psalm antiphons of the Sanctorale: only a single Gospel antiphon uses it (as an intonation) in mode 2 (this is on the Tuesday of Holy Week). On the other hand, the motive in responsories is equally divided between Temporale and Sanctorale. In mode 8 the distribution differs, favoring Gospel antiphons. (Incidentally, the motive occurs in other modes only once: in mode 6 in the Office for Thomas of Canterbury.)

How common is the variant of this motive: *DCACD* (or in general 10*01)?

Genre	Mode 2 [319 chants in all]		Mode 8 [715 chants in all]	
	Temporale	Sanctorale	Temporale	Sanctorale
R or V	14 (1)	28 (6) and 6 (4) in extended mode 1	1	1
A	6	19 (9)		2
E	7	5	2	4

The discrepancy between the number of occurrences in the two modes is even more striking. In mode 2, this slightly more ornamented version occurs more often in antiphons of the Temporale, and more often in Gospel antiphons in both Temporale and Sanctorale than its simpler counterpart, but less often in all genres in mode 8. Once again the only occurrence in another mode, and again in mode 6, is in the Thomas Office.

It is difficult to predict how useful such statistics might be. We will need to work systematically with such numbers before attempting to draw satisfactory conclusions.

Let us choose for the final example a motive that is not an intonation: the motive 13453234321 (or—to anticipate the discovery that this occurs only in modes 1 and 6—in mode 1 *DFGAFEFGFED* and in mode 6 *FABCAGABAGF*). These pitches, regardless of their repetitions or division into syllables, occur in five items, three in mode 1 and two in mode 6. The two in mode 6 may be dispensed with quickly: one is in the Office for Dominic and the other in the Office for Thomas Aquinas, modeled strictly on Dominic's. But interestingly, one of the three occurrences in mode 1 is in the Office for the *Translation* of St. Dominic.

A second occurrence is in an antiphon for Agnes, seemingly unrelated. The final occurrence is in a responsory for the Saturday of the third week of Advent (Advent.3). Its text begins *Germinaverunt campi eremi germen odoris Israel*. A chief (and quite conventional) textual motive in the Translation Office for Dominic is that of fragrance and odor; a chief (and again very appropriate) textual motive in the main Office for Dominic is the topos of distributed seed germinating, symbolizing the preaching of the word of God.

Two of the three antiphons in mode 1 are thus related textually as well as by this small musical phrase to each other, and to the remaining two in mode 6. Of five occurrences, then, four are brought close enough to raise intriguing questions. The cross-modal relations (between 1 and 6) and even more the cross-genre relations (between antiphons and a responsory) complicate the issue.

If intonations and other motives that seem to be the most stable and formulaic of chant vocabulary can reveal something interesting about the distribution and use of chant phrases, how much could even more distinctive motives reveal?

The Office of the Presentation of the Virgin. A chance discovery about the principal Office for the Presentation of the Virgin, associated with Philippe de Mézières and the late fourteenth century, suggested a possible relationship with the Office for St. Dominic.[17] Results from applying the software released with *LMLO: Sources & Chants,* and from other specially-designed programs not included with that volume, confirm a musical relationship. Rather than comparing small musical motives, as in the previous investigation described, this task focused on a comparison of melodies as complete musical pieces.

A few chants are borrowed almost verbatim: in some, complete phrases corresponding to the poetic structure are borrowed verbatim while others are modified in particular ways. The similarities are close enough and of sufficient quantity for the musical relationships to be undeniable: furthermore, they led to the discovery that the texts of the two Offices are also related, although in ways so subtle as to have escaped notice, or otherwise to have been attributed to chance. The Magnificat antiphons for Second Vespers, for instance, are:

Dominic	Presentation
O *l*umen ecclesie *doctor veritatis*	O*l*iva fructifera *mater pietatis*
rosa paciencie *ebur castitatis*	fugans mundi sclera *stella claritatis*
a*quam* sapiencie propinasti *gratis*	per *quam* cuncta prospera dantur nobis *gratis*
predicator gracie nos iunge *beatis*	nos tandem in ethera transfer cum *beatis*

Some chants, especially the antiphons of Matins, are not related to Dominic. Despite the failure to identify the source of these items, the certainty with which relations with Dominic (identified through computer searching) were established leads one to suspect that relations with other Offices, for which there is no obvious connection, may also be valid. Why, for instance, might the Presentation Office borrow from Brigid of Ireland, Edmund king and martyr, and Bernwardus of Hildesheim? Here, it seems that a proximity of the liturgical feasts might be the factor leading to use of common musical material.

But before the more tenuous connections of this kind can be confirmed, an adequate and systematic examination of much more evidence is required.

A conclusion. From a large body of evidence, features of the musical style and modal characteristics of late medieval plainsong can be revealed through analysis (statistical or otherwise) of small motives; relationships between Offices, obvious or otherwise, can be revealed through comparison of melodies. Perhaps I might risk an assertion: the distribution and frequency of what most chant scholars would regard as commonplace motives can also tell us important things. Paradoxically, many of the commonplaces of chant melody may be distinctive. Perhaps, however, they are important liturgically rather than musically. Similarities made clear through musical analysis can lead to textual and liturgical relationships that would otherwise go unsuspected.

Such investigations can be undertaken only by way of large bodies of accumulated data, including encoding of the musical chants themselves. *LMLO* begins this accumulation.

Proof and documentation. In the investigation of these matters, much subjective judgment is involved. This is especially true if minute snippets of melody are to be the objects of study, as in the investigation of Dominican plainsong motives. The selection of samples for evidence is, however, circumscribed quite strictly by criteria for "identity" and "significance." Here are some important criteria: for similarities between snippets to be convincing, they should occur in items that are the same genre, and in same position in the genre, in the same musical mode, the same service, and the same position in the service. I look particularly, too, for identity of pitch sequence and repetition and identity of notation, especially syllable division. I hope finally to find textual echoes, and regard such relationships as crucial. Given differences in the number of syllables, in the poetic structure and accentuation of different texts, it is rare for all of these criteria to be met. In fact, identity of pitch and notation and syllable division, although demonstrating the strongest links, have often to be sacrificed.

Substantial and convincing evidence must support these judgments. How might such figures be documented? Unfortunately, to support them properly calls for a huge apparatus including many music examples (the documentation for the Dominican investigation alluded to above runs to several hundred pages). Comprehensive apparatus for the first example above would require nearly a hundred musical examples. Even in the numerical representation that I adopt for encoding, *and* showing only the relevant parts of the items, several printed pages of intimidating data would be required. But if the verbal context is important, partial examples are not sufficient. Obviously samples must be chosen. Equally clearly, the need for a convincing number of samples mandates the use of a concise, compressed representation, not only of the texts and their chants, but also of the liturgical context in which they appear.

Must the necessity for short forms in all areas of this kind of research be further justified?

New Scholarship

For the flexibility of comprehensive searching and indexing of massive amounts of data, a price must be paid. The ubiquity of short forms is part of that price. Electronic research carries with it, too, the need to work in ways considerably different from traditional ones, and to accept limitations uncomfortable to those trained in conventional scholarship.

It will perhaps become a truism that computers have made it possible to deal relatively easily with huge amounts of data: inaccurately. This danger is one acknowledged in some of the sciences, which use the concept of an error bar: a percentage of error that can be tolerated because of, and made insignificant within, the vast amount of data accumulated. Accepting such a principle for scholarship in the humanities does not make me comfortable. But perhaps we have to adjust our expectations: some collections of material are so large, but potentially so useful, that we must approach them knowing their limitations, and knowing that from them can be gleaned only preliminary ideas and inspiration that must be subjected to rigorous verification by detailed research of a more conventional kind.

Furthermore, our ways of working with computers must change. Extracting and analyzing information from huge bodies of computer data cannot be done by shuffling an icon across the screen with a mouse, nor can tailor-made operations be called by clicking on a ready-made function. What icon could one devise to specify "extract Offices for confessors"? What ready-made routine? The most fundamental elements of the problem must be isolated in a rigorously logical dissection of the task into its most atomistic elements. In the next few paragraphs, I will analyze one such operation.

Firstly, the structure of the data must be thoroughly known, in all its intimidating exactitude. Secondly, the capabilities of various kinds of computer program must be thoroughly known, often necessitating the unpleasant task of careful perusal of intricate computer manuals, often barely readable. Finally, even with the help of suitable computer routines, the task may require tedious and lengthy repetitive word-processing operations.

One may naively think that such repetitive operations are precisely what the computer should be doing: but computers can do repetitively only what they have been programmed to do. Most programmers could not even imagine the kinds of operation that humanists require. This means that humanists must be prepared to undertake one of two procedures: (1) To write the programs themselves, tailor-made to the task at hand. That is an exceedingly long and complex task, fascinating for those whose minds work in such ways, frustrating and irritating otherwise. (2) To break the task into its smallest pieces, and know which of a set of ready-made routines will do each of the smaller tasks. Many such routines are available in word-processors or finding or indexing programs, or can be constructed by using the macro facilities of many word-processors. Others are to be found in tools such as those provided in the Norton Utilities.

Consider, for example, the task alluded to above: finding all the Gospel antiphons for confessors in Classical meters. Even knowing the data and the tailor-made programs available for precisely this repertory as well as I do, it took virtually a whole day to find out how this might be automated. Would it have been quicker to edit the files required and to do it piece by piece?

Here is the long-winded method, broken into separate stages: (i) load each of the 64 large files of data in a word-processor; (ii) examine the information section of each of the 1,500 Offices (a) looking for the code ,c or its more readable expansion placed between tagged parentheses (, confessor), and (b) looking in the poetic summary for V=.1 W=.1 L=.1 or V=.h W=.h L=.h (that is, Gospel antiphons for Vespers or Lauds in leonines or hexameters, leaving out of the search all other Classical meters); (iii) remember or write down all the relevant antiphons; (iv) go through the Office texts one by one, blocking each selected item and moving it or saving it into a separate file—along with as much material as necessary to identify which Office was being mined.

How long would such an operation take? How many mistakes would be made, and items missed?

Even with the tailor-made software, it proved impossible to do this particular task—to extract particular kinds of poetic text—in a single operation. To remedy this defect it was necessary to write a new program. It was possible to automate the extraction to some extent with the available routines. Here are the awful details: first it was necessary to combine the detailed poetic analysis with the data files (a program is provided to automate this operation). This linked the poetic form with each individual text by placing it adjacent to the text. All the Offices for confessors were then extracted (again with one of the routines provided): from the resulting file, it was then possible with the same program in a separate run to extract all the Gospel antiphons in hexameters. But the command line for this last operation exemplifies the very nightmare that humanists generally detest:

Snorun extract /y=source.filename /xs=": =?E:@@ h:}]:b:"

It would, of course, be possible at a huge of cost of energy and programming time to make this more user-friendly. The publisher would have to pass these expenses on to users.[18] For those who are still conscious, here is the exegesis of the last parameter of that command line: extract /xs= a block :b: beginning with a Gospel antiphon E in any service =? and ending with the characters }] and containing the string "@@ h" that signifies *hexameter*. By some means, the computer has to be made to understand these terms. To extract the other Classical meters would necessitate running the program again, replacing the letter *h* in the command line with the appropriate poetic code.

By similarly detailed and tedious operations a vast amount of varied musical information could be amassed from the encodings of the plainsongs in *LMLO*. Readers will probably be aware of the program *Humdrum,* an extraordinarily flexible set of tools for analyzing music developed by David Huron at the University of Waterloo, Ontario: describing these tools, he writes, "Like musical instruments, good research tools cannot be mastered in a day. If you are familiar with . . . UNIX . . . frequent use of *Humdrum* will lead to significant mastery in about six months."[19]

A Gloomy Conclusion . . .

Programmers have moved towards Graphical User Interfaces not involving words: user-friendly intuitive operations to make it unnecessary for workers to have to read manuals or to think about the processes involved. Such shortcuts are entirely appropriate in many contexts, especially for routine and mechanical operations. But they are antithetical to specialized research, where it may be necessary to read the individual letters and symbols, to know the manuals inside out, to know the full potential of every computer program, and to know exactly how the data are presented. Electronic data are not for the fainthearted, or for those who use the computer as a typewriter.

A different philosophy about technology has emerged, in a well-meaning attempt to make computers easier to use. The new policies may be appropriate for the routine operations usually performed by businesses. They are not appropriate for humanistic research. I doubt whether they are appropriate for many of the sciences. But scientists are used to formulas and mathematical short forms, and are happier to program special routines. It is not hard to guess which implementation attracts greater financial support.

The unfortunate and not surprising conclusion for humanists is that programs oriented toward business are not adequate for humanistic research. Those programs that are suitable—*Nota Bene, TACT, WordCruncher, Library Master,* and others—all require programming by specialists, and constant maintenance. All seem to be large projects with small resources.

... Mitigated

Most of the tasks alluded to in the preceding pages have involved the extraction of precise kinds of material from the databases, constrained by several conditions. Some of the tasks have been tendentiously complex. Specialized concordance or indexing programs, and analytical tools such as those of *Humdrum* or those provided in *LMLO* can help to achieve the required result in a single stage.

All such operations, however, can be carried out in simpler stages, using a tool familiar to all computer users: a word-processor. Since all the *LMLO* data use generic (ASCII or DOS) characters, any word-processor will serve.

Acquiring the evidence is just the first step. Somehow, meaning and understanding must follow. That involves thought and analysis, human processes not yet usurped by technology.

New opportunities. A good many large projects in music and liturgy are now under way. From several there have already emanated massive quantities of data. We have only begun to explore how to harvest what is now available. With the accumulation of vast amounts of potential evidence and, as time will surely allow, increasingly easy methods of investigating and analyzing such data, new opportunities for discovery will certainly emerge. An unexplored world of ideas and imagination will become accessible, small resources notwithstanding.

The staking of territories by impoverished pioneers may often lead to gold mines.

Postscript for 1999: Some Optimism

A young colleague in medieval studies, Steven Killings, seeing that material of *LMLO: Texts* would be of great usefulness in his literary work, and finding the electronic interface "unfriendly," decided, on his own initiative, to modify the textual data for use in a Windows environment. To complement this revision in format, he is constructing (a) a user-friendly program, and (b) an outer shell that makes my own programs easier to use.

Every so often (he now resides in New York) he shows me the results for approval. I am certainly excited by the results so far: (1) for searches requiring only the isolation of basic elements such as service and genre, the routines are excellent. To implement searches complicated by conditions such as those described on pages 540–41 a good deal more work will be necessary; (2) the programs supplied with *LMLO* will still be useful as they stand, but it will also be possible to hide the awful command lines, such as that on page 541, under a command shell in which the choices will be much more transparent.

Rather than taking up 10 to 11 megabytes of hard disk space, however, the new data may occupy some 150 megabytes. It could therefore be distributed only on CD. The publisher of *LMLO* is aware of these efforts, but we have not yet entered negotiations for any publication to proceed. Nor have financial matters been discussed, but clearly the cost of revision and programming will have to be recouped from the sale of the CD. I hope that the data can be made available in this manner for a fraction of the cost of similar databases, and that a subsequent effort can be made for *LMLO: Sources and Chants.*

Notes

1. Some two-thirds of the Offices I now have in the database to be described here were published about a century ago in about ten volumes of *AH.* This series of volumes, monumental and essential though it is, does not meet any modern standards for adequate editions.

2. I shall not argue here the appropriateness of this term: to satisfy the demands of grant applications, I have defined it as Offices using strictly rhymed and regularly accentual poetry or Classical meters.

3. For various reasons, I use the word *text* to refer to the words, and *chant* to refer to the plainsong, the music to which the words are set. The editions contain only the items sung to plainsong. I would now use the term *sungtext* to distinguish these items from the lessons and prayers. See Andrew Hughes, *Medieval Manuscripts,* 2d ed., p. xv.

4. See Andrew Hughes, *Late Medieval Liturgical Offices.*

5. As I write, do I sense a slight tone of complaint? I hope not. If so, it is directed to the paucity of funding for the humanities. Weariness, perhaps. The project has been tedious, sometimes in the extreme, and of very long gestation, some reasons for which I shall make clear. I have many times wished for easier solutions, especially with respect to the computer programs that are available. Indeed, occasionally, difficulties seemed to pile up on difficulties, sometimes threatening seriously to delay the project, and once or twice no adequate solution was apparent short of making undesirable compromises. Despite these notes of discord, I have enjoyed programming, typesetting, designing, and attempting to master the many other disciplines that have been necessary.

I discuss many features not directly related to the material itself: computer techniques, policies for choosing filenames, and the like. These matters may be of interest to scholars who might wish to pursue similar projects. Furthermore, it is conceivable that some other researcher may wish to extend or modify the data I describe. Although to include a comprehensive manual of procedures is obviously not possible here, I try to lay out the factors of most importance.

6. A long and comprehensive but still preliminary general survey of late medieval Offices was prepared in the mid-1980s as a chapter for *Musical Life and Musical Thought in Europe, 1300–1500,* ed. Reinhard Strohm, the third volume of the revised *New Oxford History of Music.* (See Hughes, Forthcoming (c).)

7. *WordPerfect,* for instance, can change the representation of tabs, even if an imported ASCII file is exported without changes. Other programs replace spaces at the

end of wrapped lines with carriage return and line feed, and the same pair of characters at the end of paragraphs with a space. Unpredictable effects of this kind are very hard if not impossible to undo.

Here are some notes about DOS or ASCII files. Although there may be an industry-wide definition of these terms, both are used to mean different things in different contexts. ASCII, in particular, technically refers to the characters from ASCII-0 to ASCII-255, including the so-called control characters. The latter are those that generally need to be excluded or greatly modified when transferring data from one word-processor to another. It is safest to define exactly what is intended.

Typewriter characters can be taken to mean all those characters to be found on the plain or shifted keyboard, including the space.

Ends of lines. To typewriter characters are normally added the characters at the ends of lines: these may differ in several ways. An exact specification must be given, as follows.

(1) What occurs at lines wrapped at the right margin? The best word-processors add nothing here other than the space normally between words, allowing the software to wrap the lines on screen or for the printer. Unfortunately very few word-processors (and none of the commonly used ones) live up to this requirement. Most insert some proprietary character(s) that can seriously affect processing by other programs.

(2) What marks the ends of lines that are not wrapped, that is, what is sometimes called the end of a paragraph? Usually a carriage return and a line feed (typewriter functions!) are both inserted by the single Enter key of the keyboard, but through the software, either of these single characters may serve both functions, leaving the other for wrapped lines, for instance. Other methods also occur. For most purposes, ignorance of this feature is of no concern, the matter being taken care of by the conversion routines of the program in use.

(3) How are paragraphs defined? By two consecutive carriage return/line feed pairs, giving a blank line? Or by a single pair?

Tabs. How are tabs managed? Is the single tab character (ASCII-9) allowed to remain, or is it replaced by the appropriate number of spaces, or by characters such as hexadecimal FF?

Extended ASCII characters. How are accented and other special symbols managed? Most sophisticated word-processors nowadays allow a very wide variety of characters, mostly by using "unprintable" codes within the text. Some allow the use of extended ASCII (from ASCII-128 to 255) for a smaller set of symbols. These may usually be treated as an extension of the typewriter set.

Control codes. Other "unprintable" codes may be used to turn on and off various formatting styles such as italics.

The simplest format to deal with is the one that uses only typewriter characters. If clean data are required, only they and spaces must be entered until the user presses Enter (i.e., every paragraph is a long line ended by the end-of-line characters, regardless of the setting of the right margin). Clearly such restrictions make it hard to change font, appearance, and other features that make a text easy to read. *Nota Bene* uses only typewriter characters, between « and », to control all such functions. Files produced in this word-processor are exceptionally easy to edit and to manage. More recent formats such as the HyperText Markup Language and the Rich Text encodings rely on similar plaintext with formatting tags between angle brackets, for example.

8. Now released with a comprehensive manual: see Lancashire et al. (1996). It is not yet clear whether this release in fact overcomes the following limitations of the version at present available: (1) The line buffer contains only 256 characters (this is my inference, from the symptoms). Consequently, the line at this limit is split in two, producing many false words, hindering the usefulness, and upsetting the statistical results. (2)

Some symbols used in the data in question here may be indexed, although the search routines will not allow all of them to be found: other symbols, if used, make some wildcard searches very hard if not impossible. (3) With really "weird" data such as that used in this project, the program will not infrequently crash or hang the system.

This program is shareware, but may be obtained free of charge by anonymous FTP from ftp.chass.utoronto.ca (subdirectory pub/tact), on the World Wide Web at www. chass.utoronto.ca/tact/, or by Gopher to gopher.chass.utoronto.ca.

9. Unfortunately, this is not 100% true. The data have now been made to conform with both *WordCruncher* and *TACT.*

10. Some of these constraints, in particular the restriction on the length of file-names, have been remedied in *Windows 95.* But, in some ways, they still remain. Using Windows, of whatever variety, brings only disadvantages to many computer operations: if loaded, the program uses vast amounts of random access memory that could other-wise be used for data. Files encoding textual data are often very large: the presence of Windows thus slows down all processing. Furthermore, the entry of long command lines may be difficult within the limitations imposed by these user-friendly shells. In fact, the command line will be the same, whether or not Windows is loaded: Windows offers few short cuts in this kind of work (but see n. 18).

11. The system used in *LMLO* is exemplified in Andrew Hughes (1993). Fuller speci-fications are in *LMLO.*

12. I had devised this system at least ten years before the appearance of *RISM,* in which the system of sigla generally accepted by musicologists first appeared.

13. The Catalogue originally ran to 450 pages with plenty of white space, and a readable 10- or 12-point type. It now occupies less than 100 pages, in 8-point type, and in dictionary and columnar format.

14. Both cataloguing and inventorying imply making lists, in lesser or greater detail. The distinction made here is as follows: a catalogue lists the manuscripts in a library; an inventory lists the contents of an individual manuscript. A group of inventories will, of course, inevitably create a catalogue of some kind. The criteria used for the prepara-tion of the inventories are also laid out concisely in my paper "Cataloguing Liturgical Manuscripts: In Order to Order," given at the conference on this topic at Wolfenbüttel, March 1996. The conference reports are being edited for publication by David Hiley; see Andrew Hughes (Forthcoming (b)).

15. An interesting suggestion has arisen recently: the release of versions of the data, both for texts and manuscript inventories, that are stripped of all material other than the essential information itself. Such data would be searchable, but most of the flexibil-ity of indexing and extraction and categorization and sifting would be lost, or at least available only with extremely tedious manipulation (for instance, by blocking, deleting, and saving) through many massive files.

16. Extended mode 1: mode 1 that incorporates plagal range and features.

17. The Office was edited by Coleman (1981). A new edition is being prepared by Coleman and Father James Boyce. See also chap. 21 above. For my study on which the following paragraphs are based, see Andrew Hughes (1999).

18. It might be possible to reduce some of the complexities of such specifications by providing various preliminary menus, in which questions in English such as "which meter do you wish to isolate" and a list of possible answers appears for the user to choose from, as in many Windows applications. But the implementation of such pro-grams is another large project, for which there are at present no financial resources. See Postscript for 1999.

19. Quoted from Professor Huron's advertising material.

CANTUS and Tonaries

LORA MATTHEWS & PAUL MERKLEY

CANTUS is a large and growing on-line database for Gregorian chant, developed under the able and vigilant directorship of its founder, Ruth Steiner.[1] CANTUS contains indexes of all the chants in selected manuscript and early printed sources of the Divine Office. At the time of final revision of this chapter, CANTUS contains the location, textual incipits, liturgical feast assignment, and musical modes and *differentiae* for the chants transmitted in 44 notated medieval service books (antiphoners and breviaries) from a wide variety of locales. The work has been accomplished over many years through the efforts of a number of scholars who have supplied the data for individual manuscripts, along with the editorial and data-entry work of the CANTUS team. The database holds a wealth of information. It allows a researcher to download the index file of an entire source or sources and to undertake comparative studies of them, both statistically (as aggregates of information by musical mode) and individually (for example, for information on feasts and transmission in various sources). Also, a search program with the database makes it possible to recover a list of manuscripts that contain a specific chant, and to retrieve the information on it from each source. All of this can be done easily and rapidly. In addition to its musicological applications, CANTUS contains a great deal of evidence concerning the liturgy, information increasingly recognized as pertinent to a broad range of historical studies.

In the field of chant studies in recent years much less attention has been paid to the search for origin or definition of the theoretical quality called mode, and more work is now being carried out in a more measurable music-historical area of inquiry: the study of the assignment of chant melodies to modal categories to support their performance with psalmody. CANTUS is a long-term project of the assembly of data on modal assignment in antiphoners and notated breviaries, the musical witnesses of the practice of antiphonal psalmody. Although these service books were not designed to list chants according to modal categories, for reasons of psalmody they must indicate the modes and the melodic subcategories, called *differentiae,* of the antiphons that they contain. This information was necessary so that the singers could perform the correct psalm intonation and *seculorum amen* formula with each antiphon. In other words, the singers needed to know how to intone the psalm and which of the many melodic termination formulas to sing to the doxology. Ruth Steiner's project is, as she herself has remarked, one of making tonaries out of antiphoners, just as the Solesmes editors of the facsimiles of the Worcester and Lucca antiphoners did (in PM 12 and 9), but in such a way that permits comparison of the modal assignments between sources.

There is ample evidence that most of the large medieval tonaries were compiled directly from antiphoners. Tonaries record the categorization of chants according to mode and *differentia,* and in many of them, the antiphons within each category are ordered roughly by liturgical feast, as if the compiler turned the pages all the way through an antiphoner, noting all of the melodies that fell into a particular category (i.e., all of the antiphons in a given mode with which a particular *seculorum amen* formula was sung), then repeated the process for each additional category. Occasional mistakes, such as the placement of the same antiphon in two categories, the duplication of an antiphon within a category, or the appending of an antiphon that had been omitted in a pass through the antiphoner, support this idea. In this way antiphoners contain an implicit categorization of melodies that is analogous to that of tonaries. In effect the CANTUS files have made antiphoners into tonaries, and for this reason the procedure rests on solid authority.

Each antiphoner that the CANTUS team analyzes, or adopts from the work of another scholar, is made into a D-Base file. At the beginning of the project Dr. Steiner had each resultant tonary published in book form and also made the files available on diskette. The biggest shortcoming was that one could not compare one antiphoner with another. But when she made the CANTUS files available through the Gopher site of The Catholic University of America, the programmer wrote a utility enabling the user to search for the modal assignments of an individual antiphon in all of the CANTUS files, i.e. in several antiphoners. The "Text" files also contain the corresponding numbers of the chants in Hesbert's *CAO,* textual incipits, and information on feast assignments. The "Text" files may be downloaded, and there are instructions for binary conversion to do this more quickly. While to date full melodies of the chants are not available on-line, it is to be hoped that melodies will be added in MIDI code in the future. For most of the sources there are "About" files, each with an inventory of the manuscript, information on provenance and origin, and bibliography.[2]

Information of this kind is valuable only if it is reliable and if it has been structured in a rational and useful way. Fortunately for the many musicologists and other medievalists who have occasion to make use of this excellent resource, its founder began with a sound conception and tended the project carefully from its inception. As in many aspects of medieval studies, computers have greatly facilitated research into many areas of chant. Repertorial, melodic-thematic, centonic (a mosaic model of the composition of the melodies), and other studies that were previously not feasible have been accomplished in recent years with the help of the digital marvel that Umberto Eco's character in *Foucault's Pendulum* called *Abulafia* and its progeny.[3]

The subject of this chapter, a comparison of the modal assignment of Office antiphons in tonaries with those in antiphoners, forms part of the larger question of theory versus practice in medieval music. Perhaps the best-known articulation of this opposition is Guido of Arezzo's epigram

> Musicorum et cantorum magna est distantia;
> Isti dicunt, illi sciunt, quae componit musica . . .[4]

The immediate context and implications of this verse are that Guido, who was a *cantor,* considered himself a learned musician, or a *musicus.* He credited himself with the development of a specific system of notation so that singers could learn the vast repertory of chant more rapidly, and the strong wording of his statement suggests the existence, even the flourishing, of a large group of singers who still continued to learn the repertory by imitation, or rote. While we cannot hope to find direct evidence of the oral tradition of chant in the Middle Ages, an indirect investigation of the tension between practice that followed written theory and practice that respected received tradition can be made in the study of modal assignment.

We have undertaken a comparison of data from CANTUS with data from our own files of modal assignments in tonaries. As a test case for the present chapter the authors have considered the antiphoner in the manuscript Piacenza, BC 65 (compiled for the cathedral of that city, while it was being built, early in the twelfth century), along with a group of antiphons identified as having conflicting modal assignments in tonaries; we have checked the assignments of this group in many antiphoners with the aid of the search feature in CANTUS. The results of these comparisons have implications for the study of both tonaries and antiphoners, two very different kinds of documents that include common information concerning chant melodies.

Our own database is a research instrument that was made in the course of extensive work on "Northern European tonaries," a project that involved hundreds of sources, including pertinent treatises, many small tonaries, and some behemoths containing thousands of antiphons (cf. Merkley 1992). With the availability of Dr. Steiner's CANTUS files, it is possible to extend the comparison of antiphon assignments much further, and this chapter should be regarded as the first part of an extended comparison to be made. Before entering into discussion of specific antiphons and their modal assignments, it is important to review briefly some aspects of our own database, and to call to mind some features of antiphons and the modal system that have often been misunderstood by medievalists outside musicology.

As is well known, after the psalms, the antiphons of the Office are generally considered to be the oldest genre of Western European chant. Their form is simple. The antiphon itself is a short, monophonic (single-line) melody followed by a psalm, which is chanted to one of eight very simple reciting formulas or tones; there is a different psalm tone for each of the eight modes. At the end of the psalm, the last six syllables of the doxology, the words *seculorum amen,* are sung to one of several termination formulas. For the music of these formulas some medieval theorists used the term *differentia,* perhaps in reference to the difference in the psalm tone. Following the *seculorum amen* formula, the antiphon is repeated. Most antiphon texts are biblical, and the texts of some were taken from a verse of the psalms with which they were sung.[5]

Almost all of the melodies from the large repertory of antiphons can be regarded as elaborations of one of a relatively small number of themes, although the precise number of these themes has been a matter of some debate. Gevaert enumerated over ninety themes, and others have suggested a much smaller number.[6] It should be noted that not all scholars accept this thematic model of the chant repertory; some, for example, hold that a model of melodic mosaics (often called *centos*) is more accurate. In any case it is of paramount importance to remember that much of the repertory of antiphon melodies grew centuries before the introduction of the modal system of melodic classification.

Together with our knowledge of the history of notation and manuscripts, the thematic model of chant, which is the most widely accepted in our discipline, has given rise to our conception of the performance of early chant and to the process of repertorial accretion; it is generally held that, before the earliest notated sources in the eighth and ninth centuries, singers improvised—or better, reconstructed—a melody by adapting its text to the designated melodic theme. Recitation (the repetition of a single note) might be increased to accommodate a longer text, or there could have been simple ornamentation. At some later period, coinciding perhaps with the employment of notated sources, and possibly associated with the imposition of the Roman rite throughout the Frankish kingdom, the notes of these melodies were codified. A period in which notated sources were used by one singer in a choir, presumably the cantor, who would have taught the melodies to the rest of the singers by rote, can be distinguished from a later period in which the choir sang together from a notated source, the distinction made by the size of the manuscripts: whether small, for individual use, or very large with huge notation, so that the whole choir could see the book at once.

The written sources of Gregorian chant show a remarkably stable tradition, with few "hard" melodic variants. As David Hughes has proven and remarked, Gregorian variants are improperly characterized by Leo Treitler's suggestion of "Gladly, the cross-eyed bear" (supposed variant for purposes of characterization of "Gladly the cross I'd bear")—anyone transmitting that variant in public would be corrected, if only on theological grounds; Hughes suggests that a more appropriate comparison would be a textual variant that can be encountered in any North American hardware store: "duct tape," and "duc tape" (D. Hughes 1987). Most chant variants are "soft"; elisions or omissions of elisions of this kind.

To return to questions of taxonomy, the Western modal system, an adaptation of the functional and formulaic Byzantine system of *oktoechoi*, has eight primary categories—the modes, and within each mode several sub-categories, or *differentiae*, each with its own *seculorum amen* formula. These categories are implicit in antiphoners, but they explicitly inform the structure of tonaries. The latter are a type of book that flourished from the ninth century through the thirteenth century, in which antiphons, and often other chants, are listed according to mode and *differentia*.[7] Some tonaries are small, giving only one or two antiphons as examples in each *differentia*, and others are large, containing thousands of antiphons in their lists. Tonaries have little or no musical notation; they contain at most the melodic incipits of antiphons. Usually at the head of each category there is the musical notation for the *seculorum amen* formula. In early tonaries, the lists of antiphons are generally in liturgical order, as if the compilers went through antiphoners and collected the antiphons of each *differentia*. In some later sources the antiphons are in alphabetical order.

As Merkley has demonstrated from his comparison of the lists of antiphons in different sources, although early compilers of large tonaries influenced each other's work in design, it is clear from the lists of antiphons that these books were independent compilations strongly influenced by local practice and individual judgment (see Merkley 1988). No one would have performed antiphons from a tonary—an antiphoner would have been much more effective—but tonaries did allow a cantor to check a modal assignment, and in this way to provide a control on musical practice, which, at least in the earlier centuries, was strongly based on learning the melodies by rote.

The study of modal assignment—the history of the placement of melodies into modal categories and sub-categories—includes the study of (1) treatises for rules of categorization, descriptions of the modal system, and arguments concerning reforms of categorization; (2) tonaries for the application of these rules and reforms to individual melodies, both with reference to treatises and as specific prescriptions for practice; and (3) service books such as antiphoners for evidence of practice.

This is a slight oversimplification of the role of tonaries, something that varies from source to source. In general tonaries that were copied into manuscripts with service books tend to have little or no theoretical commentary and exhibit a lesser degree of formality; the opposite is true for tonaries copied with treatises. Although it is not correct to refer to a tonary as solely "practical" or "theoretical," a great deal about their orientation can be learned from the manuscript environment, and we can usually tell much about the education of the scribes: whether they knew heighted musical notation, what kinds of innovation they undertook, and the types and frequency of their errors in Latin. The assessment of whether a particular tonary was prescriptive or descriptive is important, and is involved in the larger question of theory and practice in the music of the high Middle Ages. Guido of Arezzo's epigram, quoted above, is evidence as much for the flourishing of the practical, cantatorial tradition of judging the modal category of a melody by its similarity to other chants, as it is evidence of the acceptance of his own theories of assigning melodies according to their endings (final notes).

Without computers it was not conceivable to make extensive comparisons of antiphon assignments in tonaries or antiphoners.[8] In the early 1980s, after a brief foray with the cumbersome method of using knitting needles inserted into packs of index cards punched full of holes that represented antiphon assignments (which were then shaken so that cards from a specific category fell out of a pack), Merkley was driven to purchase a CPM computer and create his own Pascal programs for his research on Italian tonaries. A central list of numbers was used as place-holders for antiphons, then a list of numbers was typed in for each *differentia* in every tonary. The one drawback was the somewhat cumbersome method for making the comparisons, since the file of each *differentia* had to be intersected with every other *differentia*. Given approximately 90 *differentiae* per tonary, the task was time-consuming and prohibitively clumsy for the larger number of tonaries under consideration. In the early 1980s it took almost half an hour to run the intersection of one *differentia* in one tonary with each of the files in one other tonary. So, it took half a week to compare one pair of tonaries. It was necessary to grow accustomed to hearing the disk drive crunch the antiphons.[9]

For the northern European tonary project, a database was required for tonaries that would permit the comparison of the lists of antiphons in order to find tonaries with conflicting assignments of mode or *differentia* for the same antiphons. In addition, a central reference list with liturgical and source information was needed, and it was essential that the database be relational to other banks of data, such as those being prepared by the members of CANTUS. It was also necessary to have easy and rapid access to all of the information about individual antiphons and their assignments. This allowed on-site study, comparison, and/or entry, and greatly enriched the work in European libraries. One of the most important considerations was the scope of the project—in the final stages all extant European tonaries—and consequently the great quantity of data to be studied.

At that time we chose the FoxPro program because it also had its own programming language and was one of the few commercially available relational databases. In other words, it was possible to compare the modal assignments found in tonaries with those in the CANTUS project files or with other independent databases that might become available. The program eliminated to a great extent the possibility of error of entry. It gave the operator (Matthews) the full textual incipit of the antiphon together with information on assignments in other tonaries, a melodic incipit, feast assignment, and other source information. The modal assignment was entered as a numeral in which the tens digit stood for the mode, the units for the *differentia,* and a decimal for any subdifferential distinction (these arise frequently in tonaries—they do not imply a change of *seculorum amen* formula, but they are a distinction in classification or a taxonomy recognized and set down by the compiler and as such must be preserved in the database). In this way, for example, a chant listed in a certain source in the fifth *differentia* of the eighth mode with no subdifferential distinction was represented as 85.0.

The authors decided to store this information as numbers rather than in separate categories, as is the case in CANTUS files. For one thing, the CANTUS project has one database for each antiphoner. Our database is a master file of modal assignments in a great many tonaries. We wanted a compact method of storing the assignments, one that would be visually clear in order to display the assignments of antiphons in several columns at once: we required twenty columns of assignments on the screen in addition to many other columns of supporting information. With the advice of an engineer specializing in FoxPro it was possible to relate the Piacenza antiphoner from the CANTUS project to our database—the task was accomplished in just ten minutes, and that included the programming.[10] When the programmer asked why a numerical representation was chosen, we pointed out that it allowed for the possibility of a search within a range (for example, within authentic and plagal modes), it was compact, and it had a certain structural elegance as a solution.

Comparisons within FoxPro are very fast, even those involving large numbers of antiphons. In fact our database is almost transparent, allowing the researcher to go directly from the tonaries to the comparisons. We built rugged error-detection algorithms into the program. The only drawback found in entering the assignments was that it was impractical to look back more than one antiphon at the virtual list just created, so it was necessary to proceed in one direction only. In fact this is an almost medieval condition; it appears that compilers of large tonaries made their way through an antiphoner in one direction to collect all of the chants of one subcategory, then made succeeding passes for the other subcategories. The database allows for the efficient entry and comparison of data in a way that corresponds to the original tonary lists and keeps errors to a minimum.

Independently both the authors and the CANTUS team decided not to attempt to make a uniform numbering of the *differentiae*. The number and contents of the *differentiae* vary greatly in tonaries and significantly in antiphoners, so that it was not desirable or feasible to impose a uniform system on them; the establishment of the correspondence between categories, whether isomorphic or not, is necessarily part of any comparative study of modal assignment. This limits the immediate usefulness of searches for an antiphon in multiple CANTUS files, because it is not evident from the results of a search whether the *differentiae* correspond or not. The searching feature of CANTUS is therefore most helpful for antiphons with conflicting assignments of mode, a smaller group than those with conflicts in *differentiae*. The latter are particularly important for the question of theory and practice, because the largest, most widely disseminated treatises, such as the writings of Guido of Arezzo, did not set down rules for the assignment of melodies to *differentiae*.

Having briefly reviewed the history of the modal system and introduced the databases, we can now proceed to the specific results of the comparison. In the present chapter the comparison is limited to one antiphoner because of the scope of the questions of correspondence of subcategories and conflicts, and perhaps this is for the best. Because Dr. Steiner has made numerous antiphoners available on the Internet, the problem now facing scholars is not a lack of data, but the need for perseverance in comparison and interpretation in the face of an abundance of data. Here we will make comparisons between the modal assignment of antiphons in the Piacenza 65 antiphoner and the large tonaries in the manuscripts Bamberg, Staatsbibl. lit. 5 (Ed.V.9), here referred to as Bamberg, and Metz, Médiathèque du Pontiffroy 351, referred to as Metz, both of these early tonaries having little theoretical commentary on the modal assignments and not entered with treatises or prefaces to their tonaries.

As noted above, large tonaries occupy an important position in the spectrum of theory and practice, as expert compilations that serve as an adjunct to performance, at least as a check on errors in antiphoners. Some large tonaries have substantial theoretical commentary and others have little or none. In some cases the formality of the commentary is indicative of a theoretical orientation, and some cite specific theorists or treatises. The tonaries in the manuscripts of Metz 351 and Bamberg lit. 5 seem more closely related to musical practice as found in antiphoners. Fruitful comparisons can be made between these tonaries and other antiphoners in the CANTUS files, but these will have to be prepared for a later publication. It should be noted that the CANTUS files occasionally undergo revision, and significant revisions have been made to the Piacenza 65 text file since the publication of the volume, so that the on-line files must now be consulted for questions of mode and *differentia*. The determination of *differentia* is often a difficult task, even in a manuscript with consistent heighted notation; the misreading of a notational nuance can result in an error, and the possibility of revision is one of the greatest advantages of storage of the data on computer, which must be considered the most accurate version, rather than the published CANTUS volumes. The present chapter is based on the revised information.

First, it is necessary to establish the general correspondence of the *differentiae*. Eighty-two antiphons are in the first *differentia* of the first mode in both tonaries and the antiphoner. These are antiphons of the *Ecce nomen domini* theme that begins with the notes *dcf*, usually placed as the first *differentia* because it is the first antiphon of the church year. In addition to the conflicting assignments involving this *differentia*, there are significant differences in taxonomy. In the two tonaries there is a distinction between this group of antiphons and ten antiphons that begin *dfddc*. These make up the second *differentia* in the tonaries but they are part of the first in the antiphoner. Similarly, 18 antiphons beginning *cda* or *dac'* are placed in the third *differentia* in the tonaries, but the first in the antiphoner. In addition, 11 antiphons that begin *dcdfcd* are in the fifth *differentia* of the first mode in the tonaries but in the first *differentia* of the first mode in the antiphoner. The antiphoner has several *differentiae* with only one or two antiphons; for example, the fifth and sixth *differentiae* of the first mode in the antiphoner have only one or two antiphons and imply modal subdivisions that do not correspond in any transitive way to those of the tonaries.

As for the fourth *differentia* of the first mode in the antiphoner, those antiphons, which begin *cdf*, are split between the first and second *differentiae* of the first mode in the tonaries. Overall it seems that in the taxonomy of the antiphoner in the first mode, almost all of the antiphons are grouped into a few *differentiae*, but in the tonaries the assignments are spread out over nine *differentiae*. One possible interpretation is that the taxonomy of the antiphoner represents a simplification of the practice of *differentiae*, and therefore of *seculorum amen* formulas, perhaps with distinctive formulas preserved for antiphons taken from a small tonary, or in the preservation of a tradition.

Before moving to the other modes it is worth noting that there are several conflicts of mode in the antiphons assigned to the first mode in the antiphoner, including not only frequently encountered cases such as *Caecilia famula tua* and *Inter natos mulierum* (usually third-mode antiphons, as in fact they are in Metz, Bamberg, and the tonaries in Vienna, ÖNB 51 and the tonary in Brussels, BR 2750–65 in our database), and migrant fourth-mode antiphons such as some from the *Ex*

Aegypto theme (we mention here *Iustus germinabit,* which is in the first mode in Piacenza 65 but the fourth mode in Bamberg and Vienna 51), but also several others, including three antiphons assigned to the first *differentia* of the sixth mode in the tonaries in Metz, Bamberg, and Vienna 51.

All three sources, Piacenza, Metz, and Bamberg, have most of the antiphons of the third mode in a single category: the second *differentia* for the tonaries and the first for Piacenza. As happens between tonaries, there are several conflicts between the third and eighth modes. For example *Laetemini in domino* is in the third mode in Piacenza, but in the eighth mode in tonaries in our database. In the fourth mode there are eight *differentiae* in the antiphoner and nine in the tonaries, but most of these categories have only one or two antiphons.

In the fifth mode all of the antiphons in the antiphoner are in the first *differentia.* These are mainly divided between the second and third *differentiae* in the tonaries. The antiphoner has a fifth-mode version of *Sacerdotes dei benedicite,* an antiphon that is usually in the seventh mode and that begins *d' bd',* and similarly it has *Haurietis aquas* and *Exsultabunt omnia ligna.*

Naturally the G-modes have the most antiphons in all sources (since more antiphons end on G than on D, E, or F), and for this reason the correspondence of categories is clearer than for the other modes. In the seventh mode, of the 14 antiphons in the first *differentia* in the antiphoner that are also found in the tonaries, 11 are in the second *differentia* of Metz and the fourth of Bamberg. These begin *gd' c'.* Fifty of 58 antiphons of the second *differentia* in the antiphoner are in the seventh *differentia* in the tonaries. The antiphons of the third *differentia* in Piacenza are split between the sixth *differentia* of the tonaries, which have ten of these antiphons, and the fifth *differentia* of Metz and the third of Bamberg, which have 15. The fourth and fifth *differentiae* of Piacenza contain 59 antiphons that are assigned to the fourth mode in most other sources. The antiphons *Caro sanguis* and *Petre amas me,* for example, both for the feast of St. Peter, are in the fifth *differentia* of the seventh mode in Piacenza, but in the fourth mode in all of the sources in our database in which they are present.

In the eighth mode, 186 antiphons are in the first *differentia* of all three sources. Fourteen are in the second *differentia* of all three, and 18 that begin *c' bc'* are in the second *differentia* in the antiphoner but in the seventh *differentia* in the tonaries. This accounts for most of the antiphons in that mode. The antiphon *Circumdantes circumdederunt,* usually a first-mode antiphon, is in the eighth mode with a special *differentia* in Piacenza, and there are other conflicts with the D-modes.

Although the antiphoner in Piacenza 65 preserves many modal distinctions, many of the categories have only one or two antiphons. It appears that the taxonomy of the antiphoner represents a great simplification, or amalgamation of categories, compared with those of tonaries. We will need to consider much more data before drawing any conclusions, but it does appear that this is a promising line of investigation. This comparison of modal assignment in an antiphoner with that in tonaries demonstrates the variation in the number and content of the modal subcategories. It is evident that the application of the system of modes and *differentiae* was not uniform in these sources, and that the factors of performance tradition and theoretical innovation came into play. The differences in categorization reveal the judgments of musicians in manuscript sources—in effect, the reception of the modal system in this period.

Having compared a single antiphoner with selected tonaries, we now turn to a different type of comparison between the tonary database and the CANTUS files. Antiphons that we have identified as being involved in conflicts can be investigated for their assignments in antiphoners using the search program in the CANTUS files. As noted above, there is no uniform numbering of *differentiae,* and the results of searches of individual antiphons in CANTUS are not telling in this respect. For example, the antiphon *Appenderunt mercedem* (*CAO* 1463) is assigned to the first *differentia* of the first mode in the large tonary in Florence, BNC Conv. Sopp. F 3 565 (Tuscany, ca. 1100) (Merkley 1988, 136–41; Huglo 1971, 188–91), and in the second *differentia* of mode four in the large tonary in Oxford, Bodleian Digby 25 (mid-12th c., Italian) (Merkley 1988, 91–94). The reason for this conflict appears to have been that the two tonary compilers knew two versions of the melody, differing only in the last four pitches, one version ending on D and the other on E. The CANTUS search results for *Appenderunt mercedem* are as follows:

Source	Mode	*Differentia*
Toledo, BC 44.1	1	
Arras, BM 465	4	8
Bamberg, Staatsbibl. lit. 25	4	E1(*)
Cambrai, MM 38	4	1
Florence, Arcivescovado	4	1
Graz, UB 29	4	
Karlsruhe, Landisbibl. Aug. LX	4	
Klosterneuburg, Chorherrenstift 1017	4	
Paris, BNF n.a.l. 1535	4	
Piacenza, BC 65	4	
Cambridge, UL Mm. ii.9	4	

(*) *Seculorum amen* formula ends on E.

From the search in CANTUS there resulted first-mode versions in Toledo 44.1 and 44.2, and fourth-mode versions in Arras 465 (983) (a monastic breviary from Saint-Vaast d'Arras, 13th c.)[11]—eighth *differentia;* Bamberg lit. 25 (late 13th c., Bamberg)—*differentia* E1, referring, in the manner of the manuscript, to a fourth-mode *differentia* with the *seculorum amen* formula ending on the note E; Cambrai 38 (Cambrai Cathedral, 1230–50)—first *differentia;* Florence, Arcivescovado (made for the Cathedral of Santa Maria del Fiore in Florence in the 12th c.)[12]—first *differentia;* Graz 29 (a winter antiphoner from St. Lambert in Steiermark, 14th c.); Karlsruhe Aug. LX (late 12th c., origin unknown, monastic cursus); Klosterneuburg 1017 (Klosterneuburg, 13th or 14th c., secular cursus, winter antiphoner); Paris n.a.l. 1535 (early 13th c., Sens Cathedral); Piacenza 65; and Cambridge Mm. ii. 9 (a Sarum source in CANTUS). The antiphoners have first- and fourth-mode versions of the antiphon, but nothing can be determined concerning the *differentiae* without a comprehensive study of each manuscript, which must be postponed until later publications.

The first stage of the search proceeds quickly on CANTUS, producing a display of sources that contain a chant with the desired textual incipit, together with the genre of the chant (to distinguish, for example, between an antiphon and a responsory with the same textual incipit). To obtain the rest of the information (*CAO* number, feast assignment, location in the manuscript, mode, and *differentia*), it is necessary to open the sources one at a time. Interpretive tables are provided for the abbreviations of feasts, codes of *differentiae*, and source sigla. All of this information gives the user checks to make sure that there is no mistake in the identification of the antiphon.

A conflict between the first and fourth modes in the antiphon *Ambulabunt mecum* (*CAO* 1364), may have been caused by a similar melodic variant. A first-mode version was found in the antiphoner in Florence Arcivescovado, and fourth-mode versions in Arras 465, Graz 29, Karlsruhe Aug. LX, and Klosterneuburg 1017. One difficulty in studying tonaries is finding melodic variants in antiphons that might have given rise to particular conflicting assignments. The presence of these versions supports the assignments in the tonaries, and makes it possible to study the melodies from the manuscript locations in order to assess the conflict. Perhaps in the future transcriptions of the melodies will also be available on-line.

Circumdantes circumdederunt (*CAO* 1809), sung on Palm Sunday, is assigned to the first, sixth, and eighth modes in different tonaries (Merkley 1988, 230). From notated incipits in the tonaries it appears that the reason for the eighth-mode assignment may have been a version of the melody that began a fifth above and ended a fourth above the first-mode version. The CANTUS sources list a first-mode melody in Bamberg lit. 25, a second-mode version in Florence Arcivescovado, and eighth-mode assignments in Piacenza 65 and other antiphoners. Although this gives no witness of a sixth-mode version, it opens up possibilities for determing the variant of the eighth-mode melody. The difference between the first and second modes—the authentic and plagal versions of the D-mode—were not strictly defined in the Middle Ages, and this conflict is not surprising. Here, as in many other cases, it is important to learn that a type of variant, such as the transposition of a melody by one interval at the beginning and another at the end, is not only implied in assignments in tonaries, but actually formed part of the practice as witnessed by antiphoners. This change in the interval of transposition in turn lends credence to some of the statements of Guido of Arezzo in the *Micrologus,* those concerning the practice of changing transposition to avoid certain intervals and false similitudes.[13]

There is a conflict in tonaries between fifth- and eighth-mode assignments of *Exsultabunt omnia ligna* (*CAO* 2811), performed in Christmas week. The most probable reason for the conflict (the eighth-mode assignment in Bamberg lit. 5 is in the minority) is transposition by the interval of a second. CANTUS sources assign this antiphon to modes two, three, five, and eight:

Source	Mode
Cambrai, MM 38	2
Cambrai, MM XVI C 4	2
Graz, UB 29	3
Karlsruhe, Landesbibl. Aug. LX	3
Klosterneuburg, Chorherrenstift 1017	3
Rome, Vallicelliana C.5	3
Vienna, Diözesanarchiv C-11	3
Vorau, SB 287	3
Arras, BM 465	5
Bamberg, Staatsbibl. lit. 25	5
Benevento, BC IV, 19	5
Einsiedeln, SB 611	5
Florence, Arcivescovado	5
Florence, Laurenziana Conv. Sopp. 560	5
Montecassino, Badia 542	5
Monza, BC 15/79	5
Paris, BNF lat. 12044	5
Paris, BNF lat. 15181	5
Piazenza, BC 65	5
Stuttgart, Landesbibl. HB.I.55	5
Toledo, BC 44.1	5
Tours, BM 149	5
Utrecht, Rijksuniversiteit 406 (3 J 7)	5
Valenciennes, BM 114	5
Worcester, Cathedral F 160	5
Paris, BNF lat. 1090	8
Toledo, BC 44.2	8

Si iniquitates observaveris (*CAO* 4899), from the Office for the Dead, has an unsupported second-mode assignment in the tonary in Wolfenbüttel, HAB Helmstedt 1050 (12th c.) (Merkley 1992, 198–99). Most of the CANTUS antiphoners, like most tonaries, place the antiphon in the eighth mode, but the antiphoner in Piacenza 65 has a second-mode assignment.

In tonaries *Unum opus feci* (*CAO* 5275), for feria 3 in the fourth week of Quadragesima, is assigned to modes 3 (majority), 5, and 8 (Merkley 1992, 288). In most of the CANTUS sources this antiphon is in the third mode, but in Toledo 44.2 it is assigned to mode 7. It appears that the reason for this conflict was confusion between the incipits *fac* and *gbc'*. *Laudem dicite deo nostro* (*CAO* 3590), for All Saints, has the same melodic theme as *Unum opus feci*. In tonaries the former was assigned to the fourth and fifth modes, and there are several antiphoners for each mode in the CANTUS sources. This type of conflict, arising from variants associated with the confusion of melodic incipits, provides additional evidence for the influence of the practical tradition on the melodies themselves.

The CANTUS sources also furnish the possibility of studying variants in feast assignment. *Homo quidam fecit* (*CAO* 4536), is assigned to the third Sunday after Pentecost in the majority of sources, but to the second Sunday after Pentecost in Piacenza 65. This kind of variant may provide a clue to other local saints or idiosyncrasies of observance. Similarly, *Visionem quam vidistis* (*CAO* 5465), is assigned to the second Sunday of Quadragesima in most of the CANTUS sources, but to Saturday of the first week of Quadragesima in Bamberg lit. 25.

Some antiphons, particularly those for Marian feasts, are written out more than once in some manuscripts, or textual incipits only are provided as cues for subsequent occurrences. *Angelus domini nuntiavit* (*CAO* 1414), is written out for feria 2 of the first week of Advent. Some sources, like Florence Arcivescovado, have cues for the feast of the Annunciation or for the Conception of the Virgin, while others have the antiphon written out for those feasts.

The foregoing examples demonstrate the usefulness of the CANTUS files in the study of modal assignment, in finding melodies and melodic variants, and in gathering liturgical information. In many cases these antiphoners provide melodies that can be associated with particular, unusual modal assignments in tonaries. Additional study will naturally be required to complete these assessments, and the study of these comparisons will be greatly enhanced by relating our databases with more files of antiphoners; in this way it will be possible to establish corresponding *differentiae,* and compare the antiphons at that more precise level.

Because of the imprecision of the origins of most tonaries, it is normally not possible to associate a particular modal assignment with a melodic version in a specific source. The main exceptions to this occur in tonaries entered together with antiphoners in the same manuscript. It does, however, seem clear that it will be possible to make regional comparisons between tonaries and antiphoners, especially as more sources are added to the CANTUS project. It is also evident that the melodic variants behind some tonary assignments may never be found in antiphoners. It would be an argument out of silence to suggest on that basis that the variants never existed, but it will be necessary to consider a small group of variants attested only in tonaries.

This paper is only a pilot study of the possibility for comparisons using our database and the CANTUS files, and as such it suggests that further comparisons hold great promise. It is hoped that this also will serve as an introduction to the enormous wealth of material available on-line in CANTUS, and that it calls attention to the potential of the next phase in the study of modal assignment, a stage made possible by the determined work of Dr. Steiner and her team.

Notes

We thank the Social Sciences and Humanities Research Council for its funding of our research on tonaries. For Merkley (1992), Matthews selected a structure for the database; entered antiphon assignments into that base from the many tonaries that we studied, as well as additional materials from secondary sources (such as information on early manuscripts and feast assignments from the *CAO*); and maintained the database. Merkley chose and assessed the tonaries, devised and executed the search for the comparisons here, evaluated the modal assignments, and analyzed the data, including the correspondence of categories and conflicts.

1. We join many other scholars in thanking Ruth Steiner for her pioneering work on the CANTUS project, which she made available for all scholars on the Internet via

Gopher, fittingly, on Groundhog Day, 1994. CANTUS was conceived and developed at The Benjamin T. Rome School of Music of The Catholic University of America with funding from the National Endowment for the Humanities, the Dom Mocquereau Foundation, and The Catholic University of America.

2. CANTUS now has a new home on the World Wide Web at http://publish.uwo.ca/ ~cantus/, located at the University of Western Ontario, where the project is directed by Terence Bailey. A new search program has been installed at that site. The files moved from The Catholic University on-line site were all revised and updated as of 10 January 1998, and several new ones have been added.

For a while, the files in a state of 5 March 1998 are still available at the Catholic University of America web address http://www.cua.edu/www/musu/cantus/home.htm, where the search program operates on Gopher. (To reach the files via Gopher, find the Catholic University of America [CUA.EDU], then select option 9, Schools of the University, from that option 2, the Benjamin T. Rome School of Music, then option 2, CANTUS database of Gregorian Chant.)

The CANTUS indexes are also available on CD-ROM, published in conjunction with Thesaurus Musicarum Latinarum under the direction of Prof. Thomas Mathiesen at Indiana University (Bloomington).

3. Andrew Hughes has carried out a recent, extended study of repertory with the aid of computer technology (see chap. 22 in this volume). His *LMLO*, 2 volumes and database, allows researchers to conduct specifically targeted and extensive searches into a broad repertory of chant. Without the computer this very useful bank of data could not have been created, let alone made available for easy use. Hughes has done a great deal of work isolating and analyzing melodic mosaics in the chant repertory. The same is true for several recent and ongoing studies of melodic themes, including work on Ambrosian antiphons by Bailey and Merkley (1990).

4. "Between musicians and singers, great is the distance; the latter tell, the former know, what music comprises." Guido of Arezzo's *Regulae rhythmicae*, published in Gerbert, ed., *Scriptores*, 2:25.

5. Some musicologists, including Merkley, have argued that these made up the earliest layer of the repertory. The data for this argument are in Bailey and Merkley (1989). Merkley presented his analysis of melodic themes and temporal layers of chant repertory in a paper (Merkley 1990) to be published in the near future.

6. Gevaert (1895) is the classical source for the thematic model of the repertory of antiphons. Bailey and Merkley (1990) have argued that the Ambrosian antiphon melodies fall into only 17 categories. The relationship between the so-called standard, or Gregorian, version of chant and regional dialects is the subject of much research in musicology. For a select bibliography, see that in Cattin (1984), 215–19. One of the first dialectical questions to be taken up was the relationship of "Old-Roman" chant to the Gregorian version, called Frankish by some others. For an early treatment of the question see Hucke (1955).

7. On tonaries see Huglo (1971), Merkley (1988), and Merkley (1992).

8. Bomm (1929) made a study of the modal assignments of introits, a repertory much smaller than that of antiphons. In addition, mention must be made of Bryden and Hughes, *An Index,* affectionately known as the "medieval phonebook," a list of the textual and melodic incipits of chants and their locations in modern printed sources, which was compiled with index cards.

9. We refer here to implementation of the programs on a computer with the now nearly extinct CPM operating system, one that deserves mention for its brief but vigorous existence. At the time Merkley coined the term "antiphon crunching" for the comparison of modal assignments in tonaries, not only because of the analogy with number crunching, but because of the distinctive sound of the floppy disk drive as data were

swapped from the 64K RAM to them and back; owners of CPM computers will be easily persuaded of the aptness of the term.

10. We thank David Homa (Ottawa, Canada) for his generous help and advice.

11. The information on the origins of these antiphoners was taken from the CANTUS "About" files.

12. Liturgical reasons for the date and place of origin are in Camiciotti (1905); see also Merkley (1988), 149–50.

13. See, for example, in the eighth chapter, in particular the use of local transposition to avoid B♭ (beginning at line 17), "Quod si ipsam .b. mollem vis omnino non habere, neumas in quibus ipsa est, ita tempera, ut pro .F.G.a. et ipsa .b. habeas .G.a.b♮.c. . . ." *Micrologus,* ed. Smits van Waesberghe, 125. ("But if you wish not to have b-flat at all, alter the neumes in which it occurs, so that instead of F G a and b-flat you have G a b-natural c." Trans. by Warren Babb in Palisca, *Hucbald,* 64.)

Bibliography of Writings
by Ruth Steiner

COMPILED BY LILA COLLAMORE

Studies and Articles

1963 "Some Monophonic Latin Songs from the Tenth Fascicle of the Manuscript Florence, Biblioteca Laurenziana, Pluteus 29.1." Ph.D. diss., The Catholic University of America.

1966a "Some Monophonic Latin Songs Composed around 1200." *MQ* 52:56–70.

1966b "Some Questions about the Gregorian Offertories and Their Verses." *JAMS* 19:162–81 [= 1999a, XIII].

1967 "Alma Redemptoris Mater," "Ave Maria (antiphon)," and other entries. *NCE.* New York.

1969 "The Prosulae of the MS Paris, Bibliothèque nationale, f. lat. 1118." *JAMS* 22:367–93 [= 1999a, XV].

1970 "The Responsories and Prosa for St. Stephen's Day at Salisbury." *MQ* 56:162–82 [= 1999a, XII].

1971 Supplement to "York Pageant XLVI and Its Music." By Carolyn Wall. *Speculum* 46:698–712.

1973 "Some Melismas for Office Responsories." *JAMS* 26:108–31 [= 1999a, XI].

1974 "La musique des lais." In Tatiana Fotitch, *Les Lais du Roman de Tristan en prose,* 137–78. Münchener romanistische Arbeiten 38. Munich.

1979 "The Gregorian Chant Melismas of Christmas Matins." In *Essays on Music for Charles Warren Fox,* ed. Jerald C. Graue, 241–53. Rochester, N.Y. [= 1999a, X].

1980 Articles in *NG:*
vol. 2: "Benedicite," 471–72.
vol. 3: "Cantatorium," 718–19; "Canticle (Roman)," 724–25.
vol. 4: "Compline," 598–99.
vol. 5: "Cursus," 99–101; "Divine Office," 508–9.
vol. 6: "Fortunatus, Venantius," 725–26.
vol. 7: "Gregorian Chant," 697–8.
vol. 8: "Hrabanus Maurus," 748; "Hymn (Monophonic Latin)," 838–41.
vol. 9: "Introit (i)," 281–84; "Invitatory," 286–89; "Jerome," 606.
vol. 10: "Lauds," 544–45.

vol. 11: "Little Hours," 83; "Liturgy and Liturgical Books (General and Latin Rite)," 84–86; "Lord's Prayer," 229–30; "Magnificat" (1), 495; "Mass (Liturgy and Chant: 1. Introduction, 2. The Proper, 4. The Liturgy of the Eucharist, 5. Two Medieval Masses: Later Developments)," 770–81; "Matins," 825.

vol. 13: "Offertory" (with G. Baroffio), 513–17.

vol. 15: "Prosula," 310–12; "Preface," 208–9; "Psalter, Liturgical," 382; "Reproaches," 750–51.

vol. 18: "Te Deum (Text and Melody)," 641–43.

vol. 19: "Trope (i)," 172–87; "Troper," 187; "Vespers," 685–86.

1981   "Musicology in the United States in 1980." *AcM* 53:216–23.

1982a   "The Canticle of the Three Children as a Chant of the Roman Mass." *Schweizer Jahrbuch für Musikwissenschaft*, Neue Folge 2:81–90 [= 1999a, XVII].

1982b   "Agnus Dei (music)," *DMA* 1:74–75.

1982c   "Directions for Chant Research in the 1980s." *JM* 1:34–38.

1982d   (with Gunilla Björkvall). "Some Prosulas for Offertory Antiphons." *Journal of the Plainsong and Mediaeval Music Society* 5:13–35.

1983a   "Communion Chant." *DMA* 2:504.

1983b   "Recent Research Developments in Gregorian Chant." In *Gregorian Chant in Liturgy and Education, An International Symposium, June 19–22, 1982: Proceedings,* 59–75. Washington, D.C.

1984a   "Antiphons for the Benedicite at Lauds." *Journal of the Plainsong and Mediaeval Music Society* 7:1–17 [= 1999a, VII].

1984b   "The Music for a Cluny Office of St. Benedict." In *Monasticism and the Arts,* ed. Timothy Gregory Verdon with the assistance of John Dally, 81–113. Syracuse [= 1999a, I].

1984c   "Tones for the Psalm Sunday Invitatory." *JM* 3:142–56 [= 1999a, II].

1985a   "Gloria." *DMA* 5:564.

1985b   "Local and Regional Traditions of the Invitatory Chant." *Studia Musicologica Academiae Scientiarum Hungaricae* 27:131–38 [= 1999a, III].

1986a   "Kyrie." *DMA* 7:312–13.

1986b   "Matins Responsories and Cycles of Illustrations of Saints' Lives." In *Diakonia: Studies in Honor of Robert T. Meyer,* ed. Thomas Halton and Joseph P. Williman, 317–32. Washington, D.C. [= 1999a, IX].

1987a   "Offertory." *DMA* 9:221–22.

1987b   "Plainsong, Sources of." *DMA* 9:688–93.

1987c   "Reconstructing the Repertory of Invitatory Tones and their Uses at Cluny in the Late 11th Century." In *Musicologie médiévale: Notations et séquences. Actes de la table ronde du CNRS à l'IRHT, Orléans-La Source, 6–7 Septembre 1982,* ed. Michel Huglo, 175–82. Paris [= 1999a, IV].

1988   "The Liturgical and Musical Tradition of Bec as Revealed in the Manuscript Leningrad, Saltykov-Shchedrin State Public Library, Lat. O.v.I.6." In *Acta musicologica: Proceedings of the International Musicological Congress "Musica Antiqua Europae Orientalis" Bydgoszcz, September 5th-10th, 1988,* ed. Andrzej Szwalbe, 1:937–52. Musica Antiqua VIII. Bydgoszcz [= 1999a, XVIII].

1990   "The Parable of the Talents in Liturgy and Chant." In *Essays in Musicology: A Tribute to Alvin Johnson,* ed. Lewis Lockwood and Edward Roesner, 1–15. Philadelphia [= 1999a, VII].

1991   "Einführung und Verbreitung des lateinischen liturgischen Gesänge in der Karolingerzeit." In *Neues Handbuch des Musikwissenschaft, 2: Die Musik des Mittelalters,* ed. Hartmut Möller and Rudolf Stephan, 33–53. Laaber.

1993a   "Directions for Chant Research in the 1990s: The Impact of Chant Data Bases." *Revista de musicología* 16:697–705.

1993b "Hartker's Antiphoner and the Oral Tradition of Chant at St. Gall." In *Sangallensia in Washington*, ed. James C. King, 199–212. New York.

1993c "*Holocausta medullata:* An Offertory for St. Saturninus." In *De musica et cantu: Studien zur Geschichte der Kirchenmusik et der Oper.* Helmut Hucke zum 60. Geburtstag, ed. Peter Cahn and Ann-Katrin Heimer, 263–74. Hildesheim [= 1999a, XIV].

1993d "Marian Antiphons at Cluny and Lewes." In *Music in the Medieval English Liturgy*, ed. Susan Rankin and David Hiley, 175–204. Oxford.

1993e "Non-Psalm Verses for Introits and Communions." in *Recherches nouvelles sur les tropes liturgiques*, ed. Wulf Arlt and Gunilla Björkvall, 441–48. Corpus troporum 8. Acta Universitatis Stockholmiensis. Studia Latina Stockholmiensia 36. Stockholm [= 1999a, XVI].

1995 "Antiphons for Lauds on the Octave of Christmas." In *Laborare fratres in unum: Festschrift László Dobszay zum 60. Geburtstag*, ed. Janka Szendrei and David Hiley, 307–15. Spolia Berolinensia: Berliner Beiträge zur Mediävistik 7. Hildesheim [= 1999a, VI].

1996 "Liturgischer Gesang." *MGG* (2d ed.), ed. Ludwig Finscher. Sachteil 5, cols. 1437–46. Kassel.

1997 "The Twenty-two Invitatory Tones of the Manuscript Toledo, Biblioteca Capitular, 44.2." In *Music in Performance and Society: Essays in Honor of Roland Jackson*, ed. Malcolm Cole and John Koegel, 59–79. Detroit Monographs in Musicology / Studies in Music, No. 20. Warren, Mich. [= 1999a, V].

1999a *Studies in Gregorian Chant.* Variorum Collected Studies Series, CS651. Aldershot, Hants, and Brookfield, Vt.

1999b "Gruppen von Antiphonen zur Matutin des Afra-Offiziums." In *Die Offizien des Mittelalters: Dichtung und Musik*, ed. Walter Berschin and David Hiley, 59–67. Regensburger Studien zur Musikgeschichte 1. Tutzing.

1999c "The Cantus Database of the Divine Office in Piacenza 65." In *Il Libro del Maestro: Codice 65 dell'Archivio Capitolare della Cattedrale di Piacenza (sec. XII)*, ed. Pierre Racine, 171–80. Piacenza.

1999d "The Lessons of CANTUS." In *Die Erschliessung der Quellen des mittelalterlichen liturgischen Gesangs*, ed. David Hiley. Wolfenbütteler Mittelalter-Studien. Wolfenbüttel.

Forthcoming "On the Verses for the Offertory *Elegerunt.*" In *The Study of Medieval Chant: Paths and Bridges, East and West*, ed. Peter Jeffery. Woodbridge, 2000.

Reviews

1969 Review of Don Michael Randel, *The Responsorial Psalm Tones for the Mozarabic Office* (Princeton, 1969), in *MQ* 55: 575–80.

1971 Review of Paul Evans, *The Early Trope Repertory of Saint Martial de Limoges* (Princeton, 1970), in *Notes* 28:474–75.

1972 Review of Michel Huglo, *Les Tonaires: Inventaire, analyse, comparaison* (Paris, 1971), in *MQ* 58:672–75.

1973 Review of Hendrik van der Werf, *The Chansons of the Troubadours and Trouvères* (Utrecht, 1972), in *JAMS* 26:488–90.

1974 Review of *Gregorian Chant*, recording by Schola Cantorum of Amsterdam Students, cond. Wim van Gerven (Columbia M3X 32329), in *MQ* 60:673–77.

1977 Review of Bruno Stäblein, *Schriftbild der einstimmigen Musik*, Musikgeschichte in Bildern III/4 (Leipzig, 1975), in *MQ* 63:283–66.

1979 Review of Solange Corbin, *Die Neumen*, Palaeographie der Musik I/3 (Cologne, 1977), in *JAMS* 32:555–61.

1982   Review of *Tropes de l'Agnus Dei,* ed. Gunilla Iversen, Corpus Troporum IV (Stockholm, 1980), in *Speculum* 57:905–8.

1986   Review of Chrysogonus Waddell, *The Twelfth-Century Cistercian Hymnal,* 2 vols. Cistercian Liturgy Series I–II (Trappist, Ky., 1984), in *Hymn* 37:36–37.

1993   Review of *Lexicon musicum Latinum medii aevi / Dictionary of Medieval Latin Musical Terminology to the End of the 15th Century,* 1: *Quellenverzeichnis / Inventory of Sources,* ed. Michael Bernhard (Munich, 1992), and *Thesaurus musicarum Latinarum: A Comprehensive Database of Latin Music Theory of the Middle Ages and the Renaissance,* in course of compilation at Indiana University under the direction of Thomas J. Mathiesen, in *Speculum* 68: 721–72.

1994   Review of David Hiley, *Western Plainchant: A Handbook* (Oxford, 1993), in *Plainsong and Medieval Music* 3:212–17.

1994   Review of Christopher Page, *Discarding Images* (Oxford, 1993), in *Catholic Historical Review* 80:346–47.

1998   Review of *Ordinary Chants and Tropes for the Mass from Southern Italy: Preface Chants and Sanctus* (Beneventanum Troporum Corpus, 2: Recent Researches in the Music of the Middle Ages and Early Renaissance, 25–26), ed. John Boe (Madison, Wis., 1996); and *Early Medieval Chants from Nonantola* (Recent Researches in the Music of the Middle Ages and Early Renaissance, 30–32), ed. James Borders (Madison, Wis., 1996), in *Speculum* 73:811–13.

1998   Review of *Stiftsbibliothek Sankt Gallen, Codices 484 & 381,* ed. Wulf Arlt and Susan Rankin (Winterthur, 1996), in *Notes* 55:183–85.

1998   Review of Thomas Forrest Kelly, *The Exultet in Southern Italy* (Oxford and New York, 1996), in *Catholic Historical Review* 84: 531–32.

Publications from the CANTUS database,
edited by Ruth Steiner

1990   Lila Collamore and Joseph Metzinger. *The Bamberg Antiphoner: Staatsbibliothek, lit. 25. Printouts from an Index in Machine-Readable Form.* Introduction by Ruth Steiner. Washington, D.C.

1990   Lila Collamore and Joseph Metzinger, eds. *Frere's Index to the Antiphons of the Sarum Antiphoner.* Introduction by Ruth Steiner. London.

1992   "An Index to the Bamberg Antiphoner Staatsbibliothek, lit. 25." *International Musicological Society Study Group Cantus Planus: Papers Read at the Fourth Meeting, Pécs, Hungary, 3–8 September 1990,* ed. László Dobszay, Agnes Papp, and Ferenc Sebó, 599–605. Budapest. [= Introduction by Ruth Steiner to *The Bamberg Antiphoner,* 1990]

1992   Ronald T. Olexy et al. *An Aquitanian Antiphoner: Toledo, Biblioteca Capitular, 44.2: Printouts from an Index in Machine-Readable Form: A CANTUS Index.* Introduction by Ruth Steiner. Musicological Studies 55/1. Ottawa.

1993   Keith Glaeske et al. *Piacenza, Biblioteca Capitolare 65: Printouts from an Index in Machine-Readable Form: A CANTUS Index.* Introduction by Paul Merkley. Musicological Studies 55/2. Ottawa.

1995   Martin Czernin. *A Monastic Breviary of Austrian Provenance: Linz, Bundesstaatliche Studienbibliothek 290 (183): Printouts from an Index in Machine-Readable Form: A CANTUS Index.* Musicological Studies 55/3. Ottawa.

1995   Barbara Haggh et al. *Two Cambrai Antiphoners: Cambrai, Médiathèque Municipale, 38 and Impr. XVI C 4: Printouts from Two Indices in Machine-Readable Form: A CANTUS Index.* Musicological Studies 55/4. Ottawa.

1996   Joseph Metzinger et al. *The Zwiefalten Antiphoner: Karlsruhe, Badische Landesbibliothek, Aug. perg. LX: Printouts from an Index in Machine-Readable Form: A*

CANTUS Index. Introduction by Hartmut Möller. Musicological Studies 55/5. Ottawa. (A brief version of this index with the introduction in German appeared in *Antiphonarium: Karlsruhe, Badische Landesbibliothek, Aug. perg. 60.* Codices illuminati medii aevi 36. Munich, 1995.)

1997 Charles Downey. *An Utrecht Antiphoner: Utrecht, Bibliotheek der Rijskuniversiteit, 406 (3.J.7): Printouts from an Index in Machine-Readable Form: A CANTUS Index.* Introduction by Ruth Steiner. Musicological Studies 55/6. Ottawa.

1997 *Utrecht: Bibliotheek der Rijksuniversiteit, 406 (3.J.7): Facsimile Reproduction of the Manuscript.* Introduction by Ike de Loos, index by Charles Downey, ed. Ruth Steiner. PMMM 21. Ottawa.

1998 Debra Lacoste. *Four Klosterneuburg Antiphoners: Augustiner-Chorherren SB 1013, 1012, 1017, and 1018: Printouts from an Index in Machine-Readable Form: A CANTUS Index.* Musicological Studies 55/7. Ottawa.

1998 CANTUS: A Database for Gregorian Chant. Compiled at the Catholic University of America under the direction of Ruth Steiner. CD-ROM version: TML / CANTUS CD-ROM. Made available by the Thesaurus Musicarum Latinarum, School of Music, Indiana University.

In preparation: Susan A. Kidwell. *Paris, Bibliothèque nationale, lat. 15181 and 15182.* Introduction by Rebecca A. Baltzer.

Bibliography

The bibliography is divided into two sections, preceded by a list of abbreviations. The first section contains primary sources, indexes, catalogs, and multivolume reference works. These have been listed using author/title format. If the author's name is not known, works are listed under the editor's, and, lacking both, under the title. Works in this section of the bibliography are indicated in the notes by author and short title. In the second section of the bibliography, secondary works are listed following the author/date format. Accordingly, secondary sources in the notes are cited by author/date. It is not difficult, therefore, for the reader to know which of the two sections to consult.

Abbreviations

AASS	*Acta sanctorum.* Antwerp, 1643–1770; Brussels, 1780–86, 1845–83, and 1894– ; Tongerloo, 1794; and Paris, 1875–87.
AcM	*Acta musicologica.*
AH	*Analecta hymnica medii aevi.* 55 vols. Leipzig, 1886–1922.
ALw	*Archiv für Liturgiewissenschaft.*
AMS	*Antiphonale missarum sextuplex.* Ed. René-Jean Hesbert. Brussels, 1935.
BHL	*Bibliotheca hagiographica latina antiquae et mediae aetatis.* Ed. Socii Bollandiani. 2 vols. Brussels, 1898–1901. Subsidia hagiographica 6. 2d ed. Brussels, 1949. *Novum supplementum,* ed. H. Fros. Subsidia hagiographica 70. Brussels, 1986.
CANTUS 1990	Lila Collamore and Joseph Metzinger. *The Bamberg Antiphoner: Staatsbibliothek, lit. 25. Printouts from an Index in Machine-Readable Form.* Introduction by Ruth Steiner. Washington, D.C., 1990.
CANTUS 1992	Ronald T. Olexy et al. *An Aquitanian Antiphoner: Toledo, Biblioteca Capitular, 44.2: Printouts from an Index in Machine-Readable Form: A CANTUS Index.* Introduction by Ruth Steiner. Musicological Studies 55/1. Ottawa., 1992.
CANTUS 1993	Keith Glaeske et al. *Piacenza, Biblioteca Capitolare 65: Printouts from an Index in Machine-Readable Form: A CANTUS Index.* Introduction by Paul Merkley. Musicological Studies 55/2. Ottawa, 1993.

CAO   *Corpus antiphonalium officii*. Ed. René-Jean Hesbert. 6 vols. Rome, 1963–79.

CAO–ECE I/A   L. Dobszay. *Corpus Antiphonalium Officii–Ecclesiarum Centralis Europae*, I/A: *Salzburg (Pars Temporalis)*. Budapest.

CAO–ECE II/A   Zsuzsa Czagány. *Corpus Antiphonalium Officii–Ecclesiarum Centralis Europae*, II/A: *Bamberg (Pars Temporalis)*. Budapest.

CAO–ECE III/A   Zsuzsa Czagány. *Corpus Antiphonalium Officii–Ecclesiarum Centralis Europae*, III/A: *Prague (Pars Temporalis)*. Budapest, 1996.

CCCM   Corpus Christianorum, continuatio medievalis. Turnhout, 1964– .

CCM   Corpus consuetudinum monasticarum, ed. Kassius Hallinger. Siegburg, 1963– .

CCSL   Corpus Christianorum, series latina. Turnhout, 1954– .

CE   *The Catholic Encyclopedia*. 15 vols. and index. New York, 1907–14.

CLA   *Codices Latini antiquiores*. Ed. E. A. Lowe; James John.

CLLA   *Codices liturgici Latini antiquiores*. Ed. Klaus Gamber. 2d ed. Spicilegii Friburgensis subsidia 1. 2 parts. Freiburg, 1968. *Supplementum.* Freiburg, 1988.

CPG   Geerard, Maurice. *Clavis patrum Graecorum*. 5 vols. Turnhout, 1974–87.

CPL   *Clavis patrum Latinorum*. Ed. Eligius Dekkers. 3rd ed., ed. Emil Gaar. CCSL. Turnhout and Steenbrugge, 1995.

CSEL   Corpus scriptorum ecclesiasticorum Latinorum. Vienna, 1866– .

CT   Corpus troporum. Stockholm, 1975– . Seven volumes have appeared; several are listed individually in primary sources.

DACL   *Dictionnaire d'archéologie chrétienne et de liturgie*. Ed. Fernand Cabrol, Henri Leclercq, et al. 15 vols. in 30. Paris, 1907–53.

DHGE   *Dictionnaire d'histoire et de géographie ecclésiastiques*. Ed. A. Baudrillart et al. Paris, 1912– .

DIP   *Dizionario italiano di perfezione*. Ed. G. Pelliccia and G. Rocca. 1974– .

DMA   *Dictionary of the Middle Ages*. Ed. Joseph Strayer et al. 13 vols. New York, 1982–89.

DS   *Dictionnaire de spiritualité*. Ed. Marcel Viller et al. 16 vols. and index. Paris, 1937–95.

DTC   *Dictionnaire de théologie catholique*. 15 vols. Paris, 1908–50.

EG   *Études grégoriennes*.

EL   *Ephemerides liturgicae*.

GC   *Gallia Christiana in provincias ecclesiasticas distributa*. 16 vols. Paris, 1715–1865.

GR   *Le Graduel romain: édition critique*. 2 vols. Solesmes, 1957–62.

HBS   Henry Bradshaw Society. 1891– .

HLM   Réginald Grégoire. *Homéliaires liturgiques médiévaux: Analyse de manuscrits*. Biblioteca studi medievali 12. Spoleto, 1980.

JAMS   *Journal of the American Musicological Society*.

JM   *Journal of Musicology*.

KmJ   *Kirchenmusikalisches Jahrbuch*.

LMLO   Andrew Hughes. *Late Medieval Liturgical Offices: Resources for Electronic Research: Texts*. Subsidia mediaevalia 23. *Late Medieval Liturgical Offices: Resources for Electronic Research: Sources & Chants*. Subsidia mediaevalia 24. Toronto, 1994, 1996.

LO   Amalarius of Metz. *Amalarii episcopi opera liturgica omnia*. Ed. Jean Michel Hanssens. 3 vols. Studi e testi 138–40. Vatican City, 1948–50.

LThK   *Lexikon für Theologie und Kirche.* Freiburg, 1930–38; 2d ed. 1957–67; 3d ed. 1993–98.

MECL   James McKinnon, ed. *Music in Early Christian Literature.* Cambridge Readings in the Literature of Music. Cambridge, 1987.

MGG   *Die Musik in Geschichte und Gegenwart.*

MGH   Monumenta Germaniae historia.

MMMA   Monumenta monodica medii aevi. Kassel, 1970– .

MQ   *The Musical Quarterly.*

NCE   *The New Catholic Encyclopedia.* 14 vols. and index. New York, 1967.

NG   *The New Grove Dictionary of Music and Musicians.* Ed. Stanley Sadie. London, 1980.

NOHM   The New Oxford History of Music.

NPM*   National Association of Pastoral Musicians.

OR   *Les Ordines Romani du haut moyen âge.* Ed. Michel Andrieu. 5 vols. Spicilegium sacrum Lovaniense, Études et documents 11, 23, 24, 28, 29. Louvain, 1931–61.

PL   Patrologia Latina. Ed. J.-P. Migne. 221 vols. Paris, 1844–64.

PM   Paléographie musicale. Solesmes, 1889– .

PMMM   Publications of Mediaeval Musical Manuscripts.

RB   *Revue bénédictine.*

RB 1980   *RB 1980: The Rule of St. Benedict in Latin and English with Notes,* ed. Timothy Fry. Collegeville, Minn., 1981.

RCG   *Revue du chant grégorienne.*

RG   *Revue grégorienne.*

RH   Ulysse Chevalier. *Repertorium hymnologicum: Catalogue des chants, hymnes, proses, séquences, tropes en usage dans l'église latine depuis les origines jusqu'à nos jours.* Louvain and Brussels, 1892–1920.

SC   Sources chrétiennes.

Primary Sources, Indexes, and Multivolume Reference Works

Abelard. *Epistolae.* PL 178, cols. 113–380.

Adémar de Chabannes. *Chronicon/Chronique.* Ed. Jules Chavanon. Collection de textes pour servir à l'étude et à l'enseignement de l'histoire. Paris, 1897.

Albers, Bruno, ed. *Consuetudines monasticae.* 5 vols. Stuttgart and Monte Cassino, 1900–12.

Amalarius of Metz. *Amalarii episcopi opera liturgica omnia.* Ed. Jean Michel Hanssens. 3 vols. Studi e Testi 138–40. Vatican City, 1948–50.

Ambrose of Milan. *Hymns: Texte établi, traduit et annoté.* Ed. by Jacques Fontaine et al. Paris, 1992.

Anderson, Gordon, ed. "1 pt Conductus Transmitted in Fascicule X of the Florence Manuscript." Part 6 of *Notre Dame and Related Conductus: Opera omnia* 10. 10 parts. Institute of Mediaeval Music, Henryville, Pa., 1981.

Andrieu, Michel, ed. *Les Ordines romani du haut moyen âge.* 5 vols. Spicilegium Sacrum Lovaniense, Études et Documents 11, 23, 24, 28, 29. Louvain, 1931–61.

Anglès, Higini, ed. *El còdex musical de Las Huelgas (música a veus dels segles XIII–XIV).* 3 vols. Barcelona, 1931.

Antiphonaire de l'office monastique transcrit par Hartker: MSS. Saint-Gall 390–391 (980–1011). PM sér. 2, 1. Solesmes, 1900. See also Froger, *L'Antiphonaire de Hartker.*

L'Antiphonaire du Mont-Renaud. PM 16. Solesmes, 1955.

Antiphonaire monastique, XIIᵉ siècle: Codex 601 de la Bibliothèque Capitulaire de Lucques. PM 9. Solesmes, 1906.

Antiphonaire monastique, XIIIe siècle: Codex F. 160 de la Bibliothèque de la Cathédrale de Worcester. PM 12 (antiphonal portion only). Tournai, 1922; repr. 1971.

Antiphonarium ad usum sacri et canonici ordinis Praemonstratensis. Paris, 1934.

Antiphonarium: Karlsruhe, Badische Landesbibliothek, Aug. perg. 60. Introduction by Hartmut Möller. Codices illuminati medii aevi 36. Munich, 1995.

Arlt, Wulf, and Susan Rankin, eds., in collaboration with Cristina Hespenthal. *Stiftsbibliothek Sankt Gallen Codices 484 & 381.* 3 vols. Winterthur, 1996.

Arranz, Miguel. *Le Typicon du monastère du Saint-Sauveur à Messine.* Orientalia Christiana Analecta 185. Rome, 1965.

Augustine of Hippo. *Enarrationes in Psalmos.* CCSL 38–40. Turnhout, 1956; PL 36–37.

———. *Ordo monasterii.* In *Augustine of Hippo and His Monastic Rule,* ed. George Lawless, 74–79. Oxford, 1987.

———. *Regula.* Trans. Raymond Canning with introduction and commentary by Tarsicius J. van Bavel. Kalamazoo, 1996.

———. *Sermons for Christmas and Epiphany.* Trans. by T. C. Lawler. Ancient Christian Writers 15. Westminster, Md., 1952.

Aurelian of Arles. *Regula Aureliani.* In *Lucas Hostenii . . . Codex regularum monasticarum et canonicarum . . . collectus olim a S. Benedicto Anianensi abbate,* 1:152–53. 6 vols. in 3. Ed. M. Brockie. Augsburg, 1759.

Bannister, Henry Marriott. "Liturgical Fragments." *Journal of Theological Studies* 9 (1908): 398–427.

Baroffio, Bonifacio, et al., eds. *Biblioteca Apostolica Vaticana Archivio S. Pietro B 79: Antifonario della Basilica di S. Pietro (Sec. XII).* 2 vols. Rome, 1995.

Bede. *De temporum ratione.* In *Opera didascalia,* 2, ed. Charles W. Jones. CCSL 123B. Turnhout, 1977.

———. *Historia gentis Anglorum ecclesiastica* [Bede's Ecclesiastical History of the English People]. Ed. Bertram Colgrave and R. A. B. Mynors. Oxford, 1969.

———. *Homiliarum evangelii libri II.* Ed. David Hurst. CCSL 122. Turnhout, 1955.

———. *Homilies on the Gospels.* Trans. by L. T. Martin and David Hurst. 2 vols. Kalamazoo, 1991.

———. *Opera de temporibus.* Ed. Charles Jones. Medieval Academy of America Publications 41. Cambridge, Mass., 1943.

———. *Opera exegetica* 3. Ed. David Hurst. CCSL 120. Turnhout, 1960.

Beleth, Jean. *Summa de ecclesiasticis officiis.* Ed. Herbert Douteil. CCCM 41, 41a. Turnhout, 1976. (Cf. PL 202.)

Benedict of Nursia. *Regula monachorum.* In *La Règle de Saint Benoît,* ed. Adalbert de Vogüé and Jean Neufville. 7 vols. SC 181–86 plus one volume *hors série.* Paris, 1971–77.

———. *Regula monachorum.* In *RB 1980: The Rule of St. Benedict in Latin and English with Notes,* ed. Timothy Fry. Collegeville, Minn., 1981.

Bernard, J. H., and R. Atkinson, eds. *The Irish Liber Hymnorum,* 1: *Text and Introduction;* 2: *Translations and Notes.* HBS 13–14. London, 1898.

Bieler, Ludwig, ed. *Psalterium Graeco-Latinum: Codex Basiliensis A. VII. 3.* Umbrae Codicum Occidentalium 5. Amsterdam, 1960.

Black, Matthew, ed. *A Christian Palestinian Syriac Horologion (Berlin, MS. Or. Oct. 1019).* Texts and Studies, n.s.1. Cambridge, 1954.

Boretius, Alfred, and Victor Krause, eds. MGH: Leges, Legum, section II: Cap. regum Francorum. 2 vols. Hannover. Vol. 1, ed. A. Boretius, 1883; vol. 2/1–3, ed. A. Boretius and V. Krause, 1890, 1893, 1897.

Bovon, F., ed. *Les Actes apocryphes des apôtres: Christianisme et monde païen.* Geneva, 1981.

Breviarium Ambrosianum S. Carolo Archiepiscopo editus. 4 vols. Milan, 1902.

Brou, Louis, and José Vives, eds. *Antifonario visigótico mozárabe de la catedral de León*. Monumenta Hispaniae Sacra: Serie liturgical 5/1. Barcelona and Madrid, 1959.

—— and André Wilmart. *The Psalter Collects from V–VIth Century Sources (Three Series)*. HBS 83. London, 1949.

Bruylants, Placide. *Les Oraisons du missel romain*. 2 vols. Études liturgiques, Collection dirigée par le Centre de Pastorale Liturgique, 1. Louvain, 1952.

Bryden, John, and David Hughes. *An Index of Gregorian Chant*. 2 vols. Cambridge, Mass., 1969.

Bulst, Walther. *Hymni Latini antiquissimi LXXV, Psalmi III*. Heidelberg, 1956.

Burmester, O. H. E. *The Horologion of the Egyptian Church*. Studia Orientalia Christiana: Aegyptiaca. Cairo, 1973.

Caesarius of Arles. *Œuvres monastiques*. Ed. Adalbert de Vogüé and Joël Courreau. 2 vols. SC 345, 398. Paris, 1988–94.

——. *Regula monachorum*. In *S. Caesarii arelatensis opera varia*, 2, ed. Germain Morin. Maredsous, 1942.

——. *Regula virginum*. In *Césaire d'Arles: Œuvres monastiques*, 1: *Œuvres pour les moniales*, ed. Adalbert de Vogüé and Joël Courreau. SC 345. Paris, 1988.

——. *Sermons*. Trans. M. M. Mueller. Fathers of the Church 31, 47, 66. Washington, D.C., 1956–73.

Canals Casas, J. M. *Las colectas de salmos de la serie "Visita nos": Introducción, edición crítica e índices*. Bibliotheca Salmanticensis Estudios 26. Salamanca, 1978.

Carmichael, Alexander. *Carmina Gadelica: Hymns and Incantations with Illustrative Notes on Words, Rites, and Customs, Dying and Obsolete: Orally collected in the Highlands and Islands of Scotland and Translated into English*. 2 vols. Edinburgh, 1900. Repr. 1928, with vol. 3 continued by Elizabeth Catherine Carmichael and ed. J. Carmichael Watson, 1940; vol. 4 ed. J. Carmichael Watson, 1941; vol. 5 ed. Angus Matheson, 1954.

Cassian, John. *De institutis cenobiorum et de octo vitiorum principalium remediis libri XII*. Ed. Michael Petschenig. CSEL 17. Vienna, 1888. [Same Latin text with French translation in Jean-Claude Guy. 1965. *Institutions cénobitiques*. SC 109. English trans. by E. C. S. Gibson in Nicene and Post-Nicene Fathers, 2d ser., vol. 11. New York, 1894.]

Champeval, J.-B., ed. "Chroniques de Saint-Martial de Limoges, Supplément." *Bulletin de la Société archéologique et historique du Limousin* 42 (1894): 304–91.

Chavasse, Antoine. *Le Sacramentaire Gélasien (Vaticanus Reginensis 316)*. Tournai, 1958.

Chevalier, Ulysse, ed. *Ordinaire et coutumier de l'église cathédrale de Bayeux (XIIIe siècle)*. Bibliothèque liturgique 8. Paris, 1903.

——. *Ordinaires de l'église cathédrale de Laon (XIIe et XIIIe siècles) suivis de deux mystères liturgiques*. Bibliothèque liturgique 6. Paris, 1897.

——. *Prosolarium ecclesiae Anicensis: Office en vers de la Circoncision en usage dans l'église du Puy*. Bibliothèque liturgique 5. Paris, 1894.

——. *Sacramentaire et martyrologie . . . de la métropole de Reims (VIIIe–XIIIe siècles)*. Bibliothèque liturgique 7. Paris, 1900.

Cipolla, Carlo, ed. *Codici Bobbiesi della Biblioteca Nazionale Universitaria di Torino*. Collezione Paleografica Bobbiese 1. 2 vols. Milan, 1907.

Clarke, Hugh, O.Carm., and Bede Edwards, O.C.D., eds. *The Rule of Saint Albert*. Aylesford and Kensington, 1973.

Clément, J.-M. *Lexique des anciennes règles monastiques occidentales*. Instrumenta Patristica, VII A–B. 2 vols. Steenbrugge, 1978.

Clercq, Charles de, ed. *Les Canons des conciles mérovingiens (vi^e–viie siècles)*. 2 vols. SC 353–54. Paris, 1989.

————. *Concilia Galliae A. 511–A. 695.* CCSL 148A. Turnhout, 1963. [See also Munier, C.]

Códice de canto polifónico, Monasterio de Las Huelgas Códice 9. Madrid: Patrimonio Nacional, 1997.

Columban. *Opera.* Ed. G. S. M. Walker. Scriptores Latini Hiberniae 2. Dublin, 1957; 1970.

The Coptic Morning Service for the Lord's Day, trans. John Patrick Crichton-Stuart, Marquis of Bute. London, 1908.

Cottineau, Laurent H. *Répertoire topo-bibliographique des abbayes et prieurés.* 3 vols. Mâcon, 1935–37.

De Clerck, Paul. *La "Prière universelle" dans les liturgies latines anciennes: Témoignages patristiques et textes liturgiques.* Liturgiewissenschaftliche Quellen und Forschungen 62. Munster, 1977.

Dekkers, Eligius. *Clavis patrum Latinorum.* 3d ed. CCSL. Steenbrugge, 1995.

Delaporte, Yves, ed. *Fragments des manuscrits de Chartres.* PM 17. Solesmes, 1958.

————. *L'Ordinaire chartrain du XIIIᵉ siècle.* Mémoires de la Société archéologique d'Eure-et-Loir 19. Chartres, 1953.

Delisle, Léopold, ed. *Le Cabinet de manuscrits de la Bibliothèque impériale.* Histoire Générale de Paris. Repr. of Paris originals, 1868–81. 4 vols. Amsterdam, 1969, and New York, 1974.

————. *Inventaire des manuscrits latins conservés à la Bibliothèque Nationale sous les numéros 8823–18613.* Repr. of Paris originals, 1863–71. 4 vols. in 1. Hildesheim and New York, 1974.

Deshusses, Jean. *Le Sacramentaire grégorien.* 3 vols. Spicilegium Friburgense 16, 24, 28. Fribourg, vol. 1, 1971, 1979, 1992; vol. 2, 1979, 1988; vol. 3, 1982.

———— and Benoît Darragon. *Concordances et tableaux pour l'étude des grands sacramentaires.* 6 vols. Fribourg, 1982.

Desprez, Vincent. *Règles monastiques d'Occident (Vᵉ–VIᵉ siècle: D'Augustin à Ferréol).* Vie monastique 9. Abbaye de Bellefontaine, 1980. [French translation of the rules of Augustine (*Ordo monasterii* and *Praeceptum*), the Four Fathers and related rules, Caesarius, Aurelian, Tarnant, Ferreolus, Paul, and Stephen.]

Dewick, E. S., and W. H. Frere, eds. *The Leofric Collectar, I–II* [BL, Harley 2961]. HBS 45 and 56. London, 1914–21.

Dinter, Peter, ed. *Liber tramitis aeui Odilonis abbatis.* CCM 10. Siegburg, 1980.

Dittmer, Luther, ed. *Firenze Biblioteca Mediceo-Laurenziana, Pluteo 29.1.* Publications of Mediaeval Music Manuscripts 10–11. Institute of Mediaeval Music. Brooklyn, 1966–67.

Donatus of Besançon. *Regula ad virgines.* "La règle de Donat pour l'abbesse Gauthstrude. Texte critique et synopse des sources." Ed. Adalbert de Vogüé. *Benedictina* 25 (1967): 219–313.

Dufay, Guillaume. *Opera omnia.* Ed. Heinrich Besseler. 6 vols. Rome, 1951–66.

Dumas, A., and J. Deshusses, eds. *Liber sacramentorum Gellonensis.* CCSL 159 and 159A. Turnholt, 1981.

Dümmler, Ernst, ed. *Poetae aevi carolini.* MGH Poetae 1. Berlin, 1964.

Duplès-Agier, H., ed. *Chroniques de Saint-Martial de Limoges.* Paris, 1874.

Durand, Georges, ed. *Ordinaire de l'église Notre-Dame cathédrale d'Amiens par Raoul de Rouvroy (1291).* Mémoires de la Société des antiquaires de Picardie, Documents inédits concernant la province 22. Amiens and Paris, 1934.

Durandus of Mende. *Rationale Divinorum Officiorum I–VI.* Ed. A. Davril and T. M. Thibodeau. CCCM 140, 140a. Turnhout, 1995–98.

Eberle, Luke, ed. and trans. *The Rule of the Master.* Cistercian Studies 6. Kalamazoo, 1977.

Eclaircissemens sur quelques rits particuliers à l'église d'Auxerre en réponse aux questions d'un pieux laïc, par un chanoine de la Cathédrale d'Auxerre. n. p., 1770.

Edwards, Owain T. *Matins, Lauds and Vespers for St. David's Day: The Medieval Office of the Welsh Patron Saint in National Library of Wales MS 20.* Cambridge, 1990.

Egeria. In Geyer, *Itinera.*

———. *Egeria's Travels to the Holy Land.* [English translation by John Wilkinson.] Rev. ed. Jerusalem, 1981.

———. *Égérie: Journal de voyage (Itinéraire).* Ed. Pierre Maraval. SC 296. Paris, 1982.

———. *Itinerarium.* [*Journal de voyage*]. Ed. Hélène Pétré. SC 21. Paris, 1971.

Ekkehart IV. *Casus Sancti Galli,* ed. G. Meyer von Knonau. St. Gallische Geschichtsquellen 3. St. Gallen, 1877; Darmstadt, 1980.

Étaix, Raymond, ed. *Homéliaires patristiques latins: Recueil d'études de manuscrits médiévaux.* Turnhout, 1994.

Eugippius. *Eugipii Regula.* Ed. Fernand Villegas and Adalbert de Vogüé. CSEL 87. Vienna, 1976.

Evans, Paul, ed. *The Early Trope Repertory of Saint Martial de Limoges.* Princeton Studies in Music 2. Princeton, 1970.

Fæhn, Helge, ed. *Manuale Norwegicum ex tribus codicibus saec. XI–XIV.* Libri liturgici provinciae Nidrosiensis Medii Aevi 1. Oslo, 1962.

Ferreolus. *Regula monachorum.* In "La *Regula Ferreoli:* Texte critique," ed. Vincent Desprez. *Revue Mabillon* 60 (1982): 117–48.

Flamion, J. *Les Actes apocryphes de l'Apôtre André.* Université de Louvain, Recueil de travaux des conférences d'histoire et de philologie 33. Louvain, 1911.

Foerster, Hans, ed. *Liber diurnus Romanorum pontificum.* Bern, 1958.

Franceschini, Ezio, ed. *L'antifonario di Bangor.* Testi e documenti di storia e di letteratura latina medioevale 4. Padua, 1941.

Franklin, Camilla, et al., ed. and trans. *Early Monastic Rules: The Rules of the Fathers and the Regula Orientalis.* Collegeville, Minn., 1982.

Frere, Walter Howard, ed. *Antiphonale Sarisburiense: A Reproduction in Facsimile of a Manuscript of the Thirteenth Century.* London, 1901–24; repr. Farnborough, 1966.

———. *Graduale Sarisburiense: A Reproduction in Facsimile of a Manuscript of the Thirteenth Century . . .* London, 1894.

Froger, Jacques, ed. *L'Antiphonaire de Hartker: Manuscrits Saint-Gall 390–391.* PM II/1. Berne, 1970.

Gamber, Klaus, ed. "Ein ägyptisches Kommunionlied des 5./6. Jahrhunderts." *Ostkirchliche Studien* 8 (1959): 221–29.

———. *Codices liturgici Latini antiquiores.* 2d ed. Spicilegii Friburgensis subsidia 1. 2 parts. Freiburg, 1968.

———. *Die Messfeier nach altgallikanischem Ritus.* Studia patristica et liturgica 14. Regensburg, 1984.

———. *Ordo antiquus Gallicanus: Der gallikanische Messritus des 6. Jahrhunderts.* Textus patristici et liturgici 3. Regensburg, 1965.

——— et al., eds. *Codices liturgici Latini antiquiores. Supplementum: Ergänzungs-und Registerband.* Spicilegii Friburgensis subsidia 1A. Freiburg, 1988.

Gerbert, Martin, ed. *Scriptores ecclesiastici de musica sacra potissimum.* 3 vols. St. Blasien, 1784. Repr. Milan, 1931; Hildesheim, 1963.

Geyer, Paul, ed. *Itinera Hierosolymitana saeculi IIII–VIII.* CSEL 39. Vienna, 1898.

Gillingham, Bryan. *Cambridge, University Library, Ff.i.17(1). Facsimile Reproduction of the Manuscript.* PMMM 17. Ottawa, 1989.

———. *Paris, Bibliothèque Nationale, fonds latin 3719. Facsimile Reproduction of the MS.* PMMM 15. Ottawa, 1987.

Gjerløw, Lilli, ed. *Antiphonarium Nidrosiensis ecclesiae.* Libri liturgici provinciae Nidrosiensis medii aevi 3. Oslo, 1979.

——. *Ordo Nidrosiensis ecclesiae.* Libri liturgici provinciae Nidrosiensis medii aevi 2. Oslo, 1968.

Götz, Georgius Polycarpus, ed. *Liber Quare.* CCCM 60. Turnhout, 1983.

Le Graduel romain, édition critique par les moines de Solesmes. Vol. 2: *Les Sources.* Solesmes, 1957.

Gregory of Tours. *History of the Franks.* Trans. O. M. Dalton. Oxford, 1927.

——. *Libri historiarum X.* Ed. B. Krusch and W. Levison. 2d ed. MGH: Scriptores rerum Merovingicarum 1/1. Hannover, 1951.

Gregory the Great. *Dialogorum libri quattuor.* PL 77:149–430.

——. *Forty Gospel Homilies.* Trans. David Hurst. Kalamazoo, 1990.

——. *In evangelia homiliae.* PL 76:1075–1312.

Guibert, Louis. *Documents, analyses de pièces, extraits & notes relatifs à l'histoire municipale des deux villes de Limoges,* 1. Société des Archives Historiques du Limousin, ser. 1, Archives Anciennes 7. Limoges, 1897.

Guido of Arezzo. *Guidonis Aretini Micrologus.* Ed. Joseph Smits van Waesberghe. Corpus scriptorum de musica 4. [Rome], 1955.

——. *Regulae rhythmicae.* In Gerbert (1784), 2:25.

Gwynn, E. J. "The Rule of Tallaght." *Hermathena* 44, 2d supplemental vol., 1927.

Haggh, Barbara. *Two Offices for St. Elizabeth of Hungary: Gaudeat Hungaria and Letare Germania.* Introduction and edition by Barbara Haggh. Musicological Studies 65/1. Series: Historiae. Ottawa, 1995.

Haile, Getatchew, and William F. Macomber. *A Catalogue of Ethiopian Manuscripts* 6. Collegeville, 1982.

Hallinger, Kassius, ed. *Initia Consuetudinis Benedictinae: Consuetudines saeculi octavi et noni.* CCM 1. Siegburg, 1963.

[Hambourg], Mother Mary, and Kallistos Ware. *The Festal Menaion.* London, 1969.

Heiming, Odilo. *Das ambrosianische Sakramentar von Biasca.* Corpus ambrosiano-liturgicum 2. Münster, 1969.

Heimskringla Snorra Sturlusonar. 2 vols. Reykjavik, 1941–51.

Heiric of Auxerre. *Homiliae per circulum anni.* Ed. Riccardo Quadri. CCCM 116. Turnhout, 1992.

Hiley, David, ed. *Missale Carnotense: Chartres Codex 520.* 2 vols. Kassel and New York, 1992.

Hofmeister, Adolf, ed. *Supplementum ad voll. 1–15.* MGH: Scriptores 30/2, 3 fasc. Hannover, 1926–34.

Holstenius, Lucas. *Codex regularum.* 6 vols. in 3. Ed. M. Brockie. Augsburg, 1759.

Honorius of Autun. *Gemma animae.* PL 172, cols. 541–738.

Hughes, Andrew. *Late Medieval Liturgical Offices: Resources for Electronic Research. Text and Late Medieval Liturgical Offices.* Subsidia mediaevalia 23. *Resources for Electronic Research: Sources & Chants.* Subsidia mediaevalia 24. Toronto, 1994, 1996 (= LMLO).

——. *Medieval Manuscripts for Mass and Office: A Guide to their Organization and Terminology.* Toronto, 1982; repr. 1986; repr. 1995, with addenda.

Indebrø, G., ed. *Gammel norsk homiliebok.* [Copenhagen, KB Codex Arn. Magn, 619 Q. V.] Oslo, 1931.

Isidore of Seville. *De ecclesiasticis officiis.* Ed. Christopher M. Lawson. CCSL 113. Turnhout, 1989; PL 83:737–826.

——. *Etymologiarum sive originum libri XX.* Ed. W. M. Lindsay. 2 vols. Scriptorum Classicorum Bibliotheca Oxoniensis. Oxford, 1911; repr. 1957, 1962; PL 82, cols. 73–728.

———. *The Rule of Isidore.* Trans. A. W. Godfrey. *Monastic Studies* 18 (1988): 7–29.

Iversen, Gunilla. *Tropes du Sanctus.* CT 7. Acta Universitatis Stockholmiensis, Studia Latina Stockholmiensia 34. Stockholm, 1990.

Jocqué, Luc, and Ludo Milis, eds. *Liber ordinis Sancti Victoris Parisiensis.* CCCM 61. Turnhout, 1984.

Joinville, Jean de. *Histoire de Saint Louis.* Ed. Natalis de Wailly. Paris, 1874.

Jülicher, Adolf, et al., eds. *Itala: Das Neue Testament in altlateinischer Überlieferung.* Berlin, 1938 ff.

Kandra, Kabos, ed. *Ordinarius . . . Agriensis ecclesie. Regia in civitate Cracoviensi . . . MCCCCIX.* Eger, 1905.

Kemble, John M., ed. *Chartae Anglosaxonicae.* Codex diplomaticus aevi saxonici. London, 1839–48.

[KHS-]Burmester, O.H.E. *See* Burmester, O.H.E.

Klauser, Theodor. *Das römische Capitulare Evangeliorum.* Münster in Westf., 1935.

Krusch, Bruno, ed. *Ionae vitae Sanctorum Columbani, Vedastis Iohannis.* Scriptores rerum Germanicarum in usum scholarum ex Monumentis Germaniae historicis separatim editi. Hannover and Leipzig, 1905.

——— and W. Levison, eds. *Passiones vitaeque sanctorum aevi Merovingici.* MGH: Scriptores rerum Merovingicarum, 6. Hannover, 1913.

Labbé, Philippe, ed. *Noua bibliotheca manuscriptorum librorum, 2: Rerum aquitanarum, praesertim bituricensium, uberrima collectio.* Paris, 1657.

Laing, Samuel. *Heimskringla, Part Two: Sagas of the Norse Kings.* Rev. ed. by Peter Foote. London, 1961.

Lapidge, Michael, ed. *Anglo-Saxon Litanies of the Saints.* HBS 106. London, 1991.

Ledoyen, Henri. "La 'Regula Cassiani' du clm 28118 et la règle anonyme de l'Escorial A.I.13." *RB* 94 (1984): 154–94.

Legg, J. Wickham. "Ratio decursus qui fuerunt ex auctores: Speculations on the Divine Office by a Writer of the Eighth Century." In *Miscellanea Ceriani: Raccolta di scritti originali per onorare la memoria di M.ʳ Antonio Maria Ceriani, Prefetto della Biblioteca Ambrosiana, Nel III Centenario della Biblioteca Ambrosiana, MDCIX – 8 Dicembre – MCMIX,* 149–67. Milan, 1910.

Leo the Great. *Tractatus septem et nonaginta.* Ed. Antoine Chavasse. CCSL 138 and 138A. Turnholt, 1973.

Lépinois, Eugène de, and Lucien Merlet, eds. *Cartulaire de l'église Notre-Dame de Chartres.* 3 vols. Chartres, 1862–65.

Liber commicus, ed. Justo Pérez de Urbel and Atilano González y Ruiz-Zorrilla. Monumenta Hispaniae Sacra 2. Madrid, 1950.

Lipsius, Ricardus Adelbertus, and Maximilianus Bonnet, eds. *Acta apostolica apocrypha post Constantum Tischendorf.* 2 vols. Leipzig, 1898–1903; 3 vols. Hildesheim, 1959.

Lowe, Elias Avery, ed. *The Bobbio Missal: Facsimile.* HBS 53, 58. London, 1917–20. *Notes and Studies* by A. Wilmart, E. A. Lowe and H. A. Wilson. HBS 61. London, 1924.

Machielsen, Iohannis, ed. *Clavis Patristica pseudepigraphorum Medii Aevi.* CCSL 1- . Turnhout, 1990– .

Macomber, William F. *See* Haile, Getatchew.

Magistretti, Marco, ed. *Beroldus, sive Ecclesiae Ambrosianae Mediolanensis kalendarium et ordines, saec. XII.* Milan, 1894.

———. *Manuale Ambrosianum ex codice saec. XI olim in usum canonicae Vallis Travaliae,* part 1: *Psalterium et kalendarium.* Monumenta veteris liturgiae ambrosianae 2. Milan, 1905. Repr. Nendeln, Liechtenstein, 1971.

———. *Manuale Ambrosianum ex codice saec. XI olim in usum canonicae Vallis Travaliae,* part 2. Monumenta veteris liturgiae ambrosianae 3. Milan, 1904. Repr. Nendeln, Liechtenstein, 1971.

Mansi, G. D., ed. *Sacrorum Conciliorum nova et amplissima collectio.* 54 vols. Venice, 1776; Paris 1901–27.

Manuale continens ecclesie sacramenta et modum administrandi ea, secundum usum diocesis Carnotensis. Paris, 1492.

Marcusson, Olof, ed. *Prosules de la messe, 1: Tropes de l'alleluia.* CT 2. Studia Latina Stockholmiensia 22. Stockholm, 1976.

Martène, Edmund, ed. *De antiquis ecclesiae ritibus libri.* 2d ed. 4 vols. Antwerp, 1736–38.

Masai, François, and Léon Gilissen, eds. *Lectionarium Sancti Lamberti Leodiensis tempore Stephani episcopi paratum (901–920).* Codex Bruxellensis 14650–59. Umbrae codicum occidentalium VIII. Amsterdam, 1963. MGH I: Poetae aevi carolini I. Ed. Ernst Dümmler. Berlin, new ed., 1964.

Matéos, Juan. "Un horologion inédit de Saint-Sabas." In *Mélanges Eugène Tisserant,* 3:47–76. Studi e testi 233. Vatican City, 1964.

——. *Lelya-Ṣapra: Les offices chaldéens de la nuit et de matin.* 2d ed. Orientalia Christiana Analecta 192. Rome, 1972.

Maximus of Turin. *Collectio sermonum . . . .* CCSL 23. Turnhout, 1962.

——. *The Sermons.* Trans. by Boniface Ramsey. Ancient Christian Writers 50. New York, 1989.

Ménard, Hugh, ed. *Sancti Benedicti Abbatis Anianensis Codex Regularum.* Paris, 1638; repr. PL 103:701–1380.

Merlet, René, ed. *Cartulaire de Saint-Jean-en-Vallée de Chartres.* Chartres, 1906.

Mercenier, E., and François Paris. *La Prière des églises de rite byzantin* 1. 2d ed. Chevetogne, 1947.

Metcalfe, Frederick, ed. *Passio et miracula Beati Olaui, edited from a Twelfth-Century Manuscript in the Library of Corpus Christi College, Oxford.* Oxford, 1881.

Metzger, Marcel. *Les Constitutions apostoliques.* 3 vols. SC 320, 329, 336. Paris, 1985–87.

Meyer, Kuno. "An Old-Irish Treatise *De Arreis.*" *Revue celtique* 15 (1903): 485–98.

Milfull, Inge B. *The Hymns of the Anglo-Saxon Church: A Study and Edition of the "Durham Hymnal".* Cambridge Studies in Anglo-Saxon England 17. Cambridge, 1996.

Missale Nidrosiense. Haffnia [Copenhagen], 1519. Facs. ed. Oslo, 1959.

Mohlberg, Leo Cunibert, ed. *Liber sacramentorum Romanae aeclesiae ordinis anni circuli (Sacramentarium Gelasianum).* Rerum ecclesiasticarum documenta, ser. maior, fontes 4. Rome, 1968.

Molinier, Auguste. *Catalogue général des manuscrits des bibliothèques publiques de France. Départements,* vol. 17. Cambrai and Paris, 1891.

Möller, Hartmut. *Das Quedlinburger Antiphonar (Berlin, Staatsbibliothek Preußischer Kulturbesitz Mus. ms. 40047).* 3 vols. Mainzer Studien zur Musikwissenschaft 25. Tutzing, 1990.

Mombritius, Boninus. *Sanctuarium seu vitae sanctorum.* 2 vols. Paris, 1910.

Mommsen, Theodor, ed. *Chronica minora saec. IV, V, VI, VII.* MGH: Auctores antiquissimi 9/1–2. Berlin, 1892.

Monson, Erling. *From the Sagas of the Norse Kings, by Snorri Sturlason.* Oslo, 1967.

Munier, C., ed. *Concilia Galliae A. 314–A. 506.* CCSL 148. Turnhout, 1963. [See also Clercq, Charles de.]

Muratori, Lodovico Antonio. *Rerum Italicarum scriptores.* 25 vols. Milan, 1723–51.

Musica et Scolica enchiriadis: una cum aliquibus tractatulis adiunctis, ed. Hans Schmid. München, 1981. English translation by Raymond Erickson, ed. Claude V. Palisca. New Haven, 1985.

Neufville, J., ed. "Règle des IV Pères et Seconde Règle des Pères, texte critique." *RB* 77 (1967): 47–106. [English translation in *Monastic Studies* 12 (1976): 249–263.]

Notger of St. Gall. *Notker der Dichter und seine geistige Welt.* Ed. W. von den Steinen. Bern, 1948. 2 vols.

Odorannus of Sens. *Opera omnia.* Ed. Robert Henri Bautier, Monique Giles, Marie-Élisabeth Duchez, and Michel Huglo. Paris, 1972.

O'Keeffe, J. G. "The Rule of Patrick." *Ériu* 1 (1904): 216–24.

Olason, P. E., ed. *Heimskringla Snorra Sturlusonar.* Reykjavik, 1946.

O'Neill, Joseph. "The Rule of Ailbe of Emly." *Ériu* 3 (1907): 92–115.

Ottosen, Knud. *L'Antiphonaire latin au moyen-âge: Réorganisation des séries de Répons de l'Avent, classés par R.-J. Hesbert.* Rome, 1986.

———. *The Responsories and Versicles of the Latin Office of the Dead.* Århus, 1993.

Palisca, Claude V., ed. *Hucbald, Guido, and John on Music: Three Medieval Treatises.* Trans. Warren Babb. Music Theory Translation Series 3. New Haven and London, 1978.

Paredi, Angelo. *Sacramentarium Bergomense.* Monumenta Bergomensia 6. Bergamo, 1962.

Paschasius Radbertus. *Expositio in Matheo libri XII.* Ed. Beda Paulus. CCCM 56, 56A, 56B. Turnhout, 1984.

Passio beati Olavi gloriosi regis et martyris. [Douai, BM 295, fols. 94–108.] *Analecta Bollandia* 20: 369–70.

Paul the Deacon. *History of the Lombards.* Trans. W. D. Foulke. Philadelphia, 1907; repr. 1974.

Possidius. *Sancti Augustini vita.* Ed. and trans. H. T. Weiskotten. Princeton, 1919.

Praepositinus Cremonensis. *Tractatus de officiis.* Ed. James Corbett. Publications in Medieval Studies 21. Notre Dame, Ind., and London, 1969.

Prieur, Jean-Marc, ed. *Acta Andreae.* Corpus Christianorum, series apocryphorum 5–6. 2 vols. Turnhout, 1989.

Processional à l'usage de l'église cathédrale de Chartres suivant le nouveau bréviaire. Chartres, 1783.

Processional à l'usage de l'église cathédrale de Chartres suivant le nouveau bréviaire. Chartres, 1788.

Pseudo-Cyprian. *De pascha computus.* Ed. Wilhelm Hartel. CSEL 3/3. Vienna, 1871.

Pseudo-Dionysius. *The Complete Works.* Trans. Colm Luibheid. Foreword, Notes, and Collaboration by Paul Rorem. Mahwah, N.J., 1987.

Pseudo-Hugh of Saint-Victor. *Speculum ecclesiae.* PL 177, cols. 335–79.

Quodvultdeus. "Contra Iudaeos, Paganos et Arrianos." In *Opera,* ed. R. Braun. CCSL 60. Turnholt, 1976.

Rahlfs, Alfred, ed. *Septuaginta Societatis Scientiarum Gottingensis,* 10: *Psalmi cum Odis.* Göttingen, 1931.

———. *Septuaginta: Id est Vetus Testamentum graece iuxta LXX interpretes.* Editio minor. 2 vols. in 1. Stuttgart, 1979.

Ratcliff, E. C., ed. *Expositio antiquae liturgiae Gallicanae.* HBS 98. London, 1971.

Ratti, Achille, and Marco Magistretti, eds. *Missale Ambrosianum duplex (Proprium de Tempore) Editt. Puteobonellianae et Typicae (1751–1902) cum critico commentario continuo ex manuscriptis schedis Ant. M. Ceriani.* Monumenta sacra et profana 4. Milan: R. Ghirlanda, 1913.

Reaney, Gilbert. *Manuscripts of Polyphonic Music 11th–early 14th Century.* Répertoire international des sources musicales B IV¹. Munich and Duisburg, 1966.

Reiss, Georg. *Musiken ved den Middelalderlige Olavsdyrkelse i Norden.* Videnskapsselkapets Skrifter 5. Kristiania [Oslo], 1912.

Rituale Carnotense. Paris, 1500.

Roesner, Edward H., ed. *Le Magnus liber organi de Notre-Dame de Paris,* 1: *Les Tripla et Quadrupla.* Musica Gallica. Monaco, 1993.

The Roman Breviary Reformed by Order of the Holy Oecumenical Council of Trent. Published by Order of Pope St. Pius V, and Revised by Clement VIII, Urban VII, and Leo XIII. Trans. by John, Marquess of Bute, K. T. 4 vols. Edinburgh and London, 1908.

Royal Irish Academy. *Dictionary of the Irish Language.* 4 vols. Dublin, 1913–76.

Sabatier, Pierre, ed. *Bibliorum sacrorum Latinae versiones antiquae.* Reims, 1943; repr. Turnhout, 1981.

Salmon, Pierre, ed. *Le Lectionnaire de Luxeuil (Paris, ms. lat. 9427).* 2 vols. Collectanea biblica Latina 7 and 9. Rome and Vatican City, 1944–53.

Schenke, Hans-Martin, ed. *Das Matthäus-Evangelium im mittelägyptischen Dialekt des koptischen (Codex Scheide).* Texte und Untersuchungen zur Geschichte der altchristlichen Literatur 127. Berlin, 1981.

Schneemelcher, Wilhelm, ed. *Neutestamentliche Apokryphen in deutscher Übersetzung.* 5th ed. 2 vols. Tübingen, 1987–89.

Schneider, Heinrich. *Die altlateinischen biblischen Cantica.* Texte und Arbeiten I: Beiträge zur Ergründung des älteren lateinischen und christlichen Schrifttums und Gottesdienstes 29–30. Beuron, 1938.

Selmer, Carl, ed. *Navigatio Sancti Brendani abbatis, from Early Latin Manuscripts.* Notre Dame, Ind., 1959.

Shelemay, Kay, and Peter Jeffery, eds. *Ethiopian Christian Liturgical Chant: An Anthology.* 3 vols. Recent Researches in the Oral Traditions of Music 1–3. Madison, Wis., 1993–97.

Sickel, Theodor, ed. *Liber diurnus Romanorum pontificum.* Vienna, 1889.

Sonnet, Martin, ed. *Caeremoniale Parisiense ad usum omnium ecclesiarum collegiatarum, parochialium et aliarum urbis et dioecesis Parisiensis. Iuxta sacros et antiquos ritus sacrosanctae ecclesiae metropolitanae Parisiensis.* Paris, 1662.

Steiner, Ruth, ed. *Utrecht, Bibliotheek der Rijksuniversiteit, 406 (3.J.7).* Introduction by Ike de Loos. Ottawa, 1997.

Stevenson, James, ed. *A New Eusebius: Documents Illustrating the History of the Church to AD 337.* London, 1957. Repr. London, 1992.

Stokes, Whitley, ed. and trans. *Lives of Saints from the Book of Lismore.* Anecdota Oxoniensia, Medieval and Modern Series 5. Oxford, 1890.

Storm, Gustav. *Monumenta historica Norvegiae: Latinske Kildeskrifter til Norges Historie i Middelalderen.* Kristiania [Oslo], 1880.

Suñol, Gregorio, ed. *Antiphonale missarum juxta ritum sanctae ecclesiae Mediolanensis.* Rome, 1935.

———. *Liber vesperalis juxta ritum sanctae ecclesiae Mediolanensis.* Rome, 1939.

Szövérffy, Josef. *Die Annalen der lateinischen Hymnendichtung: Ein Handbuch, 1: Die lateinischen Hymnen bis zum Ende des 11. Jahrhunderts.* Berlin, 1964.

Thiel, Andreas, ed. *Epistolae Romanorum pontificum genuinae et quae ad eos scriptae sunt a S. Hilaro usque ad Pelagium II.* Braunsberg, 1867.

Turaev, Boris Aleksandrovič. *Časoslov efiopskoj cerkvi.* Mémoires de l'Académie Impériale des Sciences de St. Pétersbourg. 8th series, 1/7. St. Petersburg, 1897.

Vanderhoven, H., and François Masai. *Aux sources du monachisme bénédictin. Edition diplomatique des mss. latins 12205 et 12634 de Paris.* Publications du Scriptorium 3. Brussels, 1953.

Vilanova, J. Evangelista, ed. *Regula Pauli et Stephani: Edició crítica i comentari.* Scripta et documenta 2. Montserrat, 1959.

Villegas, Fernando, ed. "La 'Regula cuiusdam Patris ad monachos': Ses sources littéraires et ses rapports avec la 'Regula monachorum' de Colomban." *Revue d'histoire de la spiritualité* 49 (1973): 3–35, 135–44.

———. "La 'Regula Monasterii Tarnantensis': Texte, sources, et datation." *RB* 84 (1974): 7–65.

Villetard, Henri. *Office de Pierre de Corbeil (Office de la Circoncision) improprement appelé "Office des Fous": Texte et chant publiés d'après le manuscrit de Sens (XIIIᵉ siècle).* Bibliothèque musicologique 4. Paris, 1907.

Vives, José, et al., eds. *Concilios visigóticos e hispano-romanos.* España Cristiana: Textos 1. Barcelona and Madrid, 1963.

Vogüé, Adalbert de, ed. "La Règle de Donat." *See* Donatus above.

——. *La Règle du Maître.* 3 vols. SC 105–7. Paris, 1964–65. [English translation: see Eberle.]

——. "La 'Regula Orientalis': Texte critique et synopse des sources." *Benedictina* 23 (1976): 241–71.

——. *Les Règles des saints pères,* 1: *Trois règles de Lérins au Ve siècle.* 2: *Trois règles du VIe siècle incorporant des textes lériniens.* SC 297–98. Paris, 1982.

Voragine, Jacobus de. *The Golden Legend.* Trans. William Granger Ryan. 2 vols. Princeton, 1993.

Walpole, A. S. *Early Latin Hymns.* Cambridge, 1922.

Warner, George F., ed. *The Stowe Missal.* 2 vols. HBS 31–32. London, 1906–15.

Warren, F. E., ed. *The Antiphonary of Bangor: An Early Irish Manuscript in the Ambrosian Library at Milan.* 2 vols. HBS 4, 10. London, 1893–95.

——. *The Leofric Missal as Used in the Cathedral of Exeter During the Episcopate of Its First Bishop A. D. 1050–1072.* Oxford, 1883; repr. 1968.

——. *The Red Book of Derby* [Cambridge, CCC 422, fol. 162], appendix in *The Leofric Missal,* pp. 271–75.

Wessels, Gabriel, ed. *Acta capitulorum generalium ordinis fratrum B. V. Mariae de Monte Carmelo,* 1: *Ab anno 1318 usque ad annum 1593, cum notis B. Zimmerman, auctoritate P. M. Mayer, edidit Gabriel Wessels.* Rome, 1912.

Whitehill, Walter Muir, Germán Prado, and Jesús Carro García, eds. *Liber sancti Jacobi: Codex Calixtinus.* 3 vols. Santiago de Compostela, 1944.

Wieland, Gernot R., ed. *The Canterbury Hymnal, Edited from British Library MS. Additional 37517.* Toronto Medieval Latin Texts 12. Toronto, 1982.

Willemus Calculus. *Historiae Northmannorum libri octo.* PL 149, cols. 779–914.

Winterfeld, Paul von, ed. *Poetae aevi carolini.* MGH Poetae 4. Berlin, 1964.

Young, Karl. *The Drama of the Medieval Church.* 2 vols. Oxford, 1933.

Zimmerman, Benedict, ed. *Ordinaire de l'Ordre de Notre-Dame du Mont Carmel par Sibert de Beka (vers 1312) publié d'après le manuscrit original et collationné sur divers manuscrits et imprimés.* Paris, 1910.

Secondary Sources

Alexander, J. Neil. 1993. *The Liturgical Meaning of Advent, Christmas, Epiphany.* Washington, D.C.

Alfonzo, Pio. 1936. *I responsori biblici dell'ufficio romano.* Lateranum, n. s., year 2, no. 1. Rome.

Amann, É. 1933. "La Pénitence privée." *DTC* 12/1:845–948. Paris.

Amiet, Robert. 1982. "Manuscrits liturgiques des xve et xvie siècles acquis par la Bibliothèque municipale de Grenoble entre 1902 et 1978." *Scriptorium* 36:111–17.

Andersson, Theodore M. 1964. *The Problem of Icelandic Saga Origins: A Historical Survey.* New Haven.

Antier, Jean-Jacques. 1973. *Lérins: L'Île sainte de la Côte d'Azur.* Collections "Hauts lieux de spiritualité." Paris.

Apel, Willi. 1958. *Gregorian Chant.* Bloomington, Ind., and London.

Arens, Fritz. 1958–60. "Ein Blatt aus den Mainzer Karmeliter-Chorbüchern." *Jahrbuch für das Bistum Mainz* 8:341–45.

Arlt, Wulf. 1968. "Sakral und Profan in der Geschichte der abendländischen Musik." *ALw* 10/2:375–99.

———. 1970. *Ein Festoffizium des Mittelalters aus Beauvais in seiner liturgischen und musikalischen Bedeutung.* 2 vols. Köln.

———. 1978. "Einstimmige Lieder des 12. Jahrhunderts und Mehrstimmiges in französischen Handschriften des 16. Jahrhunderts aus Le Puy." *Schweizer Beiträge zur Musikwissenschaft* 3:7–47.

———. 1984. "Musik und Text." *Musikforschung* 37:272–80.

———. 1986. "*Nova Cantica*—Grundsätzliches und Spezielles zur Interpretation musikalischer Texte des Mittelalters." *Basler Jahrbuch für historische Musikpraxis* 10:13–62.

———. 1990a. "Das eine Lied und die vielen Lieder. Zur historischen Stellung der neuen Liedkunst des frühen 12. Jahrhunderts." In *Festschrift für Rudolf Bockholdt zum 60. Geburtstag,* ed. N. Dubowy and S. Meyer-Eller, 113–27. Munich.

———. 1990b. "A propos des notations pragmatiques: Le cas du codex Las Huelgas. Remarques générales et observations particulières." *Revista de musicología* 132:401–19.

———. 1992. Notes to CD: *Le Manuscrit du Puy,* Ensemble Gilles Binchois (Virgin Classics 077775923827).

Asketorp, Bodil. 1992. "Beobachtungen zu einigen späteren Introitustropen." In *Cantus Planus: Papers Read at the Fourth Meeting, Pécs, Hungary, 3–8 September 1990,* ed. László Dobszay, Agnes Papp, and Ferenc Sebó, 371–92. Budapest.

Aubrun, Michel. 1981. *L'Ancien Diocèse de Limoges des origines au milieu du XIe siècle.* Publications de l'Institut d'Études du Massif Central 21. Clermont-Ferrand.

Auda, Antoine. 1923. *Étienne de Liège: L'école musicale liégeoise au Xe siècle.* Académie royale de Belgique. Classe des Beaux-Arts. Mémoires. II:1. Brussels.

Auf der Maur, Franz. 1990. *Streifzüge in die Vergangenheit.* Thun.

Auger, Marie-Louise. 1985. "La Bibliothèque de Saint-Bénigne de Dijon au XVIIe siècle: Le témoignage de Dom Hugues Lanthenas." *Scriptorium* 39:234–64.

Bäumer, Suitbert. 1895. *Geschichte des Breviers.* 2 vols. Freiburg im Breisgau.

———. 1905. *Histoire du Bréviaire.* Trans. and rev. Réginald Biron. 2 vols. Paris.

Bailey, Terence. 1971. *The Processions of Sarum and the Western Church.* Studies and Texts 21. Toronto.

———. 1993. "An Ancient Psalmody without Antiphons in the Ambrosian Ferial Office." *Actas del XV Congresso de la Sociedad Internacional de Musicología,* ed. Ismael Fernández de la Cuesta and Alfonso de Vicente. *Revista de musicología* 16/2:875–82.

———. 1994. *Antiphon and Psalm in the Ambrosian Office.* Musicological Studies 50/3. Ottawa.

———. 1995. "Ambrosian Double Antiphons." *Laborare fratres in unum. Festschrift László Dobszay zum 60. Geburtstag.* Ed. David Hiley and Janka Szendrai. Hildesheim.

——— and Paul Merkley. 1989. *The Antiphons of the Ambrosian Office.* Musicological Studies 50/1. Ottawa.

———. 1990. *The Melodic Tradition of the Ambrosian Office Antiphons.* Musicological Studies 50/2. Ottawa.

Baldovin, John F. 1987. *The Urban Character of Christian Worship: The Origins, Development, and Meanings of Stational Liturgy.* Rome, 1987.

Baltzer, Rebecca A. 1985. "Performance Practice, the Notre-Dame Calendar, and the Earliest Latin Liturgical Motets." Paper presented at the conference "Das musikgeschichtliche Ereignis 'Notre-Dame,'" Wolfenbüttel.

———. 1990. "Aspects of Trope in the Earliest Motets for the Assumption of the Virgin." *Current Musicology* 45–47:5–42.

———. 1992. "The Geography of the Liturgy at Notre-Dame of Paris." In *Plainsong in the Age of Polyphony,* ed. Thomas F. Kelly, 45–64. Cambridge Studies in Performance Practice 2. Cambridge.

———. 2000 (in press). "A Royal French Breviary from the Reign of St. Louis." In *The*

Varieties of Musicology: Essays in Honor of Murray Lefkowitz, ed. John Daverio and John Ogasapian, 3–25. Warren, Mich.

Bannister, Henry Marriott. 1911. "Irish Psalters." *Journal of Theological Studies* 12: 280–84.

Barlow, Frank. 1979. *The English Church 1000–1066.* London and New York.

Barré, Henri. 1957. "Le Sermon 'Exhortatur' est-il de saint Ildefonse?" *RB* 58:10–33.

———. 1962. *Les Homiliaires carolingiens de l'école d'Auxerre. Authenticité—Inventaire—Tableaux comparatifs—Initia.* Studi e testi 225. Vatican City.

Batiffol, Pierre. 1894. "L'Origine du *Liber responsalis* de l'église romaine." *Revue des questions historiques* 55:220–28.

———. 1911. *Histoire du bréviaire romain.* 3d ed. Bibliothèque d'Histoire Religieuse. Paris.

Baumstark, Anton. 1957. *Nocturna Laus: Typen frühchristlicher Vigilienfeier und ihre Fortleben vor allem im römischen und monastischen Ritus. Aus dem Nachlass hrsg. von Odilo Heiming.* Liturgiewissenschaftliche Quellen und Forschungen 32. Münster in Westfalen. Repr. 1967.

———. 1958. *Comparative Liturgy.* Rev. by Bernard Botte. Trans. F. L. Cross. Westminster, Md.

Becker, Hansjacob. 1965. "Reform des Ferialpsalteriums." *EL* 79:17–54.

Bennett, Adelaide. 1996. "A Thirteenth-Century French Book of Hours for Marie." *Journal of the Walters Art Gallery* 54:21–50.

Bent, Margaret. 1983. "Resfacta and Cantare Super Librum." *JAMS* 36:371–91.

Benz, Suitbert. 1967. *Der Rotulus von Ravenna, nach seiner Herkunft und seiner Bedeutung für die Liturgiegeschichte kritisch untersucht.* Münster, Westfalen.

Berlière, Ursmer. 1908. "Les Hymnes dans le 'cursus' de S. Benoît." *RB* 25:367–74.

Bernard, Philippe. 1993. "Le Cantique des trois enfants (Dan. III, 52–90): Les répertoires liturgiques occidentaux dans l'antiquité tardive et le haut moyen âge." *Musica e storia* 1:231–72.

Berschin, Walter. 1981. "Sanktgallische Offiziendichtung aus ottonischer Zeit." In *Lateinische Dichtungen des X. und XI. Jahrhunderts. Festgabe Walther Bulst,* 13–48. Heidelberg.

———. 1986–91. *Biographie und Epochenstil im lateinischen Mittelalter.* 3 vols. Stuttgart.

———. 1988. "Greek Elements in Medieval Latin Manuscripts." In *The Sacred Nectar of the Greeks: The Study of Greek in the West in the Early Middle Ages,* ed. Michael W. Herren, 85–104 + 16 plates. King's College London Medieval Studies 2. London.

——— and David Hiley, eds. 1999. *Die Offizien des Mittelalters: Dichtung und Musik.* Regensburger Studien zur Musikgeschichte 1. Regensburg.

———, Peter Ochsenbein, and Hartmut Möller. 1991. "Das älteste Gallusoffizium." In *Lateinische Kultur im X. Jahrhundert. Akten des 1. Internationalen Mittellateinerkongresses,* 11–37. Heidelberg 1988. *Mittellateinisches Jahrbuch* 24/25 [1989/90]. Stuttgart.

——— ——— ———. 1999. "Das Othmaroffizium: Vier Phasen seiner Entwicklung." In Berschin and Hiley (1999), 25–57.

Bertonière, Gabriel. 1972. *The Historical Development of the Easter Vigil and Related Services in the Greek Church.* Orientalia Christiana Analecta 193. Rome.

Beyssac, G. M. 1957. "Le Graduel-antiphonaire de Mont-Renaud." *Revue de musicologie* 39:131–50.

Bhaldraithe, Eoin de. 1977. "The Morning Office of the Rule of the Master." *Regulae Benedicti Studia. Annuarium Internationale* 5 [Second International Congress on the Rule of St. Benedict]: 201–23.

Bieler, Ludwig. 1963. *Ireland: Harbinger of the Middle Ages.* London.

Bischoff, Bernhard, and Michael Lapidge, eds. 1994. *Biblical Commentaries from the Canterbury School of Theodore and Hadrian.* Cambridge.

Bishop, Edmund. 1902. "Liturgical Note." In *The Prayer Book of Aedeluald the Bishop, commonly called the Book of Cerne,* ed. A. B. Kuypers. Cambridge.

——. 1918a. "The Genius of the Roman Rite." In *Liturgica historica,* 1–19. Oxford. Repr. 1981.

——. 1918b. "Spanish Symptoms" and "More Spanish Symptoms." In *Liturgica historica,* 165–202 and 203–10. Oxford. Repr. 1981.

Bishop, W. C. 1924. *The Mozarabic and Ambrosian Rites: Four Essays in Comparative Liturgiology,* ed. C. L. Feltoe. Alcuin Club Tracts 15. London and Milwaukee.

Björkvall, Gunilla, and Andreas Haug. 1992. "Primus init Stephanus: Eine Sankt Galler Prudentius-Vertonung aus dem zehnten Jahrhundert." *Archiv für Musikwissenschaft* 49:57–78.

—— ——. 1996. "Form und Vortrag des Carmen Cantabrigiense 27." *Filologia mediolatina* 3:155–91.

—— ——. 1997. "Formauffassung und Formvermittlung: Verstechnische und versgeschichtliche Voraussetzungen der melodischen Analyse lateinicher Hymnen des Mittelalters. In *Der lateinische Hymnus im Mittelalter: Überlieferung—Ästhetik—Ausstrahlung,* ed. Andreas Haug, Christopher März, Fritz Reckow, and Lorenz Welker. Monumenta Monodica Medii Aevi. Subsidia 6. Erlangen.

—— ——. 1998. "Musik und lateinischer Vers im frühen Mittelalter." In *Musik als Text. Bericht über den internationalen Kongreß der Gesellschaft für Musikforschung, Freiburg im Breisgau 1993,* ed. Hermann Danuser and Tobias Plebuch, 2:234–40. Kassel.

—— ——. 1999a. "Text und Musik im Trinitätsoffizium Stephans von Lüttich: Beobachtungen und Überlegungen aus mittellateinischer und musikhistorischer Sicht." In Berschin and Hiley (1999), 1–24.

—— ——. 1999b. "Verslehre und Versvertonung im lateinischen Mittelalter." In *"Artes" im Mittelalter: Wissenschaft—Kunst—Kommunikation. 7. Symposium des Mediävistenverbandes, 24. bis 27. Februar 1997, an der Humboldt-Universität zu Berlin,* ed. Ursula Schaefer, 309–23. Berlin.

Blaise, Alabert. 1966. *Le Vocabulaire latin des principaux thèmes liturgiques.* Turnhout.

Bloxam, Mary Jennifer. 1987. "A Survey of Late Medieval Service Books from the Low Countries: Implications for Sacred Polyphony, 1460–1520." Ph.D. diss., Yale University.

Blum, Pamela. 1986. "Liturgical Influences on the Design of the West Front at Wells and Salisbury." *Gesta* 25:145–50.

Blume, Clemens. 1908. *Der Cursus S. Benedicti Nursini und die liturgischen Hymnen des 6.-9. Jh.* Hymnologische Beiträge 3. Leipzig.

Bomm, Urbanus. 1929. *Der Wechsel der Modalitätbestimmung in der Tradition der Messgesänge im IX. bis XIII. Jahrhundert und sein Einfluss auf die Tradition ihrer Melodien.* Einsiedeln. Repr. Hildesheim and New York, 1975.

Bonnard, Fourier. 1904–8. *Histoire de l'abbaye royale et de l'ordre des chanoines réguliers de St.-Victor de Paris.* 2 vols. Paris.

Bonniwell, W. R. 1945. *A History of the Dominican Liturgy, 1215–1945.* New York.

Borders, James. 1988. "The Northern Italian Antiphons *ante evangelium* and the Gallican Connection." *Journal of Musicological Research* 8:1–53.

Borella, Pietro. 1934. "Il capitolare ed evangelario ambrosiano di S. Giovanni Battista in Busto Arsizio." *Ambrosius* 10:212–23.

——. 1939. "La 'Missa' o 'Dimissio catechumenorum' nelle liturgie occidentali." *EL* 53:60–110.

Botte, Bernard. 1932. *Les Origines de la Noël et de l'Epiphanie: Étude historique.* Textes et études liturgiques 1. Louvain.

Bouillet, M.-E. 1965. "Le vrai 'Codex Regularum' de Saint Benoît d'Aniane." *RB* 75: 345–49.

Bourque, Emmanuel. 1958. *Étude sur les sacramentaires romains* 2/2. Studi di Antichità Cristiana 25, number 555, 424–25. Vatican City.

Boyce, James John, O.Carm. 1984. "Cantica Carmelitana: The Chants of the Carmelite Office." 2 vols. Ph.D. diss., New York University.

———. 1986. "Medieval Carmelite Office Manuscripts." *Carmelus* 33:17–34.

———. 1987. "Die Mainzer Karmeliterchorbücher und die liturgische Tradition des Karmeliterordens." *Archiv für mittelrheinische Kirchengeschichte* 39:267–303.

———. 1988a. "The Carmelite Choirbooks of Florence and the Liturgical Tradition of the Carmelite Order." *Carmelus* 35:67–93.

———. 1988b. "The Office of St. Mary of Salome." *Journal of the Plainsong and Mediaeval Music Society* 11:25–47.

———. 1989. "The Office of the Three Marys in the Carmelite Liturgy." *Journal of the Plainsong and Mediaeval Music Society* 12:1–38.

———. 1990a. "The Medieval Carmelite Office Tradition." *Acta musicologica* 62:119–51.

———. 1990b. "Two Antiphonals of Pisa: Their Place in the Carmelite Liturgy." *Manuscripta* 34:147–65.

———. 1991. "The Office of the Presentation of Mary in the Carmelite Liturgy." In *The Land of Carmel, Essays in Honor of Joachim Smet, O.Carm.*, ed. Paul Chandler and Keith J. Egan, 231–47. Rome.

———. 1993a. "The Search for the Early Carmelite Liturgy: A Templar Manuscript Reassessed." *Revista de musicología* 16:957–81.

———. 1993b. "Das Offizium der Darstellung Mariens von Philippe de Mézières, Die Handschriften und der Überlieferungsprozeß." *Kirchenmusikalisches Jahrbuch* 77: 17–38.

———. 1994. "From Rule to Rubric: The Impact of Carmelite Liturgical Legislation upon the Order's Office Tradition." *EL* 108:262–98.

———. 1996. "The Liturgy of the Carmelites." *Carmelus* 43:5–41.

———. 1997. "The Feasts of Saints Elijah and Elisha in the Carmelite Rite: A Liturgico-Musical Study." In *Master of the Sacred Page: Essays and Articles in Honor of Roland E. Murphy, O.Carm., on the Occasion of His Eightieth Birthday*, ed. Keith J. Egan and Craig E. Morrison, 155–88. Washington, D.C.

Bradshaw, Brendan. 1989. "The Wild and Wooly West: Early Irish Christianity and Latin Orthodoxy." In *The Churches, Ireland and the Irish: Papers Read at the 1987 Summer Meeting and the 1988 Winter Meeting of the Ecclesiastical History Society*, ed. W. J. Sheils and Diana Wood, 1–23. Oxford.

Bradshaw, Paul F. 1981. *Daily Prayer in the Early Church.* London, for the Alcuin Club. 2d impression: Alcuin Club Collections 63. New York.

———. 1982. "Response to Gabriele Winkler." *Worship* 56:264–66.

———. 1983. *Daily Prayer in the Early Church.* Alcuin Club Collections 63. Repr. with add. preface. New York.

———. 1990. "Cathedral vs. Monastery: The Only Alternatives for the Liturgy of the Hours?" In *Time and Community: In Honor of Thomas Julian Talley*, ed. J. Neil Alexander, 123–36. NPM Studies in Church Music and Liturgy. Washington, D.C.

———. 1992a. "The First Three Centuries." In *The Study of Liturgy*, rev. ed., ed. Cheslyn Jones, Geoffrey Wainwright, Edward Yarnold, and Paul Bradshaw, 399–403. London.

———. 1992b. *The Search for the Origins of Christian Worship.* Oxford.

———. 1993. "'Diem baptismo sollemniorem': Initiation and Easter in Christian Antiquity." In ΕΥΛΟΓΗΜΑ: Studies in Honor of Robert Taft, S.J., ed. Ephrem Carr, Stefano Parenti, Abraham-Andreas Thiermeyer, and Elena Velkovska, 41–51. Studia Anselmiana 110. Analecta Liturgica 17. Rome. Repr. in Maxwell Johnson, ed., *Living Water, Sealing Spirit: Readings on Christian Initiation* (Collegeville, Minn., 1995), 137–47.

——. 1995. "From Word to Action: The Changing Role of Psalmody in Early Christianity." In *Like a Two-Edged Sword: Word of God in Liturgy and History: Essays in Honour of Canon Donald Gray*, 21–37. Norwich.

Branner, Robert. 1969. *Chartres Cathedral*. New York.

——. 1975. "Manuscript Painting in Paris around 1200." In *The Year 1200: A Symposium*, 173–85. New York.

——. 1977. *Manuscript Painting in Paris during the Reign of Saint Louis: A Study of Styles*. Berkeley.

Bray, Dorothy Ann. 1995. "Allegory in the Navigatio Sancti Brendani." *Viator* 26:1–10.

Brooks-Leonard, John Kenn. 1988. "Easter Vespers in Early Medieval Rome: A Critical Edition and Study." Ph.D. diss., University of Notre Dame.

Brou, Louis. 1950. "L'Antiphonaire wisigothique et l'antiphonaire grégorien au début du VIIIᵉ siècle." *Anuario musical* 5:3–10.

——. 1961. "L'Ancien Office de saint Vaast, évêque d'Arras." *EG* 4:7–41.

Brown, Julian. 1993. *A Palaeographer's View: The Selected Writings of Julian Brown*, ed. Janet Bately, Michelle P. Brown, Jane Roberts. London.

Brown, Raymond E., and John P. Meier. 1983. *Antioch and Rome: New Testament Cradles of Catholic Christianity*. New York.

Bruzelius, Caroline A. 1985. *The Thirteenth-Century Church at St-Denis*. Yale Publications in the History of Art 33. New Haven.

Büttner, F. O. 1983. *Imitatio pietatis: Motive der christlichen Ikonographie als Modelle zur Verähnlichung*. Berlin.

Buisson, P., and P. Bellier de la Chavignerie. 1896. *Tableau de la ville de Chartres*. Chartres.

Bullough, Donald A. 1982. "The Missions to the English and Picts and their Heritage (to c. 800)." In Löwe 1982: 80–98.

Bulst, Walther. 1976. "Hymnologica partim Hibernica." In *Latin Script and Letters, A.D. 400–900: Festschrift presented to Ludwig Bieler on the Occasion of his 70th Birthday*, ed. John J. O'Meara and Bernd Naumann, 83–100. Leiden.

Callewaert, Camillus. 1939. *Liturgicae institutiones tractatus secundus: De breviarii romani liturgia*. 2d rev. ed. Bruges.

——. 1940. *Sacris erudiri*. Steenbrugghe. Contains:

——. 1940a. "De completorio ante s. Benedictum," 127–30.

——. 1940b. "De laudibus matutinis," 53–89.

——. 1940c. "De matutino in antiquo officio romano," 145–48.

——. 1940d. "De parvis horis Romanis ante Regulam s. Benedicti," 119–26.

——. 1940e. "Vesperae antiquae in officio praesertim romano," 91–117.

——. 1940f. "Les Prières d'introduction aux différentes heures de l'office," 135–44.

Camiciotti, M. G. 1905. "Di un antico antifonario neumatico fiorento." *Rassegna gregoriana* 4:96–124.

Camilot-Oswald, Raffaella. 1997. *Die liturgischen Musikhandschriften aus dem mittelalterlichen Patriarchat Aquileia*. Vol. 1. MMMS Subsidia, 2. Kassel.

Canal, José M., C.M.F. 1961. "Oficio parvo de la Virgen: Formas viejas y formas nuevas." *Ephemerides Mariologicae* 11:497–525.

——. 1965. "El oficio parvo de la Virgen de 1000 a 1250." *Ephemerides Mariologicae* 15: 463–75.

——. 1966. "En torno a S. Fulberto de Chartres." *EL* 80:211–25.

Capelle, Bernard. 1940. "Un plaidoyer pour la Règle du Maître." *Recherches de théologie ancienne et médiéval* 12:5–32.

Cappuyns, M. J. 1964. *Lexique de la Regula Magistri*. Instrumenta Patristica 6. Steenbrugge.

Cattin, Giulio. 1984. *Music of the Middle Ages I*, trans. Steven Botterill. Cambridge.

Chadwick, Henry. 1972. "Prayer at Midnight." In *Epektasis: Mélanges patristiques offerts au Cardinal Jean Daniélou,* ed. Jacques Fontaine and Charles Kannengiesser, 47–9. [Paris.]

——. 1974. "John Moschus and his Friend Sophronius the Sophist." *Journal of Theological Studies* n. s. 25:41–74.

Chailley, Jacques. 1957. "Les Anciens Tropaires et séquentiaires de l'école de Saint-Martial de Limoges (xᵉ–xiᵉ s.)." *EG* 2:163–88.

——. 1960. *L'École musicale de Saint Martial de Limoges jusqu'à la fin du XIᵉ siècle.* Paris.

Charles-Edwards, T. M. 1997. "The Penitential of Columbanus." In Lapidge 1997, 217–39.

Charvin, G. 1965–79. *Statuts généraux et visites de l'Ordre de Cluny.* Paris, 1965–79.

Chavasse, Antoine. 1953. "L'Avent romain, du v1ᵉ au v11ᵉ siècle." *EL* 67:297–308.

——. 1955. "Le Sermonaire des Saints-Philippe-et-Jacques." *EL* 69:17–24.

Chiarelli, Renzo. 1968. *I codici miniati del Museo di S. Marco a Firenze.* Florence.

Chitty, Derwas. 1966. *The Desert a City.* Oxford.

Claire, Jean. "Les Répertoires liturgiques latins avant l'Octoéchos. I. L'Office férial romano-franc." *EG* 15 (1975):138–63.

Clerval, Jules Alexandre. 1899. *L'Ancienne Maîtrise de Notre-Dame de Chartres.* Paris.

Clover, Carol J., and John Lindow, eds. 1985. *Old Norse-Icelandic Studies: A Critical Guide.* Ithaca, N.Y., and London.

Coathalem, Hervé, S. J. 1954. *Le Parallelisme entre la Sainte Vierge et l'Église dans la tradition latine jusqu'à la fin du XIIᵉ siècle.* Analecta Gregoriana 74. Rome.

Cockerell, Sydney C. 1905. *A Psalter and Hours Executed before 1270 for a Lady Connected with St. Louis, Probably His Sister Isabelle of France . . .* London.

Coleman, William E., ed. 1981. *Philippe de Mézières' Campaign for the Feast of Mary's Presentation.* Toronto Medieval Latin Texts 11. Toronto.

Constas, Nicolas Paul. 1994. "Four Christological Homilies of Proclus of Constantinople: Introduction, Critical Edition, Translation, and Commentary." Ph.D. thesis, Catholic University, 1994.

Corbett, P. B. 1958. *The Latin of the Regula Magistri with Particular Reference to its Colloquial Aspects.* Recueil de travaux d'histoire et de philologie 4/17. Louvain.

Crehan, Joseph H. 1976. "The Liturgical Trade Route: East to West." *Studies: An Irish Quarterly Review* 65:87–99.

Crocker, Richard L. 1986. "Matins Antiphons at St. Denis." *JAMS* 39:441–90.

——. 1990a. "Chants of the Roman Office." In *The Early Middle Ages to 1300,* ed. Richard Crocker and David Hiley, 146–73. *New Oxford History of Music,* 2d ed., vol. 2. Oxford and New York.

——. 1990b. "Liturgical Materials of Roman Chant." Ibid., 111–45.

Cullin, Olivier. 1982. "Une pièce gallicane conservée par la liturgie de Gaillac: L'offertoire Salvator Mundi pour les défunts." *Liturgie et musique (IXᵉ–XIVᵉ s.). Cahiers de Fanjeaux* 17:287–96. Toulouse.

Curran, Michael. 1984. *The Antiphonary of Bangor and the Early Irish Monastic Liturgy.* Dublin.

Curtis, Liane. 1991. "Music Manuscripts and Their Production in Fifteenth-Century Cambrai." Ph.D. diss., University of North Carolina, Chapel Hill.

Dallen, James. 1986. *The Reconciling Community: The Rite of Penance.* New York.

Daniélou, Jean. 1951. *Advent.* New York.

De Breffny, Brian. 1982. *In the Steps of St Patrick.* London.

De cultu Mariano saeculis XII–XV: acta Congressus Mariologici-Mariani Internationalis Romae anno 1975 celebrati. 1980. Vol. 4: *De cultu Mariano apud scriptores ecclesiasticos saec. XII–XIII.* Rome.

Delaporte, Yves. 1922. "Les Processions de la Fête-Dieu suivant l'usage de la cathédrale de Chartres." *La Voix de Notre-Dame* (May 1922): 197–201; (June 1922): 207–12 and 225–29.

——. 1923. "Porte Cendreuse: Souvenirs liturgiques." *La Voix de Notre-Dame* (Mar. 1922): 93–96.

——. 1924. "Une prétendue 'cérémonie bizarre' à la cathédrale de Chartres." *La Voix Notre-Dame* (July 1924): 109–13.

——. 1926. *Les Vitraux de la cathédrale de Chartres.* 3 vols. Chartres.

——. 1930. "Les Titulaires des chapelles de la crypte de Notre-Dame de Chartres." *La Voix de Notre-Dame* (Aug. 1930): 218–22; (Sept. 1930): 253–58.

——. 1931. "Une séquence en l'honneur de saint Chéron." *RG* 16:109–96.

——. 1951. "Chéron (Saint)." *DHGE* 12:634–35. Paris.

Delisle, Léopold. 1895. "Les Manuscrits de Saint-Martial de Limoges: Réimpression textuelle du Catalogue publié en 1730." *Bulletin de la Société archéologique et historique du Limousin* 43:1–60.

——. 1896. "Notice sur les manuscrits originaux d'Adémar de Chabannes." *Notices et extraits des manuscrits de la Bibliothèque Nationale et autres bibliothèques* 35:241–358. Paris.

Dickins, Bruce. 1940. "The Cult of S. Olave in the British Isles." *Saga-Book of the British Viking Society for Northern Research* 12/2:53–80. London.

Dinkler, Erich. 1970. *Der Einzug in Jerusalem.* Opladen.

Dix, Gregory. 1945. *The Shape of the Liturgy.* 2d ed. Glasgow.

Dobszay, László. 1985. "The System of the Hungarian Plainsong Sources." *Studia musicologica* 27:37–65.

——. 1988. "The Program 'CAO–ECE.'" *Studia musicologica* 30:355–60.

——. Forthcoming. "The Liturgical Position of the Hymns." In *Monumenta monodica medii aevi—subsidia.*

—— and G. Prószéky. 1988. *Corpus Antiphonalium Officii–Ecclesiarum Centralis Europae (CAO–ECE).* Budapest.

Dold, Alban. 1940. *Neue St. Galler Vorhieronymianische Propheten-Fragmente.* Hohenzollern.

Donovan, Claire. 1991. *The de Brailes Hours: Shaping the Book of Hours in Thirteenth-Century Oxford.* London.

Doyle, Peter. 1976. "The Latin Bible in Ireland: Its Origins and Growth." In *Biblical Studies: The Medieval Irish Contribution,* ed. Martin McNamara, 30–45. Proceedings of the Irish Biblical Association 1. Dublin.

Dubois, Jacques, and Jean-Loup Lemaître. 1993. *Sources et méthodes de l'hagiographie médiévale.* Paris.

Dufraigne, Pierre. 1994. *Adventus Augusti, adventus Christi: Recherche sur l'exploitation idéologique et littéraire d'un cérémonial dans l'antiquité tardive.* Paris.

Duft, Johannes. 1959. *Sankt Otmar: Die Quellen zu seinem leben; lateinisch und deutsch.* Zurich.

——. 1982. "Irische Handschriftenüberlieferung in St. Gallen." In Löwe (1982), 916–37.

Dugmore, C. W. 1944. *The Influence of the Synagogue upon the Divine Office.* Oxford.

Dumville, D. N. 1978. "Biblical Apocrypha and the Early Irish: A Preliminary Investigation." *Proceedings of the Royal Irish Academy* 73C: 299–338.

Dunn, Marilyn. 1990. "Mastering Benedict: Monastic Rules and Their Authors in the Early Medieval West." *English Historical Review* 416:567–94.

——. 1992. "The Master and St Benedict: A Rejoinder." *English Historical Review* 418:104–11.

Durand, Georges. 1901. *Monographie de l'église Notre-Dame Cathédrale d'Amiens.* 3 vols. Paris.

Dvornik, Francis. 1958. *The Idea of Apostolicity in Byzantium and the Legend of the Apos-*

tle Andrew. Cambridge, Mass.

Dyer, Joseph. 1989. "Monastic Psalmody of the Middle Ages." *RB* 99:41–74.

———. 1993. "The Schola Cantorum and its Roman Milieu in the Early Middle Ages." In *De musica et cantu: Studien zur Geschichte der Kirchenmusik und der Oper. Helmut Hucke zum 60. Geburtstag,* ed. Peter Cahn and Ann-Katrin Heimer, 19–40. Musik-wissenschaftliche Publikationen, Hochschule für Musik und Darstellende Kunst 2. Hildesheim.

———. 1999. "The Psalms in Monastic Prayer." In *The Place of the Psalms in the Intellectual Culture of the Middle Ages,* ed. Nancy van Deusen, 59–89. Albany.

Edwards, Owain T. 1992. "Chant Transference in Rhymed Offices." In *Cantus Planus: Papers Read at the Fourth Meeting, Pécs, Hungary, 3–8 September 1990,* ed. László Dobszay, Agnes Papp, and Ferenc Sebó, 503–19. Budapest.

Egan, Keith J., O.Carm. 1969. "Medieval Carmelite Houses, England and Wales." *Carmelus* 16:142–226.

———. 1972. "An Essay toward a Historiography of the Origins of the Carmelite Province in England." *Carmelus* 19:67–100.

Eisenhofer, Ludwig. 1941. *Handbuch der katholischen Liturgik.* 2 vols. Freiburg im Breisgau.

Emerson, John A. 1962. "Fragments of a Troper from Saint Martial de Limoges." *Scriptorium* 16:369–72.

———. 1965. "Two Newly Identified Offices for Saints Valeria and Austriclinianus by Adémar de Chabannes (MS BNF, Latin 909, ff. 79–85v)." *Speculum* 40:31–46.

———. 1993. "Neglected Aspects of the Oldest Full Troper (BNF, lat. 1240)." In *Recherches nouvelles sur les tropes liturgiques,* ed. Wulf Arlt and Gunilla Björkvall, 193–217. Corpus troporum 8. Acta Universitatis Stockholmiensis, Studia Latina Stockholmiensia 36. Stockholm.

Epstein, Marcy. 1978. "Ludovicus Decus Regnantium: Perspectives on the Rhymed Office." *Speculum* 53:283–334.

Evitt, Regula Meyer. 1992. "Anti-Judaism and the Medieval Prophet Plays: Exegetical Contexts for the 'Ordines Prophetarum.'" Ph.D. diss., University of Virginia.

Falck, Robert, and Martin Picker. 1980. "Contrafactum." *NG* 4:700–1.

Falk, Franz. 1902. "Zur Einfuhrung des Festes Maria Opferung in der Mainzer Kirchenprovinz 1468." *Der Katholik* 82:543–53.

Fallows, David. 1983. "Specific Information on the Ensembles for Composed Polyphony, 1400–1474." In *Studies in the Performance of Late Medieval Music,* ed. Stanley Boorman, 109–59. Cambridge.

———. 1984. "Introit Antiphon Paraphrase in the Trent Codices: Laurence Feininger's *confronto.*" *Journal of the Plainsong and Mediaeval Music Society* 7:47–77.

———. 1987. *Dufay.* London. Rev. paperback ed.

———. 1989. "The Life of Johannes Regis, ca. 1425 to 1496." *Revue belge de musicologie* 43:143–72.

Farris, Stephen. 1985. *The Hymns of Luke's Infancy Narratives; Their Origin, Meaning and Significance. Journal for the Study of the New Testament,* Supplement Series 9. Sheffield.

Fassler, Margot E. 1985. "The Office of the Cantor in Early Western Monastic Rules and Customaries: A Preliminary Investigation." *Early Music History* 5:29–51.

———. 1992. "The Feast of Fools and *Danielis ludus:* Popular Tradition in a Medieval Cathedral Play." In *Plainsong in the Age of Polyphony,* ed. Thomas Forrest Kelly, 65–99. Cambridge.

———. 1993a. *Gothic Song: Victorine Sequences and Augustinian Reform in Twelfth-Century Paris.* Cambridge Studies in Medieval and Renaissance Music. Cambridge.

——. 1993b. "Liturgy and Sacred History in the Twelfth-Century Tympana at Chartres." *Art Bulletin* 75:499–520.

——. 1994. "The Meaning of Entrance: Liturgical Commentary and the Introit Tropes." In *Reflections on the Sacred: A Musicological Perspective*, 8–18. New Haven.

——. 1995. "Liturgical Commentators." In *The Encyclopedia of Medieval France*, 553–54.

——. Forthcoming. "The First Marian Feast in Constantinople and Jerusalem: Chant Texts, Readings, and Homiletic Literature." In *The Study of Medieval Chant: Paths and Bridges, East and West*, ed. Peter Jeffery. Woodbridge.

Favazza, Joseph A. 1988. *The Order of Penitents: Historical Roots and Pastoral Future.* Collegeville, Minn.

Felder, Fr. Hilarinus. 1901. *Die liturgischen Reimoffizien auf dem hl. Franciscus und Antonius, gedichtet und componiert von F. Julian von Speier.* Freiburg.

Ferretti, Paolo M. 1935. *Estetica gregoriana: Trattato delle forme musicali del canto gregoriano*, 1. Rome.

Fischer, Bonifatius. 1964. "Zur Liturgie der lateinischen Handschriften vom Sinai." *RB* 74:284–97.

Flint, Valerie. 1982. "Heinricus of Augsburg and Honorius Augustodunensis: Are They the Same Person?" *RB* 92:148–58.

Foote, Peter. 1993. "Icelandic Historians and the Swedish Image." In *Snorre Sturlasson och de isländska källorna till Sveriges historia*, ed. Göran Dahlbäck, 9–42. Runica et mediævalia. Stockholm.

Forcadell, Augustine M., O.Carm. 1954. "The Feast of the Immaculate Conception in the Carmelite Liturgy." *The Sword* 17:184–93.

Franca, Umberto. 1977. *Le antifone bibliche dopo Pentecoste.* Studia Anselmiana 73, Analecta Liturgica 4. Rome.

Franz, Ansgar. 1993–94. "Ambrosius der Dichter: Zu dem von Jacques Fontaine herausgegebenen Kommentarwerk über die Hymnen des Ambrosius von Mailand." *ALw* 35–36:140–49.

——. 1994. *Tageslauf und Heilsgeschichte: Untersuchungen zum literarischen Text und liturgischen Kontext der Tagzeitenhymnen des Ambrosius von Mailand.* St. Ottilien.

Frei, Judith. 1974. *Das ambrosianische Sakramentar D 3–3 aus dem mailändischen Metropolitankapitel.* Corpus ambrosiano-liturgicum 3. Münster.

Frere, Walter Howard. 1894. *Biblioteca musico-liturgica: A Descriptive Handlist of the Musical and Latin-Liturgical MSS of the Middle Ages Preserved in the Libraries of Great Britain and Northern Ireland* 1. London.

——. 1930, 1934, 1935. *Studies in Early Roman Liturgy*, 1: *The Calendar*; 2: *The Roman Gospel-Lectionary*; 3: *The Roman Epistle-Lectionary.* Alcuin Club Collection 28, 30, 32. Oxford.

Froger, Jacques. 1946. *Les Origines de Prime.* Bibliotheca Ephemerides Liturgicae 19. Rome.

——. 1952. "Note pour rectifier l'interprétation de Cassien *Inst.* 3,4; 6 proposée dans *Les Origines de Prime.*" *ALw* 2:96–102.

——. 1954. "La Règle du Maître et les sources du monachisme bénédictine." *Revue d'ascétique et de mystique* 30:275–88.

——. 1962. "L'Epître de Notker sur les lettres significatives." *EG* 5:23–72.

——. 1980. "Le Lieu de destination et de provenance du 'Compendiensis.'" In *Ut mens concordet voci: Festschrift Eugène Cardine zum 75. Geburtstag*, ed. Johannes Berchmans Göschl, 338–53. Sankt Ottilien.

Fuchs, Guido, and Hans Martin Weikmann. 1992. *Das Exsultet: Geschichte, Theologie und Gestaltung der österlichen Lichtdanksagung.* Regensburg.

Fuller, Sarah. 1971. "Hidden Polyphony—A Reappraisal." *JAMS* 24:169–92.

———. 1979. "The Myth of 'Saint Martial' Polyphony: A Study of the Sources." *Musica disciplina* 33:5–26.

Gaborit-Chopin, Danielle. 1969. *La Décoration des manuscrits à Saint-Martial de Limoges et en Limousin du IXe au XIIe siècle.* Mémoirs et documents publiés par la Société de l'École des Chartres 17. Paris and Geneva.

Gamber, Klaus. 1962. "Die kampanische Lektionsordung." *Sacris erudiri* 13:155–72.

———. 1982. "Irische Liturgiebücher und ihre Verbreitung auf dem Continent." In *Die Iren und Europa im früheren Mittelalter,* Ed. Heinz Löwe, 1:536–48. Veröffentlichungen des Europa-Zentrums Tübingen, Kulturwissenschaftliche Reihe. Stuttgart.

Ganz, David. 1991. "The Luxeuil Prophets and Merovingian Missionary Strategies." *Beinecke Studies in Early Manuscripts,* Yale University Library Gazette 66 Supplement. New Haven.

Gastoué, Amédée. 1937–39. "Le Chant gallican." *RCG* 41:101–6, 131–33, 167–76; 42:5–12, 57–62, 76–80, 107–12, 146–51, 171–76; 43:7–12, 44–46. Repr. separately, 1939. Grenoble.

Gevaert, François Auguste. 1895. *La Mélopée antique dans le chant de l'église latine.* Ghent. Repr. Osnabrück, 1967.

Ghiglione, Natale. 1984. *L'evangeliario purpureo di Sarezzano (sec. V/VI).* Vicenza.

Gibert Tarruel, Jordi. 1973. "La Nouvelle Distribution du psautier dans la 'Liturgia Horarum.'" *EL* 87:325–382.

Gibson, M. T., M. Lapidge, and C. Page. 1983. "Neumed Boethian *Metra* from Canterbury: A Newly Recovered Leaf of Cambridge, University Library, Gg.5.35 (the 'Cambridge Songs' Manuscript)." *Anglo-Saxon England* 12:141–52.

Gindele, Corbinian. 1954. "Die Struktur der Nokturnen in den lateinischen Mönchsregeln vor und um St. Benedikt." *RB* 64:9–27.

———. 1955. "Zur Geschichte von Form und Abhängigkeit bei römischem und monastischem Brevier." *RB* 65:192–207.

———. 1956. "Gestalt und Dauer des vorbenediktinischen Ordo Officii." *RB* 66:3–13.

———. 1957. "Die römische und monastische Überlieferung im Ordo Officii der Regel St. Benedikts (Kap. 8–20; 45 und 52)." In *Commentationes in Regulam s. Benedicti,* 171–222. Studia Anselmiana 42. Rome.

———. 1959. "Die gallikanischen 'Laus perennis'-Klöster und ihr 'Ordo Officii.'" *RB* 69:32–48.

———. 1960. "Das Alleluia im Ordo Officii der Regula Magistri." *RB* 70:504–25.

———. 1961. "Das Problem der Offiziumsordnung in den sogennanten Mischregeln der gallischen Klöster." *Zeitschrift für Kirchengeschichte* 72:294–315.

———. 1966. "Abwechslung und Entspannung im Aufbau des Stundengebets." *RB* 76:321–26.

———. 1967. "Der 'Alleluiaticus,' ein elementares Kennzeichen vorbenediktinischer Psalmodie." *Studien und Mitteilungen zur Geschichte des Benediktiner-Ordens und seiner Zweige* 28:308–20.

———. 1974. "Die Magisterregel und ihre altmonastische Alleluia-Psalmodie." *RB* 84:176–81.

Gneuss, Helmut. 1974. "Latin Hymns in Medieval England: Future Research." In *Chaucer and Middle English Studies in Honour of Rossel Hope Robbins,* ed. Beryl Rowland, 407–24. London and Kent, Ohio.

Godel, Willibrord. 1963. "Irisches Beten im frühen Mittelalter: Eine liturgie- und frommigkeitsgeschichtliche Untersuchung." *Zeitschrift für katholische Theologie* 85:261–321, 389–439.

Gougaud, Louis. 1908. "Inventaire des règles monastiques irlandais." *RB* 25:167–84, 321–33.

———. 1927. *Devotional and Ascetic Practices in the Middle Ages,* ed. G. C. Bateman. London.

Graef, Hermann J. 1959. *Palmenweihe und Palmenprozession in der lateinischen Liturgie*. Veröffentlichungen des Missionspriesterseminars St. Augustin, Siegburg 5. Kaldenkirchen.

Graef, Hilda. 1985. *Mary: A History of Doctrine and Devotion*. Westminster, Md. Repr. of the two-vol. 1963–65 original.

Grier, James. 1990. "Some Codicological Observations on the Aquitanian Versaria." *Musica disciplina* 44:5–56.

———. 1995. "Roger de Chabannes (d. 1025), Cantor of St. Martial, Limoges." *Early Music History* 14:53–119.

———. 1997. "*Scriptio interrupta*: Adémar de Chabannes and the Production of Paris, Bibliothèque Nationale de France, MS latin 909." *Scriptorium* 51: 234–50 and plates 17–27.

Grisbrooke, W. Jardine. 1992. "The Formative Period—Cathedral and Monastic Offices." In *The Study of Liturgy*, rev. ed., ed. Cheslyn Jones, Geoffrey Wainwright, Edward Yarnold, and Paul Bradshaw, 403–20. London.

Grumel, V. 1960. "Le Problème de la date pascale aux IIIe et IVe siècles." *Revue des études byzantines* 18:163–78.

Gunnes, Erik. 1996. *Erkebiskop Øystein: statsmann og kirkebygger*. Oslo.

Gwynn, E. J., and W. J. Purton. 1911–12. "The Monastery of Tallaght." In *Proceedings of the Royal Irish Academy* 29C.

Gy, Pierre-Marie. 1991. "The Different Forms of Liturgical 'Libelli.'" In *Fountain of Life: In Memory of Niels K. Rasmussen, O. P.*, ed. Gerard Austin, 23–34. NPM Studies in Church Music and Liturgy. Washington, D.C.

Haggh, Barbara. 1987. "The Medieval Obituary and the Rise of Sacred Polyphony in the Low Countries." Paper read at the annual meeting of the American Musicological Society, New Orleans.

———. 1988. "Music, Liturgy, and Ceremony in Brussels, 1350–1500." Ph.D. diss., University of Illinois at Urbana-Champaign.

———. 1989. "The Office of the Dead by Guillaume Du Fay: Does it Survive?" Paper read at the annual conference on Medieval and Renaissance Music, Reading.

———. 1990a. "The Aostan Sources for the 'Recollectio Festorum Beatae Mariae Virginis' by Guillaume Du Fay." In *Cantus Planus: Papers Read at the Third Meeting, Tihány, Hungary, 19–24 September 1988*, ed. László Dobszay et al., 355–75. Budapest.

———. 1990b. "The Celebration of the 'Recollectio Festorum Beatae Mariae Virginis,' 1457–1987." *Atti del XIV Congresso della Società Internazionale di Musicologia, Bologna, 1987: Trasmissione e recezione delle forme di cultura musicale*, ed. Angelo Pompilio, 3:559–71. Turin.

———. 1992. "Guillaume Du Fay and the Evolution of the Liturgy at Cambrai Cathedral in the Fifteenth Century." In *Cantus Planus: Papers Read at the Fourth Meeting, Pécs, Hungary, 3–8 September 1990*, ed. László Dobszay et al., 549–69. Budapest.

———. 1995a. "The Archives of the Order of the Golden Fleece and Music." *Journal of the Royal Musical Association* 120:1–43.

———. 1995b. "Crispijne and Abertijne: Two Tenors at the Church of St. Niklaas, Brussels." *Music and Letters* 76:325–45.

———. 1995c. "Introduction." In *Two Cambrai Antiphoners: Cambrai, Médiathèque Municipale, 38 and Impr. XVI C 4. Printouts from two Indices in Machine-Readable Form. A CANTUS Index*, ed. Barbara Haggh, Charles Downey, Keith Glaeske, and Lila Collamore. Musicological Studies 55/4. Ottawa.

———. 1995d. "The Late-Medieval Liturgical Books of Cambrai Cathedral: A Brief Survey of the Evidence." In *Laborare fratres in unum: Festschrift László Dobszay zum 60. Geburtstag*, ed. Janka Szendrei and David Hiley, 79–85. Hildesheim.

———. 1995e. *Two Offices for St. Elizabeth of Hungary: Gaudeat Hungaria and Letare Germania,* ed. Barbara Haggh. Musicological Studies 65/1. Ottawa.

———. 1996a. "Foundations or Institutions? On Bringing the Middle Ages into the History of Medieval Music." *AcM* 68:87–128.

———. 1996b. "Correspondence: The Order of the Golden Fleece." *Journal of the Royal Musical Association* 121:268–70.

———. 1997a. "The Virgin Mary and the Order of the Golden Fleece." In *1454: Lille-Arras et le Voeu du Faisan. Deux capitales princières bourguignonnes face au défi de l'empire Ottoman,* ed. Denis Clauzel et al., 273–87. Arras.

———. 1997b. "An Ordinal of Ockeghem's Time from the Sainte-Chapelle of Paris: Paris, Bibliothèque de l'Arsenal, MS 114." *Tijdschrift van de Vereniging voor Nederlandse Muziekgeschiedenis* 47:33–71.

———. Forthcoming (a). "The First Printed Antiphoner of Cambrai Cathedral." In *Proceedings of the Conference: Die Entstehung einer musikalischen Quelle im 15. und 16. Jahrhundert, Wolfenbüttel, Germany, September 14–18, 1992,* ed. Martin Staehelin. Wolfenbüttel.

———. Forthcoming (b). *Du Fay's Chant for a Fifteenth-Century Marian Office from Cambrai [the Recollectio festorum beate Marie Virginis].*

Hagland, Jan Ragnar. 1990. "Olavslegender frå Bysants." In *Hellas og Norge: kontakt, komparasjon, kontrast: en artikkelsamling,* ed. Øivind Andersen and Tomas Hägg, 193–210. Bergen.

Hallberg, Peter. 1993. "Snorri Sturluson—isländsk storman och historieskrivare." In *Snorre Sturlasson och de isländska källorna till Sveriges historia,* ed. Göran Dahlbäck, 43–63. Runica et mediævalia. Stockholm.

Hallinger, Kassius, ed. 1960. "Die römischen Ordines von Lorsch, Murbach und St. Gallen." In *Universitas, Dienst an Wahrheit und Leben: Festschrift für Bischof Dr. Albert Stohr,* 1:466–77. Mainz.

Handschin, Jacques. 1954. "Trope, Sequence, and Conductus." In *Early Medieval Music up to 1300,* ed. Anselm Hughes, 128–74. NOHM 2. Oxford.

Hanssens, Jean Michel. 1952. *Nature et genèse de l'office des matines.* Analecta Gregoriana 57. Rome.

Harper, John. 1991. *The Forms and Orders of Western Liturgy from the Tenth to the Eighteenth Century: A Historical Introduction and Guide for Students and Musicians.* Oxford.

Harrán, Don. 1989. *In Defense of Music: The Case for Music as Argued by a Singer and Scholar of the Late Fifteenth Century.* Lincoln, Nebr.

Harrington, Wilfrid. 1935, repr. 1988. *The Drama of Christ's Coming.* Wilmington, Del.

Haug, Andreas, and Ritva Jacobsson. Forthcoming. "Versified Offices." *NG* (7th ed.).

Hausherr, Irénée. 1947. "Opus Dei." *Orientalia Christiana Periodica* 13:195–218. [E. T. *Monastic Studies* 11 (1975): 181–204.]

Hautcoeur, Édouard. 1881. "La Liturgie cambrésienne au XVIIIᵉ siècle, et le projet de bréviaire pour tous les diocèses des Pays-Bas." *Analectes pour servir à l'histoire ecclésiastique de la Belgique,* 2ᵉ série, 1:269–76.

Heers, Jacques. 1983. *Fêtes des fous et carnavals.* Paris.

Heiming, Odilo. 1961. "Zum monastischen Offizium von Kassianus bis Kolumbanus." *ALw* 7:89–156.

Hellemo, Geir. 1989. *Adventus Domini: Eschatological Thought in 4th Century Apses and Catecheses.* Leiden and New York.

Hennig, John. 1965. "Old Ireland and Her Liturgy." In *Old Ireland,* ed. Robert McNally, 60–89. New York.

Hertling, L. 1930. "Kanoniker, Augustinerregel und Augustinerorden." *Zeitschrift für katholische Theologie* 54:335–59.

Hesbert, René-Jean. 1947. "L'Antiphonale missarum de l'ancien rit bénéventain." *EL* 61:153–210.

——. 1980. "L'Antiphonaire d'Amalaire." *EL* 94:176–94.

Hilberry, H. H. 1959. "The Cathedral of Chartres in 1030." *Speculum* 34:561–72.

Hiley, David. 1980. "Neuma." *NG* 13:123–25.

——. 1981. "The Liturgical Music of Norman Sicily: A Study Centred on Manuscripts 288, 289, 19421 and Vitrina 20–4 of the Biblioteca Nacional, Madrid." 2 vols. Ph.D. diss. University of London, 1991.

——. 1983. "Quanto c'è di normanno nei tropari siculo-normanni." *Rivista italiana di musicologia* 18:3–28.

——. 1993. *Western Plainchant: A Handbook.* Oxford.

Hoffman, Josef. 1951. "Regula Magistri XLVII und XLVIII in St. Galler und Würzburger Caesarius-Handschriften." *RB* 61:141–66.

Hoffmann, Hartmut. 1986. *Buchkunst und Königtum im ottonischen und frühsalischen Reich.* Stuttgart.

Hofmann, J. B., and Anton Szantyr. 1965. *Lateinische Syntax und Stilistik.* Munich, 1965.

Hofmann-Brandt, Helma. 1971. *Die Tropen zu den Responsorien des Officiums.* 2 vols. Diss. Erlangen-Nürnberg.

Hohler, Christopher. 1972. "A Note on *Jacobus.*" *Journal of the Warburg and Courtauld Institutes* 35:31–80.

Hollander, Lee M. 1987. *Snorri: The Sagas of the Viking Kings of Norway—Heimskringla.* Oslo.

Homan, Frederic W. 1964. "Final and Internal Cadential Patterns in Gregorian Chant." *JAMS* 17:66–77.

Houdoy, Jules. 1880. *Histoire artistique de la Cathédrale de Cambrai.* Lille.

Hourlier, Jacques. 1951. "Remarques sur la notation clunisienne." *RG* 30:231–40.

——. 1960. *La Notation musicale des chants liturgiques latins.* Solesmes.

——. 1973. "Notes sur l'antiphonie." In *Gattungen der Musik in Einzeldarstellungen: Gedenkschrift Leo Schrade,* ed. Wulf Arlt, Ernst Lichtenhahn, and Hans Oesch, 116–43. Bern and Munich.

Hucke, Helmut. 1953. "Musikalische Formen der Officiumsantiphonen." *Kirchenmusikalisches Jahrbuch* 37:7–33.

——. 1955. "Gregorianischer Gesang in altrömischer und fränkischer Überlieferung." *Archiv für Musikwissenschaft* 12:74–87.

——. 1970. "Die Texte der Offertorien." In *Speculum musicae artis: Festgabe für Heinrich Husmann zum 60. Geburtstag am 16. Dezember 1968,* ed. Heinz Becker and Reinhard Gerlach, 193–203. Munich.

——. 1973. "Das Responsorium." In *Gattungen der Musik in Einzeldarstellungen: Gedenkschrift Leo Schrade,* ed. Wulf Arlt, Ernst Lichtenhahn, and Hans Oesch, 144–91. Bern and Munich.

Hughes, Andrew. 1983. "Modal Order and Disorder in the Rhymed Office." *Musica disciplina* 37:29–52.

——. 1988a. "Chants in the Rhymed Office of St. Thomas of Canterbury." *Early Music* 16:185–201.

——. 1988b. "Rhymed Offices." *DMA* 10:366–77.

——. 1993. "Chantword Indexes: A Tool for Plainsong Research." In *Words and Music,* ed. Paul Laird, 31–50. The Center for Medieval and Early Renaissance Studies, Acta 17. Binghamton.

——. 1995. "Literary Transformation in Post-Carolingian Saints' Offices: Using All the Evidence." In *Saints: Studies in Hagiography,* ed. Sandro Sticca, 23–50. Medieval and Renaissance Texts and Studies 141. Binghamton.

———. 1999. *"Fons hortorum*—The Office of the Presentation: Origins and Authorship." In Berschin and Hiley (1999), 153–77.

———. Forthcoming (a). "Liturgical Books: In Order to Order." In *Die Erschliessung der Quellen des mittelalterlichen liturgischen Gesangs,* Ed. David Hiley. Wolfenbütteler Mittelalter-Studien. Wolfenbüttel. In press.

———. Forthcoming (b). "The Wheat and the Chaff: Observations on the Office of St. Dominic." *Symposium on the "Prototype" of the Dominican Liturgy (Rome, 2–4 March, 1995).* Conference report, ed. Pierre-Marie Gy.

———. Forthcoming (c). "Late Medieval Office Chant: Words and Music." In *Musical Life and Musical Thought in Europe, 1300–1500,* ed. Reinhard Strohm. NOHM, 2d ed., vol. 3.

Hughes, David. 1972. "Music for St. Stephen at Laon." In *Words and Music: The Scholar's View. A Medley of Problems and Solutions Compiled in Honor of A. Tillman Merritt by Sundry Hands,* ed. Laurence Berman, 137–59. Cambridge, Mass.

———. 1985. "Another Source for the Beauvais Feast of Fools." In *Music and Context: Essays for John M. Ward,* ed. Anne Dhu Shapiro, 14–31. Cambridge, Mass.

———. 1987. "Evidence for the Traditional View of the Transmission of Gregorian Chant." *JAMS* 40:377–404.

Hughes, Kathleen. 1970. "Some Aspects of Irish Influence on Early English Private Prayer." *Studia Celtica* 5:48–61.

Huglo, Michel. 1955. "Les Preces des graduels aquitains empruntées à la liturgie hispanique." *Hispania sacra* 8:361–83.

———. 1963. "Le Domaine de la notation bretonne." *AcM* 35:54–84.

———. 1971. *Les Tonaires: Inventaire, analyse, comparaison.* Paris.

———. 1975. "Les Débuts de la polyphonie à Paris: Les premiers *organa* parisiens." *Forum musicologicum* 3:117–63.

———. 1979. "Les Réformes de l'Antiphonaire au ixᵉ siècle: Helisachar, Agobard, Amalaire", in *Culto cristiano e politica imperiale carolingia. Todi, 9–12 settembre 1977,* 89–120. Todi, 1979.

———. 1980a. "Antiphon." *NG* 1:471–81.

———. 1980b. "Gallican Rite." *NG* 7:113–25.

———. 1980c. "Processional." *NG* 15:278–81.

———. 1982. "Le Répons-graduel de la messe: Évolution de la forme, permanence de la fonction." *Schweizer Jahrbuch für Musikwissenschaft,* n. s., 2:53–73.

———. 1988. *Les Livres de chant liturgique.* Typologie des sources du moyen âge occidental 52. Turnhout.

———. 1993a. "Observations codicologiques sur l'antiphonaire de Compiègne (Paris., B. N. lat. 17436)." In *De musica et cantu: Studien zur Geschichte der Kirchenmusik und der Oper. Helmut Hucke zum 60. Geburtstag,* ed. Peter Cahn and Ann-Katrin Heimer, 177–30. Musikwissenschaftliche Publikationen, Hochschule für Musik und Darstellende Kunst 2. Hildesheim.

———. 1993b. "Remarks on the Alleluia and Responsory Series in the Winchester Troper." In *Music in the Medieval English Liturgy: Plainsong and Mediaeval Music Society Centennial Essays,* ed. Susan Rankin and David Hiley, 47–58. Oxford.

———. 1996. "Liturgische Gesangsbücher, IIa. Processionale." *MGG* (2d ed.) 5:1435–36.

———. 1999. *Les Manuscrits du Processional.* Répertoire International des Sources Musicales, B XIV, vol. 1. Munich, 1999.

Huonder, Vitus. 1992. "Der österliche Grundton in der Festtagspsalmodie der Laudes." *Ecclesia orans* 9:287–306.

Huot, Sylvia. 1987. *From Song to Book: The Poetics of Writing in Old French Lyric and Lyrical Narrative Poetry.* Ithaca, N.Y., and London.

Husmann, Heinrich. 1967. "Ein Faszikel Notre-Dame-Kompositionen auf Texte des Pariser Kanzlers Philipp in einer Dominikanerhandschrift (Rom, Santa Sabina XIV L3)." *Archiv für Musikwissenschaft* 24:1–23.

——. 1973. "Der Aufbau der byzantinischen Liturgie nach der Erzählung von der Reise der Äbte Johannes und Sophronios zum Einsiedler Nilos auf dem Berge Sinai." In Heinrich Hüschen, ed., *Scientia Musicae Collectanea: Festschrift Karl Gustav Fellerer zum siebzigsten Geburtstag am 7. Juli 1972*, 243–49. Cologne.

Ilàri, Marcella. 1980. "Il canto sublacense e cassinese dal tempo di San Benedetto alla fine del secolo XI." *Benedictina* 27:41–61.

Irtenkauf, Wolfgang. 1963. "Reimoffizium." *MGG* 9:172–76.

Izydorczyk, Zbigniew. 1997. *The Medieval Gospel of Nicodemus: Texts, Intertexts and Contexts in Western Europe.* Medieval and Renaissance Texts and Studies 158. Tempe, Ariz.

Jacobson, Paul A. 1996. "'Ad memoriam ducens': The Development of Liturgical Exegesis in Amalar of Metz's 'Expositiones Missae'." Ph.D. diss., Graduate Theological Union.

Jacobsson, Ritva. 1993. "Unica in the Cotton Caligula Troper." In *Music in the Medieval English Liturgy: Plainsong and Mediaeval Music Society Centennial Essays,* ed. Susan Rankin and David Hiley, 11–45. Oxford.

James, N. W. 1993. "Was Leo the Great the Author of Liturgical Prayers?" In *Liturgica, Second Century, Alexandria before Nicaea, Athanasius and the Arian Controversy: Papers Presented at the Eleventh International Conference on Patristic Studies Held in Oxford, 1991,* 35–40. Studia Patristica 26.

Jammers, Ewald. 1929–30. "Die Antiphonen der rheinischen Reimoffizien." *EL* 43:199–219, 425–51; 44:84–99, 342–68.

Janeras, Vincentius. 1960. "Notulae liturgicae in Regulam Magistri." *Studia Monastica* 2:359–64.

Jasmer, P. 1983. "A Comparison of the Monastic and Cathedral Vespers up to the Time of St. Benedict." *American Benedictine Review* 34:337–60.

Jaspert, B. 1977. *Die Regula Benedicti–Regula Magistri Kontroverse.* 2d ed. Hildesheim.

Jeffery, Peter. 1984. "The Introduction of Psalmody into the Roman Mass by Pope Celestine I (422–432): Reinterpreting a Passage in the *Liber Pontificalis*." *ALw* 26:147–65.

——. 1985. Review of Curran 1984 in *Worship* 59:459–61.

——. 1989. Review of Warren 1987 in *Worship* 63:172–74.

——. 1991. "The Sunday Office of Seventh-Century Jerusalem in the Georgian Chantbook (Iadgari): A Preliminary Report." *Studia liturgica* 21:52–75.

——. 1992. *Re-envisioning Past Musical Cultures: Ethnomusicology in the Study of Gregorian Chant.* Chicago.

——. 1993. "The Liturgical Year in the Ethiopian *Degg{ʷ}ā* (Chantbook)." In ΕΥΛΟΓΗΜΑ: Studies in Honor of Robert Taft, S.J., ed. Ephrem Carr, Stefano Parenti, Abraham-Andreas Thiermeyer, and Elena Velkovska, 199–234. Studia Anselmiana 110. Analecta liturgica 17. Rome.

——. 1994. "The Earliest Christian Chant Repertory Recovered: The Georgian Witnesses to Jerusalem Chant." *JAMS* 47:1–38.

——. 1995. "Rome and Jerusalem: From Oral Tradition to Written Repertory in Two Ancient Liturgical Centers." In *Essays on Medieval Music in Honor of David G. Hughes,* ed. Graeme M. Boone, 207–47. Isham Library Papers 4. Cambridge, Mass.

——. Forthcoming. "Monastic Reading and the Emerging Roman Chant Repertory." In *Western Plainchant in the First Millennium: Studies of the Medieval Liturgy and its Music in Honor of James W. McKinnon.*

Jilek, August. 1992. "Symbol und symbolisches Handeln in sakramentlicher Liturgie:

Ein Beitrag an Hand der mystagogischen Katechesen des Bischofs Ambrosius von Mailand." *Liturgisches Jahrbuch* 42:25–62.

Johnsen, Arne Odd. 1975. "Om misjonsbiskopen Grimkellus." *Norsk historisk Tidskrift* 54:22–34.

Johnson, Glenn Pierr. 1991. "Aspects of Late Medieval Music at the Cathedral of Amiens." 2 vols. Ph.D. diss., Yale University.

Jones, Charles. 1934. "The Victorian and Dionysiac Paschal Tables in the West." *Speculum* 9:408–21.

Jonsson (Jacobsson), Ritva. 1968. *Historia: Études sur la genèse des offices versifiés*. Studia Latina Stockholmiensia 15. Stockholm.

—— and Leo Treitler. 1983. "Medieval Music and Language: A Reconsideration of the Relationship." *Studies in the History of Music* 1:1–23.

Jorga, Nicolas. 1896. *Philippe de Mézières 1327–1405 et la croisade au XIVᵉ siècle*. Paris.

Jungmann, Josef A. 1951. *The Mass of the Roman Rite: Its Origins and Development (Missarum Sollemnia)*. Trans. F. A. Brunner. 2 vols. New York.

——, ed. 1958. *Brevierstudien: Referate aus der Studientagung von Assisi 14–17 September 1956*. Trier.

——. 1962. "The Pre-Monastic Morning Hour in the Gallo-Spanish Region in the 6th Century." In *Pastoral Liturgy*, 122–57. New York.

Kallenberg, Paschalis, O.Carm. 1962. *Fontes Liturgiae Carmelitanae: Investigatio in decreta, codices et Proprium sanctorum*. Rome.

Kantorowicz, Ernst. 1944. "The King's Advent." *Art Bulletin* 26:207–31.

Karnowka, G. H. 1983. *Breviarium Passaviense*. St. Ottilien.

Kasch, Elisabeth. 1974. *Das liturgische Vokabular der frühen lateinischen Mönchsregeln*. Regulae Benedicti Studia: Supplementa 1. Hildesheim.

Kaske, Robert. 1988. *Medieval Christian Literary Imagery: A Guide to Interpretation*. Toronto Medieval Bibliographies 11. Toronto.

Katzenellenbogen, Adolf. 1959. *The Sculptural Programs of Chartres Cathedral*. Baltimore.

Kelly, Aiden, et al. 1993. *Religious Holidays and Calendars: An Encyclopedic Handbook*. Detroit.

Kelly, Thomas F. 1977. "New Music from Old: The Structuring of Responsory Prosas." *JAMS* 30:366–90.

——. 1988. "Neuma Triplex." *AcM* 60:1–30.

——. 1989. *The Beneventan Chant*. Studies in Music. Cambridge.

——. 1996. *The Exultet in Southern Italy*. New York.

Kenney, James F. 1968. *The Sources for the Early History of Ireland, 1: Ecclesiastical: An Introduction and Guide*. New York, 1929. 2d ed., rev. Ludwig Bieler. Dublin, 1966, 1968. Repr. Dublin, 1978, 1993.

Kindermann, Udo. 1991. "*A la feste sui venuz*, et ostendam quare: Ein Gegenfest schafft lateinische Literatur." In *Feste und Feiern im Mittelalter: Paderborner Symposion des Mediävistenverbandes*, ed. Detlef Altenburg, Jörg Jarnut, and Hans-Hugo Steinhoff, 349–57. Sigmaringen.

Kishpaugh, Sr. Mary Jerome, O. P. 1941. *The Feast of the Presentation of the Virgin Mary in the Temple: An Historical and Literary Study*. Washington, D.C.

Klopsch, Paul. 1972. *Einführung in die mittellateinische Verslehre*. Darmstadt.

——. 1991. "Der Übergang von quantitierender zu akzentuierender lateinscher Dichtung." In *Metrik und Medienwechsel/Metrics and Media*, ed. Hildegard L. C. Tristram, 95–106. ScriptOralia 35. Tübingen.

Knowles, David. 1963. "The *Regula Magistri* and the *Rule* of St Benedict." *In Great Historical Enterprises: Problems in Monastic History*, 135–95. London.

Koester, Helmut. 1990. *Ancient Christian Gospels: Their History and Development.* Philadelphia.

Kok, Frans. 1992. "L'Office pachômien: *Psallere, orare, legere.*" *Ecclesia orans* 9:69–95.

Krusch, Bruno. 1880. *Studien zur christlich-mittelalterlichen Chronologie,* 1: *Der 84-jährige Osterzyklus und seine Quellen.* Leipzig.

Lacour, Jacques. 1985. *Chartres: Églises et chapelles.* Société archéologique d'Eure-et-Loir. Chartres.

Lair, Jules. 1899. *Études critiques sur divers textes des Xe et XIe siècles,* 2: *Historia d'Adémar de Chabannes.* Paris.

Lambert, Pierre-Yves. 1991. "Le Vocabulaire du scribe irlandais." In *Ireland and Northern France: AD 600–850,* ed. Jean-Michel Picard, 157–67. Dublin.

Lambot, Cyrille. 1930. "Un 'ordo officii' du ve siècle." *RB* 42:77–80.

Lancashire, Ian, in collaboration with John Bradley, Willard McCarty, Michael Stairs, and T. R. Wooldridge. 1996. *Using TACT with Electronic Texts: A Guide to Text-analysis Computing Tools.* New York.

Landes, Richard. 1995. *Relics, Apocalypse, and the Deceits of History: Ademar of Chabannes, 989–1034.* Harvard Historical Studies 117. Cambridge, Mass.

Langois, M. 1914. "Le Missel de Chartres imprimé en 1482." *Mémoires de la Société archéologique d'Eure-et-Loir* 14:1–54.

Lapidge, Michael. 1997. "'Precamur patrem': An Easter Hymn by Columbanus?" In Lapidge, ed. (1997), 255–63.

——, ed. 1997. *Columbanus: Studies on the Latin Writings.* Studies in Celtic History. Suffolk.

—— and Richard Sharpe. 1985. *A Bibliography of Celtic-Latin Literature, 400–1200.* Royal Irish Academy Dictionary of Medieval Latin from Celtic Sources: Ancillary Publications 1. Dublin.

Lasteyrie, Charles de. 1901. *L'Abbaye de Saint-Martial de Limoges: Étude historique, économique et archéologique précédée de recherches nouvelles sur la vie du saint.* Paris.

Lawlor, H. J. 1897. *Chapters on the Book of Mulling.* Edinburgh.

——. 1897–99. "Notes on an Irish Monastic Office." *Hermathena* 10:212–25.

——. 1916. *The Cathach of St. Columba.* Proceedings of the Royal Irish Academy 33, Sect. C, no. 11. Dublin.

Leclercq, Henri. 1937. "Pâques." *DACL* 13/2:1521–58.

Leclercq, Jean, O.S.B. 1946. *Pierre le Vénérable.* St. Wandrille.

——. 1957. "Regula magistri et Règle de saint Benoît." *Revue d'ascétique et de mystique* 33:101–5.

——. 1958. "Fragmenta Mariana." *EL* 72:292–305.

——. 1960. "Formes anciennes de l'office Marial." *EL* 74:89–102.

Leeb, Helmut. 1967. *Die Psalmodie bei Ambrosius.* Wiener Beiträge zur Theologie 18. Vienna.

Le Goff, Jacques. 1980. *Time, Work and Culture in the Middle Ages,* trans. Arthur Goldhammer. Chicago.

Lentini, Anselmo. 1967. "Note sulla lingua e lo stile della 'Regula Magistri'." *Aevum* 41:53–66.

Lépinois, Eugène de. 1854. *Histoire de Chartres.* 2 vols. Chartres.

Leroquais, Victor. 1929. *Le Bréviaire de Philippe de Bon: Bréviaire parisien du XVe siècle.* 2 vols. Paris.

——. 1934. *Les Bréviaires manuscrits des bibliothèques publiques de France.* 5 vols. and atlas of plates. Paris.

——. 1940–41. *Les Psautiers manuscrits latins des bibliothèques publiques de France.* 2 vols. plus plates. Mâcon.

Le Roux, R. 1963. "Les Répons 'de psalmis' pour les matines de l'Épiphanie à la Septuagésime." *EG* 6:39–148.

Levy, Kenneth. 1984. "Toledo, Rome and the Legacy of Gaul." *Early Music History* 4: 49–99.

———. 1990. "Latin Chant Outside the Roman Tradition." In *The Early Middle Ages to 1300*, ed. Richard Crocker and David Hiley, 69–110. NOHM, 2d ed., vol. 2. Oxford and New York.

Lidén, Anne. 1992. "St. Olav in the Beatus Initial of the Carrow Psalter." *Scripta Islandica* 43:3–27.

———. 1999. *Olav den helige i medeltida bildkonst: Legendmotiv och attribut.* Kungliga Vitterhets Historie och Antikvitets Akademien. Stockholm.

Lipphardt, Walther. 1965. *Der Karolingische Tonar von Metz.* Münster.

Longo, Augusta. 1965–66. "Il testo integrale della 'Narrazione degli abati Giovanni e Sofronio' attraverso le ' Ερμηνεῖαι di Nicone." *Rivista di studi bizantini e neoellenici,* n. s. 2–3:223–67.

López-Calo, José. 1982. *La música medieval en Galicia.* La Coruña.

Löwe, Heinz. 1982. *Die Iren und Europa im früheren Mittelalter.* 2 vols. Veröffentlichungen des Europa-Zentrums Tübingen, Kulturwissenschaftliche Reihe. Stuttgart.

MacCormick, Michael. 1986. *Eternal Victory.* Cambridge.

MacGregor, A. J. 1992. *Fire and Light in the Western Triduum: Their Use at Tenebrae and at the Paschal Vigil.* Alcuin Club Collections 71. Collegeville, Minn.

Macy, Gary. 1997. "Commentaries on the Mass During the Early Scholastic Period." In *Medieval Liturgy: A Book of Essays,* ed. Lizette Larson-Miller, 25–59. Garland Medieval Casebooks 18. Garland Reference Library of the Humanities 1884. New York and London.

Mâle, Émile. 1972. *The Gothic Image: Religious Art in France of the Thirteenth Century,* trans. Dora Nussey. New York.

Maliniemi, Aarno. 1920. "Zur Überlieferung der lateinischen Olavuslegende." *Annales Academiae Scientiarum Fennicae,* Series B: XI. Helsinki.

Manhès-Deremble, Colette. 1993. *Les Vitraux narratifs de la cathédrale de Chartres: Études iconographiques.* Corpus vitrearum. France. Études 2. Paris.

Manser, Anselm. 1930. "Aus der älteren Geschichte der Augustinusverehrung." *Benediktinische Monatsschrift* 12:289–98, 387–96.

Mansfield, Mary C. 1995. *The Humiliation of Sinners: Public Penance in Thirteenth-Century France.* Ithaca, N.Y.

Marcora, Carlo. 1954. *La vigilia nella liturgia: ricerche sulle origini e sui sviluppi (sec. I–VI).* Archivio Ambrosiano 6. Milan.

Marsden, Richard. 1995. *The Text of the Old Testament in Anglo-Saxon England.* Cambridge Studies in Anglo-Saxon England 15. Cambridge.

Martimort, Aimé-Georges. 1983. *L'Église en prière.* 4 vols. Paris.

———. 1986–88. *The Church at Prayer.* 4 vols. Collegeville. 1 vol. ed., Collegeville, Minn., 1992.

———. 1991. *Les "Ordines," les ordinaires et les cérémoniaux.* Typologie des sources du moyen âge occidental 56. Turnhout.

———. 1992. *Les Lectures liturgiques et leurs livres.* Typologie des sources du moyen âge occidental 64. Turnhout.

———. 1995. "Origine et signification du *versus* à l'office." In *Requirentes modos musicos: Mélanges offerts à Dom Jean Claire,* ed. Daniel Saulnier and Micheline Albert, 11–19. Solesmes.

Masai, François. 1947. "La Règle de saint Benoît et la Regula Magistri." *Latomus* 6:207–29.

——. 1948. "Observations sur la langue de saint Benoît et du Maître." In *Miscellanea J. Gessler*, 2:845–54. 2 vols. Antwerp.

——. 1949. "La Regula Magistri et l'historie du bréviaire." In *Miscellanea liturgica in honorem L. Cuniberti Mohlberg*, 2:423–39. Bibliotheca "Ephemerides Liturgicae" 23. 2 vols. Rome.

——. 1971. "La 'Vita patrum iurensium' et les débuts du monachisme à Saint-Maurice d'Agaune." In *Festschrift Bernhard Bischoff zu seinem 65. Gesburtstag dargebracht von Freunden, Kollegen, und Schülern*, ed. Johanne Autenrieth and Franz Brunhölzl, 43–69. Stuttgart.

Mayeski, Marie Anne. 1997. "Reading the Word in a Eucharistic Context: The Shape and Methods of Early Medieval Exegesis." In *Medieval Liturgy: A Book of Essays*, ed. Lizette Larson-Miller, 61–84. Garland Medieval Casebooks 18. Garland Reference Library of the Humanities 1884. New York and London.

McCarthy, Daniel. 1994. "The Origin of the *Latercus* Paschal Cycle of the Insular Celtic Churches." *Cambrian Medieval Celtic Studies* 28:25–49.

McDonnell, Kilian. 1981. "Prayer in Ancient Western Tradition." *Worship* 55:34–61.

McKinnon, James. 1986. "On the Question of Psalmody in the Ancient Synagogue." *Early Music History*, 6:159–91. [= 1998, VIII]

——. 1994. "Desert Monasticism and the Psalmodic Movement of the Fourth Century." *Music and Letters*, 75:505–21. [= 1998, XI]

——. 1995. "Properization: The Roman Mass." In *Cantus Planus: Papers Read at the 6th meeting, Eger, Hungary, 1993*, ed. László Dobszay, 15–22. Budapest. [= 1998, XIII]

——. 1998. *The Temple, the Church Fathers and Early Western Chant*. Variorum Collected Studies Series CS 606. Aldershot, Hants, and Brookfield, Vt.

——. Forthcoming. "Liturgical Psalmody in the Sermons of St. Augustine." In *The Study of medieval Chant: Paths and Bridges, East and West*, ed. Peter Jeffery. Woodbridge.

McLoughlin, Eleanor. 1969. "O[ld] E[nglish] *Exodus* and the *Antiphonary of Bangor*." *Neuphilologische Mitteilungen* 70:658–67.

McNamara, Martin. 1973. "Psalter Text and Psalter Study in the Early Irish Church (A.D. 600–1200)." *Proceedings of the Royal Irish Academy* 73C: 201–98.

——. 1983. "The Psalter in Early Irish Monastic Spirituality." *Monastic Studies* 14:179–205.

——. 1984. "Early Irish Exegesis: Some Facts and Tendencies." *Proceedings of the Irish Biblical Association* 8:57–96.

——. 1993. "Hiberno-Latin Bulletin." *Proceedings of the Irish Biblical Association* 16: 114–24.

McNeill, John T. 1974. "Perspectives on Celtic Church History." In *Contemporary Reflections on the Medieval Christian Tradition: Essays in Honor of Ray C. Petry*, ed. George H. Shriver, 159–82. Durham, N.C.

Mearns, James. 1914. *The Canticles of the Christian Church, Eastern and Western, in Early and Medieval Times*. Cambridge.

Merkley, Paul. 1988. *Italian Tonaries*. Musicological Studies 48. Ottawa.

——. 1990. "The Form and Type of Ambrosian Antiphons." Paper presented at the annual meeting of the American Musicological Society, Oakland.

——. 1992. *Modal Assignment in Northern Tonaries*. Musicological Studies 56. Ottawa.

Messenger, Ruth E. 1949. "Medieval Processional Hymns before 1100." *Transactions and Proceedings of the American Philological Association* 80:375–92.

Metzger, Marcel. 1994. *Les Sacramentaires*. Typologie des sources du moyen âge occidental, 70. Turnhout, 1994.

Meulen, Jan van der, with Rudiger Hoyer and Deborah Cole. 1989. *Chartres: Sources and Literary Interpretation*. Boston.

Meyer, Wilhelm. 1903. "Das Turiner Bruchstück der ältesten irischen Liturgie." *Nachrichten von der Königl. Gesellschaft der Wissenschaften Göttingen,* Philosophisch-historische Klasse, 163–214.

Meyvaert, Paul. 1963. "Toward a History of the Textual Transmission of the Regula S. Benedicti." *Scriptorium* 17:83–106.

Miskuly, Jason M., O.F.M. 1989. "Julian of Speyer: Life of St. Francis (Vita Sancti Francisci)." *Franciscan Studies* 49:93–174.

[Mitchell, Nathan]. 1981. "The Liturgical Code in the Rule of Benedict." In *RB 1980,* 379–414.

Möller, Hartmut. 1987. "Research on the Antiphoner—Problems and Perspectives." *Journal of the Plainsong and Mediaeval Music Society* 10:1–14.

———. 1991. "Zur Musik der Historia S. Galli." In Berschin, Ochsenbein, and Möller (1991), 28–37.

———. 1996. Introduction to Joseph Metzinger et al. *The Zwiefalten Antiphoner: Karlsruhe, Badische Landesbibliothek, Aug. perg. LX.: Printouts from an Index in Machine-readable Form: A CANTUS Index.* Musicological Studies 55/5. Ottawa.

———. 1999. *see* Berschin, Ochsenbein, and Möller (1999).

Moolan, John. 1985. *The Period of Annunciation–Nativity in the East Syrian Calendar: Its Background and Place in the Liturgical Year.* Kottayam.

Moreton, Bernard. 1976. *The Eighth-Century Gelasian Sacramentary.* Oxford.

Morin, Germain. 1890. "Les Témoins de la tradition grégorienne." *RB* 7:289–323. Also published as part of id., *Les Véritables Origines du chant grégorien.* Abbaye de Maredsous; 3d ed., 1912.

———. 1891. "La Liturgie de Naples au temps de Saint Grégoire." *RB* 8:481–93.

———. 1893. "Les Notes liturgiques de l'Evangélaire de Burchard." *RB* 10:113–26.

———. 1903. "Un système inédit de lectures liturgiques en usage au viie/viiie siècle dans une église inconnue de la haute Italie." *RB* 20:375–88.

———. 1905. "Fragments inédits et jusqu'à présent uniques d'antiphonaire gallican." *RB* 22:329–56.

———. 1908. "Le Lectionnaire mérovingien de Schlettstadt." *RB* 25:161–66.

———. 1911. "Liturgie et basiliques de Rome au milieu du viie siècle d'après les listes d'Évangiles de Würzburg." *RB* 28:296–330.

———. 1913. *Études, textes, découvertes: Contributions à la littérature et à l'histoire des douze premiers siècles.* Anecdota Maredsolana, 2d ser. 1. Maredsous and Paris.

Morrish, Jennifer. 1988. "Dated and Datable Manuscripts Copied in England during the Ninth Century: A Preliminary List." *Medieval Studies* 50:512–38.

Mottirani, Sergio. 1966. "Guglielmo il Grande, o di Malavalle santo." *Bibliotheca sanctorum* 7: cols. 471–73.

Moyse, Gérard. 1982. "Monachisme et réglementation monastique en Gaule avant Benoît d'Aniane." In *Sous la règle de Saint Benoît: Structures monastiques et sociétés en France du moyen âge à l'époque moderne. Abbaye bénédictine Sainte-Marie de Paris, 23–25 Octobre 1980,* 3–19. École Pratique des Hautes Études IVe Sections, Sciences historiques et philologiques V: Hautes Études médiévales et modernes 47. Geneva and Paris.

Munding, Emmanuel. 1951. *Die Kalendarien von St. Gallen: Aus XXI Handschriften; neuntes bis elftes Jahrhundert.* Beuron.

Mundó, Anscari. 1957. "L'Authenticité de la Regula Sancti Benedicti." In *Commentationes in Regulam S. Benedicti,* 105–58. Studia Anselmiana 42.

Münxelhaus, Barbara. 1982. "Der Beitrag Irlands zur Musik des frühen Mittelalters." In Löwe 1982, 630–38.

Mütherich, Florentine, and Joachim Gaehde. 1976. *Carolingian Painting.* New York.

Newton, Robert R. 1972. *Medieval Chronicles and the Rotation of the Earth.* Baltimore.

Ní Chatháin, Próinséas. 1976. "Some Early Irish Hymn Material." In *Famulus Christi: Essays in Commemoration of the Thirteenth Centenary of the Birth of the Venerable Bede*, ed. Gerald Bonner, 229–38. London.

—— and Michael Richter, eds. 1996. *Irland und Europa im früheren Mittelalter: Bildung und Literatur / Ireland and Europe in the Early Middle Ages: Learning and Literature*. Stuttgart.

Norberg, Dag. 1958. *Introduction à l'étude de la versification latine médiévale*. Acta Universitatis Stockholmiensis, Studia Latina Stockholmiensia 5. Stockholm.

——. 1988. *Les Vers latins iambiques et trochaiques au moyen âge et leurs répliques rythmiques*. Filologiskt arkiv 35. Stockholm.

Nowacki, Edward. 1995. "Antiphon." *MGG* (2d ed.), 1:636–60.

Nowak, Petrus. 1984. "Die Strukturelemente des Stundengebets der Regula Benedicti." *ALw* 26:253–304.

Oakley, Francis. 1979. *The Western Church in the Later Middle Ages*. Ithaca, N.Y.

O'Briain, Felim. 1946. "The Blessed Eucharist in Irish Liturgy and History." In *Studia Eucharistica DCC Anni a Condito Festo Sanctissimi Corporis Christi 1246–1946*, ed. Stephanus Axters, 216–45. Antwerp.

Odelman, Eva. 1975. "Comment a-t-on appelé les tropes? Observations sur les rubriques des tropes des xe et xe siècles." *Cahiers de civilisation médiévale* 18, 15–36.

O'Dwyer, Peter. 1981. *Céli Dé: Spiritual Reform in Ireland, 750–900*. Dublin.

Ó Maidín, Uinseann. 1996. *The Celtic Monk: Rules and Writings of Early Irish Monks*. Cistercian Studies 162. Kalamazoo.

Omlin, Ephrem. 1934. *Die Sankt-Gallischen Tonarbuchstaben*. Freiburg (Switzerland).

O'Neill, Timothy. 1984. *The Irish Hand: Scribes and their Manuscripts from the Earliest Times to the Seventeenth Century*. Portlaoise.

Orsy, Ladislas. 1978. *The Evolving Church and the Sacrament of Penance*. Denville, N.J.

Østrem, Eyolf. 1998. "The Early Liturgy of St Olav." In *Gregorian Chant and Medieval Music*. Papers read at the Gregorian Festival in Trondheim (July 1997), ed. A. Dybdahl, O. K. Ledang, and N. H. Petersen, 43–58. Trondheim.

Oury, Guy, and Jean de Viguerie. 1983. *Histoire religieuse de l'Orléanais*. Chambray-les-Tours.

Palazzo, Éric. 1990. "Le Role des *libelli* dans la pratique liturgique de haut moyen âge: histoire et typologie." *Revue Mabillon* n. s. 1 (= 62), 9–36.

Paredi, Angelo. 1937. *I prefazi ambrosiani*. Milan.

Pascher, Joseph. 1954. *Das Stundengebet der römischen Kirche*. Munich.

——. 1957a. "Das Psalterium der Apostelmatutin." *Münchener theologische Zeitschrift* 8:1–12.

——. 1957b. "Der Psalter für Laudes und Vesper im alten römischen Stundengebet." *Münchener Theologische Zeitschrift* 8:255–67.

——. 1958. "Das Psalterium des römischen Breviers, ein Forschungsbericht." In Jungmann 1958, 9–20.

——. 1965a. "Zur Frühgeschichte des römischen Wochenpsalteriums." *EL* 79:55–58.

——. 1965b. "De psalmodia vesperarum." *EL* 79:317–26.

——. 1971. "Die Psalmen als Grundlage des Stundengebets." *EL* 85:260–80.

Payr, Theresia. 1959. "Der Magistertext in der Überlieferungsgeschichte der Benediktinerregel." In *Regula Magistri—Regula S. Benedicti: Studia Monastica*, 1–84. Studia Anselmiana 44.

Payrard, Jean-Baptiste. 1885. "Le Prosolaire de Notre-Dame du Puy." In *Nouvelle série de mélanges historiques publiées dans l'Echo du Velay*, 1:147–55. Le Puy.

Pedersen, Olaf. 1983. "The Ecclesiastical Calendar and the Life of the Church." In *Gregorian Reform of the Calendar: Proceedings of the Vatican Conference to Commemorate its 400th Anniversary, 1582–1982*, ed. G. V. Coyne et al., 17–74, 299–321. Vatican City.

Pelikan, Jaroslav. 1996. *Mary through the Centuries: Her Place in the History of Culture.* New Haven.

Perdrizet, Paul. 1933. *Le Calendrier parisien à la fin du moyen âge d'après le bréviaire et les livres d'heures.* Paris.

Pfaff, R. W. 1970. *New Liturgical Feasts in Later Medieval England.* Oxford.

Piétresson de Saint-Aubin, Pierre, ed. 1968. *Archives départementales du Nord. Répertoire numérique. Série G (Clergé séculier),* 2: *3 G à 5 G Fascicule I.* Lille.

Pietschmann, Petrus. 1932. "Die nicht dem Psalter entnommenen Meßgesangstücke auf ihre Textgestalt untersucht." *Jahrbuch für Liturgiewissenschaft* 12:87–144.

Pinell, Jorge. 1990. *Liturgia delle ore.* Anamnesis 5. Genoa.

Planchart, Alejandro Enrique. 1972. "Guillaume Du Fay's Masses: Notes and Revisions." *MQ* 58:1–23.

———. 1981. "The Transmission of Medieval Chant." In *Music in Medieval and Early Modern Europe: Patronage, Sources and Texts,* ed. Iain Fenlon, 347–63. Cambridge.

———. 1988. "Guillaume Du Fay's Benefices and his Relationship to the Court of Burgundy." *Early Music History* 8:117–71.

———. 1993. "The Early Career of Guillaume Du Fay." *JAMS* 46:341–68.

———. 1995. "Notes on Guillaume Du Fay's Last Works." *JM* 13:55–72.

Plocek, Václav. 1985. *Zwei Studien zur ältesten geistlichen Musik in Böhmen,* unter Mitarbeit von Andreas Traub. Beisteine zur Geschichte der Literatur bei den Slaven 27. 2 vols. Giessen.

Powell, Michael. 1988. "Spacial Considerations in Liturgy: The Palm Sunday Procession at Chartres." M. A. thesis, Yale University.

Prache, Anne. 1993. *Chartres Cathedral: Image of the Heavenly Jerusalem.* Paris.

Pratesi, A. 1951–52. "Rogus=Rogatus." *Archivium latinitatis medii aevi* 22:33–62.

Prinz, Friedrich. 1965. *Frühes Mönchtum im Frankenreich: Kultur und Gesellschaft in Gallien, den Rheinlanden und Bayern am Beispiel der monastischen Entwicklung (4. bis 8. Jahrhundert).* Munich.

Prizer, William. 1985. "Music and Ceremonial in the Low Countries: Philip the Fair and the Order of the Golden Fleece." *Early Music History* 5:113–53.

Quecke, Hans. 1970. *Untersuchungen zum koptischen Stundengebet.* Publications de l'Institut Orientaliste de Louvain 3. Louvain.

Raffa, Vincenzo. 1971. "L'Ufficio divino del tempo dei Carolingi e il breviario di Innocenzo III confrontati con la liturgia delle ore di Paolo VI." *EL* 85:206–59.

Randall, Lillian M. C. 1989. *Medieval and Renaissance Manuscripts in the Walters Art Gallery,* 1: *France, 875–1420.* Baltimore and London.

Rankin, Susan. 1991. "The Earliest Sources of Notker's Sequences: St Gallen, Vadiana 317, and Paris, Bibliothèque nationale lat. 10587." *Early Music History* 10 (1991): 201–33.

———. 1993. "From Tuotilo to the First Manuscripts: The Shaping of a Trope Repertory at Saint Gall." In *Recherches nouvelles sur les tropes liturgiques,* ed. Wulf Arlt and Gunilla Björkvall, 395–413. Corpus troporum 8. Acta Universitatis Stockholmiensia. Studia Latina Stockholmiensia 36. Stockholm.

Reckow, Fritz. 1973. "Conductus." In *Handwörterbuch der musikalischen Terminologie,* ed. Hans Heinrich Eggebrecht. Wiesbaden.

Reynolds, Roger. 1984. "Divine Office." *DMA* 4:221–31.

———. 1986. "Liturgy, Treatises on." *DMA* 7:624–33.

Rivet, Bernard. 1988. *Une ville au XVIe siècle: Le Puy en Velay.* Le Puy-en-Velay.

Robertson, Anne Walters. 1988. "Benedicamus Domino: The Unwritten Tradition." *JAMS* 41:1–62.

———. 1990. "The Transmission of Music and Liturgy from Saint-Denis to Saint-Corneille of Compiègne." In *Trasmissione e recezione delle forme di cultura musicale,*

Atti del XIV Congresso della Società Internazionale di Musicologia, Bologna, 27 agusto-1° settembre 1987, 3:505–14. Bologna.

——. 1991a. *The Service-Books of the Royal Abbey of Saint-Denis: Images of Ritual and Music in the Middle Ages.* Oxford Monographs on Music. Oxford.

——. 1991b. "The Mass of Guillaume de Machaut in the Cathedral of Reims." In *Plainsong in the Age of Polyphony,* ed. Thomas Forrest Kelly, 100–39. Cambridge Studies in Performance Practice 2. Cambridge.

——. 1995. "Remembering the Annunciation in Medieval Music." *Speculum* 70:275–304.

Roper, Sally Elizabeth. 1993. *Medieval English Benedictine Liturgy: Studies in the Formation, Structure, and Content of the Monastic Votive Office, c. 950–1540.* New York and London.

Rordorf, Willy. 1981. "Origine et signification de la célébration du Dimanche dans le christianisme primitif: État actuel de la recherche." *La Maison-Dieu* 148:103–22. Repr. in Willy Rordorf, *Liturgie, foi et vie des premiers chrétiens: Études patristiques.* Théologie historique 75. Paris.

Rothe, Hans, ed. 1988. *Geistliche Lieder und Gesänge in Böhmen II, 1: Tropen und Cantiones aus böhmischen Handschriften der vorhussitischen Zeit 1300–1420,* ed. Brigitte Böse und Franz Schäfer. Cologne.

Rumar, Lars, ed. 1997. *Helgonet i Nidaros: Olavskult och kristnande i Norden.* Skrifter utgivna av Svenska Riksarkivet 3. Stockholm.

Rushe, Patrick de Saint-Joseph. 1912–13. "Antiquum Ordinis Carmelitarum Ordinale, Saec. XIII." *Études Carmelitaines* 2:5–251.

Ryan, John. 1972. *Irish Monasticism: Origins and Early Development.* Ithaca, N.Y.

Sainte-Beuve, R. de. 1928. "Les Répons de Saint Fulbert de Chartres pour la nativité de la sainte Vierge." *RG* 13:121–28; 168–74.

Salmon, Pierre. 1959. *L'Office divin: Histoire de la formation du bréviaire.* Lex Orandi 27. Paris.

——. 1962. *The Breviary through the Centuries,* trans. Sister David Mary. Collegeville, Minn.

——. 1965. "La Prière des heures." In *L'Église en prière,* ed. Aimé-Georges Martimort, 809–902. 3d ed. Paris.

——. 1967. *L'Office divin au moyen âge: Histoire de la formation du bréviaire du IXe au XVIe siècle.* Lex Orandi 43. Paris.

Saxer, Victor. 1959. *Le Culte de Marie Madeleine en occident des origines à la fin du moyen âge.* 2 vols. Cahiers d'Archéologie et d'Histoire 3. Auxerre and Paris.

Schmid, Hans. 1971. "Diastematica vocis armonia." In *Festschrift Bernhard Bischoff zu seinem 65. Geburtstag,* ed. Johanne Autenrieth and Franz Brunhölzl, 391–97. Stuttgart.

Schmidt, Christopher. 1980. "Modus und Melodiegestalt: Untersuchungen zu Offiziumsantiphonen." *Forum musicologicum* 2:13–34.

Schmidt, Hermann. 1960. *Introductio in liturgiam occidentalem.* Rome.

Schneider, Heinrich. 1949. "Die biblischen Oden im christlichen Altertum," "Die biblischen Oden seit dem sechsten Jahrhundert," "Die biblischen Oden in Jerusalem und Konstantinopel," and "Die biblischen Oden im Mittelalter." *Biblica* 30:28–65, 239–72, 433–52, 479–500.

——. 1960. "Die Psalterteilung in Fünfziger- und Zehnergruppen." In *Universitas, Dienst an Wahrheit und Leben: Festschrift für Bischof Dr. Albert Stohr,* 1:36–47. Mainz.

Schneiders, Marc. 1996. "The Origins of the Early Irish Liturgy." In Ní Chatháin and Richter, eds. (1996), 76–98.

Schumann, Otto. 1943–50. "Die jüngere Cambridger Liedersammlung." *Studi medievali* n. s. 16:48–85.

Schwab, Ute. 1992. "Das altdeutsche Lied 'Hirsch und Hinde' in seiner lateinischen Umgebung." In *Latein und Volkssprache im deutschen Mittelalter 1100–1500: Regensburger Colloquium 1988*, ed. Nikolaus Henkel and Nigel F. Palmer, 74–119. Tübingen.

Schwartz, Eduard. 1905. *Christliche und jüdische Ostertafeln.* Abhandlungen der königlichen Gesellschaft der Wissenschaften zu Göttingen, Phil.-Hist. Klasse, Neue Folge 6/6. Berlin.

Simonin, S. 1975. "Caesaris di Arles, santo." *DIP* 2:844–48.

Smet, Joachim, O.Carm. 1954. *The Life of Saint Peter Thomas by Philippe de Mézières.* Rome.

Sohn, Andreas. 1989. *Der Abbatiat Ademars von Saint-Martial de Limoges (1063–1114): Ein Beitrag zur Geschichte des cluniacensischen Klösterverbandes.* Beiträge zur Geschichte des alten Mönchtums und des Benediktinertums 37. Münster.

Souchet, J. B. 1868. *Histoire du diocèse et de la ville de Chartres.* 4 vols. Chartres.

Spanke, Hans. 1931. "St. Martial Studien: Ein Beitrag zur frühromanischen Metrik." *Zeitschrift für französische Sprache und Literatur* 54:282–317, 385–422; 56: 450–68.

Stäblein, Bruno. 1973. "Zwei Melodien der altirischen Liturgie." In Hüschen, ed. (1973), 590–97.

Steiner, Ruth. 1963. "Some Monophonic Latin Songs from the Tenth Fascicle of the Manuscript Florence, Biblioteca Laurenziana, Pluteus 29.1." Ph.D. diss., Catholic University of America.

——. 1966. "Some Monophonic Latin Songs Composed around 1200." *MQ* 52:56–70.

——. 1980b. "Compline." *NG* 4:598–99.

——. 1980c. "Magnificat (1)." *NG* 11:495.

——. 1980d. "Vespers." *NG* 19:685–86.

——. 1984. "The Music for a Cluny Office of St. Benedict." In *Monasticism and the Arts,* ed. Timothy Gregory Verdon with the assistance of John Dally, 81–113. Syracuse.

——. 1986. "Matins Responsories and Cycles of Illustrations of Saints' Lives." In *Diakonia: Studies in Honor of Robert T. Meyer,* ed. Thomas Halton and Joseph P. Williman, 317–32. Washington, D.C.

——. 1987. "Reconstructing the Repertory of Invitatory Tones and their Uses at Cluny in the Late 11th Century." In *Musicologie médiévale: Notations et séquences. Actes de la table ronde du CNRS à l'IRHT, Orléans-La Source, 6–7 septembre 1982,* ed. Michel Huglo, 175–82. Paris.

——. 1993. "Marian Antiphons at Cluny and Lewes." In *Music in the Medieval English Liturgy: Plainsong and Mediaeval Music Society Centennial Esays,* ed. Susan Rankin and David Hiley, 175–204. Oxford.

Stevens, John. 1982. Entry for Cambridge, University Library Ff.1.17, in *Cambridge Music Manuscripts, 900–1700,* ed. Iain Fenlon, 40–44. Cambridge.

——. 1986. *Words and Music in the Middle Ages.* Cambridge.

Stevenson, Jane [Barbara]. 1996. "Hiberno-Latin Hymns: Learning and Literature." In Ní Chatháin and Richter, eds. (1996), 99–135.

——. 1997. "The Monastic Rules of Columbanus." In Lapidge, ed. (1997), 203–16.

Stokes, Whitley. 1891. "Adamnan's Second Vision." *Revue celtique* 12:420–43.

Storm, Gustav. 1885. *Om en Olavs-legend fra Ribe.* Christiania Vidensk.-Selsk. Forhandlinger 3 [18 pp.]. Christiania [Oslo].

Strachan, J. 1904–5. "An Old-Irish Metrical Rule." *Ériu* 1 (1904): 191–208; 2 (1905): 58–59.

——. 1905. "Cormac's Rule." *Ériu* 2:60–68.

Strobel, August. 1977. *Ursprung und Geschichte des frühchristlichen Osterkalenders.* Texte und Untersuchungen zur Geschichte der altchristlichen Literatur 121. Berlin.

Strohm, Reinhard. 1993. *The Rise of European Music, 1380–1500.* Cambridge.

Strunk, Oliver. 1977. "The Byzantine Office at Hagia Sophia." In *Essays on Music in the Byzantine World,* 112–50. New York.

Taft, Robert. 1986. *The Liturgy of the Hours in East and West: The Origins of the Divine Office and its Meaning for Today.* Collegeville, Minn.

———. 1988. "Penance in Contemporary Scholarship." *Studia liturgica* 18:2–21.

———. 1993. *The Liturgy of the Hours in East and West: The Origins of the Divine Office and its Meaning for Today.* 2d rev. ed. Collegeville, Minn.

Talley, Thomas. 1991. *The Origins of the Liturgical Year.* 2d ed. Collegeville, Minn.

Tanner, Marie. 1993. *The Last Descendents of Aeneas: The Hapsburgs and the Mythic Image of the Emperor.* New Haven.

Tarruel. *See* Gibert Tarruel.

Taunton, Ethelred A. 1903. *The Little Office of Our Lady: A Treatise Theoretical, Practical, and Exegetical.* New York.

Teviotdale, Elizabeth. 1991. "The Cotton Troper (London, British Library, Cotton MS Caligula A.xiv, ff. 1–26: A Study of an Illustrated English Troper of the Eleventh Century." Ph.D. diss., University of North Carolina at Chapel Hill.

Thérel, Marie-Louise. 1984. *Le Triomphe de la Vierge-Église: Sources historiques, littéraires et iconographiques.* Paris.

Thompson, E. A. 1984. *Saint Germanus of Auxerre and the End of Roman Britain.* Studies in Celtic History 6. Woodbridge.

Thurian, Max. 1985. *Mary: Mother of the Lord, Figure of the Church,* trans. Neville B. Cryer. London and Oxford; repr. of the 1963 edition.

Tobiassen, Tormod. 1956–78. "Rex iustus." *Kulturhistorisk leksikon for nordisk middelalder fra vikingetid til reformationstid* 14. 22 vols. Copenhagen.

Török, József. 1977. *A magyar pálosrend liturgiájának forrásai, kialakulása és főbb sajátosságai 1225–1600.* [The Sources, Development and Peculiarities of the Liturgy of the Paulite Order in Hungary, from 1225 to 1600.] Budapest.

Tov, Emmanuel. 1992. *Textual Criticism of the Hebrew Bible.* Minneapolis and Assen/Maastricht.

Treitler, Leo. 1967. "The Aquitanian Repertories of Sacred Monody in the Eleventh and Twelfth Centuries." Ph.D. diss., Princeton Unversity.

———. 1981. "Transmission and the Study of Music History." In *International Musicological Society: Report of the Twelfth Congress Berkeley 1977,* ed. Daniel Heartz and Bonnie Wade, 202–11. Kassel.

———. 1992. "Medieval Lyric." In *Models of Musical Analysis: Music before 1600,* ed. Mark Everist, 1–19. Oxford.

Tyrer, John Walton. 1932. *Historical Survey of Holy Week: Its Services and Ceremonial.* Alcuin Club Collections 29. Oxford.

Udovich, Jo Ann. 1980. "The Magnificat Antiphons for the Ferial Office." *Journal of the Plainsong and Mediaeval Music Society* 3:1–25.

Vaassen, Elgin Van Treeck. 1973. "Die Werkstatt den Mainzer Riesenbibel in Würzburg." *Archiv für Geschichte des Buchwesens* 13: cols. 1121–1428.

Vallery-Radot, Jean. 1958. *La Cathédral de Bayeux.* 2d ed. Petites monographies des grands édifices de la France. Paris.

Vandenbroucke, François. 1952. "Sur les sources de la Règle bénédictine et de la Regula Magistri." *RB* 62:216–73.

Vanderhoven, H. 1946–47. "Les Plus Anciens Manuscrits de la Règle du Maître transmettent un texte déjà interpolé." *Scriptorium* 1:193–212.

Van Dijk, Stephen Joseph Peter. 1952. *Latin Liturgical Manuscripts and Printed Books: Guide to an Exhibition held during 1952.* Oxford.

———. 1957. *Handlist of the Latin Liturgical Manuscripts in the Bodleian Library Oxford.* (Typescript)

Vandvik, Eirik. 1959. *Latinske dokument til norsk historie fram til ar 1204.* Oslo.

Veilleux, Armand. 1968. *La Liturgie dans le cénobitisme Pachômien au quatrième siècle.* Studia Anselmiana 57. Rome.

Vellekoop, Kees. 1978. *Dies ire dies illa: Studien zur Frühgeschichte einer Sequenz.* Bilthoven.

Verbraken, Pierre-Patrick. 1988. "Vingt-cinq notices liturgiques tirées des *Retractions* inédits de Dom Germain Morin." In *Traditio et Progressio: Studi liturgici in onore del Prof. Adrien Nocent, OSB,* ed. Giustine Farnedi, 597–619. Studia Anselmiana 95. Analecta Liturgica 12. Rome.

Villetard, Henri. 1907. *Office de Pierre de Corbeil (Office de la Circoncision) improprement appelé "Office des Fous".* Bibliothèque musicologique 4. Paris.

Villette, Guy. 1975. "Saint-Cheron-des-Champs." *Recherches concernant les noms de Lieux d'Eure-et-Loir.* Unpublished typescript (in Chartres, BM, C2369).

Vodola, Elisabeth. 1986. *Excommunication in the Middle Ages.* Berkeley.

Vogel, Cyrille. 1958. "L'Hymnaire de Murbach contenu dans le manuscrit *Junius* 25 (Oxford, Bodleian 51137): Un témoin du *cursus* bénédictine ou *cursus* occidentale." *Archives de l'Église d'Alsace* 9:1–42.

——. 1979. "Les Motifs de la romanisation du culte sous Pépin le Bref (751–768) et Charlemagne (774–814)." In *Culto cristiano politica imperiale carolingia: 9–12 ottobre 1977,* 13–41. Università degli Studi di Perugia: Convegni del Centro di Studi sulla Spiritualità Medievale 18. Todi.

——. 1986. *Medieval Liturgy: An Introduction to the Sources,* trans. and rev. William Storey and Niels Rasmussen. NPM Studies in Church Music and Liturgy. Washington, D.C.

Vogt, Hermann J. 1982. "Zur Spiritualität des frühen irischen Mönchtums." In Löwe 1982, 26–51.

Vogüé, Adalbert de. 1960. "Lacunes et erreurs dans la section liturgique de la 'Regula Magistri'." *RB* 70:410–13.

——. 1961a. *La Communauté et l'abbé dans la Règle de saint Benoît.* Paris.

——. 1961b. "Le sens d''antifana' et la longueur de l'office dans la 'Regula Magistri'." *RB* 71:119–23.

——. 1965a. "Nouveaux aperçus sur une règle monastique du vie siècle." *Revue d'ascétique et de mystique* 41:19–54.

——. 1965b. "La Règle du Maître et la lettre apocryphe de saint Jérôme sur le chant de psaumes." *Studia monastica* 7:357–67.

——. 1966. "La Règle du Maître et les Dialogues de S. Grégoire." *Revue d'histoire ecclésiastique* 61:44–76.

——. 1967a. "La Règle du Maître en Italie du sud." *RB* 77:155–56.

——. 1967b. "Le Sens de l'office divin d'après la Règle de S. Benoît. II. Psalmodie et oraison." *Revue d'ascétique et de mystique* 43:21–34.

——. 1967c. "Origine et structure de l'office Bénédictine." *Collectanea Cisterciensia* 29:195–99.

——. 1967d. "Un emprunt de la Règle du Maître à la prière de Manassé." *Revue d'ascétique et de mystique* 43:200–3.

——. 1968. "Scholies sur la Règle du Maître." *Revue d'ascétique et de mystique* 44:121–59, 261–92.

——. 1972. "Saint Benoît en son temps: Règles italiennes et règles provençales au vie siècle." *Regulae Benedicti studia* 1:169–93.

——. 1977. "The Cenobitic Rules of the West." *Cistercian Studies* 12:175–83.

——. 1983. "Regula(e) Aureliani." *DIP* 7:1604–7.

——. 1985a. "La 'Regula Cassiani': Sa destination et ses rapports avec le monachisme fructuosien." *RB* 95:185–231.

———. 1985b. *Les Règles monastiques anciennes (400–700)*. Typologie des sources du moyen âge occidental 46. Turnhout.

———. 1988. "Les Offices nocturnes de Saint Colomban et des 'Catholiques.'" In *Traditio et progressio: Studi liturgici in onore del Prof. Adrien Nocent, OSB*, ed. Giustine Farnedi, 621–41. Studia Anselmiana 95. Analecta Liturgica 12. Rome.

———. 1989. "Psalmodier n'est pas prier." *Ecclesia orans* 6:7–32.

———. 1992. "The Master and St Benedict: A Reply to Marilyn Dunn." *English Historical Review* 418:95–103.

———. 1995. "Le Psaume et l'oraison: Nouveau florilège." *Ecclesia orans* 12: 325–49.

Vorgrimler, Herbert. 1978. *Busse und Krankensalbung*. Handbuch der Dogmengeschichte 4/3. Freiburg.

Waddell, Chrysogonus. 1973. "La carta 10 de Petro Abelardo y la reforma liturgica cisterciense." *Cistercium* 25:56–66.

Wagner, Peter. 1911. *Einführung in die gregorianischen Melodien: Ein Handbuch der Choralwissenschaft, 1: Ursprung und Entwicklung der liturgischen Gesangformen bis zum Ausgange des Mittelalters*. 3d edn. Leipzig.

———. 1921. *Einführung in die gregorianischen Melodien: Ein Handbuch der Choralwissenschaft, 3: Gregorianische Formenlehre: Eine choralische Stilkunde*. Leipzig.

———. 1931. *Die Gesänge der Jakobsliturgie zu Santiago de Compostela aus dem sog. Codex Calixtinus*. Freiburg.

———. 1986. *Introduction to the Gregorian Melodies, A Handbook of Plainsong*. 2d ed. Part 1: *Origin and Development of the Forms of the Liturgical Chant up to the End of the Middle Ages*, trans. Agnes Orme and E. G. P. Wyatt. New York.

Walters [Robertson], Anne. 1985. "The Reconstruction of the Abbey Church at St-Denis (1231–81): The Interplay of Music and Ceremony with Architecture and Politics." *Early Music History* 5:187–238.

Ware, R. Dean. 1992. "Medieval Chronology: Theory and Practice." In *Medieval Studies: An Introduction*, 2d ed., ed. James M. Powell, 252–77. Syracuse.

Warren, F. E. 1881. *The Liturgy and Ritual of the Celtic Church*. Oxford.

———. 1987. Reprint of Warren 1881, with a new introduction and bibliography by Jane Stevenson. Studies in Celtic History 9. Woodbridge and Wolfeboro, N.H.

Wathen, Ambrose. 1986. "The Rites of Holy Week according to the *Regula Magistri*." *Ecclesia orans* 3:289–305.

Weakland, Rembert. 1959. "The Compositions of Hucbald." *EG* 3:155–62.

Weber, Gerd W. 1988. "Intelligere historiam: Typological Perspectives of Nordic Prehistory." In *Snorri, Saxo, Widukin and Others: Tradition og Historieskrivning*. Acta Jutlandica 63.

Weber, Robert. 1947. "La Psalmodie de prime dans la Règle bénédictine." *EL* 61:335–40.

Wegman, Rob C. 1995. "*Miserere supplicanti Dufay*: The Creation and Transmission of Guillaume Dufay's *Missa Ave regina celorum*." *JM* 13:18–54.

Whakey, Diana. 1991. *Heimskringla: An Introduction*. Viking Society Text Series 8. London.

Wieck, Roger S. 1988. *Time Sanctified: The Book of Hours in Medieval Art and Life*. New York.

Wilesme, Jean Pierre. 1977. "Les Origines de l'abbaye de Saint-Victor de Paris." *Bulletin philologique et historique* 58:101–14.

Willis, Geoffrey Grimshaw. 1994. *A History of Early Roman Liturgy to the Death of Pope Gregory the Great*. HBS, Subsidia 1. London.

Winkler, Gabriele. 1970. "Das Offizium am Ende des 4. Jahrhunderts und das heutige chaldäische Offizium: Ihre strukturellen Zusammenhänge." *Ostkirchliche Studien* 19:289–311.

———. 1974. "Über die Kathedralvesper in den verschiedenen Riten des Ostens und Westens." *ALw* 16:53–102.

———. 1982a. "New Study of Early Development of the Divine Office." *Worship* 56:27–35.

———. 1982b. "Response to Paul F. Bradshaw." *Worship* 56:266–67.

———. 1987a. Review of Moolan (1985) in *Orientalia Christiana periodica* 53:234–36.

———. 1987b. "Ungelöste Fragen im Zusammenhang mit den liturgischen Gebräuchen in Jerusalem." *Handes Amsorya* 101:303–15.

———. 1988–89. "Nochmals das armenische Nachtoffizium und weitere Anmerkungen zum Myrophorenoffizium." *Revue des études arméniennes* 21:501–19.

Wright, Craig. 1975. "Dufay at Cambrai: Discoveries and Revisions." *JAMS* 28:175–229.

———. 1978. "Performance Practices at the Cathedral of Cambrai 1475–1550." *MQ* 64:295–328.

———. 1979. *Music at the Court of Burgundy 1364–1419: A Documentary History.* Musicological Studies 28. Brooklyn.

———. 1989. *Music and Ceremony at Notre Dame of Paris, 500–1500.* Cambridge Studies in Music. New York and Cambridge.

Würthwein, Ernst. 1995. *The Text of the Old Testament: An Introduction to the Biblia Hebraica.* 2d ed., trans. Erroll F. Rhodes. Grand Rapids, Michigan.

Zerfass, Rolf. 1968. *Die Schriftlesung im Kathedraloffizium Jerusalems.* Liturgiegeschichtliche Quellen und Forschungen 48. Münster.

Zufferey, Maurice. 1988. *Die Abtei Saint-Maurice d'Agaune im Hochmittelalter (830–1258).* Veröffentlichungen des Max-Planck-Instituts für Geschichte 88. Göttingen.

Index of Manuscripts

Index of Incipits

See also lists of incipits not mentioned in the text on pages 51–54, 56, 114–15, 154–55, 181, 184, 197–201, 209–212, 239–41, 306–09, 319–20, 358–64, 384, 425, 427, 436, 446–48, 468–69, 474–81, 488.

Index of Saints

General Index

Aaron's rod, 34
Abelard, Peter, 206
acolytes (*pueri*), 326
Acta Andreae, 157–66, 175 n 25, 176 n 41
Acta sancti Olavi, 404
Ad matutinam [*horam*], 119–20
Ad nocturnam [*horam*], 118–19
Adam and Christ, 336
Adam of Bremen, 404
Adamnan, *Second Vision,* 105–107
adaptations, musical, 485–518
Adomnán, *De locis sanctis,* 127
Adoration of the Cross, 348
Advent, 189
    liturgy, 464
    Office, 15–47, 49–56
    processions, 209
    responsories, 197–201
agape, 64
Agimundus (scribe), homiliary of (Vatican, BAV lat. 3835–36), 33–34, 35
Agobardus of Lyons, 147
Alan of Farfa, homiliary of, 33, 34
Alcuin
    hymn for St. Vedast, 283–84
    Lectionary of, 44 n 44
Alfonzo, Pio, 187–88
allegory, 36
alleluia, 314
    liturgical use, 5, 86, 96 n 55
    suspension of, 11 n 6, 89, 131, 141 n 88
Amalarius of Metz, 142 n 89, 147, 175 n 16, 182, 243

De ecclesiasticis officiis, 36–39, 47 nn 75, 77, 345, 365 n 12
    Prologus and *Liber de ordine antiphonarii,* 36, 174 n 9 186, 190, 191–92
    Liber officialis, 301, 302
Ambrose, St.
    commentary on Luke, 34
    De sacramentis, 71
Ambrosian chant, 257–77
Ambrosian hymns, 118, 263
Ambrosian rites, 113, 122, 129, 257–77, 303, 312, 368 n 32
Ambrosian *sanctorale,* 257–77
ambrosiana (hymns), 71, 118
Amiens
    cathedral, 300–23, 345
    processions, 361–62
Amiet, Robert, 325
Angers (church) 314
Angilbert, Abbot of Saint-Riquier, 365 n 11
Annunciation theme, 321 n 7
Antioch, 66, 68
antiphona (defined), 95 n 42
antiphonae duplae, 272 n 11
antiphonae maiores, 54
Antiphonarium Cenomannense, 447
Antiphonary of Silos (London, BL Add. 30850), 174 n 14, 203 n 17
Antiphoner of Compiègne (Paris, BNF lat. 17436), 37, 47 n 81, 147–78, 205 n 5, 248
Antiphoner of Mont-Renaud, 37–38, 151, 173, 202 n 5, 279, 292–97, 299 n 7, 460
antiphoners, indexes, 546–60